VIET ... ON
17–1

LONGMAN HISTORY OF RUSSIA

The Soviet Union
1917–1991

Second Edition

MARTIN McCAULEY

LONGMAN
London and New York

Addison Wesley Longman Limited
Edinburgh Gate
Harlow, Essex CM20 2JE, England
and Associated Companies throughout the world.

Published in the United States of America
by Addison Wesley Longman Inc., New York
© Longman Group UK Limited 1981, 1993

First published 1981
Eleventh impression 1991
Second edition 1993
Fourth impression 1996
ISBN 0582 01323 2

British Library Cataloguing-in-Publication Data

A catalogue record for this book is
available from the British Library

Library of Congress Cataloging in Publication Data

McCauley, Martin.
The Soviet Union : 1917–1991 / Martin McCauley.—2nd ed.
p.   cm. — (Longman history of Russia)
Includes bibliographical references and index.
ISBN 0–582–01323–2
1. Soviet Union — History. I. Title. II. Series.
DK266.M354 1993
947.084—dc20   92–25942
CIP

Set by 5A in Garamond 11/12pt
Produced through Longman Malaysia, VVP

Contents

List of maps and tables

Acknowledgements

I should like to take this opportunity to thank all those who have helped me during the writing of this book, especially Olga Crisp, David Holloway and Peter Reddaway, who were kind enough to read sections and comment critically on them. I am deeply indebted to them. Of course they are in no way responsible for the shortcomings of this work.

Many thanks are due to those who provided assistance, counsel, information and insight during the preparation of the Second Edition, especially Marie Broxup, John Channon and Robert Service. They are, of course, in no way responsible for the shortcomings of this volume.

We are grateful to the following for permission to reproduce copyright material:
Macmillan, London and Basingstoke and The University of North Carolina Press for a table from *Stalinist Planning for Economic Growth 1933–52* by Eugene Zaleski, translated from the French and edited by Marie-Christine MacAndrew and John H. Moore. Copyright 1980 The University of North Carolina Press; Praeger Publications Inc. for tables from *Soviet and Chinese Aid to African Nations* by W. Weinstein and T. H. Henriksen © 1980 Praeger Publications Inc.

Glossary

Agrogorod (plural *agrogoroda*) Agrotowns
Apparat Administrative apparatus of the Communist Party
ARCWC All-Russian Council of Workers' Control
AUCECB All-Union Council of Evangelical Christians and Baptists
AUCP(B) *see* CPSU
AUW All-Russian Union of Writers

Bolshevik A Party theoretical journal
Bolsheviks When the RSDRP split in 1903 those in the majority became known as Bolsheviks and those in the minority became known as Mensheviks.

CC Central Committee (of the Communist Party)
CEC Central Executive Committee (of the soviet)
CENTO Central Treaty Organisation
Cheka Political or secret police (also known as GPU, OGPU, NKVD, MVD, MGB and KGB)
CMEA Council for Mutual Economic Assistance (also Comecon)
Comecon *see* CMEA
Cominform Communist Information Bureau
Comintern Communist International
Conference Second in importance in formulating party policy to a congress. Usually at a conference not all party organisations were represented. This, however, did not apply to the XIX and last conference, convened by Gorbachev in June 1988 (sic)
Congress Supreme party policy body. After revolution convened annually but thereafter at irregular intervals. It was agreed that it should meet every five years in 1966. Under Gorbachev there were two congresses, the XXVII and XXVIII. The latter turned out to be the last. Each congress elected a new Politburo, CC and Secretariat
Cossacks Originally their task was to guard the nation's frontiers. Hence there are Don Cossacks, Kuban Cossacks and so on

CPSU Communist Party of the Soviet Union (formerly RSDRP, RCP(B) and AUCP(B))

DCs Democratic Centralists
Druzhinniki Voluntary civilian police

ECB *see* AUCECB
EDC European Defence Community

First Secretary Head of the Communist Party – this title was only used between 1953 and 1966. Also known as Secretary General. The head of a republican, krai, oblast, city and raion party organisation is also called first secretary.
FRG Federal Republic of Germany (also known as West Germany)
FYP Five-Year Plan

GDR German Democratic Republic (also known as East Germany)
GKO State Committee of Defence
Glavk (plural **glavki**) Chief department of a ministry or other central institution
GOSPLAN State Planning Commission. Had overall responsibility for the economy until 1991
GPU Main Political Administration (see Cheka)

Izvestiya Literally means 'news'. Name of the official organ of the Soviet government. In and after 1917 many soviets published their own *Izvestiya*

Kadets Constitutional Democrats (or Liberals)
Kavburo Caucasian Bureau of the CC, RCP(B). Co-ordinated activities of the CPs of Azerbaidzhan, Armenia and Georgia
KGB Committee of State Security (*see* Cheka)
Kolkhoz Literally collective economy. Collective farm
Kolkhoznik Male collective-farm peasant
Kolkhoznitsa Female collective-farm peasant
Kombedy Committees of the Poor
Kommunist A Party theoretical journal
Komsomol Communist Union of Youth
KPD Communist Party of Germany
Krai Administrative-territorial division (usually contains an autonomous oblast within its boundaries)
Kulak Well-to-do peasant (always used in a pejorative sense in Soviet writings)

Mao Zedong (Pinyin orthography) Mao Tse-tung (Wade-Giles orthography)

MBFR   Mutual and Balanced Force Reduction
Mensheviks   Those in minority when the RSDRP split in 1903
MGB   *see* Cheka
Mir   Village community
MRC   Military Revolutionary Committee
MTS   Machine Tractor Station
MVD   Ministry of Internal Affairs (*see* Cheka)

Narkomindel   People's Commissariat of Foreign Affairs
Narkomnats   People's Commissariat for Nationalities
NATO   North Atlantic Treaty Organisation
NEP   New Economic Policy
NKFD   National Committee for a Free Germany
NKVD   *see* Cheka
Novy Mir   A literary journal
NSDAP   National Socialist German Workers' Party (Nazi Party)

Oblast   Administrative-territorial division
OGPU   *see* Cheka
Oktyabr   A literary political journal
Orgburo   Organisational Bureau of the CC

Partiinost   Party-mindedness (writing from a Party point of view)
PCF   French Communist Party
PCI   Italian Communist Party
Politburo   Political Bureau of the CC. Known as the Presidium
   between 1952 and 1966. Key decision-making body for most of
   the Soviet period. It declined in significance under Stalin (1934–53)
   and Gorbachev (1990–91)
Popular Front   Tactical alliance of communists with all anti-fascists
Pravda   Literally means 'truth'. Official organ of the Communist
   party
Presidium   *see* Politburo

Rabkrin   Workers' and Peasants' Inspectorate
Raion   Administrative-territorial division
RAPP   Association of Proletarian Writers
RCP(B)   All-Russian Communist Party (Bolsheviks); CPSU 1952–91
Reds   Communists; Bolshevik forces during the Civil War
RSDRP   All-Russian Social Democratic Labour Party; founded 1898,
   split 1903; CPSU 1952–91
RSFSR   Russian Soviet Federated Socialist Republic

SALT   Strategic Arms Limitation Treaty
SEATO   South East Asia Treaty Organisation
Secretariat   The administrative centre of the communist party; second

only to the Politburo. Gorbachev deprived it of its key position at the XIX party conference in June 1988

Secretary General   Head of the Communist Party. Title used between 1922 and 1934 and between 1966 and 1991

SED   Socialist Unity Party of Germany (Communist Party in GDR)

Selkhoztekhnika   Organisation for the provision of agricultural machinery and chemicals

Selsovet   Village soviet

Social Democrats   Members of the RSDRP

Soviet   Council

Sovkhoz   Literally 'State economy'; State farm

Sovkhoznik   Male State farmworker

Sovkhoznitsa   Female State farmworker

Sovnarkhoz   Council of the National Economy (1957–65)

Sovnarkom   Council of People's Commissars (the government). In 1946 changed to the USSR Council of Ministers

SPD   Social Democratic Party of Germany

SRs   Socialist Revolutionaries

Stakhanovite   A worker who has performed extraordinary feats of endeavour; later led to raising of norms of others

State Capitalism   Name of economic order between October 1917 and June 1918

STO   Council of Labour and Defence

TPA   Territorial Production Administrations

Travopole   System of grassland management

Trudoden (plural *Trudodni*)   Labour day; a kolkhoznik could earn several *trudodni* during a day's work

Tsar   Imperial ruler (derived from Caesar)

Tsarina   Imperial ruler's wife

TSFSR   Transcaucasian Soviet Federated Socialist Republic

Uchraspred   Records and assignment division of the CC

Uezd   Administrative-territorial division

United Front   Tactical communist alliance with social democrats; united front from above was with social democratic leadership; united front from below was with social democratic rank and file over the heads of their leadership

USPD   Independent Social Democrat Party of Germany

USSR   Union of Soviet Socialist Republics

Vikzhedor   All-Russian Central Executive Committee of Railwaymen (Bolshevik)

Vikzhel   All-Russian Central Executive Committee of Railwaymen (non-Bolshevik)

Voprosy Ekonomiki   An economics journal

Vozhd   Leader (cf. Fuhrer and Duce)
VSNKh   Supreme Council of the National Economy

War Communism   Economic order between June 1918 and March
   1921
Whites   Anti-Bolshevik forces during Civil War
WO   Workers' Opposition

Zakraikom   Transcaucasian Bureau of the CC, RCP(B)
Zhou Enlai (Pinyin orthography)   Chou En-lai (Wade-Giles ortho-
   graphy)
Znamya   Journal
Zveno   Link

Introduction

The Soviet Union is no more. The great experiment has failed. The joy, ecstasy and unbridled optimism which followed the October revolution had given way to bitterness, disillusion, cynicism and despair by 1991. The brilliant tactical success of the Bolsheviks in taking power in a developing country, dominated by the peasantry, dimmed as the difficulties of transforming the country became evident. The first and greatest mistake Lenin and his cohorts made was to underestimate the task they set themselves. They believed that if they slipped into the seats of power all that was needed to modernise the country was democracy. People's power would overcome every obstacle. Sadly for them, they quickly found that human nature is not instantly malleable. Self-interest, corruption, abuse of power and all the other barriers to efficient administration reappeared, indeed had never disappeared, and vexed the Bolsheviks. Embroiled in a bloody civil war, they resorted to coercion. Democracy was a major victim. If democracy had been practised the Bolsheviks would have been swept from power. This haunted them until the demise of the USSR. They never resorted to the ballot box to measure their legitimacy.

The Civil War left an indelible imprint on Bolshevik thinking and practice. A party arranged along military lines could become a powerful force. The most efficient militaries approximate machines. The Bolsheviks were always seeking to fashion a machine which would drive the Soviet Union forward and make it a force to be reckoned with in the world. Under War Communism socialism appeared to be attainable but only for a short time. NEP was a retreat but the great offensive (military metaphors are very revealing) began at the end of the 1920s. Interlocking mechanisms were to be created so that the USSR would work like a single factory, a single machine. This goal led to a vast bureaucracy being spawned since everyone had to follow orders, otherwise the machine might break down. The market was banished but the market exacted its revenge. It can never be eliminated since an economy is a vast forum for negotiation between and among actors. It was impossible for the centre to issue all the commands necessary to achieve plan goals. Enterprises, ministries and party functionaries had to negotiate with one another to overcome bottlenecks, shortages and mistakes in planning. The centre relied on accurate information but since the penalty of failure could be death, reporting became inaccurate, to put it mildly. Hence the centre was never sure of the true potential of enterprises. The war accelerated the coming into being of industrial and regional interest groups which colluded among themselves. Whereas it was possible to co-ordinate the vast experiment in the early stages, this became progressively more difficult and eventually by the 1980s impossible. Stalin was the managing director of USSR Inc. but even he was not the master of all he surveyed by the late 1940s. Khrushchev perceived that attempts at tight control from Moscow were dysfunctional and devolved much decision-making in the sovnarkhoz reforms of 1957. He thereby strengthened the centrifugal tendencies which had been under way since the 1930s. Brezhnev recentralised, or attempted to recentralise, but he prided himself in being a master of cadres policy: promote the right man and a few women and the machine would function more efficiently. The bureaucracy waxed but the Soviet Union gradually slowed down. Khrushchev was greatly taken by mechanical solutions and Soviet space triumphs boosted his belief that the Soviet system was based on correct assumptions. All that was needed was to apply science and technology to human endeavour. Brezhnev took this up and became enamoured of scientific management. If only the advances of science and technology could be applied to running society. Cybernetics became all the rage for a while. Gradually it dawned on many scientists that the search for the perfect machine was utopian. Some planners realised that in order for everyone to behave according to scientific norms they would have to understand the whole plan perfectly. This was out of the question since everyone only knew his or her part of the plan. No one, not even the cleverest planner, actually had all the details of the plan in his head. If this task was beyond the human intellect, what about the computer? This also turned out to be a myth since there were not enough computers to cope with the task. At present no machine is capable of assimilating all the inputs and coming out with the master plan. The failures of Soviet planning led to the plan becoming a joke.

The collapse of the Soviet Union was breathtakingly fast. Gorbachev, all optimism and *bonhomie*, was convinced that it was possible to reform the Soviet Union and make Soviet socialism a phenomenon worthy of emulation. He correctly came to the conclusion that the party bureaucracy was a barrier to a more efficient system. Bar it from direct involvement in the economy, pass those functions over to local soviets and things would improve. Since the party *apparat* could not be made accountable it had to go. Democratic accountability through the soviets was to be tried but never got off the ground. The network of interest groups was so dense and regionalism so powerful that Moscow could not impose its will. The decline of the Soviet economy under Brezhnev fostered regionalism and nationalism. When Gorbachev opened the Pandora box of *glasnost* and democratisation, the floodgates opened. The pent up frustration of past decades exploded.

One of the most astonishing failures of the ruling elites in the Soviet Union was their inability to perceive the gathering storm and to find solutions to avert disaster. Soviet bureaucracy was like a dinosaur stranded on the beach of democracy, nationalism and regionalism. Eventually their only answer was coercion. The ludicrously inefficient attempted coup in August 1991 summed it all up. How were men (there were no women among the top conspirators), who could not ensure that their orders were carried out by the military and the KGB, men trained to obey orders, supposed to run a country which involved directing the lives of millions of civilians? The machine had come to a full stop. Its design was hopelessly flawed.

June 1992   MARTIN McCAULEY

For Brian and Evy Beattie

CHAPTER ONE

Revolution

'DAYS OF HOPE AND DAYS OF DESPAIR'

THE FEBRUARY REVOLUTION

The pomp and circumstance which attended the tercentenary celebrations of the Romanov dynasty in 1913 matched the occasion. The Tsar, Nicholas II, and the Tsarina, Aleksandra, glowed with pride. But pride comes before a fall. And the fall, in February 1917, was sudden, unexpected and complete. The autocrat of all the Russias passed from the scene without so much as a whisper of protest. How was this possible?

The First World War imposed intolerable strains on the State. Russia had been undergoing a process of modernisation before 1914 and the war quickened the pace but the demands were too great. By the end of 1916 public confidence in the government had evaporated, the army had been defeated and transport problems were mounting. About 80,000 metal and textile workers went on strike on 23 February. It also happened to be International Women's Day. It had not been organised by any political party, it was the spontaneous expression of increasing exasperation at the privations and shortages, exacerbated by war. There were 160,000 troops garrisoned in the capital, Petrograd. The regime did not appear to be in danger. The strike gradually spread throughout the city, bringing vast numbers of people on to the streets. On 26 February the troops fired on the demonstrators and drew blood but by the following day the mood of the army was different. The Volhynian regiment went over to the people and set out to convince others to do the same. Other regiments followed. The Cossacks, formally the most reliable of the Imperial guards, changed sides and this doomed the dynasty. The revolution had almost been bloodless; only 587 civilians, 655 soldiers and 73 policemen sealed its victory with their blood.

The leaderless crowds turned to the only authority they knew, the parliament or Duma. It had been dissolved by the Tsar but a thirteen-man Temporary Committee composed of members of all political groupings except the right, and essentially middle class, was set up on 27 February. Also established the same day and in the same building, the Tauride Palace, was the Petrograd Soviet of Workers' Deputies (when representatives arrived from the garrisons it became

1

known as the Petrograd Soviet of Workers' and Soldiers' Deputies). A descendant of the Soviet of 1905, it was brought into being largely on Menshevik initiative. The Temporary Committee wanted to preserve the monarchy, fearing anarchy if the symbol of authority passed from the scene. However, the Tsar could not be saved and he abdicated almost with a sigh of relief. He abdicated first in favour of his haemophiliac son, Aleksei, on 2 March 1917 but then changed his mind when he discovered he would have to part from the boy if the latter became Tsar. He then abdicated a second time, later the same day, in favour of his brother Grand Duke Mikhail Aleksandrovich. The latter refused the proffered crown, wisely indicating that he would only accept it if the Constituent Assembly placed it on his head. Russia had become a *de facto* republic. This was what the crowds wanted, a constitutional monarchy held little attraction for them. Already the Temporary Committee was out of step with the aspirations of the people. After all, the masses had made the revolution and not the middle classes. In the months after February they accepted that the bourgeoisie should hold the reins of government since they had no leaders of their own and the Petrograd Soviet had no desire to rule. It was dominated by the Socialist Revolutionaries (SRs) and the Mensheviks – the moderate socialists – and they reasoned that since the revolution was at its bourgeois stage the representatives of the bourgeoisie should form the administration. The Soviet would support the new government (or the Provisional Government as it became known when it took office on 2 March) against reaction but it would oppose it if it went against the goals of the February Revolution. The government was provisional or temporary until the Constituent Assembly, the first democratically elected parliament, convened. A government of national unity was never contemplated.

The first Prime Minister was Prince G. E. Lvov, a liberal but not a member of any party. The liberals, the Constitutional Democrats or Kadets, dominated the ten-man administration. There was only one surprise among the ministers, the Minister of Justice was A. F. Kerensky, an SR and a member of the Petrograd Soviet. The latter had officially voted not to participate in the new government but Kerensky's verbal wizardry, on a par with that of his contemporary David Lloyd George, won him the right to accept a portfolio.

The government immediately enacted much progressive legislation. An amnesty was declared for all political prisoners, capital punishment was abolished, the right to strike and organise was granted and all legal restrictions based on class, nationality and religion were lifted. Lenin even went so far as to state that Russia was the freest of all the belligerent countries in the world. The Kadets were in no hurry to convene the Constituent Assembly since they did not want to encourage peasant and worker radicalism. They wanted agrarian reform left until the new parliament was convened

2

and urged workers' organisations to exercise self-restraint in wage bargaining. The Kadets were ever mindful of the damage industrial and rural unrest could do to Russia's war effort. But it takes two to make a bargain. Workers and soldiers looked to the Petrograd Soviet and the myriad of other soviets to put their aspirations into practice. Soon peasants' soviets spread throughout the countryside. Dual power was a reality from the inception of the Provisional Government. Unfortunately for the government, its writ did not carry far beyond the capital. The government dismissed the tsarist governors and appointed its own commissars, but they did not last long. The police force disintegrated with the February Revolution, and law and order became the responsibility of local organisations. Free elections led to those parties based on the middle classes, such as the Kadets, losing out. The government was, understandably, reluctant to grant much autonomy to local bodies. This became more of a problem in non-Russian areas, such as the Ukraine and Finland. The Russian Orthodox Church could not be relied upon as an ally of a liberal-minded government.

War or peace proved an insoluble dilemma. Army and naval officers, on the whole, accepted the revolution, but their ability to command changed. The most unpopular were sometimes lynched. The Petrograd Soviet pushed through Order no. 1, which ended blind obedience to superiors. Soldiers did not need to salute when off duty, demanded to be addressed in the polite second person plural and the right to elect their own committees to articulate and defend their interests. The government gave in with a certain feeling of unease. Soldiers in city garrisons began to set the tone and the message which came across was a strong desire for the war to be considered defensive. Only shoot if you are attacked. In the meanwhile every effort should be undertaken to negotiate a general European peace. This severely constrained the government's room for manoeuvre. Workers and peasants also overwhelmingly favoured an end to hostilities.

But how was this to be achieved? The Soviet wanted international socialist action to secure a just peace without annexations and indemnities. Correspondingly the Soviet issued an appeal to the 'comrade proletarians and toilers of all countries'.[1] The government, on the other hand, believed that one of the reasons for the Revolution had been the inefficient manner in which the Imperial regime had prosecuted the war. Prince Lvov and his government felt that Russia had to hold to its international obligations, one of which was not to conclude a unilateral peace. To keep Russia buoyed up, the Allies had promised it the Bosphorus and Dardanelles, something the Russians had been eyeing enviously for a millennium. The gulf between the two heirs to Imperial power widened until street demonstrations, organised by the Soviet, brought down the government. The flashpoint was a note

3

which the Foreign Minister, Paul Milyukov (Kadet), had sent to the Allied Powers dated 18 April (1 May New Style). In it he expressed the hope that means would be found to 'obtain those guarantees and sanctions which were indispensable for the prevention of sanguinary conflicts in the future'.[2] This was like a red rag to a bull. To the Soviet 'guarantees and sanctions' meant imperialistic aggrandisement. The demonstrations made crystal clear who the real master of Russia was: it was the Soviet. By bringing down the government the Soviet placed itself in a quandary. The Kadet party had been chastened by the experience and plainly could not command much respect throughout the country. If reaction were not to rear its head again the Soviet would have to drop its objection to accepting governmental responsibility. The result was the first Coalition Government of 5 May 1917. Lvov stayed as Prime Minister. Kerensky became Minister of War, Viktor Chernov, the SR leader, Minister of Agriculture and two Mensheviks were included, M. I. Skobelev accepting the sensitive post of Minister of Labour.

The Kadets had the advantage in that the Mensheviks and SRs were reluctant bed partners. They hoped they would restrain the Petrograd Soviet, temper wage demands and hold back land seizures. Minority socialist ministers advocated their own policies – immediate peace, higher wages, better working conditions and more governmental intervention in the economy – but little came of them. The socialists did not leave in a huff since they were ever mindful of the threat from the right. Kadets were, after all, much preferable to a military government. This may explain why socialist ministers acceded to the government's desire to begin an offensive in late June. The Allies, launching an attack on the Western Front, had requested Russian help on the Eastern Front. The result was predictable, absolute disaster. Not only the bourgeois parties but also the moderate socialist leadership of the Soviet were now discredited. This opened the floodgates to those who had more radical ideas about ending the war, first and foremost the Bolsheviks. They, ably led by Lenin who had returned to Petrograd on 3 April from Switzerland, wanted a Soviet government, the transformation of the 'imperialist' war into a civil war and the passage of the revolution from its first bourgeois stage to its second stage, the transfer of power to the proletariat and the poor strata of the peasantry. Their slogan 'All Power to the Soviets' had instant appeal and they also championed a second explosive theme, all land to the peasants. This was SR policy and Viktor Chernov was Minister of Agriculture at the time but he could not win the government over to legalising the ever increasing land seizures before the Constituent Assembly met. The peace and land questions were intimately linked. Who were the soldiers but peasants in uniform? So the Bolshevik press, published in vast quantities and often distributed free, urged the soldiers to desert, thus robbing the Provisional Government of any armed support, and return to their villages and seize the land, thus removing one of the pillars of government support, the landlords. Lenin declared war on the Provisional Government in his April Theses, proclaimed on 4 April.

The Bolsheviks revelled in the industrial strife, rural conflict and discomfiture of the 'bourgeois' government. They were the only party who had a ready-made solution to all of society's ills, revolution. Workers tended to blame the bosses for the economic difficulties but many of these resulted from lack of inputs. Monthly coal output declined by 27 per cent between January and August 1917, and from April enterprises were receiving less than 40 per cent of the metals they needed.[3] This was partly due to transport difficulties. As revenue declined the government resorted to the printing press and inflation soared. Workers developed a greater sense of solidarity as poverty beckoned. Factory committees could take over an enterprise if they feared closure. There were also trade-union committees and often political parties had cells in factories. Most activity was defensive and one result was workers' control. This concept had many meanings but amounted in most cases to shadowing management closely.

Huge demonstrations against the June offensive, spearheaded by 20,000 very radical Kronstadt sailors, on 3–4 July, known as the July Days, came very near to transferring power to the most radical champion of the Soviet, the Bolsheviks. The government saved itself by playing a trump card. It accused Lenin of being a German agent and the Bolsheviks of accepting vast sums of money from Imperial Germany. Lenin and others had crossed Germany in a sealed train on their way home and they had accepted certain conditions. The mood of the crowd changed dramatically. *Pravda*, the Bolsheviks' newspaper, had its printing presses smashed, prominent Bolsheviks such as Trotsky were imprisoned and Lenin fled to Finland disguised as a train driver's mate. Clean shaven and wearing a blond wig he looked for all the world like a Finn. There is little doubt that the Bolsheviks did receive large sums from Berlin but they used them to pursue their main goal, revolution. Imperial Germany believed that this goal was also in its interests, a catastrophic misjudgment.

All was set fair for the second Coalition Government which took office on 24 July with Kerensky as Prime Minister. Military matters again brought it down. Kerensky reached an agreement with General Lavr Kornilov, the new C-in-C. General Krymov was to occupy and disarm the capital and dissolve the Petrograd Soviet, apparently because Bolshevik demonstrations were expected on 27 August, the half anniversary of the February Revolution.[4] When Kornilov began to move his forces on 27 August, Kerensky changed his mind and ordered him to surrender his post. Kornilov accused Kerensky of betraying Russia but could not get to Petrograd because the railwaymen would not let him through.

The Kornilov episode was the turning-point. Kerensky had to appeal to the Petrograd Soviet for help but in the event it was not needed. However, the Soviet had acquired arms to defend the capital and these weapons were not handed back. It was now possible, after the Military Revolutionary Committee of the Soviet, chaired by Lev Trotsky, had been set up to provide the Soviet with advice on military matters, for the Bolsheviks to contemplate armed insurrection. Popular exasperation at the government's ineffective showing and disillusionment after the Kornilov attack produced wave after wave of support for the radicals with the Bolsheviks gaining most. The government was helpless as more and more of the country slipped out of its control. The Finns, Georgians, Azerbaidzhanis and Armenians sought to separate from Russia and the Ukraine had its own soviet, the Rada. The military weakness of the Kerensky regime was underlined in August when the Germans advanced and took Riga without much trouble. Petrograd stood open before them but they decided not to take that prize. Had they done so it might have aroused dormant Russian nationalist feeling. Berlin preferred to have a disunited, weak Russian state rather than to occupy the country and be forced to devote men and *matériel* to imposing their authority. The Eastern Front, after all, was a side show for the Germans. They were staking all on victory in the West. The parlous state of the country led to Kerensky convening a State Conference which brought together a wide range of political parties and groups, but mutual suspiciousness paralysed the will to act. In September a democratic conference was called but those willing to attend had dwindled. Both assemblies were weak apologies for the Constituent Assembly and eventually Kerensky had to concede elections scheduled for November. In the meanwhile he cobbled together a small team to see him through the interim period. In early September the Bolsheviks gained a majority in the Petrograd Soviet and in the Moscow Soviet of Workers' Deputies. Lenin immediately called for an uprising, either in Petrograd or Moscow. The Central Committee (CC) wavered until early October. Even so two of its members, Kamenev and Zinoviev, were so opposed to the initiative that they argued against it in Maksim Gorky's newspaper *Novaya Zhizn* on 11 October. Kerensky, by then heading the third Coalition Government, could be forgiven for taking to his couch in laughter – surely a revolutionary party which proclaimed in the press that it was about to seize power need not be taken seriously.

THE POLITICAL PARTIES

The Kadet party contained both conservatives and liberals and its members came from the nobility, the civil service, the military and the professions. Large landowners were also well represented. The Kadets would have preferred a constitutional monarchy. They and those to the right of them wanted the war carried through to a victorious conclusion. This would provide them, so they thought, with the necessary prestige to remain in power. They believed in private property but were very ambivalent in their attitude to the nationalities.

The SRs were always the largest political party and eventually claimed a million members. They split, however, on their attitude towards the land. Some wanted to socialise the means of production while others, the Popular Socialists grouped around Peshekhonov, favoured a countryside of small landed proprietors.[5] Nevertheless all SRs agreed that the family farm was to be preferred to the collective in the immediate future. The agrarian problem to them was the most pressing.

They did not aspire to power in February although together with the Mensheviks they had almost complete control of the soviets. The majority of the army favoured them. However, like the Mensheviks they accepted that the revolution was only at its bourgeois stage, something which would last a long time, hence the bourgeoisie had the right to rule. The soviets, in their view, should restrict themselves to supervisory functions. The SRs also thought that it was necessary to bring the war to an end but they were of the opinion that a separate peace with Germany would only increase German power in central Europe. Socialists in the belligerent countries should bring the war to an end by applying pressure on their respective governments but this was being over-optimistic given that most socialists had accepted war in 1914.

As the SR party increased in size after February so divisions began to appear. Some landowners joined so as to influence policy from within the ranks of the party and to make the party less radical, if possible. Gradually the centre around Viktor Chernov was flanked by a group on the right, spearheaded by A. F. Kerensky, which had lost all its radical teeth, and a group on the left which became very radical, eventually finding common cause with the Bolsheviks.

Despite the fact that Viktor Chernov was Minister of Agriculture food production declined and off-farm sales dropped by almost a half by midsummer. Even the army could not be guaranteed its rations. The government decreed that all grain for sale had to be sold to the state but did not have the will-power or the means to enforce it. It tried raising prices dramatically in August but to little effect due to rampant inflation. Without reliable troops the government could not halt the dismemberment of landlord estates. Here the demonstration effect was influential. If some peasants seized land and livestock and abused a landlord and got away with it, others were encouraged to emulate them. Many landowners got the message and fled to the towns, but others were left enough land by their expropriators to feed themselves and their family.

The Mensheviks could only claim a few thousand members before the February Revolution but rapidly became a mass party and by October had about 200,000 members. They relied almost entirely on the working class for support. They were numerically stronger than the Bolsheviks in February 1917 and competition between these two factions of the Russian Social Democratic Labour Party declined afterwards as Kamenev and Stalin, the effective Bolshevik leaders while Lenin was in exile, adopted a conciliatory policy. They expected the bourgeoisie to stay in power for quite some time. This harmony was rudely shattered by Lenin on his return to Petrograd. His analysis of the situation was penetrating. The February Revolution made by the masses had placed the bourgeosie in power. However, the bourgeoisie did not control the army and the police without which it could not rule. Hence the bourgeoisie only appeared to be in power. Since most of the army and police owed allegiance to the Soviet, 'All Power to the Soviets' was a powerful slogan. Lenin also wanted no truck with the Mensheviks, but here the rank-and-file social democrat often did not follow. In October, 23 of the 163 Bolshevik committees were still composed of Mensheviks and Bolsheviks.[6] From Lenin's point of view it naturally followed that since the bourgeoisie was not really in control, revolution, placing power in the hands of the soviets, was possible in the short rather than the long term. This brought his ideas closer to those of Lev Trotsky, the apostle of permanent revolution. Trotsky, who did not become a Bolshevik until the summer, in turn moved in Lenin's direction by accepting the latter's views on the role of the party and the wisdom of the soviets taking power. This drove Bolsheviks such as Kamenev and Zinoviev away from Lenin. They regarded an attempt to seize power as much too risky and anyway how were the Bolsheviks to keep power after the revolution given that they were a minority in the land? Lenin always had a neat answer to those who asked him how the Bolsheviks would solve such and such a problem. The Mensheviks were particularly good at pointing out the difficulties which would be encountered. Lenin's reply was simply to wait and see, the creative potential of the masses was such that any problem could be solved.

The Bolshevik party grew rapidly and ordinary members, activists, officials and lower party bodies were supposed to defer to higher bodies. The situation was too volatile for this to happen. The leadership would be obeyed if it reflected lower-level opinion. Lenin, again, was not the undisputed leader. He had to convince his colleagues that his policies were correct and quite often failed to do so. Lenin's relentless war of attrition against the Mensheviks gradually paid dividends as their record in harness with the Kadets aroused hostility. Some Mensheviks crossed the floor and joined the Bolsheviks. The defeat of the July

8

Days, however, demonstrated that many in garrisons and factories favoured direct soviet rule. Workers poured into the party and they may have made up about 60 per cent of members in late 1917. Those below pushed the leadership towards action.

The Mensheviks adopted an ambivalent attitude towards the war but not Lenin. It had to be ended even if this meant a unilateral peace. If the price was military defeat, so be it. The war-weary soldiers, especially after July, rallied to his call irrespective of consequences.

Revolution to the Mensheviks meant a socialist revolution but Russia at its present stage of development was a long way from that. It was underdeveloped industrially and anyway the peasants would never allow the land to be socialised or be willing to farm in collectives. There were also Bolsheviks who thought like this, for example Kamenev.

All parties which participated in government between February and October moved to the right while the masses moved to the left. Popular support shifted to the one party which unequivocally favoured Soviet power, the Bolsheviks – only once they felt sure they could dominate them.

Mensheviks and SRs opposed the slogan 'All Power to the Soviets' in the name of democracy. They did not regard soviet power as legitimate since they thought that soviets represented classes and not the nation. As far as they were concerned only the Constituent Assembly would possess full legitimacy. Given these views and in the absence of a Constituent Assembly it is hardly surprising that they lost influence in the second half of 1917.

The Provisional Governments were broken on the rack of peace and land. One could not be solved without the other. In reality the government was in no position to prevent peasant seizures of land since it had no reliable police force. Anyway no socialist in the government would contemplate using force against other socialists.

Government policy contributed to the radicalisation of the population. Its failure to respond to peasant grievances and its inability to solve their immediate problems alienated the peasants and accelerated revolution in the countryside. This led to the distortion of the established pattern of power, property and hierarchy.[7] The peasants turned inward, only extending loyalty to the village group. This broke the normal urban–rural relationship and exacerbated the food situation which in turn contributed to the radicalisation of the urban population. Petrograd, for instance, between February and October 1917, only received by rail 43.9 per cent of the grain it had received in 1913.[8]

Although, in the main, the leaderships of the Bolshevik and Menshevik parties were middle class (in some cases, such as Lenin, they were aristocratic), middle- and lower-level representatives were usually of worker or peasant origin. It is unlikely that factory

9

committees, trade-union organisations, factory cells and the like had many middle-class members. There were middle-class representatives in the soviets since a middle-class suburb was likely to elect one of their own. However, they formed a small island in a worker and peasant sea. The masses had their first opportunity to engage in democracy and they seized it eagerly. However, those who had had experience in political parties before February had a great procedural advantage. The first all-Russian Congress of Soviets was held in June and it elected a Central Executive Committee. This was too large to react immediately to events and an inner presidium was formed. The government was alarmed by the growth of what could become a 'shadow' soviet government.

Given the Menshevik and SR majority in the Petrograd Soviet until September, and hence in the Central Executive Committee, there was no likelihood of a 'shadow' soviet government being transformed into a real government. However, the situation away from the capital was quite different. There the hesitancy about accepting the functions of authority were not so great. Kronstadt and Tsaritsyn, both strongly opposed to the Provisional Government, wanted to declare themselves independent republics but were persuaded, with difficulty, not to do so. Local soviets began to assume more and more of the functions of local government: setting up a local militia, coping with the poor and needy, intervening in the local economy, organising educational facilities. The same was true outside the Russian heartland. Cities such as Baku, on the Caspian Sea, gradually began to run their own affairs. The central government would have liked to overrule but was in a cleft stick. It could legislate but could not implement its decrees. Legitimacy, in the eyes of most people, rested with the soviets.

Why was the Constituent Assembly not called? It would have put the SR party in power and swept all the bourgeois parties off the political map. The government was always hesitant and put off all major decisions until the Constituent Assembly. It was a true caretaker government. Then there was the belief that there were no enemies on the left: danger to the Revolution could only come from the right. Ministers, into the bargain, suffered from the fact that they had had no governmental experience before February 1917. The skill, self-confidence and iron resolve of Lenin in the end placed victory in the hands of the Bolsheviks, then a very undisciplined party. Kerensky was no match for the Bolshevik leader whose political acumen and polemical gifts set him apart. Nevertheless all the political wizardry in the world would have been in vain had not the popular desire for a Soviet revolution not been so strong. Kerensky singlehandedly had discredited the SRs and the Provisional Governments. The masses wanted a complete change and Lenin was there to act on this aspiration.

THE OCTOBER REVOLUTION

The October Revolution was timed to coincide with two other revolutions: the worldwide socialist revolution and the peasant revolution in the Russian countryside. The former never materialised and the latter turned out quite differently. Hence the Russia which emerged from the Bolshevik seizure of power in Petrograd on 25 October/ 7 November 1917 was radically different from the country which Lenin had envisaged on the morrow of victory. 'We are now ready to build socialism', proclaimed the Bolshevik leader in the euphoria of victory. He did not mean that socialism would be built overnight, it would take quite a long time. In the meanwhile Soviet Russia had to modernise, industrialise and put its agricultural house in order. It would have to modernise so as to pull the country into the twentieth century and slough off all the remnants of its patriarchal and autocratic past; it would have to industrialise so as to produce a large, disciplined, skilled and cultured working class; and it would have to modernise its agriculture, transferring the twenty million-odd peasant households into large co-operative enterprises. Modernisation and industrialisation would proceed apace since international socialist revolution would put the know-how at the disposal of the Russians. The German comrades were expected to be especially helpful, proletarian internationalism in action, since Berlin was envisaged as the socialist capital of Europe. The countryside would be won over to socialism as, even after the remaining arable land had been handed over to the peasants, the poor peasants and hopefully the middle peasants, the natural allies of the working class in the rural areas, would lead a movement which would eliminate the more successful peasants, disrespectfully called kulaks, and usher in the era of co-operative farming. Socialism implied large-scale farming and the logic of this was believed to be irresistible. However, the international socialist revolution, after initial successes in Hungary and Bavaria, flattered to deceive. The poor peasant, far from being the natural ally of the worker, wanted to be a middle peasant and the middle peasant wanted to become a kulak. The Bolsheviks were thrown back on themselves; they had to undertake the building of the foundations of a socialist economy and society using only their own resources, knowing that it would be very difficult to persuade the peasants, comprising 80 per cent of the total population of 140 millions, that model and collective farms were economically more rational than small-scale peasant household farms, each sufficient to feed an extended family. The Bolshevik support base which Lenin had calculated would be very wide shrank and shrank. Extricating Russia from the First World War became an expensive business; the factory workers understood workers' control to mean that enterprises would be worked and controlled by them whereas Lenin only wanted them to have the right of inspection; after that war

11

came the Civil War and Intervention and with it an economic crisis. The cities and the Red Army needed food which could only come from the countryside. There the peasants had benefited from the revolution and harboured much good will towards Lenin and the Communist Party. This was quickly dissipated due to the desperate necessity of the time. Gradually the euphoria of victory gave way to the sober realisation that there were no short cuts to a better life for all, to justice, democracy and freedom on a national scale. A revolution whose success was based on seizing and maintaining political power gradually became one in which the needs of the economy became paramount. The desperate struggle to find the inputs to keep the wheels of industry turning; the confrontation with the peasants; the need to build a Red Army from scratch to win the Civil War; all contributed to the death of democracy. Economic necessity, the ever present shortages and urban hunger, meant that all became dissatisfied. The upsurge of idealism and hope in October when Lenin had envisaged that a republic of soviets would run Soviet Russia, rapidly gave way to a dictatorship of the Party. Factory committees, trade unions, soviets of workers' and peasants' deputies, all fell victim to the overriding, overpowering need to find an institution which would follow willingly every twist and turn of Bolshevik policy. The only institution which was capable of playing such a role was the Russian Social Democratic Labour Party (Bolsheviks) or as it became known at the VIIth Congress in March 1918, the All-Russian Communist Party (Bolsheviks). The Bolsheviks when they took power in October 1917 presented it to the IInd Congress of Soviets and thus transformed Russia into Soviet Russia. In less than a year, however, power had slipped from the soviets into the safekeeping of the Communist Party. The revolution which had signalled not socialism overnight for Lenin but the dictatorship of the proletariat revealed its true colours. Not soviet democracy but a dictatorship – and since the Communist Party claimed to be the vanguard of the proletariat – a dictatorship of the Communist Party.

THE BOLSHEVIKS SEIZE POWER

The IInd Congress of the Soviets of Workers' and Soldiers' Deputies convened in Smolny in Petrograd at 10.40 p.m. on 7 November 1917. It was late: it should have opened at 3 p.m. Even so the key figure in the dramatic events of that day, the day which had seen a declaration by the Military Revolutionary Committee (MRC) of the Petrograd Soviet that the Provisional Government had been overthrown, refused to attend. Lenin was livid, the revolution was behind schedule. Fyodor Dan, a Menshevik, at last declared the Congress open. His first proposal was to move to the election of a presidium. When a Bolshevik proposed the election of 14 Bolsheviks, 7 SRs, 3 Mensheviks and one Menshevik

Internationalist, the Mensheviks, right SRs and the Internationalists declared that they would not participate in any election. The result of this *démarche* was to deliver the presidium into the hands of the Bolsheviks and left SRs. Kamenev was then elected chairman. Yuly Martov, for the Menshevik Internationalists, was the first to speak. He proposed the formation of a delegation to negotiate with all other socialist parties to stop the bloodshed which was staining the streets of Petrograd. Lunacharsky for the Bolsheviks agreed. The moderate socialists (Mensheviks and right SRs) however declared their undying opposition to the military 'adventure' of the Bolsheviks and made clear their readiness to resist the Bolshevik seizure of power. Their first move was to march out of the Congress leaving the Bolsheviks and left SRs with an overwhelming majority. Trotsky, replying for the Congress, flung after them the famous words: 'Go where you belong, to the dustbin of history.' He was very perceptive. They were condemning themselves to oblivion. Instead of staying and challenging the Bolshevik interpretation of events from the floor of the Congress the moderate socialists opted out of the struggle. More than once in the succeeding years they were to do the same in social organisations when they believed that Bolshevik behaviour was unconstitutional. They learnt a hard lesson; all they achieved with their fastidiousness over the rule book was banishment from Soviet political life.

The news for which Lenin and his supporters had been waiting for finally arrived in the early hours of 8 November. The Winter Palace had been taken and the ministers of the Provisional Government arrested and placed in the Peter and Paul Fortress. The MRC operations, masterminded by Trotsky, had carried the day. Now the real business of the Congress could begin. It immediately assumed State power and gave the floor to Lenin to speak on the peace decree. His speech contained no surprises. Had not the Bolshevik leader declared ever since April 1917 that his party favoured an immediate end to the war? This meant that peace negotiations were to start straight away. The delegates loved it, but would the German High Command? Lenin was to discover that just as it takes two to make a fight so it takes two to conclude peace. His next speech was on the land decree. Again it surprised no Bolsheviks at home but it did some Marxists abroad, notably the German revolutionary, Rosa Luxemburg. The Bolshevik leader conceded quite openly that the decree and the land mandate, based on the 242 petitions of the local soviets of peasants' deputies, had been drafted by the SRs. What was SR land policy? Private ownership of land should be abolished. The land belonging to the *pomeshchiki* or large landowners, to the Crown and the Church should be divided among the peasants without compensation. Each person should be entitled to the fruits of his labour and have enough land to support his family. Lenin enacted this policy even though in the April Theses he had declared that land was to be nationalised and

13

model farms established on all the large estates. He was swimming with the tide of rural discontent and was actually in no position to stop the peasants parcelling up the landlord estates. To underline their belief that a man should have enough land to nourish his own family, the peasants often left the landlord sufficient land for this purpose. Once firmly in power, however, the Bolsheviks enacted their own land decree, the socialisation of the land, in February 1918. Giving the land to the peasants was a tactical move. It kept the countryside quiet while the Bolsheviks consolidated their position in urban areas.

With the peace and land decrees behind it the Congress proceeded to the election of the first provisional Soviet government, provisional until the Constituent Assembly met. The name of the new government, the Council of People's Commissars (Sovnarkom), was suggested by the ever resourceful Trotsky. A break with the old terminology had to be made and Lenin's response was instant approval: 'Council of People's Commissars, Council of People's Commissars', repeated Lenin, 'That is splendid. That smells of revolution.'9

Lenin was named Prime Minister; he in turn nominated Trotsky as Commissar of Internal Affairs but the latter did not believe it wise to have a Jew in such a sensitive post. Sverdlov, also a Jew, agreed. Trotsky was then made Commissar of Foreign Affairs and it was believed that this would afford him ample time for party affairs; A. V. Lunacharsky was made Commissar of Education and Stalin Chairman of Nationalities. Instead of one Commissar of War and the Navy there were three: V. A. Antonov-Ovseenko, N. V. Krylenko and P. E. Dybenko – all of junior commissioned rank. The Bolsheviks had read and digested the lessons of the French Revolution well: they were on their guard against the emergence of another Napoleon. No Commissar of Railways was named since the Central Executive Committee of the railwaymen's union, Vikzhel, challenged the legality of the Congress and opposed the seizure of power by one party, favouring a socialist coalition government. Vikzhel went so far as to state that if oppressive measures were taken against it, it would cut off food supplies to Petrograd. Despite this the government was accepted by an overwhelming majority. The concluding act of the Congress was to elect an All-Russian Central Executive Committee (CEC) and the Bolsheviks and left SRs occupied 90 of the 110 places. Thus the Bolsheviks had succeeded in institutionalising their seizure of power through the soviet: the CEC was the supreme legislative body and Sovnarkom was responsible to it. Lenin and his followers dominated the former and made up the latter. Henceforth all socialist opposition to Bolshevik control would have to operate outside and in opposition to the CEC and the government. The Bolsheviks had cleared the first hurdle; now they would claim legitimacy and label all opposition counter-revolutionary, as emotive a term then as it is now. Institutionalising their power had been relatively easy but the task of making their writ effective throughout the country was to prove vastly more difficult.

The two decrees aided the Bolsheviks as much as they hindered their opponents. The countryside became more chaotic than ever with everyone who believed he had a claim to some land leaving the towns. Supplies of food to the urban areas naturally became more erratic. The army virtually melted away since the soldiers were peasants in uniform. Kerensky, who had fled Petrograd for the Northern Front, could organise but feeble resistance. The army would have to regroup and reform and move to the south where the rich farmlands harboured many opponents of urban socialist rule.

Events in Petrograd produced their own reaction throughout the country. It was only on 15 November, after five days of hard fighting, that the Bolsheviks gained control of Moscow. Within a few weeks, however, most of the main Russian cities and the army on the Western Front or what was left of it were in their hands. It took more time for the waves of revolution to reach the villages but those near centres of industry and along main lines of communications were quickly under Red control. The more remote the area the longer it took. The bush telegraph spreading the news of the land decree, however, speeded up the process.

THE MASS ORGANISATIONS

Factory committees and trade unions

Lenin clarified his views on the type of economic order he envisaged after Soviet power had become a reality in 'The Impending Catastrophe and How to Combat It', his last article devoted to economic affairs before the October Revolution.[10] There were five main proposals:

1. Amalgamation of all banks into a single bank, and state control over its operations, or nationalisation of the banks.
2. Nationalisation of the syndicates, i.e. the largest monopolistic capitalist associations (sugar, oil, coal, iron and steel, and other syndicates).
3. Abolition of commercial secrecy.
4. Compulsory syndication (i.e. compulsory amalgamation into associations) of industrialists, merchants and employers generally.
5. Compulsory organisation of the population into consumers' societies, or encouragement of such organisations, and the exercise of control over it.

To Lenin these measures would introduce revolutionary democracy in the economic field. None of them is specifically socialist, however. No one was to lose his capital or his property. The main advantage of a central State bank, for Lenin, was that it would help small peasant owners to acquire credit on easy terms. What the Bolshevik leader envisaged was that the capitalist industrial economy would remain and all its activities would be co-ordinated and guided from the centre to the benefit of Soviet Russia. It is true that a few key enterprises would be nationalised but the overwhelming majority would remain in the hands of their owners. This amounted to nothing more than State capitalism. Lenin regarded this as advisable in the immediate aftermath of the revolution since Russia's position would be so parlous.

This thinking was quite out of step with the aspirations of the workers. They had played a key role in two revolutions and having taken over industry they wanted to run it themselves. The decree on workers' control (here the term 'workers' control' only means that workers have the right to supervise, not decide, what is produced) promulgated on 27 November 1917 was a compromise. However it did little to change the situation. Whereas Lenin and Trotsky were strongly in favour of State capitalism others in the CC of the Communist Party, such as Bukharin, favoured a more radical stance and wanted the beginnings of a socialist economy immediately after October.

Debate about the future was heated but economic reality was cold and harsh. Output in medium- and large-scale enterprises in 1917 dropped to two-thirds of that recorded in 1913 and in 1918 it plummeted to a half. Between November 1917 and September 1918 38 per cent of the State's large concerns had to shut down. Supply breakdowns, disruption of transport, raging inflation and labour unrest took a heavy toll. Government policy contributed to the decline. After the revolution the Bolsheviks cancelled arms contracts. Not surprisingly, most industrial enterprises had been turning out military equipment. It proved impossible to switch to producing goods for the civilian economy. The net result was further disruption of the economy. The agricultural sector fared slightly better and the 1917 harvest was only 13 per cent less than the 1909–13 average. However, this represented a shortfall of 13.3 million tonnes of grain, but this was ominous.[11] The Bolsheviks were unfortunate in that they were strong in the food deficit regions of the north and centre but their critics and opponents were becoming more influential in the food surplus zones of the Ukraine, the North Caucasus and West Siberia. Rising inflation and the drop in industrial output made off-farm sales less and less attractive. Peasants could consume more and feed more livestock. But how were the cities to be fed?

The period of State capitalism ended on 28 June 1918 with the decree on the nationalisation of industry. This ushered in War Communism which was a leap into socialism. Hence between November 1917 and June 1918 the peasants and workers were treated quite differently. The land decree afforded the peasants all they wanted from the revolution but the aspirations of the workers, the backbone of Bolshevik support, were not satisfied until June 1918.

Factory committees sprouted mushroom-like after a shower of rain, especially in the metallurgical industry. Skilled workers usually exercised considerable influence on these committees. They evolved an effective method of expressing their opposition to State capitalism. They occupied their own factories. The CC then had to decide whether or not to legalise the take-over. Since the 'left' favoured such initiatives many of them were accepted. Three-quarters of the factories nationalised by June 1918 were taken over by this wildcat method. Most were located in outlying areas, such as the Urals and the Donets basin. In Moscow and Petrograd the authorities were much more successful in curtailing this movement.[12]

The great weakness of the factory committees was that they were restricted to one enterprise. There was an All-Russian Council of Factory Committees but it envisaged factory committees eventually coming under the aegis of the All-Russian Council of Workers' Control (ARCWC). The latter organisation would be responsible for the whole economy and be dominated by representatives from the trade unions, soviets and factory committees. Hence the factory committees conceded that the trade unions, to put it no higher, were of equal status. When the decree on workers' control was eventually passed neither the factory committees nor the trade unions dominated the ARCWC. There was a sting in the tail of the decree: 'Instructions on the relationship between the ARCWC and other institutions organising and regulating the national economy will be issued separately.'[13] This meant that a central body administering the whole economy was in prospect. It turned out to be the Supreme Council of the National Economy (VSNKh) which came into being on 14 December 1917. Although Lenin seems to have turned his face against a national economic agency in November, hoping that the local soviets would keep the capitalist owners in order, he quickly changed his mind. The ARCWC, incidentally, enjoyed a very brief existence. It was merged with VSNKh in December 1917.

By November 1917 the Bolsheviks were in a strong position in the country's leading industrial trade unions and they were also important in those unions which embraced craftsmen and white-collar workers. Despite this they did not have a majority in the national trade union executive body, the All-Russian Central Council of Trade Unions.[14] The unions spoke for the particular interests of their members and, not surprisingly, regarded the improvement of their members' working conditions and pay as of paramount importance. Lenin and Trotsky, to name only two leading Bolsheviks, put the revolution and the central needs of the State first and this was bound to lead to a clash with the unions sooner or later. The unions saw themselves as the natural setters of national economic goals but so did the Communist Party and

Sovnarkom. The unions resisted the party view that the chief functions of unions, after the October Revolution, were to instil labour discipline and raise labour productivity.

A formidable opponent, in the immediate aftermath of October, was the railwaymen's union but its executive, Vikzhel, was outmanoeuvred by the Bolsheviks, who supported the union's more radical members. This led to a pro-Bolshevik executive, Vikzhedor, being set up. The Ist All-Russian Congress of Trade Unions, held from 20–27 January 1918, which claimed to represent 2.5 million men and women, revealed the strength of the Bolsheviks. The policy adopted by the Mensheviks was to argue in favour of trade-union independence. Since they did not accept that the Bolshevik dictatorship would lead to socialism they did not wish the unions to fall under state control. Their rather tame advice to their members was to participate in the great experiment going on but to seek all the time to deflect it in the direction of socialism, as they defined it. Zinoviev, speaking for the Bolsheviks, was very dismissive: 'We too are in favour of trade union independence but only from the bourgeoisie . . . . At a time when the working class and poorer peasants have succeeded in transferring power to the working class and when the unions are part of that power, what is the meaning of independence?'[15] Zinoviev's view prevailed, by 182 votes to 84. The Congress decided that unions were to 'assume the main work of organising production and restoring the country's shattered forces of production'. They were to play an active part in all the state institutions regulating production, they were to supervise workers' control, register and allocate labour and combat sabotage. All these duties, however, already fell within the competence of state organs, VSNKh or the economic commissariats. No guideline was provided on what the relationship between the central trade union body and the state apparatus was to be. The role of factory committees, on the other hand, was clearly defined at the Congress. They were to be subject to trade union leadership. In practice this meant that factory committees were fused with the factory trade-union cell. It was made clear that there could be no question of 'giving workers of an individual enterprise the right to decide matters affecting the very existence of that enterprise'. Indeed the factory could be shut down and disobedient labour dismissed. VSNKh was effective in blocking wildcat nationalisation as by restricting the supply of industrial inputs and credits it could bring the erring enterprise into line.

Before the onset of the Civil War, under the conditions of state capitalism, the unions just about held their own. It was one thing to pass regulations at a Congress but it was another to force every union to conform. Labour, on the whole, was further to the left than the Bolsheviks. The latter did not dispose of sufficient power or the economic bureaucracy to slow down the march to socialism. Lenin and Trotsky had as a result to abandon their negotiations with

Western businessmen for financial and technical assistance. Lenin's honeymoon with labour only lasted a short time and by April 1918 he was threatening draconian measures. His point of view was, arguably, quite sound. Workers could take over and run their factories when they had learned to manage them as efficiently as their former capitalist owners.

Labour's radicalism hastened the onset of War Communism. The nationalisation and militarisation of the economy, taken to safeguard the interests of the State, after June 1918, destroyed the last vestiges of independence the trade union movement had *vis-à-vis* the State. Under War Communism the interests of the State and revolution, seen through Bolshevik eyes, prevailed and the libertarian labour representatives of the early months turned almost overnight into disciplinarians.

The soviets

The Bolsheviks were ill-prepared for local government. Lenin set down some ideas in *State and Revolution* which he wrote in hiding in Finland in August 1917. He sketched out three stages for events to take: firstly the revolution, then the dictatorship of the proletariat, then communism. The State was to exist until communism had been reached and it would be highly organised.

The multiplicity of practical problems facing the Bolsheviks after the October Revolution gradually fell within the competence of the only institution which was popularly accepted, the soviets. 'Monasteries, old people's homes, tenants, passengers on long train journeys, children in primary as well as in secondary schools, all created soviets.'[16] It was all the rage in 1917. There were something like 1,200 uezd and raion soviets by the end of 1917. Decision-making thus passed from the party to the soviets at the end of 1917 and the beginning of 1918. The best party cadres went to work in the soviets since that was where power lay. The party had practically no cells in the countryside but it could work through the soviets. The soviets also had control of financial affairs. They served primarily, especially in the countryside, local interests to the detriment of the national interest. The soviets were headed by Yakov Sverdlov who was also a key party official and this confused the situation. Again, as with the other mass organisations, it was the conditions of War Communism which brought out into the open the clash of interests between local soviets and the centre.

The very success of the soviets helped to undermine them. There were so many of them that they could hardly resist the Bolshevik desire to amalgamate some of them. The communists actively sought to fuse workers' and soldiers' soviets (Moscow was a case in point – the two were not fused until the fighting was over) and wherever possible transformed the soviet into a workers', soldiers' and peasants' soviet.

This made it easier to concentrate Bolshevik activists and to increase their impact. Opponents could be harassed, shouted down, elections falsified or held again until the communists were satisfied with the mix. Not all soviets were dominated by workers and peasants. Some areas, for example in Petrograd, which were middle class produced a raion soviet with a middle-class majority. Some of these representatives then went as delegates to inter-raion conferences but were swamped there by worker and soldier delegates.

The Executive Committee of the Petrograd Soviet quickly escaped from the control of the general assembly of the Soviet. The original provisional committee had been made up of delegates representing more than a dozen parties and organisations. This had been proposed by A. G. Shlyapnikov, later Commissar for Labour, as a means of strengthening the Bolshevik position since they were very thinly represented in the group which set up the Soviet. It became the prerogative of each party to decide whom it wanted on the committee. Co-founders of the Soviet such as A. G. Shlyapnikov, P. A. Zalutsky and V. M. Molotov had later to make way for the delegates of their party, L. B. Kamenev and J. V. Stalin. The same practice was followed in the executive committees of the raion soviets. This placed the Bolsheviks in a position where they were often able to mediate between the various factions. The Mensheviks, SRs and anarchists fought one another to the eventual benefit of the Bolsheviks. Factory committees fought trade unions and trade unions fought soviets, the end result being again the same. The soviets quickly became bureaucratised. They employed their own staff and the executive committees had numerous commissions subject to them. All the organs of revolutionary democracy went the same way and the Bolsheviks skilfully aided the process of bureaucratisation and its inevitable concomitant, centralisation.

After the October Revolution the Mensheviks and right SRs, throughout Russia, when confronted with a blatant use of force or illegal behaviour on the part of the Bolsheviks very often walked out. The Bolsheviks then grasped the opportunity of replacing the moderate socialists with their own supporters. What was the result? 'Thanks to this the communists and the left SR sympathisers soon had a majority of votes in almost all soviets and executives. Within a few months the moderate socialists realised their mistake but by then it was too late to undo it.'[17]

Bolshevik tactics in the soviets accorded with Lenin's view that the soviets should be subject to central direction. The first Soviet constitution of June 1918, it only applied to the Russian Federation, placed power at the centre in the All-Russian Congress of Soviets and the CEC and thus attempted to restrict the competence of the local soviet. The Communist Party was not even mentioned. However, even if a soviet had a Bolshevik majority it did not automatically follow that Moscow was heeded. This changed under War Communism when harsh centralisation carried the day.

THE CONSTITUENT ASSEMBLY

Sovnarkom was a provisional government, provisional until the convocation of the Constituent Assembly. Pressure was exerted from all sides to force Lenin to concede a coalition government of the main socialist parties. He agreed to enter into negotiations but did not negotiate seriously. However, some members of his own CC did want the talks to achieve tangible results. On 16 November Lenin issued an ultimatum but Kamenev, Zinoviev, Rykov, Milyutin and Nogin resigned from the CC the following day; Rykov, Milyutin and Nogin quitting the government as well. This caused Lenin to change course and on 19 November serious negotiations got under way with the left SRs on the terms for their participation in a future coalition government.

Elections to the Constituent Assembly, decreed by the outgoing Provisional Government, went ahead, beginning on 25 November. Given that about four in five of the population lived on the land the result of the election was an almost foregone conclusion. The SR party gained 370 seats with the Bolsheviks trailing with 175. Even though the 40 left SRs supported them, the governing party was clearly in a minority. However, the Assembly was not due to convene until 18 January 1918 which afforded the Bolsheviks time to redress the balance.

The IInd Congress of Soviets of Peasants' Deputies convened from 9 to 24 December 1917 and it was of crucial importance. The SR party, of course, dominated the Congress' but it no longer spoke with one voice. The party had split in midsummer with the left SRs supporting the Bolsheviks. The Ist Congress of the left SRs was actually coming to an end when the Congress of Peasants' Deputies began its deliberations. Lenin and Trotsky addressed the Peasant Congress and in the end the left SRs triumphed, dominating the new executive committee. They were then invited to nominate 108 members to the CEC thus doubling its existing membership; 100 members were added from the army and navy and 50 from the trade unions. Total membership thus increased to 366. The CEC also changed its name. It became the All-Russian Central Executive Committee of the Soviet of Workers', Soldiers' and Peasants' Deputies.

Many socialists had been appalled by the composition of the first Sovnarkom government. They had welcomed the revolution and had expected a coalition socialist government. True, Lenin had invited the left SRs to join him but on his terms. Not surprisingly, they declined. The mounting political and economic tension forced Lenin's hand,

and he gave way to those Bolsheviks who also favoured a coalition government. However, the left SRs came into the government as junior partners but did not accept all of Lenin's programme. For instance, they favoured revolutionary war and adamantly opposed a peace treaty on German terms. Hence when Lenin had his way and the Brest-Litovsk peace treaty officially ended hostilities, these continued between the Bolsheviks and left SRs. It was the parting of the ways, and the left SRs were soon out of the coalition.

The left SRs received three commissariats: Agriculture, Justice, and Posts and Telegraph as well as some minor government posts. The first and only coalition government the Soviet Union has ever known was almost complete on 10 December 1917 when Vikzhel's nominee became Commissar of Transport. Agreement was reached with the left SRs on 22 December and the full government met for the first time on 25 December 1917.

The coalition with the left SRs was an astute move and gave the impression that the Bolsheviks were sharing State power with other socialists. The great SR party had split and this added weight to Lenin's argument that the party for whom so many people had voted was 'a party which no longer existed'. The Kadet party was proscribed on 11 December 1917 and this eliminated some more deputies from the Constituent Assembly. Lenin's main thrust against the Assembly, however, was that it had been overtaken by events. Soviet democracy, revolutionary democracy, was superior and 'any renunciation of the sovereign power of the soviets of the Soviet republic won by the people in favour of bourgeois parliamentar[ian]ism and the Constituent Assembly would now be a step backwards and would cause a collapse of the entire October Workers' and Peasants' Revolution'.[18] This did not convince everyone but those who demonstrated in favour of the Constituent Assembly when it was dissolved on 19 January 1918 were fired upon. Nevertheless the Constituent Assembly was a powerful symbol and would serve as the focus of anti-Bolshevik opposition during the Civil War.

THE BREST-LITOVSK TREATY

The decree on peace, the first act of the IInd Congress of Soviets, introduced something new into international relations. It called for peace without annexations and indemnities and was aimed not only at the belligerent governments but also at the people they governed. Lenin did not expect much of a response from the capitals of Europe but the intention was to go over the heads of the administration and appeal directly to the people to resolve the question of war and peace. The implementation of the decree would signal the end of multi-national empires and colonial possessions. A new international order was envisaged sweeping away traditional international society communicating at the level of government and putting in its place the people as the main actors. National self-determination promised to be a powerful rallying cry.

The Bolshevik CC was hopelessly split on the wisdom of concluding a unilateral peace with Imperial Germany. Three trends emerged, each represented by a key figure: Lenin, Bukharin and Trotsky.

During the immediate aftermath of the Revolution the Bolsheviks needed time to institutionalise their hold on power. The struggle with internal enemies, to Lenin, should take precedence over the struggle with the foreign enemy, the Germans. Hence he wanted peace with Imperial Germany from the beginning. The consolidation of the gains of the October Revolution should be given the highest priority in the short term since in the long term the Revolution would lead to the defeat of Imperial Germany. If the gains of the October Revolution were thrown carelessly away then the world socialist revolution would suffer too. Peace with Berlin was worth any sacrifice even if this meant signing away all occupied territory. These views were presented in his 'Theses on the Question of the Immediate Conclusion of a Separate and Annexationist Peace' which he drew up in January 1918.[19] Lenin also underlined the fact that the Soviet State had no army worthy of the name and that the country was war weary. It needed a breathing space to regain its strength.

The 'left' communists, led by Bukharin and supported by the left SRs, viewed matters differently. They regarded a treaty, an acknowledgement of defeat by the young Soviet republic, as unthinkable. For them there was only one course open for revolutionary democracy – a revolutionary war to further socialist revolution everywhere. Bukharin accepted that there was no army available but he wanted to appeal to the revolutionary consciousness of the Russian people. They would become a partisan army harassing and eventually defeating the German invaders. A peace treaty with Berlin would only strengthen German imperialism. It would also be a heavy blow to the working class movement.

Trotsky, ever creative, hit on a policy which would span the divide: neither war nor peace! This view was based on a debatable premise: that the German army after peace negotiations had begun on 22 December 1917 was in no shape to launch an offensive on the Eastern Front. He was wrong. On his way back from Brest-Litovsk where he had let off his verbal fireworks, Trotsky learned that the German army was on the march. By 18 February 1918 it was pushing forward with no resistance in sight. The Bolshevik CC had to make up its mind: fight or capitulate. Lenin wanted peace at any price and the war party headed by Bukharin, Radek and Dzerzhinsky wanted action. Trotsky held the balance from a middle position but finally came down on Lenin's side. On 23 February, with Trotsky abstaining, the CC accepted the new peace conditions which were more severe than those the Germans had previously demanded. The treaty was signed on 3 March. Trotsky could not face the ignominy of signing such a humiliating document and sent Sokolnikov instead. In any case he, Trotsky, had bigger fish to fry; he became Commissar of War and moved with the rest of the government to Moscow on 12 March. Sovnarkom took up residence in the Kremlin, a natural fortress. This symbolised Bolshevik determination to defend the Soviet republic, their Soviet republic, to the last drop of blood.

Brest-Litovsk was a terrible blow to the young Soviet State. It had to recognise that Georgia, Finland and the Ukraine were independent but in the German zone of influence. Poland, Lithuania, Latvia and Estonia fell under more direct German control. The Bolsheviks quit the Åland Islands, off Finland; the Turks occupied Kars, Ardahan and Batumi; the Romanians were soon to take Bessarabia. All this came to 32 per cent of the arable land, 26 per cent of the railways, 33 per cent of the factories, 75 per cent of the iron and coal mines and 62 million citizens of the old Russian Empire. There was also a huge indemnity, some of it in gold, to pay. The Bolsheviks, it is true, had exercised little control over the territory they had ceded. The Russian heartland, where they were strongest, was hardly touched. The communists could soothe their hurt pride with the hope that, come the socialist revolution in Germany, the treaty would be torn up.

The treaty broke the tenuous links which kept the Bolsheviks and left SRs together. Now the Bolsheviks were on their own and immediately changed their name to the All-Russian Communist Party (Bolsheviks). However, as before, it was a party riven with dissent; the CC only agreed on one thing, the right to rule. The left shared the urge for a revolutionary war with the left SRs and the latter began to show their impatience by quitting the government (19 March 1918) and resorting to armed violence.

The assassination of the German ambassador, von Mirbach, in Moscow on 6 July 1918 by the left SR and member of the political police, the Cheka, Blyumkin, was a flashpoint in Bolshevik – left SR relations. The aim was to provoke a fresh war between Soviet Russia and Germany. In addition the left SRs also arrested Feliks Dzerzhinsky, head of the Cheka, but only hurt his pride. The Cheka, which had been founded on 20 December 1917 to fight counter-revolution and sabotage contained many left SRs as well as Bolsheviks. It thus turned out to be very unreliable and had it not been for the tried and trusted Latvian riflemen the communists would have been perilously short of reliable troops. However the left SRs had no concerted plan and their revolt fizzled out in a few hours. Communist retribution was swift. Left SR members found themselves being removed wholesale from their elected offices, thus virtually putting an end to their party. In late July a revolt broke out in Yaroslavl and other uprisings followed across the country.

On 30 August 1918 Fanya Kaplan fired three times point blank at Lenin. She hit him twice but the bullets only accomplished their mortal mission years later. On the same day Leonid Kanegiesser, a young Jewish student, assassinated the chief of the Petrograd Cheka, Uritsky. The Kronstadt sailors replied by shooting about 500 bourgeois hostages. It was an eye for an eye and a tooth for a tooth. Lenin, who not so long before had asked almost despairingly: 'Is it possible to find among us a Fouquier-Tinville to tame our wild counter-revolutionaries?' found him in 'Iron' Feliks Dzerzhinsky, the knight who quickly transformed the Cheka into the sword and shield of the revolution. Red Terror, which dated from the peasant uprising on the Volga in June 1918, answered White Terror.

The Cheka, freed from all legal constraints, became a fearful organ of Bolshevik power. Each provincial section of the Cheka developed its own favourite methods of torture. In Kharkov Chekists scalped their prisoners and took the skin, like 'gloves', off their hands. In Voronezh they placed the naked prisoner in a barrel punctured with nails and then set it in motion. They burnt a five-pointed star into the forehead and placed a crown of barbed wire around the neck of priests. In Tsaritsyn and Kamyshin they severed bones with a saw. In Poltava they impaled eighteen monks and burnt at the stake peasants who had rebelled. In Ekaterinoslav they crucified priests and stoned them. In Odessa they boiled officers and ripped them in half. In Kiev they placed them in a coffin with a decomposing corpse, buried them alive and then after half a hour dug them out.[20]

SOVNARKOM AND THE CEC

Sovnarkom spoke in the name of the Soviet victory and was responsible to the CEC. All the decrees having 'general political significance' were to be submitted for approval to the CEC which possessed the authority to request Sovnarkom representatives to report to it and to remove and re-elect any of its members. This was not very precise and the Bolsheviks argued from the very beginning that the need to defend the revolution took precedence over all formal arrangements. The CEC met five times during the first ten days of its existence and then convened less and less frequently. Sovnarkom, in contrast, met 'almost daily and sometimes twice a day'. Gradually more and more legislation bypassed the CEC. One estimate is that of the 480 decrees promulgated during the first year of Soviet power only 68 had been forwarded to the CEC.[21]

The key role in this process was played by Yakov Sverdlov. He had been proposed for the post of chairman of the CEC as a result of Lenin's dissatisfaction with the way Lev Kamenev had handled the CEC during the contretemps with Vikzhel. Reluctant to accept the top Soviet job, which meant in effect becoming President of Soviet Russia, since he was engaged full time in the secretariat of the CC, Sverdlov was eventually prevailed upon by Lenin with whom he had worked very closely ever since the July Days and became chairman on 21 November 1917. His nomination was accepted by the presidium of the CEC which consisted entirely of Bolsheviks but there was considerable opposition within the full CEC. He was confirmed only by a margin of five votes.

Sverdlov skilfully used his position as chairman to strengthen his party's position. One way of doing this was to increase the power of the presidium and to introduce rules which restricted debate in the full CEC. He made the rules and he made them with great dexterity. With the advent of more left SRs the presidium was enlarged but the Bolsheviks were still in the majority. In the course of 1918 the presidium began more and more to speak in the name of the CEC. A decisive factor in getting the CEC to accept the Brest-Litovsk treaty was Sverdlov's unswerving support for Lenin's position. He refused Bolshevik members a free vote and reminded them of their duty to observe 'discipline and unity'.[22] This had the required effect; even opponents of the treaty, such as A. V. Lunacharsky, voted in favour. Even so the CEC accepted the peace conditions by only 112 votes to 84 with 24 abstentions on 24 February.

Sverdlov handled the IVth (March 1918, which ratified the treaty by 784 votes to 261) and the Vth Congress of Soviets (July 1918) with his usual skill. His use of the rulebook was blatantly one-sided and only a vote of no confidence could have shaken the Bolshevik position. As long as the Bolshevik faction held together this was unlikely. The Vth Congress passed the first Soviet Constitution, that of the Russian Soviet Federated Socialist Republic (RSFSR). The Constitution is notable for the fact that it omitted all mention of the most important institution, the Communist Party. The Constitution was also designed to appeal to those beyond the frontiers of Soviet Russia.

The turbulent months after the peace treaty saw the presidium increase its influence. Sverdlov increasingly dictated to the CEC and kept critics at bay by not giving them the floor. In June 1918, as a result of being accused of counter-revolutionary activities, Mensheviks and most SRs were removed from the CEC and the provincial soviet apparatus. The CEC elected at the Vth Congress reflected this turn of events; it was overwhelmingly communist. This CEC only met nine times and there was virtually no discussion even when it did meet. Hence by July 1918 the Bolsheviks were in complete control of the committee which headed the soviets and which was theoretically responsible to them. The party had triumphed as a result of Sverdlov's flexible use of electoral procedures and standing orders. He ensured that no issue central to Bolshevik policy was ever debated freely under his chairmanship.

THE CIVIL WAR

The communists were saved by something which they had previously despised and had done their utmost to discredit: the army. Founded on 23 February 1918 the Workers' and Peasants' Red Army was the creation of Trotsky. For about a year he had more or less a free hand and in that time he fashioned a fighting force. He had many formidable obstacles to overcome. There was the natural reluctance of workers and peasants to rejoin and anyway where were the officers to come from? In Trotsky's eyes there could only be one source, the old army. Most of his colleagues were outraged by this suggestion. But the situation was desperate and as Lashevich, head of the military section of the party, put it: 'The party could harness the Tsarist officers, squeeze them like lemons and then throw them away.'[23] The Commissar of War had his way and something like 50,000 officers were recruited to fight for the Reds. How was he to ensure that they remained loyal to the communist cause? Place a political commissar alongside every military officer and make all commands invalid unless signed by both. Then the officer's family could be held hostage as an earnest of his good intent. Along with the Bolshevik *volte-face* on military affairs went a *volte-face* on the command structure. They swept away the concept of elected commanders and an army run by soldiers' committees and reverted to orthodox command procedures. The Red Army was made up of conscripts and the most reliable units were normally of proletarian origin. They formed the core with peasant conscripts on the flanks. The latter often deserted *en masse*. Nevertheless the communists always had a trump card to play in the countryside; support us and keep your land, support the Whites and you bring back the landlord.

The Civil War consisted of a series of haphazard engagements on various fronts with little co-ordination among the various White commanders. The Reds had the great advantage of controlling the Russian heartland. Their lines of communications were shorter and their resolution greater. Defeat, always a possibility until 1920, spelled death for most of them, or so they believed. The Whites were scattered around the periphery; there was the Southern Front, the Eastern Front, the South Eastern Front and the Northern Front. The Red Army had a central command structure, the Whites did not. It is true that Admiral Kolchak became Supreme Ruler of Russia in November 1918 but only on paper. The Whites enjoyed considerable advantages: they attracted large numbers of officers and men from the old army; they were particularly strong in the Cossack areas; they controlled the food surplus zones of the country except for the Ukraine; they received considerable war *matériel*, advice and diplomatic support from the Interventionist powers and in the beginning the SRs were favourably disposed to them. However, the Reds turned the international support of the Whites against the latter. They labelled the Whites traitors, agents of the landlords, agents of international reaction, supporters of Tsarist autocracy and so on. The Whites were a hodge-podge of forces; SRs, Kadets and all those on the political right. They could never agree on a political and social programme. They possessed no one with the political authority of a Lenin or the acumen or ability of a Trotsky.

The Bolsheviks did not seek a civil war: they were forced to react to the attacks of the Whites who were based in areas which had previously experienced little or no communist control.

The Civil War can be divided into three chronological phases: February to November 1918; November 1918 to December 1919; and January to November 1920.

During the first phase the Eastern and South Eastern Fronts dominated events. The Czech Legion consisting of ex-prisoners-of-war and not the Whites set the ball rolling. In May 1918, on the Trans-Siberian railway, homeward bound and armed, their train was stopped. The Allies had decided to reroute them via the Arctic but had not consulted the Czechs. They suspected that the Bolsheviks intended to disarm them. Their immediate reaction was to seize many towns along the railway, from Samara to Irkutsk. They also took Ekaterinburg where the Tsar and his family were being held by the local Bolsheviks. However before they fled the Reds murdered their royal prisoners.

The Reds abandoned Kazan in August 1918 and panic set in. If the Whites could cross the Volga the road to Moscow was open. At this point Trotsky stepped in or rather he rode in on his special armed train which was to be his headquarters for the next two and a half years. By eloquence and by personal example he turned the tide. His methods were ruthless: merciless was a favourite word of his during these years. Whenever the situation on a particular front became critical Trotsky entrained for that front and threw himself into the struggle.

After the German collapse in the West the Bolsheviks could devote all their resources to the struggle with the Whites. The Allied Powers, such as Great Britain, who had landed troops, in August 1918, at Archangel and Murmansk to safeguard supplies from German attack, decided to intervene. There were British, American, Serbian and Italian troops in the north, Americans, British, Japanese and Czechs in Siberia, British troops again in the Caucasus and French troops in the Crimea – to name only the leading powers which threw in their lot with the Whites. It should be underlined, however, that these troops hardly ever engaged the Reds. Indeed this was one of their major weaknesses. If they were there to overthrow the Bolsheviks why did they not go over to the offensive? If they were there to watch the Reds win, why bother to come in the first place? The British troops, war weary and not front-line men anyway, wanted to leave almost as soon as they arrived. The ice stopped them. The following ditty summed it all up.

Note that the British Tommies had a low opinion of the local troops in an area which was officially ruled by the Whites.[24]

> We've been out here sometime in this cold Russian clime
> Now we're all looking forward to home.
> We are all feeling good, with the heartgiving food
> That the War Office sent us from home.
>
> We've had tinned crabs for breakfast and dinner as well
> For a change we've had biscuits for tea.
> Some wonder we boys are all dancing with joy
> Now we're taking a trip o'er the sea.
>
> CHORUS
>> So all the boys all smiling for they're going to be relieved
>> When the order comes from Blighty[a] with loud cheers will be received.
>> They'll gather all their rubles that they've skolkered[b] on the sly
>> Then they'll all shout Dosvidaniya which in Russia means Good Bye.
>
> Since the Armistice Day we've been fighting away
> Scrapping Bolos[c] in this Arctic Zone,
> Whilst in Blighty the bells have been ringing for peace
> We've been having a war on our own;
> We have faced all the hardships, whilst Russians looked on
> Too lazy to fight for themselves,
> So we think you'll agree, that it's high time that we
> Chucked it up and looked after ourselves.

(a) England   (b) Corruption of the Russian word *skolko*: how much?   (c) Bolsheviks

The turning-point of the Civil War came in the autumn of 1919. White forces on the Southern Front, under General Denikin, moved relentlessly forward during late summer and by 14 October his cavalry was at Orel, 300 kilometres south west of Moscow. Kolchak was advancing on the Eastern Front and Yudenich's second attack reached the suburbs of Petrograd on 22 October. It was at this decisive moment that Trotsky showed his mettle. He rushed to Petrograd to take personal command. There he found Zinoviev, party leader in the city, unprepared, to put it mildly. Trotsky is scathing in his contempt for his bitter political rival: 'Sverdlov said to me: "Zinoviev is panic personified". In quiet times when, as Lenin said, there was nothing to be afriad of, Zinoviev very easily climbed into seventh heaven. But when things were going badly Zinoviev usually lay down on a sofa – not metaphorically but literally – and sighed. Since 1917 I have convinced myself that Zinoviev does not know any intermediate moods. It is either seventh heaven or the sofa. This time I found him on the sofa.'[25]

A week later the Reds had regained the initiative. With the successful counterattack against Denikin and Kolchak forced to retreat to Irkutsk, the Civil War was all but over. Fighting dragged on but Kolchak's execution on 7 February 1920 and Denikin's retreat to the Crimea in March, where he handed over to Wrangel, almost signalled the end. The intermittent fighting between Poles and Russians flared up again in May 1920 when the Poles launched an offensive and captured Kiev. Pilsudski, the Polish leader, reasoned that only a Union of Border States, stretching from the Baltic to the Black Sea and led by Poland, could make the latter politically and economically viable. The Reds were caused a little inconvenience by Wrangel seizing the opportunity to drive north but the Reds soon regrouped. The key question for them was whether they should cross the Polish frontier when they reached it and carry the revolution to the heart of central Europe, Germany. Trotsky was against going on but Lenin was sure that the Polish workers would welcome the Russians as liberators. They did not; the 'miracle of the Vistula' saw the defeat of the Red Army and independence for Poland for two decades. At the resultant peace conference, at Riga in March 1921, the communists offered the Poles more territory than they were willing to accept. The Russians believed that the more non-Poles the young republic embraced, the less stable it would be.

The Bolshevik regime was fashioned by the exigencies of Civil War. Half measures are of little value in such times of crisis and some men accept that the end justifies the means. One of these men was Stalin. Others such as Zinoviev and Kamenev were found wanting. In more peaceful times Lenin would not have needed Stalin so much but in the desperate days of 1918–20 he came to rely on him and to regard him as indispensable. To Lenin, Stalin was a true Bolshevik, ruthless to the core. Given the important task of securing grain in the south for the north which was a food deficit zone, Stalin wrote to Lenin on 7 July 1918: 'I am driving and bullying all those who need it; you can rest assured that we shall spare nobody, ourselves or others, and the grain will be obtained.'[26] It was. Grain, *en route* to the starving city of Baku, was commandeered by Stalin's men. They justified the seizure by saying: 'If we do not obtain grain and go back to Stalin empty-handed, we shall be shot.' The others pleaded for the grain and took the matter to Stalin personally. Stalin was adamant: 'What nonsense you are talking. If we lose Baku, it is nothing. We shall take it again within a few months or a year at the most. If we lose Moscow, we lose everything. Then the revolution is over.' The grain went to Moscow.

Stalin was not content with just finding grain, he involved himself in military preparations as well. He became the chief commissar on the Southern Front in late summer 1918 and this brought him into conflict with the Commissar of War, Trotsky. Their festering hostility began on the plains before Tsaritsyn and ended in Trotsky's study in Mexico. The victor was always Stalin; he engaged in strategic retreats from time to time but the end result was always the same. The main trouble was the Tenth Army. It was being nurtured by Stalin, with Voroshilov as his aide. Stalin's interference in the defence of Tsaritsyn infuriated Trotsky: 'I insist categorically on Stalin's recall', he telegraphed Lenin on 4 October 1918. 'Things are going badly on the Tsaritsyn Front despite a superabundance of forces .... Tsaritsyn must either obey or get out of the way.'[27] The next day Trotsky wrote: 'The activities of Stalin are wrecking my plans.' Lenin recalled Stalin. But back in Moscow Stalin could work on Lenin and it paid off: 'Stalin is anxious to work on the Southern Front .... As for me, I think it is necessary to make every effort to work in conjunction with Stalin.' Thus Lenin to Trotsky.

Stalin stalked and slighted the Commissar of War at every turn. It was left to Lenin to forward some important dispatches to Trotsky. Stalin had not sent the Commissar of War a copy! Lenin held the ring and tried to solve the problem by sending the following note to Trotsky: 'Address all military communications to Trotsky as well, otherwise there may be a dangerous gap.' Trotsky was then told to forward the note to Stalin over Lenin's signature.

WAR COMMUNISM

The communists won the war to secure political control: they won the Civil War but they lost the economic war. More than anything else it was the lack of Bolshevik success in the economic sphere, under the conditions of civil war, which shaped and fashioned the Soviet regime. Shortages, cold, hunger and disease racked the communist body politic in the terrible years 1918–20. The only thing that kept them warm was their ideological fervour. They were convinced that there would be light at the end of the dark tunnel of deprivation and sacrifice.

War Communism, a retrospective appellation, refers to the period from June 1918, which saw large-scale nationalisation of industry, to March 1921 when the New Economic Policy, (NEP), saw the light of day. During this period the market economy was smashed and the illegal black market made its appearance and saved many urban dwellers from starvation. Money became valueless, whether this was by design or by accident has still not been resolved, and barter again appeared on a large scale. The whole of the Russian economy can be compared, during these years, to a farm where the father directs his sons' labour and then decides what each shall get according to his need. No money is necessary and everything is shared. The Russian Post Office did not charge for its services, the trams in Petrograd when they were running were free. Each factory produced its goods, passed them on to the next factory and so on until the final product appeared.

What were the Bolsheviks trying to achieve by introducing War Communism? They were attempting to secure central control of economic processes in order to impose their priorities. They accorded the highest preference in resource allocation to defence institutions; the nationalisation and militarisation of almost all enterprises; the forcible requisition of food from the peasants to feed themselves and their supporters; the central allocation of labour; the raising of labour discipline through a system of rewards, propaganda and force and the rationing of producer and consumer goods. Resources were channelled into bottlenecks in the military economy irrespective of cost.

The apostles of the left, communists such as Bukharin and Preobrazhensky, welcomed War Communism as a leap into social- ism. The chaos was inevitable, the dying capitalist mode of pro- duction had to give way to the nascent socialist one.

The large-scale nationalisation of June 1918, partly in response to the fear that vital industrial plants could fall under German control if left in private hands, saw all important enterprises placed under the control of VSNKh. Although Lenin would have preferred a mixed economy he finally accepted what most workers wanted, a socialist economy. This did not mean that the communist leader thought that workers should run the factories and the trade unions the economy. As before he held to the view that the party was the supreme arbiter of the nation's destiny. It alone could overcome sectional interests and speak for the whole working class.

The most important good was food and the Bolsheviks did not control its production. The land decree confirmed the peasants' right to the land they had seized. The average increase *per capita* came to between 0.1 and 1 hectare. But it did end payments to the landlord and mortgage arrears. Thus the 'big grab' did not solve the problem of land shortage. The socialisation of the land, on 9 February 1918, abolished all private ownership and made it the property of the whole nation. It also made it incumbent on local soviets to develop collective farms at the expense of individual homesteads, arguing that the former were more profitable because of their more efficient use of labour and materials, 'with a view of passing on to a socialist economy'. This had very little impact at the time and it was only in 1929 that the peasants felt its full impact. According to data from thirty two *gubernii* in 1919, 4.6 per cent of the land fund was in state farms and only 1.7 per cent in kolkhozes or collective farms. A decree in February 1919 even spoke of a transition to collective farming but it was a mirage, as the above data show. In his April Theses Lenin had looked forward to Soviets of Poor Peasants in the countryside. They would wage war on the other peasants and do the work of the communists with whom they had a natural community of interest.

32

This again was far from reality and in many places the richer peasants dominated the Soviets of Peasants' Deputies. If soviets of the poor could not be set up, committees of the poor (*Kombedy*) could be and were set up on 11 June 1918. Their task – about 122,000 came into existence – was to uncover surpluses and help the Bolsheviks feed the towns. They failed. The peasants were more interested in helping themselves than the centre. If the peasant would not work with the Bolsheviks then coercion would have to be used, so reasoned the leaders. Workers' detachments were dispatched to the countryside and they were very successful during War Communism. The main reason was that they had machine-guns. However the communists paid a heavy price for their success. War Communism with its compulsory requisitions, called *prodrazverstka*, cast a long shadow over relations with the rural sector. The peasants had always believed that the fruits of their labour belonged to them: the ownership of land was immaterial. The honeymoon with the peasants was over, it had not lasted even one harvest. The peasant responded in the only way he knew: he reduced production, subdivided his farm among his sons and attempted to make everything himself. In 1919 the cultivated area was 16.5 per cent less than in 1917; in 1921 it was 40 per cent less. The towns emptied. Could the Bolsheviks have avoided their war against the peasants? The peasant responded to the market, but given inflation and the dearth of industrial and consumer goods there was little incentive to sell. The Bolsheviks needed to feed the towns and the Red Army. Inflation worked in their favour since it wiped out bourgeois wealth held in notes. They could have attempted to impose a minimal grain tax, arguing that it was to feed the towns and the army and to keep the landlord away. They never seriously discussed this option. In the euphoria of victory the proletarian interest took precedence over peasant interest. There were 2.6 million workers in 1917 but only 1.2 million in 1920. The black market expanded. In 1918–19, 60 per cent of city bread passed through illegal channels. In provincial cities only 29 per cent of all food in April 1920 came from the official system.[28] Yet the government continued to inveigh against speculators. The failure to feed the cities also affected industrial discipline. During the first half of 1920 there were strikes in 77 per cent of large and medium-sized factories, mostly over the lack of food. Conditions in the factories also deteriorated. The working day, where it was possible to work, lengthened to ten or eleven hours. In January 1919 the mobilisation of workers made the labour situation so tight that those left behind were not permitted to change their jobs. In May 1920 the penalties for absenteeism became very harsh. The Bolsheviks could no longer rely on the working class and had to discipline it as they were disciplining the peasants. The soviets in the countryside increasingly refused to acknowledge the authority of the centre and often barred the Red Army from their villages, fearing that all their food and animals would be taken. In many cities Mensheviks and SRs were voted on to the soviets by an exasperated populace and places such as Kazan and Kaluga declared themselves autonomous. One small group of men prospered under War Communism: the bagmen. They carried the much desired food in sacks on their backs and made their way illegally into the towns to ask incredible prices for their life-giving products. Urban impoverishment was almost total.

Something like eight million people perished during the years 1918-20, seven and a half million due to hunger and disease. The working class was decimated, the cities lost many of their inhabitants and the intelligentsia was either dead or had emigrated. Culturally Russia was at a very low ebb.

Lenin and among others Bukharin drew lessons from the conflict and chaos. The Bolshevik leader was still for abolishing money when the programme of the Communist Party was being drawn up in 1919 but by early 1921 he had changed his mind. He also became much more aware of the complexities of the agrarian problem. In his last years he was convinced that coercion could not succeed and argued in favour of co-operation based on genuine peasant conviction. He became much more humanitarian at the moment when the reins of political leadership were slipping from his grasp. Bukharin was also caught by the same mood and from being an apostle of the left swung right over and became a devoted Leninist.

THE PARTY AND THE STATE

'The party is the mind, honour and conscience of our epoch.' In saying this Lenin implied that the party encompassed all that was good and progressive in mankind. This, to him, meant the working class. Would membership of the party be restricted solely to those of proletarian origin? Plainly not, since this would have eliminated practically all Bolshevik leaders in 1917. Just what the mix should be has always been a problem. When a revolutionary party sloughs off its clandestine garb and becomes a ruling party, a state party, it must of necessity include in its ranks administrators, specialists, managers and so on, in short those people against whom the revolution was made in the first place.

Bolshevik party membership, in February 1917, amounted to 23,600.[29] It had climbed to 200,000 by August 1917 but by March 1919 it was still only 350,000. The main reasons for this were the restrictions placed on recruitment in an attempt to keep the party free of 'careerist elements'. Nevertheless at the VIIIth Party Congress, in March 1919, complaints were voiced that local communists were fusing with top soviet officials to form a new privileged stratum, using their party membership to secure for themselves, their friends and their relatives extra rations, preference in housing and job promotion.[30] The Congress decided to throw the door open to workers but at the same time to re-register everyone. This was aimed particularly at those who had joined since the October Revolution. The vicissitudes of the Civil War with its loss of life, plus the cleansing of the party, reduced party ranks from 350,000 in March 1919 to about 150,000 in August 1919. Lenin was pleased that the 'cowards and good-for-nothings had run away from the party'. This was the nadir; by March 1920, the IXth Congress, membership had climbed to 611,978 and at the Xth Congress, in March 1921, it was 732,521. How did this influx affect the social composition of the party? Not surprisingly it reduced the proportion of workers. Whereas in 1917, 60.2 per cent of party members were of proletarian origin, this figure had dropped to 41 per cent in 1921. The proportion of white-collar workers was almost constant over the same period; it was the influx of peasants which forced the percentage of workers down. Peasants accounted for 7.5 per cent of membership in 1917 but 28.2 per cent in 1921.[31] Many workers when they entered the party were immediately transferred to work in the bureaucracy, thus considerably reducing the number of party workers still actually at the factory bench.

Control of the Communist Party began to slip away from Lenin in late 1922. For the previous two decades he had dominated the party and had always jealously guarded his position. He had sought successfully to restrict decision-making to himself and a few close colleagues. By 1919 such a system was no longer viable. One reason why the old framework survived until early 1919 was that Yakov Sverdlov was a man after Vladimir Ilich's heart – a comrade who believed in the need for a centralised party with each local committee bound by the decisions of a higher one and the whole subordinated to the CC. Sverdlov acted as secretary of the CC after November 1917. He played an important role as chairman of the VIIth Party Congress, skilfully suppressing criticism of the CC. Such was his ability to anticipate problems that when he was instructed by Lenin to act he was often able to tell him that the matter had already been dealt with. Sverdlov's authority to act independently of his leader testifies to the closeness of their organisational views. Indeed Sverdlov, head of the Soviets, and Lenin, head of Sovnarkom, formed the core of the central Soviet government. Eventually Sverdlov's overwork led to his premature death on 16 March 1919. His passing was a shattering personal blow to Lenin who said that no single person could ever replace him.

The organisational question became critical in the spring of 1919. A Political Bureau (Politburo) was set up at the VIIIth Congress, in March 1919, although it had been functioning unofficially since December 1918. The Politburo was only to deal with urgent matters and to give a full account of its activities to the CC. From 1919 to

1921 it consisted of Lenin, Kamenev, Trotsky, Stalin and Krestinsky. In 1921 Zinoviev took over from Krestinsky and in 1922 Rykov and Tomsky joined. The Politburo had become necessary due to the ever increasing size of the CC.

An Organisational Bureau (Orgburo) had been set up on 19 January 1919 but it was junior to the Politburo. Lenin declared that the general principle was that 'the Orgburo allocates forces, while the Politburo decides policy'.[32]

The Secretariat of the CC was also expanded. Until his death Sverdlov had been the only secretary. He was succeeded by the mild-mannered Krestinsky but at the IXth Congress in March – April 1920 Preobrazhensky and Serebryakov were added. The Secretariat also became independent of the Orgburo, of which it had previously been a part, at the IXth Congress. Each of the secretaries was responsible for a group of CC departments and in 1921 it was stated that 'in the absence of an objection by the members of the Orgburo ... the Secretariat's decision is to be regarded as a decision of the Orgburo'.[33]

The outcome of these administrative changes was that the creatures of the CC usurped the power of the CC and when, in April 1922, Stalin became not a secretary but Secretary General of the party, he was the only person who was a member of the CC and its three offshoots. He took to organisational work very quickly but he understood organisation primarily as the placement of personnel. Just find the right person; one who was a dedicated, able, unshakeable supporter of the Bolshevik regime and above all loyal to the Secretary General himself. This was something new and many welcomed the prospect of tying their future to that of Stalin. Given that the bodies on which Stalin sat embraced most of national life, the opportunities for self-aggrandisement through a loyal clientele were vast. Stalin possessed the ability to make the most of them. He was aided, in part, by the need of local communists to turn to the centre for personnel and by the natural authority of the centre, reinforced by Russian tradition.

All the while the State was becoming stronger and stronger. Sovnarkom's responsibilities, at the end of 1920, were enlarged when the Council of Labour and Defence (STO), set up in 1918 to provision the army, was transformed into a People's Commissariat. It had cut deep into the competence of local soviets. Other centripetal tendencies affected the soviets. As of 1919 VSNKh intervened locally without reference to the soviets and soviets were subordinated, from the autumn of 1919, to the revolutionary committees, set up in areas where Soviet power was in peril. Two other forces, independent of local control, made the State increasingly formidable: the army and the police.

This centralisation, or bureaucratisation, caused increasing problems. The VIIIth Party Congress devoted much attention to the evils of bureaucratism and in April 1919 a decree established a People's Commissariat for State Control, with Stalin as the commissar. It was renamed the Workers' and Peasants' Inspectorate (Rabkrin) in February 1920.

THE NATIONALITIES

'A nation which oppresses another can never be free.' This statement by Marx was taken to heart by Lenin and the multi-national nature of the Russian Empire made it imperative to devise a formula which would attract non-Russians to the Bolshevik cause. National self-determination was Lenin's answer and it meant that all nationalities would be free to choose, after the revolution, if they wished to join and share the common destiny of Soviet Russia or become independent and go their own way. Lenin's views were vehemently opposed by Bolsheviks such as Pyatakov who wanted nothing to do with national self-determination. As a Marxist he clung to the internationalist concept of a world socialist revolution. To him nations were becoming increasingly anachronistic. Why bring new ones into existence? Of course Lenin, as a Marxist, was also an internationalist but he was thinking dialectically: increasing the number of nations was heading in the wrong direction but, on the other hand, if it furthered the prospects of revolution then it was justified. The colonial possessions of the European capitalist powers were a primary target. If they became independent then the prospects of revolution in the metropolitan countries would be enhanced, so thought Lenin.

The Bolshevik leader's view prevailed and two pieces of legislation touched on the problem. The Declaration of the Rights of the Peoples of Russia of 15 November 1917[34] contained the principles of the new revolutionary power. The frontiers of the new Soviet state were not drawn in since the decree afforded any nation who wished to secede the right to do so and to establish its own independent state. The Declaration of the Rights of the Toiling and Exploited People of January 1918 stated that all nationalities had the right to determine on what basis they wished to participate in the federal government and in federal Soviet institutions. In line with Lenin's thinking Soviet Russia had to be a federal state.

Bolshevik nationality policy was expressed through the People's Commissariat for Nationalities (Narkomnats), headed by Stalin, by birth a Georgian. It was made up of sections, also called commissariats, each devoted to a particular nation; the commissariat for Polish affairs, the commissariat for Lithuanian affairs and so on. As of 1918 nineteen commissariats were in operation and their heads formed the board of Narkomnats. In 1920 Narkomnats was transformed into a type of parliament where elected national representatives debated their problems and the centre had an opportunity of establishing closer contact with them. Narkomnats gradually lost its significance. The Constitution of 1924 abolished it when representation was elevated to the Union level.

The Bolsheviks had expected the revolution to bring many nationalities to their side and the world socialist revolution to increase the number of fraternal nations. However events turned out otherwise and the Bolsheviks were taken aback by the number of non-Russians who wanted to secede. Poland was the first to go immediately after the revolution; then came Finland on 31 December 1917. Lenin did not expect either nation to secede for very long. The Ukraine was recognised as an independent state by the Bolsheviks in December 1917. The Ukrainians soon threw their support behind General Kaledin who was organising opposition to the Bolsheviks among the Don Cossacks. This was a rude awakening: self-determination could actually lead a nation into the camp of the adversary. Georgia, in turn, elected a Menshevik government. Stalin and the 'left' communists, especially Bukharin, favoured the view that self-determination should be restricted to workers. Lenin opposed this stating that it had to be national and not workers' self-determination as long as there was no bourgeois revolution. Once the bourgeois revolution had started the right to decide passed to the workers. However the VIIIth Party Congress, in March 1919, conferred the right of decision on the party. When a Socialist Workers' Republic was set up in south Finland in January 1918 it was recognised by Petrograd and a treaty of friendship was signed with it. This policy was also adopted towards the socialist republics set up in the Baltic States in 1918–19 and towards the Ukrainian government in Kharkov.[35] Hence Lenin saw three stages: first the nation had the right to secede and if it chose independence the Soviet government would acknowledge its sovereignty. Then workers could set up a socialist republic which would be recognised by Petrograd. The Communist Party there, when it felt strong enough, would then request admission to the Soviet Russian federal state.

The war against Poland, ongoing since 1918, was a turning-point. In July 1920 Lenin agreed to push into Poland. He thought that the Polish workers would see the Red Army soldiers as brothers who had come to help them liberate themselves from the capitalist yoke. This would be workers' self-determination in action. The Poles looked at it quite differently, seeing the Russians as mere invaders come to reclaim their slice of Poland. The defeat of the Red Army ended the prospects of physically aiding revolution in central Europe. It also convinced Lenin that his concept of national self-determination had been correct. However it meant too that Soviet Russia was alone. The interests of the Soviet state would have to be afforded more weight in the future when implementing nationality policy. Just how euphoric the Bolsheviks were about the prospect of victory in Poland can be gauged from the fact that during the conflict Ordzhonikidze requested permission to invade Persia to promote revolution there. The Politburo declined to sanction such a *démarche*.

SECURING THE FRONTIERS

During War Communism Soviet Russia waited impatiently for aid from the proletariat of the Western nations. By 1921, however, the Bolsheviks had to admit that the revolutionary flood had ebbed. The fate of the Red Army in Poland, the failure of the policy of occupying factories in Italy in September 1920, the downright defeat of the German communists in March 1921 and the suppression of Soviet Republics in Hungary and Bavaria all underlined the same point.

If the revolution had failed in the West it was also not going according to plan from a Bolshevik point of view in the East. The Congress of the Peoples of the East, held in Baku in September 1920, brought home to the Bolsheviks that revolution in the East would not be based on opposition to the bourgeoisie, on class solidarity with the Russian workers, but on common hostility to the colonial or Western powers. Hence the Comintern drew back from giving support to such an eventuality and concentrated on promoting revolution based on the Marxist principle of class struggle. Baulked in the West and in the East Moscow's first priority was now to secure its own national frontiers.

The Soviet state from the beginning had two faces, one looked outward and promoted revolution, the other looked inward and consolidated the Bolshevik position. Trotsky, as Commissar of Foreign Affairs, negotiated as a representative of the revolutionary proletariat. Soviet Russia was seen as a purely temporary phenomenon. G. V. Chicherin, who took over from Trotsky in March 1918, took a more traditional view of state interests. When the Comintern came into being Zinoviev represented the revolution in motion.

The Commissariat of Foreign Affairs began to play an important role in 1920 and to act independently of the Comintern. Treaties were signed with Estonia on 2 February 1920, with Lithuania on 12 July 1920, with Latvia on 11 August 1920, with Finland on 14 October 1920, with Poland on 18 March 1921, with Iran on 26 February 1921, with Afghanistan on 28 February 1921, with Turkey on 16 March 1921 and a trade agreement was signed with Great Britain on 16 March 1921. Relations with the countries in the Far East were not regulated until 1924–25.

CRITICAL CHOICES

Hunger was a constant companion in the cities and was especially severe during the winter of 1920–21. It exacerbated production difficulties and added to the disunity of the party. So concerned was Lenin that the supported measures at the IXth Party Congress, in April 1920, which sharply reduced the involvement of the work force in decision-making. Non-communist specialists were to be employed, one-man management introduced and membership of party and trade union committees were to be filled from above and not elected from below. These measures, necessitated by the seriousness of the situation, were strongly challenged by what became known as the Workers' Opposition (WO) led by Aleksandr Shlyapnikov, one of the few proletarians in the Bolshevik leadership and a candidate member of the CC in 1918, and I. Lutovinov. They were convinced that industry should be run by the trade unions and that the party should be purged of non-proletarian elements. They also wanted a return to genuine elections. Another group who became known as the Democratic Centralists (DCs) formed around V. Osinsky, T. Sapronov and V. Smirnov argued in favour of democracy within the party. They deplored the progressive centralisation of party decision-making. The situation was made worse by the measures adopted by Trotsky on being made responsible for transport in late 1919. It was in utter chaos and Trotsky thought that the only way to impose order was to introduce the same tactics which had proved successful in licking the Red Army into shape. He was simply proposing the militarisation of labour. Lenin did not hesitate to attack the WO and the DCs but held back where Trotsky was concerned. Zinoviev stepped into the breach and vented his spleen on the Commissar. Such dissent within the highest ranks boded ill for the party and it was left to the Xth Party Congress, in March 1921, to decide the issue. Early 1921 saw events which had a lasting impact on the nature of the Soviet regime: revolts at Tambov and Kronstadt, the introduction of the New Economic Policy (NEP) and the reshaping of the party at the Xth Congress.

The peasants of the Tambov region, on the Volga, not only refused to provide the grain demanded by the State but also stopped the grain convoys heading towards the Russian heartland and seized their contents. Troops in the vicinity were not numerous or reliable enough to quell the revolt. The Bolsheviks were wary of applying too much force lest they provoke a general peasant uprising. The situation in the countryside was pitiable, yields were down 40 per cent compared with 1913, much arable land was unworked and farm implements and equipment were suffering from overuse.

At the same time the sailors of Kronstadt, situated on an island in the Gulf of Finland, raised the flag of revolt. Trotsky, the Commissar of War, was ineffective; Zinoviev's vehement attack on him in connection with his views on labour had helped to undermine his authority among the sailors of the Baltic Fleet. The mutineers formed a Provisional Revolutionary Committee, published their own newspaper, demanded free elections to the soviets, the right of all socialist parties, anarchists and syndicalists to assemble and publish, the right of peasants to dispose of their grain as they thought fit, the abolition of the grain detachment squads and the right of those artisans who employed no labour to work where they pleased.

The examples of Kronstadt and Tambov sparked off more violence; everyone identified as a communist in Saratov was massacred. Peasants and workers called for soviets without communists.

Lenin, in a moment of frankness about the Kronstadt sailors, conceded: 'They do not want the White Guards but neither do they want our power.' Notwithstanding the Bolshevik riposte was military violence, but it took from 7 to 18 March to subdue the garrison. The Red Army which had to attack over ice, lost something like 10,000 killed, wounded or missing. Fifteen delegates from the Xth Party Congress, who had come to help, perished. The Kronstadt rebels were dealt with savagely. The Reds blamed the White Guards aided by the Mensheviks and SRs. In reality the SRs and the anarchists were the driving force behind the revolt.

On 15 March 1921, that is during the fighting at Kronstadt, the Xth Party Congress stopped the grain requisitions, imposed a progressive tax in kind, later expressed in money, and restored the peasant's right to dispose of his surplus as he liked. Trade was again legal. NEP was launched. It helped to bring the Kronstadt revolt to a close and removed the danger of a countrywide peasant revolt. NEP was not the consequence of Kronstadt, it can be traced back to early 1920. It was Trotsky who first put forward the idea, in February 1920, but his proposals fell on stony ground. At the IXth Congress of Soviets, in December 1920, Mensheviks and SRs joined in the chorus advocating an end to requisitioning. Lenin put the new policy before the Politburo on 8 February 1921 and on 24 February the CC discussed it and it was placed on the agenda for the Xth Party Congress. The delegates would have preferred to avoid reintroducing capitalism to Soviet Russia had they had the choice. The decisive factor in convincing Lenin that NEP should be introduced was the Tambov revolt which revealed how precarious food supplies really were. The Bolshevik leadership was not unnerved by the Kronstadt revolt since it could solve it by using force. Force in the countryside had turned out to be counter-productive. The vast majority of the population, the peasants, were overjoyed by the change in direction but the working-class element in the party was profoundly unhappy. These communists must have been bewildered by the change in course since as recently as 20 November 1920 all remaining factories in private hands employing more than ten workers (five if mechanised) had been expropriated. NEP gave these owners back much of light industry. Lenin appears to have thought that NEP would last quite a long time, an unwelcome prospect for the working class. To sugar the pill, however, he insisted that the commanding heights of the economy remain in the hands of the State and that the foreign trade monopoly be left intact.

The Xth Party Congress which opened on 8 March 1921 was faced with the problem of deciding which role the trade unions should play in the Soviet state. Since the nineteen-man CC was split on the question the issue had been taken to the party at large in January 1921 and demarcation lines had been drawn up expressed as platforms. Trotsky held to the view that the trade unions should be integrated into the administrative apparatus and given production tasks. The WO, on the other hand, wanted the economy to be run by committees of producers and favoured the independence of the trade unions. Lenin and Trotsky split on this issue. The Bolshevik leader took umbrage at Trotsky's methods rather than his ideas. The very aggressive Trotsky favoured calling a spade a spade whereas the astute, verbally skilled Lenin was adept at camouflaging the real meaning of his words. The WO, in the meanwhile, had acquired the support of an illustrious lady, Aleksandra Kollontai, but it had to battle against the bulk of the party, with Trotsky as the villain of the piece. On the question of the militarisation of labour, Trotsky, Bukharin and Dzerzhinsky were ranged against Lenin, Stalin and Zinoviev. The latters' views were presented in the 'platform of ten'. A third confrontation was also under way, the DCs against all the centralists.

With the tragic events of Kronstadt as a backdrop, the Reds there killing their own, the party closed ranks and the WO and the DCs were swept aside. The 'platform of ten's' proposals were accepted overwhelmingly. Lenin had some soothing words for the injured *amour-propre* of the trade unions and promised them a fuller say in government.

Two resolutions, of great import, were passed on the last day of the Congress. The first, 'On the Syndicalist and Anarchist Deviation in our Party', outlawed the views of the WO and stated that the propagation of these ideas was incompatible with party membership. Congress delegates had been listed according to platforms and Zinoviev had promoted this before the Congress but at the Congress he denounced it as amounting to factionalism. This even further embittered relations between Zinoviev and many others. The second, 'On the Unity of the Party', banned all factionalism in the party. Issues could be discussed by party members but the formation of groups with platforms of their own was forbidden. Once a decision had been taken complete obedience was demanded. Defeated proposals could not be defended within the party and infringement of this rule could mean expulsion from the party. Also passed was a clause, kept secret at the time and first published only three years later, that CC members could also be expelled if two thirds of their colleagues voted for their removal. This was to have momentous consequences, sensed at the time by some, including Radek. Lenin did not envisage the ban staying for ever, but only until things became 'normal'. He also foresaw the possibility of the party, at some time in the future, falling into error. In such an eventuality it would be the duty of a comrade to point this out to the whole party.

What would have happened if Shlyapnikov and the WO had carried the day? They recognised the problems which faced the party in industry and proposed solutions. They were conscious of the fact that the working and living conditions of the mass of non-Bolshevik factory employees had a profound indirect impact on the party. However, their rejection of the party's desire to dominate all the institutions of state would surely have resulted in even more administrative chaos.[36] This in turn would have encouraged bureaucratic centralist solutions. One way of countering Soviet Russia's political, economic and administrative underdevelopment was to run her from the centre. The only body which could hold the State together, in 1921, was the party. Even then it was a party riven with dissent. This resulted in decision-making being restricted to a handful of men and their decisions had to be imposed on a reluctant party membership.

The WO and the DCs were very concerned about democracy but they bore some of the responsibility for the state of affairs they disliked so much. They had not protested when undemocratic practices were used to remove non-communist political opponents in the past. Indeed many of them owed their present positions to such practices.

The ban on factionalism was needed to impose NEP on the party. If communists could not voice opposition to the leadership's policies then the other two parties the Bolsheviks feared, the Mensheviks and the SRs, had to be silenced as well. The Mensheviks and right SRs had been banned in June 1918 for associating with 'notorious counter-revolutionaries'. The ban on the Mensheviks was lifted in November 1918 and that on the SRs in February 1919. During the Civil War the Mensheviks consistently and the SRs less so denounced the Whites and the Interventionist Powers. Many Mensheviks and SRs fought in the Civil War, others joined the administration and some even joined the Communist Party. Something like 2,000 Mensheviks, including the entire CC, were apparently arrested on the eve of the introduction of NEP.[37] Many of these were later released and the leading Mensheviks went into emigration. A number of SR leaders were put on trial in 1922 and sentenced to death or life imprisonment. The death penalty was not applied partly due to international pressure.

THE KEY DECISION-MAKING BODY

By the time the capital was moved to Moscow in March 1918 Sovnarkom had established itself as the chief decision-making body in the Soviet Union. This was primarily due to Lenin's drive and initiative. He was fascinated by administrative detail and really enjoyed being boss of the government machine. Nevertheless by 1921–22 the Politburo had become the chief decision-making body. This was a development which Lenin viewed with some dismay and attempted to reverse. However, his health failed him and Trotsky, who also shared his leader's view that the party bureaucracy should divest itself of some of its government duties, proved an ineffective political infighter. Just how did the party bureaucracy erode the government's power?

Lenin's willingness to take over the existing structure of government, banks, factories and so on was based on the Marxist assumption that the ownership of institutions, not their structure, is of key importance. The areas of competence assigned to the commissariats was quite traditional. This obviously facilitated the survival of elements of the old society in the new. Administrative detail was the real stuff of government to Lenin; in 1918 Sovnarkom met 203 times. Such was the volume of work that a little Sovnarkom was set up at the end of 1917 to decide 'minor questions, not involving matters of principle'. Soviet bureaucracy was following in the footsteps of the Tsarist bureaucracy which had had a similar institution for various periods throughout the nineteenth century.

Sovnarkom never evolved into a cabinet system of government since Lenin was biased against such a development. For him it smacked too much of the cabinet-parliamentary system with influence being exerted from below. It was always difficult to define which work came within the competence of the government and which rightfully belonged to the Politburo. The party, to Lenin, was of course the supreme centre of authority and a commissar could go over the head of Sovnarkom and appeal to the Central Committee of the party. The Bolsheviks were after all the only government party. Despite this Lenin and Trotsky did not think that the party apparatus should get too involved in administration. The party held the reins of power but it was the task of the government to run the country. Other Bolshevik leaders such as Stalin, Zinoviev and Kamenev took a radically different point of view. A key factor in the rise of the party bureaucracy was its prerogative of making appointments not only in the party but in the government and mass organisations as well. For instance between April 1920 and February 1921 the central party organs appointed 1,715 persons to Sovnarkom positions in Moscow and filled 202 key trade union posts.[38] Such was Lenin's involvement in the minutiae of government that he was often ill informed about developments in the party. He was much more willing to delegate party than government responsibilities to others. Just as Sovnarkom was influenced by Tsarist practices so the party bureaucracy in turn gradually acquired more and more traditional Russian attitudes to administration.

Had Sovnarkom developed into a cabinet system of government it would have been able to compete more effectively with the Politburo. Lenin's domination of it was part of its undoing. When he fell ill his deputies either waited for him to get well or passed important items to the Politburo for decision. Due to the pressure of work the practice grew up that commissars could send their deputies and so it became the exception rather than the rule for commissars to attend in person. This inevitably affected the standing of Sovnarkom. Lenin resisted for a long time the thought that power would accumulate where final authority lay, in the Politburo. This process was speeded up by the Secretariat. Neither Lenin nor Trotsky occupied an executive position in the party, hence they were late to perceive that a formidable party machine was coming into being. All along Lenin thought that government administration was more important than party administration, and he devoted the greater part of his working day and his energies to government work. However, he misjudged the situation totally.

THE COMINTERN

Ever since the Second International had failed to stop the First World War Lenin had been convinced that a Third International, a Communist International, was necessary. The Zimmerwald Union was a beginning. When the Bolsheviks heard that the British Labour Party had proposed an international socialist conference they prepared frantically to upstage the event.

The Ist Congress of the Communist International (Comintern) began its deliberations in the Kremlin on 2 March 1919. There were only fifty-two delegates. The main difficulty had been to contact Lenin's sympathisers abroad. One tactic employed was to sew invitations into the clothing of twenty-four prisoners-of-war who were then sent home with instructions to contact the desired person. The vast majority, however, did a Lenin. Just to get home they agreed to all conditions, took the money and forgot everything when over the Russian frontier. So short of delegates was the Congress that one Rutgers represented Holland, the USA and even Japan, on the strength of having once spent two months in that country. The main foreign communist party then in existence, the Communist Party of Germany (KPD), instructed its delegate, Hugo Eberlein, to oppose the setting up of the International. However, the deaths of the first leaders of the party, Karl Liebknecht and Rosa Luxemburg, weakened his resolve and he failed to protest.

The IInd Congress met on 19 July 1920 in Petrograd but removed to Moscow and remained in session until 7 August 1920. This Congress was much more representative of left-wing opinion and delegates from forty-one countries attended. The Congress adopted the famous twenty-one conditions of admission which, although signed by Zinoviev, head of the Comintern, had really been penned by Lenin. Communist parties were to be set up in each country and modelled on the Russian party. Implacable opposition was declared to social democracy everywhere.

The formation of communist parties left behind dissident groups and nourished resentment of the communists and of the Comintern. In Germany the Independent Social Democrat Party (USPD) voted by a small majority to merge with the KPD. Besides those who refused to go along with this move there was also the largest Marxist party, the Social Democratic Party (SPD), opposed to the KPD. Hence the communists could only claim the allegiance of a minority of the German working class. When the KPD launched an armed uprising in March 1921 with the blessing of the Comintern their weakness became all too apparent and the uprising was easily suppressed.

The French Communist Party (PCF) was founded in December 1920 and again many socialists did not join. The same happened in Italy. The upshot was that the rift between the communist party (PCI) and the socialists so weakened the left that it was in no position to resist effectively the rise of fascism.

NOTES

1. Martin McCauley (ed.) *The Russian Revolution and the Soviet State 1917–1921: Documents* pp. 24–6.
2. Ibid. p. 47.
3. P. V. Volobuev *Ekonomicheskaya politika vremennogo pravitelstva* p. 289; Robert Service *The Russian Revolution 1900–1927* 2nd ed. p. 35.
4. L. S. Gaponenko (ed.) *Revolyutsionnoe dvizhenie v russkoi armii 27 fevralya – 24 oktyabrya 1917 goda: Sbornik dokumentov* pp. 352–4; Evan Mawdsley *The Russian Revolution and the Baltic Fleet* p. 76.
5. Hélène Carrère d'Encausse *Une Revolution Une Victoire: L'Union Sovietique de Lénine à Staline 1917–1953* p. 66.
6. Ibid. p. 68.
7. Graeme J. Gill *Peasants and Government in the Russian Revolution* p. 187.
8. Ibid. p. 174.
9. Leon Trotsky *Lenin* p. 132.
10. V. I. Lenin *Collected Works* 4th edn, vol. 25, pp. 323–65. It is dated 10–14 September (OS).
11. Service, op. cit. p. 49.
12. J. L. H. Keep *The Russian Revolution: A Study in Mass Mobilization* p. 187.
13. McCauley, op. cit. p. 234.
14. Keep, op. cit. p. 288.
15. *Pervii Vserossiiskii S'ezd professionalnykh Soyuzov, 7–14 yanvarya 1918 g* (Moscow 1918) quoted in Keep, op. cit. p. 301.

16. Quoted in Chris Goodey, 'Factory committees and the dictatorship of the proletariat' *Critique* no. 3, p. 35.
17. Keep, op. cit. p. 343.
18. McCauley, op. cit. p. 185.
19. Lenin, op. cit. vol. 26, pp. 442–50.
20. P. Milyukov *Rossiya na Perelome* vol. 1, p. 193.
21. B. M. Morozov *Partiya i Sovety v Oktyabrskoi Revolyutsii* p. 96; Keep, op. cit. p. 321.
22. Charles Duval, 'Iakov Mikhailovich Sverdlov: Founder of the Bolshevik Party Machine' in Ralph Carter Elwood (ed.) *Reconsiderations on the Russian Revolution* p. 226. Sverdlov's handling of the CEC can be followed in John L. H. Keep *The Debate on Soviet Power: Minutes of the All-Russian Central Executive Committee of Soviets: Second Convocation October 1917–January 1918.*
23. J. Carmichael *Trotsky: An Appreciation of His Life* p. 238.
24. I am indebted to Jack Simmons, a veteran of the campaign, for this song. The words are by J. H. Connor and it was sung to the tune 'When Irish Eyes Are Smiling'.
25. L. Trotsky *Moya Zhizn* vol. 2, p. 158.
26. I. V. Stalin *Sochineniya* vol. 4, p. 118.
27. McCauley, op. cit. p. 149.
28. Alec Nove *An Economic History of the USSR* p. 62.
29. T. H. Rigby *Communist Party Membership in the USSR 1917–1967* p. 59. Unless otherwise stated all membership figures are taken from this book.
30. Ibid. p. 75.
31. Ibid. p. 85.
32. V. I. Lenin *Polnoe Sobranie Sochinenii* vol. 40, p. 262; Leonard Schapiro *The Communist Party of the Soviet Union* p. 240.
33. Schapiro, op. cit. p. 241.
34. McCauley, op. cit. pp. 191–2.
35. Carrère d'Encausse, op. cit. p. 116. Cf. Hélène Carrère d'Encausse *Decline of an Empire: The Soviet Socialist Republics in Revolt.*
36. Robert Service *The Bolshevik Party in Revolution 1917–1923: A Study in Organisational Change* p. 210.
37. E. H. Carr *The Russian Revolution from Lenin to Stalin 1917–1929* p. 35.
38. T. H. Rigby *Lenin's Government: Sovnarkom 1917–1922* p. 185.

CHAPTER TWO

The New Economic Policy

'RECULER POUR MIEUX SAUTER'

INTRODUCTION

If War Communism was a leap into socialism then the New Economic Policy (NEP) was a leap out of socialism. The extreme egalitarianism, the ever expanding role of the State, the breakneck speed of the attempt to make the economic life of the country socialist and the concomitant rejection of economic laws gave way to the legitimisation of small-scale commodity production and the acceptance of the market. The commanding heights of the economy, i.e. large-scale industry, especially energy and machine building, essential services and so on remained firmly in Bolshevik hands. At first the peasants paid a tax in kind but with the stabilisation of the currency in 1923, this could be paid in money – Soviet Russia was back to a money economy. The economic planning of State industry remained but it had to be within the constraints of the market.

The party leadership accepted NEP in 1921 as a necessary evil but by 1924 a majority favoured its continuance. The party rank and file, however, were never in favour of it. It marked a retreat from the heroic days of War Communism, it favoured the peasant and capitalism, and it put off the advent of socialism in Soviet Russia.

The October insurrection had placed power in the hands of the soviets but it soon slipped away. Lenin, with that characteristic frankness which sets him apart from most of his colleagues, put the matter quite bluntly at the VIIIth Party Congress in March 1919: 'the soviets, which according to their programme are organs of government *by the workers* are in reality only organs of government *for the workers* by the most advanced stratum of the proletariat, but not by the working masses themselves'.[1] Power had passed to the party and it became responsible for building up local and central government. The party began to promote a state machine. Where, however, were the myriads of necessary officials to come from? The lamentable level of education of the average party member, something which continued to pain Lenin until the end of his days, opened the floodgates to the only available source, former Tsarist bureaucrats. The Bolshevik leader was vexed by what he saw:

At the top we have, I do not know exactly how many, but at least a few thousand, and at the most a few tens of thousands, of our own people. But at the base, hundreds of thousands of former officials whom we have inherited from the Tsar and bourgeois society, are working, partly consciously and partly unconsciously, against us.[2]

The picture was not as black as Lenin painted it. Trotsky tells us that:

The demobilisation of five million Red Army men played no small role in the formation of the bureaucracy. The victorious commanders obtained leading posts in the local soviets, in the economy, in education and they persistently introduced the regime which had ensured victory in the civil war. Thus on all sides the masses were cut off from actual participation in the leadership of the country.[3]

Lenin was becoming very disillusioned with the working class. On 19 October 1921 he stated that the Russian industrial working class 'owing to the war and to the desperate poverty and ruin, has become declassed, i.e. dislodged from its class groove and has ceased to exist as a proletariat'.[4] Taken literally this would mean that the socialist (proletarian) revolution of October 1917 had been rendered null and void. In seizing power in October 1917 in the name of an underdeveloped proletariat Lenin had overcome the determinism in Marxism. Until then it had been held that such a revolution could only take place in an advanced industrial state. However there was a penalty to pay: in Soviet Russia Marxism thereby forfeited all its predictive validity. Lenin's next step, one may argue, should have been to disband the Communist Party since there was no proletariat to lead.

Be that as it may, the dictatorship of the proletariat had become the dictatorship of the leadership elite. 'It must be recognised', wrote Lenin in March 1922, 'that the proletarian policy of the party is determined, at present, not by its rank and file but by the immense and undivided authority of the most minute section which might be called the party's old guard'.[5] This abnormal situation gradually became the norm or rule. As the centripetal tendencies increased it became the norm to appoint a secretary from above and this expanded to take in non-party posts as well. The exigencies of civil war had forged this behaviour but the advent of peace and NEP did not dissipate it. The insecurity of the party did not permit that and within a short period the central appointment of officials, through the agency of the Organisational Bureau (Orgburo), became a natural way of doing things.

The local party organisation did not always welcome the centre sending someone to take over however. A. I. Mikoyan, in his memoirs, relates how the Orgburo sent him to become secretary in Nizhny Novgorod *guberniya* in 1920. It was a tough assignment since the previous nominee, V. M. Molotov, had failed to impose his authority. Mikoyan proved himself a more skilful politician and eventually overcame the local opposition in which supporters of Trotsky, the Workers' Opposition and the Democratic Centralists were very strong. By 1922 he was completely in charge and was then transferred to Rostov-on-Don as party secretary of the South East Bureau. The task there was quite different as he had to impose Bolshevik authority over an area which had supported the Whites during the Civil War. Mikoyan's close links with Stalin were forged in these formative experiences in the early 1920s.

As chairman of Sovnarkom Lenin invested that institution with great authority but gradually it became the custom to discuss more and more government business in the Politburo. With the onset of his illness in December 1921, his three strokes in 1922 culminating in semi-paralysis and loss of speech on 10 March 1923, this tendency was accelerated and Sovnarkom's authority declined accordingly. Hence by 1922 the Politburo and the Central Committee with its Secretariat constituted the brain of Soviet Russia; every key decision and every major appointment was made by them.

Stalin became Secretary General of the CC at the XIth Congress in April 1922. At the time he was also Commissar for Nationalities (responsible for about half of the population) and Commissar for the Workers' and Peasants' Inspectorate (Rabkrin), a body responsible for the struggle against bureaucratism and corruption in Soviet institutions. His heart, however, belonged to the party and the fact that he was the only person who was a member of the Politburo, the Orgburo and the Secretariat, as well as being on Sovnarkom, excited little comment. After all Lenin towered above all and Stalin's duties were mainly secretarial. Information provided at the XIth Congress should have given pause for thought. The number of officials subordinate to the CC Secretariat was revealed for the first time: in Moscow there were 325, in the *gubernii* 2,000 and in the raions 8,000; there were also 5,000 full-time secretaries in the provinces and in large industrial undertakings, a total of 15,325 persons.[6] The records and assignment department (Uchraspred) of the CC nominated over 10,000 persons for posts in 1922 and in the following year seven commissions (industry, co-operatives, transport, etc.) were set up in Uchraspred. In 1924 Uchraspred was merged with the Orgburo.

It was only in late 1922, by which time Stalin had clashed with his leader on several issues, that Lenin changed his mind and endorsed the criticism of the small minority who saw the Secretary General's accumulation of offices as potentially dangerous for the party.

Lenin was the natural leader of the party but he had to reaffirm his credentials repeatedly. Not by nature a dictator, he never sought to silence his critics by institutional means. He expected and accepted opposition from his colleagues. Every member of the Politburo during Lenin's active political life (up to 1922) disagreed with him on a major issue. How could it be otherwise with the party attempting to build a new society on Russian soil? However, this lack of consensus on many major issues imposed a heavy burden on the leader. Lenin, moreover, had very definite views on which policies should be adopted and he characteristically fought to have them accepted and implemented. Although factionalism was officially banned after March 1921 he was a master factionalist. If he was in a minority in the Politburo he did not submit, he fought on. Factionalism only became a heinous crime in the Politburo once Lenin had passed from the scene. Since the Politburo conferred enormous prestige and privilege, its members could cultivate their own constituencies. Zinoviev was party leader in Leningrad and president of the Comintern; Kamenev headed the Moscow party organisation; Trotsky was Commissar for War; A. I. Rykov was Lenin's deputy on Sovnarkom; M. P. Tomsky headed the trade unions and there was also Stalin. Some were more politically skilled than others and with Lenin's health deteriorating there was every likelihood that a successor would soon be needed. Pretenders were legion but only three could be taken seriously: Trotsky, Zinoviev and Stalin. That left three other members of the Politburo, men whose support or opposition would decide who succeeded Lenin. Had Lenin died after his first stroke Trotsky would almost certainly have succeeded him as party leader. This made clear who the front runner was, thus permitting his two main contenders to devise a strategy to stop Trotsky seizing the prize. Stalin especially used the time afforded him to good effect and in his haste to outflank Trotsky and cement his position in the government and party, he chose to challenge his leader on two fronts, foreign trade and nationalities, areas where Lenin had very decided views.

THE FOREIGN TRADE MONOPOLY

Towards the end of 1921 and throughout 1922 the question of whether there should be a foreign trade monopoly aroused passions in the Politburo and the Central Committee. On the face of it this appears strange since all that was at stake was how to conduct foreign trade. But in the context of Soviet Russia every economic question was at source a political question. Lenin held tenaciously to the view that all trade with foreign businessmen should be conducted through the Commissariat of Foreign Trade, in other words, indirectly. There must be no direct dealing between the peasant (agricultural products were what Soviet Russia had to export in the main) and the representatives of foreign capital. Surely this would not have happened. The peasant would not have dealt directly with the foreign merchant but would have sold his produce to a Russian trading firm. Trotsky had his own ideas based on expanding the role of the state planning commission,

Gosplan, to embrace foreign trade, but basically he was on Lenin's side. Practically everyone else was against the monopoly. Lenin's opponents started from the premise that foreign trade was of key importance to the survival of Soviet Russia. They just did not believe that the Commissariat of Foreign Trade could successfully and quickly negotiate foreign trade deals. Therefore they advocated a relaxation or the abolition of the monopoly. Lenin vehemently opposed these views arguing that if the foreign businessmen entered into direct relations with the peasant the result would be that Soviet Russia would be fleeced and then bled white. The monopoly was not just a matter of agricultural exports. The industrial trusts resented it since they wished to enter into direct contact with foreign suppliers and markets.

The CC, in Lenin's absence due to illness, watered down the monopoly on 6 October 1922. When Lenin was well enough he demanded, in a letter, that the Politburo should reverse its decision. Stalin, a key figure in the clutch of opponents of the monopoly, appended to the letter the laconic statement: 'Comrade Lenin's letter has not made me change my mind.'[7] Since Lenin was too ill to argue his case personally he invited Trotsky to speak for him and notified the CC accordingly: 'I have also come to an arrangement with Trotsky on the defence of my views on the foreign trade monopoly.'[8] The CC capitulated on 18 December 1922. Since Lenin had also revealed that he was planning to retire, his move in speaking through Trotsky could only mean one thing: he saw Trotsky as his natural successor. This was sensational and the blow pierced Stalin to the core. So the bumptious, overbearing Commissar of War, a non-Bolshevik until 1917, was to lead the party of Lenin! This rankled with Stalin and of course Zinoviev, whose hatred of Trotsky was ill-concealed, but also with many of the old Bolsheviks, those who had been members before 1917. Thus a cabal came into being, composed of Zinoviev, Kamenev and Stalin, with Zinoviev as the apparent leader, the prime objective of which was simply to keep Trotsky out.

THE GEORGIAN AFFAIR

Initially Soviet Russia consisted of the Russian Soviet Federal Socialist Republic (RSFSR), then the Ukraine and Belorussia were added and, as a result of military action in Azerbaidzhan in April 1920, in Armenia in December 1920 and in Georgia in February/March 1921, the number of Soviet republics rose to six. Relations between the RSFSR and the other republics were regulated by bilateral treaties but many areas of competence remained unclear. Stalin, as Commissar for Nationalities, was responsible for the autonomous regions and republics of the RSFSR. To all intents and purposes these areas had no autonomy and were administered from Moscow. When the three Transcaucasian republics were taken over the question of their relationship *vis-à-vis* the RSFSR became acute. Economically and politically the best way of administering them was to merge them in a Transcaucasian Federation but whereas Azerbaidzhan and Armenia could be counted upon to raise few objections to such an initiative, Georgia had to be treated very diplomatically. This was due to the fact that the Menshevik government which had ruled Georgia until February 1921 had enjoyed considerable support, and local pride and national consciousness were well developed.

The Communist Party of Georgia, as a constituent part of the Russian Communist Party (Bolsheviks), was duty bound to follow the directives of Moscow. In order to co-ordinate the activities of the three communist parties, a Caucasian Bureau (Kavburo) of the RCP(B) had been established. This was headed by Sergo Ordzhonikidze, a Georgian, most of whose revolutionary career had been spent as a Bolshevik in Lenin's organisation, and who paid scant attention to the *amour-propre* of Georgian communists, considering it within his prerogative (with Stalin's backing in Moscow) to present the Georgian CC with *faits accomplis*. Despite the protests of the Georgian CC a Federal Union of the Soviet Socialist Republics of Transcaucasia was set up on 12 March 1922 and the Kavburo was correspondingly renamed the Zakraikom (Transcaucasian Regional Committee). Relations with the RSFSR were to be left to a separate agreement. This was the hub of the matter and it led to a sharp disagreement between Lenin and Stalin. On a purely administrative level some autonomy could be granted to the various republics but as democratic centralism prevailed in the RCP(B) the CP of Georgia could expect no concessions.

On 10 August 1922 the Politburo called on the Orgburo to draft proposals to regulate relations between the RSFSR and the other five republics. The resulting plan, drawn up by Stalin, recommended the incorporation of the five republics in the RSFSR as autonomous republics. This would have meant ruling them directly from Moscow by making the decrees of the CEC, Sovnarkom and the Council of Labour and Defence (STO) binding on them. Only the CPs of Azerbaidzhan and Armenia concurred, Belorussia preferred the existing system, the Ukraine could not make up its mind, and the response of the Georgians was predictable: total opposition. To make matters worse Stalin apparently sent a telegram to Georgia on 29 August 1922, before the plan had been discussed by the CC in Moscow, informing them that the decisions of the CEC, Sovnarkom and STO were binding on all republics.[9]

Lenin reacted by proposing that a Union of the Soviet Republics of Europe and Asia be established with a new Federal Executive Committee of the Union of Soviet Republics and a new federal Sovnarkom to which the Russian government would be subject. Stalin was unimpressed by the 'old man's' comments and on 27 September

53

1922 circulated Lenin's proposals and his own comments. He dismissed his leader's views as amounting to nothing more than 'national liberalism'.[10] But Stalin had miscalculated; Lenin had also been drumming up support and this proved decisive on 6 October 1922 when the CC ratified Lenin's version.

The Georgians, however, would not let matters lie and protested again against the existence of the Transcaucasian Federation. They wished to join the new Union of Soviet Socialist Republics as a separate republic. When Lenin, relying on the good offices of the Secretariat, rejected their plea, nine of the eleven members of the CC of the CP of Georgia resigned. This disturbed Lenin and a committee of enquiry was set up to look into the conflict. He was as perplexed by the Georgians' behaviour as Ordzhonikidze and Stalin were furious. As loyal party men they afforded Moscow precedence so why were they making such a fuss over an administrative arrangement? The problem touched the very core of Lenin's nationality policy and his thinking about the Communist Party. He wished some genuine autonomy for the republics but at the same time denied this to the local communist party. Since the party fiat had precedence all real autonomy vanished. It would have taken a fundamental change in the relationship between the RCP(B) and the other communist parties to have guaranteed any real autonomy and this Lenin would not countenance. Hence the row with the Georgians revealed the weakness of his nationality policy.

The committee of enquiry did not resolve the dispute although non-Russians such as Ordzhonikidze, Stalin and Dzerzhinsky dominated it. Lenin belatedly recognised this and railed against their behaviour in a memorandum on the nationalities, dictated on 30 December 1922. But the lion was mortally wounded and it was not Lenin's views which prevailed but those of the 'assimilated Great Russian chauvinists' – Lenin's words – Ordzhonikidze, Stalin and Dzerzhinsky.

The USSR came into existence on 30 December 1922 when the Ist Congress of Soviets passed the Treaty of the Union. Its constitution was ready on 6 July 1923 and it was ratified on 31 January 1924. Georgia entered as part of the Transcaucasian Soviet Federated Socialist Republic (TSFSR) and not as a separate republic. The TSFSR was dissolved on 5 December 1936 and only then could Georgia enter the USSR as a republic in its own right but by then the change was merely formal since it was Stalin's nationality policy, with its emphasis on strict control from Moscow, and not Lenin's which prevailed.

THE GREAT DEBATE

The 1920s were a period of extraordinary economic and social experimentation. Although the Civil War was over some of its ideas lingered on. The Marxist concept of the moneyless economy was still a desired goal. Cash, prices, markets and wages were perceived as distinctly capitalist phenomena and not suitable components of socialist relations of production. The disintegration of the market economy during the Civil War as a result of severe inflation, disruption, state military demands and labour unrest demonstrated how fragile it could be. The primary goal of maintaining State power, however, convinced Lenin that further experimentation had to be put off for a few decades at least.

NEP conceded, during the transitional period until the march to socialism could begin once again, the legitimate existence of private and public sectors of the economy – in other words, a mixed economy. The commanding heights of the economy – heavy industry, banking, energy, fuel, transport and communications remained in the State's hands. Small-scale enterprises and shops were privatised. Foreign entrepreneurs were invited to invest and set up business in Soviet Russia. One of those who took up Lenin's invitation was Armand Hammer. Thus began a relationship which was to last for almost seventy years. Wholesale and retail trade were also privatised, as was, of course, agriculture.

NEP was a gamble but Lenin struck it lucky. Its beginnings were inauspicious. The 1921 harvest was a disappointment and more people left the towns while hundreds of thousands of peasants in the Volga region starved to death. However, by about 1926 State and small-scale industrial, handicrafts and agricultural output was back to the average level achieved over the years 1909–13. One advantage which favoured recovery was the annulling of Russia's foreign debts by the Bolsheviks. Only under Gorbachev were settlements reached with aggrieved creditors. Trade with the developed world expanded. Then as now, oil was the chief commodity exported and machinery the main product imported.

The Bolsheviks did not take to business easily. The money economy, especially profits, seemed unethical to them. Lenin, for ever the realist, saw no alternative and forced *khozraschet*, or accounting on State enterprises in 1922. They now had to operate seriously in a market economy, balance their books and achieve profits wherever possible.

The State sector of the economy quickly acquired some of the less attractive traits of the market economy. It did not produce enough goods to satisfy demand and its prices were high. This meant a sharp decline in the purchasing power of agricultural goods relative to the purchasing power of industrial goods. Farmers in 1923 may have been paying three times as much for industrial goods as in 1913. Soviet economists calculated an index of agricultural goods relative to industrial goods and vice versa. To Trotsky the two curves looked like scissors. So it became known as the scissors crisis. The explanation given was that agriculture had recovered more rapidly than industry after 1921 and that enterprises were engaging in monopolistic practices.

The Bolsheviks feared that the peasants would withdraw from the market until prices dropped. By 1924 they had forced down prices by combating monopolistic practices. It is not clear if peasants did in fact withdraw from the market in protest at high prices. What is significant, however, is that the Bolsheviks believed that they did and acted accordingly. This perception was to influence significantly the debate on economic growth that was just beginning.

Hence the key question was how peasants would react to adverse terms of trade with the State sector of the economy. Various debates were going on among Bolshevik theorists, but that between Evgeny Preobrazhensky and Nikolai Bukharin achieved notoriety since the latter was the 'darling of the party'. In order to industrialise Soviet Russia needed capital. Since peasants made up 80 per cent of the population it was natural that they would provide the lion's share. From a Marxist point of view the net profit which peasants made represented surplus value. This was due to the peasants paying their hired labour less than their productivity merited. Bolsheviks set about ending this 'unethical' state of affairs. Preobrazhensky developed the concept of primitive socialist accumulation – inspired by Marx's theory of primitive capitalist accumulation. He argued in favour of turning the terms of trade against the peasant: in simple language, charge them exorbitant prices for industrial goods. Bukharin was appalled by this and opposed it on two grounds: it was unethical and the peasants would not go along with it, they would simply withdraw from the market until prices came down. The weakness of Preobrazhensky's case was that even he conceded that the peasant might withdraw from the market. The great disadvantage of Bukharin's position was that socialist industrialisation would be 'tied to the peasant's nag'. Bukharin's position is also referred to as the organic or genetic approach to economic development whereas Preobrazhensky's can be called the teleological approach. The latter wanted to set goals for accumulation and hence industrial investment, whereas the former would allow the market to decide.

A major concern for the government was keeping bread prices in the towns down. There was also unemployment. Over a million were registered as unemployed in 1928. Support for the Bolsheviks was centred in urban areas and they regarded private agriculture as strengthening capitalism in rural areas. Hence their policy of depressing prices paid by the State for peasant grain was understandable but self-defeating. Predictably, the peasant marketed less and this led to grain crises in the late 1920s. The percentage of the harvest which left the countryside may have dropped from 20 to 10 per cent between 1913 and 1927.

Animal husbandry was recovering its vitality and meat and milk products brought good returns and prices were uncontrolled. The peasant fed more grain to his livestock and also produced more home-brewed alcohol. Arguably he was not withdrawing from the market but adjusting to a change in the relative terms of trade. However, it was not every peasant who enjoyed the luxury of reacting in a sophisticated manner to relative price changes. The majority of farms operated at or just above subsistence level. A farming elite was, however, emerging. In 1926–27 about 11 per cent of farms accounted for 56 per cent of net off-farm sales of grain in European Russia.[11]

Many Bolsheviks were wont to see it as a conspiracy. Stalin, in 1928, reacting to the 1927 harvest marketings, identified small-scale agriculture under NEP as a major constraint on economic growth. He complained that the amount of marketed grain was only half of what it had been in 1913 although gross output was on a par with 1913. The inevitable conclusion was that small-scale agricultural production should be replaced by large-scale production and the surplus appropriated by the State. However, Stalin himself had contributed to the crisis. In 1927 he was responsible for cutting the price paid for state deliveries and for increasing the price of industrial goods to the peasant. The Politburo became alarmed at the consequences of Stalin's policies, and State grain procurement prices rose in July 1928. Just in case, 250,000 tonnes of grain were imported between June and August 1928. When the 1928 harvest turned out to be good but grain marketings were again disappointingly inadequate, the reflex reaction of the Bolsheviks was to blame the peasants. If industrialisation was to get under way successfully grain for the cities had to be guaranteed. Stalin set gangs of toughs and enraged urban dwellers on the peasants and the 'Urals-Siberian method' proved very effective. The seeds of enforced collectivisation had been sown. In retrospect the way out of the grain crisis of 1928 was to have changed the relative prices of grain, meat and alcohol in favour of grain. This was never seriously considered since it stuck in the Bolsheviks' gullet to defer to peasants.

Another reason why Stalin needed grain was to expand exports so as to be able to import industrial equipment for the first FYP. Molotov, close to Stalin on agriculture, made a very significant remark in early 1928. Referring to the reluctance of peasants to sell grain to the State he stated that the Bolsheviks should deal the kulaks such a blow that the 'middle peasants would jump to attention'. Molotov had correctly identified the problem. In 1927 middle peasants made up 62.7 per cent of the peasantry, a rapid jump from 20 per cent in 1913. There were only about a million kulak households or 3.9 per cent of all peasants. About 13 million peasant households were members of co-operatives. Hence it would appear that Stalin's policy was to create tension by cutting procurement prices. This, in turn, allowed him to apply coercive measures. As a consequence, the kulaks and middle peasants held back grain and the coercive cycle began again. Stalin was not seeking an economic solution but was giving priority to the political dimension. The better-off peasants were incorrigibly petty bourgeois so they had to be driven into collectives where the State could appropriate a much higher proportion of their output than under NEP. The Soviet Union was heading for violent confrontation in the countryside but Stalin was willing to sacrifice anything to obtain control over agrarian surpluses. The cost to the country in terms of waste of resources, human suffering, and a sullen peasantry was immense, and the bill is still being paid today.

THE STRUGGLE FOR THE SUCCESSION

Lenin's ill health made everyone in the Politburo a factionalist, thus making the problems which the leader perceived more acute. From 1922 to 1930 a relentless struggle for supremacy was waged by Politburo members. They regularly forged and then abandoned alliances. This reduced the impact of the leadership on the problems of the day but the dissent at the top had to be concealed. After all, factionalism had been banned in 1921 and the Politburo could not be seen to disagree. This testified to the insecurity of the party and to the depth of disagreement at the top. A more united and composed leadership could have entered into a debate, albeit circumscribed, with party members on the momentous decisions to be taken. And the decisions were momentous in their implications. NEP was a reverse, a retreat from socialism. Just how long should the retreat last? Perhaps decades, thought Lenin. Did that mean that the building of socialism had to be struck off the agenda for the time being? Since socialism in the Bolshevik mind was linked to industrialisation could the foundations of socialism, by developing state-run industry, be laid during NEP? What rate of industrial growth should be aimed at, where was the necessary capital to come from? Some capital might come from abroad but the lion's share could only emanate from one other source, the peasantry. So the leadership's attitude to the rural dwellers who made up the vast majority of the population became the heart of the matter. Could socialism be achieved in alliance with the peasantry or were they incorrigibly petty bourgeois and thus anti-socialist? Put another way, would socialism be built with bricks provided voluntarily by a prosperous peasantry or with bricks squeezed out of a recalcitrant, impoverished peasantry? To speak of the leadership here is misleading: there were as many solutions to the above problems as there were members of the Politburo. It was Stalin's special talents and political manoeuvring, infighting and forming of tactical alliances which made him the supreme arbiter of the Soviet Union's destiny. He could not have achieved what he did had the Soviet Union not been in transition and had there not been genuine disagreements over major issues. He flitted about from faction to faction, espousing differing views at different times. His overriding objective was to make his own position unassailable while most of his colleagues were taken up by the intricacies of ideological debate. He made it his business to be very well informed. His secretary, Bazhanov, caught him listening in to the conversations of his colleagues on the Kremlin internal telephone network, the Vertushka, as early as 1923.[12]

Against Trotsky

Lenin's physical weakness meant that he had to find a reliable ally to fight his political battles for him. The master tactician chose Trotsky but in so doing condemned himself to ineffectiveness as Trotsky possessed neither the ability nor the will-power for political infighting. Lenin misread Trotsky completely. In confiding in him and attempting to speak through him he multiplied opposition to his own views since they were identified with those of Trotsky as well. For a man of ambition the Commissar for War displayed a lamentable lack of political judgment; three times in 1922 Lenin invited him to become a deputy chairman of Sovnarkom and three times he refused. On the last occasion, in December 1922, Lenin offered him a 'bloc against bureaucratism in general and the Orgburo in particular'. Trotsky did not understand the ground rules of politics, that a power base has to be built up before an attack can be launched. Indeed such was Trotsky's lack of perception that it took him a long time to realise that a triumvirate (Zinoviev, Kamenev and Stalin) was operating against him. He took each issue as it came and attacked as the urge took him: he had no understanding of political timing. He was popular with the rank and file and with the army and was a national figure whereas Stalin was not well known outside the CC. But since the triumvirate only needed one more vote in the Politburo to defeat Trotsky on any issue, the latter's great popularity availed him nothing. Zinoviev and Kamenev, who chaired Politburo meetings when Lenin was absent, were convinced that the discomfiture of Trotsky could only work in their favour. They had no objection to Stalin removing Trotsky's supporters in the party *apparat* and anywhere else for that matter and replacing them with 'his' men, who surely must also be 'their' men. Bazhanov, one of Stalin's secretaries, relates how surprised he was that men of Zinoviev's and Kamenev's intelligence should not regard the fact that Stalin was making all the key appointments throughout the country as important.[13] Just who should be appointed required considerable skill on the part of those in line for promotion and on the part of Stalin. The latter could only hint at the views expected of a new incumbent, he could not openly indicate his preferences. Those who had excellent antennae picked up the message without anyone articulating it.

The greatest threat ever posed to Stalin's political advance, and concomitantly the greatest opportunity ever presented to Trotsky to establish his own pre-eminence, was contained in a note dictated by Lenin on 4 January 1923. This was one of several in which he gave expression to his thoughts and anguish at developments in the party and government between December 1922 and January 1923: collectively they are known as his Testament. Lenin's first doubts about Stalin are contained in a note dictated on 24–25 December 1922 in which the Bolshevik leader ruminated on the abilities and defects of the party leadership. He divided it into three groups of two. The top group consisted of Stalin and Trotsky. 'Comrade Stalin, having become Secretary General, has concentrated *unlimited authority* in his hands and I am not certain *whether he will always be capable of using that authority with sufficient caution.*' Trotsky also came in for criticism. 'As a person, he is probably *the most capable man on the CC at present* but he has revealed excessive self-assurance and shown excessive preoccupation with the purely administrative side of the work.'[14] In other words Trotsky was arrogant, overbearing and did not get on with people. The second layer consisted of Zinoviev and Kamenev and the third of Bukharin and Pyatakov. Lenin saw that Stalin and Trotsky did not complement one another, they excluded one another. In his January note Lenin finally lost patience with Stalin. 'Stalin is too rude and this defect, although quite tolerable in our midst and in relations among us communists, becomes intolerable in the post of Secretary General. That is why I suggest that comrades think of a way of removing Stalin from that post.'[15] It would appear that Stalin's handling of the Georgian affair was the turning-point in their relationship. There could now only be one logical successor to Lenin as head of the party: Trotsky.

The Bolshevik leader had expected his Testament to be on the agenda of the XIIth Congress in April 1923 but his wife, Krupskaya, only forwarded it to the Politburo a few days before the XIIIth Congress was due to convene on 23 May 1924. However, it was never mentioned. Bazhanov states that the notes were read by Kamenev to a CC plenum just before the Congress. 'A painful confusion paralysed the audience, Stalin . . . felt himself small and pitiable . . . . In spite of his self-control and enforced calm one could see clearly from his face that his fate was in the balance.'[16] It was Zinoviev, according to Bazhanov, who saved Stalin by arguing that the common endeavours of the leadership in the previous months had proved Lenin's fears to be groundless. The Congress itself was determined to show to the world the face of unanimity in the light of the shock announcement of Lenin's passing on 21 January 1924. Stalin was his old self again at a CC meeting after the Congress, going so far as to offer his resignation which was refused by all, including Trotsky. So much for the legacy of Lenin. The triumvirate held together and not even the dead pharaoh could prise it apart.

The passing of Lenin left a political void. Since his pre-eminence had not been based on the incumbency of any office those who aspired to his mantle could not set their sights on capturing a recognised position. They had to acquire some of Lenin's authority to flesh out the bare bones of an office. Even before the 'old man' was dead Zinoviev, for example, made a bid to capture some of his authority. There were various ways his followers could claim his legitimacy. They could place him on a pedestal and quote his views to buttress and give credibility to their own, as did Zinoviev and to a certain extent Kamenev. They could treat him as an equal and demonstrate how important their contribution had been to Lenin's thought and tactics, even on occasion claim that they had put the master right, as did Trotsky, or they could claim that everything that Lenin had written or said was infallible and that they were his chief disciples, as did Stalin.

Stalin's speech on 26 January 1924 to the IInd All-Union Congress of Soviets was stunningly effective. He was the only speaker to depart from the orthodox rhetoric of Marxism. Instead he drew on his own theological training and expressed his own and the nation's fidelity in the form of a liturgy. 'Leaving us, comrade Lenin bequeathed to us the duty of holding high and keeping pure the great calling of member of the party. We swear to thee, comrade Lenin, that we shall fulfil this thy commandment with honour.' Five other oaths followed. Besides sanctifying Lenin Stalin had a word for mortal man:

Comrades! We communists are people of a special mould. We are made of special stuff. We are they who form the army of the great proletarian general, the army of comrade Lenin. There is nothing above the honour of belonging to this army. There is nothing higher than the calling of a member of the party whose founder and leader is comrade Lenin. It is not given to every man to be a member of such a party.[17]

How party members must have glowed with pride! The next step was to define Leninism in terms which the average member could grasp and memorise. Stalin attempted to do this in his *Foundations of Leninism*, first delivered as lectures at Sverdlov University in Moscow in April 1924. He was much more ambitious than Bukharin and Zinoviev who were attempting the same task but who had not got beyond the preliminary stage. Stalin was rewarded for his industry and timing. His formulation struck the right chord with the large number of new party members who were to all intents and purposes politically uneducated.

Trotsky, as brilliant a writer as he was an orator, had to respond. However, he got off on the wrong foot. He committed the cardinal sin of missing Lenin's funeral: he had been sunning himself in Sukhumi instead. True, Stalin had misinformed him about the date, but he should have known Stalin and his ways by 1924! In the *New Course* (January 1924) Trotsky warned that 'Lenin could not be chopped up into quotations suitable for every possible occasion'. In other words he was opposed to the systematisation of Lenin's thought. On the eve of the seventh anniversary of the revolution he published *Lessons of October* and all his opponents found enough ammunition in it to riddle Trotsky's reputation. He castigated Zinoviev and Kamenev for their opposition to the seizure of power, which permitted Stalin to step neatly in and defend the erring comrades and take Trotsky to task over his portrayal of Lenin. Stalin argued that Trotsky had failed to present Lenin as he really was – the greatest Marxist of the present age. He had painted 'a portrait not of a giant but of some kind of . . . dwarf'.[18] Trotsky, in attacking the revolutionary record of Zinoviev and Kamenev, was establishing a dangerous precedent since it would be child's play for Stalin or anyone else to demonstrate that Trotsky not only was a non-Bolshevik before 1917 but had carried on a running ideological battle with Lenin between 1904 and 1917. Trotsky linked the fate of the revolution at home to the success of revolution abroad but this could be construed as betraying a lack of faith in Soviet Russia. Stalin appeared to change his mind so as to buffet Trotsky on this point. In *Foundations of Leninism* (April 1924) he had asked: 'Can the final victory of socialism in one country be achieved without the joint efforts of the proletarians in several advanced countries?' and answered: 'No, it cannot.' However in *October Revolution and the Tactics of the Russian Communists* (December 1924) he wrote: 'On the basis of Lenin's pamphlet *On Co-operation* . . . we have all that is necessary for building a complete socialist society.'[19]

The triumvirate discovered that it had another ally in the struggle against Trotsky, Nikolai Bukharin. His credentials for Leninist orthodoxy were even flimsier than those of Zinoviev and Kamenev. As a former left communist he revealed that the left communists and the left SRs had thought of arresting Lenin in 1918, but by 1921 he was a devoted disciple.

Bukharin, the leading economist among the party leaders, knew that the economic difficulties of 1923 portended a crisis. Industrial prices were very high due to the monopolistic position of state industry and agricultural prices were low, producing the so-called scissors crisis. Rural demand for industrial products dropped, massive stocks accumulated and strikes broke out in the summer and autumn in large cities.[20] In this tense situation forty-six prominent Bolsheviks chose to forward, in October 1923, a memorandum to the CC voicing sharp criticism of official policy. They also called for a change in leadership. Gradually a left opposition was forming, feeding on the economic thinking of Evgeny Preobrazhensky and Georgy Pyatakov. Such factionalism, which could only endanger the standing of the party in the country, was anathema to Bukharin. Trotsky was linked with this opposition because of his emphasis on the rapid expansion of industry. When the triumvirs raised agricultural and lowered industrial prices, thus confirming the continuance of NEP, Bukharin became a natural ally.

When Trotsky resigned his last great government office, that of Commissar of War, in January 1925, he was consigning himself to political impotence. He gave up his last power base without a fight.

Rather late in the day Zinoviev and Kamenev realised that Stalin was the person who had gained most from Trotsky's discomfiture and had become dangerously powerful. In their innocence they launched an attack on Stalin at the XIVth Congress, in December 1925, but lost by 559 votes to 65, a shattering defeat. As a result Kamenev was demoted to candidate member of the Politburo and Molotov, Voroshilov and Kalinin, all Stalin's men, stepped up to full membership.

Against Trotsky, Zinoviev and Kamenev

So the three lame ducks came together. They were referred to as the united opposition or the left opposition, terms which hung like albatrosses round their necks from the beginning. One major issue was at the centre of their battle with Stalin – socialism in one country. The question was whether Soviet Russia could build a socialist society by herself or whether the world socialist revolution was necessary before socialism could flower at home. Everyone was involved in the debate since it turned on the economic strategy to be adopted to secure a better future. Opinion split into two camps – the right and the left.

Trotsky was very emphatic on the key role of the international connection, arguing that: 'the contradictions in the position of a workers' government in a backward country with an overwhelming peasant population can only be solved on an international scale, in the arena of the world proletarian revolution'.[21] Zinoviev rejected the notion of socialism in one country since the 'final victory of socialism in one country is impossible. The theory of final victory in one country is wrong. We are building and will build socialism in the USSR with the aid of the world proletariat in alliance with the main mass of our peasantry. We shall win final victory because revolution in other countries is inevitable'.[22]

Stalin's approach to the problem was quite subtle. He made a distinction between 'building a complete socialist society' and the 'final victory of socialism' in the Soviet Union. The country was quite capable of performing the first task but final victory depended on breaking the capitalist encirclement of the Soviet Union. This would be effected by the victory of the proletariat in at least a few countries. Armed with this fine distinction, Stalin went forth to war with Trotsky. His approach was to declare his own position to be Leninist and Trotsky's to be anti-Leninist: it was as simple as that. Trotsky could be accused of lacking faith in the Soviet working class, of preaching permanent revolution – very dangerous for the stability of the infant Soviet state and of discarding Lenin's last writings with the advocacy of a worker–peasant alliance. Trotsky, into the bargain, had begun to speak of the 'degeneration' of the party.

Stalin's belief in the 'internal forces of the revolution' and the Soviet proletariat's capacity to build socialism struck a responsive chord in the party. He had the knack of communicating easily with the unsophisticated run-of-the-mill party member whereas Trotsky appeared to be addressing the angels most of the time as no one on earth could follow him. Stalin saw himself, although born a Georgian, as a Russian. He so identified with his adopted country that he believed it could show the world the way forward to socialism. The Russians had changed history in 1917 and could now build socialism on their own. His Russian nationalism contained elements of chauvinism, excessive national pride and a feeling of superiority over other nations. This had alarmed Lenin but he was by then too ill to act decisively. Stalin injected passion into his advocacy of socialism in one country. His Russian nationalism was also exclusive: it was anti-Semitic. In the mid 1920s he made covert use of anti-Semitism in his struggle against the left opposition whose leading members, Trotsky, Zinoviev and Kamenev, were all Jews. He promoted the baiting of the opposition leaders as Jews in factory party cell meetings. He deliberately promoted his faction as the party's Russian faction and Trotsky and his supporters as the Jewish one. He seems to have considered that Jews, despite how assimilated and cultured, could never become really Russian. Bolshevism was not a Jewish conspiracy but a national Russian phenomenon. A Russian who was a Bolshevik should feel proud. This was what many Russians wanted to hear.[23]

By the mid 1920s industry and agriculture were back to their 1913 production levels, and hence the socialism or no socialism in one country debate touched everyone. The party wanted socialism and potentially Trotsky and the left opposition with their demand for rapid industrial growth rates had a large following. It was Stalin's political skill, aided by the economic expertise of Bukharin, which turned the tide. The party's deepseated suspicion of the kulak, or rich peasant, surfaced in the left's pronouncements. Stalin had to argue that the private farmer posed no political threat to the regime.

The formal demolition of the left took place at the XVth Congress in December 1927, but it was a spent force long before that. Zinoviev had lost his seat on the Politburo in July 1926 and his position as chairman of the Comintern in October 1926. Kamenev and Trotsky were expelled from the Politburo in the same month.

Trotsky's humiliation at the hands of Stalin, given the character and political ability of the two men, was almost inevitable. Trotsky, the brilliant hare, was outmanoeuvred by the pedestrian tortoise. What lay behind Stalin's stunning success? Trotsky, for all his intellectual gifts, was ill at ease in the political whirlpool. He was reluctant to sully his hands in the mire of political infighting. Revealingly he was quite incapable of devising political tactics to match his military exploits. His lack of rapport with his party comrades led to his elevating the concept of the party to metaphysical heights. 'The party in the last resort is always right . . . . One can only be right with the party and through the party since there is no other way for correctness to be expressed. The English have a famous saying: "My country right or wrong." With much greater historical justification we may say: "My party right or wrong." '24

Trotsky's character was ill-suited to the political round. Lunacharsky catches it well: 'A sort of inability or unwillingness to be in the least caressing or attentive to people, an absence of that charm that always enveloped Lenin, condemned Trotsky to a certain solitude.'25 Yet Trotsky wanted to communicate: 'Exchanging visits, assiduously attending the ballet, the collective drinking sessions with the gossip about those absent, could by no means attract me . . . group discussions would cease whenever I appeared and the participants would separate in slight embarrassment and with some hostility towards me.'26 So Trotsky's arrogance and highhandedness was nothing but a mask, a mask desperately trying to cover up his innate shyness.

A striking fact about Trotsky's career is the number of times illness intervened. This meant that meetings often took place in his flat. Natalya Sedova, his wife, describes them.

He [Trotsky] spoke with his whole being; it seemed as though with every speech he lost some of his strength – he spoke to them with so much 'blood' . . . . After such a meeting L. D. [Lev Davidovich] developed a temperature, he would come out of his study soaked to the skin, get undressed and go to bed. His clothes had to be dried as if he had just been drenched in a storm.27

Natalya also recalls: 'He suffered from gastric troubles, often on the eve of speaking in public. He was never cured of the fevers which laid him low at times in the course of the struggle with the Politburo, the party.'28 Together with the fever went lassitude and insomnia. Illness struck at key moments, for example just before Lenin's death, whereupon Lev Davidovich and Natalya packed a bag and made for the Caucasus. Trotsky spent months there annually after 1921 and even went to Berlin, in April 1926, but not even the German doctors could exorcise the spectre which was haunting him, the spectre of Stalin. Was this what was at the bottom of all his ill health? Were his afflictions psychosomatic? Just why did Stalin have such a paralysing effect on him?

This is one way of looking at Trotsky. One could also argue that Trotsky never came to terms with the daily round of government business. He was really only engaged when he was involved in solving desperate crises in an heroic manner. He was capable of organisational excellence over a short period but his interest flagged when the problem dragged on. He invested those tasks which he perceived as revolutionary with enormous energy but such an expenditure of creative power drained him after a short period. He had ambitions to be a creative writer and this conflicted with his role as a politician. One has the impression that at times he was indecisive because he saw the myriad possibilities which presented themselves. The creative writer in him, therefore, could hinder his capacity to act. He was always in conflict with his colleagues but it was Stalin, who appeared on the surface to be so ponderous, whom he came to dread.

The foreign policy context

In repudiating the debts of Imperial Russia, taking over foreign-owned industrial concerns and publishing the secret treaties, the Bolshevik leaders broke all the unwritten laws of pre-1914 diplomatic and commercial relations. The Comintern gave guidance to the proletariat of Great Britain, France, Germany and other countries in an effort to further revolution. On the face of it Soviet Russia seemed to have abandoned contact with the surrounding capitalist powers. However, stemming from Lenin's belief that foreign trade was vital to the survival of his government, commercial and by extension diplomatic relations were sought avidly with the capitalist powers. This surely was a paradox. A state which declared the capitalist world to be its enemy, wished and needed to trade with that world. Surely in so doing Soviet Russia was shoring up capitalism abroad by providing markets for its products and thereby lessening the 'internal contradictions of the capitalist system'? Were the goals of the Comintern in conflict with foreign trade since the latter kept workers in jobs? So thought the left communists before the Comintern was born but they were politically outmanoeuvred in early 1918.

The introduction of NEP led to Soviet Russia rethinking its national security strategy. During War Communism national security had been based on strong armed services but the country could no longer afford the defence burden. The Red Army was run down from its peak of 5 million in 1920 to 562,000 in 1924. The high command was reformed and military doctrine was amended. The army was made up of a core of regular troops supplemented by territorial (consisting of 16 per cent regulars and 84 per cent reservists) or national troops and the defence sector was run down. A less hostile view of the outside world was adopted and greater emphasis was placed on threat reduction measures such as propaganda, diplomacy, espionage and disarmament. Defence economics was vigorously debated and was on the agenda of party congresses and conferences. Getting more value for money was their goal although they would not have used such language. The Bolsheviks faced the formidable task of discovering what new weapons were being developed by their opponents and how to counter them. By the mid 1920s specialists were placing their analyses less and less in an ideological framework. It took until 1923–24 to achieve macroeconomic stabilisation (balanced budget, tight credit policy and sound currency) and even then the military came off second best in budgetary allocations. This led to many talented officers abandoning the service. Defence expenditure, however, began to rise relentlessly from the late 1920s onwards.

Trade with the capitalist world was avidly sought for various reasons: access to advanced technology and capital goods; under the cover of commerce military and economic espionage could be conducted; revolution could be promoted abroad by channelling money through Western bank accounts; and commercial relations paved the way for diplomatic relations.

The first trade breakthrough was negotiated by Leonid Krasin (an old Bolshevik of an independent turn of mind who did not involve himself in infighting and instead concentrated on international trade) and resulted in the Anglo-Soviet treaty of 1921. A modest beginning but better was to follow. Only a year later Soviet Russia was able to break out of her diplomatic isolation and appropriately enough she exchanged ambassadors with the country she believed held the key to socialism in Europe, Germany. This was not the first occasion, of course, that the two countries had exchanged missions. After Brest-Litovsk Germany and Soviet Russia had exchanged ambassadors for a short period but relations had been broken by the German government just at the moment, maddeningly for the Bolsheviks, when the German revolution was getting under way. The two outcasts came together again at Rapallo on 16 April 1922. This was possible because a Soviet delegation was attending the Genoa conference, held to find ways of revitalising the European economies. The Soviet-German treaty led to an agreement in August 1922 between the two states which permitted the Reichswehr to use bases in the Soviet Union to train forces in aviation, motorised and chemical weapons tactics and the testing of weapons. This neatly circumvented the limits placed on the German military by the Treaty of Versailles. There were joint exercises and regular exchanges of officers. The Soviet Union received compensation for the lease of bases, the training of personnel and access to the results of German tests and training. An aerodrome at Lipetsk was put at the Germans' disposal in 1924 and tank crews were trained at Kama. Gradually cordial relations developed between the two armies cemented by a common hostility to Poland. Both countries believed that Poland held territory which rightfully belonged to them and officers began to speak of creating a common German-Soviet frontier as in 1914. Voroshilov, Commissar for War, even asked von Blomberg what Germany would do in the event of a Soviet-Polish war. All this came to an end in the spring of 1933. After that Hitler did not need aerodromes in the Soviet Union: the Luftwaffe could use German ones instead.

If Soviet relations with Germany, cemented by the treaty of 24 April 1926, were reasonably satisfactory, those with Great Britain and China were certainly not.

Relations with the British government were coldly formal but there were high hopes that proletarian internationalism would stir the passions of the British working class. A policy of the united front from above, i.e. with labour leaders, was adopted and the breakthrough came with the establishment of the Anglo-Russian committee, voted into being at the Trades Union Congress in September 1925. Tomsky, chairman of the All-Union Council of Trade Unions, a speaker at the Congress, was delighted as was Stalin in Moscow. The general strike of May 1926 was a miserable failure, however, and it dealt the Anglo-Russian committee a mortal blow, the latter expiring in September 1927.

The united front from above in China meant collaborating with the Kuomintang, led after Sun Yat-sen's death in 1925 by Chiang Kai-shek. Ever since 1923 Chinese communists had been encouraged to join the ranks of this nationalist organisation whose aims were to unify China and rid her of warlords and foreign capitalists. The Soviets provided weapons and military advisers. Great hopes were placed on China by Bukharin and Stalin following Lenin's views in *Imperialism, the Highest Stage of Capitalism* that 'national liberation movements' should be fostered since their success would undermine the vitality of capitalism in the metropolitan country, thus increasing the prospects of revolution there. But disaster struck at Shanghai on 12 April 1927 when Chiang's forces, having just taken the city with the aid of communists, turned on the local communists and their supporters and put them to the sword.

The massacre was due to the very success of the communists. Chiang had come to the decision that they were becoming dangerously influential and when he struck he caught Moscow completely off guard. So sure was the Comintern that events were flowing in its direction that shortly before the killings it had made Chiang an honorary member of its executive committee. Now its policy lay in ruins and opprobrium was heaped on the heads of Bukharin and Stalin for their failures in foreign policy. The chief accusers? The left with Trotsky and Zinoviev in the van. They and eighty-one of their supporters in the CC, Central Control Commission and the Executive Committee of the Comintern wrote to the CC that the failures were the outcome of the 'petty bourgeois theory of socialism in one country'. They also thought that the Chinese débâcle would strengthen the sinews of world imperialism and lead to aggression against the Soviet Union. To add verisimilitude to this gloomy prognosis, Great Britain broke off diplomatic relations and cancelled the 1921 trade treaty in May 1927; Canada followed suit and declared the trade treaty with the USSR null and void; and the Soviet envoy in Warsaw, P. L. Voikov, was murdered by a White Russian émigré in June 1927.

Stalin seized the opportunity of giving expression to the prevailing mood. He claimed that there was a 'real and imminent threat of a new war in general and of a war against the Soviet Union in particular'. The instigator was the 'British Tory government' which 'had definitely and resolutely undertaken to start a war against the Soviet Union'.[29] This dramatic statement had predictable consequences at home. A house which is divided against itself will fall, so those guilty of sowing dissent had to be silenced. This meant that Trotsky, Zinoviev and their supporters were not to breathe another word about the Comintern and the party under Bukharin and Stalin betraying the revolution abroad and at home.

Ironically the person who had started the scare was Bukharin, in a speech at the Vth Moscow Regional Party Conference in January 1927: 'We possess no guarantee against an invasion of our country. It is of course not a question of today or tomorrow, or even of next month, but we have no guarantee whatever that it may not come in the spring or the autumn.' Stalin in March 1927 denied that war was a real possibility and remained silent between March and July. It would appear that he used the war scare in his campaign against the left. They appeared to be claiming that they would only offer full support if there was a change in the party regime. This could be construed as a refusal to defend the revolution, thus providing Stalin and his supporters with more ammunition to destroy the left.

With war clouds supposedly on the horizon Trotsky and Zinoviev were expelled from the CC and they and their supporters put themselves beyond the pale when they took to the streets on 7 November 1927 in a forlorn attempt to whip up opposition to NEP. Retribution followed as prescribed by the resolution on party unity passed at the Xth Congress. The factionalists, Trotsky and Zinoviev, were expelled from the party on 15 November. Trotsky was sent packing to Alma Ata on the Chinese frontier, in January 1928, since in those days nothing ever happened there. He found out too late that in a one-party state, which he had helped to build, there is no legal way of voicing dissent.

Against Bukharin, Rykov and Tomsky

At the XVth Congress in December 1927 the rout of the left was complete and the Politburo could feel satisfied. However, whereas the right thought the events at the Congress were the last move, Stalin regarded them as the penultimate move in the grand game for the control of the Soviet Union's destiny. As the only politician with a grasp of games theory he took the right completely by surprise. Stalin had succeeded in scattering the left to the four winds in order to steal their clothes, or rather their ideas. In 1927 almost everyone was moving leftwards and even Bukharin caught the mood. In October 1927 he called for an 'offensive against the kulak' so as to restrict 'his exploiting tendencies'.[30] Just how numerous were the kulaks in 1927? There were about 750,000 homesteads, about 3.4 per cent of all farms, employing about one million labourers. The most prosperous peasants had two to three cows and up to ten hectares of land under crops for an average family of seven persons.[31] This represented a *per capita* annual income of 239 rubles 80 kopeks for the members of the kulak's family compared to a rural official's 297 rubles.[32] The kulak earned twice as much as the middle peasant but the belief that there was a powerful kulak capitalist class in the countryside was a myth.

The State now felt itself strong enough to challenge the successful farmers. One way of doing this was to increase the taxes they had to pay. Simultaneously taxes on poor and middle peasants were reduced. However, as the goal of these peasants was to become rich peasants who were seen as class enemies, the party found itself in a *cul de sac*. Action against private producers, NEP-men, had already been taken in 1926 when swingeing taxes had been imposed, among other things. A serious goods shortage also appeared in 1926, for the first time since 1923, and this favoured those who lived in towns since they snapped up state-produced articles. The peasant, on the other hand, had to rely on the private manufacturer and hence had to pay higher prices. The government's answer to the goods famine was to cut prices, which only exacerbated the situation. Grain prices fell as well, dropping 20 per cent in 1926–27. Another reason for the shortage was the war scare of 1927 which had led to peasants hoarding grain and flour. In January and February 1928 Stalin, some officials and police, descended on the Urals and Siberia. They made use of the technique, then in existence, afterwards called the Urals-Siberian method, to close down markets, arbitrarily and illegally seize grain and arrest peasants. This Stalin said could be done by invoking article 107 of the Criminal Code adopted in 1926, which provided for drastic measures against 'speculators'. The whole manoeuvre was a great success, if the procurement of grain by the State at minimal cost irrespective of the law and of the effect on producers can be regarded as a success. When the policy was debated in the Politburo the right because of the shortage of grain had reluctantly agreed to the 'extraordinary measures'. What they had not agreed to were the excesses. They could extract a promise from Stalin, at the CC plenum in April 1928, that the exercise would not be repeated (in the months following the plenum it was repeated, this time hitting the middle peasant) but the damage had been done.

The mir had been losing power during the 1920s and this made it easier to promote collectivisation. The village soviet (selsovet) was established in 1918 to control the distribution of land, thereby depriving the village of some of its prerogatives. In 1924 the selsovet acquired administrative functions and in 1926 it became responsible for the communal budget, a key move in weakening the autonomy of the village community. Hence in 1929 when collectivisation arrived the mir had lost its administrative and economic functions to the selsovet. The kolkhoz became the economic arm of the government in the countryside and the selsovet the administrative arm. The mir, therefore, was in no position to resist collectivisation.

The first Five-Year Plan (FYP) operated as of 1 October 1928. Drafting such a novel exercise in inducing economic growth was so complex that the plan was only submitted to the XVIth Party Conference in April 1929, and even then in two versions, the first version and the optimal version – the latter being adopted. The first version was ambitious enough, for example industrial production was to grow by 130 per cent, but the optimal version was utterly unrealistic. In it industrial production was to go up by 180 per cent. The immensity of the task of formulating the plan was such that much detailed work had still to be done in April 1929. Part of the blame for this must rest with Bukharin. As the protagonist of planned proportional growth he had failed to provide an economic defence of his view. Economists in Gosplan and the Supreme Council of the National Economy found themselves under greater and greater pressure from committed planners who believed, in the words of S. G. Strumilin, that: 'We are bound by no laws. There are no fortresses the Bolsheviks cannot storm.'[33] Industrial goals were dear to the hearts of the Bolsheviks as to them the industrial sector represented the socialist sector.

The goals set agriculture in the first FYP were much more modest than those set for industry, 44 per cent growth in the first version and 55 per cent in the optimal version. Unlike the situation in industry, these targets were perfectly feasible, provided prices were right. But planning did not envisage the use of the market but the abolition of the market in agricultural goods. The market was to be phased out in agriculture, but how was this to be done? The XVth Congress in December 1927, adopted a resolution stating that the current task of the party in the countryside was to unite and transform the small individual peasant farms into large collectives. This would be a ten- to fifteen-year process – a leap into collectivisation was not envisaged. The immensity of this task will be evident from the fact that in 1928 only 1.2 per cent of the sown area was inside collective farms and a further 1.5 per cent in state farms. By the end of the plan the goal was to have 26 million hectares in state and collective farms, accounting for 15 per cent of total agricultural output. On the face of it it was a perfectly reasonable target. Just why collectives should suddenly appeal to peasants was not explained. Entry to collectives was to be on a voluntary basis – even Stalin said that – so presumably the incentives were to be considerable in order to achieve the goals of the plan.

In the meanwhile, however, the grain crisis would not go away. The resolution adopted by the CC plenum in July 1928 appeared to vindicate the thinking of the right. The peasant farms were to remain the backbone of NEP, the emergency measures were to cease and prices were to rise. It was all a chimera, notwithstanding. The right found themselves in a minority in the Politburo and in the CC and the resolution was passed to paper over the cracks in the façade of party unity. The suffocating political climate, the war scare and the grain difficulties meant that discord had to be concealed.

The struggle moved to the VIth Congress of the Comintern which opened in Moscow on 17 July 1928. Here Bukharin's authority and record in the Comintern were put to the test. The Stalinists asserted that capitalism was near to breakdown and it was up to communist parties to go over to the offensive, hitting also at social democrats, labelled social fascists, whereas Bukharin believed that capitalism was stabilising and entering a higher phase. The Congress programme warned that the deepening imperialist antagonisms would also lead to a fresh round of imperialist wars. Hence Bukharin had to concede ground to Stalin. Moreover, Stalinist factions had been formed in foreign communist parties and Bukharin unwisely conceded Stalin's point that 'the right deviation represents the main danger'.

The support base of the right was gradually chipped away. The Moscow organisation fell to Stalin; Bukharin, although still editor of *Pravda*, no longer decided policy as his supporters among the editors were removed; a witchhunt was conducted in the executive committee of the Comintern and in foreign communist parties against Bukharinites; and Tomsky was outgunned at the VIIIth Trades Union Congress in December 1928. In December 1928 Bukharin resigned as editor of *Pravda* and political secretary of Comintern and Tomsky as head of the trade unions. The right was prostrate and the advocates of rapid industrialisation at the expense of the peasant took over. All that remained to be done was some institutional tidying up. Bukharin was expelled from the CC in November 1929; Tomsky was not re-elected to the Politburo after the XVIth Congress in July 1930; and Rykov was expelled from the CC in December 1930. With the political death of the right went the demise of NEP. In December 1929 Stalin opted for collectivisation 'without limitations', the 'liquidation of the kulaks as a class' and the concomitant view that anyone who refused to join a collective had to be an enemy of the Soviet regime.

CULTURE

If the goal of War Communism was the hegemony of the proletariat then the goal of NEP was to effect a reconciliation with the peasantry and the remnants of the bourgeoisie. The compromise had already commenced under War Communism when military specialists and technical experts were needed to bolster Bolshevik power. In the 1920s it extended to all branches of endeavour, to science, medicine and technology and then to education, literature and the arts.[34] The only exceptions were philosophy and history where party tolerance did not extend to the propagation of non-materialist philosophies or the glorification of pre-1917 Russia. This led in all fields to the formation of groups of 'fellow travellers' of revolution. They were not for or against the proletariat, indeed they did not address themselves to such a problem. Their concern was their own discipline, be they painters or geologists, and they wished to promote their own speciality, free of the fetters of censorship. However there were some Bolsheviks with expertise, notably among the writers, whose goal coincided with that of the party – the building of socialism. They wanted state and party intervention in culture and science but their voices were muted in the early years of NEP and it was not until the end of the 1920s that their influence was felt.

The party first kept aloof from direct involvement in culture and Trotsky summed up the mood when he wrote that in the realm of culture the 'party is not called upon to command'.[35] Even Stalin accepted that literature was non-party and covered a wider area than politics. This however did not please the radicals and the artists, musicians and writers among them formed their own associations in the course of 1922–23.[36] They were very critical of Anatoly Lunacharsky, Commissar of Enlightenment, but as long as he maintained his influence he was quite determined to prevent his commissariat discriminating in favour of any one group.

The situation changed after the defeat of Trotsky and the left at the XVth Party Congress. The proponents of the hegemony of the proletariat in culture could now assert themselves. This they did at party conferences and by the summer of 1928 the Institute of Red Professors and other centres were in their hands. Stalin's conflict with Bukharin, long known as the protector of the non-party intelligentsia,[37] spilled over into the cultural arena. The defeat of Bukharin was the death-knell of an apolitical cultural and scientific policy. Stalin's 'revolution from above' in the short term meant the resurrection of the concept of the hegemony of the proletariat in all walks of life.

SUMMARY

From the peasant point of view NEP was the golden era of Soviet history. The land was theirs, the landlord was gone and real income was probably higher than in 1913. True, the government had acted against the better off elements, the kulaks, and non-farm goods were in short supply and more expensive than in the towns. The flow from the countryside to the towns slowed to a trickle and the presence of one and a half million unemployed in urban areas by 1928 did not go unnoticed in the village. The peasant was eating better; whereas 12 million tonnes of grain were exported in 1913, less than 3 million tonnes were sent abroad during the best years of NEP. There were strong regional disparities however. Surplus grain areas were much better off than grain deficit areas. NEP agriculture represented a fat hen ready to be plucked. The very success of the agrarian sector made it a tempting source for the capital investment necessary to build the foundations of a socialist industrial economy. The peasants were unable to resist the onslaught since, although they had some economic power, they had no political power.

Political power had been restricted to fewer and fewer hands during the 1920s and the trend of the early years of the revolution continued. In 1917 the need to defend the revolution had led to the strengthening of the state with its concomitant centripetal tendencies. The soviets and the mass organisations had suffered as the arena of policy formation diminished more and more. The party followed the same evolution. Democratic centralism, meaning that there is free discussion at all levels until a decision has been reached and this decision is then binding on all members, is arguably democratic. However, the desperate Civil War years, the low level of political culture not to say literacy of most party members, and the near extinction of members who could claim impeccable working-class origins, led to decision-making becoming more and more the prerogative of the CC and then of the Politburo. Sovnarkom and the CEC suffered. With Lenin gone it was uncertain which institution would dominate. Constitutionally the CEC and its presidium were superior to Sovnarkom and it managed to claw back some of its lost influence. The presidium of the CEC held joint meetings with the government and discussed matters formerly the prerogative of Sovnarkom. This affected the position of Rykov, chairman of Sovnarkom. Furthermore the election in 1926, to the Politburo of Mikhail Kalinin, chairman of the CEC, multiplied the pressure on Rykov.

It was the party which expanded its apparatus and influence most rapidly during NEP and this benefited the Secretariat most. A tactic employed by Stalin to challenge opposition in the Politburo was to call joint sessions of the CC and the Central Control Commission and use them as a forum to apply pressure, thus restoring to the CC some of its lost authority.[38] In the meanwhile party membership increased rapidly; there were of 472,000 members in January 1924 but 1,535,362 members in January 1929.[39] The rawness of these recruits and their desire for guidance from above can be gauged from the fact that 91.3 per cent of members in January 1927 had only enjoyed a primary school education or even less.[40]

One of the institutions which grew in importance during NEP was the political police. Renamed the GPU (Main Political Administration) in February 1922, it had *carte blanche* to investigate the political orthodoxy of all communists and non-communists, including members of the Politburo. Lenin could not have foreseen this nefarious consequence of his ban on factionalism at the Xth Congress. The skeleton of the coercive system of the 1930s came into being during this period, including the corrective labour camps.

If the arena of political decision-making contracted during NEP so did that of science, culture and the media. Here more and more conformity was the order of the day but it should be stressed that the pressure was often from below, from those who wished to establish a monopoly for the proletarian point of view, as they understood it.

The death-knell of NEP was probably the XVth Congress which paved the way for the first FYP. Planning will sooner or later collide with the market and one or the other must cede primacy. However, at the time, the desire for planning and the gradual collectivisation of agriculture were not seen as a revolutionary change in economic policy.

How does one explain the fact that members of the Politburo were so blind that they did not perceive that the political infighting was benefiting only one of them, Stalin? Bukharin epitomises this, in 1928, when he still felt that the defeat of the left benefited him most.

Politburo opponents of Stalin had had little practical experience of politics before 1917. They had not mounted the party ladder step by step and had not had to claw their way up; 1917 had made them, at a stroke, key political figures. They were singularly ill-equipped to recognise a party climber when they saw one. They were all superior to Stalin, or so they thought, despite what Lenin had written in his Testament. Their fierce intellectual independence ill prepared them for caucus politics. Stalin was moderate and methodical, not to say pedestrian, but he was the only one skilled at building tactical alliances and this put him head and shoulders above the rest. This did not automatically guarantee success: he had to reflect the aspirations of the party and that party wanted socialism. On the face of it the left should have won between 1925 and 1927 and in any case the distance between the right and the left was narrow in 1927 when Bukharin moved against the kulak. Convergence might have resulted if domestic and foreign peace had been guaranteed. However, Stalin used the imaginary threat of war in 1927 to stifle debate and exaggerate the differences with the left.

Some of the responsibility for the rise of Stalin must attach to Bukharin. He, like many other men of ideas, was so fired by the challenge to forge and bend theory to his will that he failed to observe the shadow which was approaching, the shadow of a man who was imbued by the challenge to forge and bend men's minds to his will.

Politburo members also suffered from the old blight of the Russian intelligentsia, personal animosity. The extraordinary virulence of the exchanges and the depth of antipathy are all the more startling in that the actors involved were Marxists, men to whom the role of personality in history was minimal and social forces almost all. Zinoviev hated Trotsky, Trotsky hated Zinoviev, Bukharin hated Trotsky, Trotsky hated Stalin, Stalin hated Trotsky, and Bukharin came to hate Stalin. As Lenin remarked in his Testament: 'In politics spite generally plays the basest of roles.'[41] In this, as in many other things, the 'old man' was right but in no position to rectify the situation. The end of NEP was the end of an era.

NOTES

1. V. I. Lenin *Polnoe Sobranie Sochinenii* vol. 38, p. 170.
2. Ibid. vol. 45, p. 290.
3. Leon Trotsky *The Revolution Betrayed* pp. 89–90; Moshe Lewin *Lenin's Last Struggle* p. 9.
4. Lenin, op. cit. vol. 44, p. 161.
5. Ibid. vol. 45, p. 20.
6. *VKP(b) v Resolyutsiyakh* vol. 1, p. 729.
7. L. A. Fotieva *Iz Vospominanii o Lenine* pp. 28–9; Lewin, op. cit. pp. 151–2.
8. Lenin, op. cit. vol. 45, p. 338.
9. Lewin, op. cit. p. 50.
10. Leon Trotsky *The Stalin School of Falsification* p. 67; Lewin, op. cit. p. 52.
11. R. W. Davies *The Socialist Offensive: The Collectivisation of Soviet Agriculture, 1929–1930* pp. 26–7; Service, op. cit. p. 66.
12. Boris Baschanow *Ich war Stalins Sekretär* pp. 50–1.
13. Boris Bajanov *Avec Stalin dans le Kremlin* p. 51.
14. Martin McCauley *The Russian Revolution and the Soviet State 1917–1921: Documents* p. 295.
15. Ibid. p. 296.
16. Bajanov, op. cit. pp. 43–4. Trotsky, on the other hand, states that the notes were only read, with suitable comments, to leaders of delegations to the Congress: Leon Trotsky *The Suppressed Testament of Lenin* pp. 11–12, 17; Leonard Schapiro *The Communist Party of the Soviet Union* p. 283.
17. I. V. Stalin *Sochineniya* vol. 6, pp. 46–51.
18. *Za Leninizm Sbornik Statei* (Moscow–Leningrad 1925) pp. 107–8; Robert C. Tucker *Stalin as Revolutionary* p. 353.
19. Joseph Stalin *Leninism* p. 154.

20. Stephen F. Cohen *Bukharin and the Bolshevik Revolution: A Political Biography* p. 156.
21. Leon Trotsky *Permanent Revolution and Results and Prospects* p. 247; Tucker, op. cit. p. 381.
22. *XV Konferentsiya Vsesoyuznoi Kommunisticheskoi Partii (b) 26 Oktyabrya – 3 Noyabrya 1926 g* pp. 564, 566; Tucker, op. cit. p. 384.
23. *Trinadtsatyi Sezd VKP (b) Mai 1924 goda* p. 158.
24. Robert C. Tucker *Stalin in Power: The Revolution from Above 1928–1941* p. 41.
25. A. Lunacharsky *Revolyutsionnie Siluety* p. 25; Joel Carmichael *Trotsky: An Appreciation of His Life* p. 296.
26. Leon Trotsky *Ma Vie* vol. 3, p. 234.
27. Ibid. p. 229.
28. V. Serge *Vie et Mort de Trotsky* p. 187; Carmichael, op. cit. p. 311.
29. *Pravda* 28 July 1927.
30. *International Press Correspondence* VII (1927), p. 1422.
31. Yu. V. Arutyunyan *Sotsialnaya Struktura Selskogo Naseleniya SSSR;* Moshe Lewin 'Society, State and Ideology during the First Five Year Plan' in Sheila Fitzpatrick (ed.) *Cultural Revolution in Russia 1928–1931* p. 49.
32. *Statisticheskii Spravochnik SSSR za 1928 god* (Moscow 1929) p. 42; Lewin, op. cit. p. 49.
33. P. J. D. Wiles *The Political Economy of Communism* p. 47.
34. A. Kemp-Welch 'New economic policy in culture and its enemies' in *Journal of Contemporary History* vol. 13 (1978) p. 449.
35. L. D. Trotsky *Literatura i Revolyutsiya* pp. 161–2; Kemp-Welch, op. cit. p. 453.
36. Kemp-Welch, op. cit. p. 454.
37. N. Mandelstam *Hope against Hope* pp. 115–16; Kemp-Welch, op. cit. p. 463.
38. T. H. Rigby 'Stalin and the Mono-Organizational Society' in Robert C. Tucker (ed.) *Stalinism: Essays in Historical Interpretation* p. 72.
39. T. H. Rigby *Communist Party Membership in the USSR 1917–1967* p. 52.
40. Ibid. p. 401.
41. McCauley, op. cit. p. 299.

CHAPTER THREE

The Thirties

'LIFE HAS BECOME BETTER, COMRADES, LIFE HAS BECOME MORE JOYOUS'

INDUSTRIALISATION AND COLLECTIVISATION

The panorama of life in the Soviet Union during the years which link the first FYP (1 October 1928) and the German attack on 22 June 1941 almost defies description and comprehension. Heroic self-sacrifice, unflinching devotion, patriotism, the neglect of the material well-being of today because a better tomorrow was being constructed, incredible industrial achievements, sadistic, corrupt party and police officials maltreating and murdering thousands if not millions, starving children left to die only because they had a kulak as a father, man-made famines claiming countless lives, ecstatic joy and bottomless misery and sadness, all co-existed and ran parallel – it was heaven and hell cheek by jowl. Extremes no longer appear to be extremes: they become commonplace.

Stalin, the cult of whose personality can be dated from his fiftieth birthday in December 1929, stands astride the period. He never appears to rest, he urges, he cajoles, he is brutal, he is affectionate, he is a hero, he is a devil. His vaulting ambition to make the Soviet Union a world power overnight knew no bounds. In December 1929 it was decided to fulfil the plan in four years and indeed 31 December 1932 saw the termination of the first FYP. It became fashionable to increase goals repeatedly as if mathematics had ceased to function. This was great fun for those who set the goals but no fun at all for those who were required to meet the targets. The impossible goals, the daily fight to secure vital raw materials and parts (and here success for one enterprise spelled failure for another), the harassment by party and police officials began to take their toll and timid voices began to ask if the tempo could not be slackened a little. 'No, comrades, it is not possible. The tempo must not be reduced. On the contrary we must increase it as much as is within our powers and capabilities.' Thus Stalin in a speech to the first conference of workers in Moscow on 4 February 1931. He continued: 'To slow the tempo would mean falling behind. And those who fall behind get beaten. But we do not want to be seen to be beaten. No, we refuse to be beaten.' Then he listed the foreign armies which had beaten Russia in the past, curiously omitting all mention of the Germans. 'Do you want our socialist fatherland to be beaten and to lose its independence? If you do not want this then you must end its backwardness in the shortest possible time . . . . We are fifty or a hundred years behind the advanced countries. We must make good this distance in ten years. Either we do this or they will crush us.'[1] Such nationalist fervour begets miracles – and 1941 was ten years away!

This kind of pressure produced breakdowns of machinery and conflict between ambitious technically unsophisticated communists and those who knew that a quart could not be squeezed out of a pint pot, 'bourgeois' specialists. Although the threat of an interventionist war had receded another threat was on the horizon – that of economic intervention, in the form of wrecking, crises in various industries, and so on. So said Stalin in April 1928.[2] Such was the mood after the public prosecutor had announced the uncovering of a large-scale conspiracy of engineers in the Shakhty area of the Donbass. Fifty-three engineers, including three Germans, were accused of wrecking or sabotage. The defendants were subjected to physical and mental coercion, first and foremost deprivation of sleep, to encourage them to incriminate themselves and their co-defendants. However, only ten made full confessions and implicated the others. The system became more efficient in the 1930s! The trial was staged as drama and was given star billing in the press. Stalin's political aim in promoting such a trial was to undermine confidence in 'bourgeois' specialists. In so doing he was chipping away at his opponents on the right who favoured using such specialists. The techniques elaborated by the team of interrogators were to be developed later in the 1930s. Many of the team were to be promoted by Stalin. Furthermore, Stalin told Komsomol members the following month: 'No, comrades, our class enemies do exist. And they not only exist but are growing and trying to act against Soviet power.'[3] The 'industrial party' trial in November–December 1930, when industrial experts confessed to wrecking, gave the date for ostensible foreign military intervention (1930), the name of the leading power involved (France) and the membership of a future government, heightened tension as did the trial of Menshevik Internationalists in March 1931. However the mass arrests of 'bourgeois' engineers after the Shakhty trial was counter-productive, occurring at a time when their skills were desperately needed to boost production. The distrust of native and foreign specialists was exacerbated by industrial countries campaigning against Soviet 'dumping' and refusing to handle timber alleging that it had been prepared by forced labour. Given that the terms of trade after 1929 swung against the Soviet Union, as an exporter of raw materials and grain, and since it now had to export more to buy the same amount of machinery, it was a short step to seeing capitalist conspirators abroad and capitalist wreckers at home in league with one another.

One determined opponent of the campaign against 'bourgeois' engineers was Sergo Ordzhonikidze, who became head of the

Supreme Council of the National Economy at the end of 1930 and was therefore the *de facto* chief of the industrialisation drive. The house newspaper, *Za Industrializatsiyu*, argued for the restoration of order in administration, an end to OGPU interference in industry and the rehabilitation of 'bourgeois' specialists. Stalin sided with Ordzhonikidze on 23 June 1931 when he acquitted 'bourgeois' specialists of the collective charge of treason. This brought the class against class war which had characterised the early years of the first FYP to an end. However Metro-Vickers engineers were still put on trial in 1933 – a desperate year for the Soviet economy. The Soviets congratulated themselves on 'having overcome the threat of economic intervention' by the early 1930s. They believed this to be the result of Soviet power, the outcome of rapid industrialisation.

The goals of the first FYP can be likened to utopia, unattainable but nonetheless worth aiming at. More was achieved in the end than if 'sound' advice had been taken.[4] Planning was not very realistic. The determination to force industrialisation and collectivisation was very great. There was a belief that product exchange would take over from money after NEP was phased out; indeed in 1930 it was thought that this stage was approaching fast. Socialism then was conceived of as a moneyless economy. It was also thought in 1930 that society could be transformed very rapidly. Workers would be motivated by enthusiasm so that piece rates could be phased out. It was only in 1931–32 that the outlines of the socialist economy became visible: a stable currency, wage rates based on incentives, the kolkhoznik's private plot, the free market for his private produce and socialist trade for the rest of the economy.

The industrial expansion of the first FYP was due mainly to using the existing plant at higher capacity and the extra plant which became available as a result of investment from 1925 onwards. New plants begun during the first FYP did not really come on stream until 1934–36.

Very few of the targets expressed in physical terms in the first FYP were met but those expressed in 1926–27 rubles were often reached. Gross industrial production was just overfulfilled, producers' goods overfulfilling by 27.6 per cent and consumers' goods failing by about 19.5 per cent (see Table 3.2). Here the Stalinist pattern of industrialisation is evident. Where resources were available they were channelled into heavy industry and away from light industry. But these ruble figures are suspect: there was considerable inflation over the period and many of the machines produced during the plan did not exist in 1926–27, so what 1926–27 price was allocated to them? Generally it erred on the high side. Nevertheless heroics were performed. Magnitogorsk and Komsomolsk-on-the-Amur, to name only two cities, rose from the virgin soil. Great new industrial centres in the Urals, Kuzbass and the Volga took shape and the traditional areas such as Leningrad,

Moscow and the Donbass also expanded. Technology and engineering were taken to remote areas such as Kazakhstan and the Caucasus. The great Dnieper dam was completed and provided vital electrical power for bourgeoning industries. Electricity output by 1932 had almost trebled since 1928, hard coal and oil had almost doubled and iron ore had more than doubled its output. So energy was a great success although no branch actually fulfilled its plan. Steel output however was disappointing. Production only climbed from 4 million tonnes in 1927–28 to 5.9 million tonnes in 1932; pig iron, on the other hand, jumped from 3.3 million tonnes in 1927–28 to 6.2 million tonnes in 1932. Yet it was claimed that machinery output quadrupled over the same period. This was just not possible.

The number of peasants in collective farms of all types doubled between June and October 1929 and between October and December 1929 another 2.4 million households were added. This meant that by the end of 1929 over 25 million peasants or about 20 per cent of the peasant population had been collectivised. The main reason for this remarkable phenomenon was the decision of the Stalin leadership to speed up the process. Five years was too long. Why not see what could be achieved in five months? Stalin, in an article in *Pravda* on 7 November 1929, characterised 1929 as a great turning-point. One reason for this was that peasants were now entering collectives not in families or groups, but whole villages and regions were turning to the collectives. He signally failed to mention the coercion being applied by local party and soviet officials. Poor peasants and farm labourers were much more easily persuaded but middle peasants were hanging on hoping they could weather the storm. The great majority of those in collectives came from the poor peasantry but they only made up about 30 per cent of the peasantry. The middle peasants accounted for about two-thirds of the peasantry. How was Stalin to convince the middle peasant that he had no option but to enter the collective? There was no economic argument so the Soviet leader had to use coercion or the threat of coercion. He targeted the kulaks and in so doing made it abundantly clear to all middle peasants that there was no future for private farming. The only possible avenue for expansion was the collective. If they resisted they would be next on the hit list. Molotov, the faithful mouthpiece of Stalin, put it very succinctly in early 1928 when addressing party officials in the Urals. The kulaks had to be dealt such a blow that the middle peasants would immediately jump to attention! Stalin used this metaphor again in December 1929 in a speech to agrarian Marxists:

Taking the offensive against the kulaks means preparing for action to deal the kulak class such a blow that it will no longer rise to its feet. That's what we Bolsheviks call an offensive .... When the head is off, one does not grieve for the hair. There is another question no less ridiculous: whether kulaks should be allowed to join collective farms? Of course not, for they are the sworn enemies of the collective farm movement.[5]

What was to become of these kulaks and their families if they could not continue farming privately or join collectives? There may have been about 1.1 million households, comprising 7 million persons expropriated. Half of these may have been deported to labour camps in the frozen north and Siberia. Another estimate puts the number of peasant households liquidated between 1929 and 1933 at about 3 million, involving 15 million persons. Whatever the numbers involved the story is horrendous, and the cruelty and suffering numbing. The kulaks were almost completely liquidated in the course of 1930.

Middle and poor peasants were pushed headlong into collectives in early 1930. By 1 March 55 per cent of these peasants had been collectivised. Some areas reported almost total collectivisation while in others, such as Kazakhstan, Uzbekistan and the Caucasus the percentage was much lower. No attempt was made to persuade the peasants by rational argument that collective life would be better than private existence. There was no point, it had failed in the past. Party officials were under enormous pressure. They were instructed to collectivise by voluntary means! If they failed they could be accused of being pro-kulak and enemies of Soviet power. They were forwarded contradictory instructions, their guidelines were vague, deliberately vague. That way more local initiative could be displayed. The peasant resisted, blood flowed and the survivors destroyed everything they could. It was relatively easy to form a collective, just declare a village or two a kolkhoz, as the artel or most common form of collective became known. The trouble started when the officials began to collectivise livestock and implements. More blood flowed and the peasants often chose to slaughter their animals and break their implements rather than allow them to be put in a common pool. When some animals and implements were collectivised there was nowhere to store them since collectivisation preceded the building of the necessary infrastructure. So many of the animals died and the implements rotted or rusted.

Stalin called a temporary halt to the mayhem in an article in *Pravda* on 2 March 1930. With sublime condescension he put the blame on the local officials who had become 'dizzy with success'. This from someone who had encouraged coercion, arbitrariness and violence by the man on the spot! Then a small concession was made: the house, a small vegetable garden and orchard and some livestock were not to be socialised. Such was the stampede out of the collectives (since practically no one had joined voluntarily) that some local party men became demoralised. Regions such as Moscow and areas to the west almost decollectivised. The proportion of peasants in collectives dropped to 23 per cent on 1 June 1930. But Stalin had not changed his mind, he merely wanted to ensure that the spring sowing took place. Afterwards the offensive was again resumed and the peasants reacted as before, destroying and slaughtering everything they thought would be of use to a kolkhoz. 'Slaughter, you won't get meat in the kolkhoz, crept the insidious rumours. And they slaughtered. They ate until they could eat no more. Young and old suffered from indigestion. At dinner time tables groaned under boiled and roasted meat. Everyone had a greasy mouth, everyone hiccoughed as if at a wake. Everyone blinked like an owl, as if inebriated from eating.'[6] The peasants had a feast. Between 1928 and 1933 they slaughtered 26.6 million cattle or 46.6 per cent of the total Soviet herd, 15.3 million horses or 47 per cent of the total and 63.4 million sheep or 65.1 per cent of the total. Such desperation, such irrational destruction: these same peasants were inviting famine in the near future. Such was the breakdown of communication between the urban mind which wanted cornucopia and the peasant mind which also wanted cornucopia. Both shared common goals but were quite unable to find a common language to define the route to be taken. The urban–rural divide in the Soviet Union was deep before collectivisation but afterwards it became a chasm with mutual suspicion elevated to the natural order of things.

The second FYP (1933–37) got off to a very inauspicious start. The country seemed to be exhausted in 1933 from the gargantuan efforts of the previous years. There was a terrible famine as well as a crisis in transport and severe shortages in many industries. Gross industrial production only rose by 15 per cent compared with the 20 per cent annually claimed for the years 1929–32. Consequently the whole plan was redrafted and adopted by the XVIIth Party Congress in January–February 1934.

The goals of the plan were now consolidation, meaning the bringing into effective operation of industrial plant, mastering techniques and raising living standards.[7] Soviet planning had become more realistic. Consumer goods' industries, badly neglected during the first FYP, were to be accorded higher priority, though certainly not given preference over heavy industry. These high hopes, however, were not fulfilled, and the plans for consumer goods, housing and real wages were not achieved. The Stalinist economic order took firm shape instead with its emphasis on heavy industry, energy and defence and detailed command planning from the centre. The defence sector devoured more and more resources: 3.4 per cent of total budget expenditure in 1933 but 16.5 per cent in 1937 and 32.6 per cent in 1940. Over the period 1933–38 the output of the defence sector almost trebled and between 1934 and 1939 the armed forces doubled in size.[8] This was a development a young industrialising nation could ill afford since it depressed living standards and reduced the efficiency of consumer goods' industries and agriculture by creaming off the best scientists, engineers and workers for the defence sector. The threat from national socialist Germany was felt to be very real and it put off raising living standards for a whole generation.

The industrial performance during the years 1934–36 was as impressive as 1937 was disappointing, due in part to the purges. However it made the Soviet Union much less dependent on imported capital goods and, also, the debts contracted during the first FYP could be paid off.

The third FYP was elaborated during 1937–38 and formally adopted at the XVIIIth Party Congress, in 1939, but it was cut short after three and a half years by the German invasion. It continued the trend of the previous plans, giving priority to producers' goods over consumer goods. Hence by the outbreak of war the foundations of heavy industry, including defence, had been well and truly laid.

The mayhem of collectivisation and the poor yields of 1932 resulted in famine in many areas in 1933. Those worst affected were the Ukraine, the North Caucasus, the Lower and Middle Volga and Kazakhstan. The situation was exacerbated by the need to seize grain from the peasants to build stocks to feed the Red Army in the eventuality of a conflict with Japan in the Far East. There was also the need to service the USSR's hard currency debt which had risen sharply after 1928. Grain exports rose to 4.8 million tonnes in 1930 but fell back to 1.8 million tonnes in 1932 and 1.7 million tonnes in 1933. They even reached 800,000 tonnes in 1934. This was harsh *realpolitik* by Stalin. He exported grain knowing that condemned some to hunger and death. Importing foreign technology took precedence with 1.5 billion rubles worth of equipment for heavy industry being acquired between 1928 and 1933. The Great Depression ensured that grain prices were low, compounding the Soviet Union's difficulties.

The famine of 1933 was man-made. If collective-farm peasants evaded bringing in part of the crop, as they did in 1932, they had to pay the penalty. A new way of measuring the harvest was imposed – biological yield. The State estimated the harvest according to the standing grain, and deliveries were based on this. (Khrushchev was to admit later that it overestimated barn yield by about 40 per cent.) Stalin's logic was ruthless. Those who don't gather in the harvest don't eat. He prevented food being taken to the stricken areas and, unlike the previous Soviet famine of 1920–21, there was no foreign help. The myth was maintained that there was no need for help since there was no famine. Foreign admirers of Stalin colluded, most of them unknowingly, in this charade. One of these was George Bernard Shaw. Over 3 million died of starvation, and this may be an underestimate.

Published statistics had to maintain the myth that there were no famine deaths. The purges also took a heavy toll of human life. The 1937 census results were never fully published, but a hitherto secret document provides some guidance as to the number who died unnatural deaths. It is dated 21 March 1939 and is signed by Stalin, an official of Gosplan reporting to Molotov. The actual Soviet urban and rural population in 1939 is given as 161.1 million but 2.7 million should be added. They are presumably in the gulag. This gives a total of 163.8 million. However, the published figure for 1939 is 170.1 million. According to this estimate the undeclared victims of Stalin's famine and purges during the 1930s come to 6.3 million.

Agriculture hit rock bottom in 1933, but thereafter it was upwards all the way. Although there were still about nine million peasants outside collectives in 1934 the great majority had been dragooned into the socialist sector by 1937 by imposing taxes and compulsory deliveries to the State which the individual peasants could not possibly meet. When they inevitably failed their property was sold to meet the deficit. By 1937 almost all cultivated land was in collective farms (kolkhozes) or state farms (sovkhozes). The latter were run as state enterprises, factories without a roof, and employees were classified as workers and not as collective farm peasants. State farm workers were paid a guaranteed wage but collective farm peasants only attained this in 1966. State farms could and did run up substantial losses which had to be borne by the State, whereas the kolkhoz peasants had to bear the losses of the kolkhozes themselves. Sovkhozes were set up in regions where there had previously been little or no settled agriculture and were often enormous. State farms, or grain factories, became very popular during the second FYP, especially in the east, but many of them failed.

Table 3.1   Soviet grain production and procurement 1929–38

Year	Grain production (million tonnes)	Grain procurement (million tonnes)	Percentage
1929	66.8	10.8	16.2
1930	71.0	16.0	22.5
1931	65.0	22.1	34.0
1932	65.0	23.7	36.5
1933	71.0	23.3	32.8
1934	77.5	28.4	36.6
1935	63.0	25.7	40.8
1936	63.0	25.7	40.8
1937	97.5	31.8	32.6
1938	73.0	31.5	43.1

Source: Paul R. Gregory and Robert C. Stuart (eds) Soviet Economic Structure and Performance 4th edn, p. 117

Livestock numbers recovered reasonably quickly from the depredations of the 1930–33 era. This was due to a large extent to the willingness of the State to permit the private ownership of animals by kolkhozniks and workers, within certain limits. The socialist sector grew as well but the majority of meat and milk products, eggs,

Table 3.2   Fulfilment of principal goals of Stalinist Five-Year Plans 1928–50 (per cent)

	First Five-Year Plan (1928–1932)	Second Five-Year Plan (1933–1937)	Fourth Five-Year Plan (1946–1950)
National income			
Official Soviet estimate (1926/27 prices)	91.5	96.1	118.9
Jasny estimate (1926/27 'real' prices)	70.2	66.5	
Bergson estimate			89.9
Nutter estimate			84.1
Industrial production			
Official Soviet estimate (1926/27 prices)	100.7	103.0	116.9
Jasny estimate	69.9	81.2	
Nutter estimate	59.7	93.1	83.8
Kaplan and Moorsteen estimate	65.3	75.7	94.9
Official Soviet estimate, producer goods (1926/27 prices)	127.6	121.3	127.5
Official Soviet estimate, consumer goods (1926/27 prices)	80.5	85.4	95.7
Agricultural production			
Official Soviet estimates (1926/27 prices)	57.8	62.6–76.9	89.9
Jasny estimate	49.6	76.7	
Nutter estimate	50.7	69.0	76.4
Johnson and Kahan estimates	52.4	66.1–69.0	79.4
Transport			
Railway freight traffic (tonne-km)	104.0		113.2
Employment			
National economy, workers and employees	144.9	93.4	116.1
Industry, workers and employees	173.9		118.9
Wages (workers and employees, nat. economy)			
Average money wage	143.9	173.6	127.8
Average real wage, official Soviet estimate	31.9	102.6	89.1
Average real wage, Zaleski estimate	26.0	65.8	
Labour productivity, industry			
Official Soviet estimate	65.1		100.7
Jasny estimate	41.8		
Nutter estimate	36.3		
Kaplan and Moorsteen estimate			80.0
Cost of production			
Industry (current prices)	146.1	121.1	134.2
Investment			
In constant prices	54.		122

Source: E. Zaleski *Stalinist Planning for Economic Growth 1933–1952* p. 503. Jasny, Bergson, Nutter, Kaplan, Moorsteen, Johnson and Kahan are Western economists.

vegetables and fruit was still produced by the private owner. The latter fed the countryside and gradually provided more and more for the towns. Whereas the kolkhozes and sovkhozes dominated grain, cotton, sugar beet and flax production, the private sector accounted for most of the rest.

One of the goals of collectivisation was to ensure a guaranteed flow of food to the cities and the Red Army. On this score collectivisation was a signal success. During 1926–28 State procurements of grain at modest prices had been about 14 per cent of the harvest. However, this rose to 22.5 per cent in 1930, to 34 per cent in 1931 and 40.8 per cent by 1936 (see Table 3.1). Procurements of meat, milk and eggs rose while output declined. Peasants retaliated by helping themselves to stalks of corn, potatoes and other crops before and after harvesting. Stalin's response was savage. A law dated 7 August 1932, in his own handwriting, prescribed the death penalty or ten years' jail for stealing kolkhoz or sovkhoz property. No amount was specified so it was possible to be shot for stealing a few ears of corn.

Table 3.3 Structural change of the Soviet economy in the 1930s

	1928	1937
Sector shares of NNP[1] (%)		
Agriculture	49	31
Industry	28	45
Services	23	24
End use shares of NNP (%)		
Consumption	82	55
Government	8	22
Net domestic investment	10	23
Foreign Trade		
Exports + imports/NNP	6.2	1
Economic growth (average annual, %)		
Total product: 1928–40	5.1	
Per capita product: 1928–40	3.9	

1 Net National Product
Source: Gregory and Stuart op. cit. p. 121

Since the kolkhoz had taken firm shape by 1935 a congress was convened to adopt a model statute to regulate the economy of the collective farm until the early 1970s. The kolkhoz was defined as a voluntary co-operative on land which was allotted by the State rent free in perpetuity. The chairman was elected by the members but the farm had to obey the instructions of the local party and government organs which meant that it had very little operational autonomy. The mechanical work on the farm was carried out by the local Machine Tractor Station (MTS) to whom payment was made in kind. This was another way by which the State could increase procurements and control the kolkhozes. Labour was rewarded at the end of the year, according to a complicated labour-day system (*trudodni*). If the farm was not very prosperous, and given the fact that procurement prices remained more or less the same until the

1950s, there was often very little to pay out at the end of the year. The peasant was sustained by his private plot which varied between 0.25 and 0.5 hectare. He could also own a cow and followers, one sow and litter, four sheep and unlimited numbers of rabbits and poultry. Livestock usually found their way on to kolkhoz grazing land and the ripening crops also made a contribution, all strictly illegal of course. It was overwhelmingly the women of the household who looked after the private plot.

SOCIAL POLICY

The forging of the industrial worker out of the wayward peasant was a painful process. The latter, used to working flat out twice a year, at sowing time and at harvest, as long as the light lasted, was to be turned into a disciplined, punctual, regular worker giving of his best six days a week throughout the year. Such was the surge out of the countryside during the first FYP that the labour plan was grossly overfulfilled. Whereas the plan looked for an increase of labour in all state enterprises and concerns from 11.4 million in 1927–28 to 15.8 million in 1932–33, the actual number in 1932 reached 22.8 million. In industry there were 6.4 million workers instead of the planned 3.9 million in 1932. This exacerbated the already tight housing situation in the cities. The housing plan was based, of course, on the economists' own projections, which turned out to be underestimates. Moreover, even the modest housing plan was not met, living space increased only by 16 per cent, so overcrowding, shared kitchens, frayed nerves, limited sanitation and poorly maintained buildings became a way of life for a whole generation of Soviet people.

Another consequence of the overfulfilment of the labour supply plan was that more wages were paid out and hence there was more money in circulation chasing the few goods that were available. Also, average wages throughout the economy, excluding agriculture, exceeded the plan for 1932 by 43.9 per cent.

Bread rationing was introduced in early 1929 and then spread to other foodstuffs and scarce consumer goods. By 1940, forty million persons were receiving their bread ration from 'centralised sources' and a further ten million from local sources.[9] This helped to keep the prices down for those fortunate enough to have ration cards but the latter did not guarantee that the goods would be available when needed. This gave rise to a host of other sources of supply, some state run but many not. The black market flourished, as it will do when there is an acute shortage of anything, and there was also the kolkhoz market where the peasants sold the goods they produced on their private plots. Private or free market prices rocketed between 1928 and 1932; for instance the price of flour in 1932 was twenty-three times that of 1928. Even the prices of rationed goods increased sharply in January 1932 as the government attempted to mop up surplus purchasing power and increase its financial resources for the industrialisation of the country. Then in an effort to reduce the difference in price between rationed goods and the free market price, with a view to abolishing rationing, prices of rationed and other scarce goods were substantially increased in 1933 and again in 1934 when, for instance, the price of rye bread, the staple diet in the north, was doubled.[10] The rural sector bore the full brunt of the price increases as the government did not provide the collective farm peasants with ration cards. Procurement prices, the prices paid by the State for farm produce, stagnated. The procurement price of wheat in the Ukraine was only increased in 1934 and beef prices in 1931–32 were actually below those of 1928–29 but pork levels were a little higher.[11] The only bright spot for the kolkhozes was the substantial increase in 1934 in the prices paid for industrial crops, flax, cotton, sunflower, sugar beet and others.

Kolkhozniks were second-class citizens in all but name. They were denied the social security which workers and employees received from the state; they could be called up to build roads, move timber, etc. (something from which the urban dweller was exempt), and they could not obtain an internal passport as long as they lived in the countryside. By permitting kolkhozniks to own some livestock and work a private plot the State acknowledged that it could not pay them a living wage for their work on the kolkhoz. Selling their private produce on the kolkhoz market meant that they continued to trade, thus underlining the fact that under collectivisation the State accepted that the kolkhoznik should remain part peasant. The organisational problems in agriculture were so formidable that the State simply could not cope. So a retreat was ordered in the campaign to employ the peasant in full-time socialist labour. Real living standards dropped in industry and agriculture during the first FYP. They hit their lowest level during the famine year of 1933 but climbed steadily afterwards. Since such emphasis was placed on physical plan goals, quantity took preference over quality. Shop assistants, faced with long queues, could tell customers to take what was offered to go somewhere else. Complaints were inadvisable since they could be construed as a criticism of Soviet life. If anyone doubted that life was getting better he had to remember Stalin's words uttered at a CC plenum on 7–12 January 1933 and devoted to the results of the first FYP: 'But we have without doubt achieved a situation in which the material conditions of workers and peasants are improving year by year. The only people who doubt this are the sworn enemies of Soviet power.'[12]

The rapid rise in employment meant that unemployment in the cities had disappeared by 1932. This was a signal success but the planners were disappointed by the slow rise in labour productivity. With millions of peasants coming in from the countryside the traditional industrial labour force was swamped. The country lads practised on the available machinery and had to learn to be punctual and to accept discipline the hard way. The miserable housing conditions and the shortage of food led to a huge turnover of labour. In a bid to curb this fluidity labour laws became more and more strict after 1930.

The first legislation imposing prison sentences on those who violated labour discipline was passed in January 1931. Labour books or records were introduced for all industrial and transport workers in February 1931 and the theft of state or collective farm property became a capital offence as of 7 August 1932. Absenteeism, if only for a day, led to instant dismissal from November 1932 and the internal passport was introduced on 27 December 1932 to restrict movement and facilitate control. The passport was a feature of Imperial Russia but in the Soviet case it was not issued to the rural population. Trade unions became merely state institutions geared to raising labour productivity and discipline.

In order to keep vitally needed workers enterprises had to concern themselves with accommodation and food supplies and special shops were set up where only those with the requisite pass could buy goods unobtainable outside. Stalin attacked the concept of egalitarianism in wages in 1931 and did away with the maxim that party members were not to earn more than skilled workers. Differentials now established a yawning gap between the incomes of the skilled and the unskilled and more and more competition was introduced. Shock workers were used to show what could be achieved and their exploits were then translated into higher norms for everyone else. No wonder some of them were stuffed down shafts!

Total employment (those employed by state institutions and enterprises) during the second FYP rose to 27 million in 1937 and the industrial labour force grew to 10.1 million but in both cases the planned goals for 1937 were not achieved. This was a gratifying development as it indicated that the plan had been achieved, if one accepts the official figures, with a smaller labour force, thus demonstrating a healthy rise in labour productivity. Workers were becoming more skilled and also better educated although the technical colleges were unable to turn out the numbers of skilled craftsmen required. Another reason for the improved performance was the impact of the Stakhanovite movement. It was named after Aleksei Stakhanov who on 30–31 August 1935 mined 102 tonnes of coal in five hours and 45 minutes or the equivalent of fourteen norms in the Zentralnaya-Irmino mine in the Donbass. Of course he had optimal conditions, he had assistants and all the machinery worked. An even more extraordinary claim was made for Nikita Isotov who was stated to have mined 240 tonnes of coal or the equivalent of thirty-three norms in just one shift. In other words he had done the work of thirty-three miners all by himself.

In January 1936 Sergo Ordzhonikidze, Commissar for Heavy Industry, placed Aleksei Gastev in charge of preparing cadres for the Stakhanovite movement. Gastev was an enthusiastic supporter of the ideas of F. W. Taylor, the American time and motion innovator. Hence the latter's concept of 'scientific management', which has been used to determine wages ever since 1931, became firmly embedded in Soviet industry. The settling of wage rates passed mainly into the hands of technical experts and industrial managers, thus eliminating collective bargaining and the right to strike.

Money wages of workers and employees almost doubled between 1933 and 1937, which again was ahead of the plan so that inflationary pressures continued. The government did its best to control increases and to favour workers in those sectors of the economy which were accorded high priority. Rationing was phased out in 1935 and gradually state and free market prices approached one another. State prices rose by 110.2 per cent between 1932 and 1937 and free market prices dropped considerably, producing an increase of 80 per cent in the retail price index.[13] Average real wages rose over the same period, exceeding the plan by 2.6 per cent (see table 3.2). However real wages (the sum of money left after deducting the rate of inflation) were lower in 1937 than in 1928 and in that year were little better than in 1913.

Life down on the farm improved during the second FYP. The number of livestock owned by kolkhozniks increased and the kolkhoz market was a valuable source of additional income. Migration to the towns slowed and the technically minded could be placed on the machinery in the MTS. The low wages of the unskilled industrial workers and the chronic overcrowding in the cities, only 6 per cent of families in Moscow in 1935 had more than one room, helped to lessen the attraction of urban life. Nevertheless there were still many who wanted to migrate from the comparatively infertile regions. As late as 1939, 15,700 kolkhozes out of a total of over 240,000 did not make any cash payments to their members and a further 46,000 paid the miserable sum of 20 kopeks per workday unit (*trudoden*).[14]

Living standards of workers and employees stagnated during the third FYP, 1938 to June 1941, and may even have dropped slightly by 1941. Government policy appears to have been based on the assumption that living standards were of secondary importance, that labour discipline was too lax and had therefore to be greatly improved, and that everyone should consciously place state goals ahead of private preferences. During 1940 labour law became even more restrictive. Officially there was to be no labour market and no worker could change jobs without permission, indeed skilled workers and specialists could be directed anywhere by the authorities. Absenteeism, which could be interpreted as being more than twenty minutes late for work, became a criminal offence. The working day was stretched from seven to eight hours and the seven-day week, six days of labour out of seven, again become standard.

This legislation stayed on the statute book until 1956 but lost most of its sting with the death of Stalin in 1953. It is without precedent in a peacetime economy and its only advantage was that it needed little amendment when war actually came. It was vigorously enforced; if judges were soft on the offenders they were put in the dock! Absences which were quite legitimate were reported by factory managers. In one case a woman was sentenced while she was in a maternity home; another with a sick breast-fed baby and five months pregnant got four months, and this sentence was confirmed by the republican supreme court.[15] Other measures, not designed to win public approval, cut social benefits for most workers and fees were charged for students in tertiary education and for pupils in senior forms in secondary schools. This latter move actually contravened the provisions of the 1936 constitution. There must have been general bewilderment at these measures since the impact of them was not cushioned by claiming that they were necessary given the probability of war. Indeed the danger of war, it was claimed, had receded as a result of the German–Soviet non-aggression pact.

Peasants were treated in the same manner. In 1939, 2.5 million hectares of land in private plots was taken away and private livestock numbers were also cut. Compulsory deliveries of meat and milk products were levied on the kolkhoznik – this at a time when his income from kolkhoz work was declining.

This new, hard policy towards all segments of the population, very noticeable in 1939 and 1940, seems to have been decided upon by Stalin at a time when he believed that the risk of open rebellion was past. It cannot have been born of the need to gird the Soviet Union for war since no attempt was made to win hearts and minds and to ask for voluntary sacrifices. It was as if administrative fiat, alloyed to force and coercion, were regarded as capable of producing the desired product, the *vir sovieticus* and the *femina sovietica*. Perhaps Stalin thought that the savage measures just adopted would be regarded as abnormal only in the short run and that they would be seen as normal and commonplace in the near future. Such policies were a dreadful waste of human initiative and talent and could only be applied to an unsophisticated labour force. Coercion, on the same scale, in an advanced economy would have been economically disastrous.

Lenin had proclaimed, during his last years, the need for a cultural revolution in the Soviet Union. A revolution did occur during the 1930s but it was a technical revolution. Science and technology acquired a dominant position in the tertiary sector, a position they still occupy. Applied knowledge was at a premium in a state undergoing industrialisation and collectivisation. There were certain barriers to be overcome, however. Very few of the technical experts who possessed the coveted knowledge were open advocates of Stalin's policy – that the sky was the limit as far as growth rates were concerned. Aware of the difficulties involved, they were the natural allies of Stalin's critics in the Politburo after 1928. Stalin and his supporters, and here Molotov played a key role, wanted to tap the abilities of workers and peasants and thereby swamp the 'old' technical intelligentsia with the new. The Stalinists accepted that technical standards might fall in the short run but in the long run a dedicated cohort of specialists would be created who would form the backbone of Soviet industrial society. Consequently specialist baiting became a sport, almost a blood sport, in 1928. The old exclusive technical societies, restricted to graduates, were dissolved in 1930 and new organisations appeared which offered membership to all interested in technology. This was a move in the direction of undermining the authority of the traditional specialists, thus making it less likely that the new intelligentsia would be under their sway. There was the added bonus that the new organisations would make political control much easier.

A pronounced class policy was adopted towards science and technology between 1928 and 1931. Specialist baiting and trials of engineers for alleged wrecking, sabotage and espionage were commonplace. The Shakhty trial in 1928, for instance, and the 'industrial-party' trial in late 1930, involving 2,000 engineers, were part of a deliberate campaign to break down resistance to central directives. By 1931 half of all the engineers and technical workers in the Donbass, a key industrial zone, had been arrested.[16] If a machine broke down, which given the unskilled nature of the labour force happened quite often, it could be construed as wrecking. If imported machinery was not effectively used, this again could be called wrecking.

This aggressive attitude towards the engineer went hand in hand with a determined bid to pick the right students for higher technical education. Selection by social origin, and not by ability, was decreed in July 1928 and in 1929 class quotas were introduced together with shorter courses, narrow specialisation and an increase in practical work. Lunacharsky and his Commissariat of Enlightenment opposed these measures since it meant that quality was being sacrificed to quantity. Unfortunately for Lunacharsky his commissariat was stronger on non-technical subjects and this led to technical education being transferred to the Supreme Council of the National Economy and economic agencies. This was the end of Lunacharsky and he was succeeded by Aleksandr Bubnov, a member of the party secretariat, who was unlikely to disagree with Stalin. After July 1928 technical education in the commissariat was entrusted to Andrei Vyshinsky who was to transfer his schoolmasterly qualities to a different milieu in the course of the 1930s.

Cultural radicalism, however, did not last. A marked change appeared in 1932 and 1933 which reversed many of the previous policies. Class quotas went, there was a retreat from narrow specialisation and renewed emphasis on scientific theory and polytechnical education.[17] Quality took over from quantity and ability reasserted itself, replacing a proletarian class background as the guarantee of success. The long battle, begun in 1918, waged between those who believed that access to higher education should be based on ability and those who thought that class should determine entry was almost over. By 1935 the contest had been decided in favour of the former. This was another indication of the de-emphasis of class after the first FYP.

Just why did this turnabout take place? It would appear that a moderate group in the Politburo crystallised around Ordzhonikidze, head of the Supreme Council of the National Economy in late 1930 and then Commissar for Heavy Industry in 1932 when the Supreme Council was broken up, and Sergei Kirov, party secretary in Leningrad, an important industrial area. Ordzhonikidze was effectively head of the industrialisation drive. They were conscious of the damage that impossibly high growth targets were having, especially on quality. The second FYP was to concentrate on bringing into operation existing plants and the mastering of techniques, so growth rates were scaled down. At the XVIIth Party Congress in January–February 1934 Molotov proposed an annual growth rate of 19 per cent whereupon Ordzhonikidze suggested 16.5 per cent and this lower figure was eventually incorporated into the plan. This revealed a lack of consensus in the Politburo and flew in the face of Stalin's dictum at the XVIth Party Congress in June–July 1930 that those who proposed lower growth rates were 'enemies of socialism, agents of our class enemies'. Stalin was deprived of his title of Secretary General at the XVIIth Congress and simply became a secretary. However the murder of Kirov on 1 December 1934 and the suicide of Ordzhonikidze in February 1937 removed the opposition to faster growth rates. One of the chief targets of the purges was the group of moderates advocating slower economic expansion.

There was a rush of students into higher education during the first FYP and numbers peaked in 1932 when 295,600 were registered. Of these 62,200 were aiming at becoming agricultural specialists.[18] Due to the renewed emphasis on quality after 1932 numbers dropped but began to climb again in 1938–41 without reaching the high 1932 figure.

It was one thing to start a course and another to finish it and the emphasis on class rather than formal qualifications between 1928–32 led to a heavy drop-out rate. Probably 70 per cent failed to complete their courses. The re-emphasis on ability cut this to 45 per cent during the second FYP.[19] Students had their greatest impact on curricula and teaching methods during the first FYP but the disappointing results led to a rethink by the authorities. During this period higher technical education was mainly in the hands of enterprises which were to train specialists in the various sectors of industry. However the pressures on managers were so great that few resources were channelled into education. Moreover an enterprise was only concerned about training someone in its own particular field and this led to narrow specialisation with technicians being produced instead of engineers. During the second FYP education was recentralised and the teachers were restored to their former position of authority, relegating the students to organising socialist competition and depriving them of any real influence on the curriculum.

Between 1928 and 1940 a new generation of Soviet specialists was trained; 291,100 graduated with engineering and industrial and 103,400 with agricultural qualifications.[20] How did technical students affect the composition of the Soviet student body during these years?

Table 3.4 Breakdown of graduates in higher education (per cent)[21]

	First FYP	Second FYP	1938–40
Engineering/Industrial	39.8	36.3	27.4
Agriculture	18.0	11.2	9.5
Social Sciences	10.5	19.9	7.1
Educational/Cultural	20.4	22.8	42.6
Health/Medicine	11.3	9.8	13.4

It can be seen that technical graduates accounted for over half of the total in the first FYP but their proportion dropped thereafter. Great stress was placed on turning out teachers in the immediate pre-war years which pulled down the share of engineers and agricultural specialists.

The July 1928 CC plenum decreed that 65 per cent of new entrants to higher technical education were to be of working-class origin and this was raised to 70 per cent in November 1929. This was just about double the proportion of such students in 1928. However the very high figure of 70 per cent was only attained once, in 1929–30, and thereafter never rose above 62 per cent before the quota system based on social origin was abolished in 1935.[22] The consequence of this was that the proportion of students of working-class origin declined to 44 per cent in 1939. Students of peasant background were at a disadvantage as long as the quota system was in operation. They found it more difficult than before to enrol for engineering courses but prospects in agriculture, medicine and education improved.

The group which gained most from the abolition of the quota system was, not surprisingly, the intelligentsia. In 1938 students from non-working-class or peasant backgrounds accounted for 53 per cent of engineering students even though the intelligentsia made up less than 10 per cent of the population. The marked advantage of this social group has continued to the present day.

The proportion of women in higher education jumped as a result of the expansion of the economy. The CC decree in February 1929 stipulated that 20 per cent of places in higher technical education be reserved for women. This was a modest improvement on the 14 per cent of places occupied by women in 1928. In the 1930s women made up about a quarter of engineering students and just under a third of agricultural students. However in 1940 women occupied 40.3 per cent of the engineering places, 46.1 per cent of agricultural places and 58 per cent of all places in higher education.[23] This breakthrough owed more to the call-up of one million young male school leavers in 1940, than to any fundamental change in policy. Significantly in 1941 only 15 per cent of graduate engineers were female.

The ethnic composition of the student body is of considerable interest. Whereas the percentage of Russians in higher education and in the population tallies that of Jews is dramatically different. They made up 1.8 per cent of the Soviet population in 1939 but 13.3 per cent of students in 1935. The only other major nationalities to be overrepresented were Georgians and Armenians. Nevertheless Russians, Ukrainians and Jews made up 80 per cent of those in higher education in the 1930s.

Those with party connections naturally had a better chance of getting a coveted place in higher education. The party was particularly aware of its underrepresentation among technical specialists; it only counted 138 graduate engineers among its members in 1928. By 1937 this number had jumped to 47,000. More significantly, about 70 per cent of all new members recruited between 1939 and 1941 came from the administrative or technical intelligentsia.[24] Such were the pressures on engineers engaged in direct production that many chose to leave the factory and make for other fields. There was a great influx of engineers into the party *apparat* and into the ranks of the political police after 1938. The effect of this was to improve immeasurably the technical efficiency of these two institutions but it meant that only 31.8 per cent of engineers in 1941 were involved directly in production, a sharp drop compared with previous years. The largest proportion, 37.2 per cent, were engaged purely in administration.[25]

CULTURE

Towards the end of his life Lenin was much exercised by the low level of culture in Soviet Russia. He came to see that a cultural revolution was absolutely essential. What he meant were the three Rs, reading, writing and arithmetic. Until this happened it would not be possible to speak of proletarian culture and of narrowing the gap between art and the masses. The divide between the artist and the worker had to be bridged, thus ending the concept of a cultured and artistic elite. The artist had to play his part and put his shoulder to the wheel. There could be no art for art's sake. Art had to serve the construction of socialism.

The party did not attempt to control all aspects of culture during the 1920s and its 1925 decree made clear that no particular group would be afforded primacy. However the defeat of the right had repercussions on the cultural scene and the proponents of proletarian culture, of the hegemony of working-class views, the Association of Proletarian Writers (RAPP), appeared to have won the day. There was only one main obstacle to RAPP dominance in 1929, the All-Russian Union of Writers (AUW). The latter was a loose group of fellow-travellers and as non-political as it was possible to be in the 1920s but it contained many of the big names in Russian literature. Fired with the enthusiasm of religious believers RAPP set out to demolish the AUW by forcing the fellow-travellers to decide on which side of the fence they belonged. Those who did not submit to the proletarian point of view, and by extension to the *avant-garde* of the working class, the party, would be drummed out of literary life. The technique chosen was to accuse Boris Pilnyak, the AUW chairman, and Evgeny Zamyatin, head of the Leningrad branch, of publishing works abroad which had not been passed by the Soviet censor. When this charge was refuted without much difficulty the attackers changed their tack and claimed that the works in question were anti-Soviet. Pilnyak and Zamyatin were found guilty and they lost their posts, as did the whole of the leadership of the AUW. The organisation was renamed the All-Russian Union of Soviet Writers and something like one half of AUW members were refused admission. Pilnyak succumbed and recanted but Zamyatin, made of sterner stuff, requested and was given an exit visa.

RAPP now appeared to have achieved its goal. It thought that the CC approved of its stand and from time to time invited Stalin to intervene in the cultural scene, on its side of course. However, what it had done in destroying the fellow-travellers was to restrict creative freedom even further. RAPP was genuinely concerned about literature and literary values and believed that the writer had a responsibility to tell the whole truth, warts and all. Not only workers but class enemies had to be portrayed objectively and humanely. It is clear that RAPP failed to understand the claims made by the party to be the dominant force in the transformation of the Soviet Union. By inviting the intervention of the party leadership in literary affairs they were tacitly accepting that the party knew best. Nevertheless RAPP was shocked in 1932 when a CC decree disbanded it and set up one organisation, the Union of Soviet Writers, for all those who wished to publish in the USSR. This was in line with what was happening to organisations in other fields of endeavour. The goal was to have just one organisation catering for all involved in a particular pursuit with the party cell giving direction to its activities.

The end of RAPP was also the end of an era in Russian literature. The years 1928–31 had seen the glorification of the man in the street. The first FYP had underlined the need to pull together as a family so as to build a brave new world. The heroes were small men with few skills and little education. Managers and technical experts faded into the background although technology was worshipped. Shock workers and shock brigades achieved wonders and there was an absence of hierarchy. Indeed these years were rich in worker initiative and the labour force exercised an influence on production never again to be equalled. Stalin's attack on egalitarianism in July 1931, the introduction of large differentials and the return of the technical expert to a position of authority, changed all that.

The economic switch from quantity to quality was mirrored in the cultural field. In literature there was a move away from the sheer quantity produced by just any worker who had something to share to the belief that writers should be skilled since they were the 'engineers of the human soul', as Stalin graphically put it. The hero also had to change. The manager, the specialist, the party official, in short the decision-makers, took over. They were portrayed as men and women worthy of emulation, set above the ordinary person.

Party thinking about the role of literature under socialism was spelled out for the first time at the Ist Congress of the Union of Soviet Writers in April 1934. Andrei Zhdanov, speaking for Stalin, called for Bolshevik tendentiousness in literature and art. Writing was to be optimistic, heroic and to serve the goals of socialist construction. Revolutionary romanticism was welcome provided it had both feet firmly planted on the factory floor or farm. The name given to the new framework inside which all writers and artists had to work was socialist realism. This is not the same as social realism, the criticism of existing shortcomings in society. The intellectual, that paid sceptic or Cassandra, was declared redundant in the Soviet Union of the 1930s. Socialist realism was socialist in so far as it was in accordance with the goals of the Communist Party. Realism means the comprehensive depiction and interpretation of life by art from the point of view of social relations.[26] Hence the format became openly didactic; compulsory optimism was the order of the day. Excessive introspection, psychoanalysis, self-doubt and flights into the world of fantasy or the sub-conscious had no place in the new cultural milieu.

Socialist realism did not spring, hydra like, out of Zhdanov's head. It was held to be a continuation and development of classical traditions, the distilled experience of progressive mankind. Since there were no mechanical rules to be followed to produce a work of socialist realist art, considerable latitude was still afforded the artist. However, everyone who wished to publish had to belong to the Union of Soviet Writers and that meant accepting the statutes of the Union, statutes which were mainly political. Party members had the duty of dominating the Union and they in turn were subject to the guidance of the section for culture and propaganda of the Secretariat of the CC. Hence creative expression could be put on a loose rein or restricted according to the mood of the party leadership. Literature, theatre and the cinema were accorded great significance in the 1930s since a new society was coming into existence and the right attitudes had to be propagated.

However the rise of fascism and the policy of the popular front was accompanied by a change in attitude towards foreign writers. In the mid 1930s there was a great deal of contact between Soviet writers and their counterparts in the outside world, which meant that the real impact of socialist realism was not felt until the late 1930s.

The switch after 1932 to the cult of the big hero was given added impetus by the rising tide of Russian nationalism. In 1934 one of the victims of this wave was the Pokrovsky school of history which had almost submerged the national in the international. Suddenly the Russian past was rediscovered and the nation builders and soldiers were accorded star treatment. Two historians in disgrace, E. V. Tarle and B. R. Vipper, were brought back to add to the output. The most impressive achievement was the biography of Peter the Great by Aleksei Tolstoy. There was also a flood of novels on the early years of the Soviet State, especially on the Civil War. The classic is, of course, *And Quiet Flows the Don* by Mikhail Sholokhov, which is concerned with the life of peasants and Cossacks. A striking fact about the novel is that its hero, Gregor Melekhov, is a tragic person who eventually turns against the Soviet regime. He is far removed from the leather jacketed, motorcycle riding communist functionary whose iron will and dedication solves every problem – the hero with whom the party identified.

The most positive hero, from the party point of view, is probably Pavel Korchagin in *How the Steel was Tempered* by Nikolai Ostrovsky. Korchagin, a Ukrainian boy of humble background, battles against impossible odds during the formative years of Soviet power. His unswerving loyalty to the party keeps him going. Knowing that he has only a short time to live he decides to put down on paper his experiences so that they can inspire future generations.

Many Stakhanovites published their life stories in the same vein. They dared to do the unthinkable and thus pushed back the limits of the possible. These autobiographies consistently fail to mention the considerable aid extended to the record-breaker by his manager and workmates.

The struggle with the elements was also a popular theme. The fight to fly higher and faster can be followed through the exploits of the most successful pilot, V. Chkalov. Expeditions to the Arctic were widely covered, possibly to underline Stalin's feat of surviving exile there before 1917. The military significance of such events requires no emphasis but it is striking how technology and technical exploits were used to legitimise the role played by Stalin and the party in the 1930s. Stalin becomes the extraordinary hero, the superman who inspires, guides and cares for all the record breakers. They claim that a meeting with Stalin gives them more resolve and makes it more likely that they will succeed. Stalin, as leader of the Soviet Union, is seen as superior to any capitalist head of state in the outside world. This again is a reflection of the rise of Russian nationalism with the Soviet Union being seen as the centre of the universe.

Folk art and culture were not forgotten. Folk singers and raconteurs were invited to Moscow to sing and declaim the glories of the FYPs. One who fitted contemporary political realities into her art was M. S. Kryukova. In the *Tale of Lenin* she introduced Vladimir Ilich (the red sun), Klimenty Voroshilov (the magic knight), Stalin-svet (light), Dora Kaplan (the furious viper) and Trotsky (wait for it – the villain).[27] The climax of the tale is Lenin on his deathbed sending Stalin out into the world to carry on his work.

THE PURGES

Careful preparation was necessary to make the Show Trials of the 1930s a success. The accusations made by the State had to appear credible to the internal audience of the Soviet population and to the external audience of world opinion. Whereas the trial of Socialist Revolutionaries in 1921 and 1922, since the accused made no secret of their opposition to the Soviet regime, were unexceptional, the first major Show Trial, that of the Shakhty engineers in 1928, involved some of the standard elements which were to become so familiar in the thirties: the written confessions, the non-appearance of some of the accused (one had become insane, another had committed suicide, or so it was said), the bullying, sarcastic behaviour of Andrei Vyshinsky, a clever, cynical lawyer and ex-Menshevik who had arrested Bolsheviks in Moscow in the summer of 1917, the complete absence of any rules of evidence and the inevitable judgment. In this case eleven death sentences were handed down but only five engineers were actually shot. A favourite sport during the years 1928–31, as has been observed, was specialist baiting. Politically specialists were linked to Bukharin and economically they could be blamed for shortages and breakdowns. During 1930 and 1931 there were many secret trials and executions which hit bacteriologists, food scientists and even historians. There were two Show Trials during this period as well, the 'industrial-party' trial in November–December 1930 in which the chief accused was Professor Ramzin and the Menshevik trial in March 1931. The former trial was characterised by the usual confessions. Much was made of the contacts with a former industrialist, one Ryabushinsky, including a long list of his sabotage instructions. This piece of evidence was startling given the fact that the accused had been communicating with the other world since Ryabushinsky was dead. Nor was this the only example of spiritualist power: the party's future Minister of Finance, Vyshnegradsky, a former Tsarist minister, was also no longer in the land of the living. Despite the ineptitude of the prosecutor's frame-up, five death sentences were announced but all were commuted and Professor Ramzin returned to his post a few years later.

The Menshevik trial aimed at discrediting not only Mensheviks but all those who had had contact with them and their ideas. A special target were the Menshevik planners who had helped to draw up the initial lower variant of the first FYP.

The disastrous state of agriculture in 1933 led to two secret trials in March 1933 in which seventy State farm and People's Commissariat of Agriculture officials were executed.

The last of the Show Trials before the Great Purge really got under way was directed against Metro-Vickers engineers in April 1933. Six of the eighteen accused were British and they were said to have organised a sabotage network. The sentences were light, reflecting the lack of convincing evidence and the Soviet Union's sensitivity to British public opinion.

A common denominator in all the above trials was the connection of the accused with the economy. The only major trial with political overtones which took place before 1934 was the one involving the group around M. N. Ryutin. He had put together a 200-page indictment of Stalin and the regime, called the 'Ryutin Platform', from a Bukharinist point of view in late summer 1932.[28] He characterised Stalin as 'the evil genius of the Russian revolution who, motivated by a personal desire for power and revenge, had brought the revolution to the brink of destruction'. Needless to say he wanted Stalin removed before the revolution perished. Stalin in turn took this to mean that Ryutin and his associates were planning his assassination. Other members of the Politburo, notably Kirov, did not read it this way and a majority of the Politburo, it would appear, opposed the use of the death penalty against Ryutin or any other party member. The Ryutin group was expelled from the party, and since many party members had seen the offending document without reporting it, the opportunity was taken to sweep the party clean. Zinoviev and Kamenev, for example, were expelled again from the party and sent packing to the Urals. One estimate puts the number of members purged at 800,000 in 1933 and 340,000 in 1934.[29]

The Ryutin affair appears to have played a key role in convincing Stalin that oppositionists were out to get him and that he had to strike first. Time and time again during the Great Purge trials of 1936–38 the accused were linked to the Ryutin affair. It is seen as the first attempt to shed blood as a way of settling intra-party disputes. However, in 1932 Stalin could not convince his colleagues of this and so the party did not devour any of its own. It would take the assassination of one of the moderates to convince the waverers that Stalin was right when he claimed that the opposition within the party wanted blood. After that it was a short step to the fateful decision to shed the royal red blood of the Bolsheviks, if necessary.

The suicide of Nadezhda Alliluyeva, Stalin's second wife, on 9 November 1932, affected him deeply. She was deeply unhappy with the course the revolution was taking, especially the horrors of forced collectivisation. After the celebrations marking the October Revolution Stalin, and others, had gone to Kliment Voroshilov's flat to dine and drink. Stalin then moved on to a dacha with an officer's beautiful wife. Nadezhda, very concerned about his lateness, phoned around and was told the full story. When Stalin arrived home in the morning Nadezhda was dead. She had shot herself. Stalin's unfaithfulness was the final straw. She left behind a bitter denunciation of his personal and political failings. He was outraged by her suicide and never visited her grave in Novodevichy cemetery. However, his feelings were mixed with guilt. She and he had moved easily in society but those days were now over. He preferred male company afterwards. Although he never remarried he did not give up women. Lavrenty Beria procured luscious lovelies for him in private. Khrushchev remembers catching a glimpse once of a black-eyed Caucasian beauty who on encountering him scurried away 'like a mouse'.

The murder of Sergei Kirov, party chief in Leningrad, in the corridor outside his office in Smolny on the afternoon of 1 December 1934 was a rapier thrust which penetrated to the heart of the party and the nation. This one blow was to lead to the death of millions. The circumstances surrounding the assassination are still mysterious. All that can be determined with certainty is the name of the executioner, Leonid Nikolaev. It was Nikolaev's third attempt. Nevertheless he found Kirov without a bodyguard and no guards were patrolling the fateful corridor, which was highly irregular. Nikolaev and thirteen accomplices were tried in camera and all were executed on 29 December 1934. Significantly they were also accused of plotting to assassinate Stalin as well as Molotov and Kaganovich.

The killing could not have occurred at a more propitious moment for Stalin. Kirov, one of the stars of the XVIIth Party Congress in January–February 1934, the 'congress of victors', at which he had been elected a secretary, was a credible alternative to Stalin. The latter lost his title of Secretary General and reverted to that of secretary. During the voting for membership of the Politburo Kirov received almost 300 votes more than Stalin. A group of delegates approached Kirov and asked if he would stand for the post of General Secretary. He refused and immediately informed Stalin of the *démarche*. It is tempting to see this move as signing Kirov's death warrant. A moderate majority appears to have coalesced in the Politburo and this influenced the goals of the second FYP. The moderates were also against blood letting. Nevertheless there was much blood letting; 1,108 of the 1,966 delegates were executed and 98 of the 139 members of the CC elected at the congress were shot in the years following. Hence the XVIIth Party Congress was not the 'congress of victors' but rather the 'congress of the condemned'. It was the XVIIIth Party Congress which was the real 'congress of [Stalinist] victors'.

Was the death of Kirov just another example of the good fortune which attended the career of Stalin? The death of Sverdlov, the natural secretary general of the party had he lived, the death of Lenin and the death of Dzerzhinsky had all occurred at propitious moments for Stalin. Although it cannot be proved, it would appear that in Kirov's case Stalin made his own luck. One pointer was the fusion of the OGPU and the All-Union NKVD with Genrikh Yagoda in charge. Another was the haste with which Stalin had a decree enacted which speeded up and simplified procedures in political cases. It was published on 2 December 1934 and approved by the Politburo a day later. Since Stalin only heard of Kirov's murder about 5 p.m. on 1 December and then took the overnight train to Leningrad, it would appear that he had drawn up the decree before the death of Kirov. He then phoned from Leningrad on the morning of 2 December giving orders for its publication. The legislation had an immediate effect, resulting in the arrests of former oppositionists. Among those sentenced were Zinoviev to ten years' and Kamenev to five years' imprisonment. Then, paradoxically, there followed a lull until the onset of the Great Purge proper, in August 1936. With the wisdom of hindsight it is clear that Stalin and the NKVD were sharpening their knives for the final showdown but not all the legislation passed then pointed in this direction. On the same point, it is true that what was later to become the notorious article 58 of the Criminal Code of the RSFSR was passed. This defined counter-revolution and was to be used extensively in the Purge trials. It also provided for the execution of civilian and military personnel who fled abroad and for the imprisonment or exile of the families of military absconders even if they were unaware of the intention to defect. Also in 1935 a law was passed which lowered the age of criminal responsibility. This meant that the death penalty could be applied to twelve-year-old children. This severe legislation accorded well with Stalin's understanding of the class struggle. Classes would fade away 'not as a result of the slackening of class conflict but as a result of its intensification'. The

State would wither away 'not through the weakening of its power but through its becoming as strong as possible so as to defeat the remnants of the dying classes and to defend it against capitalist encirclement'.

On the other hand the 'most democratic constitution in the world', the Stalin constitution of 1936, largely penned by Bukharin, came into effect. A bicameral legislature, the Soviet of the Union and the Soviet of Nationalities, was set up. The constitution guaranteed freedom of speech, of assembly and of the press (article 125), freedom of religious worship (article 124), inviolability of the person (article 127), the home and the privacy of correspondence (article 128). Even a Union republic was guaranteed the right to secede from the USSR (article 17). The foundations of socialism had been laid and exploiting classes had ceased to exist. Only two fraternal classes, the working class and the collective farm peasantry, now existed together with the intelligentsia which was defined as a stratum since it owned no property. The party was defined as the 'vanguard of the working people in their struggle to build a communist society and the leading core of all organisations of the working people, both government and non-government' (article 126).

The constitution was a new departure in many ways. Previously it had been argued that soviets were peculiar to the stage of the dictatorship of the proletariat. They were simultaneously legislative and executive organs and even local soviets were not considered to be merely local authorities but organs of state power. All together they constituted a unified system of equal links of varying sizes. As such they represented true progress and were far in advance of the bourgeois parliamentary system. The 1936 constitution shattered this unity. Local organs – soviets and their executive committees – became local authorities; the 'supreme organs of state power' – the Supreme Soviets – became legislative organs and the 'supreme organs of state administration' – Sovnarkom (or the Council of Ministers as of 1946) became executive organs. The Supreme Soviets even began to describe themselves as 'Soviet parliaments' despite Lenin's strictures on 'parliamentary cretinism'.

Though it was obvious to anyone reading the constitution that the interests of the party were to supersede those of any individual or group, the USSR nevertheless appeared to be moving in the right direction with the prospect of an end to the arbitrariness of the previous years. In line with this, law as a discipline staged a comeback at this time.

But all this flattered to deceive; it was purely cosmetic and accentuated the ugliness of the body politic. The face of the Soviet Union during the dreadful Purge years of 1936–38 revealed the suffering and travail of a whole nation. Anguish, despair, pain and death were constant companions. No one could feel secure, not even Stalin himself.

There were three great Show Trials during these years. The first, in

August 1936, starred Zinoviev and Kamenev with a supporting cast of minor officials. Confessions played a key role in proving that the accused had all been behind the murder of Kirov and would have killed Stalin as well had they had the opportunity. The bogey man of the 1930s, Trotsky, was introduced and shown to have ordered assassinations and wrecking. The tone of the proceedings can be neatly illustrated by quoting from Vyshinsky's closing speech for the prosecution: 'I demand that these mad dogs be shot, every last one of them!' He had his way, they were all shot. But it was not Vyshinsky who decided their fate, the decision had been taken outside the courtroom, in the Kremlin. This was quite constitutional as the party took precedence over the court though it obviously violated other aspects of the same constitution.

The second great Show Trial should have involved Bukharin, Rykov and Tomsky but *Pravda* announced on 10 September 1936 that charges against the first two had been dropped due to lack of evidence. Tomsky did not need to be acquitted since he had already cheated the executioner by executing himself on 22 August. The acquittals point to opposition within the Politburo and the CC and to the fact that Bukharin and Rykov were not willing to make the confessions demanded of them, at least not yet. Yagoda, possibly as a result, lost his position as head of the NKVD on 26 September and was replaced by Nikolai Ezhov. He was to give his name to the terrible events of the next two years. The *Ezhovshchina*, or 'Ezhov times', were red years when rivers of blood were shed.

The second great Show Trial, in January 1937, turned out to involve mainly Pyatakov, mentioned in Lenin's 'Testament', Sokolnikov, a signatory of the Treaty of Brest-Litovsk, Radek, an important early figure in the Comintern and Serebryakov, a former secretary of the CC. They were all welded together to form an 'Anti-Soviet Trotskyite Centre', with predictable goals. They were spying for Germany and Japan and Trotsky was stated to have met Rudolf Hess to agree plans to sabotage Soviet industry and military preparations in case of war. Pyatakov debased himself and made the most abject confession but it availed him nothing. He and Serebryakov were shot and the other two lost their lives in labour camps in 1939.

The most incredible of all the charges hurled about during the *Ezhovshchina* was that Marshal Tukhachevsky, a leading strategic thinker and deputy commissar of defence, and a host of other military were guilty of treason. In Tukhachevsky's case there was evidence that he was in league with the national socialists but it had been fabricated in Berlin and arguably Stalin was aware of this. He never allowed the incriminating evidence to be published.

The slaughter of the armed forces began on 12 June 1937 when Tukhachevsky and some top army men were executed, then spread to lower ranks, then to the political commissars whose head Yan

Gamarnik had committed suicide on 1 June. A posting to Spain turned out to be invariably fatal, not when the officer was fighting for the Spanish republic, but when he returned. The navy was completely decapitated, all eight admirals perishing. A roll call of the top dead makes sombre reading:

3 out of 5 Marshals
14 out of 16 Army Commanders Class I and II
8 out of 8 Admirals
60 out of 67 Corps Commanders
136 out of 199 Divisional Commanders
221 out of 397 Brigade Commanders

All 11 deputy commissars of defence and 75 out of 80 members of the Supreme Military Council were executed. In all 35,000, half of the officer corps, were either shot or imprisoned.[30] And it was all a ghastly mistake. As Khrushchev admitted later the charges were unfounded.

The last great Show Trial opened to a packed house on 2 March 1938. The key accused were the pair who had slipped through the net before, Bukharin and Rykov. Krestinsky, a Politburo member under Lenin was also thrown in as was Yagoda, getting a taste of his own medicine. Two Uzbek communists were also indicted on charges of 'bourgeois nationalism', reflecting the clamp-down on the nationalities. The national elites were simply wiped out. Krestinsky actually retracted his confession but the next day he thought better of it. They were all lumped together in a 'bloc of right wingers and Trotskyites', something which only existed in Vyshinsky's head. The inevitable death sentences followed.

When Ezhov had served his purpose he departed the stage. On 8 December 1938 Lavrenty Beria stepped up to become People's Commissar for Internal Affairs and held the post until 1946. However, until Stalin's death he had Politburo responsibility for the police. A fellow Georgian, he was just as hard as Stalin.

Foreign communists exiled in the Soviet Union were in a particularly unenviable position. The NKVD decimated their number, being especially hard on the Germans and Poles. However, the greatest prize of all, Trotsky, eluded Beria's men until 21 August 1940.

Those who were not executed were dragged off to labour camps in outlandish places such as northern Siberia and northern Kazakhstan, venues, in other words, where no one would normally head for. In the labour camps the daily food ration depended on fulfilling labour norms. In this way much useful work was rendered the Soviet State in regions where voluntary labour was almost non-existent. Prisoners worked also on major projects in the rest of the country, for instance on the Volga–White Sea canal. Here the mortality rate was very high but Stalin is reported to have said that man is after all mortal but that the canal would last for ever.

Stalin once confided to Churchill that the kulaks had been his greatest problem. Many of these were in labour camps in 1933–35, probably about 3.5 million or 70 per cent of the then total.[31] By 1937 the camp population had risen to perhaps 6 million.

Stalin signed many of the death sentences. In total, Stalin, with Molotov counter-signing, had placed before him 383 lists of names for execution. They were divided into four categories: general, military, NKVD and wives of enemies of the people. During 1937–38 these lists contained about 40,000 names. During the whole Stalin period 230,000 appeared on these death lists. On one day alone, 12 December 1937, Stalin and Molotov sentenced 3,167 to death and then went off to the cinema. Even after the beginning of the war Stalin was still settling scores. On 5 September 1941 he confirmed 170 death sentences. These included survivors of the Show Trials such as Rakovsky. Also executed was the famous left SR Maria Spiridonova. The following month four generals were shot without trial. And so it went on.

After such a catalogue of methodical madness the question must arise why Stalin deemed it all necessary. It is instructive that two opponents of incestuous murder, V. V. Kuibyshev, a Politburo member and head of Gosplan, and Maksim Gorky, the writer, both died before the first Show Trial of the Great Purge. It is difficult to believe that Stalin took the confessions at face value knowing that they had been exacted under physical and psychological torture. One case will suffice. Mironov had reported to Stalin that he had been unable to break Kamenev. Stalin's reply was very direct: 'Now then don't tell me any more about Kamenev . . . . Don't come to report to me until you have in this briefcase the confession of Kamenev!'[32] Often the accused admitted to the most preposterous deeds in an attempt to save their families. Some accused, Zinoviev and Kamenev for instance, believed that their lives would be spared if they co-operated fully and some communists thought they were doing it for the good of the party.

The tales of wrecking, sabotage, assassination attempts, efforts to restore capitalism and weaken the defences of the USSR had a great impact on the population, repeated as they were *ad nauseam*. The confessions implicated hordes of others and the family of each accused was automatically in disgrace. The economic hardships, the shortage of food, indeed every mishap could be blamed on these 'enemies of the people'. The tense atmosphere was such that people took to denouncing others in the hope of deflecting suspicion away from themselves. Many sought to overfulfil their plan of denunciations.

Stalinist policy between 1928 and 1941 can be interpreted as a series of offensives. The first FYP was the initial offensive, which was accompanied by intense politicisation and mobilisation of the population. Specialists became scapegoats for economic failure. Stalin had to take cognisance of his fellow oligarchs. From 1932 onwards a period of consolidation set in and plan targets were pitched a little lower and living standards improved. However, politicisation became even more intense with every nook and cranny of life subject to Bolshevik examination. Efforts were made to develop a new science of Soviet success. All this was a preparation for the purges of 1936–38 which launched the second offensive. By 1936 Stalin was unquestionably dictator and so could set about devouring his other oligarchs. Stalin's inner group appears to have believed that there was considerable opposition within the country to the modernisation drive under way. This offensive sees the Politburo and Central Committee losing effective power to Stalin, the enormous extension of the NKVD's coercive power and the deliberate use of terror and the promotion to leading positions of the Stalinist nomenklatura. This elite was essentially of peasant origin. During this offensive economic goals were sharply raised; political opponents were hounded, often to their deaths; there was a renewed campaign against bourgeois specialists; concomitantly, there was a concerted effort made to educate a generation of 'new' specialists; discipline, especially of labour, became harsh. A motivation for the purges may have been the belief that the 'old' governmental and party apparatus would hold back growth. If this is so the leadership took the tremendous risk of annihilating it and ensconcing a new elite in record time. The elimination of the military leadership was part of this process. This underlines Stalin's lack of understanding of expertise. He evidently believed that it could be garnered very quickly.

PARTY AND GOVERNMENT

Lenin was fascinated by the apparatus of government and invested great energy in the running of Sovnarkom. Stalin had to choose another route to power. He made the party machine his base, and when he proved victorious in the post-Lenin power struggle it was inevitable that he would set out to transform Sovnarkom. The XVIth Party Conference in April 1929 ordered a purge of the governmental bureaucracy. In 1930 Rykov was replaced by Molotov as Prime Minister and this sealed the defeat of the right. Stalin, unlike Lenin, did not favour strong, independently minded commissars. Lenin respected comrades who stood up to him and argued their cases cogently but left the final policy-making prerogative to him. Gone were the days when ministers could make policy and argue their case for implementation. One of the exceptions was Maksim Litvinov, who remained Commissar for Foreign Affairs. His knowledge and authority abroad were valuable assets but another reason for his remaining *en poste* was that foreign affairs were of secondary importance to Stalin during the 1930s.

The party Politburo was the senior policy-making body, but Stalin did not control it until after the murder of Kirov in December 1934.

Sovnarkom was responsible for implementing the Five Year Plans but, given the declared aim of eliminating the market economy, an agency to supervise the implementation of policy was needed. The party became this agency. In 1930 Stalin completely reorganised the party apparatus to perform its new task.[33] The Central Committee now consisted of a Secret Department servicing the Politburo, the Orgburo, and the Secretariat; an Organisational Instructor Department to select officials and supervise party organisations throughout the country; an Assignments Department to select and place administrative, economic, and trade-union officials; a department of Culture and Propaganda to supervise the press, education, party propaganda and general culture; a Department of Agitation and Mass Campaigns; and the Institute of Lenin. Gradually, however, the party apparatus began to influence more and more policy-making. This is evident in the greatly expanded functions of the Orgburo by 1932. It moved from supervising party organisations to overall responsibility for securing the fulfilment of all party and governmental decrees. The party-state was becoming a reality. Lenin had shied away from the party playing the leading role in the State and, had he lived, would have cut back the party's role. Stalin deliberately set out to establish a 'government within a government'. The 'outer' government was Sovnarkom, but the more important became the 'inner' government, fashioned within the party apparatus.

During the 1920s Stalin had been building up his own party 'government'. The Secret Department was headed by Ivan Tovstukha, his chief assistant. One of the Politburo secretaries was Georgy Malenkov. The very important Secretariat bureau of the Central Committee had more than 100 members by 1925. Stalin's own exclusive bureau was the Special Sector, which was part of the Secret Department. This was headed by Aleksandr Poskrebyshev until 1953. Stalin's assistants could also be insinuated into party and governmental posts through the mechanism of the nomenklatura. This was both a list of State posts which could not be filled without party approval and a list of suitable candidates. The Secret Department–Secret Sector was thus in a prime position to influence who filled leading, sensitive posts. It also supervised the security police and foreign affairs as well as domestic life. Each republic had its own Secret Department–Special Sector subordinate to Moscow. This applied also to the Young Communist League, the Komsomol.

Stalin cultivated relations with OGPU, the security police, after the death of Dzerzhinsky but did not gain control over them until the mid 1930s. Stalin had the party Control Commission, responsible for party discipline, comb the tsarist Okhrana archives for evidence which could be used against his colleagues and opponents. Telephone lines were tapped as a matter of course.

The Five Year Plans required a rapid expansion of the governmental system.[34] Under the Soviet constitution of 1924 there were five All-Union Commissariats (Foreign Affairs, Military and Naval Affairs, Foreign Trade, Transport, and Posts and Telegraph) which ran everything from one institution in Moscow; and five Union-Republican Commissariats (Food Supply, Labour, Finance, Worker-Peasant Inspectorate, and the Supreme Economic Council) with commissariats in each republic but all co-ordinated at the centre. In late 1929, thirty-five associations were set up in the Supreme Economic Council to plan and run various branches of the economy. In 1930 Ordzhonikidze succeeded Kuibyshev as head of the Supreme Economic Council – he became head of Gosplan – and formed groups consisting of various associations. Running the economy proved beyond the capabilities of the Council. In early 1932 the Council was subdivided into an All-Union Commissariat for Heavy Industry – headed by Ordzhonikidze, an All-Union Commissariat for the Timber Industry, and a Union-Republican Commissariat for Light Industry, which was swiftly transformed into an All-Union Commissariat. Insignificant sectors of the economy were left under the jurisdiction of republican commissariats. The associations developed into chief administrations (*glavki*), each responsible for hundreds and eventually thousands of enterprises in their sector of the economy. The *glavki* evolved into separate central commissariats; for example, for coal, chemicals, textiles and so on. They in turn spawned their own *glavki* within their own commissariats.

The All-Union Commissariat for Transport split in 1931 into a Commissariat for Railways, a Commissariat for Water Transport and a Central Administration of Road and Automobile Transport. The Commissariat for the Food Industry emerged from the Commissariat for Supply, and it became responsible for the food industry when the Supreme Economic Council was wound up in 1932. Government trusts were established for grain, cattle, sheep, and other products and presented with the massive task of co-ordinating the activities of thousands of kolkhozes and sovkhozes. A USSR Commissariat for Agriculture came into being in 1929. It gave birth to a Commissariat for Grain and Livestock Sovkhozes in 1932. The State procured its products through a Commissariat for Procurement. The All-Union Academy of Agricultural Sciences, headed by the eminent plant biologist Nikolai Vavilov, was established in Moscow in 1929 and became responsible for initiating and co-ordinating all agricultural research throughout the country.

Part of the inspiration behind the rapid industrialisation and collectivisation drive was to enhance the security of the Soviet Union. Heavy industry produced the war *matériel* but the country had to evolve a military doctrine which made maximum use of its limited resources. This was crafted during the 1920s by, among others, Marshal Mikhail Tukhachevsky, Chief of Staff of the Red Army between 1925 and 1928.

The strength of the armed forces rose from 586,000 in 1927 to over 1.4 million a decade later. The Council of Labour and Defence (STO) was transformed into the Council for Defence. The Revolutionary Military Council (*revvoensovet*) was dissolved and replaced by an advisory Military Council under the Commissariat for Military and Naval Affairs. This became the Commissariat of Defence in 1934. The various commissariats concerned with producing war *matériel* were brought together in the Commissariat of the Defence Industry in 1936. This became the Soviet military-industrial complex. In 1937 a Commissariat of the Navy was detached from the Commissariat of Defence as a consequence of the greatly enhanced navy which had been built over the previous decade.

Where was the locus of decision-making? When asked by an American journalist in 1931 if he were a dictator, Stalin, of course, denied it. He maintained that decisions were taken by the party and implemented by the Central Committee and the Politburo. A German journalist returned to the question the following year, but this time Stalin stated that policy was made in the seventy-member Central Committee. It represented the best minds in the country, and members had the opportunity of commenting on and improving proposals laid before them. It would thus appear that the Central Committee played a consultative role with final decision-making the prerogative of a small Politburo group, headed by Stalin.

NATIONALITIES

Lenin's nationality policy accepted that nations had the right to secede from Soviet Russia but took it for granted that a large centralised State would emerge from the revolution. Stalin put it succinctly in 1920 when he stated that it was not in the interests of the people to leave since in so doing they would signal the victory of counter-revolution. Military force was deployed to keep the new State together but the Bolsheviks (Stalin was Commissar for Nationalities until the Commissariat was dissolved in 1924) also revealed great tactical skill in making concessions to national and religious sentiment. They pursued two goals. One was the development of the non-Russian peoples within their own national framework. The goal was to have all organs of government and the party staffed by locals. This policy can be called *korenizatsiya*. This term is related to the word for 'root'. Hence locals were to form the roots of the Soviet tree. This would permit the party in Moscow to guide developments indirectly since direct intervention was bound to occasion protest and resentment. This was the short-term goal. It was expected that gradually, due to the integrating influence of the party and industrialisation, all nations would converge into one Soviet nation, headed by the Russians.

Bolsheviks concentrated their attention on creating and developing a working class in non-Russian areas.[35] This was a formidable undertaking since, among non-Russians, only a Ukrainian, Azerbaidzhani, Jewish and Tatar proletariat existed. The beginning of the Five Year Plans led to a rapid increase in the proletariat but it fell far behind the natural increase of the indigenous population. However, the industrial working class, outside Russia and the Ukraine, remained relatively small. The number of industrial workers in Georgia, Armenia, Azerbaidzhan, Belorussia, Uzbekistan. Tadzhikistan and Turkmenistan rose from 115,000 in 1928 to 350,000 at the end of the first FYP in 1932. Numbers in the sixteen autonomous territories in the RSFSR more than doubled to 140,000 in 1932. Since there were about 6 million industrial workers in the USSR in 1932, this means that only about 8 per cent of workers were outside Russia and the Ukraine. Another difficulty was that it was proving quite difficult to attract the indigenous population into industry. Apart from Belorussia, Kazakhstan and the Tatar and Volga German autonomous republics, the titular nationality was very poorly represented among industrial workers. In the Middle Volga region in 1932 only 13.4 per cent of the 800,000 workers were non-Russians, who made up 28.1 per cent of the population. However, by the mid 1930s the proportion of indigenous workers in the Ukraine, Belorussia, Georgia and Kazakhstan was almost the same as their percentage of the republican population. In Armenia the proportion of workers was higher than that of Armenians in Armenia. Non-Russians were almost all unskilled, with Russians dominant in skilled positions. Russians numerically dominated the industrial labour force and this situation had only slightly changed by 1959. Whereas the proletariat expanded quite rapidly in non-Russian republics, the proportion of industrial workers remained low. In Kazakhstan in 1959 workers made up 58 per cent of the labour force but only 6 per cent of workers were in industry. In Central Asia the proportion was only 4 per cent. In the RSFSR it was 23 per cent.

Most Bolsheviks were Russian, and in 1922 they accounted for about 72 per cent of party members. Others who had a higher percentage in the party than in the population were Jews, Georgians, Armenians, Poles and Latvians. Jews, Georgians and Armenians were overrepresented in the party leadership, and this remained the case until 1953. In the early 1920s there were very few Ukrainians, Belorussians and Muslims in the party. There were about 15,000 Muslims in the party in 1922 and of these about 11,500 were Tatars or Kazakhs. This meant that the Muslims of Central Asia were to all intents and purposes outside the party. A concerted campaign to recruit party members changed the situation. The proportion of indigenous communists in territorial organisations rose from 46.6 per cent in 1927 to 53.8 per cent in 1932 (582,000 members). However, by 1937 this had dropped back to 45 per cent. The percentage of Russians declined from about 72 per cent in 1922 to 65 per cent in 1927 and dropped further during the 1930s. In 1946 it was stated that 67.8 per cent of communists were Russian.

A goal of party policy was to achieve the same representation of non-Russians within the party as in the territory they inhabited. This was not achieved overall, but in 1932 90 per cent of communists in Armenia were Armenian, although they only made up about 83 per cent of the population of Armenia. The lowest score was by Crimean Tatars, who only made up 14 per cent of party membership in 1932. Party recruitment changed in 1933, with much less emphasis on attracting non-Russians. The party purge of 1933–34 resulted in about one-third, or 1.2 million members and candidates being excluded. The purge was especially severe in rural areas. This was a consequence of opposition to collectivisation, and resulted in expulsions in non-Russian republics being 12–14 per cent higher than in industrial regions. When recruitment got under way again in 1937 the party switched to attracting those with technical qualifications. Very few non-Russian people had a technical intelligentsia.

Georgia and Armenia are an exception to the general rule. Even before 1930 the percentage of Georgians and Armenians in the party exceeded their representation in the population. Kazakhs were the only Muslim people overrepresented in the party. This was partly due to the rapid industrialisation of northern Kazakhstan although most workers were Slavs. The most overrepresented in the party were the Jews. They had played an important role before and during the revolution, were highly urbanised and well qualified. In 1922 5.2 per cent of party members were Jews, while they made up 1.82 per cent of the Soviet population (1926). This dropped to 4.3 per cent in 1927 and was still at this level in 1940, when they accounted for 1.78 per cent of the population (1939). Even after war losses and the anti-Semitic campaigns over the years 1948–53 they still accounted for 2.8 per cent of members in 1961, while their proportion in the Soviet population had dropped to 1.09 per cent by 1959.

Russians dominated the party leadership. Of the thirty-four members of the Politburo and Secretariat between 1919 and 1935 65 per cent were Russian, 18 per cent Jewish, 6 per cent Georgian and 3 per cent Armenian. The proportion of Russians in these two bodies rose to 81 per cent between 1939 and 1952. Of the sixty-three members of the party's top body, the Politburo (before 1919 the Central Committee), before 1930, thirty-eight were Russians and ten Jews. Between 1930 and 1939, of the thirty members, twenty-one were Russians.

Non-Russians made more progress in local government. By 1930 Georgians and Armenians dominated the local and republican soviet apparatus. At the raion soviet level the Azerbaidzhanis were over-represented, with Ukrainians and Belorussians almost up to their proportion in the republic's population. The situation was least satisfactory in Turkmenistan, where only 24.1 per cent of officials at the raion level were Uzbek. At the republican level the percentage of Turkmens among governmental and soviet officials was only 8.4 per cent. The other extreme was Armenia, where 93.5 per cent of State officials were Armenian. In Georgia 74.1 per cent of State officials were Georgian, but in all other republics locals were underrepresented. In Uzbekistan and Tadzhikistan the situation was only marginally better than in Turkmenistan. The picture which emerges is that in Belorussia, the Ukraine and the three Transcaucasian republics locals occupied over three-quarters of administrative posts at the raion level but in Central Asia Russians provided the leadership even at the raion level.

Since the party and Soviet goal for the whole country was re-presentation of all nationalities in accordance at least with their representation in the local population, the situation was quite unsatis-factory. The Uzbeks decided that direct action was called for. The Central Executive Committee of Uzbekistan decreed the Uzbekisation of all top governmental and soviet posts by 1 September 1930. The Central Asian Bureau of the party Central Committee in Moscow confirmed the decree. However, it was only 22.6 per cent fulfilled. All non-Uzbeks were to learn Uzbek. This has still not been achieved. The Uzbek Commissariat of Education went over to Uzbek as its official language in 1931, but, contrary to the orders of the Uzbek government, all other commissariats, including the Railways, and Posts and Telegraph retained Russian. This reveals quite clearly that these commissariats were Russian-dominated. This was the pattern throughout Central Asia. A survey in 1931 revealed that in 118 central soviet organs there only 10.5 per cent of officials were indigenous. Only 6.4 per cent of the non-locals could speak a local language.

The situation in the Ukraine was much more satisfactory. In 1933, at the height of the campaign to promote local cadres, 87.6 per cent of village soviet deputies, 70 per cent of raion executive committees and 58.4 per cent of city soviets were Ukrainian. The Ukrainian language was used as the official language in practically all local soviets and in many commissariats. The situation in Belorussia was broadly similar.

In the Russian Federation non-Russian participation was greatest at the village soviet level. Here representation in 1931 was greater than the percentage in the local community in all autonomous republics and regions except in North Ossetia. However, in 1933, only in Bashkiria was this pattern repeated at central governmental and soviet level. Even in the Volga German autonomous republic only 39.2 per cent of officials at the centre were German, whereas Germans made up 66.4 per cent of the population (1926). The rule seemed to be that the longer the region had been part of Russia the greater the representation. Muslim areas were grossly underrepresented. The higher the post, the less likely a local was to fill it. However, a policy of positive discrimination was practised and this led to some locals being in high positions. Those positions requiring technical expertise were almost entirely occupied by Russians or other Europeans. In the North Caucasus and in Central Asia the number of local technical specialists was extremely low. There were very few locals in the economic and planning bodies of the RSFSR autonomous republics. During the 1930s the number of qualified Muslim agronomists, engineers, doctors and accountants in the Soviet Union was very small.

Another important tenet of nationality policy was the use of the local language as the official language of communication. The All-Russian Soviet Central Executive Committee decreed on 10 May 1931 that all national territories should go over to using the indigenous language. This goal was never achieved, but already in 1931 all Crimean Tatar and 90 per cent of Yakut village soviets conducted their affairs in the native language. In 1931 about a third of village soviets in national territories corresponded in the local language. At the autonomous republican level Russian still prevailed, but locals could hand in requests and receive information in their mother tongue.

One of the areas where most progress was made was the law. At the beginning of the 1930s almost 70 per cent of law officials in RSFSR autonomous republics were locals. All raions in the Tatar autonomous republic corresponded in Tatar.

The campaign to promote local cadres and local languages continued until 1936. A decree of the Presidium of the USSR Central Executive Committee of 7 January 1936 sharply criticised the slow progress achieved in promoting locals in the North Caucasus. Of 1,310 officials employed by central State organisations, only seventeen were locals although they made up about 65 per cent of the population. Russian was used as the language of communication almost everywhere even when the local population did not understand it. The regional soviet executive committee was instructed to employ not less than one-third locals within two years, and all Russians were obliged to learn the indigenous language. All village and raion soviets were to go over to the local language within the following two years. Moscow also demanded that by 1937 one-half of industrial workers should be indigenous. At that time, the oil industry in Grozny employed practically no locals.

The 1920s and 1930s were a golden era for the development of the non-Russian languages and national consciousness. Forty-eight languages appeared in written form for the first time. These included Turkmen, Kirgiz, and Karakalpak in Central Asia. In the Ukraine, Ukrainian was promoted vigorously, especially in cities dominated by Russians. Ukrainians often could not read and write their mother tongue. In 1926 only 6.3 million out of 23.2 million were literate. In Belorussia, Belorussian was promoted although the educated elite favoured Russian or Polish. The preference given to Ukrainian and Belorussian was also of significance for foreign policy. Many Ukrainians and Belorussians found themselves in Poland after the Treaty of Riga in 1921 and were subject to Polonisation. In Bashkiria, a Bashkirian language was fashioned out of Tatar and declared the official 'state' language. After the revolution Central Asia was generally referred to as Turkestan, but Moscow set out to create separate nations with their own distinct languages. One of the reasons for this was to block the development of pan-Islamic and pan-Turkic movements.

The modernisation of indigenous languages led to the promotion of the Latin alphabet. This affected first and foremost the sixteen Muslim peoples who used the Arabic script. These included the Azerbaidzhanis, Uzbeks, Kazakhs and Tatars. Buryat and Kalmyk, which used the Mongolian script, were also Latinised. Enthusiasts promoted the Latin script as the only genuine revolutionary one and the alphabet of world communist society. There were even plans for Russian to go over to the Latin alphabet. Udmurt, Komi, Ossetian and Yakut, written until 1930 in Cyrillic, also went over to the Latin script. In all, seventy languages, including Chinese, went over to the Latin alphabet. This affected over 36 million people. The adoption of the Latin script led to bitter conflict, especially in Azerbaidzhan and Tatarstan, where religious leaders wished to preserve Arabic since it is the language of Islam. The policy of Latinisation was abruptly reversed in 1937, when Moscow ordered that all languages in the Soviet Union should go over to the Cyrillic script within three years.

The number of books, journals and newspapers published in non-Russian languages expanded very rapidly during the 1920s. Whereas only 7.5 per cent of all books in 1913 were published in languages other than Russian, this grew to 14.5 per cent in 1927 and 26.6 per cent in 1933. However, this had dropped to 21.2 per cent by 1938 and to 17.2 per cent in 1956. In 1933, 37.5 per cent of all Soviet newspapers were in non-Russian languages. Thereafter, the same decline as with books set in. In 1938 it was 23 per cent and in 1956 only 21.6 per cent. The advance was particularly significant in the Ukraine. In 1933, 70 per cent of books and 84.5 per cent of newspapers were published in Ukrainian, but this fell to 52 per cent and 58.7 per cent respectively in 1938.

Even though publications in non-Russian languages were cut back from the mid 1930s onwards, language policy must be judged a great success. During this period two peoples who now have their own Union republics (the Kirgiz and Uzbeks) adopted a written language for the first time. (Chagatay had been used by Uzbeks since the fifteenth century but was very different from modern Uzbek.) The same is true of a whole range of peoples in autonomous republics (for example, the Bashkirs, Mordovians, Chechens and Ingushi). This led to the rapid development of national consciousness and communication between peoples in writing for the first time. They became more and more self-confident in expressing their national point of view. This became apparent during the collectivisation campaign, when

116

most non-Russian raion newspapers ignored the subject. Far from promoting class struggle in the village, they overwhelmingly refused to acknowledge that there was a class struggle going on. They preferred to underline the national unity of the non-Russian village. Only about 15 per cent of the non-Russian local press supported the party line. The locals had a habit of interpreting Moscow directives in their own way. Tatar anti-religious literature consisted of declaring that Islam was superior to Christianity.

Compulsory school attendance was decreed in 1930 and considerable progress in eliminating illiteracy was achieved. In 1935, 50 per cent of Kazakhs were literate, but among Uigurs, for example, only 10 per cent could read and write. Illiteracy was only officially declared to have been eliminated in 1959. Which language should act as the vehicle of literacy? Attempts to use Russian in the 1920s were dismissed as 'great power chauvinism'. Instead, the mother tongue was used as the language of instruction in primary schools. There were no schools before 1917 which taught in Ukrainian or Belorussian, but by 1927 over 90 per cent of Ukrainian and Belorussian children were being instructed in their mother tongue. The picture was the same in many other republics. The RSFSR Commissariat of Education decreed in 1930 that all secondary and tertiary education should use the native language by 1934. There were far fewer schools for national minorities who lived outside their republics – 20 million in 1926. Nevertheless, primary education was conducted in eighty languages in the RSFSR in 1935. This should be compared with the fact that in 1980 primary education was provided only in forty-five languages throughout the Soviet Union. Such a rapid expansion of local schools inevitably resulted in very low standards. Most teachers were unqualified and there were few books and buildings available. Even in 1939 in Kirgizia 81 per cent of teachers in secondary schools had not completed a secondary school course themselves. However, by the mid 1930s the number of children in non-Russian schools corresponded well with the proportion of non-Russian children in the population. All this changed in the second half of the 1930s when quite different priorities took over. For instance, the expansion of tertiary education in the mother tongue ceased, and much vocational training reverted to instruction in Russian. The number of non-Russians attending secondary schools varied greatly. In Tatarstan in 1936 it was about the same as the proportion in the population, but in Kirgizia it was only 2 per cent. In further education, quotas for non-Russians (with more modest entry qualifications) were observed until 1934. Afterwards their numbers dropped.

Concern for those who did not belong to the dominant nationality in a given republic led by the mid 1930s to the establishment of 250 raions or about 10 per cent of the total and 5,300 village soviets to cater for the diaspora. About a half of these were in the RSFSR. For instance, in the Ukraine in 1930 there were 28 non-Ukrainian raions:

9 Russian; 8 German; 4 Bulgarian, 3 Greek, 3 Jewish and one Polish. In Belorussia in 1934 there were 93 non-Belorussian village soviets: 40 Polish; 24 Jewish; 15 Russian; 6 Ukrainian; 5 Latvian; 2 German and one Lithuanian.

Policy towards the diaspora changed dramatically in 1937. Between then and 1939 most national raions, schools, legal institutions and village soviets were dissolved. For example, all seven German raions which still existed in the Ukraine disappeared in 1939. A few dozen national raions survived in the Far North until the 1950s. Gradually during the 1930s the institutions which catered for national minorities ceased to function. That phase of Soviet policy which had aimed to protect and develop them was now over. Assimilation was now the goal. Specially affected were Ukrainians in the RSFSR, Germans in the Ukraine, Jews and Finns. Most Jewish schools, newspapers and theatres had closed down by 1940.

Leninist nationality policy deliberately promoted the formation of nations and the development of national languages and cultures. It was believed that these new nations would be socialist-orientated and would therefore support the building of socialism in the Soviet Union as defined by the party in Moscow. Little thought was given to how much autonomy these nations should be afforded. Not surprisingly, they demanded more and more, and this led to more and more friction with the central authorities. Until the 1930s Stalin argued that all the problems which had arisen were due to great Russian chauvinism. When this had been overcome there would be no reason for nationality problems. There were difficulties with Russian officials. Many of them resolutely opposed the formation of non-Russian nations and the use of the local language. Remarkably few appear to have been willing to learn it. Officials simply offered passive resistance. They failed to carry out decrees they did not agree with and also omitted to collect the statistical data required by Moscow. This was particularly disappointing for the planning authorities. Russian economists argued that the promotion of nations and national cadres hindered industrialisation. Those best-qualified should get the job. This, of course, favoured Russians and Ukrainians. National sensibilities should take second place. This view grew stronger during the first and second FYPs and was eventually to triumph. Industrial enterprises and sovkhozes simply omitted to collect data on nationality and in this way circumvented their responsibilities to develop a local proletariat. Nationality policy fell victim to the demands of production. Everything was trampled upon in the rush to produce more. Industrialisation led to the migration of many non-Russians. They were unskilled, were paid less than a Russian for the same work, were excluded from factory meetings since they did not understand Russian and were at the bottom of the pile for housing and social services. Tensions between Russians and non-Russians were described in considerable detail in the press until the mid 1930s.

The battle against Great Russian nationalism was fought until the mid 1930s without much lasting success. That against local nationalism was more successful.[36] In 1923, Sultan Galiev, a Tatar and close associate of Stalin, became the first leading functionary to be excluded from the party for nationalism and was arrested. He and other non-Russian communists hoped that they could unite the struggle for social revolution in their own nations with that against Russian imperialism. These national communists favoured a weak central authority and wide-ranging autonomy in political, economic, social and cultural affairs for each nation. They also wanted to stop Russian immigration into their territories. Sultan Galiev was accused of pan-Turkism and pan-Islamism and of placing the interests of Muslims above those of the party. However, he was released in 1924 and devoted his energy to establishing a socialist and nationalist-Turkic Turan which was to include Turkestan and other Muslim regions. Moscow acted. It dissolved Turkestan and set up the republics of Uzbekistan and Turkmenistan, the autonomous republic of Tadzhikistan and the Karakirgiz autonomous region. Tadzhikistan became a Union republic in 1929, Kirgizia and Kazakhstan in 1936. This flew in the face of what Muslim communists wanted. They opposed the division of the Turkic peoples into separate small nations and proposed the establishment of a Turkic Soviet republic. Sultan Galiev was arrested in 1928 and sentenced to ten years' imprisonment. At the same time a wide-ranging purge of party and government officials in the Tatar autonomous republic began. The chairman of the soviet central executive committee was removed, also in 1928, tried and executed for nationalism. This was the first time that a communist had been executed for nationalism. There was a wholesale purge in the Crimea which affected at least 3,500 people. Some were shot, others arrested and yet others deported. The Crimean Tatars, who had a well-developed sense of national identity, had proved too ethnically self-aware for Moscow. The centre was clearly alarmed at the pretensions to autonomy which some nations were revealing and was quite determined to demonstrate that local nationalism would not be tolerated. In Uzbekistan officials, teachers and writers were accused of basing cultural policy on Western and Turkish models, propagating pan-Turkism and pan-Islamism in schools, and favouring the establishment of a bourgeois state in Central Asia. Many other secret Muslim organisations were 'uncovered' by Soviet police in Tatarstan and elsewhere and members arraigned before the courts. In the Ukraine, in 1930, forty-five leading members of the intelligentsia were accused of belonging to an organisation whose goal was an independent Ukraine and sentenced to imprisonment. In Belorussia many Academy officials lost their positions. Some were accused of belonging to a 'counter-revolutionary, bourgeois' organisation, but no trial took place.

Great Russian chauvinism was represented as the greatest danger to the party's nationality policy until 1933. Afterwards local nationalism, referred to as 'bourgeois' nationalism, takes over as the main threat. Since its goal is perceived to be the re-establishment of a bourgeois, capitalist state, it is always coupled with alleged support for intervention by 'imperialist powers'. After 1936 the Soviet press dropped all discussion of locals being discriminated against and of falling victim to Russian nationalism.

The turning-point in the Ukraine came in 1932–33 as a direct result of opposition to collectivisation. Famine followed, and there was considerable anti-Russian feeling. Stalin appears to have mistrusted the Ukrainians from the late 1920s onwards, and this was to remain with him to his death. He much preferred Russians. In January 1933 the party in Moscow severely criticised the economic performance and the work of the Ukrainian party. Heads rolled, and the most far-reaching purge ever to hit a republic until then was set in train. Prime targets were culture, education and agriculture. Ukrainian functionaries were replaced by Russians. Almost 6,000 Russians had arrived by 1934. The accusation that some Ukrainians were planning the intervention of 'international fascism' makes its appearance. The struggle against 'bourgeois nationalism' was extended to many republics and went hand in hand with the extensive party purge of 1933–34. Culture and education were of considerable concern to Moscow. The formation of the USSR Writers' Union in 1934 and the adoption of socialist realism provided the centre with instruments with which to promote Russian views and to combat local views. Non-Russian writers were directed to Soviet themes and away from their own national themes and traditions. In the same year the teaching of history changed and placed the evolution of Russia in the foreground. The history of the Soviet Union was the history of Russia. Hence Soviet history began with the beginnings of Rus, over a thousand years ago. The history of the non-Russians was seen in the context of their becoming part of the Russian Empire and the Soviet Union. Stalin spoke of the friendship of the peoples of the Soviet Union, and Soviet patriotism made its appearance. Its critics saw it as a thin veil for Russian nationalism. The Russians became the elder brother and non-Russians the younger brothers.

Resistance to collectivisation was generally stronger than in the Russian republic. It was most marked in the Ukraine, the Middle Volga, Kazakhstan, Uzbekistan and Turkmenistan. Losses were greatest where collectivisation was carried through most rapidly. In Dagestan and in Transcaucasia collectivisation was not as all-embracing as elsewhere. There was no famine in these regions. Most Azerbaidzhani, Armenian and Georgian peasants joined kolkhozes only in 1936 and 1937, and private farming in Georgia remained significant, contributing 40 per cent of global agricultural output in 1970. As a concession to non-Russians most kolkhozes were nationally homogenous. For example, in 1931, in Belorussia over 90 per cent of kolkhozes were Belorussian. In some autonomous republics mixed kolkhozes were established from the beginning. This, however, led to much conflict and the dissolution of the kolkhozes. Single nationality collectives became the rule in 1932. This policy was abruptly changed at the end of the 1930s. The very strong family and clan loyalties in Muslim areas forced the Soviet authorities to concede the establishment of collectives along family lines. After 1932, the heads of families in the collectives were expelled as 'kulaks'. In many Muslim areas and in the Far North it was impossible to found kolkhozes, so artels or associations for the communal working of land were established. In the second half of the 1930s these were transformed into kolkhozes.

Opposition to collectivisation had been broken by the summer of 1932 but it was followed by a terrible hunger. Stalin conducted a war against the peasants to force collective farming on them. Losses of lives ran into millions. Especially badly hit were the Ukraine and Kazakhstan. The number of Ukrainians declined by 9.9 per cent, but Kazakhs dropped by 21.9 per cent between 1926 and 1939. The latter were particularly badly affected by the forcible settlement of about 4 million nomads. Many nomads died of hunger because of the mass slaughter of their animals by the State.

Industrialisation during the first FYP concentrated on regions inhabited by Russians.[37] Iron ore in the Urals, the raw materials of West Siberia and northern Kazakhstan led to the emergence of new industrial centres there. However, they were mainly inhabited by Russians. Large oil reserves were discovered in Bashkiria in the early 1930s but again were mainly worked by Russians. The autonomous regions of the RSFSR only received about 2 per cent of the republic's investment during the years 1928–32. More progress was made during the second FYP but from a low starting-base. The same is true of the non-Slav republics. Per capita investment over the years 1933–40 in the non-Russian republics was only 63 per cent of that in the RSFSR. Over the years 1928–40, as regards investment, Kazakhstan and the Transcaucasian republics were favoured. Belorussia and the Ukraine were at a considerable disadvantage. Ukrainian economists and planners argued for heavy industry to be expanded rapidly in their republic and not in the Urals, where the coal had to be brought from West Siberia. The Urals won.

Industrialisation led to rapid urbanisation and population movement. This was most marked in the Russian republic. It also led to Russians and Ukrainians moving outside their republics. Between 1926 and 1939 the number of Russians outside the RSFSR rose from 5.1 million to 9.3 million. They made up 14.9 per cent of the population outside the Russian republic in 1939. Over the years 1926–39 1.7 million persons, overwhelmingly Russian, migrated to Kazakhstan and Central

Asia. In the RSFSR the Russian population east of the Urals grew rapidly. This led to a steep rise in the proportion of Russians in many autonomous regions. This was particularly marked in the North Caucasus and the Kalmyk autonomous republic. In the latter the percentage of Russians in the republic rose from 10.7 per cent in 1926 to 48.6 per cent in 1939. Russian migration to Kazakhstan and Central Asia changed the demographic pattern significantly. In Kazakhstan the proportion of Russians rose from 19.7 per cent in 1926 to 40.3 per cent in 1939, but that of the Kazakhs fell from 57.1 per cent to 38.2 per cent. The latter percentage was also heavily influenced by the large nomadic losses. In Kirgizia locals had dropped to 51.7 per cent of the population by 1939, and in Tadzhikistan and Turkmenistan their percentage fell to 59.6 per cent and 59.2 per cent respectively. This process continued in some republics. In Kazakhstan locals only made up 30 per cent of the population in 1959 and in Kirgizia it was 40.5 per cent. Russians were mainly to be found in cities.

The difficulties encountered by Moscow in its nationality policy underlined the flaws inherent in Leninist theory. From the Bolshevik point of view socialism was a higher stage of development than nationalism. The October Revolution had drawn the fangs of nationalism and rendered it harmless. This was because nationalism was perceived as the product of class conflict within bourgeois society. Because antagonistic class conflict ceased under socialism, nationalism had nothing to feed on. Hence nationalism was of minor significance in a socialist state. The victory of socialism worldwide would see the merging of nations into one world society. If nations were doomed to extinction, why did Lenin seek to create new nations within the Soviet Union? He characterised the Russian Empire as the prison of nationalities, and believed that if non-Russians were encouraged to found their own nations and develop their potential it could only work for the benefit of the USSR. The right to secede, granted republics in every Soviet constitution, was to convince them that a Soviet State could never be imperialist. Non-Russian nations would flourish for a season. Then industrialisation and modernisation would lead to the expansion of the working class. This, in turn, would strengthen class solidarity on an All-Union basis. The belief was that the working class could never be nationalist. Those sentiments could only emanate from the bourgeoisie and the goal of nationalism could only be counter-revolution.

The problems posed by rising nationalism caused Stalin, in 1929, to examine and develop Leninist theory. He came up with the concept of the socialist nation and the bourgeois nation. He argued that a bourgeois nation oppressed its minorities but a socialist nation promoted their flowering. This belonged to the first stage of the world dictatorship of the proletariat. The second stage would see the merging of nations. A socialist nation would always seek closer union with other socialist nations. Attempts at separatism revealed that the nation was not socialist. Reality turned out to be different. The flowering of the nations led to the creation of intelligentsias whose goals were to achieve as much autonomy as possible. This led Stalin to change tack completely in the mid 1930s. His new policy can be described as the promotion of assimilation and Russification.

The onset of the planned economy in 1928 saw economic power and influence pass to the centre. This was given concrete form in 1932 with the dissolution of USSR Sovnarkhoz and all the republican and local sovnarkhozes and the creation of Commissariats for Heavy Industry, the Timber Industry and Light Industry. Their *glavki*, or sections, acquired responsibility for the whole Soviet Union. Republics and autonomous republics were left to run such things as brewing – in other words, everything that Moscow afforded low priority. Hence key economic decisions affecting the development of the non-Russian republics and regions passed from them to Moscow. In agriculture collectivisation led to the establishment of the USSR Commissariat of Agriculture, organised on a Union-republican basis. This meant that the republican commissariats were all subordinate to Moscow and the relative autonomy which these commissariats had enjoyed during the 1920s vanished. A unified school system was introduced in May 1934. It laid down only three types of school: the primary, with four classes; the incomplete secondary, with seven classes; and the middle school, with ten classes. In September 1935 a school plan, outlining the use of every minute of the school day, was made obligatory. Technical education was made uniform throughout the country in 1928, and a Union Committee for Higher Technical Education was established in 1933. It became a Union Committee for Further Education in 1936 and decided personnel policy, the content of courses and textbooks, and thereby ensured a unified system throughout the USSR.

Soviet federalism flowered at a time when more and more decision-making was being transferred from the periphery to the centre. The 1924 constitution listed four Union republics, sixteen autonomous republics and seventeen autonomous regions, but the 1936 constitution included eleven Union republics, twenty-two autonomous republics, nine autonomous regions and nine national areas. Hence many territories were upgraded in 1936. The dissolution of the Transcaucasian Soviet Federal Socialist Republic led to Azerbaidzhan, Armenia and Georgia becoming Union republics. Kazakhstan and Kirgizia, autonomous republics, became Union republics. The Kabardino-Balkar, Komi, Mari, North Ossetia, Chechen-Ingush autonomous regions were elevated to autonomous republics. Some autonomous regions had been raised to autonomous republics before the 1936 constitution. This affected Karakalpak region in 1932; the Mordovian and Udmurt regions in 1934 and the Kalmyk region in 1935. This process ended with the 1936 constitution. Afterwards new republics appeared only through annexation.

Soviet federalism was an artificial bloom. On paper it appeared that non-Russians were acquiring greater control over their development, but in reality Moscow rule prevailed. Another move by Stalin was the establishment of the bicameral USSR Supreme Soviet by the 1936 constitution. The two houses were the Soviet of the Union, directly elected according to population – hence Russians were in the majority – and the Soviet of Nationalities. Each Union republic provided twenty-five deputies, each autonomous republic eleven, each autonomous region five, and each national area one. The non-Russians dominated this house and the two houses had equal authority. However, real power rested elsewhere. The constitution, however, reflected the realities of governmental power. Four of the six republican commissariats (Interior, Justice, Health and Agriculture) became Union-republican commissariats. Only education and social security remained exclusively in the hands of the republics, but commissariats for local industry, and the economy, were added.

The 1936 constitution strengthened the Soviet State. This followed the rediscovery of the concepts of the homeland and the fatherland. Soviet patriotism took the place of revolutionary idealism. This came to mean the leading role of the Russian nation in the Soviet Union. In 1937 the 'Great Russian people' becomes the 'great, Russian people', first among equals among Soviet nations. A theme during the building of socialism was the help which the 'great Russian people' extended the 'backward' peoples of the USSR. It was even maintained that the freedom and independence of the Ukrainian people had been 'bought with the streams of blood of the best sons of the Russian people'. The expressions 'Russian toilers' and 'Russian working class' began to cede primacy to the 'great, Russian people' extending 'unselfish' and 'constant' help to every other nation. It was stated that Russians felt limitless love for the Uzbek people. Stalin used the expression 'friendship of the peoples' for the first time in public in 1935. It was stated that this friendship was not only strong but eternal – a clear warning to those who dreamed of separation. Needless to say, the Soviet Union was held up as a model for emulation for mankind since it represented the apogee of achievement in nationality affairs.

Although Stalin never officially stated during the second half of the 1930s that the Soviet Union had reached the phase when Soviet nations would begin to merge, clear evidence of Russification is evident. In 1938 Russian became a compulsory subject in all non-Russian schools in Union and autonomous republics. A knowledge of Russian was necessary to promote contacts between and among nationalities, to create cadres in science and technology and for national service. The implications of this were profound. Science and technology would quickly become the preserve of those with first-class Russian and the military had been, until then, proud of its national units and multi-lingualism. National units were also abolished in 1938. Non-Russian military schools and other establishments were closed as well. The chances of non-Russians becoming officers and non-commissioned officers declined. The promotion of local languages in further education, except in Transcaucasia, was abandoned. This forced greater attention for Russian in secondary schools. Another consequence was that Russian students enjoyed an advantage when it came to applying for further education. The numbers of non-Russians in tertiary education dropped. The overall impact of Stalin's change in policy was to favour Russians and discriminate against all others. Between 1937 and 1940 all languages which had adopted the Latin script were obliged to go over again to the Cyrillic. More than 40 million persons were affected, and progress in education was halted. Only Georgian, Armenian and Yiddish, untouched by Latinisation in the 1920s, retained their own alphabets. Going over to the Cyrillic alphabet made learning Russian easier but it also cut non-Russians off from the outside world.

The rationale behind the savage purges of the years 1936–38 is still unclear. Stalin demolished the old revolutionary leadership and scythed down millions of communists, non-communists, military personnel and so on. One by-product of the bloodletting was that it prepared the way for the rapid advance of a new generation of specialists and politicians. Of those who graduated during the first FYP about 90 per cent were in leading positions by 1941, and of those who obtained their diplomas during the second FYP about 70 per cent were in top positions. This can be referred to as the Brezhnev generation. In 1979 about half of the full members of the Politburo came from this group.

The purges began in the autumn of 1936 and were carried out systematically and with precision in non-Russian areas. Initially top party functionaries were not affected. It was they who carried out purges in the middle and lower levels of their administrations. They did this with gusto believing that this would prove their limitless loyalty to Stalin and deflect suspicion away from them. Alas, Stalin had other ideas. He, in turn, encouraged the little people to attack and denounce the bosses under whom they had suffered. Before 1937 there had to be a grain of truth in the accusation. Afterwards anything would do.

The object of the purges was quite clear: decapitate the non-Russian national elites. In the Chechen-Ingush autonomous republic 14,000 were arrested. This represented 2 per cent of the population and must have amounted to practically the whole educated elite. In Georgia, of the 644 delegates who attended the Xth Georgian Party Congress in May 1937, 425 were shortly afterwards arrested, deported or shot. In 1937–38, 4,238 persons were promoted to leading party, state and economic positions. Many party leaderships were decimated in September 1937. Stalin's cynicism was boundless. The Armenian leadership was accused of murdering one of their number and arrested. In reality, Lavrenty Beria had shot the comrade himself, clearly at Stalin's behest. The two most prominent Muslim leaders in the Soviet Union were deemed so important that they were included in the last great Moscow Show Trial in March 1938. Faizulla Khodzhaev, chairman of the Uzbek Sovnarkom or Prime Minister, and Akmal Ikramov, first Uzbek party secretary. Both had been in office since 1925. As a result many in the Uzbek leadership were implicated. The curtain also came down on Sultan Galiev. He did not serve his full term of imprisonment after 1928 but was rearrested in early 1938, interrogated and imprisoned. In December 1939 he was sentenced to death and was executed on 28 January 1940.

In the Ukraine the purges began in the spring of 1937 with 20 per cent of party members being expelled and two-thirds at the oblast level and one-third at the primary level losing their posts. In August 1937 Stalin sent Molotov, Ezhov and Khrushchev to Kiev to demand the sacking of the Ukrainian party and government leadership. The Ukrainian party refused, whereupon the Politburo was invited to Moscow. Some were arrested, others returned to Kiev but disappeared and the Prime Minister committed suicide. By the summer of 1938 the whole Politburo, Orgburo and CC Secretariat and all seventeen People's Commissars had been arrested. One third of the 102 members of the Ukrainian CC survived. All oblast first secretaries lost their posts and most their lives. The only leading Ukrainian politician to survive was Petrovsky, who had been a Bolshevik member of the pre-1917 Duma. Indeed, no Bolshevik member of the Duma was arrested. Was it an oversight on Stalin's part, or did he regard these men as a protected species? Stalin's executioner was Nikita Khrushchev who, together with a dozen officials from the CC apparatus in Moscow, devastated the Ukrainian party and government. In May and June 1938 the whole Ukrainian government was replaced. The party apparatus was transformed: 1,600 raion and city secretaries were replaced in 1938. Among the new appointees were Leonid Brezhnev and Andrei Kirilenko. The purge embraced education and culture since they were important bearers of the national culture. Stalin presumably picked Khrushchev, a Russian, to carry out his ruthless policies in the Ukraine since there was no Ukrainian around who was fit to do the job.

Who replaced the purged officials? The great majority of leading positions in the republics were filled by Russian appointees sent from the Moscow CC apparatus or other institutions. The goal was that the party and governmental leadership in the republics should not represent the republics but the policy of the centre in the republics. The proportion of Russians in the CC rose to 66.2 per cent in 1939. This was to rise to 71.5 per cent at the XIXth Party Congress in 1952. In 1939 there were no Kazakhs, Kirgiz, Turkmen and Tadzhiks in the CC even though they had Union republics. The number of locals in the party declined and that of Russians rose. In 1940 about 40 per cent of party members were Tadzhiks. Only 34 per cent of party members in Kirgizia in 1953 were Kirgiz. One consequence of this was that the role of Russians in national party and governmental leaderships grew. The only exception to this was in Armenia and Georgia, where locals continued to dominate the party and government.

WOMEN AND REVOLUTION

Red women played an important role during the Bolshevik Revolution and the Civil War. Nadezhda Krupskaya, Lenin's wife, Angelica Balabanova and Aleksandra Kollontai, to name only some of the most prominent, held important propaganda posts during the Civil War. Women had been drafted into the war effort before 1917 but afterwards expanded their theatre of action. Propaganda, psychological warfare, espionage and police functions, which had previously involved extremely few females, now recruited large numbers of women.[38] The party's own women's section, the Zhenotdel, co-ordinated efforts and helped to recruit systematically. By the end of the Civil War in 1920 conscription of young women for non-combatant duties was well under way. Women occupied leading posts in the Military Revolutionary Committees and Political Departments of the Red Army. Some women also saw active service. This had already happened in the tsarist army, but there were certainly more women soldiers in the Red Army. They usually formed company-sized detachments of 300 or more. They were called upon in cases of siege but also saw front-line service. The Red Army missed an opportunity to recruit women for a specialised area of warfare for which many proved skilled during the Great Fatherland War – sniping. The most famous was Lyudmila Pavlichenko, who disposed of 309 German and other enemy officers and men. (The highest was 346 by Filipp Yakovlevich.) She relates that when she joined the army in 1941 women were not yet accepted, especially not as snipers. However, women were so skilled at dispatching Germans that the central Women's School for Sniper Training was set up in Moscow in May 1943. In all about 2,000 were trained and they claimed 12,000 German lives. The military impact of women during the Civil War seems to have faded away during the two decades before the next conflict.

Women were also active in the Cheka and revealed talents for deception, intelligence-gathering but also brutality. One estimate puts the number of women participants in the Civil War at 73,858, with casualties accounting for 1,854. Most high-ranking women had already achieved prominence in the revolutionary movement.

Politically, a tight group of women played an important role during the immediate post-revolutionary years. However, during NEP women become less visible, and by the mid 1920s they are on the periphery of political life. Whereas some men emerge who did not play roles during the 1917 Revolution, no woman joins them in the late 1920s and 1930s. The revolutionary cohort consisted of Elena Stasova, who was the first 'general' secretary of the party before and shortly after the revolution until she was replaced by Yakov Sverdlov; Inessa Armand, who had founded and led Zhenotdel until she died of cholera in 1920 and also played a significant role in rallying support for the Third International; and Angelica Balabanova, who had been active in the European socialist movement before 1917 and after the revolution took on, among other duties, the posts of Ukrainian Foreign Minister and secretary of the Comintern but was to fall out with the course of the revolution and abandoned Soviet Russia in 1921. Aleksandra Kollontai was the woman with the highest revolutionary profile. A member of the party CC in October 1917, she was made Commissar of Public Welfare. Her marriage to Pavel Dybenko, a Military and Naval Commissar, and a comrade of radical and unpredictable views, lost her the confidence of Lenin. Among other things, she was head of Zhenotdel. Siding with the Workers' Opposition at the Xth Party Congress cost her dear. She was packed off as a diplomat to Norway but later became ambassador to Sweden. Stalin shared Lenin's lack of respect for her integrity and in 1941 dispatched Vladimir Semonov, a German specialist and later to become ambassador to Bonn, to Stockholm as her minder. He was to ensure that no one with an offer of a separate peace involving the Soviet Union got near Kollontai. Semonov did an exemplary job. Nadezhda Krupskaya had an abiding interest in propaganda and education, where her ideas were liberal. Her reminiscences of Lenin do not reveal her as an acute observer of the everyday political scene. Stalin knew how to intimidate her, and the opposition's hopes that she could become a focal point for protest were in vain. She was a faithful foot soldier of revolution, not a general.

The revolution proclaimed equality for the sexes, and the statute book was replete with legislation to this effect. The implementation proved much more difficult. Political power proceeded from the party. Apart from Stasova, who was head of the Secretariat between 1918 and 1919, no woman had been elected to the key bodies, the Politburo, the CC, the Orgburo and the Secretariat by Lenin's death in 1924. Between 1924 and 1939 only four women made the CC, and three of them were head of Zhenotdel. Less than 2 per cent of CC members were female. Stalin's influence was of some importance. There were no women in his inner group. Women would have to wait to the Khrushchev era before one of them, Elena Furtseva, was elected to the Politburo. At lower party levels women did much better and occupied about one-sixth of administrative posts by the 1930s. However, the proportion of women in party posts declined during the 1930s. No woman played a prominent role as victim during the Show Trials.

Women only accounted for 8.2 per cent of party members in 1924, but this had doubled by 1932. It hardly rose afterwards, and even in 1945 after the gargantuan male bloodletting of the purges and the war, women only made up 17 per cent. Women communists were almost entirely urban and Russian, with a smattering of Poles, Balts and Jews. In non-Russian regions indigenous women accounted for only 40 per cent of female communists.

Women fared no better in government. Kollontai became the first female commissar but only held on for a few months. Elena Furtseva, when she became USSR Minister of Culture in 1956, was the next woman minister. No woman has ever been Soviet or republican President or Prime Minister. Kollontai's wry comment, in 1922, that the Soviet State was run by men with women kept in their place, still rings true today. At local soviet level women made some progress. In 1926 they made up 18 per cent of urban and 9 per cent of rural soviet deputies. In the 1950s women only accounted for about 20 per cent of all soviet deputies.

Women communists found a great wall of hostility to them and their ideals. Most women feared that the Bolsheviks would break up families, drag children off to homes, destroy the Church and cultural tradition. Zenotdel worked indefatigably to educate women about the goals of socialism. It was an uphill task. Lenin did not want it to become a fount of feminism. Suggestions to improve the image of woman included banning the word '*baba*', the meaning of which in Russia ranges from 'grandma' to 'old biddy'. Zhenotdel organisers adopted the leather attire of their male colleagues. Leather-coated and booted Zhenotdel women would tramp around the factories and organise women, hold meetings and set up reading rooms. Agit-trains and agit-boats were also used to penetrate the countryside. Collectivisation aroused great hostility. Rumours swept the Ukraine that in the kolkhozes young women would be handed around by the men and old ones boiled down to make soap. Men everywhere fought attempts to politicise their wives. Outrage was greatest in Muslim areas. Women leaving a club in Baku had wild dogs turned on them and boiling water poured over them. There were 300 murders in Central Asia in three months in 1929. Despite these risks, thousands of Muslim women became involved in Zhenotdel and celebrated May Day by tearing off their veils. Zhenotdel did have a social impact on traditional societies. However, despite the considerable political and social work the organisation was doing it was dissolved in 1930. Opposition came from the party and trade unions. The party thought that there was a danger that Zhenotdel could become feminist and that women workers would split from the men. Interestingly enough, the International Women's Secretariat (usually dominated by Zhenotdel) had been abolished and replaced by a Women's Department of the Executive Committee of the Comintern. The onset of industrialisation and collectivisation brought criticism to a head. There had always been those male party officials who had viewed Zhenotdel as superfluous. In the reorganisation of the CC Secretariat in 1929, the women's and village sections were abolished and subsumed under Agitation and Mass Campaigns. However, in some non-Russian areas women's sections were retained in the party until the 1950s. Although International Women's Day on 8 March was retained as a major holiday, it became just another forum for campaigning. In 1930 the slogan was 'full collectivisation!'. The male view was that by 1930 the woman question had been solved. Women were to be mobilised by men in the race for modernisation and industrialisation. The days when women had their own voice were gone. It was part of the centripetal flow of power – to the centre – which was so evident in the 1930s. Perhaps it was linked to the emergence of the new elites, which were predominantly from the countryside. The rural male is more conservative in his attitude to women than the urban male.

As the party turned its back on separate organisations for women, so did it also on all the libertarian theories which had been floated since the revolution. The main inspiration of the ideas of free love, sex, the liberation of women from the tyranny of the kitchen and household chores was Aleksandra Kollontai. Practically all the ideas had been expressed before the revolution. One goal was the separation of the kitchen from marriage. Kollontai's dislike was echoed by Lenin's total opposition to individual kitchens. Communal kitchens were to become the norm, and communal living quarters were designed to share all duties involved with child rearing. The household chores were to be done by cleaning ladies.

The revolution was physically very demanding. Did it leave any energy over for sex? Most revolutionaries maintained that it had weakened their sex drive. The revolution was just too important for time and effort to be expended on love and sex. It became fashionable to denigrate all finer feelings: love does not exist – it is just a sex urge, ran one widely held view. Ties, combs, a careful coiffure, neat clothing clearly revealed 'bourgeois' leanings. To be a revolutionary was to be wild. Any woman who resisted was 'petty bourgeois'. Mixed dormitories were widespread. This resulted, as one journalist put it, in liberty, equality and maternity – equality for the sexes, liberty for the men and maternity for the women. Free love was a myth. Women paid.

Marriage was simplified. Civil marriage became the norm by a decree in December 1917, and this was enlarged upon in the Family Code of 1918. The Church lost its legal status and marriage was to be a partnership of two equal parties. But some things did not change. Unhappy marriages were often due to the husband's penchant for vodka. Had the Bolsheviks been able to abolish the bottle they would indeed have been revolutionary! Many husbands took strong exception to wives devoting time to Zhenotdel or other social activities if it meant that their dinner was not ready when they got home or their socks had not been darned. A cold bed was also nothing to look forward to in the evenings.

Revolution and civil war put about 7 million orphans on the streets or, more accurately, into the fields. Adoption was not permitted under the Family Code of 1918. These *besprizorniki* roamed the countryside and the towns. They were unwashed, uncivilised and unloved. Their numbers grew as marriages broke up and parents could not support their offspring. Divorce was made simple. The new divorce law of 1927 tried to protect the wife and children after divorce. Alimony was to be paid. Children could now be adopted. Common-law marriages were widespread and more fragile. By the end of the 1920s cities were full of deserted and destitute wives. It had proved extremely difficult to collect alimony and average incomes were low. Prostitution flourished under NEP. The number of prostitutes in Leningrad was back to its pre-revolution heyday in 1922.

Lenin was no revolutionary when it came to sex. He found concentration on sexual matters objectionable and called the attitude of youth to sex the modern disease. Promiscuity was bourgeois and a waste of health and strength. He rejected the glass of water theory of sex. This held that it was as natural as wanting to slake one's thirst. August Bebel, the German social democrat, wrote that after eating and drinking, man's greatest natural demand was sex. Lenin hoped that vigorous sport, physical exercise of every kind and intellectual stimulation would keep the minds of the young off sex. If Lenin was a conservative Aron Zalkind was an arch-conservative. He drew up twelve commandments which owed very little to the Old Testament. Purely physical sexual desire was quite impermissible from a revolutionary-proletarian point of view. Sexual attraction to a class enemy was as depraved as a crocodile and an orang-utan trying to mate. Sex outside marriage was forbidden. Sex was for reproduction. Sex should not be indulged in too often during marriage. The energy saved could be devoted to furthering revolutionary goals.

Abortion was covered by the law of 1920 which sought to combat back-street abortions. Abortion on demand ended in 1936 when Stalin came down very hard against it. He wanted more males to be born. The 1936 law also made it more difficult to divorce and marked a return to more traditional views on marriage and the family. However, this law did not act against common-law marriages and it was still possible to get a divorce. War losses caused the State to look again at the family. It was praised as an institution by *Pravda*. The party newspaper stressed the 'spiritual' side of marriage and parenthood and the contribution they made to the development of the full-blown personality. There was a special message for women: 'A woman who has not yet known the joy of motherhood has not yet realised the greatness of her calling.' In simple language, childless women were not women at all.

The reform of family law of 8 July 1944 increased the judicial procedures for divorce, thus making it more difficult and expensive to obtain one. This was balanced, however, by laying down that a child born out of wedlock was no longer to be considered the father's child. Illegitimacy was therefore reintroduced in 1944. The father of such a child was no longer to be held responsible for it. Maternity leave was extended from 63 to 77 calendar days – and to 112 calendar days in 1956. Since the paternity suit had now disappeared from Soviet law the unmarried mother was to receive a state allowance for her child until it reached the age of twelve years: if she had three or more children she was to receive further allowances. Medals were struck; a mother of ten or more children received a medal and the title of Mother Heroine, one with five children got a Motherhood medal and so on. Childless couples, bachelors and spinsters were to be taxed.

The goal of this pro-natal policy was clear: increase the birth-rate so that the ravages of war could be quickly overcome. The legislation was loaded in favour of the male. Women had carried a heavy burden during the war and many of them had acquired positions of responsibility. What was to happen when the ex-soldier returned? The women had to step down. Every woman was informed, on the highest authority, that child-bearing was the apogee of her calling. But there were not enough males to go round, and many women could only have their child out of wedlock. The woman of the 1930s, who devoted herself selflessly to the party and the economy and neglected her family life, was no longer in vogue. The family was back in favour with a vengeance. Add to this the 1943 law abolishing inheritance tax; accumulation by the family and others was being encouraged. All in all, the male was king after 1945; never had the party and the law been so openly on his side.

FOREIGN POLICY

The great depression which afflicted the advanced industrial states after 1929 was watched with quiet satisfaction in Moscow. After all it appeared to vindicate Soviet predictions about the internal contradictions of capitalism.

The real threat to Soviet interests, however, emerged in the east. An expansionist Japan wanted sources of food and raw materials which were unavailable at home. Manchuria was an obvious target and Japan invaded in 1931, renamed it Manchukoa, and declared it independent. It was, nevertheless, about as independent as an apple on a tree. This was a direct blow at the Soviet Union who had railway interests in Manchuria and at Chiang Kai-shek's China. Moscow's nightmare was that the Japanese would reach an agreement with Chiang Kai-shek, thus directing Japanese military power against Outer Mongolia, a Soviet zone of influence, and the Soviet Union. If strategic goods, food and raw materials were uppermost in Japanese minds then she would strike against China since Soviet Asia was little developed, but if military goals were paramount then she might find Siberia irresistible.

While the Japanese were pondering their alternatives Moscow managed to restore diplomatic relations with Nanking and resumed deliveries of war *matériel* to Chiang Kai-shek.

The rise of national socialism in Germany appeared to pose as little threat to the Soviet Union as fascism in Italy. If the Weimar republic collapsed then the social democrats, the main supporters of the republic, would lose as well. Hence the chief target of the KPD were the 'social fascists' and not the national socialists. Indeed, on occasions, communists linked up with Nazis to oppose the SPD. The Comintern, and by extension the KPD, regarded national socialism as the most rapacious expression of finance capital which could not long survive in power since it had practically no social base. A fascist government would exacerbate social tensions thus hastening the advent of a socialist revolution. Nationalism was not regarded as having much appeal to the German working class.

Just in case events in Germany did not turn out as favourably as the Comintern hoped, the Soviet Union skilfully negotiated non-aggression pacts with France, Poland, Finland and Estonia in 1932. They had already signed an agreement with Lithuania and Romania. The French army was regarded as the most powerful in Europe and Poland, the Baltic States, Finland and Romania had frontiers with the Soviet Union across which German armies might march to attack the USSR. Japan had refused to sign a non-aggression pact but Italy had signed one in 1933.

Communists were not alone in misjudging the staying power of the NSDAP when it took over in January 1933. Some opponents moved to Paris and awaited the expected telegram informing them that it was safe again to return to Berlin since Hitler was no longer Chancellor.

The termination of the Reichswehr–Red Army agreement in late 1933 was wholly predictable since Hitler had promised to challenge the provisions of the Versailles treaty. It was also not in the Soviet Union's interests to afford German officers the opportunity of judging Soviet military potential at first hand given Hitler's clear anti-communist views.

The breathtaking ease with which the Nazis swept the German communists from the political stage, the abject surrender of the other political parties and the Night of the Long Knives, 30 June 1934, when Hitler disposed of Ernst Röhm and his SA plus a few politicians as well,[39] as part of a deal with the Reichswehr, revealed the true potential of the NSDAP. This forced a rethink on the Comintern and it decided on a *volte-face* on fascism. It called for a popular front to stem the tide of fascist advance in Europe and this became official policy at the VIIth Comintern Congress in July–August 1935. This was the popular front from above and it had been preceded, until 1934, by the united front from below, whose aim had been to appeal to rank and file social democrats over the heads of their leaders. The popular front was more ambitious than the united front since it sought to enlist the help of all anti-fascists, from the left to the right. Just as many social democrats and anti-fascists could not see why they should trust communists and help them to political power and influence, so the Soviet Union had no intention of strengthening Great Britain and France, making them even more formidable than before. This mutual suspicion did not augur well for the success of the popular front but the Soviet Union set about improving its international situation so as to make itself a potentially more attractive ally. It joined the League of Nations, in 1934, while Germany left it and, into the bargain, renounced the Treaty of Versailles. Then the League was faced with the invasion by Italy of Ethiopia, in 1935, and its response was summed up by an Abyssinian who wryly remarked amid the popping of champagne corks at a reception: 'Just listen to the artillery of the League of Nations!'

The Soviet Union argued strongly for collective security but did not only rely on the League. Its search for closer military relations with the capitalist powers resulted in the Franco-Soviet treaty of mutual assistance, signed on 2 May 1935. This was a replay of the Franco-Russian alliance of 1894 but again it was difficult to see what the Soviet Union could do to help France in the case of German aggression since Poland stood between the USSR and Germany. Poland had signed a declaration not to resort to force against Germany, in 1934.

The Franco-Soviet treaty was widened on 16 May 1935 to embrace Czechoslovakia but here the Soviets only committed themselves to come to Czechoslovakia's aid if France did so as well. Again the Soviet Union had no common frontier with Czechoslovakia and coming to her aid would have meant crossing Polish and/or Romanian territory whereas France had a common frontier with Germany, the obvious aggressor.

The respectability of the Soviet Union was further enhanced by the 1936 constitution which was partly for external consumption. The apparent movement of the USSR towards becoming a model democratic state stood out in stark contrast to what was happening in the rest of Europe.

Nevertheless 1936 was a bad year for the Soviet Union. The German remilitarisation of the Rhineland on 7 March, the onset of the Spanish Civil War, in July, and the signing of the Anti-Comintern pact by Germany, Italy and Japan in November, revealed the vitality of the fascists and the pusillanimity of Great Britain and France. The Soviets found themselves the main supporters of the Spanish republic as France and Great Britain stood idly by. However Moscow was in a cleft stick as it did not want a socialist republic. This might have driven France and Great Britain to the right and the USSR did not wish to become embroiled in a conflict with Germany and Italy, the main backers of Franco. As of 1937 the Soviet Union concentrated on disposing of Trotskyites and anti-communists, thus effectively reducing the republic's chances of victory.

The situation in the Far East took a turn for the better, from the Soviet point of view, when on 7 July 1937 Japan attacked the Kuomintang while Chiang Kai-shek was negotiating with his communist compatriots. A united front was now imperative for communists and non-communists in China and moreover the Soviet Union signed a non-aggression treaty with China in August 1937. This replaced German advisers with Soviet ones and provided for military supplies. Plainly it was in the interests of the Soviet Union for Japan to become bogged down in a long war with China and anyway no power could ever hope to occupy the whole of China. This did not prevent the Japanese from probing and testing Soviet defences between 1937 and 1939 and Soviet resistance was strong enough to convince the Japanese that considerable forces would be required if they wished to penetrate deep into Soviet territory. Soviet victories over the Japanese at Lake Khasan, in the Maritime krai near the Chinese and Korean borders, in July–August 1938 and at Khalkhin-Gol, in Mongolia, in July–August 1939, when the Japanese suffered 61,000 casualties, including prisoners-of-war, were the turning-points.

Germany's remilitarisation of the Rhineland and the *Anschluss* with Austria, in March 1938, enlarged her territory and expanded her influence but it only affected German speakers. There were, however, two large concentrations of German speakers outside the Reich; in the Sudetenland in Czechoslovakia and in Danzig, now a Free City but previously in Germany. If Austrians could join Grossdeutschland why should the Sudeten Germans not do so as well? Hitler had a case and France and Great Britain accepted it at Munich, in September 1938, but in so doing abandoned and dismembered Czechoslovakia. France was pledged to come to the aid of Czechoslovakia as was the Soviet Union, but the latter was excluded from the Munich negotiations. The USSR made much capital out of the affair and appeared to many Czechoslovaks to be the only country willing to defend the republic.

In October 1938 Hitler turned his eyes towards Danzig and proposed to the Poles that the Free City should become part of the Reich and that a German-controlled road and rail link between Danzig and West Prussia be permitted. It would appear that he had no desire to go to war with Poland at this stage but the Poles had the spectre of the break-up of Czechoslovakia before their eyes. Hitler did not wait to resolve the Danzig question before annexing Bohemia and Moravia, in March 1939. Hungary and Poland acquired what was left of the former Czechoslovak state. The annexation was a fatal step since it revealed for the first time that Germany's ambitions included ruling non-Germans. It was precisely at this moment that Poland chose to reveal the German proposals and this led the British and French governments to overturn their policy of appeasement and to guarantee Poland's frontiers. The two governments hoped that the guarantee would frighten off Germany since neither was in a position to aid Poland without defeating Germany first. France and Great Britain also began discussions with the Soviet Union aimed at establishing a common front against Germany. This was the move for which Stalin had been waiting. He was now presented with a choice, an agreement with France and Great Britain or one with Germany. Stalin had been toying with a pact with Berlin ever since 1936 but Hitler had shown no interest. Now after Germany had renounced the German–Polish pact of 1934 and the Anglo-German naval agreement of 1935 there was every likelihood of hostilities. Stalin hinted at what he wanted at the XVIIIth Party Congress, in March 1939; replaced Litvinov, a Jew, as commissar for foreign affairs with Molotov on 3 May and the breakthrough eventually came. On 23 August 1939 von Ribbentrop and Molotov signed the German–Soviet non-aggression pact in Moscow. A secret protocol, amended and supplemented by another on 27–28 September 1939, divided up the loot. The treaty became not merely one of non-aggression but also one of friendship. Poland east of the Narew, Vistula and San rivers, inhabited mainly by Belorussians and Ukrainians but including a slice of ethnic Poland, Estonia, Latvia and Finland were to pass into the Soviet sphere and Lithuania into the German sphere. Germany acknowledged Soviet interest in Bessarabia, then part of Romania.

This pact made war in Europe inevitable. Why did Stalin not opt for an agreement with France and Great Britain? Such an arrangement would arguably have halted Germany in her tracks as she would have been faced with a war on two fronts. Stalin appears to have decided that a war was almost inevitable, with Germany the aggressor, so he set out to make sure that the Soviet Union came out on top. One option was to join Great Britain and France and if Germany did go to war then all three would defeat her. But at the back of Stalin's mind was the suspicion that when the decisive moment came the western powers might opt out and leave the USSR alone with the German wolf. Great Britain especially negotiated with little finesse. She sent a second-string team by slow boat to Leningrad to explore terms. This was because British diplomats did not believe that Stalin had any room for manoeuvre. The idea of a German–Soviet agreement could only emanate from a madhouse. Also Poland adamantly refused to permit Soviet troops to penetrate its territory. If the Soviet Union were to link up with Britain and France to oppose Germany, how was the Red Army to get to Germany if not through Poland?

Germany unleashed the dogs of war against Poland on 1 September 1939 and the western powers declared war on 3 September. The rapid German advance caused the Soviets some anxiety and still the French armies did not move. Stalin even feared that the Wehrmacht might not stop but might invade the Soviet Union. He was faced with a cruel choice: invade Poland and run the risk of the western powers declaring war on the USSR or stand back and hand the initiative to the Germans. Stalin eventually decided that the Germans were the greater risk and invaded Poland on 17 September 1939. The western powers very obligingly did nothing. A rich harvest fell into the Soviet Union's lap and, into the bargain, most of Lithuania was exchanged for the Soviet slice of ethnic Poland.

Since Finland was within her zone of influence the USSR could act with impunity there. The Soviets decided they would like to move the Finnish frontier further away from Leningrad and offered the Finns some Soviet territory in return. The Finns made some concessions but would not agree to Soviet naval bases on their soil so the Soviet Union renounced the non-aggression pact and attacked Finland on 30 November 1939. The Winter War cost the Red Army some 175,000–200,000 dead and 200,000–300,000 wounded and the Finns 23,000 dead.[40] The longer the war continued the more likely France and Great Britain were to intervene so a lenient peace was concluded on 12 March 1940. The war revealed the incompetence of the Red Army and Stalin moved quickly to remedy the situation. Voroshilov handed over to Timoshenko as People's Commissar for Defence. The rank of general was restored and some of the purge victims rejoined the army.

If the Red Army had demonstrated its ineptitude in Finland the Wehrmacht startled everyone with the pace and panache of its occupation of Denmark and Norway, in April 1940, and its defeat of France, in June 1940, engulfing the Low Countries as well. Victory in the west brought Stalin's strategic thinking into question. He had expected that the Second World War would be a re-run of the First with the belligerents exhausting one another. Eventually the USSR could step in and pick up the pieces. Göring added to Stalin's discomfiture by claiming that Soviet deliveries of materials had speeded up Germany's advance in the west.

During the war in the west the Soviet Union moved substantial forces to the Soviet German frontier in the hope of diverting some German units to the east. The speed of the Blitzkreig, or lightning war, was such that the Soviet move only irritated Hitler and produced the opposite effect from the one intended. As it could not be trusted he determined to attack the USSR in 1941.

It was at this moment that the Soviet Union swallowed up the Baltic States and Bessarabia, taking northern Bukovina for good measure. Just under 20 million new citizens were added and they made the ethnic composition of the Soviet Union more and more like that of Imperial Russia.

When Molotov visited Berlin in November 1940 there was still a possibility that Germany could be deflected from attacking the Soviet Union. Hitler proposed that the USSR should join Germany in finishing off Britain and join the Tripartite Pact which allied Germany, Italy and Japan to Berlin's east European satellites. The Soviets were promised gains in the Black Sea area and in central Asia. The Germans attempted to convince Molotov that Great Britain was almost on its last legs but it was at precisely that moment that the RAF chose to visit Berlin. Molotov had a point when he asked what he was doing hiding in a bunker if Britain was almost finished.

Molotov parried Hitler's proposals and asked for time to consult his government. (The Soviet Union later agreed to join the Tripartite Pact.) Then he produced an astonishing shopping list of demands: Finland and southern Bukovina were to come within the Soviet orbit; Bulgaria was to be regarded as being within the Soviet security zone; Sweden was also placed there; Moscow expressed long-term ambitions in Hungary, Yugoslavia, Greece and even in a part of Poland currently under German occupation; the Soviets wanted military bases in the Dardanelles; and they requested a Soviet–Danish condominium over the Skagerrak and the Kattegat which would have given them control over the Baltic.

Just why Stalin decided to make such demands at a time when he was appeasing Hitler and doing everything in his power to avoid war is very difficult for a non-Russian to understand. Possibly he believed that if he did not make counter-demands the USSR would be taken to be weak. All he did achieve was to irritate Hitler and fuel his suspicions that the Soviet Union was an unreliable ally. Stalin's move was a diplomatic *faux pas* of the first magnitude.

Without bothering to deal Great Britain the final blow, Hitler, on 18 December 1940, signed Operation Barbarossa, the invasion of the USSR. Everything was to be ready by 15 May 1941. This afforded the Führer the option of picking any date he pleased after that date. Fortunately for the Soviet Union the Wehrmacht was not ready since it was detained elsewhere, in Greece and Yugoslavia to be precise. On 25 March a *coup d'état* had removed the pro-German government in Belgrade but German reaction was swift. German forces also moved into Greece because of the ineffectual showing of the Italians there. The net result was that the Wehrmacht was delayed five and a half weeks, a delay which arguably saved the Red Army from defeat in 1941. The Wehrmacht could have attacked earlier but Hitler was so confident of victory, reinforced by the superb showing of his forces in Yugoslavia, that he took his time over the decision. He did not consider the other option, that of putting pressure on Stalin to see what concessions he was willing to make. All the indications point in one direction, that Stalin would have made far-reaching concessions to preserve peace. However to Hitler a struggle was inevitable so since the Red Army was expected to take another four years to recover its pre-purge effectiveness the earlier the Wehrmacht struck the easier it would be.

STALINISM TRIUMPHANT

The onset of the cult of Stalin's personality dates from his fiftieth birthday, in December 1929. For the first time his persona was eulogised and praised to the skies. His command of the media meant that he had an almost unfettered right to have his thoughts and exhortations beamed to every corner of the country. But Stalinism is more than Stalin. Without willing cohorts in all aspects of human endeavour Stalinism would not have flowered. It was his ability to inspire, respond to and ensnare a whole generation that makes Stalin a consummate political actor.

The revolution from above, industrialisation and collectivisation, set in train events which developed their own momentum. The party was full of raw recruits and many cadres failed the test in the early harsh years of collectivisation. Workers enjoyed, between 1929 and 1931, the golden years of their dominance over management. However by 1933 another revolution had taken place and they had been cowed. The social revolution which had promised to give the working class dominance turned sour as the era of the manager, the specialist and labour discipline came in with a vengeance. This was hard for party cadres to take, especially 'old' (pre-1917) Bolsheviks who accounted for 69 per cent of local party secretaries in 1930.[41] Nevertheless by the end of the first FYP the party had produced a body of men and women, battle scarred but reliable, and they became the core of the Stalinist cadres. Of predominantly peasant origin, dedicated to the party and to the person of Stalin and willing to act on any order without demur, they put their stamp on a whole epoch. The squeamish had passed from the scene and there was no going back. Ambition, idealism, ruthlessness fired these men and women. They really were people of a special mould. However, few as yet were in leading positions. At the XVIIth Party Congress in 1934 80 per cent of delegates had joined the party before 1920. Hence the Leninist elite was still in place and it would take the purges to sweep it away so as to allow the Stalinist elite to take over. When technical specialists joined the Stalinist elite in the late 1930s it became invincible.

The early years of the first FYP were the golden era of the little man, which had another function as well. It allowed the Bolshevik or would-be specialist to challenge the existing specialists. In this way a new type of specialist could be fashioned, one who was willing to accept the goals of the FYPs. Men and women of ambition could climb to influence on the backs of their former teachers. Folk leaders sprang up in various fields: Makarenko in education, Vilyams in grassland management, Lysenko in agrobiology, Marr in linguistics, Michurin in fruit farming and so on. The aim was to demystify learning: anyone with the right attitude could become a specialist. Stalin regarded experts as those with special technical or other qualifications. Expertise could be garnered quite quickly. Hence he did not afford experience any great significance. This is probably because he never studied a technical discipline. He was very cavalier in disposing of experts, even military experts. They could, after all, be replaced.

Concomitant with this went the exaltation of Russian achievements and the downgrading of foreign experience. The various independent technical associations were replaced by party-linked organisations. Choice was systematically eliminated as government and party ambitions to invade every sector of human endeavour grew.

The way Stalin projected himself is instructive. During the 1920s he presented himself as the true disciple of Lenin and branded Trotsky, Zinoviev and Kamenev and others as anti-Leninists. The view of the October Revolution was that it was inconceivable without the first Bolshevik leader. In the course of the 1930s, changes appeared. Stalin gradually became the equal of Lenin, writers spoke of the Lenin–Stalin partnership and the two came to be seen as the engineers of the October Revolution. 'Stalin is the Lenin of today' marks the next phase when Stalin superseded Lenin in the world of the 1930s. Stalin becomes the father of the nation, he is above party, indeed he is above everyone. In this new guise he is acclaimed as the fount of all wisdom, he is the coryphaeus of science, he is the most learned of men. Lenin steps backward as Stalin steps forward in the affections of the people. The epithet Stalinist becomes synonymous with everything that is good, if it is Stalinist it will succeed. The party suffered in consequence. The last occasion on which Stalin's position was under assault was the XVIIth Party Congress at which an attempt was made to elevate Stalin into the stratosphere well above mere diurnal problems so as to leave the world to Kirov, Ordzhonikidze and other mere mortals. Once Stalin had overcome this threat he was unassailable and became the source of all proletarian thought. Stalin, and he alone, knows what is in the mind of the working class and consequently is the only one who knows what is best. Following his guidelines in turn enriches the individual. The party loses its key role in Soviet society and the proof of *partiinost*, or party-mindedness, is the ability to comprehend and act on Stalin's words.

This scenario links opposition to Stalin to opposition to the party and the nation. Hence treason is a common accusation during the purges. Since many old Bolsheviks were aware of the cracks in the Stalinist edifice they had to be silenced. Only when there was no one who could and would contradict Stalin's skilful version of past events could he rest assured that he was untouchable.

Stalin's power was based on control of government, party and the security police. The government was formally in control but there was a parallel government, the party. The police supervised both. Stalin liked to use military metaphors when talking about the party. At the CC plenum on 3 March 1937 he described the commanding heights of the party: there were 3,000–4,000 senior leaders who were the generals; the 30,000–40,000 middle-level officials made up the officer corps, and the 100,000–150,000 lower-level leaders were the NCOs.[42] This provides a revealing insight into Stalin's hierarchical way of thinking.

Stalin, of course, could not rule the country singlehanded. He sought out different sources of information and needed assistants to sift through the mass of material which flowed on to his desk, to help him reach decisions and to check that decisions were implemented. A secret chancellery was set up to perform these tasks.[43] Collectively the secretaries and assistants in the secret chancellery knew all the secrets of the Soviet Union but individually they only knew some of them. Stalin was the only person who was privy to everything and only he was able to fit the jigsaw completely together. When he needed advice he consulted individuals or small groups. Information flow was deliberately restricted to ensure Stalin's monopoly. He became very skilled at playing his subordinates off against one another. It gradually became unnecessary for higher party organs to meet formally very often. For instance, there were only two party congresses between 1935 and 1953. No wonder Khrushchev, in his Memoirs, complained that even top party officials found it very difficult to discover what was going on.

Probably the outstanding feature of the system in the 1930s was its arbitrariness. No official, no specialist, no policeman could ever feel absolutely safe in his position. Since there was no personal security, there was no institutional security. No group or institution was ever permitted to congeal into a potential opposition.

Such a system was only possible in a country undergoing industrialisation and modernisation. The tremendous waste of talent and human lives could be sustained since labour productivity was low and industry relatively unsophisticated. Ideology, paradoxically, played an important role since advice in *Pravda* was couched in vague terms, the right ideological attitude would produce the desired results and so on. This was not very helpful if the problem was to repair combine harvesters. This led to a situation that a person who succeeded in solving technical problems would be invested also with ideological rectitude. Extraordinary lengths were resorted to in the 1930s to link the legitimacy of the regime to technical success, at home and abroad. Pilots would claim that a personal meeting with Stalin had made it possible for them to overcome almost insurmountable difficulties. Besides providing great satisfaction these achievements fanned the flames of Great Russian nationalism. The Russian was second to none.

Not all the coercion in the world would have driven the Soviet Union forward had the population not been in sympathy with the goals of the FYPs. There was enormous suffering but Stalin was able to detach himself, in the common mind, from this and to become the beloved leader of the nation. Many went to their deaths believing that had Comrade Stalin only known what was going on he would have saved them from injustice.

Stalinism flowered in the 1930s in a responsive soil. It owes more to Russian political culture than to the westernising tradition of social democracy. It is different from Leninism, which contained some of its elements, but which was less demanding and a less severe judge of human frailty. Stalinism was demotic but not democratic, and pitiless in subjecting men and women to material goals. The needs of the State and the economy took precedence over every private desire. Stalin, by 1941, had mown down the harvest of potential opponents and left himself as the only stalk standing. He had become the charismatic leader and as such was indispensable.

Is it possible to decipher a pattern in the revolution from above and mass mobilisation from below? Stalinist policy between 1928 and 1941 can be interpreted as a series of offensives. The first FYP was the initial offensive, which was accompanied by intense politicisation and mobilisation of the population. Specialists became scapegoats for economic failure. Stalin had to take cognisance of his fellow oligarchs. From 1932 onwards a period of consolidation set in and plan targets were pitched a little lower and living standards improved. However, politicisation became even more intense, with every nook and cranny of life subject to Bolshevik examination. Efforts were made to develop a new science of Soviet success. All this was a preparation for the purges of 1936–38, which launched the second offensive. By 1936 Stalin was unquestionably dictator and so could set about devouring his other oligarchs. Stalin's inner group appears to have believed that there was considerable opposition within the country to the modernisation drive under way. This offensive sees the Politburo and Central Committee losing effective power to Stalin, the enormous extension of the NKVD's coercive power and the deliberate use of terror and the promotion to leading positions of the Stalinist nomenklatura. This elite was essentially of peasant origin. During this offensive economic goals were sharply raised; political opponents were hounded, often to their deaths; there was a renewed campaign against bourgeois specialists; concomitantly, there was a concerted effort made to educate a generation of 'new' specialists; discipline, especially of labour, became harsh. A motivation for the purges may have been the belief that the 'old' governmental and party apparatus would hold back growth. If this is so, the leadership took the tremendous risk of annihilating it and ensconcing a new elite in record time. The elimination of the military leadership was part of this process. This underlines Stalin's lack of understanding of expertise. He evidently believed that it could be garnered very quickly. If the will-power was there Bolsheviks could achieve anything, appears to have been his thinking. He wanted to breed a generation of like-minded comrades. No wonder the educated blanched at his aspirations.

NOTES

1. I. V. Stalin *Sochineniya* vol. 13 pp. 38–9.
2. Ibid. vol. 11, p. 54.
3. Ibid. p. 69.
4. Alec Nove *An Economic History of the USSR* p. 190.
5. Stalin, op. cit. vol. 12, pp. 176–7.
6. Mikhail Sholokhov *The Soil Upturned* p. 152. There were 70.5 million head of cattle in the Soviet Union in 1928 but only 38.4 million in 1933; pigs declined from 26 million to 12.1 million over the same period; sheep and goats from 146.7 million to 50.2 million; horses from 33.5 million to 16.6 million (*Sotsialisticheskoe Stroitelstvo SSSR* (Moscow 1936) p. 354). The serious reduction in draught power meant that more resources had to be switched to the production of tractors than planned. The loss of so many cattle and sheep reduced the amount of leather and wool available for consumer goods.
7. Nove, op. cit. p. 227.
8. Ibid. pp. 227–8.
9. Ibid. p. 201.
10. Ibid. p. 205.
11. Ibid. p. 208.
12. Stalin, op. cit. vol. 13, p. 200.
13. Nove, op. cit. p. 249.
14. Ibid. p. 246. Only 4.2 per cent of kolkhozes had electricity in 1940.
15. Ibid. p. 262.
16. Kendall E. Bailes *Technology and Society under Lenin and Stalin: Origins of the Soviet Technical Intelligentsia 1917–1941* p. 150.
17. Ibid. p. 173.
18. Ibid. p. 219.
19. Ibid. p. 226.
20. Ibid. p. 221.
21. Nicholas De Witt *Education and Professional Employment in the USSR* p. 336.
22. Bailes, op. cit. p. 194.
23. Ibid. p. 202.
24. Ibid. p. 335.
25. Ibid. p. 336.
26. C. Vaughan James *Soviet Socialist Realism: Origins and Theory* p. 88. Also useful are: Max Hayward and Leopold Labedz (eds) *Literature and Revolution in Soviet Russia 1917–62* especially chapters 3–5; and Katerina

Clark 'Utopian Anthropology as a Context for Stalinist Literature' in Robert C. Tucker (ed.) *Stalinism: Essays in Historical Interpretation* pp. 180–98.

27. Clark, op. cit. p. 196.
28. Robert Conquest *The Great Terror: Stalin's Purge of the Thirties* p. 28.
29. Ibid. p. 30.
30. Ibid. p. 485.
31. Ibid. p. 335.
32. Alexander Orlov *The Secret History of Stalin's Crimes* p. 130.
33. Robert Tucker, *Stalin in Power: The Revolution from Above 1928–1941* pp. 107–10.
34. Tucker, *Stalinism: Essays in Historical Interpretation* pp. 120–6.
35. Gerhard Simon, *Nationalismus and Nationalitätenpolitik in der Sowjetunion*, pp. 41–82.
36. Ibid. pp. 91–129.
37. Ibid. pp. 130–94.
38. Richard Stites, *The Women's Liberation Movement in Russia: Feminism, Nihilism and Bolshevism 1860–1930* pp. 317–45.
39. The Nazi executioners were not always very careful in identifying their victims. One unfortunate, a music critic in Munich, was dumped on his widow's doorstep with the laconic remark: 'Sorry, madam, the wrong Willy Schmidt.'
40. A. F. Chew *The White Death* p. 212. The official Soviet estimate is 48,745 dead and 158,863 wounded. Khrushchev, in his Memoirs, speaks of one million casualties.
41. *XVI Sezd VKP(b)* pp. 749–67.
42. I. V. Stalin *Sochineniya* vol. 1 (XIV) 1934–1940 (Stanford edn) pp. 220–1.
43. Cf. Niels Erik Rosenfeldt *Knowledge and Power. The Role of Stalin's Secret Chancellery in the Soviet System of Government.*

CHAPTER FOUR

The Great Fatherland War

'EITHER THIS COUNTRY WINS OR EVERYONE WILL DIE'

INVASION

At 3.15 Berlin time (4.15 Moscow time) on the morning of Sunday 22 June 1941 the frontier from the Baltic to the Carpathians, separating the Wehrmacht and the Red Army, belched with fire and fury. The fragile pact was at an end and a titanic struggle was under way. Operation Barbarossa (Red Beard) launched Army Group North against the Baltic States and Leningrad, Army Group Centre against Belorussia and Moscow and Army Group South against the Ukraine and Kiev. The Romanians and the German 11th Army were to come in as reinforcements and the Finns were to be ready to join the German thrust against Leningrad, beginning on 11 July. Hungarian, Slovak, Italian and Spanish troops added their contribution after 24 June.

The German goal in 1941 was to reach a line running from Archangel to Kuibyshev and then down the Volga to Astrakhan. This would then permit the German air force, the Luftwaffe, to bomb industrial centres in the Urals.

The Wehrmacht attacked with 3,200,000 men, 600,000 lorries, 600,000 horses, 3,350 tanks and 2,000 combat aircraft.[1] The Soviet forces included 2,900,000 men, 1,800 tanks (excluding light tanks) and 1,540 combat aircraft (new types).[2] If all types are counted the Soviets probably possessed 20,000 tanks (most of them obsolete) and 6,000 aircraft (again mostly obsolete).

The Red Army and air force were quite unprepared for war. As late as 14 June a TASS communiqué reiterated the view that there was not going to be an attack. Great sporting activities had been planned for 22 June and because of this some of the troops, including tank men, had been sent off for special coaching and training. Amateur theatricals were also in full swing. Some commanders were absent and many divisional artillery regiments were undergoing special training at camps far from the front.[3]

On the eve of the invasion Beria ordered some of his spies who had provided precise information about the attack to be 'ground into dust' in labour camps for attempting to deceive systematically the Soviet leadership. Among those to be disciplined were the Soviet ambassador and military attaché in Berlin. Beria reported to Stalin:

'My colleagues and I, Iosef Vissarionovich, steadfastly remember your wise assessment: Hitler will not attack us in 1941.'

Despite precise intelligence information on the timing of the Wehrmacht onslaught,[4] instructions to Soviet forces to 'man secretly the fire-points of the fortified districts on the frontier . . . have all units brought to a state of combat readiness'[5] were dispatched at 12.30 a.m. but many did not receive them before the Wehrmacht struck. The dispatch ended: 'No other measures are to be taken without special orders.' Information on the exact timing of the attack came from German deserters and from diplomatic and NKVD sources. Hence when the Germans attacked Red Army commanders could not react and had to ask for instructions. It took up to two hours for the order to fight back to come through and even then Soviet troops were not permitted to advance into enemy territory. Moscow simply did not believe that a full-scale attack was under way and it took several hours for it to sink in that it was not just border provocations by undisciplined German commanders.

The turn of events stunned Stalin and his fear of the adversary caused him to lose his nerve. He remained prostrate at his dacha while the running of the war passed to his subordinates. It was left to Molotov to reveal to the nation, at noon, the true course of events.

A key element in the rapid advance of the Wehrmacht was air power. The Luftwaffe achieved almost total supremacy by destroying 1,200 Soviet machines by noon on 22 June. The Germans knew that they could not conquer and occupy the whole of the Soviet Union. They also realised that they could only win by means of a Blitzkrieg, a lightning war. The resources of the Soviet Union were so great, in men and *matériel*, that a long-drawn-out affair was bound to favour Moscow. Hence the plan was to annihilate the Red Army in pitched battles. If the Soviet forces could extricate themselves and retreat behind a defensive wall initial German victories would be nullified. Time was of the essence: the Soviets had to buy time but the Germans could not afford to waste a minute. Therefore any desperate rearguard action, irrespective of cost and inevitable defeat, was a valuable contribution to the Soviet war effort.

The invasion led to a restructuring of the Soviet military command. Stavka was established on 23 June and was responsible for all land, sea and air operations. Its original members were: Stalin (chairman), Molotov, Timoshenko, Commissar for Defence, Voroshilov, Budenny, Shaposhnikov, Zhukov and Admiral N. G. Kuznetsov. Timoshenko was the *de facto* chairman during the first two weeks. It had a permanent council of advisers on whom it could draw for reports and advice.[6] Stalin supervised all major military operations. His link with the front was strengthened by sending a Stavka representative to check on operations and report back to him. As well as this military information Stalin also received, of course, reports from the political police.

The more important committee, the State Committee of Defence (GKO), was set up on 30 June. The initiative to set up the GKO came from Nikolai Voznesensky, a minor official but who was to play an important economic role during hostilities, proposed to Molotov that the whole leadership go to see Stalin at his dacha at Kuntsevo. When they arrived Stalin remained seated in a corner by the window. He greeted them with a question: 'Why have you come?' It was as if he had expected them to arrest him. When they proposed the GKO, Stalin merely agreed. According to Molotov, Stalin's 'paralysis' gradually wore off as he pitched himself back into the fray, but he remained very gloomy about the outcome of the war. In typically crude language he complained that they had screwed up Lenin's legacy. Stalin chaired the GKO, and the other original members were Molotov (vice-chairman), Malenkov, Voroshilov and Beria, head of the NKVD. The GKO had a wide brief, overseeing the military, political and economic life of the nation. Molotov appears to have been the *de facto* leader of the country during the first week of the war.

Stalin had regained sufficient composure to address the nation on 3 July and tell the terrible truth about the war. Until then official communiqués had been pure fiction. He addressed his compatriots as brothers, sisters, friends and appealed to them not in the name of the Communist Party but in the name of the motherland. 'Hitler's troops have captured Lithuania, most of Latvia, the western part of Belorussia and part of the western Ukraine.'[7] If the Red Army was forced to retreat it had to destroy everything which might be of use to the Germans, a scorched earth policy which would mean that occupied territory would be a vast wilderness and the hand of destruction would be Soviet.

Stalin operated from the Kremlin with a personal secretariat, headed by Poskrebyshev. Through him he could keep in contact with field commanders. This provided him with a vital independent source of information. It also meant that he was sometimes better informed than front-line commanders. He only visited the front on one occasion, in August 1943. He became Commissar of Defence in mid July and on 8 August the Supreme Soviet made him Supreme Commander of the Soviet Armed Forces.

The most successful German thrust was made by Army Group Centre. It swept ahead and took Smolensk on 16 July. Army Group North was behind schedule but did reasonably well, taking Pskov on 8 July. Army Group South had the most difficult task because of the large area and the number of natural barriers. Most Soviet forces were able to retreat and evade capture. The first stage of Barbarossa was completely successful. Fortunately for the Red Army the Germans could not make up their minds about the next target. Hitler thought of Leningrad, the General Staff wanted Moscow but on 21 August Hitler caused consternation among his generals by deciding to go south to take the Ukraine. A decisive factor was the industrial and agricultural potential of the republic and further south the oil of Baku. The Wehrmacht could live off the Ukraine but not off the northern part of the country.

Kiev fell on 19 September with huge Soviet losses including 655,000 prisoners, but the autumn rains and the quagmire they produced bogged the army down and made the original goals unattainable. A push in the north brought the Germans to the outskirts of Leningrad but on 17 September when the city was at his mercy Hitler withdrew his armour and bombers. His new plan was to surround and take Moscow, continue the advance in the Ukraine, take the Crimea and the oilfields of Baku and starve Leningrad into submission by surrounding it with infantry.

These goals were demanded of troops who had suffered 534,000 casualties by 26 September, about one in six of total establishment on the Eastern Front. Men and equipment needed a rest as natural conditions worsened. However, the Wehrmacht was not equipped for a winter campaign.

Operation Typhoon, the attack on Moscow, launched on 30 September, caught the Soviet High Command by surprise. Desperately they sought every available soldier to establish defensive lines. In anticipation of a German attack the civilian population of Moscow, ever since mid July, had been drafted to build two great earthwork systems running for about 250 km, the forward one about 300 km and the rear one about 120 km west of Moscow. Nevertheless the Wehrmacht advanced about 100 km during the first day and on 3 October Orel fell. Disaster overtook the Red Army around Vyazma and Bryansk, the former netting the Germans 650,000 prisoners or the loss of forty-five divisions.[8] Despite the rain, the mud, illness and disease the German army reached out for Moscow. Embassies and many government offices were evacuated to Kuibyshev, on the Volga, other departments to twenty-one different cities in the east. Only those people essential to the defence of Moscow stayed in the capital. With the German units on the outskirts Stalin panicked once again. On the night of 16–17 October he left Moscow and only returned on 18 October. The capital was at the mercy of the invader. The underground stopped, the NKVD and police disappeared, the bakeries stopped baking and communists tore up their party cards. Astonishingly the Wehrmacht failed to realise this and the opportunity once missed was never to recur.

The failure to seal the fate of Moscow was compensated for by successes in the south. Odessa fell on 16 October but 80,000 troops and many civilians were evacuated by sea to help in the defence of the Crimea; Kharkov on 24 October and Rostov-on-Don, the gateway to the Caucasus, on 20 November. Some of these gains, however, were shortlived. The exhausted Germans, soaked by day and frozen by night, were soon to feel the impact of the Soviet winter offensive.

The Red Army's attack began during the night of 5 December with the aim of saving Moscow, underlining once again Hitler's mistaken tactics in not giving top priority to the capture of the Soviet nerve centre. When they discovered how weak the Germans really were the Soviet High Command launched a counter-offensive over a 1,000-kilometre front, involving sixteen armies. Disaster might have overtaken the Germans had not Hitler demanded that every man should stand and fight and not retreat. Nevertheless the Soviet offensive threw the Wehrmacht back 200 and 300 kilometres in places and at one time the liberation of Smolensk even appeared a possibility.

Zhukov's offensive west of Moscow[9] was more successful than other thrusts in the north, in the Ukraine and in the Crimea. However, the Red Army could be satisfied with its achievement. German casualties, between 27 November 1941 and 31 March 1942, amounted to 108,000 killed or missing, 268,000 wounded, over 500,000 ill (of whom 228,000 were suffering from frostbite), making a total of 900,000.[10] Huge quantities of *matériel* were lost, including 74,000 motor vehicles. Equipment losses could be made up but not personnel losses. By April 1942 the Wehrmacht was short of 625,000 men.

The blocking of the German offensive before Moscow was a turning-point in the war. Was the failure of the Blitzkrieg due to the Wehrmacht's shortcomings or to the Red Army's strengths? Hitler had only planned a short campaign and intended to withdraw and leave only fifteen to twenty divisions in the USSR. Hence neither men nor machines were prepared for a winter campaign. The clinging mud meant that only tracked vehicles could move but most German vehicles were wheeled. Carts fell apart on Soviet terrain but the Russian cart carried on. German horses died in their thousands but the scraggy Russian animal lived. When the first frosts arrived there was no anti-freeze for vehicle radiators. Jackboots afforded no protection at −30°C; toes and heels were prone to frostbite. The Red Army issued leather boots a couple of sizes too large so that they could be stuffed with paper.

German military intelligence was very inaccurate. The Wehrmacht had no knowledge of the KV1, KV2 and T34 tanks and the Katyusha rocket launcher. The KV2 weighed 52 tonnes and the KV1 and KV2 were impervious to a 150 mm howitzer at 300 metres, and a 37 mm anti-tank gun could not dent the armour of a T34. None of this equipment, superior to anything the Germans had, had been used in the Winter War against Finland.

Even had estimates of Soviet equipment and men been nearer the mark Hitler would have swept them from the table. He was in no mood to believe that the Soviet Union could hold out very long, otherwise the original offensive would never have been launched. Had

Leningrad and Moscow fallen the war would not have been over, the Red Army would have retreated to the Urals and beyond and fought on. The knowledge that the Japanese were not planning to attack Siberia, obtained through Dr Richard Sorge, a communist spy with contacts in the German embassy in Tokyo and friends among highly placed Japanese, was of incalculable value. Stalin was able to withdraw about half the divisional strength of the Far Eastern command together with 1,000 tanks and 1,000 aircraft to protect Moscow.[11] Hence Japan's decision to strike east and south saved the Soviet Union.

Soviet losses were much higher than necessary. The true cost of the purges had now to be paid. After the initial débacle Marshal Voroshilov was put in charge of the North Western, Marshal Timoshenko of the Western and Marshal Budenny of the South Western Front on 10 July 1941 but Voroshilov and Budenny were out of their depth. Allied to this were the new orders from Stalin not to concede a centimetre of territory; this led to many Soviet units being encircled. Marshal Zhukov took over command of the Western Front on 19 October 1941 and made a considerable difference. He had the good fortune to have at his disposal fresh Siberian troops and they helped him to become the victor of Moscow.

Morale was not very high in the Red Army. About two million prisoners were taken in the first year of the war. The total reached five million in November 1943, and there was widespread defeatism among the public, for example in Moscow in October 1941.

Hitler was always in dispute with his generals which meant that decisive leadership was lacking. After the failure before Moscow he dismissed von Brauchitsch and made himself Commander-in-Chief on 19 December 1941. Leningrad and Moscow could have been taken had they been afforded priority early on. The longer the Germans remained in the field the more exhausted they became. They were quite unprepared for the mud, the frost, the snow and the steppe. The endless Ukrainian steppe induced illness and despair.

GERMAN WAR GOALS[12]

The German attack on the Soviet Union was not a preventive war. It was not based on a deep fear of an imminent attack but was rather the expression of the policy of aggression which had been practised ever since 1938. Hitler wanted the Soviet Union to be 'severely beaten' and several states to be set up such as the Ukraine, a Baltic States Federation and Belorussia. The USSR was seen as the key to the control of Europe. The Wehrmacht envisaged a campaign lasting three to five months. The Russians were to be reduced to a 'leaderless people performing labour'. The war in the east was seen as more than a struggle between different

Weltanschauungen. It was not enough to defeat the Red Army; the whole of the USSR had to be broken up into states headed by their own governments with which Germany could conclude peace. This demanded great political skill and well-thought-out principles. It would not be possible to eradicate socialism so the new states and governments would be socialist. However the 'Jewish-Bolshevik intelligentsia', seen as the 'oppressor' of the people had to be 'removed' and the 'government machinery of the Russian Empire destroyed'. Since the former 'aristocratic-bourgeois intelligentsia' was anti-German it had also to be pushed aside. A 'national Russian state' must not come into being since it would inevitably become anti-German. Socialist states 'dependent on Germany' were to be established using the minimum of military force. The influence of Alfred Rosenberg, the chief Nazi ideologist, can be seen in these proposals.

The 'most brutal violence' was to be practised in the 'Great Russian area'. Political administrations were to be introduced as quickly as possible so as to conduct ideological warfare. Hitler saw communism as a great future danger. The war was to be one of annihilation: 'We are not waging war to conserve the enemy', he declared. The Führer was not thinking of establishing socialist states dependent on Germany and then of leaving the Soviet Union. The Nazis saw the area as Lebensraum and wanted to 'dominate, rule and exploit' it ruthlessly. Any concern for the feelings and way of life of the Russian people was dismissed as sentimental drivel. Heinrich Himmler, the head of the SS, made himself very clear: 'I am totally indifferent to the fate of the Russians, Czechs . . . whether they live well or are wracked by hunger only interests me in so far as we need them as slaves for our culture, otherwise they don't interest me.' According to the 'Generalplan Ost' about 75 per cent of the Slav population was to be moved later to Siberia. Germans, Norwegians, Swedes, Danes and Dutch were to colonise the land vacated by the Slavs.

In the Caucasus the Wehrmacht supported national governments which sprang up in the wake of the retreating Red Army. A Karachai national government, for instance, came into being. The experiment was, however, not repeated in the Slav areas. Favouring the nationalities against the Great Russian nation was opposed by some leading military figures such as General Jodl. He favoured an appeal to the Great Russians over the heads of their rulers. The goal was to separate them from their rulers and hasten the break-up of the Soviet Union.

Politically German policy was almost suicidal. The *Kommissarbefehl* or commissar order of 6 June 1941 ordered the execution of all Red Army political commissars taken prisoner. It was extended to include other party and government officials and, of course, Jews were also shot. Some units just ignored these orders but most carried them out. German treatment of Red Army prisoners was short-sighted and criminal. Out of 5.7 million prisoners taken during the war, 3.3 million perished, most of hunger and disease. The huge bag of prisoners in the early stages of the war found the army unprepared and rations to feed them were not diverted from German mouths. The mass deaths of Soviet prisoners occurred without Hitler's knowledge and many of the extreme measures adopted in the Soviet Union never came to the knowledge of the top leadership.[13] So demoralising did some units find the task of shooting communists and Jews after they had been taken prisoner that they decided to take no prisoners whenever possible.

The Wehrmacht's senseless brutality soon turned the Soviet population against them. The population had many grievances. The peasants wanted their land back, the non-Russian nationalities wanted more autonomy and everyone favoured less oppression. The Germans were welcomed in some places and many Soviet citizens would have fought against the Communist Party but this reservoir of goodwill was hardly touched. The Germans did change their mind later but by 1944 it was too late.

THE PROGRESS OF THE WAR

The Germans scored a notable victory near Kharkov on 29 May 1942 and bagged 214,000 Red Army prisoners-of-war, 1,200 tanks and 2,000 guns.[14] Disasters at Kerch in May and Sevastopol in June 1942 were but a prelude to the death and destruction caused by the German summer offensive of 1942 in the southern Ukraine. Operation Blue directives fell into Soviet hands and were in front of Stalin several days before the attack of 28 June but he did not believe them. Rostov-on-Don fell on 23 July, giving the Germans control of the Donbass, and the road to the Caucasus appeared to be open once again. In this desperate situation Stalin issued an order on 28 July ordering every Soviet soldier to fight to the last drop of blood and to hold his ground to the bitter end. 'Not a step backwards' became more than a rallying cry, it was vital necessity. Maikop and Krasnodar were lost in early August and the Wehrmacht reached Stalingrad in early September. Thence followed one of the epic battles of history when every centimetre of the city was fought over. The Germans took ninety per cent of the city on one occasion but could never quite reduce it totally. The battle was unnecessary since Stalingrad was not of primary strategic importance, the Volga could have been cut between the city and Astrakhan with the same effect. The name hypnotised Hitler and when his armies appeared to be in danger of encirclement, he refused to permit a tactical withdrawal. He promoted Paulus to Field-Marshal on the battlefield in the belief that no German field-marshal would ever surrender. The Soviet counter-offensive began on 19 November 1942 and gouged into Romanian formations and encircled the German Sixth Army with its 284,000 troops. Despite efforts to relieve the beleaguered troops, especially by von Manstein, by the end of December their fate was sealed. Paulus and his staff were captured on 31 January 1943 together with 91,000 prisoners of whom twenty-four were generals; hence almost 200,000 Germans lost their lives in the ruins of Stalingrad. The prisoners were disowned by Hitler, the German population being led to believe that all had perished. A crack in the edifice of trust between Hitler and his fighting men appeared for the first time.

Nothing should detract from the magnificent Soviet victory even though Hitler's refusal to allow the Sixth Army to withdraw doomed it. The battle was an incalculable boost to Red Army morale, the High Command learned how to wage a modern battle and never again would Soviet formations abjectly surrender or flee the field of battle.

Germany's greatest defeat was a turning-point. From now on it was not a matter of how the war would end but when.

A Soviet offensive secured Kharkov but by 18 March 1943 Kharkov and Belgorod had fallen again to a German counter-attack. Nevertheless the Red Army could feel satisfied at having destroyed the strongest German army, the Sixth, and four armies of Germany's allies, Romania, Hungary and Italy. The enemy had been thrown back 800 kilometres from Stalingrad. Hitler's rigid defence had cost the Wehrmacht dear but it was still a match for the Red Army. Nevertheless even though man for man the German Army was superior its lead in equipment was disappearing. On 23 January 1943 only 495 tanks were fit for battle on the Eastern Front. Soviet KV and T34 tanks were superior to the German Mark III and IV and the Germans had nothing to compare with the quarter-tonne jeep for commanders or messengers and the Studebaker or Dodge six-wheel-drive truck.[15] The Red Army became motorised in 1943, partly through Lend Lease, and this was to have momentous consequences.

German defeats at Stalingrad and in North Africa and Japanese defeats in the Pacific, together with the increasing strength of the Anglo-American and Soviet forces meant that the Nazis could only win the war if the Allies fell out amongst themselves. The prospect of a second front in Europe was becoming a real possibility. In these circumstances Hitler believed the best course was to launch an offensive on the Eastern Front to repair the reputation of German arms. The chosen site was Kursk, the Soviets came to the same conclusion, and there developed the greatest, until then, tank battle of all time. Hitler decided to commit all his heavy tanks, including his new Mark V Panthers and his Mark VI Tigers, which weighed about 56 tonnes and mounted an 88 mm gun, and Ferdinands. Battle was joined on 4 July 1943. The fate of the encounter hung like a thread with the Germans tantalisingly near success. On 13 July Hitler decided to break off the engagement so as to counter the Anglo-American landings in Sicily. The Wehrmacht had finally lost the initiative in the east: henceforth it was only able to react to Red Army manoeuvres.

The Soviets took Belgorod on 5 August, Kharkov on 23 August. Donetsk on 8 September and Mariupol on 10 September 1943. And so the victorious march continued, checked now and then, but finally irresistible. Poltava and Smolensk were liberated by the end of September and Kiev on 6 November.

The year 1944 was one during which the Soviet cup of victory was full to overflowing. In January Soviet attacks led to the German stranglehold on Leningrad being finally broken and Finland later asked Moscow for armistice terms. Soviet successes in the Ukraine were such that by late March they were near the Czechoslovak and Romanian frontiers. Fighting became even fiercer and Zhukov felt strong enough to deliver an ultimatum, on 2 April 1944, to the first Panzer Army with between 200,000 and 300,000 men, surrounded near Kamenets Podolsk, stating that if all resistance did not cease that day one third of those subsequently captured would be shot. A second ultimatum followed saying that all German officers who did not surrender immediately would be shot on capture. This spurred the Germans on no end and they succeeded in fighting their way out of encirclement. Zhukov was subsequently blamed for not wiping out the German army. This temporary setback was more than compensated for by the retaking of the Crimea in May.

A massive Soviet offensive over a 700 kilometre front was launched on 22 June 1944, just over two weeks after the Anglo-American landings in Normandy. Minsk was taken on 4 July, Vilnius on 13 July and the Germans lost 300,000 men, a more terrible loss than at Stalingrad.

On 20 July 1944 Count von Stauffenberg planted a bomb in Hitler's HQ at Rastenburg in East Prussia but it failed to kill the Führer. A terrible vengeance was wreaked on the High Command and General Staff by Hitler who had never had a high opinion of the army. He was doing Stalin's work for him, the German version of the purge of the Red Army. The army was destroyed from the inside at the moment of its greatest peril.

Soviet forces had reached the outskirts of Warsaw on 1 August when the Warsaw Uprising broke out. No Soviet help, however, was extended until mid September but by then the underground army of predominantly nationalist, non-communist forces and the city had been smashed by the Germans. The key role in applying the *coup de grâce* was assigned to the SS and they committed abominations and bestialities in the streets of Warsaw.

Further south the Red Army reached the San and Vistula rivers and the Carpathians in early August. Romania surrendered on 23 August 1944 and changed sides. Although Bulgaria was not a belligerent, war was declared on her and Sofia occupied on 16 September. Belgrade was taken on 19 October and Budapest was within sight in early November.

The final massive offensive running from the Baltic to the Carpathians was launched on 12–14 January 1945. The remnants of Warsaw were occupied on 17 January, Krakow and Łodz on 19 January 1945. Resistance in east Prussia was very spirited and Königsberg did not fall until 9 April. Further south Budapest was taken by the Red Army on 13 February and Vienna on 13 April 1945. The final push against Berlin began in April and the city fell on 2 May. The German acknowledgement of defeat on 8 May 1945 (9 May 1945 in Moscow due to the time difference) ended the war on the battlefield but the war of words about the shape of the post-war world was only just beginning. With Germany defeated and Great Britain bled white by the war, the Soviet Union became the main military and political power in Europe and as such was certain to play a key role in decision-making. The centre of gravity of European power had thus moved further eastwards.

ADMINISTRATION

Since Stalin was convinced that there would be no German attack in 1941 there were no contingency plans to run the State under wartime conditions. However, there was something on which to build: experience during the Civil War and Intervention. The Soviet leadership had to fashion a new system of decision-making and implementation which maximised human initiative but which also allowed Stalin and his coterie to retain overall central control of the war effort. The State Defence Committee (GKO), chaired by Stalin, was operational from 30 June 1941. It had a basic membership of eight but its task was immense; win the war by providing everything the fighting man and woman needed. The command-administrative system had to become efficient as never before. Its resolutions had the force of law. It also covered social order and security and, when necessary, set up committees to promote military-economic and defence construction. In addition, it was involved in the appointment and replacement of higher-ranking military commanders; the preparation of reserves for the armies in the field; the solution of military-strategic questions; putting industry, transport and agriculture on a war footing; providing the military and the population with food and other necessities; the acquisition of fuel; the training and allocation of labour and the battle against spies.[16] It quickly generated plenipotentiaries whose task was to solve specific problems and to set up local defence committees. The GKO was superior to all party, komsomol, soviet and military organs. It decided policy but it had no executive apparatus. The implementation of decrees became the responsibility of the party and governmental apparatus. The GKO and *Stavka* very quickly came together. GKO members had the right to attend and be part of *Stavka*. The establishment of the GKO brought Stalin's name back into prominence. Since the outbreak of hostilities decrees had been issued in the names of the Soviet government or the Central Committee. Stalin's door was always open to GKO members delivering reports and making a suggestion if they deemed it necessary. There was genuine debate in GKO since the situation was so critical. Once something had been agreed and signed by Stalin, all the usual round of negotiating with Gosplan, the commissariats, and so on to obtain the necessary inputs became superfluous. The order was simply handed to the competent authority and it became responsible for its implementation. Progress was checked by the GKO member responsible. Woe betide any organisation which fell down on its task! Each GKO member was responsible for a specific area of policy. It was up to him to find a technical solution to any new problem which arose. This was often done by calling a group of experts together and mulling over the situation until a solution suggested itself. When a sector became critical, such as transport in February 1942, a subcommittee was set up to find the optimal solution. Stalin was a good chairman since he had a phenomenal memory and was skilled at putting rapier-like questions which struck to the heart of the matter. Depending on his mood, his mind could be changed by a convincing argument. In April 1945 Stalin summoned Marshals Konev and Zhukov to decide who should take Berlin. Both submitted their proposals and Stalin accepted both. Although the Council for Evacuation responsible for transferring Soviet industry to the rear, and local city defence councils in front-line areas played key roles, no systematic reorganisation of the country's administration was ever undertaken. Stalin got round this problem by appointing plenipotentiaries. These trouble-shooters – such as Kaganovich and Malenkov – had the authority to play Stalin in their respective area of responsibility. It was not very efficient but it got things done.

THE NATIONALITIES

The war was mainly fought on non-Russian territory. Over two-thirds of occupied territory was in non-Russian Union republics and autonomous republics. German civil government was only set up in non-Russian areas. Many of these peoples were accused of collaboration with the fascist enemy and deported in 1944.

The greatest expansion of the Soviet Union since its foundation occurred as a result of the Non-Aggression Pact of 23 August 1939 and the German–Soviet Border and Friendship Treaty of 28 September 1939. The Soviets were given a free hand to incorporate the territories of the former Russian Empire: Finland, Estonia, Latvia, Lithuania, western Belorussia and Bessarabia. They also acquired East Galicia (West Ukraine and Lvov), and northern Bukovina, which had never previously been under Russian rule and had been part of the Austro-Hungarian Empire in 1918. Moscow acquired all the territories above except Finland. This was due to the vigorous war which the Finns waged against the Red Army and the ever-increasing threat of Western intervention. Stalin had to be content with some Finnish concessions of territory. The annexations brought in more than 23 million new citizens, the overwhelming proportion non-Russian. Of these, 13.4 million had previously been under Polish rule, 3.2 million in Bessarabia, 500,000 in northern Bukovina, 1.1 million in Estonia, 2 million in Latvia and 3 million in Lithuania. Stalin tried to curry some favour with the Lithuanians by returning Vilnius to them (from Poland) in September 1939. The incorporation of all Ukrainians had always been Soviet policy and was also Comintern policy from 1924. The newly acquired Finnish territory was added to the Karelian autonomous republic and the new territory became the Karelo-Finnish Union republic in March 1940. However, most Karelians left the new Soviet territory and moved to Finland. Presumably Stalin's long-term goal was the incorporation of the whole of Finland in the new republic. The transfer of Bessarabia also permitted Moscow to upgrade the Moldavian autonomous republic to Union status in August 1940. However, about two-thirds of the territory of the old autonomous republic was returned to the Ukraine since the population was overwhelmingly Ukrainian.[17]

By 1940 Moscow was skilled at assimilation and Russification. After the territory was occupied by the Red Army, a provisional government was established. The Communist Party and mass organisations were declared the only legal bodies and all other parties, organisations and trade unions were banned. Elections, with a single list of candidates, were held; the Supreme Soviet which resulted petitioned for annexation and the USSR Supreme Soviet acceded to this wish; the republic's industry was nationalised and its banking and trade became part of the Soviet planned economy; top positions in all areas of activity were filled by Moscow nominees, often local communists; land reform resulted in estates being divided among land-poor and landless peasants; the political elite and intelligentsia became special targets for mass deportations and agriculture was collectivised and kulaks deported. Considerable effort was devoted to fulfilling this programme, but by June 1941 collectivisation had hardly got under way. In the new Ukrainian territories the Ukrainian language and culture were promoted, and this was warmly welcomed. In Moldavia 230,000 ha were distributed among 185,000 families. About 40 per cent of peasants benefited. However such holdings were not economically viable and the preconditions for collectivisation were being prepared. In February 1941 the Moldavian language went over to the Cyrillic script. One consequence of the German–Soviet agreements was that Soviet Germans could return to Germany if they wished. About 80,000 left Moldavia. Another 390,000 left other newly annexed regions. Deportations, executions and drafting into the Red Army affected 65,000 persons in Estonia, 35,000 in Latvia and 34,000 in Lithuania. There were four major deportations from ex-Polish territory between 11 February 1940 and 4 June 1941 affecting 980,000–1,080,000 persons. Over the period 1939–41 about 1,450,000 inhabitants and refugees were removed to the USSR. Of these 58 per cent were Polish; 19.4 per cent Jewish; 14.9 per cent Ukrainian; 6.3 per cent Belorussian; and 1.4 per cent other.

Stalin presented the German invasion as the greatest challenge the nation had ever faced – the Russian nation. On the anniversary of the revolution on 7 November 1941 he drank deep at the fount of Russian national heroes: Aleksandr Nevsky, Dmitri Donskoi, Kuzma Minin, Dmitri Pozharsky, Aleksandr Suvorov and Mikhail Kutuzov. Stalin wanted to be seen as the successor of Ivan Grozny and Peter the Great. He was ceasing to be a Soviet socialist leader and becoming a Russian imperialist *vozhd*. The mammoth task ahead was a struggle for survival – of the Russian people, of Russian culture, of old Russian cathedrals and churches against the fascist barbarians. It was Russian against German, to the death. Class solidarity, of Russian and German worker, was forgotten. The non-Russian peoples were presented as the supporting cast, under the leadership of the great Russian brother. Bogdan Khmelnitsky, the Cossack hetman who had sought and been granted protection for the Ukraine by the Russian tsar in the seventeenth century was one of the few non-Russian heroes to be celebrated. This was understandable, since most of the non-Russian national heroes had fought for independence from Russia and not to remain part of Russia.

The surge of Russian nationalism and patriotism was mirrored in other nationalities and contradicted the Stalinist line which had been operative since 1937. The Kazakhs once again presented their recent history as a struggle against the imperialist ambitions of Russia. The official Soviet view was that Russian conquest was a lesser evil than being subjugated by other foreign powers or sinking into oblivion. Moscow tolerated non-Russian nationalism in the interests of the war effort but acted when victory was assured. The party in Tatarstan was severely criticised in a decree of 9 August 1944 for the idealisation of the Golden Horde and Tatar national history.

National military units reappeared. In August 1941 a Latvian infantry division was established, and in December 1941 preparations got under way to set up Estonian and Lithuanian divisions. Besides the military function these units had also a political one. They were to play a key role in the liberation of their homelands. Afterwards many members occupied leading economic and cultural posts in the Baltic area. The exact number of national divisions is difficult to assess. The number began to decline after 1943. Besides the Baltic republics, there were Azerbaidzhani, Armenian, Georgian, Uzbek, Tadzhik, Kirgiz, Kazakh, Turkmen, Bashkir, Kalmyk, Chechen-Ingush and

Kabardino-Balkar divisions. There were many other smaller national units. The costs of mobilisation and training of these troops were borne by the republics. Officers were normally Russian with locals providing the NCOs. Losses were high and were normally replenished from standing units so that the national component in these units declined. In the eight Transcaucasian divisions in 1943–44 it had dropped to 1–1.5 per cent. It is striking that apparently no Ukrainian or Belorussian national units were established. Only about 10 per cent of non-Russians called up served in national units. The overwhelming majority fought in mixed units.

Evacuation to the east was a high priority, and during the first month of the war 1.4 million left Moscow and 400,000 Leningrad. Industry went with them to the Urals, the Volga region, Kazakhstan, Siberia and Central Asia. Refugees swelled the flood. About 1.5 million fled Belorussia and 3.5 million the Ukraine. During the war years about 25 million were evacuated to the east and of these 17 million moved between June and December 1941. Evacuees were almost entirely Slav. Many returned after the war, but others stayed and thereby increased the Slav presence in the east. Central Asian workers were sent to work in Urals and Siberian industry and presumably returned home after 1945.

Soviet republics gained substantially from the amendments to the Soviet constitution, promulgated on 1 February 1944. Republics were afforded the right to establish national military units, to enter into direct relations with foreign states and to exchange diplomatic and consular missions. The People's Commissariats for Defence, and Foreign Affairs became Union-republican organisations. Each republic was to set up its own Commissariats for Defence, and Foreign Affairs. This was a spectacular change in policy. Ever since the founding of the USSR in 1922 Moscow had always claimed a monopoly of these two policy areas. Why did Stalin change his mind? He had his eye on the United Nations and wanted all sixteen Union republics to become members. American opposition led the Soviets, at the Yalta conference in February 1945, to ask merely for three places: the USSR, the Ukraine and Belorussia. Hence only the Slavs were directly represented in the UN. The centre remained strong enough to prevent the Union republics developing independent links with the outside world until the Gorbachev era. No Commissariats for Defence were ever established. There was a Ukrainian Commissar until 1947 but he had no commissariat to head. No new national units were established and the Constitution of 1977 dropped all mention of them.

The Soviet leadership feared that the Germans would seize hold of the national antagonisms in the Soviet Union to fashion effective collaboration. Hitler was not interested and had no contingency plan for military or political collaboration. However, the Germans soon found they needed local help. Those who did side with the Wehrmacht did so for two main reasons: survival and the hope that their nation could exact independence as an eventual reward. The most important group among the politically motivated were the Ukrainian nationalists. The Organisation of Ukrainian Nationalists was especially strong in the west Ukraine where attempted Polonisation had strengthened it. the NKVD decimated it before June 1941, but it was weakened by a split in 1940 into a Melnik group and a Bandera group. The latter advocated the use of terrorism. They worked with the Germans before the invasion and two Ukrainian units were set up. When the Bandera group reached Lvov on 30 June 1941, they unilaterally proclaimed a sovereign all-Ukrainian state and elected a government. This was too much for Berlin, and the SS moved swiftly to smother the new state at birth. However, members of the Melnik group were appointed to many leading positions in the administration established by the Germans. They published newspapers and opened theatres and literary clubs. German policy changed, and in 1942 Ukrainian national organisations were suppressed by the SS. About forty Ukrainian nationalists were executed in Kiev in 1942. Ukrainian partisans coalesced in 1943 into the Ukrainian Revolutionary Army (URA). German policy added quickly to the ranks of the URA. In 1944 over 1.5 million Ukrainians were sent for forced labour to Germany, there were harvest requisitions and hostages were shot. In the autumn of 1943 the UPA controlled the rural areas of Volhynia with the Germans running the cities. The UPA began to establish schools, hospitals and military camps. There may have been 40,000 UPA members by the end of 1943. So strong was the desire of the West Ukrainians to defend their territory against reconquest by the Red Army that the SS changed its policy and promoted the formation of Ukrainian units. There was an appeal in May 1943 for volunteers for the SS Galicia division. Politicians and the Church supported the appeal and 100,000 turned up and 30,000 were taken on. The division saw action for the first time near Brody in Galicia in July 1944 but was almost annihilated. The Committee for the Liberation of the Peoples of Russia was founded by the Vlasov movement on 14 November 1944. The Vlasov army had about 300,000 men in January 1945 and of these 35–40 per cent were Ukrainian. Since the committee did not advocate Ukrainian independence it was vigorously opposed by Ukrainian nationalists but found some support among Ukrainian POWs in Germany.

In the Baltic states a similar pattern emerged. Red Army units formed predominantly of locals surrendered without a fight to the Wehrmacht. A Lithuanian Activists' Front had been formed in 1940 and had set up a provisional government but this was disbanded by the Germans in August 1941. Locals occupied leading posts in the civil administration in the Baltic states in stark contrast to the Ukraine, where they were only entrusted with minor posts. Many from the

Baltic served in the Wehrmacht and the Waffen-SS. National units were formed and performed mainly guard duties but were also used against partisans. The Waffen-SS began recruiting in the autumn of 1942 and two Latvian and one Estonian SS division were formed. Lithuanians refused to serve in a division under SS command. In mid 1944 about 60,000 Latvians and 60,000 Estonians were fighting on the German side against the Red Army.

The Germans revealed more sympathy for the national aspirations of the North Caucasian, Crimean and Kalmyk peoples. During the two and a half years of German occupation the Crimean Tatars were able to reopen about fifty mosques and to set up Islamic committees. They were not permitted to establish a Tatar political movement. Tatar units were formed and used against Soviet partisans in the Crimea. German control of the western part of the Kalmyk autonomous republic led to the formation of a Kalmyk cavalry corps. It operated against partisans and, like the Crimean units, retreated with the Wehrmacht. In the North Caucasus a Karachai national committee was founded and enjoyed a certain autonomy. In the Kabardino-Balkar autonomous republic the Muslim Balkars were more willing to collaborate than the Kabardins. An important factor here was the kolkhozes were actually dissolved instead of, as elsewhere, promising this sometime in the future. There was practically no partisan activity in this region as a result. A Cossack region, with some autonomy, was established in the Kuban in October 1942 and included 160,000 people. When the Wehrmacht began to retreat many Cossacks accompanied them. About 20,000 Cossacks were fighting on the German side at the end of 1943.

In early 1942 the Germans began to recruit Muslims, Armenians and Georgians for special 'eastern legions' (*Ostlegionen*) among Red Army POWs in Germany. They were formed into battalions (1,000 men), provided with German officers and sent into action separately. There were 53 battalions (14 Turkestani, 8 Azerbaidzhani, 7 North Caucasian, 9 Armenian, 8 Georgian and 7 Volga Tatar) in Poland. Until May 1943 there were 25 battalions and other groups in the Ukraine, but most of the soldiers were Muslim.

Soviet Germans had a special role to play in the Germanisation of the conquered territories. About 100,000 Germans had been deported to the east by the Soviets before the Wehrmacht arrived but another 320,000 found themselves under German rule. They enjoyed many privileges. A large number of them worked for the Wehrmacht, SS and civil administration as interpreters and others were appointed village mayors, kolkhoz chairmen, auxiliary police and so on. However, the German occupation regime did not regard them as having either the right *Weltanschauung* or the qualifications to occupy leading posts in the Ukraine. German SS units were set up by the end of 1941 in Transnistria (between the rivers Dniester and Bug, north of

Odessa) to combat the partisans. Some of these units took part in the executions of tens of thousands of Jews who had been deported from Odessa and Romania. All Ukrainian and Black Sea Germans retreated with the Wehrmacht and were to resettle in Poland but were overrun by the Red Army. They were deported to Siberia and Central Asia.

Stalin had always regarded the probability of collaboration by non-Russians with an invader as very high. As a result, deportation of peoples who belonged to potential enemies began. In 1932–33 1,200 German forced labour deportee families were deported from the border regions of the Ukraine to the Karelo-Finnish ASSR. (They were deported to the Komi ASSR in July 1941.) In April 1935, 2,000 Finnish peasant families near the Finnish and Estonian borders were deported to the Urals and Central Asia. In May and June 1936, another 20,000 persons in the eastern part of Leningrad region were sent to the east. Germans and Poles living in a 100-km-wide strip along the Polish frontier were forced out in 1935. The Germans were sent to Murmansk. A Polish and a German raion in Zhitomir region were dissolved. In the Ukrainian border region in 1937 the NKVD shot thousands who were regarded as unreliable. One mass grave near Vinnitsa, discovered by the Germans in 1943, contained almost 10,000 corpses. There were mass executions in other Ukrainian cities. Over 122,000 Koreans were removed from border regions in the Far East and sent to Kazakhstan and Central Asia. Well-laid plans to deport Germans to the east were put into operation in July 1941. All males between 16 and 60 years were called into labour armies and sent to work in mines, oil refineries and forestry. Only those between the rivers Dniester and Bug escaped because of the rapid advance of the Wehrmacht. Women, children and old people were loaded without warning into cattle wagons. Many died during the long journey to Siberia and Kazakhstan. When they arrived they were left in open terrain and had to dig holes in the ground to seek shelter. With the process well under way the USSR Supreme Soviet passed a decree on 28 August 1941 stating they were being deported because there were 'thousands of subversives and spies among them'. Stalin left nothing to chance. Soviet parachutists in German uniforms had landed in the Volga region in August 1941 and those Germans who welcomed them were shot on the spot. Between July and October 1941, 945,468 Germans were deported and lost everything. These included 438,280 (according to other sources 446,480) from the Volga; 26,614 from Stalingrad oblast; 46,706 from Saratov oblast; 2,544 from Gorky oblast; 8,640 from Moscow and Moscow oblast; 38,288 from Rostov oblast; 70,790 from the Ukraine; 23,580 from Georgia; 212 from Armenia; 7,306 from Dagestan; 819 from the Chechen-Ingush ASSR; 5,965 from the Kalmyk ASSR; 8,665 from Kuibyshev oblast; 18,895 from the Leningrad suburbs; 40,636 from Krasnodar krai; 95,489 from Ordzhonikidze (Stavropol) krai; 2,702 from Tula oblast; 22,841 from Azerbaidzhan; and 64,233 from the Crimean ASSR. Of these, more than 560,000 were deported to Kazakhstan, and about 100,000 to Novosibirsk oblast; the rest were sent to Krasnoyarsk krai, Altai krai, Omsk oblast, Komi ASSR and Yakut ASSR. Deportation was carried out by the NKVD and the Red Army: 1,200 NKVD officers and 2,000 militia officials, and 7,350 Red Army men were sent to the Volga-German ASSR to carry out the operation. The USSR Supreme Soviet dissolved the Volga-German autonomous republic on 7 September 1941 and all traces of its German connections were erased. German party members, soviet functionaries and Stakhanovite workers were not exempt. Germans who held responsible posts in Soviet life were arrested and most of them executed. German officers and men in the Red Army were dismissed and sent to labour armies. If commanders and commissars of formations wished to retain servicemen of German nationality they could appeal to the USSR NKVD through the military councils of the fronts, okrugs and individual armies.

The above deportations were preventive measures, but those that came after territory was recaptured from the Wehrmacht were punitive measures. Whole nations were deported as punishment for allegedly collaborating with the Germans. Again it affected party members, soviet officials, Red partisans, those who had worked with the Germans and those who had resisted their occupation. All that mattered was that a person belonged to a certain nationality. Collective guilt was the norm. Wives who were Russian or Ukrainian were given a choice: go with their families or stay behind. In November 1943, 63,938 Karachai were deported from Stavropol krai. The Germans had organised the Karachai into bands and they harassed the Soviet rear. After the Red Army retook the krai, 8,673 persons were arrested and 286 killed in the operation against the insurrectionary bands. Among the equipment confiscated from the bands were 339 mortars and machine guns, 5,851 rifles and 4,515 grenades. Also netted were 5,953 Red Army deserters and 7,238 men who had evaded military service. After the deportation was carried out the NKVD swept through Stavropol krai in an attempt to capture any remaining bands. During this operation the NKVD and military lost more than forty officers and men. The Kalmyks were deported in December 1943; by February 1944, 92,983 Kalmyks had been deported, almost all to Omsk and Novosibirsk oblasts and Krasnoyarsk and Altai krais. In February 1944, 478,489 Chechens and Ingushi were transported east; 40,900 Balkars (some Kabardins were also included) were sent to Kazakhstan and Kirgizia in April 1944 (the NKVD arrested forty-seven armed bands – 800 persons – in August 1943 and confiscated their weapons). Between May and August 1943 there had been 32 armed raids on kolkhozes, 8 kolkhozniks attacked and robbed, 7 attacks on Communist Party activists and 207 head of cattle stolen. In May 1944, 191,044 Crimean Tatars were deported, mainly to the Mari ASSR and Uzbekistan. During the German occupation a Tatar national committee had been set up and about 20,000 Tatars served in the Wehrmacht. Armed Tatar bands resisted deportation and 7,739 persons were arrested. Among the weapons confiscated were 449 machine guns, 7,238 rifles and 10,000 grenades. Also deported from the Crimea were 37,000 Bulgarians, Greeks and Armenians found guilty of collaborating with the Germans. In November 1944, 86,000 Turks, Kurds and Khemshins (Muslim Armenians) were transported form Georgia to Kazakhstan, Uzbekistan and Kirgizia. They had been living along the frontier with Turkey and were regarded as a security risk. Meskhetians were also deported from Georgia at the same time. Beria supervised the whole operation. Probably about a million people were sent to Kazakhstan and Central Asia, with possibly a quarter dying *en route* or soon after. The Chechens and Ingushi were included, even though the Germans had only occupied a minute part of their territory. Deportations on such a scale required considerable human and material resources which Stalin was prepared to divert from the front. About 6,000 lorries were deployed during the first phase of the Chechen-Ingush deportation, while overall 15,200 railway wagons were withdrawn for over a month from transporting Red Army troops and supplies. Stalin seems to have seized the opportunity to be rid of a fractious people. They had a long history of resistance to Soviet rule. The Chechen-Ingush autonomous republic became Grozny region and Russians and many others moved in. However, Russians were to pay a price for this injustice. While in Kazakhstan and Central Asia Muslim clans were forced to collaborate to survive. When permitted to return after 1956 they forged networks throughout the country which afforded them great influence over private trade, especially in Moscow.

Whereas the Soviet population declined during the war by about 10 per cent, the number of Jews dropped by about 60 per cent. The heavy toll suffered by the Jews was due in part to the fact that most Jews, about 3 million out of a total population of 17 million, lived in precisely those areas which fell under German control.

When the Germans invaded, about one million Jews lived in the RSFSR. About 250,000 found themselves in German-occupied territory, and of these about 100,000 perished. Losses in the Ukraine and Belorussia were so great that the 1959 census revealed that there were only 840,000 Jews in the Ukraine compared to the 1,533,000 recorded by the 1939 census. The comparable figures for Belorussia are 150,000 and 375,000. The overall impact of the war was to scatter Jews over the country, but in the post-war period Jews hastened to return to their former homes. Nevertheless, the Jewish population in the RSFSR in 1959 was still only 875,000.

THE CIVIL SCENE: THE ECONOMY

The headlong Soviet retreat had cost the country dear. By November 1941 territories which accounted for 63 per cent of coal production, 68 per cent of iron, 58 per cent of steel, 60 per cent of aluminium, 41 per cent of the railway network and 47 per cent of land under grain had fallen to the Wehrmacht. Almost half the population and one third of Soviet productive capacity was lost or threatened.

The picture, however, was not one of totally unalloyed gloom. Miracles were achieved in moving equipment and plant eastwards. By November 1941 over 1,500 enterprises had been transported. In Moscow alone, in October 1941, 80,000 wagons took out 498 factories and industrial installations, leaving only 21,000 of the capital's metal-cutting lathes. The Urals, West Siberia, Kazakhstan and Central Asia were common location areas for the reconstituted factories. With the equipment went skilled labour, and millions of persons moved as well.

The situation demanded that production be accorded the highest priority and improvisation, ingenuity and dedication led to remarkable results. Despite shortages of practically everything, especially clothing and food, output rose, above all in armaments industries. Women and the unskilled had to put their hands to new tasks and succeeded in raising production in 1942 to 77 per cent and by 1944 to 104 per cent of global industrial output in 1940. The command economy came into its own under the direction of the GKO. The proportion of national income devoted to defence in 1942 rose to 55 per cent and this was reflected in the output of tanks, guns and aircraft which gradually turned the Red Army from being an ill-equipped force in 1941 into a better equipped army than the German in 1944. Over 18 million rifles, carbines and sub-machine-guns, 95,099 tanks and self-propelled guns and 108,028 combat aircraft were turned out during the war.[18]

With some of the best agricultural land lost to the Germans and industry given preference food production inevitably suffered. Yields of grain in 1942 and 1943 were miserably low, about half the 1940 figure. Draught power, where possible, went to the army where losses were heavy. The number of horses was cut by half between 1940 and 1945; this meant that women had to farm under the most primitive conditions. The cow population was only 13.9 million in 1942, half the 1940 figure, but it rose to 22.9 million in 1945. The country simply went hungry during the war years.

CULTURE

'Reading *Pravda* after the German invasion was a terrible shock. Up to then you could safely assume that everything you read was pure fiction but now you were face to face with the awful truth, *Pravda* was describing the real world.' This sentiment tartly sums up what many Soviet citizens felt after having been assured for so long that war was not a remote possibility. The desperate nature of the situation had a beneficial effect on the printed word. Since everything was in short supply, every published page had to have the maximum effect. Patriotism was at a premium as the Russian nation was again being put to the test. It had survived many invasions before and had produced great national heroes. What was more natural than to see comrade Stalin as the latest in a long line of saviours of national virtue?

The two years which followed the invasion were the least encumbered with censorship since the 1920s. They produced a tidal wave of poetry, novels, short stories and articles on the war. Writers took to the front to describe the raw courage, fortitude, death and destruction they encountered there. The scribe was exempted from active military service but he was expected to and did contribute his all to the common war effort.

The output was deeply patriotic and virulently anti-German. If there exists a love-hate relationship between Russians and Germans then it was now all hate and no love. The writers who had never accepted the Soviet–German Pact could now give vent to their emotions and have their pre-June 1941 work published. A notable case in point was Ilya Ehrenburg's *Fall of Paris* which was bitterly critical of the Germans. Their behaviour in France, however, was exemplary when compared with their demeanour in the Soviet Union.

The long-drawn-out agony of the Leningrad siege, where in the dreadful winter of 1941–42 alone over 600,000 civilians succumbed to starvation and cold, produced emotional and moving literature. A. A. Fadeev's *Leningrad in the Days of the Blockade*, Vera Inber's *About Three Years: A Leningrad Diary*, and Margarita Aliger's narrative poem *Zoya*, relating the fate of a young Leningrad girl communist who was active in the underground but who was caught and hanged by the Germans, transcended the confines of place and time.

The theatre is a natural forum of nationalistic sentimentality during a period of crisis because of the powerful impact of the spoken word. Some explanation had to be forthcoming for the appalling leadership record of the Red Army and Aleksandr Korneichuk's *The Front*, published in *Pravda* from 24–27 August 1942, put the blame fairly and squarely on the shoulders of the older generation of war leaders. The advent of the younger generation who were more in tune with the demands of mechanised warfare would turn the tide.

The common soldier was not forgotten and his wit, ingenuity and fortitude were celebrated on every stage. Another powerful theme was the national hero. Every Russian hero of the past was put on stage and his exploits glorified so as to inspire the audience to similar deeds. Alexander Nevsky, Kutuzov, Bagration and Brusilov walked the stage of history once again, liberties quite naturally being taken with the historical record.

This theme found expression in many novels and films. Stalin liked to compare himself with the makers of the Russian State such as Ivan the Terrible and Peter the Great. This continued a trend evident in the late 1930s when leadership was extolled and the leader seen as someone quite out of the ordinary.

The party hardly needed to coax writers to choose acceptable topics: the overwhelming impact of the war was felt by everyone. It began to reassert some authority in late 1943 when the noted satirist M. M. Zoshchenko came under attack. His *Before Sunrise* was regarded as too subjective, too pessimistic and lacking in patriotism. K. A. Fedin also came in for some savage treatment. The offending work was the second volume of his Gorky anthology and such was the furore that the third volume was never published. All this took place in 1944 when the war was almost won but it revealed that Gorky's criticisms of the regime had been neither forgotten nor forgiven. It was a harbinger of things to come. The war had loosened the bonds which had tied the Soviet state and society together. Its very nature had put a premium on initiative and willingness to take risks. The State would have to reassert its authority once again and this could only mean that creative writers and artists would have to guide their talents into channels charted by the authorities.

THE CHURCH

The war changed the fortunes of an age-old institution, the church. To encourage the full co-operation of the faithful churches were reopened, the League of Militant Atheists was dissolved, anti-religious propaganda was toned down, indeed if a man's faith made him a better soldier or worker then so be it. Stalin received church dignitaries in the Kremlin on 4 September 1943 and agreed to the election of a new patriarch[19] and synod. The patriarch was installed three days later and immediately called on all Christians everywhere to fight against Hitler. In October 1943 a Council for the Affairs of the Orthodox Church was set up, instruction was again permitted in theological seminaries and the rules governing the religious instruction of children were eased. The faithful responded with vigour and contributed their full share to the nation's war effort.

THE PARTY

If party losses during the 1930s were mainly self-inflicted or endo-genous, those during the war were exogenous. Communists were needed to occupy key positions in the civil and military economy and in the armed forces. As losses mounted new recruits had to be found and the turnover in party membership exceeded 50 per cent, surpassing the 50 per cent turnover of the years 1933–39. Due to the need to find the most able, irrespective of social origin, recruitment was heaviest among the intelligentsia. During the war 32.1 per cent of new members were workers, 25.3 per cent peasants but 42.6 per cent members of the intelligentsia.[20]

Over 5 million new candidate members and 3.6 million new members were added to the ranks of the party during the war. Of these 3.9 million candidate members and 2.5 million members were serving in the army or navy.[21] By May 1945 25 per cent of men and women in the armed forces were communists and a further 20 per cent were Komsomol members. Service personnel accounted for just over half of all party members at the end of the war. This militarisation of the party was a new phenomenon as party membership among the military ever since the late 1920s had been modest. It had only been 15 per cent in June 1941.

Membership was highest in key sectors. For instance in the navy the proportion of communists was higher than in the army and the highest percentage was found among submarine crews.

An extraordinarily high number of those decorated were commun-ists: 74 per cent of the Heroes of the Soviet Union were party members and a further 11 per cent belonged to the Komsomol.[22]

The party operating on the home front underwent cataclysmic changes during the war years. Casualties would have been higher had it not been for the fact that about 350,000 were transferred to the rear. Many of these were engineers and managers and they helped to maintain the size of party organisations in the Urals and Siberia, the only areas to achieve this during the first year of mobilisation.[23] The more rural an area the higher proportion of communists who were seconded to the armed forces. Those with technical skills were held back. It would appear that in Moscow only 48 per cent of communists were sent to the armed forces, only 43 per cent in the Ukraine and only 44 per cent in Leningrad. Communists had the task of organising resistance in occupied areas but only about 7 or 8 per cent of partisans were party members.[24] Partisans were active from late 1941 and tied down about 10 per cent of German troops at the peak of their effectiveness.

The war had a powerful formative influence on those who joined between 1941 and 1945. There was a bond between them and the party and the State which was stronger than that of members recruited during the 1930s. The latter too were changed by their experience so that the post-war USSR was dominated to quite an extraordinary extent by the memories, disputes and mentality of the war years.

THE GRAND ALLIANCE

For Winston Churchill the German invasion of the Soviet Union was the turning-point of the war. It afforded Great Britain a breathing space and the British Prime Minister's first thought was to extend help to the USSR. This he did on the day of the attack in a radio talk but there was no immediate response from Moscow. When Sir Stafford Cripps, the British Ambassador, returned to Moscow on 28 June it was Molotov who received him. With Stalin back at the helm things changed dramatically. Six days after the Anglo-Soviet diplomatic agreement Stalin wrote to Churchill on 18 July 1941 and suggested the establishment of a front in northern France and another in the Arctic.[25] When Harry Hopkins, President Roosevelt's personal envoy, discussed the situation with Stalin at the end of July Stalin produced a long shopping list, asking for among others 20,000 anti-aircraft guns, aluminium and steel.

The deteriorating position of the Red Army was reflected in Stalin's note to Churchill, sent on 3 September 1941. He wanted a second front in the Balkans or in France in 1941 and '30,000 tonnes of aluminium by the beginning of October and a minimum *monthly* aid of 400 aeroplanes and 500 tanks'. Stalin's pessimism came to the fore when he stated that without these two kinds of aid the Soviet Union would 'either be defeated or weakened to the extent that it would lose for a long time the ability to help its allies'.[26] On 13 September he suggested that Great Britain should land twenty-five to thirty divisions at Archangel or ship them to the southern areas of the USSR via Iran for military co-operation with Soviet troops on Soviet soil.[27] Things were black indeed.

In order to cover supplies of war *matériel* and commodities the United States extended the Lend–Lease Act to include the Soviet Union in September 1941. The USSR was granted a credit of US$1,000 million, to be repayable over a ten-year period commencing five years after the end of the war.[28]

One of the reasons why Roosevelt was so generous to Moscow was his assessment of Stalin. This was influenced by Harry Hopkins' rosy view of the Soviet dictator. The President had sent Hopkins on a special mission to Moscow in July 1941. William Bullitt, an ex-US ambassador to the USSR, told Roosevelt that the Soviets were imperialists and that, in return for Lend–Lease, the Soviets should be asked to pledge that they would not expand into Eastern and Western Europe and Asia after the war. Roosevelt replied that he was going to play a hunch. 'I think if I give him everything I possibly can and ask for nothing in return . . . he won't try to annex anything and will work with me for a world of democracy and peace.' Some hunch! Britain's answer to Harry Hopkins was Lord Beaverbrook. The latter judged Stalin to be a 'kindly man'. General (later Lord) Ismay, head of the British Military Mission, was hard-boiled and perceptive in his assessment of Stalin. 'He moved stealthily like a wild animal in search of prey, and his eyes were shrewd and full of cunning. He never looked one in the face . . . As he entered the room, every Russian froze into silence, and the hunted look in the eyes of the generals showed all too plainly the constant fear in which they lived.' Had specialists like Bullitt and Ismay, with hands-on experience of Stalin, been listened to, many of the misunderstandings of the Grand Alliance could have been avoided.

In December 1941 Anthony Eden, British Foreign Secretary, went to Moscow to begin negotiations on a treaty between the two countries and such were Soviet objections to some British proposals that V. M. Molotov was sent to London in May 1942 to discuss them. He went on to Washington to discuss the feasibility of a second front in Europe with President Roosevelt. The US was now in the war as a result of the declaration of war on the US by Germany on 11 December 1941. This move was a major error of judgment by Hitler as it was quite unnecessary. Had Germany not declared war there is every likelihood that the US would have confined herself to the Pacific until Japan had been defeated. Only then would she have committed herself fully to the war against Germany.

A sticking-point in London was the recognition of the Soviet gains of 1940–41. The USSR wanted the post-war western frontier to be the same as that of 22 June 1941. This involved Poland ceding territory which the Polish government-in-exile in London refused to do. In exchange the Soviet Union suggested that the British secure bases in France, the Benelux countries and Scandinavia. Churchill would probably have conceded the Soviets the western frontiers they wanted had not the Americans objected to making any binding agreements on post-war frontiers. Consequently the clause was omitted from the Anglo-Soviet treaty which was signed in London on 26 May 1942. This highlighted the problem of Poland which was to become one of the most bitter during the war. It is worth noting that at a time when the Soviet Union was waging a life and death struggle with the Wehrmacht Stalin was thinking of territorial gains. The US, being in the stronger position, could have laid down the post-war western frontiers then and there had she so desired.

A second front was forthcoming in 1942 but not in Europe. When Churchill informed Stalin in August 1942 in Moscow that Anglo-American forces would invade North Africa the Soviet leader became very offensive. On one of the few occasions on which he lost his

170

temper in front of a Western statesman Stalin asked if British soldiers were afraid to fight Germans? Stalin's behaviour was the outward manifestation of the enormous strain he was under due to the terrible mauling the Red Army was suffering at that time.

The victory of Stalingrad was a turning-point in Soviet diplomatic activity. Prior to the battle the USSR was a suppliant, almost begging for help; afterwards, in the knowledge that the tide at long last was turning, she could manoeuvre for maximum advantage and make the most of the fact that it was the Red Army which was doing most to defeat the Wehrmacht. The Soviet position was strengthened by the feelings of guilt in the Anglo-American camp that they had not done enough to help the Soviet Union. Pro-Soviet sentiment welled up and the avuncular Soviet leader became a hero to many. Time was playing into the hands of the Soviets: there was no pressing need to reach agreement on anything.

The Germans stated, on 13 April 1943, that they had discovered a mass grave of Polish officers in the Katyn forest near Smolensk. They took them to be corpses of the 15,000 Polish officers who had been captured during the Soviet push into eastern Poland in September 1939 and who had subsequently disappeared. The Polish government-in-exile in London immediately asked for an independent inquiry by the International Red Cross. The Soviet reaction was to break off relations with the Poles. This afforded the Soviet Union the opportunity of recognising an alternative Polish government. One was available in embryo, the Union of Polish Patriots, which had come into existence in Moscow on 1 March 1943. These Poles were willing to accept the Soviet view on Katyn and on the location of the future Polish-Soviet frontier.

It was only in 1990 that Moscow finally laid the blame for the massacre at Stalin's door. Hitherto Beria and the NKVD were presented as the perpetrators. Beria, according to one story, had misunderstood Stalin and knocked the Poles off himself. It is now quite clear that Stalin deliberately liquidated the officers for political reasons. They were shot in batches of 250. Their deaths were intended to deprive post-war Poland of the cream of its aristocracy, gentry and leaders. It was to cause Stalin much trouble later but will haunt Polish-Soviet and Polish-Russian relations for decades to come.

The key to the future of post-war Europe, Germany, was not forgotten. A National Committee for a Free Germany (NKFD) was founded on 12 July 1943 near Moscow and comprised leading members of the Communist Party of Germany (KPD) in exile and German prisoners-of-war. A League of German Officers (BDO) was set up on 13 September 1943 to attract those who found the NKFD too overtly political. The NKFD was active in front-line propaganda and its policy in 1943 was to advocate an end to the war and the retreat of the Wehrmacht to the frontiers of the German Reich. In the same year

KPD working groups were formed to work out guidelines for post-war German development.

To allay Western suspicions that the Soviet Union was planning subversion and revolution everywhere the Comintern was dissolved on 15 May 1943. This surprised some Western observers but it shocked foreign communists in the USSR. They need not have worried. Such was Soviet control over the world communist movement, to be enhanced by Soviet military victory, that an overt organisation was no longer necessary.

Defeat at Kursk ended the capacity of the Wehrmacht to launch any more large-scale offensives. The initiative passed henceforth to the Red Army. The Anglo-American invasion of Italy, where they opted for the western littoral instead of the eastern, the wrong decision, led to the Allied armies becoming bogged down.

The Tehran Conference of the Big Three, the first time they had met together, in November 1943, was a signal Soviet diplomatic victory. On Poland, neither Churchill nor Roosevelt put up much of a fight to retain the pre-war frontiers and Stalin could infer from this that the 1941 frontiers would eventually be accepted. This affected Germany and it was actually Churchill who suggested that Poland be compensated in the west, receiving German territory up to the river Oder. A firm commitment was also made to launch the second front in Europe in the spring of 1944. Roosevelt gave Stalin the impression that he was very keen to meet Soviet wishes and to show that he and Churchill were not in accord on many issues. The Soviet Union, for her part, agreed to join the United Nations and to enter the war against Japan once Germany had been defeated.

After the satisfaction of Tehran came the gratification of a visit to Moscow by Edvard Beneš, the dominant figure among Czechoslovak exiles in London. Without any pressure from Stalin or Gottwald, the exiled leader of the Communist Party of Czechoslovakia, Beneš proceeded to guarantee the communists key portfolios in the post-war government and told Gottwald that the communists 'would be the strongest element in the new regime'.[29] All this to a party which had only polled 10 per cent of the votes in the elections of 1935. Hints that the Soviets wanted frontier changes involving sub-Carpathian Ukraine brought the response from Beneš that he would consider cession of the territory favourably after the war. A treaty of friendship, alliance and mutual assistance was signed on 12 December 1943 and this put the seal on the new relationship. Beneš, of his own volition, had placed his country firmly on the orbit of Soviet influence. Stalin must have been most pleased. If Czechoslovakia, a country which had suffered German aggression, could change sides without any real pressure, what could he not expect from Romania and Hungary, two countries still fighting on the Nazi side in the Soviet Union.

The year 1944 was one of unalloyed victory for the Soviet Union.

The destruction was watched with despair from London but there was little either Churchill or the London Poles could do. Stalin even went so far as to label those who had unleashed the uprising as 'criminals'. Poland was but one country: if the Allies fell out what would happen to the rest of eastern and south-eastern Europe?

The most direct route to the heart of the Reich was through Poland but Stalin decided to deflect troops to the Balkans so as to strike at Romania, Bulgaria, Hungary, Yugoslavia and Austria. He plainly had political as well as military goals in mind.

Finland was the first country to leave the war. On 19 September 1944 she signed an interim peace treaty with the USSR and the UK. The country was not occupied but Soviet troops were installed at Porkkala, near Helsinki, and the Allied Control Commission was dominated by the Soviets. War reparations had to be paid but the general impression abroad was that Finland had been let off lightly. It was important to the Soviet Union to give the impresssion of magnanimity so as to lessen opposition to her playing a key role in other belligerent countries.

The inevitability of Red Army penetration of Romania, coupled with the possibility of a communist victory in Greece, led Churchill to suggest to the Soviets that they should take the lead in Romania while Britain did the same in Greece, in May 1944. Churchill was emotionally involved in the fate of Greece and got Roosevelt to agree to the deal. When he visited Moscow in October Churchill attempted to widen the agreement to include Bulgaria, Hungary and Yugoslavia. All Stalin did was to put a large tick against the percentages presented to him. Nevertheless Stalin kept to his agreement on Greece and did not intervene in the civil war there. Churchill, in turn, was much gratified by this. Greece was saved but given the eventual military presence of the Red Army in south-eastern Europe it was clear to Churchill that there was little that the Western Allies could do to check Soviet influence there.

Britain had consistently supported Tito and his partisans in Yugoslavia and when the country was liberated, in the autumn of 1944, with Soviet help, he and the communists were in a strong position to take power. Only in one other country were the communists to come to power mainly through their own efforts: Albania.

The Union of Polish Patriots joined other Poles in Lublin, in eastern Poland, on 21 July 1944 to form the Polish Committee of National Liberation. This body declared itself the provisional government of Poland on 31 December 1944 and was recognised as such by the Soviet Union on 5 January 1945. The London Poles had been neatly outmanoeuvred and did not even enjoy diplomatic relations with the Soviet Union.

When the Big Three met for the first time on Soviet soil, at Yalta in the Crimea in February 1945, the Red Army was master of most of eastern and south-eastern Europe and was only a hundred kilometres from Berlin.

Although Yalta did not give Stalin all he wanted he could still feel moderately satisfied. Poland's eastern frontier was to be drawn in accordance with Soviet wishes, compensation would include territory up to the Oder–Neisse line and part of East Prussia. This meant expelling millions of Germans from territory they had occupied for centuries and ensured that post-war Poland would have a frontier problem since Germany could not be expected to accept the unilateral loss of so much wealth. Hence Poland would need an ally to counterbalance German strength. The provisional government of Poland was accepted as such but some London Poles were to be added. Germany was to be divided into zones of occupation and Berlin to be placed under four-power occupation. The USSR asked for and got southern Sakhalin and the Kuril islands as a reward for joining the war against Japan after the defeat of Germany. What concessions did the Soviet Union make to compensate for these enormous gains? She dropped her demand that the Great Powers should be able to veto procedural matters and accepted three UN seats, the USSR, Belorussia and the Ukraine, instead of the original sixteen demanded. The US could have claimed forty-nine seats in return but made do with one. This neatly illustrates Roosevelt's thinking at that time. He believed that concessions to the USSR would demonstrate to her that she was being treated as an equal. This was important since Soviet participation and goodwill in shaping the post-war world were considered absolutely vital. Roosevelt, like Beneš and many others, thought that the war had profoundly changed the USSR.

There was, however, considerable friction between Moscow and Washington over the reshaping of the provisional Polish government. Stalin was just not willing to accept changes which would affect the leading role of communists and fellow-travellers in it. Then Stalin heard that the Allies were negotiating the surrender of German forces in northern Italy. It was rather late in the day but Stalin still feared that the Allies might negotiate a separate peace with Germany. On the same tack one reason for Churchill's willingness to meet Soviet demands in the past had been the fear, quite unfounded, that the Soviet Union might come to terms unilaterally with Germany. The death of Roosevelt, on 12 April 1945, was a sad blow and it helped to smooth the ruffled feathers. The Soviet flag flying over the Reichstag on 2 May 1945 symbolised the new situation. Victory on 9 May placed the Red Army astride central and south-eastern Europe as well as in a position to influence directly the future evolution of Germany. The war against Japan imposed little strain on the USSR and Soviet troops rapidly overran Manchuria. The Soviet Union as a world power had arrived.

NOTES

1. John Erickson *The Road to Stalingrad: Stalin's War with Germany* p. 98.
2. P. N. Pospelov *et al. Great Patriotic War of the Soviet Union 1941–1945* p. 449.
3. It was thought that Great Britain had to fall before Germany would attack elsewhere. The second half of June was considered too late for an attack on the USSR.
4. The Soviet intelligence network in Germany and elsewhere in Europe was superbly organised. Leopold Trepper, 'Grand Chef', Viktor Sokolov, 'Kent', and Rudolf Rossler, 'Lucy', who operated from Switzerland, were members of the *Rote Kapelle* (Red Orchestra) which however was liquidated in the summer of 1942. Nevertheless the Soviet espionage network in Germany quickly recovered. The valuable Soviet espionage organisation in Switzerland remained untouched. The information sent to Moscow was detailed and correct but in the beginning Stalin did not believe it, seeing it as a plant by his enemies. He changed his mind in the light of its acccuracy and during the war obtained a massive amount of information on German military intentions, for example he had accurate accounts of the operational plans of the Wehrmacht at Kursk. One of the Soviet sources was in the German High Command which meant sometimes that Moscow learned of German orders before front line commanders received their instructions. In contrast German intelligence on the Soviet Union was third-rate.
5. Erickson, op. cit. p. 110. One of the German deserters, Wilhelm Korpik, was immediately shot, on Stalin's orders, for his pains. When Churchill warned Stalin of an imminent attack, the latter responded by calling it a 'dirty provocation'.
6. These included Vatutin, Vasilevsky, Antonov, Voronov, Shtemenko, Fedorenko, Golovanov and Novikov. From time to time, at critical moments, some of these officers were put in command or given the task of co-ordination in the field. Vasilevsky thought that Stalin did not master the modern methods of war until the battle of Kursk.
7. Not all the Soviet casualties were due to German bullets and bombs. Colonel-General D. G. Pavlov, commander of the Western Front, his chief of staff and some other senior officers were called to Moscow, court-martialled and shot on 30 June 1941 for incompetence. They were unfairly treated, as was later admitted. Stalin loosed the NKVD on the military, reminiscent of 1937, and the political police exacted savage retribution on anyone who did not fulfil orders or who had carried out his orders unsuccessfully.
8. Zhukov was recalled from Leningrad to Moscow on 7 October and dispatched by Stalin to discover what was happening to Konev's Western Front and Budenny's Reserve Front. Konev was easy to find but

Budenny was not. When Zhukov finally found him, Budenny had to admit that he had lost his troops, he did not know where they had moved to!

9. Albert Seaton *The Russo-German War 1941–45* p. 228n.

10. So confident was the Politburo that the tide had turned and that Moscow was now safe that the Central Committee and the main departments of government were recalled from Kuibyshev; Stavka, split into a group in Moscow and one outside since 17 October, was reunited after 16 December.

11. Seaton, op. cit. p. 261.

12. Based on Hans-Adolf Jacobsen 'Kommissarbefehl und Massenexekutionen sowjetischer Kriegsgefangener' in *Anatomie des SS-Staates* vol. 2 (Munich 1967), pp. 137–65.

13. Christian Streit *Keine Kameraden: Die Wehrmacht und die sowjetischen Kriegsgefangenen 1941–1945*. More than one million German prisoners-of-war died in Soviet camps.

14. Erickson, op. cit. p. 239.

15. Seaton, op. cit. p. 352.

16. Sanford R. Lieberman 'Crisis Management in the USSR: The Wartime System of Administration and Control' in Susan J. Linz (ed.) *The Impact of World War II on the Soviet Union* pp. 59–76.

17. Simon, op. cit. pp. 195–233.

18. Seaton, op. cit. p. 425.

19. The patriarchate had been abolished by Peter the Great, reinstated by the Provisional Government and when the patriarch died in 1925 the office was left unfilled until 1943.

20. Pospelov, op. cit. p. 441. Output covers the period 1 July 1941 to 30 June 1945.

21. T. H. Rigby *Communist Party Membership in the USSR 1917–1967* p. 239.

22. Ibid. p. 260n.

23. William O. McCagg Jr. *Stalin Embattled 1943–1948* p. 87.

24. John A. Armstrong *The Politics of Totalitarianism* p. 163.

25. *Correspondence between the Chairman of the Council of Ministers of the USSR and the Presidents of the USA and the Prime Ministers of Great Britain during the Great Patriotic War of 1941–1945* 2nd edn, vol. 1, p. 21.

26. Ibid. p. 28.

27. Ibid. p. 31.

28. Ibid. vol. 2, p. 10. The USSR received Lend-Lease Aid worth US$10,982 million during the course of the war. The following items proved of great value: 2,000 railway engines, 540,000 tons of railway lines, 15 million pairs of felt boots and 375,000 Dodge trucks. British aid, delivered often at appalling cost, was not as influential. However, the West supplied the USSR with over 14,000 aircraft. The Red Army's artillery was overwhelmingly of Soviet manufacture but its transport was almost entirely American. Stalin conceded that without this help victory would have been in doubt. Recent Soviet analysts state quite

openly that without foreign supplies the Red Army would not have been victorious.

29. Vladimir V. Kusin, 'Czechoslovakia' in Martin McCauley (ed.) *Communist Power in Europe 1944–1949* rev. edn p. 75.

CHAPTER FIVE

The Last Years of Stalin

INTERNAL POLITICS

'The mountains and hills burst into song and the trees of the fields clapped their hands.' And the people were happy too, overjoyed in fact. It would be impossible to overstate the immediate and lasting effects of victory on Soviet society. Nothing would ever be the same again. The sacrifices, the heroics, the agony, the excitement and the fear had been indelibly imprinted on the Soviet mind, first and foremost on the Great Russian mind. Two groups had made outstanding contributions to victory: peasants and women. The fighting man had been predominantly the peasant in uniform, 76 per cent of the population was rural in 1939. The gaps in the home front had been manned by women; during the day they worked in the economy, during the evening they brought up the next generation. It was only after the war that they had time to reflect on the tragic losses of human life, something like 25 million dead, worse than the 17 million corpses of the First World War and the Civil War. The air was heavy with the sorrow of women. The dead cried out to the living, the disabled and the maimed from their graves from Moscow to Berlin. Their deaths must not be in vain, they had given their all for a better future, for everyone.

Stalin's authority reached a new peak in 1945 but not his control of the country. The State Defence Committee (GKO) had become very powerful and the armed forces were full of the wine of victory. GKO was dissolved on 4 September 1945 and its functions passed to various commissariats, soon to be extensively reorganised. Most of the country was again placed under civilian control. As of October 1944 the party ceased granting membership as a reward for feats of valour on the battlefield and launched a campaign to raise the ideological standards of members in uniform. The announcement of demobilisation in June 1945 was accompanied by Stalin's elevation to the rank of Generalissimo. As demobilisation was stepped up in 1946 so the party's role in the armed forces increased. On 22 August 1946 the CC stated that party secretaries were not subject to military control and that they were henceforth to be elected and not appointed. The system of political commissars was thereby reintroduced. Such was

178

the emphasis placed on ideological training that any independence from party control that the armed forces may have acquired during the war was effectively ended. Stalin also acted against the generals. They had been exuding self-confidence if not arrogance at the end of the war. N. A. Bulganin proved to be an effective watchdog. A political general, he replaced Voroshilov as chief representative of the armed forces on GKO in November 1944. He also replaced Stalin as Minister of Defence in March 1947. He entered the Politburo as a candidate member in March 1946 and advanced to full membership in January 1948. Marshal Zhukov was censured in June 1946 for not showing due deference to his Commander-in-Chief (Stalin) and of 'awarding himself the laurels of principal victor'. A case making him out to be a British spy was even put together. But Stalin thought better of liquidating the general and he was merely transferred to a minor command. Other less renowned figures, including some of Zhukov's commanders, did not fare as well. Several generals were arrested and imprisoned. In early 1948 five admirals were incarcerated as Anglo-American spies. In 1950 Marshal Kulik, Stalin's unfailingly incompetent crony, was shot. Not a word of these purges appeared in the press. There were almost no promotions to the higher ranks of the armed forces between 1945 and Stalin's death.

When the war ended, police ranks were brought into line with those of the military and L. P. Beria became a Marshal. However, Stalin appears to have been concerned about Beria's power base and in January 1946 Beria lost control of the Commissariat of Internal Affairs.

The rejuvenation of the party from the doldrums of the war was capped in December 1945 when the Politburo began to meet fortnightly. The CC met in March 1946 and elected a new Politburo, Secretariat and Orgburo.[1] Then in August 1946 the Politburo laid down that the Orgburo was to supervise all party affairs and to meet at least once a week.

Never a garrulous man in public, Stalin kept his official utterances to a minimum after 1945. For 1947 there are only three and for 1949 only two entries in his collected works. This meant that the party and government elite had little to go on but it also allowed Stalin to intervene in the ensuing discussions when he judged it opportune. The party would have liked a flowering of Marxist-Leninist ideology reminiscent of Lenin's time but this was not favoured by Stalin since there was no guarantee that he could control it. From 1948 onwards the aridity of the immediate post-war years returned.

Stalin's reading of the intentions of the United States appears to have had a considerable impact on his internal policies. The increasingly critical stance of President Truman and his administration towards the Soviet Union, especially over Poland, and the explosion of the first atomic bomb in New Mexico on 16 July 1945, providing the Americans with a nuclear monopoly for the time being, were factors whose implications had to be assessed. There were basically two ways of viewing the US after the Second World War. Either the country and capitalism had been irreparably weakened by the travails of war, leading to a sharpening of class tensions and the advent of a socialist revolution, or the war had made the US stronger and provided her with a world role, something which she had previously lacked. This would not fit ideologically since it was held that the advent of Soviet power had weakened capitalism, and the stronger the USSR, the weaker capitalism became, hastening the world-wide socialist revolution. Stalin, one can argue, hit on a third evaluation which in turn could be given a Marxist-Leninist gloss. Capitalism was dying but in so doing had become even more predatory, aggressive and dangerously seductive. The smiling, conciliatory face of capitalism was but a mask. This is reminiscent of the Comintern's assessment of national socialism, it too was seen as capitalism at its most aggressive but nevertheless on its last legs. Also class struggle intensifies as the remnants of capitalism in the Soviet Union die.

Above all the Soviet Union had to be seen to be strong. It had to blow itself up like a bull frog so as to intimidate any predator.

Stalin appears always to have viewed the West through ideological spectacles. Underlying hostility is detectable in his private and some-times public utterances. He told the Yugoslavs in April 1945 that the USSR would need fifteen to twenty years to recover from the war. 'Then we'll have another go at it.' This did not make war inevitable – Stalin's grasp of how far he could go in provoking the West served him well – but it revealed the expansionism that was endemic to Soviet socialism. At the XVIIIth Party Congress, in 1939, Mekhlis, clearly reflecting Stalin's thinking, stated that a major task for the Red Army in an eventual war would be to increase the number of Soviet republics. Understandably, this portion of his speech was not published at the time. The West was warned about Stalin's inplacable hostility by Maxim Litvinov. In November 1945, Averill Harriman asked what the West could do to satisfy Stalin. 'Nothing,' replied the former Soviet Commissar for Foreign affairs. He told an American journalist in June 1946 – he was by then a Deputy Minister of Foreign Affairs – that the prevailing view in Moscow was that the communist and capitalist worlds were bound to collide. Concessions would not pacify Stalin. What if the West conceded all Stalin's demands? He would soon come back with another list of demands. Litvinov was taking risks in being so frank, but he favoured co-operation between the USA and the USSR and wanted the Americans to base their policies on hard-headed realism.

Stalin set about resurrecting the 1939–41 regime again. Coercive measures were taken against critics of his person, and this policy was applied before the war ended, Solzhenitsyn being a case in point.

Practically all those who had had any contact with the outside world were separated from the rest of the population. Those who had survived German camps and forced labour and returned home voluntarily were often marched off straight to labour camps. About 2 million were sent back against their will by the Allies and presumably most of them perished. The Allies had agreed at Yalta to the repatriation of Soviet prisoners-of-war. Stalin was mindful of the fact that 800,000 Soviet citizens had served in the German forces so perhaps he feared that the two million could spearhead an invasion army.

The Soviet leadership saw Western models and Western modes of thought and life as too attractive to be resisted by the average Soviet citizen and so it took the decision to cut off access to them. Another aspect of this policy was that the average Russian was garrulous and his eloquence tended to increase with his intake of alcohol so the outside world would become well acquainted with the strengths and weaknesses of the USSR. Stop the contact and the enemy would be left speculating about the Soviet scene. Scholars were told not to refer to Western publications and kowtowing to foreign expertise was taboo. In place of the foreign idols Russian ones, in the main, were pressed into service. It was suddenly found that Russians had discovered everything worth discovering. Anything their geniuses had not hit upon was not worth knowing or was simply false. Relativity theory, quantum mechanics, genetics were nothing more than pseudo-science!

Stalin spelled out the lessons of the war and the consequences to be drawn from them in a major speech at an election meeting in the Bolshoi Theatre in Moscow on 9 February 1946. 'Our victory demonstrates, first and foremost, the victory of our Soviet *social* system . . . secondly, the victory of our Soviet *state*.'[2] He then went on to justify the 'Soviet method of industrialisation' and to state that without collectivisation the age-old backwardness of agriculture could not have been overcome. The message was as plain as a pikestaff: there would be no letting up on the hard road of industrialisation and collectivisation, scotching numerous rumours to the contrary. To drive home his message Stalin made clear the dimensions of the task: 50 million tonnes of iron, 60 million tonnes of steel, 500 million tonnes of coal, 60 million tonnes of oil, annually by 1960.[3] Stalin promised that rationing would be abolished in the near future and that special attention would be paid to the expansion of consumer goods but everyone knew that the latter would be accorded low priority. Significantly enough he expressed the tasks of the party in economic terms.

The party had sacrificed itself during the war so the number of experienced cadres was quite inadequate for peacetime conditions. Only one third of the party's 5.8 million full and candidate members, in January 1946, had been in the party before the German invasion and of these less than half had been members before 1938.[4] The wartime emphasis had been on practical necessities and patriotism rather than on theory. As well a whole new post-war generation of party activists had to be trained. Since the party was larger than ever before there was no pressing need to increase numbers significantly until existing members had been ideologically schooled. This huge task, of necessity, meant that the intellectual content of their training was modest. Given that the main tangible task of the party, after 1945, was economic, it followed that it needed to recruit those with professional skills. Engineers, technicians, members of the intelligentsia, skilled workers, especially in industry, and leading cadres in the MTS and on the farm were especially desirable. In short the party was looking for decision-makers, those who had the competence to lead and inspire their co-workers. These key persons would have to be rewarded and given a large share of the scarce consumer goods available. Privilege would have to increase so as to compensate for the lack of material rewards. Hence the trend which had begun in the 1930s was continued, the trend of increasing differentials. A new ruling stratum was forming, conservative, concerned with its own wellbeing, seeking security, not very interested in ideology or dangerous intellectual ideas and devoted to the leader rather than the party. In this regard the striking increase in the number of ministries (commissariats were renamed ministries in March 1946) after the war is of special interest. Some ministries were later reunited but the expansion nevertheless continued. Gosplan, for instance, was split into three in 1947–48. One explanation would be to see the administrative reforms as removing the promotion blockage and allowing ever increasing numbers of bureaucrats to enjoy the fruits of high office. This all helped to widen the gulf between the ruling class and the working class.

Party membership grew very slowly after 1945 and by 1953 was only about 20 per cent above the 1945 fig.re. Selective recruitment went hand in hand with expulsions. The last years of Stalin were characterised by a permanent purge which saw about 100,000 expelled annually.[5] Many of these fell victim to the numerous plots and accusations fabricated by the political police, again a feature of the period.

The party's advance in the countryside was very striking. Whereas in 1941 only one kolkhoz in eight had a party cell, the proportion had jumped to five out of six by 1953.[6] This transformation had come about mainly because of the large number of soldiers who had become party members at the front and who had settled in the countryside after demobilisation and the sharp reduction in the number of kolkhozes due to amalgamation.

Andrei Zhdanov, who headed the party in Leningrad during the blockade, headed the campaign away from a universal world of science, learning and culture to a specifically Soviet one. This may seem obscurantist, even xenophobic, but if the Soviet population was to be galvanised into the frenetic activity necessary to rebuild and strengthen the economy then all comparisons with the outside world, which put the USSR at a disadvantage, had to stop. Zhdanov began his campaign by attacking two Leningrad literary journals denigrating the prominent poetess, Anna Akhmatova and the satirist Mikhail Zoshchenko, both Leningraders. The war had not mellowed Zhdanov but had made him more intolerant. The period from 1946 to August 1948, when Zhdanov died, is referred to as the *Zhdanovshchina*, the Zhdanov times. Repression spread to almost every discipline as the spirit of the late 1930s was conjured up.

Zhdanov vied with Malenkov and Molotov to be Stalin's most influential adviser and his competence extended to the world communist movement. He it was who made the key speech at the constituent meeting of the Communist Information Bureau, the Cominform, at Szklarska Poręba, in Poland, in September 1947. There he divided the world into two hostile camps, the capitalist and the socialist, but placed countries such as India and Indonesia in neither. This accorded well with his and Stalin's views on internal Soviet developments.

The repression somewhat abated after Zhdanov's death but it took a new turn. Strident Russian nationalism, given a boost by Stalin at a victory banquet in the Kremlin on 24 May 1945, when he raised his glass and drank to the people who had contributed most to victory, the Great Russians, 'who are the most prominent nation in the Soviet Union',[7] was bound sooner or later to have an impact on other nationalities. He did not hold the Ukraine in very high regard, even stating, according to one report, that every Ukrainian would have been deported after the war had there not been so many of them.

The second capital's travails continued when what became known as the Leningrad Affair erupted in 1949. A contributing factor was the expulsion of Tito from the Cominform, in June 1948, for opposing Stalin. Zhdanov had enjoyed particularly good relations with the Yugoslav leader, culminating in a successful visit by Tito to Leningrad. With Tito a heretic and Zhdanov dead the Leningrad party apparatus was very vulnerable. The blow fell in July 1949 when all five secretaries of the city committee, all five secretaries of the oblast committee, the top four officials of the city soviet, the leading officials of the oblast soviet and A. A. Kuznetsov, secretary of the Central Committee, M. I. Rodionov, chairman of the RSFSR Council of Ministers, A. A. Voznesensky, RSFSR Minister of Education, and many others were arrested and later executed. The most prominent victim was N. A. Voznesensky, Politburo member, chairman of Gosplan and author of *War Economy of the USSR in the Period of the Patriotic War*, which had been awarded a Stalin prize in 1948. The background of the affair still remains murky but the only clear things to emerge were the advance of Malenkov, who appears to have been involved in the frame-ups, and the fact that Leningrad had lost another contest in its perpetual struggle with Moscow.

The infighting during the Leningrad affair proved lethal and illustrated the nature of relations at the top. The remaining years of the
Stalin era were characterised by considerable personnel changes. The
reasons for this are not clear to an outsider but the end result appears
to have been the same as after a game of musical chairs. It was as
if the ageing dictator was shuffling and reshuffling his pack so as
to increase mutual suspicion and to maximise his own security. For
example, Molotov was replaced by Andrei Vyshinsky as Minister of
Foreign Affairs and A. I. Mikoyan lost the Ministry of Foreign Trade,
all on 4 March 1949. Both dismissed ministers, however, returned to
their positions as deputy chairmen of the USSR Council of Ministers.
Then N. A. Bulganin ceded the Ministry of the Armed Forces to
Marshal A. M. Vasilevsky on 24 March 1949. N. S. Khrushchev,
who had been given the formidable task of bringing the Ukraine
back into the Soviet fold in 1944, was relieved as First Secretary of
the Ukrainian party by L. M. Kaganovich in March 1947 but returned
to Kiev in December 1947 when Kaganovich was recalled to Moscow.
Khrushchev came to the capital in December 1949 to become a
secretary of the CC and first secretary of the Moscow party committee.
He appears to have replaced A. A. Andreev as the secretariat's
spokesman on agriculture since a long article by him on collective
farms appeared in *Pravda* on 25 April 1950. Kolkhoz numbers were
to be drastically reduced by amalgamation. This was unexceptional
but then Khrushchev went on, in January 1951, to float the idea of
agrogoroda or agrotowns. This found its way into *Pravda* on 4 March
but on the following day the newspaper stated that due to an oversight
it had omitted to mention that the article was for discussion only. This
effectively killed the *agrogorod* scheme. Malenkov appears to have
played a key role in convincing Stalin that Khrushchev was purveying
dangerous ideas. He was to criticise the scheme openly and sharply
at the XIXth Party Congress in October 1952. Khrushchev did not
fall out of favour, however, as he delivered the report on the party
statutes at the congress. Ekaterina Kalinin, the wife of the Soviet head
of state until his death in 1946, was in a labour camp after being
beaten unconscious by a female NKVD officer in the presence of
Laverenty Beria. Poskrebyshev's wife was imprisoned for three years
before being shot despite her husband's pleas. Kaganovich's brother,
accused of conspiring with the Nazis and held to be their nominee
to head a fascist Russia, had managed to commit suicide in Mikoyan's
WC. What an accusation to make against a Jew! A Jew as head of
Hitler's Russia – he should be so lucky! Molotov's wife, Polina,
was also arrested and jailed. This behaviour certainly did not lead
to intimacy between the top elite and Stalin. The *vozhd* (boss) appears
to have regarded his tactics as another way of ensuring servility. No
one could complain that he was victimising only the families of his
top comrades. He meted out even more barbarous punishment to

his own family. Not surprisingly, family life with his close relatives hardly existed. The best that they could hope for was that the boss had forgotten them.

V. S. Abakumov, the Minister of State Security, was replaced by S. D. Ignatev in late 1951. At that time the Mingrelian affair erupted in Georgia.[8] It involved a group of Mingrelians who were prominent in Georgian politics and they were accused of attempting to 'liquidate Soviet power in the republic'. This appears exaggerated, to say the least, since only the United States with atomic bombs could have achieved this, something the Americans did not have in mind, so the target was clearly Beria. Stalin instructed the interrogators who were dealing with the little Mingrelians not to forget the 'big Mingrelian'. The only big Mingrelian around was Lavrenty. It led to a considerable turnover of party officials in Georgia.

Access to information was restricted by Stalin even to members of the Politburo. Before 1952 his tactic was to convene small committees composed of members of the Politburo, excluding those who were not then in favour. This led to very few being aware of all that was going on and added to this the division of responsibilities was very unclear. The meeting of the CC, in August 1952, must have been an experience for many, it was the first time that body had met in plenary session for over five years. It convened, at long last, at the XIXth Party Congress for October 1952. This again had been long awaited. Malenkov, at the founding meeting of the Cominform, in 1947, had referred to preparations for a new congress.

The congress spoke of the need for vigilance in the face of the 'threat of a new war' and dedicated endeavour, and confirmed the fifth FYP, covering the years 1951–55, almost two years late. It changed the name of the party from the All-Union Communist Party (Bolsheviks) to the Communist Party of the Soviet Union (CPSU). The party was defined as a 'voluntary, militant union of like-minded communists, formed of persons of the working class, the toiling peasantry and the working intelligentsia'.[9]

Stalin was not fit enough to deliver the report of the CC: Malenkov did it instead. Khrushchev, in delivering the report of the party statutes, lamented the fact that criticism at the local level was often stifled. How did this come about?

There are quite a few officials who consider that they are not subject to the law. Conceited enough to think that they can do as they please, these officials turn the enterprises or institutions under their control into their own fief where they introduce their own 'order' and their own 'discipline' . . . . There are many scandalous practices of this kind wherever such bureaucrats with a party card in their pockets are active.[10]

He introduced some excitement into the proceedings by announcing the disappearance of the Politburo and the Orgburo. Party conferences were no longer considered necessary. The new top body was called a Presidium and had twenty-five full and eleven candidate members, more than twice that of the old Politburo; the secretariat jumped from five to ten members and the CC almost doubled in size. Stalin was evidently planning more personnel changes and getting ready to introduce some new blood.

The most bizarre news of the late Stalin era was carried by *Pravda* on 13 January 1953. The Soviet public and the world were told that a 'group of saboteur-doctors' had been arrested. These specialists had worked in the Kremlin medical centre, where top Soviet leaders receive treatment, and most were Jewish. They had confessed to the medical murder of A. A. Zhdanov and A. S. Shcherbakov, who had died in 1945. Most of them were linked to the Jewish organisation 'Joint' which was stated to be under American direction. One of the accused had stated that he had received orders to 'wipe out the leading cadres of the USSR'. Three of them also turned out to be agents of British intelligence. *Pravda* drove home its point by stating that 'documentary evidence, investigations, the conclusions of medical experts and the confession of the accused' had established the above. What, readers must have asked themselves, had the security forces been doing ever since 1945? Screening for the Kremlin hospital was especially strict and the word was that ideological orthodoxy was accorded a higher rating than medical skill!

The whole episode was blown up and it became a dark time for Jews, now also accused of 'cosmopolitanism and zionism'. Besides Jews other targets were ministries for slackness, and party and Komsomol organisations for lack of vigilance. Evidently a new purge in the state and party apparatus was imminent and the fate of the Jews in the USSR hung in the balance. The campaign ended on 23 February 1953 as suddenly as it had begun. The master was no longer in control. He was paralysed by a stroke during the night of 1–2 March and died on 5 March.[11]

Inside a month the 'doctors' plot' was officially recognised as a fabrication and the surviving doctors rehabilitated. The official blamed was Mikhail Ryumin, deputy Minister of State Security. He was duly executed in July 1954.

ECONOMIC POLICY

It would have taken a miracle to have restored the Soviet Union, during the fourth FYP, to its pre-invasion state. The losses were so immense that they were almost incalculable: 70,000 villages, 98,000 kolkhozes completely or partly destroyed, 1,876 sovkhozes, 17 million head of cattle and 7 million horses driven away;[12] 65,000 kilometres of railway track, half of all the railway bridges in occupied territory, over half of all urban living space there, 1.2 million houses destroyed as well as 3.5 million rural homes.[13] And then there was the greatest loss of all, the 20 million dead, as well as the maimed in body and in mind.

A minor economic miracle was forthcoming during the period but only in industry. The first year of the plan, 1946, was a very poor one: there was a drought and industrial targets were not reached. The returning soldiers had to settle down, acquire new peacetime skills, the mines and factories put out of operation by the retreating enemy had to be reactivated and the war industries switched to peacetime activities. After 1946 industry took off and by 1950 the official claim was that industrial production was 73 per cent above the 1940 level.[14] This figure is exaggerated due to the continued use of 1926–27 prices but the overall picture is one of astonishing achievement. The Ukraine managed to equal its 1940 output of metallurgical products by about 1950 and electricity generation in that year was higher than in 1940,[15] a formidable achievement.

Down on the farm it was quite a different tale. It was the return of the bad old days of the 1930s; no incentives, the centralisation of every decision which could be centralised, a harsh paternalistic attitude towards the rural sector, with the farms regarded as the milch cows of the cities and industry. And it was all unnecessary. A case could be made for strict central control in the 1930s but there was no justification for the leadership's treatment of agriculture during Stalin's last years. Since there were precious few resources to channel into agriculture local initiative should have been encouraged to fill the gap. The returning soldiers and the women left in the countryside would surely have responded with enthusiasm.

The immediate post-war state of agriculture was critical. The ravages of the war, the removal of practically all mechanical and horse draught power, the run-down nature of the farms in the non-occupied areas, due in part to the absence of male labour and the lack of rural party cadres, had led to the collective system being neglected, to put it mildly. The private plot had flourished as had the private animals of the kolkhozniks.

The government reasserted its authority in a decree on 19 September 1946 which set out to reclaim all that the kolkhoznik or any statutory body had filched. About 14 million hectares were returned; 456,000 kolkhozniki were transferred from administrative to productive work; another 182,000 were struck off kolkhoz payrolls; 140,000 head of cattle and 15 million rubles were recovered.[16] Much of the recovered land, however, lay fallow since the kolkhozes had neither the labour nor the machinery to work it. The year 1946 was a dreadful one with drought afflicting many areas. Soviet agriculture is fortunate in that drought never affects the whole of the country in any one year, as the USSR spans too many climatic zones. The grain harvest was a miserable

39.6 million tonnes in 1946,[17] just over 40 per cent of the 1940 crop. Many must have gone hungry. Afterwards things picked up but the harvest in 1950 was still about 15 per cent below that of 1940.

If crop husbandry had not fully recovered by 1950 then there was no prospect of the other vital sector of agriculture, animal husbandry, doing better. The shortage of grain for human consumption meant that little was left over for animals. Procurements of meat by the state, in 1946, were about 700,000 tonnes deadweight for a population of over 165 millions. However by 1950 procurements were back to their 1940 levels. State procurements were predominantly for the cities and the countryside was left to fend for itself. In 1950, 44 per cent of cattle, including 66 per cent of cows and 35 per cent of pigs, were in private hands.[18] In the same year between 40 and 50 per cent of global agricultural production originated in the private sector. This at a time when determined efforts were being made by the State to curtail private production.

Kolkhozes saw their taxes rise, as well as procurements, and on 20 October 1948 a government and party decree introduced the 'Stalin plan for the transformation of nature'. If Stalin never visited the countryside he certainly thought about it – about how much it could contribute to state finances and to feeding the cities. Protective tree belts were to be planted on 5,709,000 hectares, of which the kolkhozes were to be responsible for 3,592,500 hectares, over the years 1945–68.[19] Since there were plenty of trees, indeed there were too many, in areas of adequate precipitation, the burden was to fall on farms in drier areas. The idea was good, many of the trees are to be seen in the southern Ukraine today, but the scheme was far too ambitious. Too many trees were planted with the inevitable result. It was just another burden for the farmer to bear.

The year 1948 saw the death of D. N. Pryanishnikov, an advocate of mineral fertilisers and a formidable defender of his views. With this death the *travopole* system, associated with the name of V. R. Vilyams, who had died in 1939, came to the fore. It was a grassland system which led to the favouring of spring wheat over winter wheat and the rejection of mineral fertilisers. At the same time T. D. Lysenko, who can charitably be called an enthusiastic amateur, became the leading light in agrobiology. One of his special targets was genetics and he, with the help of some colleagues, including philosophers, succeeded in driving the discipline underground until it was rehabilitated by Brezhnev in 1966. He fitted the pattern of the little Stalins of the 1930s. Enthusiastic to the point of ignoring evidence to the contrary he was dedicated to achieving agricultural advance but was, in reality, the farmers' worst enemy. One idea that struck him was that if a cow, giving a high milk yield, was crossed with a good beef bull, the result would be cows which provided large amounts of milk and beef. If only genetics were so simple!

Collectivisation in the Baltic States and the other new territories did not begin until 1947 and took three years to complete. The response of the local farmers was predictable, exacerbated by strong local national feeling. To them the whole exercise was a latter day version of russification. Large numbers were deported as a result.

Kolkhoz numbers dropped rapidly after 1950 in the wake of Khrushchev's policy of amalgamation. The 254,000 on 1 January 1950 had become 97,000 by October 1952. He then began to speak of *agrogoroda*. The idea had its attractions for the kolkhoznik but there was a serious drawback. Only 0.01–0.15 hectare was to be permitted around the block of flats while the rest of the kolkhoznik's plot would be further away. It was a move to wean the kolkhoznik away from his private plot but Khrushchev was too optimistic in thinking that a farmer would voluntarily prefer a fourth-floor flat with the lift out of action to a house with a garden around it.

Raising labour productivity, without the necessary machinery and incentives, was an uphill task. A. A. Andreev, USSR Minister of Agriculture and Politburo member responsible for the rural sector, had favoured the link (*zveno*) system over the brigade. The former permitted small groups to be set up and these were paid by results at the end of the harvest. However, the brigade or large group remained in favour.

The link favours the strong, young males with technical skills. These young men tend to acquire most of the farm's technical resources for their own work. They are rewarded according to the amount of produce they grow, not the number of labour days worked. Hence the others, mostly women, feel themselves disadvantaged. A small proportion of the labour force is highly paid but the great majority poorly paid. The brigade is a much larger unit and involves men and women of all ages. Its members are paid according to the amount of labour they have contributed, calculated in labour days.

Andreev suffered as a result but Khrushchev gained. The latter was to return to this perennial problem during his period in office and the link *v.* brigade debate is still continuing.

Stalin's last major publication, *The Economic Problems of Socialism in the USSR*, contained a clear warning to economists to stay out of politics and had much to say about the future of the countryside. Stalin envisaged kolkhozes gradually being transformed into state farms, and commodity circulation, the buying and selling of products by kolkhozes for money, giving way to products' exchange. Nevertheless he rejected the notion that machinery from the MTS should be sold to kolkhozes and nothing was done before his death to raise kolkhozes to the status of sovkhozes.

The fifth FYP, 1951–55, passed by the XIXth Party Congress was not as ambitious as the fourth. Almost all factories were again on stream but the atmosphere of the time was inimical to scientific and technical innovation except in some areas of the defence industry. The Soviet Union had acquired her own atomic bomb and had, as of 1949, been increasing defence expenditure and the size of her armed forces so Stalin could feel that the country, in 1953, had never been stronger.

Table 5.1 The Soviet economy 1940–50

	1940	1945	1946	1950
National Income (1940=100)	100	83	–	161
Industrial production	100	91	76	172
Heavy industry	100	112	82	204
Light industry	100	59	67	122
Gross agricultural product	100	60	–	99
Steel (million tonnes)	18.3	12.3	13.3	27.3
Oil (million tonnes)	31.1	19.4	21.7	37.9
Grain (million tonnes)	95.6	47.3	39.6	81.2
Wages (rubles per month)	33.1	–	48.1	64.2

Source: Narodnoe Khozyaistvo SSSR za 60 let (Moscow 1977)

SOCIAL POLICY

Life was harsh for the worker in the immediate post-war years. Basic commodities were rationed, and prices were raised considerably in 1946, but free market prices were considerably higher, reflecting the prevailing scarcity. Rationing should have ended in 1946 but the poor harvest postponed it for a year. Even so real wages in 1947 may only have been 51 per cent of the 1940 level.[20]

Such was Stalin's trust in the security organs and his utter confidence that the population would accept almost any decree that he pushed through a punitive currency reform on 14 December 1947, abolishing rationing at the same time. The target was the person with large personal savings in cash, in other words the peasant, first and foremost. There was precious little to spend the wartime profits on so peasants were caught unawares and their hoards lost most of their value overnight. Savings bank deposits below 3,000 rubles were exchanged at 1:1 and the face value of state loans was cut by two thirds, as they were exchanged at a ratio of 1:3. The rate of interest they carried was also reduced.[21] Cash was exchanged at the rate of one new ruble for ten old rubles. Anyone who went to the bank with a sackful of rubles was in trouble so the peasant and anyone else with lots of cash had to find other uses for it. They could always light their cigarettes with it! Wages however stayed the same: 500 rubles in 1947 still meant 500 rubles in 1948. The rationale behind the reform was to cut disposable income to the level where it did not greatly exceed the value of goods and services on offer. It had a powerful levelling effect on the population. However, only a Stalin could have got away with such a reform.

But the worst was over: workers' real wages rose appreciably between 1948 and 1952 and overtook the 1940 level. Nevertheless real wages in 1952 were about the same as in 1928. The 1948–52 increases led to wages in priority industries rising much faster than in other sectors with the result that differentials continued to increase.

If the worker could feel, by 1953, that life had improved and would continue to improve, not so the kolkhoznik. He or more often she had every right to feel aggrieved. Labour on the collective farm was rewarded according to the income of the farm and this in turn was heavily influenced by procurement prices. The State did not increase procurement prices between 1940 and 1947 while the retail price index rose to 2,045 (1928 = 100). In 1952 the average prices paid for grain, beef and pigs were actually below those of 1940.[22] Hence given the fact that the more the kolkhoz produced the greater its loss, the only reasonable policy was to run the farm down so as to minimise state deliveries. The party official on the spot could see what was wrong but if he sided with the kolkhoz he could be labelled a Populist.

Peasants got by because of their private plot. Almost certainly the majority of their income came from it between 1945 and 1953. However, taxes and procurements on the private plot increased so peasants reduced their output and livestock numbers after 1949. Cattle numbers per household, in 1952, were lower than in 1940. Nevertheless peasants were taxed on notional output. If they had no milk they had to acquire it so as to meet their deliveries – only just over half the households had a cow.[23]

Those kolkhozes which were near large conurbations or where the soil and climate were good were the best off. Generally speaking the European part of the Russian Federation was the place not to be. When Stalin toasted the Great Russians for playing the major role in victory over Germany he was not thinking of the soldier as a peasant: the Great Russian peasant received no recognition and precious little material reward over the years 1945–53. No wonder the number of workers and employees in the state sector was 39.2 million instead of the planned 33.5 million in 1950.

Urban life in the post-war years was harder than it had been during the 1930s. In Moscow, for example, in 1945, about 90 per cent of central heating and 48 per cent of water and sewerage systems were out of operation. By 1950 the Soviet urban population was 6 million higher than in 1940 and the construction of housing and repairs came a poor second to industrial construction. Housing space per person dropped from 4.09 square metres in 1940 to 3.98 square metres in 1950. Nine square metres was the acceptable sanitary minimum.

Rationing of food and manufactured goods began at the outbreak of war and remained until 1947. Rationing was the norm. It had been introduced at the beginning of the first FYP and was only lifted in 1935. The drought of 1946 made food shortages more severe, the

191

prices of rationed goods tripled in September 1946. Only in 1949 did the standard of living of the urban dweller begin to improve.

Many women stayed in the labour force after the war, probably out of necessity because of the high food prices and low incomes. They made up 47 per cent of the total labour force in 1950 compared to 39 per cent in 1940. The very large increase in the labour force of 11.6 million between 1945 and 1959 led to the creation of *orgnabor*. Its function was to direct mainly unskilled labour to high priority sectors of heavy industry and energy in the north, Siberia and the Urals. There was a Ministry of Labour Reserves, set up in 1947.

CULTURE

Gifted figures in the world of culture may be compared to research scientists in the technical world. A country, if it wishes to progress internationally, cannot get by without them. The talented are by instinct innovators and their inspiration cannot be programmed beforehand. Stalin, as the 'engineer of human souls', regarded training as more important than education. Gradually as competent engineers were trained an expanding technical intelligentsia came into being. There was no conflict between these specialists and the cult of Stalin as the fount of all knowledge and wisdom in the Soviet Union. A person's material needs were being progressively satisfied; that left the cultural and spiritual needs to be catered for. The 'engineer' of the cultural world, the artist, who could be trained in socialist realism and could draw in the contours of the society the party desired was available, but because he relied on others for inspiration he was not genuinely creative. The greatly gifted, creative writers, painters, musicians and so on would not fit into any scheme drafted by the party. They are paralleled by the research scientists, men and women who vault over existing knowledge and views to reach new shores. They cannot accept that Stalin or the party can guide them in their discipline since what they are researching into has not yet become known or perhaps even formulated. They must think heretical thoughts and challenge received opinions and it is the party which must follow them.

The perennial problem of creativity and the acquisition of new knowledge is one which the CPSU never solved: indeed it is insoluble in any ideological system. The church in medieval and modern Europe did not solve it either.

Stalin's speech of 9 February 1946 which heralded a turning away from the wartime alliance and the onset of austerity in the short term was bound to have repercussions on cultural and scientific life. The field chosen for the first attack was literature. A CC decree of 14 August 1946 pilloried the magazines *Zvezda* and *Leningrad*.[24] The former was accused of publishing 'ideologically harmful works' and of providing a tribune for Mikhail Zoshchenko. His story *Adventures of a Monkey* especially raised the ire of the party. In this satire a monkey escapes from the zoo and after experiencing Soviet life returns gratefully to his cage where he can breathe more freely. Also violently attacked was Anna Akhmatova, a celebrated poetess, who had written much on the themes of love and religion. *Leningrad* was upbraided for publishing works which 'were permeated with the spirit of servility towards everything foreign'. *Zvezda* was ordered to mend its ways and *Leningrad* was closed down.

A week later Zhdanov spelled out party thinking on literature and art and was at his vituperative best.[25] After pouring scorn on Zoshchenko, 'the scum of the literary world', he turned his attention to Akhmatova. 'It would be hard to say if she is a nun or a whore; better perhaps to say that she is a little of both, her lusts and her prayers intertwine.' Zhdanov went out of his way to denigrate 'kowtowing to the West' or indeed praising anything foreign. Soviet literature represented a higher culture and had the right to reach the world. Soviet writers were seen as being in the front line of the ideological battle then under way. Another task of Soviet writers was to 'help the State to educate youth properly'.

Then the CC moved to the theatre and the cinema. Its main complaint in its decree 'On the Repertoire of the Theatre and Measures for its Improvement', dated 26 August 1946,[26] was that only 25 out of 119 current productions were plays by Soviet writers on contemporary themes and even some of these were ideologically worthless. Putting on so many plays by Western writers was tantamount to trying to 'poison the consciousness of the Soviet people with hostile ideology and to revive the remnants of capitalism in consciousness and life'. The true task of the theatre was to put on plays which furthered the 'development of the best aspects of the character of Soviet man and Soviet woman'.

The CC attack on the cinema came on 4 September 1946 and was entitled 'On the Film *Bolshaya Zhizn* (The Great Life)'.[27] The party thought that Pavel Nilin's film gave a 'false, distorted picture of Soviet people'. It seemed to be objecting to the portrayal of life as it really was; the film showed workers, some of whom were barely literate, enjoying their vodka and sex.

Among other films to be savaged was the second part of Sergei Eisenstein's *Ivan the Terrible*. Eisenstein stood condemned for his 'ignorance of historical facts by portraying Ivan the Terrible's progressive army, the *Oprichnina*, as a band of degenerates, comparable to the American Ku Klux Klan, and Ivan the Terrible, a man of strong will and character, as weak and irresolute, akin to Hamlet'. This was a devastating blow for the great film maker and he died a broken man in 1948.

The message was crystal clear. Russia's historical past was so glorious that there were no warts or blemishes to be seen. Historical accuracy took second place to national myth-making.

The stress on the greatness of Russian literature boded ill for the specialists in comparative literature. A natural extension of the derision of all things foreign was to belittle the achievements of other cultures. This included attacking the notion that many great Russian writers had been influenced by foreign literati. The first shot in this battle was fired by Aleksandr Fadeev, the new first secretary of the Union of Soviet Writers, in the spring of 1947. He chose as his target *Pushkin and World Literature* by Isaac Nusimov, published in 1941.[28] Nusimov, a prominent orthodox Soviet critic during the 1930s, had presented Pushkin as a 'European' and as someone who had been greatly influenced by foreign ideas. 'The book is based on the view that light shines from the West and that Russia is an "oriental" country.' Fadeev's audience could not fail to understand that such a formulation placed Russia in an inferior position *vis-à-vis* the West. The debate on where Russia belonged had reverberated down the centuries and memories of Chaadaev, the Slavophiles and Westernisers, Populists and Marxists were present in every Russian mind.

Fadeev then anathematised the work of A. N. Veselovsky, who had died in 1918, divining in him the roots of the trouble. Veselovsky, a major scholar of comparative literature, was accused of preaching the superiority of Western literature and the inferiority of Russian literature. A veritable hurricane of abuse was hurled at him and his followers in Soviet publications. Anyone who hinted that a Russian writer owed something to a foreign writer was set upon. One such case was linking Gorky to the English writer Henry Fielding – what apostasy!

Music's turn came on 10 February 1948 when the CC turned its ire on the opera *Velikaya Druzhba* (The Great Friendship) by V. Muradeli and on many leading Soviet composers.[29] The opera portrays the struggle to establish Soviet power in North Caucasus during 1918–20 and is centred on life of Sergo Ordzhonikidze. The opera had been a sensational success during the winter of 1947 but then the sky fell on Muradeli. Possibly Stalin objected to everyone being reminded that he was a Georgian and even more to anyone singing the praises of Ordzhonikidze, with whom he had not always seen eye to eye. Zhdanov also disliked it because of its modestly modern music. The complaint was that there was not a single tune or aria which stayed in the memory, it was all pure disharmony and dissonance: in short a cacophony. A combination of Stalin and Zhdanov disliking it was enough to kill it, irrespective of what the musicians and the public thought.

Shostakovich, Prokofiev, Khachaturyan and other leading Soviet composers were not spared. They were accused of being formalistic and anti-national.

Science, where T. D. Lysenko played the role of Zhdanov, was also under assault at the same time, as has already been mentioned.

Philosophy took the stage in early 1947 and the debate centred around *The History of West European Philosophy* by G. F. Aleksandrov. Zhdanov made a major speech at a meeting held to discuss the book on 24 June 1947.[30] His aides had ransacked the book to provide him with ample ammunition to accuse Aleksandrov of not being savage enough in his criticism. The drift of Zhdanov's meaning was palpably clear: there was no wisdom in the West, except for the writings of and Marx and Engels.

The emphasis on the greatness of Russian and by extension of Soviet culture fanned the flames of Russian nationalism. As everything Western was denigrated and authors competed with one another to pour scorn on things foreign eyes turned inwards towards the multi-national Soviet Union. 'Bourgeois nationalists' were discovered lurking in many places and duly attacked. Only Russian nationalism which was co-terminous with Soviet nationalism flowered but in turn it had to be centred on Moscow, Leningrad regionalism was taboo. Another term roams the period, anti-cosmopolitanism. It reached a crescendo on 28 January 1949 when *Pravda* attacked a group of theatre critics for dipping their pens in poison to destroy the 'best plays which depict Soviet patriotism'. A witchhunt followed and scores of critics, many of them Jews, rootless cosmopolitans, lost their positions.

It is one thing to attack writers but it is quite another to put something readable in the shops. Soviet literature is a failure, irrespective of the contents, if it does not sell. Drama, art and music are failures if the theatres, galleries and concert halls are empty. The party cannot tolerate such a state of affairs since it is evidence that it is failing in its cultural mission. There are limits to what the public will tolerate. The Zhdanov period is remarkable more for what the talented writers did not write than for what was produced.

This said, much literature was still published and some of it proved popular. What themes run through Zhdanovite literature?[31] Status, social climbing and the desire for material satisfaction, denied during the war years, appear often. The mores of the Soviet ruling class are being formed and they have something in common with those of the traditional lower middle class in English society. The desire is overwhelmingly to imitate, copy what those above you have and do. The new intelligentsia, managers, state and party bureaucrats and more important their wives and families, are seeking to acquire objects, especially to wear, which will advertise to everyone that they have arrived in Soviet society.

The returning war hero is inevitably a major theme. The difficulties of readjustment, especially in the countryside, are explored. Family responsibilities are underlined. The woman scientist who neglects her child and husband in the pursuit of science and the plan is criticised. If she is hard on her returning husband, the war had made innumerable women old at thirty, the novelist is usually on the husband's side. Women have to learn to adjust. They have to help to rebuild human lives and souls as well as the towns and villages they live in.

Technical expertise is celebrated since socialism cannot be built without a material base and it in turn requires managerial and personnel skills. The engineer or manager, however, who lives by production alone is portrayed negatively: he must also be able to solve the problems of his private life.

The party official who is insensitive and bullies everyone is a target for criticism. The best known example is in a study by V. Ovechkin which was an overnight sensation when first published in *Novy Mir* in September 1952. The villain Borzov is a Stalinist party apparatchik and Martynov, his deputy, is the good bureaucrat. The outcome of the confrontation, however, remains unclear. So well known was Borzov that the term Borzovism was coined to describe the behaviour of his spiritual brethren.

Literature is intensely Russian and Soviet and the campaign against cosmopolitanism and formalism (the representation of objects in terms of abstract geometrical form rather than of natural appearance; it should however be underlined that Soviet critics used this term very loosely when seeking to attack a writer) ensured that if a foreigner stepped on the page he left behind a negative imprint.

Plots were not very strong and convincing. Conflict is not between the hero and the villain but rather between the hero and the super-hero. Serious everyday problems melt away and the future tends to take over. Under these conditions even a genius of the calibre of Tolstoy would find it difficult to write riveting dialogue and invent powerful plots.

Zhdanov's campaign against the world of learning was a success. It achieved its object of turning Soviet minds inwards and away from Western ideas and models. It was, in reality, an assault on the mind. It did not try to convince but to frighten. Since little satisfaction could be achieved in the cultural and spiritual fields energies were concentrated on improving the material. In a significant sense, however, the whole episode was self-defeating. Creative scientists, if they are to continue to innovate, cannot be cut off from the scientific world outside. The creative writer can be frightened into silence but cannot be made to produce the works desired by the party. He simply works and does not offer his material for publication, it is 'for the bottom drawer', as the saying goes. He goes into internal migration, he is silent, ready to surface when the intellectual climate becomes more hospitable. For a living many of them took temporary refuge in translating, Pasternak being the most distinguished. These are the cultural figures who gain international recognition, when they do reveal their output, thus enhancing the standing of the Soviet Union throughout the world.

The party can decide to do without them and the USSR only loses some international literary prestige. However, the country cannot do without the troublesome scientists since they are vitally necessary to industrial growth and by extension to USSR military strength on this criterion, Lysenko and the Lysenko-ites in the scientific field are much more lethal than Fadeev and his friends in the cultural world.

RELIGION

The favourable treatment accorded the Russian Orthodox Church, in return for its co-operation in the war effort, continued after 1945. By 1948 the number of parishes had risen to 22,000 and there were eighty-nine monastic institutions.[32] Metropolitan Nikolai informed a delegation of British women that the Church had over 20,000 churches, about ninety monasteries and nunneries, two academies and eight seminaries.[33]

The Orthodox Church paid a heavy price for the tolerance which the State extended to it. Part of the price was to support uncritically Soviet foreign policy initiatives. This cost it some members, those who did not agree with its acceptance of the *status quo*. Persecution between 1948 and 1952 scattered these believers to the four winds.

The party tolerated the Church but moved against it when the anti-religious article of the Soviet Constitution was again highlighted. Some forty-nine members of the CP of Georgia were expelled for 'observing religious rites', in 1948, and the Komsomol made clear that a person could not be a member and harbour religious convictions. The party was thereby confirming that religious belief was on the increase.

The Roman Catholic Church, centred in Lithuania, was under severe pressure during the last years of Stalin. Recognising as it did a spiritual leader who lives outside the country it was especially suspect and was the target of many accusations of spying, subversion and so on. The sharp anti-Western trend after 1946 inevitably involved the Vatican and anti-Papal propaganda was very virulent.

Muslims fared quite well during and after the war and some even made the pilgrimage to Mecca in 1945. Mosques were reopened during the war and officially there were 3,000 mosques in the USSR in October 1947.[34] Islamic theological training recommenced in Bokhara in 1948. This toleration of Islam is puzzling since it occurred at the moment the *Zhdanovshchina* was reaching a peak. Evidently Moscow did not regard Islam as much of a threat since at that time there were few independent Islamic states. Four of these states were near neighbours. Afghanistan, Iran and Turkey shared a common frontier with the USSR and Pakistan was not far away. It would appear that Moscow was concerned with improving the attractiveness of the Soviet model of Islamic development especially to Muslims living on her southern frontier.

NATIONALITIES

As soon as the Red Army liberated Soviet territory the NKVD moved swiftly in to search for collaborators. Thousands were shot and hundreds of thousands sent to labour camps. The Ukraine was a special case and in April 1944 3,000 officials from the Russian east were given leading positions. By the end of 1946 half the leading party and governmental officials in the Ukraine were new.

Zhdanov's attacks on Russian culture during the summer of 1946 were the signal for parallel assaults on 'bourgeois nationalism' in the non-Russian republics. Khrushchev, at a CC Plenum of the Communist Party of the Ukraine (CPUk) in August 1946, sharply criticised a recently published book on Ukrainian literature for containing 'serious nationalist errors'. The CC, CPUk promulgated six decrees between August and November 1946 on 'bourgeois-nationalist deviations' in Ukrainian culture. The elements were also against the Ukrainians. Drought led to famine during the winter of 1946–47, but it also afflicted the Volga and central Russia. Hundreds of thousands died.

The *Zhdanovshchina* affected all republics and attempted to achieve the same goals: development of a Soviet-orientated political and historical consciousness; suppression of local national traditions in education and culture; stress on links between the local nations and the Russian nation; promotion of Russian culture as the dominant world culture and hence the one to play the role model.

In Armenia it was claimed that historians preferred to write about Armenia's golden age long ago and avoid the present. This was not confined to Armenia. Many a Russian historian took refuge in the past, as far back as possible, so as not to become entwined in ideological arguments. The anti-nationalist watchdogs were very vigilant. They even found evidence of 'bourgeois' leanings in Buryat-Mongolia. It was claimed that local historians had failed to appreciate the value of the Russian contribution to local development, especially in the Soviet period. The authorities banned Muslim epics in an effort to eliminate specific national traditions. The epics are one of the mainsprings of the culture of the Muslim peoples. The Azerbaidzhani epic *Dede-Korkut* was lauded and published by the Academy of Sciences, but the party leader discovered in 1951 that it contained the 'poison of nationalism' in its verses. The locals did not give up without a fight, especially in Kirgizia. But it was an unequal struggle, and Moscow was determined to banish all the forms of culture which celebrated resistance to Russian domination. Only Russian epics were excluded. Stalin's toast to Russia as the leading nation in the USSR in May 1945 led to specialists being given the task of glorifying Russian achievements worldwide. Historians were to research the influence of Kievan Rus on Western Europe, and the Norman theory of the origins of Rus was to be banished. The history of non-Russian nations only had relevance in the context of their relations with Russia. Only 'rootless cosmopolitans' could maintain that Russia was of Norman origin, backward and lacked national tradition. Everything Russian was number one in the world. Whereas hitherto the peoples of the Soviet Union had regarded Russians as their elder brother, this was now extended to Eastern Europe. In contrast, Western culture and life were diseased and decadent.

The Soviet Union welcomed the establishment of the State of Israel in May 1948, but Stalin did not take kindly to Soviet Jews looking to Israel. Attitudes began to change in September 1948 as Jews were accused of 'national nihilism', of kowtowing to the West and being subversives and spies. Jewish cultural organisations and publications were closed down. A Jewish anti-fascist committee had come into being in April 1942 to mobilise support for the war. It was dissolved in November 1948. The last Jewish schools in Vilnius, Kovno and in Birobidzhan closed. The only Yiddish newspaper left was in Birobidzhan. Leading Jewish writers, intellectuals and party officials in Moscow and elsewhere were arrested at the end of 1948. All members of the anti-fascist committee except Ilya Ehrenburg were rounded up. Many of those arrested were executed. Solomon Mikhoels, a leading Yiddish actor and theatre director and an active participant in the committee, was murdered in circumstances strongly suggesting MVD involvement. He and others had proposed the Crimea as a Jewish homeland. In a secret trial in July 1952 twenty-five Jewish writers were sentenced to death and shot. This was in direct contrast to the show trials of the 1930s when Stalin was seeking maximum publicity. Among the nine doctors accused in the Doctors' Plot in January 1953 there were seven Jews.

The Soviets were aware of the magnitude of their task in integrating the 'new' territories after their recapture. The West Ukrainians, Moldavians and Balts did not welcome Soviet rule and had armed underground units who were capable of resisting. The only territory populated predominantly by Ukrainians which had escaped the net of 1939–41 was the Subcarpathian Ukraine in Czechoslovakia. President Beneš obligingly offered the area to Stalin, and half a million Ukrainians joined the Ukraine on 29 June 1945. There was no armed revolt against incorporation. Party and governmental officials from the eastern Ukraine were sent to the new areas to integrate them into the Soviet order of things. Since Stalin gave way to Western pressure to move the Soviet-Polish border eastwards to the Curzon Line, some Ukrainian territory reverted to Poland. Lithuanians, Russians, Belorussians and Ukrainians (but not Jews) west of the Curzon Line were permitted to move to the Soviet republics, and the Poles and Jews (but not other nationalities) who had been Polish citizens before 17 September 1939 and who had resided east of the Line could cross to Poland. Altogether, about 520,000 Ukrainians left Poland, and by December 1946 1.5 million Poles had moved back to Poland. In 1950 there were 2.1 million in Poland who had come from the areas which had become part of the USSR. Many Jews got out of the Soviet Union through the exchange, but a large proportion of them subsequently left Poland for Palestine and elsewhere. The incoming Ukrainians and Belorussians were not resettled in the border regions of western Ukraine and western Belorussia which the Poles and Jews had vacated. Most of the Ukrainians were settled in the southern Ukraine, while Russians and Ukrainians who had been living in Siberia and Kazakhstan were brought in to populate the border districts. Despite Belorussia's heavy wartime losses Belorussian peasants were directed to work in industry and construction in Karelia, Altai, Siberia and the Far East. The Jews who were deported during the anti-cosmopolitan campaign of the late 1940s were not sent to Birobidzhan but Yakutia. Some Crimean Tatars were deported to Birobidzhan. There was clearly a deliberate policy to mix the Soviet population.

Ukrainian nationalists continued their armed opposition to the Sovietisation of the Ukraine and operated from Polish territory. In 1948 there were about 6,000 armed Ukrainians engaging in mainly guerrilla raids along the Polish-Ukrainian border. Soviet control was achieved only at the end of the 1940s, but they paid a price. According to Khrushchev, the Soviets lost thousands of men. Ukrainian railway tunnels were still guarded in 1957. Collectivisation was forced through over the years 1948–50 and gradually removed the social base of support for the partisans. Another blow against Ukrainian national identity was the campaign against the Ukrainian Catholic Church, the Uniates. They observed the Orthodox rite but acknowledged the Pope as their spiritual leader. In April 1945 the metropolitan and all bishops were arrested and accused of collaborating with the Germans, and were imprisoned. An initiative group was set up, inspired by the NKVD, and a council was held in Lvov in March 1946. It declared the Union of Brest (1596) to be at an end and voted to fuse with the Russian Orthodox Church. Half of the priests went over, others were deported and some went underground. The Uniate priest Kostelnik, who had played the leading role in the transfer, aroused such intense opposition among the faithful that he was murdered on 20 September 1948 in Lvov. During the Moscow conference of Autocephalous Orthodox Churches, in the summer of 1948, he had drawn up a sharply anti-Vatican resolution which had been duly passed at the conference. Almost all the 4 million believers still regarded themselves as members of the Catholic Church. The Uniate Church in Subcarpathian Ukraine totally opposed joining the Orthodox Church. The bishop, Mgr Romza, was murdered on 27 October 1947. When a collision between his carriage and a lorry load of police and soldiers failed to remove him to the next world he was set upon and beaten to death with iron bars. The Uniates were merged with the Moscow Patriarchate in August 1949. The re-emergence of this Church in the late 1980s and its present vitality reveal that the 'conversion' was cosmetic.

Moscow promoted rapid industrialisation in the west Ukraine, concentrating on Lvov. Here the number of industrial workers rose from 43,000 in 1945 to 148,000 in 1959. Most of the skilled labour, engineers and management came from the eastern Ukraine and Russia. Between 1944 and 1949 about 16,000 Russian specialists arrived. Nevertheless, the inflow could not match the outflow of Poles and Jews who had returned to Poland. The Ukrainian population in Lvov region rose from 59.3 per cent in 1931 to 86.3 per cent in 1959. The cities lost their Polish and Jewish aspects and a Ukrainian intelligentsia developed. They demanded more and more autonomy as the years passed. Russification failed here.

The Baltic states resisted Russification even more vigorously than the west Ukrainians. It was more difficult for the Soviets since they had been independent states until 1940. Lithuania put up the greatest struggle with their partisans more effective than those in the Ukraine. Since there were so few locals who had the requisite qualifications, thousands of officials came from outside. The first source was the Baltic units in the Red Army. There were practically no Lithuanians who had been living in exile in the USSR, so Russians, Belorussians and others were called upon. Russians accounted for half of party members in Estonia and two-thirds in Lithuania, and overall in the Baltic parties only a third of members were indigenous. However, almost all of these had been living in exile in the USSR. Only 0.3 per cent of Lithuanian and 0.7 per cent of Latvian and Estonian party members were really natives. Deportations followed reconquest. The first category were those who had served in the Wehrmacht; more than 30,000 Estonians and 38,000 Latvians were dispatched by early 1945. Another 100,000 Lithuanians and 60,000 Lativans followed by spring 1946. Partisans were most active between 1945 and 1948, when there were about 30,000 in Lithuania, 15,000 in Latvia and 10,000 in Estonia. Possibly more than 100,000 Lithuanians were at some time or another active as partisans. Their own casualties were high, but they assassinated between 4,000 and 13,000 over the years 1945–52. As in the Ukraine, collectivisation broke the partisan movement. The overwhelming resources of the NKVD and the Red Army were bound to prevail. On 15 March 1945, 2,257 NKVD and army operations were carried out in Lithuania. As a result, 497 bands (16,982 persons) were liquidated, 5,364 partisans killed, 10,929 persons seized, 71,674 arrested of whom 11,412 were nationalist underground members; 33,670 deserters were apprehended and 9,376 gave themselves up. Among the equipment confiscated were 662 light machine guns, 912 sub-machine guns and 7,606 rifles. At the end of 1947 about 70,000 Lithuanians were deported and another 70,000 followed in May 1948 for resisting the formation of kolkhozes. Beginning in March 1949, about 60,000 Estonians, 50,000 Latvians and 40,000 Lithuanians were transported east. Another 40,000 were removed from Lithuania in the summer of 1949. Many died *en route* to West Siberia and Kazakhstan. As was usual, the males were put in labour camps and the women and children in kolkhozes. Industrialisation was given priority, and this brought in many Russians. This affected Lithuania less than Latvia and Estonia. Between 1944 and 1947 about 180,000 immigrants arrived in Estonia. More than 400,000 Russians and 100,000 others settled in Latvia between 1945 and 1959. The proportion of Latvians in the republic dropped from 83 per cent in 1945 to about 60 per cent in 1953. In Estonia it was down to 72 per cent by 1953. Lithuania was an exception. The partisan movement and the slow pace of industrialisation resulted in the population remaining overwhelmingly Lithuanian.

FOREIGN POLICY

Soviet foreign policy during the last years of Stalin was defensive, as it had been ever since 1917. This was so in spite of the USSR emerging as a victorious great power from the war. The Americans were convinced that world peace could only be secured if the Soviet Union played a leading international role. Churchill thought that Great Britain had to acknowledge USSR hegemony in the countries liberated or occupied by the Red Army; there was no point in entering into a hostile confrontation with Moscow since the British were bound to lose. The US did not favour conflict either. When Churchill suggested that the Americans and British use the fact that they were in occupation of about one third of the agreed Soviet occupation zone in Germany as a bargaining counter with the Soviets, the Americans refused. The British were quite incapable of playing the card on their own, they had to acknowledge the US as the senior partner.

The mood of 1945 blinded the US and Great Britain to the economic weakness of the Soviet Union. Since the Soviets read British and American intentions correctly they seized as much as possible and kept on asking for more – knowing that the other side would not resort to armed action. Stalin must have realised that such a policy could not last for ever but was justifiably upset when the Western Powers, after 1947, attempted to claw back part of what had been conceded in eastern Europe in 1944–45.

Given that there was little likelihood of the West attacking the USSR and indeed the Soviets stood to gain a great deal by co-operating with their war-time allies, why did Stalin, in early 1946, signal to the world that the cosy relationship with the capitalist world was coming to an end? The warm Crimean sun, he made clear, was to give way to an icy Siberian winter.

The most probable reason is that Stalin was pessimistic about the Soviet Union's chances of victory in a contest with the US. His system, geared to forcing the country to become economically strong at a breakneck pace, was not mature enough to compete on equal terms with the richer, more vital capitalist societies. It would have been very nice to welcome foreign capital: recovery would have been swifter but the end product would not have been a Stalinist society. American capital brings American ideas and the Soviet Union was like a fat chicken ready to be plucked; abundant raw materials, a plentiful supply of docile labour and a tremendous thirst for things foreign. No, Stalin had to reject the soft option.

Soviet policy was, understandably, to hang on to the fruits of war. Retreat from one country could lead to others and turn into a rout.[35] The USSR had to show herself hard and uncompromising and wholly capable of defending her interests. Her behaviour was quite unfathomable to the Americans. They wished to build a brave new world on American-Soviet foundations but the Soviets could not believe this. The administration of occupied Germany was a testing ground and no common language could be found there. Recriminations had begun even before Germany capitulated.

Stalin's speech in Moscow on 9 February 1946, Churchill's in Fulton, Missouri, on 5 March 1946, the articulation of the Truman Doctrine on 12 March 1947 – promising support for all regimes threatened by communism, originally designed to help Greece and Turkey since Great Britain could no longer afford the expense – the onset of the Marshall Plan in June 1947, are only some of the bricks which built the edifice of mutual hostility and recrimination known as the Cold War. Initially it cemented the division of Germany, the country at the heart of Soviet concern in Europe, and led to the creation of two German states, one facing east and the other west. Then followed the North Atlantic Treaty Organisation (NATO) and in 1955 the Warsaw Pact.

The accession of China to the world social camp, in October 1949, meant that the Soviets numerically only made up a minority of the world communist movement.

At the end of the war Stalin launched a number of major military research and development programmes (nuclear weapons, rockets, and jet engine technology for example) which were very expensive. This could be read as indicating that Stalin feared a conflict with the West in the not too distant future. About 9 million men were demobilised and according to Khrushchev the armed forces numbered 2.8 million in 1948. Then a build-up began because of the Berlin Blockade, the formation of NATO and the onset of the Korean war. Moreover the

USSR acquired her own atomic bomb in 1949. All this set in train a pattern which has continued to the present day: military spending should keep in step with economic growth and from time to time may increase its proportion of total investment. As of 1949 the Soviet Union could hardly have been defeated militarily on her own soil. For the first time the USSR could consider the option of adding a military dimension to her foreign policy.

By 1953 the USSR was stronger than ever before but arguably foreign policy between 1945 and 1953 was a failure since it had produced two hostile military camps and united the main capitalist powers in NATO. Only the West could win an arms race in the quarter century after 1949 and only the West could afford one. The Soviet Union needed desperately to restrict defence expenditure so as to build up her civilian economy and concentrate the best brains on the task of making the country bloom. A large army was an awful waste: the soldiers could have been more productively employed in industry and agriculture. Stalin set in motion the pattern which continued until the collapse of the USSR, of creaming off the most able scientists and engineers for the defence sector and giving the military first priority. The lop-sided development of the USSR, so evident today, was a natural consequence. Since the Soviet target was what the Americans had they worked very hard to catch up. In catching up they made the Americans nervous. They began to fear that their lead was disappearing so they spent more on defence which in turn forced the USSR to do the same. The Soviets thus became trapped in a vicious circle, with goals always being set by their opponents.

The centre of Soviet concern in Europe and a key factor in East–West relations during Stalin's last years was Germany. From the USSR's point of view the coming to power of governments which were well disposed towards her in eastern Europe would be nullified if a future German government turned hostile. Hence Soviet policy towards Germany was both positive and negative – positive in the sense of promoting socialism in all four occupation zones and negative in the sense of ensuring that capitalism, if it proved victorious in the three Western zones, did not penetrate the Soviet zone. No Great Power, with the possible exception of France, wanted the division of Germany. The Potsdam Conference (July–August 1945) agreed on demilitarisation, denazification and the democratisation of Germany. Since it was held that German industrial capacity was greater than a civilian economy required, dismantling and reparations were to be exacted so as to prune the capital stock to the required peacetime level. The Soviet Union asked for US$10,000 million (1938 prices).

East–West relations over Germany were reasonable in 1945, strained in 1946 and bad after 1947. Given this scenario the Soviet Union had to hang on to its occupation zone and this in turn required it to dominate Poland since the road to Berlin ran through Warsaw. In

Czechoslovakia the composition of the government had been agreed in Moscow in March 1945. The country was soon free of foreign troops but the Soviet Union could exert pressure through the Communist Party. That left the Balkans. Hungary and Romania were ex-enemy countries and Bulgaria was treated like one. Heavy reparation payments were imposed on them and the USSR dismantled large numbers of enterprises and equipment into the bargain, claiming that they were only taking ex-German property.[36] This was of considerable value to the Soviet Union but it also aided the local communist parties since it sapped any vitality the local capitalist economy might have possessed.

Exiled communists returned to their homelands clinging to the coat-tails of the Red Army. They were keen to set in motion their own national 1917 but Stalin restrained them. On the analogy of 1917 the east European states had to achieve first their February Revolution before they started thinking about their own October. This applied not only to countries with a Red Army presence but it extended to the other countries of Europe as well. Various reasons to explain this phenomenon suggest themselves. The economic weakness of the USSR meant that everything, including goods, which could be shipped back home was of great value. A rapid socialist revolution forced through by the local communists and the Soviet soldier would have halted the transfer of goods and equipment. The locals would have simply nationalised ex-German and local capitalist enterprises. A premature revolution would have placed the problems of hunger and reconstruction fairly and squarely on the shoulders of the local communists and Moscow could ill afford any aid. It would also have made the Communist Party and by extension Moscow the target of resentment. Since communists, in 1945, were not in control of all those with fire power, the army, the police and the partisans, a civil war might break out. Probably the key reason for holding back the indigenous communists was the desire not to cause the Western Powers offence. At Yalta Stalin had not given the impression that he expected socialist regimes in eastern Europe. The USSR needed reparations and time to consolidate her position. The policy of ripping off everything worth taking was counter-productive, however, since it increased local hostility which could then lead to an appeal to the West for support. It is possible that the Soviet Union only expected to be in Germany and eastern Europe a short time.

The Soviet zone of Germany set the pace. The refounded Communist Party of Germany (KPD) declared that its immediate goal was an anti-fascist democratic parliamentary republic. What 1848 had failed to do, 1945 would complete. It refused the offer of the Social Democratic Party of Germany (SPD) to set up a united party of the left. This lead was followed elsewhere. There were to be separate communist and socialist parties, no united working-class parties. This phase did not last long in the Soviet zone and Wilhelm Pieck launched the campaign to fuse the KPD and SPD in September 1945. This was achieved in April 1946 when the Socialist Unity Party of Germany (SED) came into being. A significant part of the SPD leadership opposed the fusion but probably a majority of the rank and file were in favour. This pattern was not followed immediately by the other countries: united working-class parties only came into being there in 1948. The German *démarche* revealed the nervousness of the Kremlin at the rising tide of support for the SPD in 1945. However, as of April 1946, the SED was the most powerful party in Germany and one which was loyal to Moscow. This alarmed the other occupying powers. They simply refused to permit an SED party in their zones, the only exception being West Berlin. The US was becoming increasingly aware that the Soviet zone was sliding towards communism. Unless the Western zones improved economically socialism would become more and more appealing as a way out of the existing misery. One policy adopted was to create Bizonia, fusing the US and British zones economically, in January 1947, but in doing so relations with the Soviet Union became more and more strained. The advent of the Marshall Plan in June 1947, which was to be extended to all war damaged countries in Europe, exacerbated the situation further. The currency reform of June 1948, without which the Western zones could not take off economically, sealed the division of Germany. The desperate, defensive Soviet reaction was to declare all access routes to Berlin closed, a direct challenge to US power. The Americans decided against calling Stalin's bluff, if they had he would surely have given way and instead started the air lift which kept the Western sectors of the city doing until the blockade was lifted in May 1949. Hence by 1948 the Cold War had reached such a pitch that a common language no longer existed between the US and the USSR. If the trend towards a separate west German state was slowly crystallising before the blockade of Berlin it was speeded up by the Soviet *démarche*. Soviet policy produced what it was trying to prevent, the formation of a west German state which would gradually become part of the Western world. The Berlin blockade was a particularly inept piece of diplomacy. It resulted from the Soviet Union allowing herself to be forced into a corner over Germany and then having to react to American initiatives so as to underline her Great Power status. The creation of two German states during 1949, the German Democratic Republic in the east and the Federal Republic of Germany in the west, followed as a matter of course. The German problem had not been solved, it had been shelved.

Could the USSR have arrested the division of Germany? She could have, had she been willing to accept a demilitarised, neutral Germany. The Americans pushed this solution in 1946 with the safeguard that the US and USSR could intervene if they agreed that Germany was becoming dangerous. The Soviet Union refused to leave her zone since she had a shrewd idea that a unified neutral Germany, under a market economy, would inevitably look westwards. Such a Germany would want the return of the territories east of the Oder–Neisse rivers and this could place Poland in a quandary. Khrushchev summed up Soviet thinking, in 1957, probably representing what Stalin would have said when he told a visiting French delegation that the reality of 17 million Germans living under socialism was preferable to 70 million unpredictable Germans in a neutral state.

The Soviet Union used her own zone as a sounding-board for Western reaction. Reform after reform, several indeed before the Potsdam Conference convened, including the refounding of political parties, were pushed through without consulting the Allies. Stalin wanted to see what the West would tolerate and hence he needed to keep the revolutionary ardour of the KPD and later of the SED under control. In 1947 the SED received the signal to become a 'party of a new type', a Marxist-Leninist party, and the road was also clear for socialism. If a reform was acceptable in the Soviet zone of Germany then it was acceptable in the countries of eastern Europe. Since the Americans were not going to use force to push through their policies in Germany they were not going to use force in eastern Europe. Stalin knew that the Soviet military presence there meant that the initiative was his.

The Soviets showed great diplomatic skill in dealing with the east European states. By mid 1947 a network of treaties, economic agreements on military aid, on the exchange of experts and the extension of technical aid had been signed. Besides this the national communist parties played an important role in state, economic and national life. Even had the various countries tried to break away from this pattern which was guiding them towards people's democracies they would have found it very difficult to do so.

The setting up of the Cominform, in 1947, and Zhdanov's division of the world into two hostile camps with some developing countries outside signalled the transfer of the hard internal line to the outside world. The French (PCF) and Italian (PCI) communist parties were violently attacked for not having achieved more since 1945. This was hard on them as Moscow had not favoured violent revolution after liberation and had done little to aid them in their struggle. The French had been in a very promising position in 1945, having spearheaded resistance during the German occupation. Many non-communists were changing sides and had a socialist Germany emerged, a socialist France would not have been far behind. Again Germany was the trend-setter: a socialist Germany would have meant a socialist Europe.

The Comintern strategy, establishing people's democracies, took two years, 1947–49, to achieve. The aim was to turn the local communist parties into carbon copies of the Soviet, to begin to build socialism, to introduce planning and to eliminate bourgeois parties and politics from national life. In February 1948 the last plum, Czechoslovakia, fell into communist hands. There were no Soviet troops in the country so the communists came to power by astute political manoeuvring, aided by inept social democratic tactics.

The Cominform drummed Tito out of the communist movement in June 1948. It was an admission of failure and ended the myth of the monolithic nature of the communist world. Tito, since he had not ridden to power on the backs of the Red Army, had set his own pace towards socialism. A people's republic was proclaimed in November 1945. In a flash of zeal Edvard Kardelj had declared on 5 June 1945 that the CP of Yugoslavia was now a part of the AUCP(B) and that Yugoslavia would later become a republic of the Soviet Union. Stalin did not agree but it gradually became clear that he could do little to hold the Yugoslavs in check. Tito's independent behaviour plus his discussions with Bulgaria on a Bulgarian–Yugoslav customs and currency union and his popularity, not least in Leningrad, led to the break. Stalin was convinced that Yugoslavia would collapse but instead she received considerable American aid.

The defection of Tito resulted in a quickening of the pace of sovietisation in eastern Europe. The hunt was on for the overt or covert supporters of the 'hangman of the Yugoslav people'. As in the Soviet Union in the mid 1930s many of those who fell victim made preposterous confessions. The only country in which show trials did not take place was the German Democratic Republic (GDR). They were on the agenda but never staged. Had Stalin lived longer even Ulbricht might have been forced to sacrifice a few old comrades. It is noticeable that many of the defendants in the Prague trial of 1952 were Jews and indeed in the GDR many of the top Jews in the SED lost their positions, but unlike Rudolf Slansky in Czechoslovakia kept hold of their lives.

The increasingly close political relationship between eastern Europe and the Soviet Union was given an economic dimension in January 1949 when the Council for Mutual Economic Assistance (CMEA or Comecon) was set up in Moscow. It was a belated response to the Marshall Plan but it did not really come to life until the mid 1950s. Meanwhile practically all trade was on a bilateral basis.

In an attempt to prevent the Federal Republic of Germany (FRG) joining the European Defence Community (EDC), the Soviets proposed the negotiation of a German peace treaty, in a note on 10 March 1952. A united, independent, democratic and peace-loving Germany was the declared goal. All occupying powers were to leave the country one year after the signing of the treaty, at the latest. The Western Powers replied on 25 March stating that an all-German government could only emerge from secret, free elections. The exchanges continued until August but the joining of the EDC by the FRG on 27 May 1952 made it almost impossible for the Western Powers to negotiate seriously on a unified, neutral Germany. One of the stumbling-blocks was the Soviet desire to unify the country first and then hold elections. In other words they wanted unification then integration, but the Western Allies wanted the reverse.

The Soviet initiative failed partly because of Western scepticism, partly because Konrad Adenauer, the FRG chancellor, opposed it and partly because Moscow was not flexible enough in its response to the Western notes. An interesting question is who was making foreign policy *vis-à-vis* Germany in March 1952 in the Kremlin? Certainly Stalin was losing his grip and this may mean that the initiative originated from someone else. One criticism of the way the Soviets handled the whole affair would be their failure to make additional concessions which might have enticed the Western Powers to rethink their German policy. If the original goal was to prevent the integration of th FRG in the Western defence network, the Soviet Union handled the affair very badly.

The civil war in China between the nationalist regime of Chiang Kai-shek and the communists under Mao Zedong gradually turned in favour of the communists. In 1947 their confidence was such that they dropped partisan tactics and engaged in full scale battles with the Kuomintang. Even so China appeared too vast for the communists to capture militarily: it was more likely that Mao would establish himself in the key eastern parts of the country and then slowly move westwards. However such was the disintegration of the Kuomintang, linked to increasing American reluctance to help, that in the summer of 1948 the possibility arose of China becoming a people's republic in the not too distant future. The Soviets did very little to promote Mao's chances, they were embroiled in a confrontation with the US in Germany at that time.

The People's Republic of China was proclaimed on 1 October 1949 and another state came into being in which local communists had come to power largely due to their own efforts. Stalin's reaction was less than enthusiastic and when Mao came to Moscow in December he found the Soviets tough negotiators. Mao, heartened by the Yugoslav example, knew that the Soviet Union was not all-powerful and proposed that the USSR should abandon her special position in Manchuria. The Sino-Soviet treaty of 14 February 1950 enhanced the position of China. The USSR gave up the special concession which Chiang Kai-shek had made in the years after 1945. If Mao was happy with his diplomatic success he must have been very unhappy about the economic terms he had to accept. Instead of the enormous aid he needed, China was extended a US$300 million loan over five years at one per cent interest. He also had to countenance mixed companies as a way of attracting Soviet technical expertise. Mao asked for the atomic bomb and Stalin said no. Mao had also to acknowledge the independence of Outer Mongolia. Stalin did, however, give the Chinese a parting gift, his man in the Chinese Politburo, Kao Kang. Kao was immediately marched out and shot. (Was Kao really a Soviet agent or was Stalin fingering someone he wanted liquidated?) Stalin was prepared for some Chinese ill-will but he needed to bind the Communist Party of China (CPC) very closely to the CPSU if Moscow was to retain its hegemony in the world communist movement. Economic development was the key to control. Stalin wished to limit the CPC's capacity to act independently in Asia.

Among other foreign visitors to Moscow was Ho Chi Minh, the Vietnamese leader. Ho was very deferential, but Stalin treated him with scant respect. He annoyed the *vozhd* by asking for his autograph. He gave it to him but instructed the MGB to extract it from Ho's luggage before it left Moscow. Presumably Stalin was concerned about what Ho might write above his signature.

The outbreak of the Korean War on 25 June 1950 offered the US her first opportunity since the outbreak of the Cold War of militarily stemming the advance of communism. It was presumed at the time that the war had been instigated by Moscow to test Western resolve, but the moving spirit was North Korea. Kim Il Sung travelled to Moscow to confer with Stalin. He gave his assent but made it clear that the Soviet Union would not be drawn into the conflict. China was kept in the dark about the impending attack.

The matter was taken to the UN, and the Security Council decided to send a UN force to resist the North Korean attack. Hence the US-led force fought under the UN flag. The Soviet Union did not use its veto because it had been boycotting the UN ever since January 1950, arguing that the People's Republic of China should occupy the seat assigned to China. Moscow deliberately abstained in the Korean affair since Stalin did not desire a confrontation with the United States.

Besides intervening in Korea the US also decided to defend Taiwan against attack by the People's Republic. China entered the Korean War in November 1950, withdrew, but then came in again when the Americans continued their advance. By early 1951 the two sides were back to the old pre-1950 frontier. Fighting continued for another two years until an armistice was signed after Stalin's death acknowledging the *status quo ante*.

The Korean War and the American decision to side with Chiang Kai-shek produced the bitter hostility between China and the US which was to last a generation. The US attitude towards communism in Asia hardened during the war and the momentous decision to intervene in Indo-China and elsewhere if necessary was almost automatic.

Looking back it is clear that the Soviet Union's primary goal in foreign policy was security and this involved penetrating countries on the periphery. This was not a new departure on the part of Stalin but was part and parcel of a traditional Russian concern with the open frontier. Peter the Great expanded into northern

Persia (hence Stalin was just repeating a move previously tried and found wanting). Catherine the Great acquired the Crimea; during the nineteenth century Russia took over Central Asia, was rebuffed in the Balkans and needlessly went to war with Japan over control of Korea in 1940–5. Stalin did not trust to the goodwill of his neighbours and sought control. What did he understand by control? Simply the same level of control as in the USSR. As a Bolshevik Stalin had minimum and maximum goals. The latter represented complete control. He preferred to deal with four types of person when seeking to achieve his minimum goal: compromised bourgeois leaders and politicians; careerist minded non-proletarians; idealistic communists; and official communist party members. Idealistic communists were recruited to provide an additional source of information and they were flattered by being told that since their first loyalty was to socialism, represented by the USSR, they should report only to the Soviets since if they relayed their information to the local communist party there was a possibility that an enemy of socialism in the apparatus could suppress it.

Stalin's views on democracy and on non-Russian communists were coloured by his experience in the Soviet Union during the 1920s. He had a low opinion of pluralistic democracy as a result of his years on the Politburo before 1929. The Politburo was the only body in the USSR which actually practised democracy up to 1929. Stalin thought that democracy merely meant that intellectuals could form factions to sabotage party decisions with which they disagreed. Stalin thought that if the party had an agreed goal one point of view should prevail. As Commissar for Nationalities he had an intimate knowledge of the thinking of non-Russian communists and this had led him to liquidate national communists in the USSR during the 1930s. Hence the propagation of different roads to socialism – there were Polish, German, Czechoslovak and Hungarian roads to socialism – was only tactical but very few communists realised this at the time. There was only one socialism as far as Stalin was concerned. He did not favour autonomous Marxist-Leninist states since they would inevitably have become national communist states.

Soviet preference after liberation or defeat of the enemy was to have weak bourgeois governments. During secret negotiations with the Badoglio government in Italy in February 1944 Moscow revealed its liking for such an unpopular administration since it would attempt to act as the intermediary between the government and popular demand – articulated by the Italian Communist Party. Palmiro Togliatti prepared to leave for his homeland to head the PCI at this time. In Germany the Soviets attempted to reach an agreement with the Dönitz government but failed.

Even before VE Day the Soviets had garnered much experience in Allied Control Commissions: in Italy, Romania and Bulgaria. To all intents and purposes Romania and Bulgaria were communist states on

8 May 1945. The percentages agreement placed Romania, Bulgaria and Hungary within the Soviet zone of influence, Greece in the British and Yugoslavia fifty–fifty. Any help the Greek communists received during the Second Round of the Civil War (December 1944) was channelled through Yugoslavia and Albania. In 1946 during the Third Round a zone on the Bulgarian side of the border with Greece was established to provide refuge and training facilities for Greek communists. Moscow never physically intervened in Greece and this is what gratified Churchill.

The Soviets skilfully used the precedent of Italy where the British and Americans had negotiated surrender but in the name of all three powers. Great Britain and the US took the lead in Italy and kept the Soviet representative informed. The USSR did the same in Romania and Bulgaria. After the suppression of the Greek communists during the Second Round by the British the Soviets could plausibly argue that their activities in Romania and Bulgaria were geared towards keeping those countries safe for democracy. It is worth noting that the British Mission in Bucharest does not appear to have been aware of the percentages agreement, at least not until the end of the war.

As a former Commissar of Nationalities Stalin was acutely aware of the political potential of national antagonisms. Transylvania could be offered to Romania; the Hungarian minority could be expelled from Slovakia; the Sudetenland could be returned to Czechoslovakia and the Germans expelled; Poland could acquire Upper and Lower Silesia, Pomerania and part of East Prussia, again at the expense of the German population; Yugoslavia and Bulgaria both claimed Macedonia. Then there was land to be distributed. The large estates could be parcelled up; the Poles could take over German land; the Sudetenland was also in need of settlers; the Agrarian Party was banned in Czechoslovakia thus permitting the Communist Party to play a key role in agrarian change and to distribute land among its supporters. All the states needed an ally among the Great Powers in order to hang on to their gains or to seek redress. The Soviet Union could play this role. Moscow as not above exploiting national discord. Slovaks were incited against Hungarians and vice versa between 1945 and 1948. Prearranged roles were played by the respective communist parties.

There was considerable goodwill towards the Red Army and the Soviet Union in such countries as Yugoslavia and Czechoslovakia in 1945. There was widespread support for fundamental social changes in the region. People yearned for a new start, a more just distribution of wealth, general access to education and culture and an end to the German threat. The communists were determined to be the party which would bring all this about. However, Stalin was not content with the national communist parties achieving these goals in their own indigenous ways. Many communists became disillusioned after 1947 and it was only in Yugoslavia that the national communist solution won the day. The Yugoslavs were deeply offended by the tactics adopted by Moscow. This included successfully blackmailing a member of the Politburo of the CP of Yugoslavia. The most skilled Soviet personnel were sent to Germany. On the whole they acted throughout the region as they would have done in the USSR. Given the radically different political traditions of eastern and south-eastern Europe this caused considerable offence.

Sloppy diplomacy led to unnecessary misunderstandings between East and West. Had Winston Churchill and Anthony Eden negotiated with more finesse during the war the Soviets would have had a much clearer picture of what their allies were willing to countenance after the war. The advent of Ernest Bevin as British Secretary in 1945 added some steel to British diplomacy. As a social democrat and trade-union leader he had had long experience of negotiating with communists.

Lack of Soviet diplomatic skill when dealing with stronger nations was another reason for the outbreak of the Cold War. Molotov's shopping list in November 1940 is the classic example. The Berlin Blockade is another. It hastened the formation of NATO and divided Europe into two hostile blocs.

Another reason for the Cold War was that in 1945 everyone saw Germany as the main threat. By 1947 it was clear that this judgment was quite false. From containment of Germany the Western Allies switched to containment of the USSR. Beneš also misread the situation. He had based his policy on the need to have the Soviet Union as an ally against Germany after the war. By the time he had realised his mistake it was too late.

NOTES

1. *Pravda* 20 March 1946; William O. McCagg Jr *Stalin Embattled 1943–48* p. 206.
2. I. V. Stalin *Sochineniya* vol. 3 (XVI) 1946–1953 pp. 6–7. Italics in the original.
3. Ibid. p. 20. Actual production in 1960 was: iron, 46.8 million tonnes; steel 65.3 million tonnes; coal, 444.3 million tonnes; oil, 147.9 million tonnes, *Narodnoe Khozyaistvo SSSR v 1961 gody* (Moscow 1962) pp. 196, 205, 209. Astonishingly Stalin underestimated the capacity of some sectors of the economy to expand!
4. T. H. Rigby *Communist Party Membership in the USSR 1917–1967* p. 276.
5. Ibid. p. 281.
6. Ibid. p. 290.
7. *Pravda* 25 May 1945.
8. R. Conquest *Power and Policy in the USSR* pp. 129–53.
9. *Pravda* 13 October 1952.
10. Ibid.

11. Stalin died at his dacha at Kuntsevo, just outside Moscow. According to his daughter Svetlana, who is convinced that his death was natural, he was found on the floor next to where he slept at 3 a.m. on 2 March. He was not moved to hospital but instead specialists were called. Stalin's end was sad and lonely and it was almost certainly natural. His personal physician, Professor Vinogradov, was not at the dacha when Stalin was struck down. The eminent doctor was in the Lubyanka in chains and was beaten from time to time on Stalin's personal orders. There were many however who had reason to help Stalin on his way to the next world. He lived surrounded by security police and Beria was increasingly under pressure at that time. Molotov and Mikoyan had reason to fear demotion or even death. The 'doctors' plot' showed that any evidence could be forged so no one was safe. At the top it was plot and counterplot and Beria certainly came out of it all very well. He earned Svetlana's undying hatred by failing to hide the fact that he was extremely pleased at the dictator's death. Svetlana Alliluyeva *20 Letters to a Friend* pp. 14–16.
12. Leonid I. Brezhnev *Tselina* p. 31.
13. N. Voznesensky *War Economy of the USSR in the Period of the Patriotic War* pp. 128–9. He puts the cost of the damage at 679,000 million rubles or US$128,000 million. This amounted to two thirds of the pre-war national wealth of the occupied territories. Ibid. p. 129.
14. Alec Nove *An Economic History of the USSR* p. 291. Producers' goods were put at 205 (1940 = 100) and consumers' goods at 123.
15. Ibid. p. 293.
16. *Partiinaya Zhizn* no 4, 1947, pp. 50–76; *Pravda* 18 September 1947; McCagg, op. cit. p. 246.
17. *Narodnoe Khozyaistvo SSSR v 1964 g.* (Moscow 1965) p. 295.
18. Karl-Eugen Wädekin *Privatproduzenten in der sowjetischen Landwirt-schaft* p. 19. In 1950, 73 per cent of potatoes, 44 per cent of vegetables, 67 per cent of meat, 75 per cent of milk and 89 per cent of eggs were produced on the private plot. Ibid. p. 24.
19. *Izvestiya* 24 October 1948.
20. Nove, op. cit. p. 309.
21. Ibid. p. 308.
22. Ibid. p. 299.
23. Ibid. p. 302. Khrushchev put the amount paid kolkhozniks in 1952 for social work on the kolkhoz at 12,400 million rubles or about 620 (old) rubles each (*Pravda* 25 January 1958). This is equivalent to about £45 sterling in 1979 prices.
24. *Bolshevik* no 15, 1946, pp. 11–14.
25. A. A. Zhdanov *On Literature, Music and Philosophy* pp. 19–51.
26. *Bolshevik* no 16, 1946, pp. 45–9.
27. Ibid. pp. 50–3.
28. *Bolshevik* no 13, 1947, pp. 20–35.
29. *Bolshevik* no 16, 1947, pp. 7–23.
30. *Bolshevik* no 3, 1948, pp. 10–14.
31. This is based on Vera S. Dunham *In Stalin's Time: Middle Class Values in Soviet Fiction.*
32. Robert Conquest (ed.) *Religion in the USSR* p. 38.
33. Ibid.

34. Ibid. p. 74.
35. The only exception to this took place in Iran, in March 1946, when the Soviet Union declared that she would withdraw her forces, and did so quickly, having previously given the impression that they were there to stay. The retreat occurred shortly after Churchill's famous speech at Fulton, Missouri. The Soviet Union also adopted a belligerent attitude towards Turkey in an attempt to secure territorial adjustments. The result was the Truman Doctrine which accorded Turkey the support she needed to withstand Soviet pressure. Turkey joined NATO in 1952. Stalin must have found it difficult to pick the country on which to apply pressure and to gauge Western reaction to his moves. In 1945 he got almost everything he wanted but in 1946 it was quite a different story.
36. Romania was especially severely treated. Between 23 August and 12 September 1944 equipment, cars, railway rolling stock, etc. to the value of US$2,000 million were seized by the Soviet Union. The Romanians also had to deliver 300 million gold dollars' worth of industrial and agricultural output. Reparation payments accounted for 37.5 per cent of the Romanian budget in 1946–47 and 46.6 per cent in 1947.

    Hungary's reparations amounted to 200 million gold dollars to the USSR, 70 million to Czechoslovakia and 30 million to Yugoslavia. This came to 26.4 per cent of expenditure in the 1946–47 Hungarian budget. Bulgaria had to pay 50 million gold dollars to Greece and 25 million to Yugoslavia (Jörg K. Hoensch *Sowjetische Osteuropa–Politik 1945–1975* pp. 16–19).

    On German reparations, which may have reached US$17,100 million (current prices) between 1945 and 1953, see Martin McCauley *Marxism-Leninism in the German Democratic Republic: The Socialist Unity Party (SED)* pp. 69–74, 80–1. Another profitable line for the Soviets were the mixed companies in east European countries, including Yugoslavia. The output was regarded as Soviet and the monopoly position of many of the enterprises in their respective countries was put to full advantage. Mixed companies were later sold back to the respective governments.

The Khrushchev Era

'THIS GENERATION WILL LIVE UNDER COMMUNISM'

INTERNAL POLITICS

Like Stalin in the early 1920s, Khrushchev was not seen as the eventual leader in 1953 and 1954. However, like Stalin he climbed to power on the back of the party and proved himself a master of political infighting. In the early years his political opponents underestimated him and again in 1957 but he in turn, as if he had learnt nothing from his victories, was to underestimate the force of opposition in 1964. A dedicated Stalinist in the 1930s, and this meant spilling blood, he ascended to the CC in 1934 but the war changed him. He mellowed and a genuine concern about the human cost of the modernisation of the Soviet Union developed in him. Khrushchev had his ups and downs in the Ukraine and Moscow during Stalin's last years but he was not under a cloud, unlike Beria, Molotov, Mikoyan and others when Stalin died.

There were two realms in which Khrushchev was convinced that he was first class: party work and agriculture. Although Prime Minister of the Ukraine and after 1958 Prime Minister of the USSR he was not really an administrator. His forte was the spoken word and his ability to communicate with others. Since he eschewed mass terror as a motivator he exhorted, cajoled and tried to persuade orally. He was dynamic and innovative and wished to make others the same. He was fortunate in that neither of his two main competitors for supreme office was in the party secretariat after 14 March 1953. Again neither was an agricultural specialist nor keen to become involved in the rural sector, an Irish bog for aspiring politicians, in 1953.

Such was the nervousness of the party and of Malenkov, the USSR Prime Minister, about the ambitions of Beria, head of the Ministry of Internal Affairs and of the security police, that a tactical union led to the arrest of Beria in June 1953. Now the way was clear for a straight contest between Malenkov, head of the government, and Khrushchev, head of the party, as of September 1953.

The dispute produced the first open policy debates in the Soviet Union since the 1920s. The subject-matter was economic. Two recipes for raising living standards were on offer. Malenkov's New Course favoured less emphasis on heavy industry to the advantage of light industry. More food would come through the mechanisation of agriculture and the use of chemical fertilisers. Khrushchev countered by arguing that the way to raise living standards was to start with the basic essential, food. Agricultural output could be rapidly expanded by increasing the area cultivated, there was plenty of virgin and idle land in Siberia, Kazakhstan, the Volga and so on. The capital expended would be recouped in two to three years, Khrushchev's favourite time span, through increased output. Grain production, in turn, would provide more fodder for animals, thus increasing the amount of meat and milk products available. Also the increased cattle population would expand the number of hides going to industry so more shoes and leather goods would flow from the factories. More cotton, sugar beet and so on would allow the light and food industries to meet the demands of the consumer. The primacy of heavy industry, and with it defence, could be left intact. It all sounded so simple, if only the weather, the soil and the peasants would co-operate. The weather was kind to Khrushchev in 1953, the harvest was poor and Malenkov was blamed.

The turning-point came in the summer of 1954 when it became obvious that the 1954 harvest, especially in the virgin lands, was going to be a record. Malenkov resigned in February 1955 as USSR Prime Minister and Marshal Bulganin, a political Marshal, took his place. It soon transpired that Bulganin was nothing more than a velvety-voiced, more grammatically correct, version of the First Secretary.

One of the hallmarks of a good politician is his ability to assimilate the best ideas of his opponents, especially defeated opponents. Khrushchev was to prove himself a past master at this art and he stripped Malenkov bare. He continued Malenkov's policy of seeking better relations with the outside. This went hand in hand with an internal policy which aimed at raising living standards in the short rather than the long term. Khrushchev needed time to get his hand in but the first-fruits, the Austrian peace treaty and a reconciliation with Tito, fell quickly into his lap. Khrushchev's ignorance of foreign affairs was a direct result of Stalin's technique of government. As he remarked later, if you were not told you presumed that you were not supposed to know. Under no circumstances did you ask. Since Khrushchev's province was the number of cows in the country the intricacies of the Berlin situation or the state of Sino-Soviet relations were mysteries to him.

Khrushchev was very ambitious and was probably as vain as Stalin. He wanted to carve himself a niche in history and to go down as a benefactor. He harboured a genuine desire to better the lot of the average Soviet citizen. As someone who had never had his mind deformed by education Khrushchev looked askance at the dominance of the intelligentsia. As a former Prime Minister of the Ukraine he had had close contact with the governmental bureaucracy and had a shrewd idea of the mentality of the average ministry man. One thing was clear, he did not like what he saw.

In the realm of administration Khrushchev suffered from what may be called the *Iskra* complex reminiscent of Lenin's early revolutionary organisation in the first years of the century. Find the right administrative set-up and everything will be fine; this to Khrushchev meant that the economic growth of the country would be faster than before. Theory to him was only of value if it made two blades grow where only one had grown before. Since his view of administration was simplistic, he usually left out the human factor, and he found he needed a reform to put right the defects of the previous reform. He gradually became addicted to reform.

He had, however, much to reform. He wanted to break the Stalinist mould, the conservative, non-decision-making attitude of bureaucrats, managers and labour alike. The wherewithal was there for rapid growth, the only trouble was finding the key which would unlock the true potential of the population. The Stalinist system had given great power to the ruling group which included government and party officials, managers and those with technical skills. Stalinism was efficient from the point of view of ruling the country but was economically and administratively inefficient. During Stalin's last years middle-level officials in ministries had elaborated proposals, often by involving specialists in consultations, as a means of putting pressure on the men at the top. This generation of officials, after 1953, expected promotion and a strengthening of the administrative machine which they were adept at manipulating. Khrushchev did not share their confidence in the efficacy of the existing ministerial machinery. He knew that the dominance of Moscow and the fact that every important decision had to be taken there stultified local initiative. Indeed such were the penalties, under Stalin, for local initiatives which went wrong that very few were willing to take the risk. Stagnation and inertia had descended and Khrushchev was aware of this. The idea struck him that if decision-making were located nearer the centre of operations, the economy might become more efficient. He wanted to move the ministries out of Moscow and set up local economic councils. Such an innovation was bound to face enormous opposition. Before launching it he took what was probably the most far-reaching decision he ever made: he toppled Stalin from his omniscient perch.

The telling speech was made at a closed session of the XXth Party Congress in February 1956. Khrushchev, speaking in the name of the party, laid bare some of Stalin's crimes. Just as Stalin had taken Lenin as his model and then risen above him, so Khrushchev followed Stalin until he decided he could do without the old monster. The motives behind the move are very complex since Khrushchev wanted to be a Stalin himself. However, he wanted to be an enlightened, civilised, democratic, lovable version of the former dictator. Mass terror as an instrument of power was to be dropped and the political police cut down to size. Khrushchev was as dictatorial as the next man, politicians usually take after their mentors, but genuinely wanted to break the Stalinist mould and produce a richer, happier Soviet Union. Whereas Stalin was quite happy if foreigners feared him, Khrushchev wanted the world to love the USSR.

So he set in motion reform after reform. With the father of the previous system gone it was now easier to innovate. Education (here Khrushchev was especially keen to prevent the intelligentsia becoming a self-perpetuating elite), industry, agriculture, military thinking, foreign policy, literature and the other arts all felt the wind of change. Reforms were a convenient way of removing Stalinists and replacing them with keen, energetic Khrushchev men. He revivified existing institutions, encouraged change, but when all is said and done he did not fundamentally alter Soviet institutions.

Khrushchev soon discovered that it was one thing to promulgate a law and quite another to have it carried out. His assault on the ministries quickly backfired. They proved redoubtable opponents, they could no longer be ordered to do something they disagreed with. The crisis reached a head in June 1957 when the so-called Anti-Party Group, consisting of Malenkov, Molotov, Kaganovich and Shepilov was defeated in deft manoeuvring in the CC. The government bureaucracy was against Khrushchev but he outflanked it in the upper councils of the party.

After 1958, when he pushed Bulganin aside and added the post of Prime Minister to his list, he did not think it worth the trouble of becoming President, the Presidium restraints of the previous years were gone. Khrushchev's imagination was given full scope at home and abroad. The great model, the US, was in economic difficulties during the late 1950s and this led Khrushchev, buoyed up by good harvests and industrial results at home, to launch the Soviet ship of state into communist waters. The *per capita* production of meat and milk products was to be stepped up and everyone could look forward to the advent of communism around 1981. Communism meant almost entirely food and consumer goods. The material again was the master.

Soviet agricultural and industrial growth slowed and the US spurted ahead, such was the reality of the early 1960s. The First Secretary's solution was by now predictable: reform after reform. Even the party was not immune to his scythe. It was split into industrial and non-industrial wings. The object was to force the local official to concentrate on one particular sector of the economy, a testimony to the disappointing level of industrial and agricultural activity. In trying to outwit the new US President, John F. Kennedy, the USSR placed medium-range rockets on Cuba, thus nullifying the intercontinental ballistic missile lead of the US. In the ensuing confrontation Khrushchev took some decisions on his own without consulting the military but he lost. Then there were the terrible Chinese, he was losing the war of words with them as well. Perplexed at home he took to foreign travel and left his opponents, legion in 1964, all the time in the world to prepare a coup. He was convinced that he was unassailable but he discovered that after all he was a mere mortal. The Presidium replaced him as First Secretary of the party with Leonid Brezhnev and as Prime Minister with Aleksei Kosygin in October 1964.

Khrushchev's leadership style was unique: whereas Stalin had kept to the Kremlin or his dacha and observed the world from there Khrushchev went out to discover the world at first hand. He and his court, which often included T. D. Lysenko, the agrobiologist, and A. V. Shevchenko, an expert who shared his mentor's craze for maize and a man of phenomenal memory who provided Khrushchev with much valuable *ad lib* material, peregrinated around the Soviet Union, often to the discomfiture of local officials, farmers and managers.

Khrushchev was very quick witted and preferred to hear an argument. Hence someone who wanted to influence him had to meet him. He listened attentively to what was being said and then if he liked the ideas would assimilate them and later reproduce them as his own. His penchant for the spoken word meant that he was not given to much reading. Here is a clue to the ineffectiveness of many of his innovations. Had he sat down and read the small print of the new decrees he would have been forced to rethink his ideas. Many of the decrees were so complex that they must have been put together by a committee or failing that by someone who was not clear in his own mind what the desired goal was. No wonder party officials were pulling out their hair after 1958; lines of competence were vaguely drawn, if at all. Khrushchev as a man brimming with ideas expressed them orally but never worked them out on paper. His personal style of leadership was acceptable in an underdeveloped country but the Soviet Union of his day had outgrown him. The power of the ministries, the party *apparat* and the managers was such that new departures could only be implemented if almost everyone was in agreement. Not even the KGB can force through economic reforms and he had expressly given up terror as an instrument of rule. The Khrushchev era saw the coming of age of the ruling class and it proved itself capable of containing an obstreperous First Secretary. If Stalin was a calculating ruler, Khrushchev led by inspiration and flashes of intuition. Stalin was a master committee man, so much so that he dispensed with committees. Khrushchev proved a poor committee man, he lacked the patience. Since the skilled committee men removed him his successor had to be one of them. They in turn, having suffered under Stalin and often been ignored by Khrushchev were in no mood to permit the emergence of a Stalin or a Khrushchev. The end of Khrushchev was the end of an era. He had sought commendably to remove fear as a driving force in Soviet administration but this in turn meant that his opponents became more daring and by 1964, apart from Adzhubei, his son-in-law and editor of *Izvestiya*, there was probably no one who had a good word to say about him. He was out of touch with the times. The Soviet Union had become too complex to be headed by such a pre-industrial figure.

1953–55

Many Russians love to remember suffering; they had ample opportunity during the four days of official mourning for Joseph Vissarionovich Stalin. Others were disturbed by what the future might have in store for them, with the leader gone who was going to do the thinking? A few had been doing some thinking while Stalin lay dying and on 7 March 1953 the first post-Stalin division of power became known. The major benefactors were Lavrenty Beria, out of favour at the end of Stalin's life, who became First Deputy Chairman of the USSR Council of Ministers and head of the amalgamated Ministry of State Security and Ministry of Internal Affairs; G. M. Malenkov who became Prime Minister, and V. M. Molotov who became another First Deputy Chairman. Many ministerial changes were made as the new broom swept clean. Molotov recovered foreign affairs, Bulganin defence and Mikoyan trade. The government, since Stalin had been Prime Minister at his death, was held at the time to be the key institution. There were two other pillars on which Stalin had built his power, the party and the security police.

No head of the party was named since the CC secretaries had managed to have the post of secretary general of the CC abolished in 1952. Stalin, after all, had been signing himself secretary of the CC for some time. This move prevented Malenkov from nominating himself secretary general and hence head of the party.

The Presidium reverted to its pre-October 1952 size and the order of precedence of the top five was: Malenkov, Beria, Molotov, Voroshilov and Khrushchev. Nikita Sergeevich was transferred from his post as head of the Moscow party organisation to work in the secretariat.

With Beria now in control of the civilian police as well as the security organs he was one of the three key figures. Malenkov, Molotov and Beria formed the collective leadership of the country; they would 'prevent any kind of disorder or panic'.[1] As Prime Minister, Malenkov had the right to chair meetings of the Presidium following the practice set by Stalin. The Presidium agreed that Malenkov and Khrushchev should be responsible for setting the agenda of its meetings. Khrushchev was to help Malenkov guide the Presidium through its business. Malenkov and Beria took to inviting Khrushchev to discuss policy options during strolls in the Kremlin. Beria made no secret of his low opinion of Malenkov to Khrushchev. On 10 March 1953 a falsified photograph of Malenkov appeared in *Pravda*, greatly enhancing the role he had played while Mao Zedong had been in Moscow in 1950. Malenkov's reaction was to propose to the Presidium that the cult of the personality be discontinued. Khrushchev was given the task of overseeing all material relating to the reputation of Stalin.

This cosy collective only held together one week. On 14 March Malenkov abandoned his position in the secretariat while remaining Prime Minister.[2] It is still unclear whether he was given a choice of concentrating his energies in the government or the party. What is clear is that the post-Stalin leadership quickly agreed that the same person should not hold both offices. If Malenkov did choose then he made a mistake, even though he was following in the footsteps of Lenin and Stalin. More than likely he was not afforded the luxury of choice but informed by the Presidium that his role as Prime Minister excluded him from the secretariat. A moving force behind this manoeuvre may have been Khrushchev who thereby became the leading secretary in the CC, his name was placed at the top of the list of five secretaries, even though he was not formally nominated First Secretary until September 1953.

The new arrangement lasted until 26 June when Beria was arrested, although this was not made known officially until 10 July.

In dying Stalin took some people with him. At his elaborate state funeral on 9 March such was the crush in the approaches to Red Square that many mourners succumbed while others were injured. Lenin's chief disciple was placed beside the first Bolshevik leader in what was now known as the Lenin-Stalin mausoleum on Red Square. The two Soviet leaders fitted well together, both were short, modestly built men. The following day *Pravda* published a photograph of Stalin, Mao Zedong and Malenkov hinting that Malenkov was the natural successor. The photograph, however, was not genuine. Taken at the official signing of the Sino-Soviet pact in 1950 it had originally included several other leading figures. This may have provided some of the impetus behind the move to ease the new Prime Minister out of the secretariat.

An amnesty on 27 March freed many prisoners in labour camps and permitted exiles to return to the city of their choice. As regards others, Beria had proposed in the Presidium that all those who had completed their sentences and exile should seek the permission of the MVD to return and that the MVD should decide where they were to live. This did not go down very well and was rejected. Molotov got his wife back, Mikoyan his son, and so on. Lyubov Khrushcheva, the widow of Leonid, Khrushchev's son, also returned. He had died in aerial combat near Voronezh in 1943. He was never found as his plane had disappeared into a bog. Lyubov was arrested and condemned as a Swedish spy. There was also a promise to dismantle the worst excesses of the Stalinist legal system. Socialist legality was to be the fashionable phrase to describe this process. All this produced a spirit of optimism among the Soviet population. The amnesty only affected the elite, their families and friends. About 1,000 had returned to civilian life by the end of 1953. The new mood was given impetus by the expectation, aroused by the leadership, that living standards would rise. The New Course was to concentrate more investment in light industry, thus deflecting some from heavy industry and defence and provide more mechanisation in agriculture. To make this possible peaceful co-existence with the capitalist world was to be pursued and Malenkov held out the hand of friendship conceding that in an atomic war both sides would be wiped out.

If Malenkov was active so was Beria. The latter set about refurbishing the image of the security forces and spoke of socialist legality being respected. He struck the right note with the nationalities by advocating that nationals should occupy leading positions in their area. He may even have suggested that the kolkhoznik's private plot be extended. Nevertheless the memory of his and his predecessors' role under Stalin was ever present in the minds of government and party functionaries. They could not feel secure until the security forces were again firmly under party control. The riots and disorders in east Germany, culminating in the events of 17 June 1953, adversely affected his position. He was the minister responsible, in the last regard, for security in the GDR. The fact that his subordinate, Wilhelm Zaisser, the Minister of State Security, had together with Rudolf Herrnstadt attempted to topple the incumbent First Secretary, Walter Ulbricht, and failed, had repercussions in Moscow. Beria was even said to favour a unified, neutral Germany. He was arrested on 26 June 1953, questioned and put on trial between 16 and 23 December 1953. (The material runs to some forty volumes.) There was a lot of dirty linen to be washed and Beria was keen to get on with the job. His testimony reveals that he claimed to have regretted his malodorous behaviour. The police chief was known as Stalin's procurer and he was wont to pick a few beauties for himself. He had a particular passion for redheads and liked to frolic in black bedsheets. The list of outraged mothers wishing him ill was legion. Among his confessions were details of his sexual perversions. He described how he had personally interrogated many prisoners, delighting in inflicting pain. He was accused of 'sowing the seeds of discord among the nationalities', slowing down the solution of all urgent agricultural problems, of doing his best to disrupt the kolkhozes and create difficulties in the provisioning of the country and of being a British agent since 1919. Beria, a 'careerist, adventurer and Bonapartist' was found guilty and immediately executed. Facing death, he revealed himself a coward and begged for mercy. A rag had to be pushed into his mouth to prevent him spilling any more embarrassing political beans.

Beria did Khrushchev a service by pouring mud on all his associates, including Malenkov. Light was thrown on the murky Leningrad Affair and this was used against Georgy Maksimilianovich later.

The CC plenum which met on 2–7 July 1953 to condemn Beria discussed many other matters. During it the first concerted attack on Stalin since his death was made, albeit tame compared with the exposé of 1956. It was restricted to the post-1945 period and lamented the dictator's inability to work with his subordinates due to his increasing paranoia. Interestingly enough the decree passed at the plenum was never published. Its contents were communicated orally to party officials and foreign communists.

Beria's fall brought others down with him. About six accomplices were shot with him as well as some eighteen security officers during the next three years. As late as 1956 Bagirov and some others were executed. Khrushchev and the party vented their anger on Beria and his subordinates and took their revenge. As far as is known the 1956 executions are the only political killings to have occurred since Stalin's death. The party was willing to shed the blood of policemen but not its own blood.

Until the XXth Party Congress Beria served as a convenient scapegoat for all the crimes of the late Stalin era. The security organs lost some of their impact and in 1954 the Ministry of Internal Affairs was again split from the Committee of State Security (KGB). It was to be responsible for state security at home and abroad and to continue to guard all state and party personnel. However, a subtle change was engineered. Henceforth, instead of taking orders from the head of the security forces, guards were to obey the instructions of those they were looking after. Khrushchev managed to influence the selection of the first head of the KGB, General Ivan Serov. He had known him from his days in the Ukraine where Serov had been Minister of Internal Affairs. Although Nikita Sergeevich trusted him, he had an unsavoury reputation. When he arrived in London ahead of Khrushchev and Bulganin in 1956, the popular press savaged him and he had to be recalled. Khrushchev did not know Kruglov, the Minister of Internal Affairs (MVD). Revealingly, this meant that Nikita Sergeevich did not trust him.

Government ministries were streamlined immediately after Stalin's death, their number falling from fifty-five to twenty-five. Until August 1954 the government took precedence in all government and party decrees. Malenkov was therefore the front runner and Khrushchev had to hold up the party apparatus as a credible alternative. Here again, as in Stalin's early days, there were many aspiring party officials keen to make a career for themselves. It was up to Khrushchev to harness this enormous potential.

In order to restrict Khrushchev's position in the secretariat Malenkov took to referring to himself as 'acting chairman' of the Presidium of the CC (although this never appeared in the press).[3] One of the reasons for appointing Khrushchev First Secretary of the CC in September 1953 was that the Presidium did not believe that he had the ability to outmanoeuvre Malenkov. The latter set up large departments in the

USSR Council of Ministers which were to assume the duties of their counterparts in the CC secretariat.

The Malenkov-Khrushchev confrontation took place mainly on the economic plane. Malenkov, at the Vth session of the USSR Supreme Soviet in August 1953, launched his economic policy. He assured everyone that the country was being provided with sufficient grain, he had said the same at the XIXth Party Congress in October 1952. He proposed the abolition of the system whereby grain production was assessed according to the biological yield. This overstated output by about a third. The peasant was informed that taxes would be cut, his compulsory deliveries reduced and his tax arrears cancelled. Mechanisation and electrification were to be promoted in agriculture and more mineral fertiliser made available. Procurement prices for meat, milk, wool, potatoes and vegetables were to be raised. Malenkov's policy may be called the intensification of agriculture; producing higher yields on the existing cultivated area. The expansion of light industry would be aided by switching some machine building and other heavy industry enterprises to consumer goods production.

The initiative now passed to Khrushchev and he launched his policy from his party base. A special CC on agriculture, called at Khrushchev's request, convened on 3 September 1953. He advocated the expansion of wheat production in south-east European Russia, West Siberia and Kazakhstan. He laid bare the appalling situation in the livestock sector, promoted maize for silage, proposed that 100,000 specialists should be sent to the Machine Tractor Stations (MTS) to provide technical aid to the kolkhozes and berated the Ministry of Agriculture and Procurements, and the Ministry of Sovkhozes. The long unhappy relationship with the agricultural ministries began at this plenum. The CC decree, adopted on 7 September, however, did not support all of the First Secretary's strictures. A consequence of the plenum was the abolition of the raion agricultural department, the local agency of the Ministry of Agriculture and the appointment to the MTS of a raion party secretary. The raion party committee was to manage the entire economic and social life of the raion.

During the plenum Khrushchev seized the opportunity of meeting leading party officials from Kazakhstan and pressed on them the need to expand the production of wheat in their republic. The outlines of what later became the virgin land programme were taking place in Khrushchev's mind. The initiative stemmed from the First Secretary since he later made clear that the Kazakh party leadership was cool towards the whole idea.

The CC plenum was quite an occasion for the participants, policy-forming debates were taking place and members had the feeling that they were in a position to influence developments. This was a direct consequence of Khrushchev's need to use the party as his base since Malenkov dominated the governmental apparatus.

If Malenkov was satisfied that the cultivated area was adequate to feed the Soviet population, Khrushchev was not. His grand initiative which caught the imagination of many young people is called the virgin and idle land programme.[4] The former is land which has not been farmed before and the latter is land which has previously been in cultivation but has been abandoned for at least five years. The programme was launched at a CC plenum which met between 23 February and 2 March 1954. The government and party decree which followed, only published on 28 March, spoke of assimilating 13 million hectares in the north Caucasus, the Volga, west Siberia, north Kazakhstan, east Siberia and the Far East. It was a truly nation wide plan.

The tactics used by Khrushchev in promoting the programme provide insights into the policy-making process in the Soviet Union. From September 1953 onwards numerous articles appeared in newspapers and journals such as *Pravda*, the party organ and *Kommunist*, the party theoretical journal. Party officials pointed out that much new land was available for cultivation in the east and elsewhere. Khrushchev, for his part, kept on talking about the need to expand the sown area, then forwarded a memorandum entitled 'Ways of Solving the Grain Problem' to the party Presidium on 22 January 1954. In it he openly challenged Malenkov's statement, made at the XIXth Party Congress, that the grain problem had been solved 'definitely and finally'. Afterwards meetings of MTS workers, sovkhoz workers, leading agricultural specialists in the RSFSR and the Komsomols took place to promote the proposal. It was not all plain sailing. Khrushchev's speech at the MTS workers' conference on 28 January 1954 was not carried by *Pravda* or *Izvestiya*. I. A. Benediktov, the USSR Minister of Agriculture, signally failed to mention the programme in his speech to the conference. At the conference of sovkhoz workers on 5 February 1954 Khrushchev delivered the key speech but it went unreported in *Pravda* and *Izvestiya*. This happened to another speech later in the month. The collective leadership obviously did not favour publication. Nevertheless the breakthrough came shortly afterwards and a CC plenum afforded the First Secretary the national platform he needed to attack the government over the poor state of agriculture.

Since the Kazakh leadership was plainly lukewarm towards the whole project, and proposals from Moscow to the Kazakh CC had not been acted upon, the first and second secretaries were dismissed and replaced by P. K. Ponomarenko and L. I. Brezhnev respectively. Kazakhstan had been in the news in early 1953 when 'bourgeois nationalists' had been unmasked. Obviously the Kazakhs felt that such a major new initiative would bring large numbers of non-Kazakhs to the republic and this could only mean that the proportion of Kazakhs would drop. The industrialisation drive of the early FYPs had, already by 1939, placed the Kazakhs in a minority. The 1959 census revealed that Kazakhs only made up 30 per cent of the population in their own republic.

Khrushchev could not defeat Malenkov by agriculture alone. He needed to find allies in the industrial struggle. A consumer goods approach, in reality Malenkov's proposals were very modest, was guaranteed to raise many hackles. The military, the Stalinist party leadership and many managers had been brought up on the primacy of heavy industry, especially the machine-building industry. Khrushchev's extensive agricultural programme promised to leave heavy industry alone, and he was also able to mobilise the willing medium- and lower-level party officials into activity. However, it was more difficult than it sounded. Molotov and Kaganovich, for example, strongly orthodox in their economic views, opposed the virgin lands initiative, arguing that it would be money wasted. Their opinions carried weight. Until the summer of 1954 it appeared that Malenkov's economic policy would carry the day. *Izvestiya* and *Voprosy Ekonomiki* trumpeted its virtues and indeed the mass of the population was probably in agreement.

A major speech by Khrushchev at a CC plenum in June 1954, calling for the assimilation of an extra 15 million hectares, went unreported in the national press. The CC decree announced reductions in compulsory deliveries and increased prices for deliveries of grain and oil crops and all arrears of grain payments to the MTS were cancelled. The kolkhoznik was also freed of the need to deliver grain from his private plot. Another speech by Khrushchev, in Novosibirsk in July 1954, was again not carried by *Pravda* or *Izvestiya*, even though he was First Secretary and *Pravda* was the party's organ.

A breakthrough occurred on 13 August 1954 when a joint party and government decree, the first time the party took precedence in the post-Stalin era, raised the original goal of 13 million hectares to 28–30 million hectares by 1956. Now the virgin land programme was really under way. The ideal date for this decree, from Khrushchev's point of view, would have been March since the new lands were predominantly spring grain areas. It was too late to have much impact in 1954 but it would be felt in 1955.

The *dénouement* of the controversy between the two attitudes to economic growth occurred between November 1954 and January 1955. A key blow was struck in *Pravda* by the editor, D. T. Shepilov, on 24 January 1955, when he attacked several economists, whom he named, for spreading false theories about Marxist economic development. Shepilov, aided by copious references from Marx, Lenin and Stalin, demonstrated that priority had to be afforded heavy industry.

Malenkov resigned at a joint session of the Soviet of the Union and the Soviet of Nationalities on 8 February 1955. His letter of resignation was read by the chairman. He confessed his 'guilt and responsibility' for the 'unsatisfactory state of affairs which had arisen in agriculture'. He put this down to his 'lack of experience in local work and supervision of industrial branches of the economy'. Malenkov was defeated but not disgraced. He was demoted to deputy USSR Prime Minister and made Minister of Power Stations. Khrushchev was not strong enough to head the government, the post went to Marshal Bulganin.

Khrushchev's victory was the victory of the party. It had reasserted its position as the leading institution in the country and retained it until Gorbachev demoted it in 1990.

The tactics adopted by Khrushchev to build up the party apparatus as his power base had been refined under Stalin. It consisted of recruiting and keeping officials loyal to himself. The officials were known as his 'tail'. The higher he ascended the political ladder, the longer the 'tail'. There were five main types of person Khrushchev was seeking to attract to his 'tail'. Those who had served successfully under him in Moscow and the Ukraine; those whose patrons had lost ground in the post-Stalin power struggles, such as Beria's men after June 1953 and Malenkov's entourage after February 1955; those who had been Stalin's men until his death and who had not found a successful patron; those who had been losers in the factional infighting of the late Stalin era – for example, the Leningrad Affair; bright, ambitious young officials who could be promoted over the heads of their superiors.

The group which did best after Khrushchev entered the secretariat were, not surprisingly, those who had been in his team in Moscow and the Ukraine. Many of them became first party secretaries at oblast and krai level, and others moved into the central party apparatus in Moscow. One informed estimate is that by the XXth Party Congress in February 1956 Khrushchev's Moscow and Ukrainian 'tail' and the others listed above accounted for about a third of the full members of the Central Committee. After consolidating his victory over the Anti-Party group, Nikita Sergeevich's team from the above groups made up the overwhelming majority of full CC members.

Besides growing his 'tail' in Moscow, Khrushchev was quietly doing the same in the republican communist parties. Each of the republics had its own Communist Party with the exception of the Russian Federation. Republican parties were subject to close control from the centre. It is reasonable to assume that Khrushchev's web of patronage took in republican, oblast and krai government leaders, top-ranking police officers and officials in agricultural ministries. However, the majority of senior posts in the central governmental apparatus were still beyond his reach.

1955–57

The removal of Malenkov allowed the initiative to pass to Khrushchev. The new Prime Minister, Bulganin, was not anxious or able to engage in any far-reaching reform and he and the other conservatives in the Presidium, Molotov, Kaganovich and so on, were content to guide the country along familiar paths. Khrushchev, since he was ambitious and wanted to transform the USSR according to his own vision, acted through the one institution which provided him with a platform, the party. Life was being breathed back into the party after the long years of Stalin's leadership when the conventional wisdom had been that the *vozhd* was the brain of the party. Ideology was to become a mobilising force once again. The economic role was becoming more significant as the party's task was to find the new men and women to run the virgin lands as well as organising the migration of over 300,000 young people to work on the new farms.

The CPSU also enjoyed relations with foreign communist parties and indeed saw itself as the father of the movement. This relationship had not always been a happy one, as the expulsion of Tito from the Cominform in 1948 had demonstrated.

Khrushchev was quick to seize the initiative and set off, in September 1954, at the head of a top-level Soviet delegation for Beijing. Bulganin and Mikoyan came along but Molotov, the Minister for Foreign Affairs, was left at home. Had Mao come to Moscow Khrushchev would only have been one of the top Soviet officials but in the Chinese capital he was able to dominate the Soviet side of the proceedings. He found the Chinese tough negotiators. Nikita Sergeevich and Mao had several conversations, some of them lounging around a swimming pool. This must have been an obscene sight given the mountains of flesh on view! Khrushchev records in his memoirs that many of Mao's statements were so complex that they were opaque. Others were so mundane that they amounted to the obvious. Mao clearly enjoyed bamboozling Nikita Sergeevich. The Soviets agreed to hand back Port Arthur and Dalny and to leave their bases on Chinese territory as well as to wind up the joint Sino-Soviet companies which had been exploiting China. Mao even asked for Outer Mongolia (the Mongolian People's Republic, Chinese until 1911) to revert to China. Nikita Sergeevich must have returned from his first trip to China in a rather chastened mood and unhappy that the first round had gone so clearly to the Chinese. With Stalin gone Mao Zedong and Zhou Enlai obviously did not hold his successors in awe and as time passed they stepped up their demands. They must have been gratified at the ease with which they had obtained so many Soviet concessions.

Next Khrushchev boldly set out to heal the breach with Yugoslavia and welcome her back into the socialist commonwealth. However this was entering the world of foreign affairs again and not surprisingly Molotov, the relevant minister, was offended. The First Secretary nevertheless had his way and he and Bulganin but not Molotov, who opposed the whole venture, went to Belgrade in May 1955 to woo Tito. The Soviet delegation was thankful to set foot on terra firma since their pilot did not know the airport and found landing difficult. Tito welcomed them and switched the microphones off so that few could hear Nikita Sergeevich. Tito ensured that there was no Serbo-Croat translation. Khrushchev placed the blame for the seven years of calumny, during which Tito had been referred to as the 'fascist hangman of the Yugoslav people' and the 'chained dog of imperialism', fairly and squarely on Beria's shoulders. Tito was not taken in but in 1955 the real progenitor of the vilification of the Yugoslavs, Stalin, could not be openly named. At the evening reception at the White Palace the debonair Yugoslav leaders and their elegant ladies in Parisian dresses looked down their noses at the ill-dressed Soviets, some of whom looked as if they had been pulled through a hedge backwards. At the return reception Nikita Sergeevich got carried away and imbibed too much. Sir Frank Roberts, the British ambassador observed the scene.

He had to be carried out between rows of diplomats and other guests on the arms of Tito and Rankovic, with his feet sketching out the motions of walking without ever touching the ground.

Nikita Sergeevich wanted to restore inter-party relations but Tito would have none of it. He knew that the Soviets would require the primacy of the CPSU to be acknowledged. He offered to restore inter-state relations instead. Tito was important because of his influence in the Third World and Moscow wanted a united world communist movement. Since the Presidium was not of one mind on Yugoslavia, the question was passed to the CC for discussion and it even went to the CCs of some republican parties.[5] Things had changed.

Another startling move in foreign policy in 1955 saw the Soviet Union leave Austria and sign a peace treaty, again against the wishes of Molotov. Porkkala naval base was returned to the Finns and a new spirit was abroad. It was called the 'spirit of Geneva' after the meeting of the heads of state in that city in July 1955. Although Molotov attended he did not participate in any of the major discussions. This was a good move since Vyacheslav Mikhailovich was known as Comrade Nyet or Mr No. The atmosphere was always frosty when he was negotiating. Molotov was also rebuffed over his proposals to establish the Warsaw Treaty Organisation in May 1955. His original draft had omitted Yugoslavia, which was understandable. However, Albania and the GDR were also excluded. The former was 'far away' and had no common frontier with the USSR. As regards the GDR Molotov put the question: 'Why should we fight with the West over the GDR?'. Khrushchev's riposte was that if these two countries were omitted it would amount to an invitation to the West to take them over. This view prevailed. At Geneva the main topic was Germany since the Federal Republic had just joined NATO and the GDR the Warsaw Pact. No agreement was reached, but the Soviets conceded that all-German elections were possible. On his way home Nikita

Sergeevich dropped in on Walter Ulbricht in East Berlin and assured him that such elections would only take place with his consent, which, of course, would not be forthcoming. Khrushchev also stated for the first time that the 'socialist achievements' of the GDR would have to be preserved. This marked a change in the Kremlin's German policy. This was linked to the Soviet desire to establish diplomatic relations with Bonn. The West German Chancellor, Konrad Adenauer, travelled to Moscow in September 1955. In a 'strictly secret' letter to Ulbricht dated 14 July 1955 Khrushchev informed him that the decision had been taken to release all the German prisoners-of-war and civilians who were still being held in the Soviet Union. This was to include those who were classified as war criminals. The negotiations were hard, and threatened to collapse over the issue of repatriation. The First Secretary pretended to be annoyed when Adenauer mentioned the German prisoners-of-war. He stamped his foot on the floor, indicating where they were, six feet under. This was a negotiating ploy to encourage Adenauer to establish diplomatic relations. These were established and the repatriation of the 9,626 who remained began soon afterwards, some going to the GDR. The Soviets were after beneficial trade links with Bonn. Adenauer, in turn, tried to 'buy' the GDR from Moscow by offering generous credits and reparations. Nikita Sergeevich resisted the temptation, remarking, 'Once you start retreating, it's difficult to stop.'

One of the byproducts of the First Secretary's encounter with the German Chancellor was a story which he greatly enjoyed telling his male guests.

Adenauer likes to speak in the name of the two Germanies and to raise the German question in Europe as though we couldn't survive without accepting what Adenauer proposes. But Adenauer himself does not reveal the true state of affairs and himself demonstrates that what he says is not true. If you strip Adenauer naked and look at him from the rear then you can see clearly that Germany is divided into two parts. But if you look at Adenauer from the front, then it is equally clear that his view of the German question never did stand up, doesn't stand up and never will stand up.

Khrushchev's travels took him to India, Burma and Afghanistan and revealed that the Soviet Union was taking the Third World seriously for the first time. Soviet arms found their way to the Middle East, signalling Soviet intent to challenge Western hegemony there.

If 1955 was diplomatically very successful, economically it was a disappointment. The total harvest was up but the virgin lands were a dismal failure. Those such as Molotov[6] and Kaganovich who begrudged any extra investment in agriculture were provided with ammunition and could plausibly argue that had the money been invested in the traditional areas returns would have been higher. This was Malenkov's plan but it is unlikely that the extra 600 million rubles invested in the new lands annually between 1954 and 1958 would have been forthcoming for the old areas.

Throughout 1955 Khrushchev was availing himself of his prerogative to make middle and lower ranking changes in the party *apparat*. With a weak Prime Minister, Bulganin, in charge, the real power now rested with the Presidium, but Khrushchev could not change its composition at will. Only a congress could do that. The XXth Party Congress was convened in February 1956, six months ahead of schedule. The 1956 Congress was breaking new ground, no one was certain beforehand about its power or its influence. The changes since 1953 were reflected in the composition of the congress, in which over one-third of the 1,355 voting delegates were new to the upper ranks of the party and just under a half of CC members were new. Over a half of the new CC was, significantly, made up of oblast and krai first secretaries.[7]

The congress turned out to be of seminal importance and it made Khrushchev a household name throughout the world. He boldly reformulated Soviet thinking on foreign policy and ushered in the era of peaceful co-existence. This concept held that war between the Soviet Union and the capitalist powers was not inevitable: the growing strength of the anti-war forces and the Third World would prevent it. It differed from Lenin's 'co-habitation' and Stalin's popular front tactics in that it was seen as a long-term policy. It signalled the Soviet desire for better and closer relations in all fields except one, ideology. There could never be peaceful co-existence between socialism and capitalism, the class struggle would continue. Peaceful co-existence was there under Malenkov but it was Khrushchev who spelled out its implications. The First Secretary had perceived that there was a technological gap between the USSR and the West and wanted to close it by importing technology and know-how. This spilled over into scientific and technical fields, and Western ideas were welcome provided they speeded up Soviet growth. Gone were the days when if someone complained to a shop assistant that a bottle of milk was off he could be suspected of anti-Soviet activities. However, measuring the Soviet Union against the capitalist powers was potentially very dangerous. Whereas the measuring stick previously had always been Soviet achievements, Khrushchev was now inviting comparisons with advanced industrial economies which in the short run at least were bound to relegate the USSR to a second position. The First Secretary was entering the marketplace of ideas. Since the USSR was not a market economy she would have to learn how to compete economically and culturally with the West. Such a move could only have been initiated by Khrushchev and accepted by the party if everyone concerned was certain that the final victor would be the Soviet Union. Hence peaceful co-existence was an expression of optimism and faith in the potential of the Soviet people.

If peaceful co-existence surprised some then Khrushchev's secret speech, not on the agenda but delivered technically when the congress was over, must have stunned everyone. It was a 26,000-word four-hour tirade about the evil deeds of Stalin. The great leader, the coryphaeus of science, the omniscient, benevolent father of the nation was unceremoniously dethroned. For the prescient there had been some straws in the wind beforehand; no Stalin prizes were handed out in 1953 (indeed his birthday went unrecorded), Lenin's Testament with its criticisms of Stalin was published in *Kommunist* in 1955 but on the other hand the *Short Course* was republished in 1955 and his birthday was celebrated in the same year. Mikoyan's was the only set speech which openly criticised the old demi-god at the congress, accusing him of abuse of power, distorting party history in favour of himself and so on. Khrushchev was careful to exclude the period before 1934 from his strictures, otherwise he would have been bringing the whole Soviet planned economy into question. In other words the 'cult of the personality', the Soviet Russian euphemism for Stalinism, only appeared after collectivisation and industrialisation, both praised by Khrushchev, had got into their stride. Only Khrushchev and Mikoyan were credited with having stood up to Stalin, and Marshal Zhukov, Minister of Defence who became a full member of the Presidium at the congress, also emerged with credit. This led to Stalin's wartime role being downgraded and the victims of the military purge of 1937 being rehabilitated. But, it may be objected, Khrushchev and Mikoyan, the most skilful ballet dancer in top party circles, were as guilty as anyone. Quite true, but then the condemnation of Stalin was politically motivated and was used as a weapon by the First Secretary for his own ends.

Why did he do it? Why start sawing at the branch on which Stalin had placed the ruling elite of the Soviet Union? One explanation would be that if Stalin's capricious, undemocratic behaviour were condemned then no party leader could imitate him afterwards. Collective leadership meant un-Stalinist modes of behaviour. By villifying Stalin for his shedding of innocent blood Soviet leaders could feel the bloodletting was over. Another explanation would be that Khrushchev believed that the Stalinist mould was holding back the development of the country. Breaking the spell of psychological subservience to Stalin was the only way to release the pent-up creative energies of the people. The party would assume the task of guiding all these talents into productive channels, thus opening up exciting prospects for party functionaries and members. Khrushchev saw himself as the conductor of the whole enterprise: he sought Stalin's power but he wished to use it responsibly and humanely. He wanted to rule as Lenin would have done in a period of internal stability, as an enlightened dictator.

Destalinisation was a double-edged sword, it could remove much of the dead wood in Soviet life but it could also undermine the base on which society rested, the party. Khrushchev discovered that his room for manoeuvre was very limited. At home writers, historians, artists and others were keen to evade party control, abroad foreign communist leaders were in a difficult position – if Stalin had been toppled why should they, his minions, not go as well?

The first phase of destalinisation lasted until the summer of 1956. It saw a new spirit abroad in the USSR, as the camps emptied and rehabilitations got under way (about 10,000 were affected – some posthumously – but practically all were party apparatchiks), the security forces were kept on a tighter rein, Kaganovich left the USSR Council of Ministers and Molotov the Ministry of Foreign Affairs, the Cominform was dissolved in April 1956 and Tito came to Moscow in June.

The October events in Poland and Hungary stopped Khrushchev in his tracks. He could justifiably be blamed for them as he had called in question the whole nature of the regimes in eastern Europe. They had never had a Lenin and the revolution had come about thanks mainly to the Red Army. Hence the ice of legitimacy was very thin, it cracked in Poland but broke in Hungary. The key question in Soviet minds was: was the primacy of the party under threat? In Poland the party elected Władysław Gomulka as leader and the Poles stood their ground and won greater control over their internal affairs while promising to support Soviet foreign and defence policies. In Hungary Imre Nagy's new government sought to take the country out of the Warsaw Pact and the party lost its dominating role. The Soviets invaded. The lesson for everyone was clear, the new Soviet leaders would tolerate no new Titos in eastern Europe. They had acted as Stalin would have acted: loss of party or international face took second place to Soviet security needs.

Khrushchev had to mount the Stalin bandwagon again until things had cooled down. The Hungarian episode especially was costly as Budapest had to be repaired as quickly as possible and the new party leader János Kádár provided with goods to improve the Hungarian standard of living. It was a burden the USSR could ill afford to bear and it meant less investment in agriculture, for example. Hence the astonishingly bountiful harvest of 1956 in the virgin lands obviously helped Khrushchev.

The First Secretary launched his major economic reform at a CC plenum in February 1957 and it was breathtaking in its boldness. He proposed that the central industrial ministries should be dissolved and their powers passed to over one hundred economic councils or *sovnarkhozy*. The economic rationale behind the reform was to shift decision-making nearer the enterprise. On first glance it appears praiseworthy but Khrushchev failed to understand that without a rational pricing system the major increases in productivity would not come. Not all ministries were to go to the provinces, of course, and the defence-related ministries stayed in Moscow.

The CC loved the idea because it would increase the power of the oblast and krai first secretaries and would mean that economic development would come more and more under party control. If the CC was all in favour, the Presidium was not. It contained many top government personnel and they predictably did not want any change. How did Khrushchev outmanoeuvre the opposition in the Presidium? He took the issue to the country and the population seized upon the opportunity of participating in policy-making. The vast majority was in favour and Khrushchev was able to argue that the nation was behind him. The reform was pushed through and thousands of bureaucrats and their families had to leave Moscow. The wives were the most critical as they felt the drop in living standards the most keenly.

The Ministries of Agriculture were greatly discomfited by the change. They were dispatched to sovkhozes, often with only rudimentary communications with the rest of the country, and had to grow crops. They were only to make recommendations to farms based on their own experimental results. All officials were expected to do some work in the fields. The USSR Ministry of Agriculture, for example, was located on a sovkhoz about a hundred kilometres from Moscow and most officials made the journey, two or three hours each way, daily.[8] Not surprisingly the majority of the staff soon found other jobs in Moscow and handed the ministry over to untrained personnel.

Khrushchev was often away from Moscow and his critics in the Presidium waited until he and Bulganin returned from a trip to Finland before forcing a showdown. Khrushchev sensed from the Prime Minister's behaviour in Finland that something was in the air.[9] On the afternoons of 18 June 1957 Khrushchev, at home, received a phone call from Bulganin, in the Kremlin, asking him to convene the Presidium. 'We have decided', insisted Bulganin. 'Who are we?', asked Khrushchev. Bulganin explained that a group of Presidium members were lunching in the Kremlin. Khrushchev's response was that neither in the party statutes nor in party practice was there a 'luncheon club' to be found. Hence the Presidium meeting would take place as planned but not on the 18th. Nevertheless it did take place on the 18th and Bulganin was put in the chair. The others present were Voroshilov, Molotov, Malenkov, Kaganovich, Pervukhin and Mikoyan. Suslov was on holiday outside Moscow, Saburov was attending a Comecon meeting in Warsaw and Kirichenko was in the Ukraine. Khrushchev asked for the absent members to be invited to attend the session and this request was granted. He hoped to redress some of the imbalance in the Presidium since only Mikoyan sided with him. When they arrived it turned out that Suslov and Kirichenko supported Khrushchev and Saburov opposed him. Various accusations were made against the First Secretary: there was no unity in the Presidium and the party, Khrushchev travelled about as he liked, interfered in foreign affairs, he was to be the key speaker at the celebrations marking the 250th anniversary of the founding of Leningrad (to take place on 22–24 June), and the majority opposed Khrushchev's plan to catch up with the US in *per capita* output of milk, butter and meat by 1961. Khrushchev imposed himself on foreign delegations and so on. It was not all one-way traffic, however. Khrushchev hit back at Malenkov by accusing him of being directly to blame for the shooting of Kuznetsov and of strangling Voznesensky (during the Leningrad affair). The plan was to make Nikita Sergeevich USSR Minister of Agriculture. Bulganin was the front man and would stay as Prime Minister but Khrushchev suspected that Malenkov would soon take over the post. Molotov, the real leader of the group, was to head the party.

On 19 June a group of twenty CC members, headed by Marshal Konev, arrived and demanded to be present at the Presidium session. Marshal Zhukov and the other candidate members had joined the meeting by this time. Brezhnev sided with Khrushchev but was very rudely interrupted by Kagonovich. Leonid Ilich was so shocked that he almost fainted. Voroshilov told the session that the CC members could even bring up tanks if they pleased. Zhukov sharply reminded him that the tanks would only move on his, Zhukov's, orders. Khrushchev reminded the Presidium that every CC member had the right to be present at Presidium sessions. This was a very old practice and had only lapsed during the purges of the 1930s. No permission was required. Nevertheless the Presidium refused to allow the twenty CC members in. A compromise was reached and Bulganin and Khrushchev were sent out to talk to them. Bulganin was incoherent and Khrushchev seized the opportunity to argue that a plenary session of the CC should decide the issues at stake. On 21 June another group, this time numbering thirty, arrived and banged on the door demanding to be admitted. Khrushchev's conservative opponents had to agree to a CC plenary session and it began on 22 June and lasted until 29 June 1957. The First Secretary was in magnificent form and he deployed great political and tactical skills. His opponents were still convinced that they would win in the CC. Gradually Khrushchev detached Voroshilov from the group and the hard core of opposition centred on Malenkov, Molotov, Kaganovich and Shepilov, a candidate member. When defeat stared them in the face only Molotov had the character to fight on. Khrushchev was especially angry at Bulganin's behaviour. He had suggested him as Prime Minister in 1955. Bulganin, according to Khrushchev, was a fool who could not see that he was being used and that he would soon cease to be Prime Minister after Khrushchev had gone. The 'Anti-Party group', as they were labelled, also wanted to remove Serov from the Ministry of Internal Affairs so as to destroy archival evidence against them.

The Anti-Party group was accused of opposing peaceful co-existence, destalinisation, the *sovnarkhozy* and the more relaxed policy towards the collective farms. For the first time defeated political opponents were not accused of being in the pay of foreign powers.

When the Presidium met at the end of the affair Malenkov, Kaganovich, Saburov and Shepilov voted for their own removal but Molotov abstained. All five lost their places on the CC as well and their government offices a few days later. Voroshilov stayed for the moment as did Bulganin as it was deemed politic not to remove him at that juncture lest it adversely affect the international standing of the USSR. Khrushchev's anger and Bulganin's pathetic performance marked him down, however, for removal when the dust had settled. Kaganovich was so fearful that he phoned Khrushchev and asked whether it was true that Stalin's methods would no longer be employed. Khrushchev assured him that the spilling of the blood of defeated political opponents was a thing of the past.

Molotov and his friends handled the affair badly. With a large majority in the Presidium they became too self-confident and should never have allowed the CC to convene. The role of the military was significant it was firmly behind Khrushchev and ferried his CC supporters to Moscow. The ten army and air force marshals, appointed in March 1955, were Khrushchev men.

It was not the CC, however, which saved Khrushchev, but the secretariat with Zhukov's help. It got the First Secretary's supporters to the Kremlin on time. The one CC secretary who changed sides, Shepilov, was dealt with very harshly as a lesson to others. He was removed from the secretariat, the party and the USSR Academy of Sciences. The secretariat had developed once again into a formidable instrument and in this particular instance proved that it was capable of defeating the Presidium.

The Presidium was completely refashioned. Nine new members were elected, including Marshal Zhukov, the first professional soldier to climb to the top of the party, and Leonid Ilich Brezhnev. Eight new candidate members were announced, including Kosygin and Kirilenko. The nature of the Presidium had changed; whereas previously it had been government dominated it was now party dominated and this enhanced the standing of the secretariat since it serviced the top institution. Again Khrushchev's victory was the victory of the party.

Zhukov's forceful personality was used to enlarge the compass of military interests. He wanted less time spent on ideological affairs and more time on professional military training. Besides this the military wanted the party's representatives in the armed forces, the political officers, to be subordinate to them.

Soviet military strength was reduced by 640,000 men in 1955 but despite this defence spending rose by 12 per cent. However, spending was down in 1956 when it accounted for 18.2 per cent of the budget compared with 19.9 per cent in 1955. Zhukov was bound to argue strongly for a more powerful Soviet military establishment. His sharp rejoinder to Voroshilov that tanks only moved on his orders and the fact that he had mobilised transport in support of Khrushchev when the latter was in a minority in the Presidium made him potentially dangerous to the party.

He was sent off on an official visit to Yugoslavia and Albania in October 1957 and removed from the Presidium and Ministry of Defence while in Albania. Marshal Malinovsky, his less dynamic successor, welcomed him on his return. He had to confess to Bonapartist tendencies and the party stepped up its control of the armed forces.

Bulganin, only in name Prime Minister, went in March 1958 and left the Presidium in September 1958. Khrushchev became the new Prime Minister and thereby headed both party and government. He had attained his goal, successor to Lenin and Stalin, in just five years. He exuded self-confidence, as well he might. Internationally the prestige of the USSR had soared as the first sputnik orbited the earth in October 1957. The USSR was to score other firsts in space, the first manned flight and the first to photograph the 'blind' side of the moon. Genuinely believing in the potency of Marxism-Leninism at home and abroad and in the imminence of an economic take-off which would leave the capitalist world in her wake, Khrushchev was on top of the world.

1958–64

Khrushchev's pre-eminence flattered to deceive. Head of the party and government, he could initiate action and push through much legislation and many changes. In the last resort, however, others had to carry out his policies. If the majority of the *apparat* or bureaucracy, plus some in the Presidium and the CC, opposed an innovation, there was little likelihood that it would have much effect. Since Khrushchev did not wish to or would never have been allowed to resort to Stalin's methods of removing opposition, persuasion and the reshuffling of personnel were the only ways open to him. Even here the officials wanted security: everyone wanted security and tranquility after the nerve-racking years under Stalin, and objected to constant change. Khrushchev soon discovered the limits of his power. He needed a talented supporter who could bring order to the confusion of his economic thought. Aleksei Kosygin could have played this role but the opportunity was let slip in 1958. Much of the legislation of the post-1958 period was ill conceived, ill digested and doomed to failure before the ink was dry on the documents. There was no overall plan, no strategy of reform. New legislation usually began with Nikita Sergeevich having a wizard idea. He was brilliant at lateral thinking

– coming up with several solutions to the same problem. He would dictate his inspirational thoughts, make amendments and then hand them over for drafting as a decree. There were great institutional barriers to change – Gorbachev can testify to that – but it must be said that the personal factor also played an important role. Khrushchev believed passionately that he had a mission – to transform the Soviet Union into a land of plenty where justice and democracy would prevail. As an evangelist he was as full of eloquence as he was empty of doubt about the communist goal. Unfortunately, the number of doubters increased to such an extent that by 1964 there were precious few believers left.

His vision of economic cornucopia called for more technical expertise and higher qualifications from everyone. Ideology was fine but if it was not accompanied by a capacity to solve problems then the comrade was of limited potential. Khrushchev was appalled to discover that about 80 per cent of the students at Moscow University were the sons and daughters of the intelligentsia. He determined to broaden the intake, permitting more social mobility but furthering the prospects of the working class. The 1958 education reform was the result but it soon ran into the sand since few of those with higher education were in favour of it.

Khrushchev initiated a far-reaching reform in agriculture in January 1958 when he announced the phasing out of the Machine Tractor Stations (MTS). They had been valuable in the days when there had been little farm machinery and skilled personnel very hard to find. Khrushchev decided that machinery should be sold to the kolkhozes, contrary to what Stalin had written in the *Economic Problems of Socialism in the USSR*. Instead of two masters in the countryside there was now to be one, the kolkhoz. The move was precipitate and ill-thought-out. Many of the farms were obliged to buy useless machinery in order to get the good, and many farms sank deep into debt. Who was going to work and repair the machines? Repair Tractor Stations were set up but they were phased out after 1961 in favour of the *Selkhoztekhnika*, an organisation that sold farm equipment, machinery and fertilisers to the kolkhozes. Gradually farms built up their own repair bases.

Despite this the immediate results must have warmed Khrushchev's heart. The 1958 harvest was a record one. Industrially the country was not doing so well so it was decided to scrap the 1956–60 FYP, which could not be achieved anyway, and substitute the 1959–65 Seven-Year Plan.

The Seven-Year Plan was launched at the 'extraordinary' XXIst Party Congress, in January 1959, extraordinary since the congress was not due until 1960. A great expansion of capital and consumer goods was to be set in train which could lead to the US being passed in *per capita* output in 1970. Khrushchev was praised to the skies but he was not able to apply the *coup de grace* to the remaining members of the Anti-Party group. None of them was demoted and no promotions of Khrushchev's followers occurred.

In 1959 Khrushchev discovered America. He went on a highly successful tour in September and had talks with President Eisenhower in Camp David. Wide-eyed, he looked and learned a good deal, especially about agriculture. He gave as good as he got. When put under pressure in Washington about human rights he retorted: 'If you throw dead rats at me, I'll throw dead rats at you!' in Los Angeles he was riled by the mayor's speech which was sharp and wounding. Nikita Sergeevich then performed his exploding act. He made it clear he represented a great power and should be treated as such. He enquired if his plane was ready. After all, it was not very far to Vladivostok. Later the lugubrious Andrei Gromyko was despatched to convey the same message to Henry Cabot Lodge, who was accompanying the Soviet delegation around the country. The next day, in San Francisco, all was sweetness and light. Nikita Sergeevich's act had worked. He was very impressed by the role of maize as a cattle feed and determined to popularise the crop back home. This was continuing his love affair with the crop, as he had always been a champion of it in the Ukraine. About the only disappointment he suffered was the refusal of his hosts to take him around Disneyland – for security reasons. The tour was given massive publicity in the Soviet Union, something which the vast majority of the population welcomed. It was the heyday of peaceful co-existence but there were powerful opponents of a *rapprochement* with the 'heartland of capitalism'. All those responsible for party control saw that it would make life more difficult for them. Increased contact with the US would stimulate consumer demand which the economy could not cope with, and the military establishment looked askance.

The drop in the birth rate during the war was now beginning to manifest itself in lower additions to the labour force annually. There was a source of manpower and Khrushchev seized on it. In January 1960 he announced that the Soviet armed forces were to be reduced from 3.6 million to 2.4 million men. This was possible because of the USSR's increasing nuclear missile force. 'The airforce and the navy have lost their previous importance', asserted Khrushchev, revealing his lack of understanding of strategic matters. Something like 250,000 officers, those who were not regarded as capable of acquiring the requisite technical knowledge, were released and found jobs. As before agriculture was lumbered with many of these reluctant civilians.

The honeymoon with the US came to an end on 1 May 1960 when an American reconnaissance aircraft was shot down near Sverdlovsk. The pilot, Francis Gary Powers, was under orders to blow up the aircraft but he failed to do this and most of it fell into Soviet hands. US planes had been flying over the USSR for a long time but hitherto Soviet anti-aircraft techniques had not been sufficiently advanced to bring one down. The incident led to the scuttling of the Paris summit meeting, which opened on 16 May. Khrushchev asked for an apology from Eisenhower which, as Harold Macmillan pointed out to the Soviet leader, the US President could not make. The top level meeting between the USSR, the US, the UK and France thus came to nought.

The Chinese had all along been making it clear that they had reservations about the policy of peaceful co-existence. Khrushchev, who was never able to find a common language with Mao Zedong, angered the Chinese at every turn. The Soviet Union, in June 1959, decided not to help China become a nuclear power and went back on a 1957 agreement. Since there was no way the Soviets could stop the Chinese developing a nuclear capacity, short of annihilation, the only result of this *démarche* was to delay the process and incur lasting Chinese enmity. The Sino-Indian border war led to further acerbic exchanges and in July 1960 Khrushchev decided really to teach the Chinee a lesson. He withdrew Soviet and East European technicians and specialists and all the blueprints as well. This was a body blow to the Chinese economy but again it nurtured in the Chinese the desire never again to become dependent on a single source of technical know-how.

The Chinese took umbrage at Khrushchev's thesis on the non-inevitability of war and in the course of 1960 made it abundantly clear that they believed that a lasting world peace could only come when the capitalists had been defeated. Khrushchev had also to appear militant. 'We are going to make the imperialists dance like hens on a griddle but without war', he assured delegates to the Bucharest Congress of twelve ruling communist parties in June 1960. This included threatening nuclear strikes against any country, such as Norway or Pakistan, which allowed US reconnaissance aircraft to use its territory.

At the Ist conference of communist and workers' parties in Moscow in December 1960 the Chinese again criticised the Soviets but the final document was a victory for the CPSU. The Sino-Soviet dispute became public knowledge at the XXIInd Party Congress, in October 1961, when Khrushchev vigorously attacked Albania as a haven of Stalinism and Zhou Enlai defended the Albanians.

If internationally things were not going well for the First Secretary, the same could be said of his internal policies. The *sovnarkhozy* were gradually losing more and more of their power to the central authorities and Khrushchev was having the same trouble as Malenkov with the partisans of capital goods expansion (he called them the metal eaters). His foreign policy adventures inadvertently strengthened the hand of the defence lobby. Thought had now to be given to the Chinese frontier. As a result an end was made to demobilisation, defence expenditure was to expand by a quarter in 1961 and the Soviet Union ended her nuclear test moratorium, exploding two of the most powerful devices ever. All this was bad news for the non-heavy industry section of the economy. Agriculture, into the bargain, was limping along and the much vaunted programme of matching US *per capita* output of milk, butter and meat by 1961 had to be buried. Little went right after the record 1958 harvest and heads rolled. N. I. Belyaev not only lost his position as first secretary of the CP of Kazakhstan but also his seat on the Presidium in Moscow. Belyaev had been rash enough, at the XXIst Party Congress in January 1959, to promise a record crop in the virgin lands in northern Kazakhstan. His contact with the Almighty must have been faulty since early winter snows in September meant that huge amounts of grain could not be harvested.

There was considerable movement in the Presidium and the secretariat at the same time but Khrushchev benefited little from the changes, demonstrating that the top level of the *apparat* was able to contain him and protect its own interests.

Khrushchev had a vision for the USSR, a country which would see communism within a generation. At the XXIInd Party Congress, in October 1961, he launched a new party programme and party statute. His programme superseded the second, adopted in 1919 during the desperate days of War Communism. (The first dated from 1903.) It was ambitious, challenging and geared to rekindling the revolutionary enthusiasm and ardour of the Soviet population, something which had been lost in the late Stalin period. The base was economic, a Twenty-Year Plan was to see a 'communist society, on the whole, built in the USSR'. Over the years 1961–70 the Soviet Union was to surpass the US in *per capita* production and by 1970 everyone 'would be living in easy circumstances'. Between 1971 and 1980 Soviet society would 'come close to a state where it can introduce the principle of distribution according to need'. There was one caveat however: the programme could only be realised 'under conditions of peace'.

The Chinese claim, in 1958, that they were leaping ahead to communism may have stimulated the First Secretary to draw in the contours of the industrial communist society. The State ceased to be a 'state of the dictatorship of the proletariat' and became a 'state of the whole people'. The State would not wither away *en route* to communism but would 'survive until the complete victory of communism'. As socialist democracy developed the 'organs of state power will gradually be transformed into organs of public self-government'. Soviets were to expand and involve more and more citizens, one third of members at each election were to be new. This led to many voluntary organisations being created to maintain law and order such as the *druzhinniki* or part-time police. Sports organisations were encouraged to run their own affairs.

The party was to be the key institution on the march towards communism. It was defined as the 'wisdom, the honour and conscience of our epoch, of the Soviet people'. It ceased to be the party of the working class, collective farm peasantry and intelligentsia and became the party of the 'militant, tested vanguard of the Soviet people' – a party of the whole people. Its cadres were to become more accountable to the membership. Leading officials of union, republican and local bodies were to be elected, as a rule, for not more than three consecutive terms. The only exception to this, doubtless to include the top leadership, were those officials whose 'personal gifts' made their continuation in office 'useful and necessary'. Half of the members of party committees at the lower levels, one third at the higher levels and one quarter of the Presidium and the CC, CPSU were to be replaced at each election. The programme ended: 'The party solemnly proclaims that the present generation of Soviet people shall live under communism!'

Khrushchev doubtless had ulterior motives in launching the programme. He wanted to exert more and more influence over Soviet development and to be applauded as the man who spearheaded the victory over capitalism. Not all the economic goals were unrealistic, for instance the target for mineral fertilisers was below that achieved in 1980. Given the difficulties of the US economy in the late 1950s and the performance of the Soviet economy over the same period Khrushchev became too sanguine about Soviet prospects. In reality the US economy took off under Kennedy and the Soviet economy did not continue its rapid march forward.

Khrushchev looked back as well as forward at the congress. He pilloried Stalin once again and large numbers of delegates followed his lead. D. A. Lazurkina, a Leningrad party member, said: 'Yesterday I asked Ilich (Lenin) for advice and it was as if he stood before me alive and said: "I do not like being beside Stalin who inflicted so much harm on the party." '[10] After such a revelation Stalin had to go and he was removed from the mausoleum and buried nearby. A headstone was added several years later. This was about the only tangible piece of destalinistation which emerged from the congress. The First Secretary's desire to continue exposing Stalin's crimes and by extension to punish the guilty ones was evidently not shared by many at the top. Nevertheless Stalin's name was gradually disappearing from the map, Stalingrad became Volgograd, Stalinabad, Dushanbe, and so on.

Agriculture was constantly on Khrushchev's mind, not because it was prosperous but because it was 'in serious danger' of not fulfilling the goals of the Seven-Year Plan. In March 1962 territorial production administrations (TPA) were established at the local level to 'plan and supervise the production of state and collective farms and the purchases of food from them for the state'.[11] The TPA would be staffed by farm and party officials. Agricultural management committees, operating at oblast, republican and USSR level, were to 'plan and supervise the agricultural system as part of the Soviet economy'. Party officials were to run these committees.

Agriculture was crying out for more farm machinery and chemicals but the investment was just not available. It was officially stated that money would not be diverted from defence to agriculture. The only way out was to raise food prices, so meat went up 30 per cent and butter 25 per cent on 1 June 1962. The consumer did not like it. There were riots in several cities, notably Novocherkassk where the authorities killed some demonstrators.

The most startling innovation in the administration of agriculture occurred at the end of 1962 and was approved in January 1963. The party was split into industrial and non-industrial wings. The reform had come about due to party officials, on being upbraided for agricultural failure, arguing that they had had to concentrate their energies on industry in their area. Khrushchev wanted to improve the efficiency of agricultural management and the only way he knew was to make party officials responsible for it. Needless to say there was a stampede out of the agricultural wing since success could only really be registered in the industrial wing. Not only the party but the soviets, Komsomol and the trade unions were likewise split.

With little success at home Khrushchev looked to foreign policy to redeem his position. Berlin was always a favourite topic but little success had been achieved there. He hit on the idea of directly challenging the US on nuclear weapons. Install short-range missiles on Cuba and nullify the lead of the US in intercontinental ballistic missiles: it appeared so inviting.

On 18 October 1962 the Americans discovered what was afoot and Dean Rusk, the Secretary of State, confronted Andrei Gromyko. According to Khrushchev, his Foreign Minister answered, 'like a gypsy who's been caught stealing a horse: it's not me, and it's not my horse. I don't know anything'. On 22 October President John F. Kennedy imposed a naval blockade on Cuba to prevent more missiles being located there. Castro informed Khrushchev that his intelligence sources revealed that the US was planning to strike against the missile sites. The Cuban leader proposed a pre-emptive strike against the US. From 23 to 28 October Khrushchev and Kennedy exchanged letters. The US leader warned that if the missiles were not withdrawn action would be taken. The Soviet leader argued that the missiles were merely there to protect Cuba and were therefore defensive. This was quite untrue. In his memoirs, Khrushchev states: 'We picked targets in the US to inflict the maximum damage. We saw that our weapons could inspire terror. The two nuclear weapons the US used against Japan at the end of the war were toys by comparison.' It later transpired that the Soviet forces had had thirty-six nuclear warheads and twenty-four intermediate-range missiles capable of hitting the US. The CIA informed the President that it did not believe that there were any nuclear warheads on the island. The CIA also estimated that there were about 10,000 Soviet troops in Cuba, whereas there were, in reality, 42,000. The

Soviet field commanders in Cuba were authorised to use the nuclear warheads without further authorisation from Moscow in the event of an American invasion. The USSR had deployed six dual-purpose tactical launchers supported by nine tactical missiles and nine nuclear warheads to be used against an American invasion force. The situation became very tense after an American reconnaissance aircraft was shot down over Cuba. Then Khrushchev, without consulting or informing Castro, agreed to remove the missiles. In return, the US promised not to invade Cuba. Castro was angry with the Soviets, and did not believe the Americans would keep their side of the bargain. The USSR removed their missiles and forty IL-28 jet medium-range bombers from Cuba and the US ended its blockade. It had been a close thing. Had the US invaded the Soviets would have used their nuclear weapons and the US would have responded in kind. The first nuclear war would have been under way. The world had held its breath as war appeared imminent. Khrushchev had gambled and lost and was very exposed. The Chinese grasped the heaven-sent opportunity and berated him for his handling of the crisis and his climb down.

The VIth Congress of the SED in east Berlin, in January 1963, saw the exacerbation of the Sino-Soviet conflict. Khrushchev and his socialist allies pilloried the Chinese, accusing them of wanting a continuation of Stalinism and thermonuclear war. The Chinese delegate was jeered when he sought to refute Khrushchev's strictures. The agreement by the Soviet, American and British governments to ban nuclear weapons testing in the earth's atmosphere, in space and under water, signed in Moscow on 5 August 1963, added fuel to Chinese indignation. Talks aimed at reaching further agreements got under way.

On the home front the Seven-Year Plan was abandoned and a Supreme Council of the National Economy set up in March 1963. New plans were to be worked out for 1964 and 1965. The Supreme Council was to supervise the activities of Gosplan, the Council of National Economy – responsible for the industrial sector of the economy, the state construction committee and other specialised bodies. It was also to oversee electric power, natural gas and geological surveys. In February 1962 the USSR had been divided into seventeen economic regions, ten in the RSFSR, three in the Ukraine and one each in the Baltic republics, Transcaucasia, Kazakhstan and the Central Asian republics.

All this did not satisfy Nikita Sergeevich. In March 1963 he acquired a new USSR Minister of Agriculture and proposed among other things that the fifteen republican Ministries of Agriculture be abolished since they duplicated the work of the USSR Ministry, *Selkhoztekhnika* employees be remunerated according to the performance of the farms they serviced and state farm workers not be permitted to own their own livestock. It did not prevent the worst harvest since 1955 as well as the lowest virgin land harvest. Only 107.5 million tonnes were gathered in, far short of the planned 172–180.2 million tonnes. The First Secretary was faced with a choice of either making do with the limited amount of grain available and slaughtering all the livestock which could not be fed, or importing the shortfall from the West. To his credit he convinced his colleagues that the grain had to be imported, and so began the now traditional grain purchases in North America. About 20 million tonnes of grain was imported.

Khrushchev's frustrations with the Presidium may be illustrated by reference to the tactics he adopted to promote his agricultural ideas. He spent much time travelling the country with his court and on his return was wont to propose some new reform. He forwarded two memoranda to the Presidium in 1960, two in 1961, but nine in 1962 and seven in 1963. It is difficult to resist the conclusion that had he enjoyed the confidence of the Presidium he would have put his proposals on the agenda and had them adopted. Interestingly enough he forwarded no memoranda in 1964 but this was not because he had run out of ideas. He could also not get the amount of investment he needed for agriculture. For instance it was only in 1962 that the 1958 level of investment for electrification was surpassed and 1963 for farm machinery.

The First Secretary was quite unaware that the foundations on which his power rested were crumbling in 1964. He had antagonised practically all those who had saved him in 1957. The party was grateful for its new position which allowed it to control the political police and exert more influence over the military as well as the economy. Its numbers jumped from 7 million in 1955 to 11 million in 1964. The type of member being recruited changed. Khrushchev, in his desire to reduce the role of bureaucrats and the intelligentsia in the party, brought in more and more workers and peasants. By 1964 these two classes accounted for 60 per cent of new recruits. Khrushchev was emotionally committed to the revolution and its goals and tended to see workers and peasants, like Lenin, as the source of new inspiration. This was partly due to the lack of *rapport* with the intelligentsia and the bureaucrats. Khrushchev was given to inviting non-members to meetings of the CC and the gatherings at the XXIst and XXIInd Party Congresses were very large and included many who would not normally have attended such an event. Of course he was courting support as well as drawing more people into the decision-making process. In fact the consultation of 'outsiders' by the party, government and the Supreme Soviet became a feature of the Khrushchev period. These tactics, however finally helped to alienate the basis of his support, the *apparat*. His plan to replace some members of each committee at each election also rankled.

He had little time for the governmental apparatus. The military was put out by his defence cuts and his mishandling of the Cuban affair. The intelligentsia were successfully blocking the 1958 education reform. The professional diplomats disliked, as did the party *apparat*, the role played by Aleksei Adzhubei, his son-in-law and editor in chief of *Izvestiya*. He was sent to Czechoslovakia and West Germany in the summer of 1964 to prepare the ground for a Khrushchev initiative. There was practically no one left who had a good word for the First Secretary.

The campaign to remove him, according to Vladimir Semichastny, head of the KGB at the time, began in February 1964. Its genesis may have been the CC plenum in February. Podgorny, Brezhnev, Shelepin and Polyansky were the conspirators. Their task of discrediting Khrushchev was made easier by Nikita Sergeevich's blundering leadership. Pyotr Shelest, Presidium member and party leader in the Ukraine, dates the conspiracy from 14 March 1964. It was his birthday and Podgorny and Brezhnev drove over to congratulate him. He sensed that he was being sounded out. The cult of Khrushchev's personality reached new heights and Podgorny and Brezhnev vied with one another to be the sycophant of the month. When it became clear that Frol Kozlov, whom Khrushchev regarded as a possible successor, would not recover from a stroke Nikita Sergeevich decided to move Brezhnev full-time into the secretariat and make Anastas Mikoyan president. This annoyed Brezhnev, who loved the trappings of office. According to Semichastny, Brezhnev thought up various ways of removing Nikita Sergeevich. These included poisoning him, causing the plane bringing him back from Cairo to crash and arranging a car accident. Brezhnev, who was an enthusiastic hunter, enjoyed duck shooting at Zavidovo, outside Moscow. However, in August 1964 his mind was not on the ducks but on power. Gennady Voronov, then a member of the Presidium, thought that all the threats led to Zavidovo. 'Brezhnev himself would put down a plus (next to the names of those who were ready to support him in the fight against Khrushchev) or minus. Each man would be worked on individually.' Brezhnev's supporters in the apparat had the task of approaching CC members in their area in order to win them over. Shelest looked after the Ukraine, Mzhavanadze Transcaucasia, Egorychev, the Moscow First Secretary, the Moscow members, and so on. This reveals the authority of regional party officials under Khrushchev. Hence many people must have been privy to the plan. Also the conspirators sought to avoid the impression that a coup was being instigated. In September Khrushchev set off to attend some rocket tests but his son, Sergei, a rocket engineer, could not accompany him. He got a phone call from an associate of Nikolai Ignatov (chairman of the Presidium of the RSFSR Supreme Soviet) that the latter was involved in a conspiracy against Sergei's father. He informed his father when he returned. Nikita Sergeevich thought it over and rejected the whole story. Just in case, he asked Podgorny about it! He just did not want to believe that his life-long colleagues were staging a coup. Two other Khrushchev supporters tried to reach him to warn him but the KGB made sure they did not contact him. Nikita Sergeevich's daughter was told of what was afoot but afforded the revelation little credence. Brezhnev was in the GDR when he was informed that Khrushchev had got wind of the coup. He did not want to return. As 'Second' Secretary he was supposed to tell Khrushchev that he had to go. He funked it and Suslov took over. (Another version states that Brezhnev was dragged to the phone and eventually made the call to the First Secretary.) Khrushchev, who was on holiday at Pitsunda on the Black Sea coast, and Mikoyan, were brought back to Moscow on 13 October. Semichastny met them and whisked them off to the Kremlin. At the Presidium meeting Khrushchev tried to defend himself and to make one last request. He was rudely interrupted by Brezhnev. 'Tears appeared in Nikita Sergeevich's eyes and then he simply broke down and cried. It was sad to see.' The CC plenum convened on 14 October. Two of Khrushchev's supporters were excluded from it. Semichastny was brutally frank: 'The Presidium decided everything for the CC and having decided, prepared, chewed it over, and then chewed it over again, and then threw it to the CC, saying, Vote.' The Presidium report, delivered by Suslov (again it should have been Brezhnev) indicted Nikita Sergeevich on fifteen counts. Among the accusations were that his leadership had been erratic; many decisions had been hasty and ill-considered; he had slighted and ignored his colleagues; he had turned Aleksei Adzhubei, his 'obsequious, incompetent and irresponsible' son-in-law, who, among other things had insulted Walter Ulbricht, into a shadow foreign minister; his bifurcation of the party apparatus had led to considerable confusion; he believed himself to be an expert on all he surveyed; he lacked diplomatic tact and referred once to Mao Zedong as an 'old boot' and told Todor Zhivkov, the Bulgarian party leader, that all Bulgarians were parasites; he had distributed too much largesse to Third World states; and of course, his agricultural policies were a disaster. Many of these criticisms were justified. Mikoyan was dispatched to inform Nikita Sergeevich about his future. His city flat and dacha were to be his for life. There was a 500-ruble-a-month pension and a car and he would have guards and domestic staff as well. Mikoyan had suggested to the Presidium that Khrushchev be appointed consultant to the Presidium, but not surprisingly this was turned down. Before leaving Mikoyan embraced Nikita Sergeevich and kissed him. They were never to meet again, but Mikoyan did manage to get to Khrushchev's funeral. On 14 October Leonid Ilich Brezhnev became First Secretary and the following day Aleksei Kosygin put on the Prime Minister's mantle. Adzhubei went on 16 October as editor of *Izvestiya*, and lesser lights went out as well.

The removal of Khrushchev was motivated by many factors: lust for power; the desire to ensure stability of cadres; fear that the authority of the party was being undermined by Khrushchev's erratic leadership, which would inevitably lead to social unrest; the party in 1964 yearned for a manager rather than a leader at the top. Brezhnev was viewed, correctly, as lacking leadership qualities, and hence was, potentially, a good manager of the party and State.

ECONOMIC POLICY

Industry by the end of the fifth FYP (1955) was quite unable to meet the increased demand generated by retail price cuts and the large rises in procurement prices paid by the State for agricultural products over the previous two years. Consumer goods' output grew faster than would have been the case under Stalin but Malenkov's economic policies were too ambitious and paid too little attention to the actual production problems involved.

The most startling innovation in agriculture over the years 1953–55 was the virgin and idle land programme. The original goal of 13 million hectares in 1954 was left far behind as 29.7 million hectares were ploughed up by the end of 1955. Of this 18 million hectares were in northern Kazakhstan and 5 million hectares in west Siberia. However such was the pace of assimilation that not all the land was sown to crops. In Kazakhstan, for instance, only an extra 11 million hectares were sown to crops in 1954 and 1955. This was typical of the programme: haste took precedence over sober contemplation. To make matters more difficult 1955 was a year of drought and the problem of wind erosion in dry farming areas, places where the annual precipitation is less than 250 mm, reared its head. Khrushchev, for political reasons, would not acknowledge it as a problem at all.

The original plan had envisaged that most of the new land would be assimilated by kolkhozes but the expansion of the programme meant that areas never before inhabited had to be farmed. This led to state farms dominating the new lands. The party launched an ambitious drive to recruit young people and the fact that they would be going to sovkhozes with a guaranteed wage was an added incentive. Over 300,000 went. Many returned, but a solid phalanx of European farm workers settled in northern Kazakhstan, for instance. Conditions in the beginning were primitive, with all amenities lacking.

The dominant crop was spring wheat since the climate was too severe to grow winter wheat. Khrushchev saw the new lands growing so much wheat that the Ukraine, for example, would be free to plant maize, which is much superior as a fodder crop. In this way animal husbandry could bloom.

The 1954–58 quinquennium were the good years for the virgin lands and Soviet agriculture in general. Farm incomes were rising, the private plot was no longer subject to compulsory deliveries – as of 1 January 1958, the MTS had been abolished, farms were being encouraged to take the initiative as never before, indeed a campaign was launched, in 1957, to catch up with the US '*per capita* output of milk and butter in 1958' and 'meat production in 1960 or 1961'. Everything in the garden seemed rosy especially after the wonderful harvest of 1958. But nothing in agriculture is ever as it seems.

The pattern of agriculture also changed. Many weak kolkhozes with little prospect of economic advance were taken over by the State and became state farms. This benefited the kolkhozniks who were now elevated to the status of workers, paid a wage, secured social benefits and a pension. It made food, however, more expensive. Other kolkhozes transformed into state farms were those near large cities, and envious workers could claim that they enjoyed an unfair advantage, being so close to their market. A network of sovkhozes producing vegetables, milk, butter and so on around each large city came into existence in this way. Add the virgin lands and the net result was that the area cultivated by State farms was almost equal to that cultivated in kolkhozes. The USSR is the only socialist country with such a high proportion of arable land in the state farm sector.

The XXth Party Congress, besides providing a stunning finale with Khrushchev's anti-Stalin speech, also passed the sixth FYP (1956–60). The inspiration for the *sovnarkhozy* appears to have been political in origin. They were a counter to the proposal, advanced in December 1956, to set up a state economic commission with powers to issue orders to all economic ministries.

The Seven-Year Plan had several goals. Khrushchev wanted to expand rapidly the chemical industry which in turn would provide more mineral fertilisers for agriculture. It would permit more emphasis to be placed on hydrocarbons, oil and natural gas, and a greater proportion of national investment could be concentrated east of the Urals.

The ambitious goals were not met for a host of reasons. There were just too many demands on the available investment. After the launching of the first sputnik on 4 October 1957 the space race occupied a high position on the list of priorities. In Stalin's day heavy industry had been afforded primacy and everything else suffered. Now there was no clearcut distinction between primary and secondary objectives. Growth rates suffered and in 1963 only 8.2 per cent was achieved and in 1964 7.4 per cent, the lowest in peacetime since planning began. All Nikita Sergeevich could do was to move people around and introduce one administrative reform after the other. By 1964 few knew the boundaries of their field of competence.

Agriculturally the years after 1958 did not come up to expectations. The goal of raising production by 70 per cent between 1959 and 1965 remained unattainable. The two best years were 1964 and 1965 but they did not concern Khrushchev. The dismal 1963 performance saw global agricultural output dip below the 1958 level. Nikita Sergeevich was full of bright ideas, all borrowed from somewhere else, usually the US. He favoured the intensification of agriculture, Malenkov's brainchild, the rapid expansion of mineral fertilisers, taken from Pryanishnikov, the sweeping away of Vilyam's *travopole* system, the reduction of fallow, the expansion of irrigation and drainage, to name only the economic campaigns. The average kolkhoznik benefited little from the post-1958 innovations so he reverted to his private plot. This is turn forced the First Secretary to place more restrictions on it. It was a vicious circle. Khrushchev saw problems from the production side and overlooked cost. Animal husbandry, despite the many campaigns, was and still is a loss-making enterprise for the vast majority of farms. So the incentive to increase meat and milk products was absent. So much pressure was put on farms to produce good results to be sent to Moscow that wholesale fraud and padding resulted. In Ryazan oblast, for instance, meat deliveries tripled in 1959 and more was promised for 1960. The method employed was to borrow or buy the kolkhoznik's animals, scour the countryside for additional livestock, paying high prices for any beast that could be obtained and then deliver them to the State – inevitably at a loss. However, one oblast's overfulfilment of the plan was another oblast's underfulfilment. There was also the unimportant point that the more meat the farms delivered the greater their losses were. The balloon went up in 1960 when only one sixth of the planned deliveries arrived. The farms were bankrupt, they could not afford to buy any more animals. Ryazan oblast's first secretary went the way of his animals; he shot himself.

Table 6.1   Economic performance 1951–65 (%)

	Average annual growth		
	1951–55	*1956–60*	*1961–65*
Population growth (%)	1.4	1.4	1.4
Gross National Product	5.5	5.9	5.0
Industry	10.2	8.3	6.6
Agriculture	3.5	4.2	2.8
Services	1.9	3.5	4.4
Consumption	4.9	5.7	3.7
Investment	12.4	10.5	7.6

Source: US Congress, Joint Economic Committee, *USSR: Measures of Economic growth and development, 1950–80* (Washington DC 1982). Population calculated from *Narodnoe Khozyaistvo SSSR v 1965 g.* (Moscow 1966)

SOCIAL POLICY[12]

The living standards of the Soviet population in 1953 were depressingly low; it is probable that most people were below the poverty line. The

Khrushchev years altered that. Between 1960 and 1965 *per capita* real personal disposable income increased by a commendable 4.1 per cent annually; the 1953–59 figure may have been just as good. If the poverty line is taken at 50 rubles per person per month in 1965, then *per capita* personal income (34 rubles 89 kopeks) in 1960 was only 79.6 per cent of this figure, adjusting for inflation. In 1965 it was still just below 50 rubles. Thus a substantial improvement had been achieved but living standards were still very modest.

State employees – industrial workers, office staff, sovkhoz operatives and so on – fared better than the collective farm peasant. Nevertheless, in 1958, 62.1 per cent of state employees were in need, but if 25–30 rubles is taken as subsistence level then those in poverty drop to about 26 per cent. Their earnings increased annually by 2.6 per cent between 1955 and 1964 but only by 1.4 per cent when adjusted for inflation. In 1960 the standard of living of industrial workers, 20.6 per cent of the labour force, was about 30 per cent above that of the population as a whole but in 1965 it was only 20 per cent above. Hence industrial workers were just above the poverty line in 1960.

Kolkhozniks, not unexpectedly, were at the bottom of the incomes tree. In 1960 the average total monthly income per collective farm peasant was about 32 rubles and by 1965 it had risen to about 46 rubles. Only Latvia and Estonia, in 1960, had incomes exceeding 50 rubles. Tadzhikistan was the poorest, only recording 18 rubles and Azerbaidzhan, Moldavia, Kirgizia and Turkmenistan all managed just over 22 rubles. In Lithuania, the other Baltic republic, the kolkhoznik earned about 45 rubles a month. This reveals the great disparities in farm income in various parts of the country; in 1960 *per capita* income in Latvia was 3.3 times that of Tadzhikistan.

Incomes increased rapidly between 1960 and 1965 with the greatest improvement coming in Moldavia, Kirgizia and Turkmenistan. Worst off was Azerbaidzhan with only 25 rubles, half of the minimum necessary for a normal consumption pattern. The clear leader was Estonia, with about 97 rubles, and Latvia and Lithuania were not far behind. All the Baltic republics had incomes about the level of the Soviet population as a whole. Indeed in Latvia and Lithuania the kolkhoznik was better off than the industrial worker in 1960–65. However, the kolkhozniks in the Baltic republics only accounted for about 3 per cent of all collective farm peasants while the five poorest republics contained about 20 per cent. In 1960, in the Soviet Union as a whole, the disposable personal income of kolkhozniks was about 70 per cent of that of state employees but this rose to about 80 per cent in 1965.

The breakdown of the kolkhoznik's income is very instructive. In 1960, 52.5 per cent of income came from the private plot in the USSR as a whole. In Lithuania it was as high as 75.6 per cent, in Georgia it was 66 per cent, in Latvia 65.3 per cent, in Belorussia 64.8 per cent and in Estonia 59.6 per cent. Kolkhoz labour payments only accounted for 17.1 per cent in Lithuania but 27.1 per cent in Latvia. In only three republics did labour payments account for more than half of income.

By 1965 the private plot had declined in significance and contributed only 42.3 per cent of USSR income. Nevertheless in Belorussia, Georgia, Lithuania, Latvia and Estonia it still provided only 50 per cent. The figures are eloquent testimony to the fact that under Khrushchev the peasants' interests lay in cultivating their private plots and go a long way to explain reluctance to put their backs into social labour. The disparities between the richer and poorer republics also increased during the Khrushchev years.

Kolkhozniks remained, as before, second-class citizens. They did not receive state retirement pensions until 1965; no maternity benefits were paid to female kolkhozniks (*kolkhoznitsy*) before 1965 and no sickness benefits before 1970. Since they did not have an internal passport they were effectively rooted in the countryside and did not benefit from state subsidised housing. They had to make do with their own dwelling places. Medical and educational facilities were not as good as in urban areas and given the fact that there were 67.3 million kolkhozniks and their dependants (31.7 per cent of the labour force) in 1960, there was evidently much suffering and hardship in the countryside. This led to many leaving and in 1965 kolkhozniks and their dependants only made up 24.7 per cent of the labour force.

Wages account for the lion's share of incomes but social benefits increased markedly under Khrushchev. These included holiday pay, pensions, allowances, education, medical care and the housing subsidy. State expenditure on these increased by 3 per cent annually between 1950 and 1955 but by 8 per cent annually over the period 1956–65. In 1955 this came to 7 rubles a month per head of the population but by 1965 it was 15 rubles 20 kopeks a month or 26.9 per cent of total *per capita* income.

Since social benefits were tied to wages and not to need they did little to reduce disparities in income throughout the country. This was especially true of the collective farm sector since it was effectively excluded from the welfare state until the second half of the 1960s.

Much social legislation was passed under Khrushchev. The swingeing legislation against absenteeism and changing jobs without permission was repealed, fees were no longer charged for secondary and tertiary education, the minimum wage was set at 27 rubles in the countryside and 35 rubles in the towns in June 1956, it was again raised to 40–45 rubles in February 1959, the seven-hour day (six-hour day underground) was in operation in 1960, adding up to a 41-hour week, and the non-productive spheres received a much needed boost in May 1964 when those in education, health and trade were awarded increases ranging from 19 to 26 per cent.

Substantial additions to the housing stock were also made. Soviet engineers pioneered the construction of large blocks of flats composed of prefabricated units. These often left a lot to be desired as many of the units did not fit properly and the quality of workmanship was low. The building craftsman no longer existed in the 1950s. Wits could refer to them as Khrushchev's slums but nevertheless they were a great improvement on no home at all. Private co-operative building also expanded and the desire and ability to own one's own flat (practically no houses were built) was especially strong among the intelligentsia.

Further education and medical facilities also expanded so that when Khrushchev had to go he could look back on some solid achievements. The difference between social classes had been reduced, wage differentials were smaller and the gulf between town and countryside and between industry and agriculture was slowly being closed.

CULTURE

No creative writer or thinker who was well known was imprisoned or exiled for his work between the death of Stalin and 1962. Many were upbraided for their outpourings but it was tacitly accepted that they could experiment. Since the top political leaders were hardly men of culture their judgements in this field were greatly influenced by their advisers. Many and manifold were the jokes about the lack of culture of the only top woman, the Minister of Culture, E. A. Furtseva. This was somewhat unfair as she did enjoy the circus. The Khrushchev period is marked by great fluctuations in the approach to culture with decisions being taken essentially on political rather than on artistic grounds.

With Stalin gone writers and artists were quick to seize the initiative. Olga Berggolts expressed the view that poetry could not be written without the individuality of the author finding expression. The most daring outburst came from Vladimir Pomerantsev in *Novy Mir* in December 1953. He attacked the lack of sincerity and truth displayed in Soviet literature and, by extension, called for writing to reflect unvarnished reality. Ovechkin published another story which laid bare village and raion life. The sensation of the period, however, was the novel which gives its name to the period, *The Thaw* by Ilya Ehrenburg, published in *Znamya* in May and then in book form in September 1954. People read into it what they wanted: it appeared to champion the true artist and to speak up for the wronged and oppressed. This was really throwing down the gauntlet and the conservative response was swift. After all they still manned all the fortresses of literary power and privilege. The convocation of the IInd Congress of Soviet Writers, in December 1954, was an event in itself and indicated that the authorities were thinking of pointing Soviet literature in a new direction. Members eagerly grasped the opportunity of expressing themselves. They harboured the hope that eventually their views would influence policy. Ovechkin made the apt point that there should be fewer meetings to discuss writing and life and more writing and living.

Rehabilitation of writers flowed like a current through 1955. Babel, Bulgakov and Meyerhold were the most prominent. Dostoevsky again became permitted reading and Hemingway and other Western writers reappeared in translation. This should have led to a revision of Soviet literary history but there were too many conservatives in high places to permit this. By 1956 two schools of thought were plainly visible and Khrushchev's denunciation of Stalin passed the initiative to the reformers. The most biting attack on the Union of Writers and its secretary general, Aleksandr Fadeev, was made by Mikhail Sholokhov at the XXth Party Congress. He claimed that only a few really good books had been published in the previous twenty years, the vast majority of the output was 'grey rubbish'. Fadeev had passed from being a writer to being a bureaucrat and this had ruined him as a writer. 'Neither as secretary general nor as a writer has he [Fadeev] achieved anything in the last fifteen years', claimed Sholokhov. This cut Fadeev to the quick. The burden of the past weighed heavily on his mind and he took his own life in May 1956.

Open dissent about literature in public thus appeared after a hiatus of three decades. Journals and newspapers were full of the debate and works flowed from the presses. A new peak was reached with the serialisation of *Not by Bread Alone* by Vladimir Dudintsev in *Novy Mir* in August, September and October 1956. The novel is populated by the new ruling class, party officials, generals, engineers and bureaucrats but it is the lonely, unrecognised engineer inventor Lopatkin who is the hero. The individual is preferred to the mass. It was unfortunate for Dudintsev that his novel should have appeared at the time of the Hungarian revolution. Khrushchev and the party were frightened by the events which owed their origin to the toppling of Stalin. The First Secretary was also aware of the role played by the Petöfi Circle of intellectuals in Hungary. He turned on Dudintsev and viciously attacked him. Writers were called to his dacha outside Moscow, in 1957, and officially warned that the party would not tolerate literature which undermined the foundations of Soviet society. Although Khrushchev knew and loved the Russian classics and enjoyed going to the theatre, he lacked confidence in cultural matters. So voluble in other spheres, he was reluctant to pass an artistic judgment. In retirement, he regretted not having read many of the heavily criticised works for himself. Instead, he was misled by the cultural bureaucrats who wished to stifle independent talent.

The polemics which greeted the publication in Italy of *Dr Zhivago* by Boris Pasternak were of an intensity and reached a pitch reminiscent of the Stalin years. One doctor even accused the author of slandering the medical profession! And this without having read the novel which was certainly not available officially in Moscow. Pasternak was awarded the Nobel Prize for literature in October 1958 but declined when he realised that if he left the Soviet Union he would never be allowed to return. Zhivago means living, in pre-1918 orthography to boot, and Pasternak knew that exile would mean artistic death. He was convinced that he could do more for Soviet letters by staying but he was over-sanguine: he never published another word in the USSR during his lifetime.

Khrushchev vilified Stalin at the XXIst Party Congress, in January 1959, and so took a flexible stance on literature since he could hardly attack his old mentor and at the same time threaten writers with doom. Aleksandr Tvardovsky, editor of *Novy Mir*, made an eloquent plea for truth at the congress but he was counterpoised by Vsevolod Kochetov, a writer known for his establishment line. Khrushchev again played the sage at the IIIrd Congress of Soviet Writers, in May 1958, and encouraged writers to decide among themselves if a manuscript was worth publishing and not to 'bother the government'.

Some remarkable poets emerged as a result of the changed atmosphere, the most prominent being Evgeny Evtushenko, Andrei Voznesensky and Bella Akhmadullina. They spoke for their generation (all three were in their twenties) and the first two became well known abroad. Evtushenko touched on matters which had hitherto been taboo. In *Babi Yar* (1961) it was anti-Semitism. The party was embarrassed but in *Stalin's Heirs* (1962) Evtushenko expressed the current line when he asked for the guards at Stalin's grave to be doubled and tripled lest the old dictator and his times be resurrected. In the same year Evtushenko went too far, publishing his autobiography in France without first submitting it to the Soviet censors. He had his wings clipped and was not permitted to travel abroad for a time.

The appearance in *Novy Mir* in November 1962, of *One Day in the Life of Ivan Denisovich* by a hitherto unknown writer, Aleksandr Solzhenitsyn, was a sensation at home and abroad which put *Dr Zhivago* in the shade. Whereas the latter could be faulted for not dealing with Soviet society the former treated one of its open sores, the labour camps. The story is an account of one day in the life of a prisoner, unjustly sentenced under Stalin, in the cold north. Solzhenitsyn had first-hand knowledge of the subject. The novel ends by stating that the day described was like all the 3,653 days he spent there. Solzhenitsyn published more stories in 1963 and then nothing more appeared until 1967, obviously a decision taken higher up.

Aleksandr Tvardovsky's poem *Tyorkin in Paradise*, written in 1953, was published in 1963. It is a satire on the absurdities of everyday life in the post-1945 period. Anna Akhmatova's moving poem *Requiem*, a memorial to the suffering of mothers left behind when their loved ones were exiled and imprisoned, also appeared in 1963.

Just how conservative Khrushchev was in cultural affairs can be gauged from remarks he made at an exhibition of modern paintings in Moscow in December 1962. Stopping in front of a painting which depicted a lemon, Khruschchev thought that it consisted of 'messy yellow lines which look, if you will excuse me, as though some child has done his business on the canvas when his mother was away and then spread it around with his hands'.[13] Of another picture: 'What's the good of a picture like this? To cover urinals with?' Another painting was 'dog shit'.

Revealing comments on music also flowed from Nikita Sergeevich. He did not like jazz but then many sane men don't. Ballet dancers, when he first saw them, were indecently dressed girls in petticoats.

Given that the First Secretary was a traditionalist in the world of culture how did it come about that so many literary works appeared which owed so little to socialist realism as the party understood it? On the face of it Leonid Ilichev, Khrushchev's answer to the even more conservative Mikhail Suslov, and the establishment writers and officials should have won hands down.

The key to the question lies in Khrushchev's desire to denigrate Stalin. If a work showed the blackest side of Stalin and his malefactions it stood a good chance of being published. However, Khrushchev was only willing to loosen the reins of party control very slightly, since the printed word was very potent. So how did a daring work appear in print? Through the intervention of someone whom the First Secretary trusted. Nikita Sergeevich was not a man given to much reading, he preferred the spoken word. An influential figure was V. S. Lebedev. He arranged for the work to be read to the First Secretary but he had to choose the opportune moment. Usually Khrushchev was at his dacha outside Moscow or vacationing on the Black Sea coast, especially at Gagri, a particularly beautiful spot. This technique was tried in 1962 and resulted in the publication of *One Day in the Life of Ivan Denisovich*. The reading of it so impressed Khrushchev that he was able to push publication through the Presidium.[14] Tvardovsky read *Tyorkin in Paradise* so well that Khrushchev was hugely amused at the maltreatment of Stalin. The First Secretary was much more careful before 1958 but his victory over the anti-party group increased his boldness.

Just why should novels and poems, often of modest literary merit, arouse such passions? Literature in the USSR expresses thoughts which are not articulated in the official political culture. Hence literature envelops politics, economics, indeed any discipline which cannot find overt expression. Soviet citizens are avid readers, they need to be, and they search for instances of unofficial views. Poetry plays an especially important role and poets such as Evtushenko and Voznesensky can fill a stadium. The audience often knows the poems by heart and it listens for inflections of the voice which communicate shades of meaning. The audience is young, the poets are young, a special phenomenon of the Khrushchev period. Youth emerged and journals were founded to express their aspirations.

Themes explored in the literature are instructive: love is emphasised and often it is lost or wasted love, sometimes between a married and an unmarried person. The stony bureaucrats and those who ride roughshod over the people, even in pursuit of the plan, are negatively portrayed. Much literature reflects real life, often the hard, grinding everyday existence of some people. Wide-spread social and economic abuses are portrayed. The 'new' literature was most popular among the young, but authors were attempting especially to influence that segment of the young who would join the party and become part of the ruling class. This class could change Soviet society in the future if it collectively wished to do so.

The fragility of the Thaw period was plain for all to see. Publication depended on political circumstances, considerable political skill on the part of Tvardovsky and others and sometimes on getting the nod from Khrushchev. Moscow was the hotbed of 'new' writers. Sometimes it was possible to publish in some provincial city where the pressures were not so great. But this could backfire. Konstantin Paustovsky's *Pages from Tarusa* came out in 1961 in Kaluga. Such was the reaction of the CC in Moscow that the second party secretary in Kaluga was dismissed for permitting publication and the local editor was sacked for wasting scarce paper.

On the scientific front the most important event occurred at the XXth Party Congress when Khrushchev transferred science from the superstructure to the base. It became a force of production and as such had a greater claim of investment. Cybernetics, hitherto a bourgeois pseudo-science, was welcomed and management science emerged. The windows to the West were then wide open. The goal was to assimilate everything of scientific value to the Soviet Union. Learning from the capitalists was acceptable provided only technical and scientific ideas were adopted. The party as before wished to exclude 'bourgeois life styles'.

RELIGION

The Christian churches, by 1959, were extending their influence on Soviet society to the extent that Khrushchev and the CPSU became alarmed. The years 1960–64 saw a vehement anti-religious propaganda war in the USSR with the result that the institutional churches were in danger of sinking under the blows administered by the State.

The Russian Orthodox Church came under special fire. In 1958 the Moscow Patriarchate stated that there were sixty-nine monasteries and convents in the Soviet Union. Within six years there were only ten at the outside, with only a few monks or nuns in each. Over the same period the number of theological seminaries dropped from eight to three.[15] The number of churches shrank from 22,000 to 20,000 before 1959 to 11,500 at the beginning of 1962. Numbers dropped to 7,500 soon afterwards.[16]

An important step in weakening the church was taken at a synod at Zagorsk, in July 1961. A document was rushed through which freed the parish priest from his responsibility for the 'preservation of the buildings and the properties of the church' and transferred it to the parish church council. The priest was to concentrate on conducting church services and on the spiritual welfare of the parish. Thus in effect the priest ceased to be the central figure in the parish. Each priest had to be registered according to Soviet law. Since church buildings are not the property of the church but the State they are in fact leased to the believers. A common procedure by the State was to cancel the priest's registration and refuse to accept a successor. Then the church could be handed over to say a kolkhoz for use as a club, the State claiming that the congregation had dispersed. Often the opposition was so strong that the church was physically destroyed, making it impossible for worship to continue. The believers could not adjourn to a private house since permission had to be obtained to hold such a meeting. It was normally not granted, and hence believers could not legally worship together. The penal code of the RSFSR was tightened at the same time, giving the authorities even more power.

It was one thing to close the churches but quite another to reduce the number of believers. The leadership of the Orthodox Church did not publicly, at home or abroad, protest against the behaviour of the authorities. There were, however, priests and believers who were not prepared to be so reticent. Out of persecution came those who wanted the 1961 legislation repealed and who protested that according to Soviet law the behaviour of local authorities was illegal. It was, but the local party and soviet received unpublished instructions which gave rise to their actions. In the summer of 1965 Archbishop Ermogen, then of Kaluga, led a delegation of eight Russian Orthodox bishops to the Moscow Patriarchate to appeal for the revision of the 1961 regulations.[17] Ermogen was dispatched to a remote monastery but his writings and those of two priests, Nikolai Eshliman and Gleb Yakunin,[18] who were then relieved of their duties, penetrated to the West and brought the struggle inside the church to the light of day.

The Baptist Church was thrown into turmoil as a result of the increasing demands of the State. New statutes were accepted by the All-Union Council of Evangelical Christians and Baptists (AUCECB), in 1960. A letter of instruction was also sent out to all senior presbyters.[19] This had the effect of bringing to a head opposition to the AUCECB for leaning too far in the State's direction. The main objective of the reformers, the Action Group, was to convene a congress to reform the ECB church. The reformers were against the church performing any state function. They wanted to free the church from state control, although this was never overtly stated, and to alter the leadership of the church so as to revitalise it spiritually.[20] The official church attempted to win over the protesters but failed. The authorities then acted against the critics in the same way as against the Orthodox. They deregistered churches and pastors and when the believers met arrested them. Many leaders of these illegal Baptist churches were imprisoned.

An ECB Congress did meet in Moscow in 1963 but the reformers were not adequately represented and so were defeated. This deepened the schism between the two branches of the church. As the number of prisoners increased a council of prisoners' relatives came into being and gradually more and more contact was made with Christians abroad. The plight of believers in the USSR was taking on an international dimension. Leonid Ilichev, the key party man in the fight against religion, was particularly incensed by the ability of Baptists, and significantly also of Muslims, to organise evening meetings for young people.

NATIONALITIES

In the struggle for the succession nationality affairs played an important role. Georgy Malenkov's power base was the central government and hence he did not regard it as incumbent upon him to make concessions to the union republics. Lavrenty Beria and Nikita Khrushchev both set out to undermine Malenkov by promoting the claims of the non-Russian nationalities. The predominance of Russia and Russians in the administration of the Soviet Union was a fertile source of resentment on which to play. Beria seized the initiative, and in early June 1953 presented various memoranda to the Politburo condemning Stalin's nationality policy and advocating a return to the Leninist policy of the 1920s. He underlined repeatedly that the preponderance of Russians in the leaderships of the non-Russian republics had to end. The predominantly Russian party Presidium accepted this. A Presidium decree of 12 June 1953 ordered all party and state organs in the non-Russian republics to end the distortions in nationality policy; to groom and promote locals for leading positions; those officials who did not speak the local language were to be dismissed and put at the disposal of the CC, CPSU; and the local language was again to become the norm in communications within the republic. It was probably also laid down that the First Party Secretary had to be a local.

The first republic to be affected was the Ukraine. The Presidium immediately dismissed L. G. Melnikov as First Secretary and replaced him with Andrei Kirichenko, hitherto Second Secretary. A plenum of the CC, Communist Party of the Ukraine (CPUk), ratified these appointments and went on to criticise severely the 'distortions of Leninist-Stalinist nationality policy' which had resulted in cadres from other parts of the Ukraine being promoted to leading party and soviet positions in the western regions of the Ukraine as well as the imposition of Russian as the language of further education. Party policy was thereby turned on its head. Almost the same language was used by the party in the Baltic republics. As a result, in the summer of 1953, the Second Secretary in all three parties was replaced by a local. The Second Secretary is responsible for personnel policy. However, a Russian was again appointed to this key position in Lithuania in 1955, in Latvia in 1956 and in Estonia in 1971. A process got under way which was to see the grooming and promotion of thousands of locals for leading party, governmental and soviet positions. This made more rapid progress in the western parts of the Soviet Union than in Central Asia. The party began to use language reminiscent of the 1920s. Each nation was to develop its language, culture and traditions and the material and cultural level of the working masses of all national republics and regions was to be raised. However, attacks on Great Russian chauvinism ended with Beria's arrest. Afterwards Russians again were held up as the leading nation. Beria was accused by Khrushchev at the Presidium session at which he was arrested, on 26 June 1953, of interfering in party affairs in the Baltic republics, Belorussia and the Ukraine. He had played on 'national antagonisms' in order to undermine Soviet unity. When he was sentenced to death in December 1953 it was claimed that he had tried to 'activate bourgeois-nationalist elements' in the Union republics, 'enmity among the peoples of the USSR' and to 'undermine the friendship of the Soviet peoples and the Great Russian people'. The case against him may have been exaggerated, but the general drift appears to be that Beria, a Georgian, was playing the non-Russian card in his struggle against the two Great Russians, Malenkov and Khrushchev.

Khrushchev became heir to Beria's nationality policy. The party was his power base and the Ukraine his favourite non-Russian republic. The number of full and candidate Ukrainian members in the CC, CPSU rose from 16 (6.8 per cent) in 1952 to 39 (15.5 per cent) in 1956 and 59 (18.5 per cent) in 1961. As they made up only 17.7 per cent of the Soviet population in 1959 they were now overrepresented in the CC at the expense of those nations which had been preferred by Stalin, the Russians, Georgians and Armenians. Russian CC full and candidate members dropped from 71.5 per cent to 62.7 per cent in 1961. Georgians and Armenians fell back from 5.6 per cent in 1952 to 2.4 per cent in 1961. The CPUk pursued a conscious policy of recruiting Ukrainians and they accounted for 74.2 per cent in 1956. Whereas only 40 per cent of leading party positions in the Ukraine were held by locals in 1940, this had risen to 67.8 per cent in 1956. In the same year, 76 per cent of Ukrainian Supreme Soviet deputies and 84 per cent of all local soviet deputies were Ukrainian. A different tendency is observable in the economy. In 1957, 56.8 per cent of all graduates employed in the economy were Ukrainian, but this only rose to 58.1 per cent in 1964. Over the same period the proportion of Russians rose from 25 per cent to 28.1 per cent.

Khrushchev's victory over the Anti-Party group in June 1957 resulted in an unprecedented promotion of Ukrainians to top posts. Never before or since have Ukrainians attained such prominence as between 1957 and 1964. Khrushchev's 'tail' in the Ukraine was quite long since he had been party boss there. He had a penchant for Ukrainian military officers. In October 1957, Marshal Rodion Malinovsky replaced Marshal Zhukov as Defence Minister, and when he died he was followed by another Ukrainian marshal, Andrei Grechko. In 1960 Marshal Moskalenko became deputy Minister of Defence and commander-in-chief of the Strategic Rocket Forces. Andrei Kirichenko became a secretary of the CC, CPSU and responsible for cadre policy in December 1957. Nikolai Podgorny took over as Ukrainian party leader. Kirichenko would have pushed the claims of non-Russians in the CPSU apparatus. He was dismissed from all his posts and banished from political life in May 1960. This was connected with Khrushchev's radical revision of his nationality policy in the late 1950s.

The celebration of the tercentenary of the 'reunification of the Ukraine and Russia' in 1954 was an elaborate affair. To mark the occasion the Russian republic presented the Crimea to the Ukraine. This certainly could not be justified on population grounds. In 1959 Ukrainians made up 22.3 per cent of the population but Russians accounted for 71.4 per cent.

Khrushchev's promotion of the non-Russian republics fulfilled two functions. One was the desire to weaken the central government power and the other was to build 'tails' in the various republics. Economically he believed that decision-making by local party and government elites would be more efficient. Despite the fact that Malenkov was Prime Minister and one of the beneficiaries of over-centralisation, he had to concede that decentralisation of governmental functions was necessary. A wide-ranging transfer of functions to the republican level got under way in 1954. Many All-Union ministries were dissolved or transformed into Union-republican entities. In April 1954, the USSR Ministry of Coal was changed into a Union-republican ministry. A Ukrainian Ministry of Coal was set up. Before the end of 1954 the USSR Ministries of the Oil Industry, Communications, and Further Education ceased to be merely All-Union ministries. The USSR Ministry of Paper and Woodworking followed the same pattern in August 1955, and in 1956 geology, mining and chemical equipment, coal equipment, and grain products were added. In May 1956 enterprises and organisations concerned with the food, meat and milk, fish, grain procurement, light, textile, building materials, paper and woodworking, automobile transport and roads, inland navigation, health and retail and catering trades were transferred from central to republican control. The USSR Ministry for Inland Navigation and the Union-republican Ministries for Automobile Transport and Roads, and Justice were dissolved in May 1956. New Ministries for Inland Navigation, and Automobile Transport and Roads were created in the Union republics. The republican Ministries of Justice assumed sole responsibility for justice in their territory. This recreated the situation established by the first Soviet constitution in 1924. This situation, however, did not last very long. The Ministries of Justice were dissolved in the autonomous republics between 1957 and 1958 and in the Union republics between 1959 and 1963. Their functions were taken over by the Supreme Courts of the territories and by the newly created juridical commission of the Council of Ministers.

Decentralisation of industry increased substantially the influence of the republics. Whereas in 1950 enterprises subject to republican authorities were responsible for a third of industrial output, this had risen to 55 per cent in 1956. This was even more marked in the Ukraine, where republican-administered industry contributed 36 per cent of republican production. This increased to 76 per cent in 1956. The planning and financing of the republican economies also had to change. Legislation in May 1955 increased substantially the competence of governments and ministries. Henceforth the USSR State Plan was to be handed down to the republics and they then became responsible for devising ways of fulfilling the plan. The republic was to decide what its enterprises were to produce. New investment became the responsibility of the republican government. When this concerned Union-republican ministries, it had to be agreed with Moscow. Indicators such as the size of the labour force and wages were passed down in global terms and the republic became responsible for keeping to them. Republican governments determined expenditure as the centre handed over a global sum to cover all activities. This also included the means of support of the government itself. The republic, in turn, apportioned a global sum to cover expenditure in autonomous republics, raion, krai, oblast and city soviets. The local authority apportioned the resources according to its own lights. They were, in addition, responsible for agreeing the plans of their enterprises and cooperatives.

The republics needed to influence decision-making at the centre. The above changes concerned plans handed down by the centre. Republican input into plan formation was promised by the establishment, in February 1957, of an economic commission of the Soviet of Nationalities, the second house of the USSR Supreme Soviet. It consisted of a chairman and thirty representatives, two from each republic. Supreme Soviet deputies from autonomous republics and other national areas could participate when their area was under discussion. The commission was responsible for elaborating plans for economic and cultural development. These functions had been performed by the Presidium of the Soviet of Nationalities before the 1936 constitution abolished it. The commission, in turn, was dissolved in 1966. Also in February 1957 republics obtained the exclusive right to make administrative changes within their republics. They could set up autonomous republics and oblasts and alter existing raion and oblast boundaries. At the same time, republics gained jurisdiction over enactment of law and judicial procedure. They could also pass their own civil and criminal codes, but they were not to infringe the USSR civil and criminal codes. This had been the situation until 1936. When there were no USSR guidelines, criminal law varied from republic to republic, especially in the definition of what constituted a crime. The Chairman of the Supreme Court of a republic became, *ex officio*, a member of the USSR Supreme Court. Republican courts could hear all cases. Only when cases affected other republics or where the judgment was contrary to All-Union law were they referred to Moscow.

Decentralisation of economic decision-making reached its apogee with the reform of May 1957. Central ministries and organisations were replaced by 105 (101 from 1961) councils of the national economy (sovnarkhozes). All industry and construction sites of a region were subordinate to its sovnarkhoz. Each had an economic council, and it, in turn, was under the jurisdiction of the republican government. The USSR Council of Ministers administered the activities of the sovnarkhozes through the republican governments. This placed great influence in the hands of the republics. Prime Ministers became, *ex officio*, members of the USSR Council of Ministers. Ten All-Union and 15 Union-republican industrial ministries were liquidated. Similar republican ministries also disappeared. Over 140 All-Union, Union-republican and republican ministries were swept away. In 1960, republican economic councils were set up to co-ordinate and supervise the activities of local sovnarkhozes in the three largest republics: the RSFSR, the Ukraine and Kazakhstan. The other twelve republics, and autonomous republics, had one economic council each. In this way the non-Russian territories obtained direct access to economic management for the first time. Three All-Union ministries, all concerned with the defence economy, remained. By the early 1960s, about 94 per cent of Soviet industrial output was coming from the sovnarkhozes. The central government only accounted for 40.3 per cent of the Soviet budget in 1961, the lowest ever recorded.

Among the charges levelled at Khrushchev by the Anti-Party group in June 1957 were that decentralisation would foster economic *mestnichestvo* or localism, a centrifugal flow of power from the centre to the periphery and bourgeois nationalism. The Anti-Party group – essentially Malenkov, Kaganovich and Molotov – were accused, in turn, of hindering the party in its struggle to remove the deformations in its Leninist nationality policy. They also opposed the republics acquiring greater economic, legal and cultural autonomy, and the strengthening of local soviets. The Union republics welcomed Khrushchev's victory, with the greatest plaudits coming from the Ukraine. The Ukrainians exulted in the downfall of Lazar Kaganovich, who had become a symbol of hatred for his ruthlessness there. Nikolai Podgorny, Ukrainian First Secretary, referred to him as a 'real sadist'.

Khrushchev grasped the nettle of the deported peoples in his secret speech to the XXth Party Congress. He called the policy of removing all the men, women, children, party and Komsomol members of a particular nation 'monstrous'. However, he only rehabilitated the Kalmyks, the Chechens and Ingushi, the Karachai and the Balkars. He omitted deliberately the two largest deported nations: the Crimean Tatars and the Germans. The position of the banished, however, had been improving since a July 1954 decree had improved their legal status. In December 1955, the Germans became the first people to be released from labour camps. This move was probably linked to the establishment of diplomatic relations with the Federal Republic of Germany. However, Germans were required, on leaving the camps, to guarantee that they would not seek to return to their former homes in the Volga, the Ukraine and the Caucasus and not to make any claim for restitution of property. In April 1956 Crimean Tatars, Balkars, Meskhetians, Khemshins and Kurds were released from labour camps. The last three peoples had been deported to Central Asia in November 1944. They had had no contact with the Wehrmacht but lived in Georgia along the border with Turkey. Stalin appears to have considered them a security risk. The relaxing of controls in the summer of 1954 led to many Caucasians, especially the Chechens and Ingushi, heading for their homeland. Despite renewed deportations to Central Asia the stream became a flood and Moscow relented. It re-established the national territories of the Chechens and Ingushi, the Kalmyks, the Karachai and the Balkars. Had the Crimean Tatars and Germans followed the example of the above peoples and ignored Soviet directives and moved *en masse* back to their former homes, they might have got their territory back. In January 1957 the Chechen-Ingush autonomous republic reappeared, the Kalmyk autonomous oblast was formed, the Kabardin autonomous republic became once again the Kabardino-Balkar autonomous republic and the Cherkess autonomous oblast reverted to the Karachai and Cherkess autonomous oblast. Moscow was to provide compensation for all the injustices caused but, according to the nationalities involved, never did. In July 1958 the Kalmyk autonomous oblast was upgraded to autonomous republic, its former status. There was bound to be friction between the returnees and those who had taken over their homes and property. It was most severe in the Chechen-Ingush automous republic where about half a million demanded the *status quo ante*. In early 1957, about 77,000 post-1944 residents asked to be repatriated to Dagestan and Ossetia. Over 36,000 Russians left in haste for Russia. A four-day riot in August 1958 between Russians, and Chechens and Ingushi was a clear manifestation of the tension. Some Chechens and Ingushi, on returning, found themselves in the North Ossetian autonomous republic since the boundaries of the new autonomous republic were not exactly the same as the old. Demonstrations protesting against the discrimination practised against Chechens and Ingushi in North Ossetia began in Grozny in February 1973 and lasted several days. The Germans had to wait until August 1964 to be rehabilitated and to be cleared of the accusations of having aided the 'fascist-German aggressor'. The Crimean Tatars were the last to be rehabilitated – in September 1967.

Khrushchev's nationality policy was not a carbon copy of the 1920s. In two important instances it diverged – in language and cultural policies. Russian was to be the medium for the modernisation of the USSR. When communism was reached, everyone would be fluent in Russian. Great emphasis on the learning of Russian as a second language emerges with the education reform of 1958. It was also stated that the end goal was the merging of nations, something which had disappeared in the post-Stalin period. The education reform led to considerable conflict over the language of instruction in schools. The new decree proposed that parents should choose which language was used. The Ukraine, Transcaucasia and the Baltic republics wanted Russian to be made an obligatory subject. They foresaw the risk of the republican language being dropped from some schools. In the end, the All-Union decree made no provision about language. However, Moscow instructed the republics to allow parents to choose the language. Nevertheless, Azerbaidzhan and Latvia refused to toe the line. This infuriated Khrushchev, and he went to Riga in July 1959 to supervise a purge of party and government officials. In Azerbaidzhan many officials also lost their posts. Despite all the changes, the language reform had little impact and was not implemented. Parents were not permitted to choose. The non-Russian republics wanted Russians living and working there to learn the local language, but Moscow would not agree. In the RSFSR, in non-Russian areas, Russian was adopted more and more as the language of instruction. In the school year 1962–63, 27 per cent of RSFSR non-Russian children in the first four classes, 53 per cent of those in classes five to eight and 66 per cent of those in the final two classes were taught in Russian. Karelians lost their native language school in 1958, the Balkars in 1965–66 and the Kalmyks in 1968. Russian made great strides during the 1960s and was helped by autonomous republics, autonomous oblasts and national areas going over to Russian as the language of correspondence in the economy, administration and law.

Purges of officials began in Turkmenistan in 1958 and affected other republics until 1961. Those affected lost their positions but not their lives. Some of them were given minor jobs. This turnabout in national policy disillusioned many, and it was all the greater because of the high hopes placed in Khrushchev. By 1961 the Soviet party and government leader had lost almost all support in the non-Russian republics. Pro-Moscow locals took over the leadership. One of the benefactors was the new Uzbek First Secretary, Rashidov. He replaced scores of Uzbek officials with Russians and Ukrainians. Uzbek Russians in the KGB and Ministry of Justice made way for Russians from the RSFSR. The purge in Latvia was very extensive and involved the expulsion of thousands of members from the party. Latvian economists opposed the rapid expansion of heavy industry in Riga, which involved bringing in outside labour. Almost 27,000 moved to Latvia in 1956, more than during the previous six years put together. In Latvia and elsewhere purges were accompanied by sharp attacks on the local intelligentsia for exhibiting 'nationalist tendencies'. One republic is an exception to the above 'rotation of cadres' – the Ukraine. Once again Khrushchev revealed it to be the apple of his eye.

Recentralisation of the economy began in November 1962 when the USSR Economic Council was set up to coordinate the activities of all economic councils. Whereas there were only twelve industrial state committees, there were thirty by 1963. They were organised on the branch principle and performed the same functions as industrial ministries before 1957. A Central Asian Economic Council also made its appearance in November 1962. It was to co-ordinate the activities of the economic councils in Uzbekistan, Kirgizia, Tadzhikistan and Turkmenistan. A party CC bureau for Central Asia, and for Transcaucasia were also set up. In March 1963 a USSR Supreme Economic Council was established in an effort to make co-ordination of the economy more efficient. Besides the economic councils, Gosplan, the State Committee for Construction (Gosstroi) and all industrial state committees were subordinate to it. This reform brought republican economic councils back under the jurisdiction of the centre and greatly reduced their autonomy. However, the net result of Khrushchev's many reforms was bureaucratic confusion. In 1965, under Brezhnev, the whole edifice of decentralisation of economic decision-making was brought crashing down and everyone reverted to ministries. Recentralisation cost the republics control over law and order. In January 1960 the Ministry of the Interior ceased to be a Union-republican ministry and became a purely republican ministry. In July 1966 it reverted to being a Union-republican ministry. In August 1966 the first ever All-Union Ministry of Education was established, and the republican ministries, hitherto wholly responsible for education, were transformed into Union-republican ministries.

Sblizhenie or sliyanie?

The Khrushchev leadership backed away from its rather liberal nation-alities policy after 1956. Its policy of *sblizhenie*, or the drawing together of nations, gradually gave way to *sliyanie*, or the fusing of nations. The latter policy implied the assimilation of all non-Russian nations. This course was confirmed at the XXIIth Party Congress in October 1961 and found its way into the new party programme approved by the delegates. The new programme sketched out the route to communism in the near future. The offending term *sliyanie* did not appear, but the goal under communism was clearly the creation of a Russian-speaking, socially homogeneous, communist State. The programme stated: 'Comprehensive communist construction signifies a new stage in the development of national relations in the USSR in which the nations will draw more closely together and their complete unity will be achieved.' It also spoke of the party promoting the 'socialist content of the cultures of the peoples of the USSR'. This would lead to an 'international culture common to all the Soviet nations'. Russian would 'in effect, become the common medium of intercourse and co-operation among all the peoples of the USSR'. Khrushchev, at the Congress, gave short shrift to those who 'complain about the elimination of national distinctions'. He declared that the party's task waas to demonstrate 'uncompromising Bolshevik implacability' in the struggle to eradicate 'even the slightest manifestation of nationalist survival'. Did this mean that the party was going to stamp out national cultures? No. Khrushchev reached for the dialectic to legitimise his policy. Nations would continue to flourish but at the same time they would grow together. National languages could develop providing they did not 'reinforce barriers between peoples' but rather fostered the 'coming together of nations'. The debate on the flourishing or the merging of nations was given new impetus. Non-Russians vigorously opposed *sliyanie* and they were also supported by Russian nationalists, who were fearful of the effect of this policy on their own nation, culture and language.

FOREIGN POLICY

The US and China

Strictly speaking a socialist state should not need a foreign policy. Marx had envisaged the socialist revolution being victorious on a world scale and hence relations between these new states would be on a fraternal basis. Foreign policy became necessary only when the advanced capitalist world did not go socialist. Since socialist states believe that capitalist states will one day also become socialist, foreign policy is a temporary phenomenon. Its main goal is to strengthen the socialist state and to weaken the capitalist state. Lenin coined the expression peaceful cohabitation to describe the unequal relationship which existed in his day between the infant Soviet state and the outside world. He accepted that just as revolution is attended by violence so armed conflict between the socialist and capitalist camps was inevitable. The arrival of the atomic bomb in 1945 in the US and 1949 in the USSR and the thermonuclear bomb in 1952 in the US and in 1953 in the USSR conjured up the spectre that inevitable war, using nuclear weapons, could destroy all life on the planet. Malenkov began the rethink, war was not inevitable, and Khrushchev publicised the concept, now called peaceful co-existence, at the XXth Party Congress. An argument in favour of peaceful co-existence was that the increasing power of the socialist camp made the prevention of war possible. In the Soviet mind peaceful co-existence was a temporary policy, one which ultimately will be superseded by the era of socialism. Hence the element of competition was still there, seen as a form of historic contest on a world scale between capitalism and socialism, linked with the revolutionary process and the accompanying class struggle. Despite this, mutually advantageous co-operation was also envisaged. Co-operation, however close, would always be accompanied by an ideological and economic contest designed to reveal the systems' relative merits. The fundamental need for peaceful co-existence between states with differing social systems stems from the inadmissibility of nuclear war and the fact that the worldwide socialist revolution was slow to materialise.

The horrendous implications of nuclear war would be sufficient to prevent it provided nuclear nations acted rationally. There were two approaches to this goal. The first was that the existing nuclear powers, the USSR, the US, the UK and France, could retain their nuclear monopoly and prevent proliferation. The second was to allow all nations to acquire the weapons so that no state would be tempted into unilateral action to secure an advantage. Given the events in eastern Europe in 1953–56 it was quite clear which alternative the Soviet Union would choose. Hence its foreign policy ever since has been directed at preventing the proliferation of nuclear weapons. Translated into

269

material terms, the two countries which Khrushchev saw as potentially the most dangerous to the Soviet Union if they ever acquired a nuclear capability were China and Germany.

In the first flush of ideological enthusiasm the Chinese were keen on ideological solidarity and a determined stance *vis-à-vis* the US. Since they did not have the atomic bomb they were less frightened of its impact during a war. They were convinced that socialism would prove victorious even if casualties were high. They looked askance at Malenkov's New Course, the *rapprochement* with the Yugoslavs in 1955 and the doctrine of peaceful co-existence – 'a bourgeois pacifist notion' to them. Yugoslavia, as far as they were concerned, was still a heretic. What rankled with the Chinese was that the Soviets had taken all these initiatives without even consulting them. Khrushchev's anti-Stalin speech was another case in point.

Khrushchev's first taste of Chinese diplomacy was in September 1954 when he, Bulganin, Mikoyan and D. T. Shepilov but not Molotov, the Foreign Minister, went to see Mao and Zhou. The Chinese quickly took the measure of the Soviets and it was all one-way traffic. Chinese self-confidence had received a boost at the Geneva Conference which had been held shortly before the visit and which had brought the war in Indo-China to a halt. China had been treated as a Great Power and Ho Chi Minh would continue to need Chinese help in the struggle to take over south Vietnam.[21]

Soviet and Chinese thinking about the US diverged sharply. Whereas the former sought improved relations to strengthen peace and permit the flow of technology and know-how, the latter was an implacable enemy of Washington. The Chinese were actively seeking to extend their revolution to the numerous offshore islands and Taiwan.

Disagreement became discord, then covert hostility, then overt hostility by 1960. Part of the blame must rest with Khrushchev. By temperament he was quite incapable of coping with the refined, astute Mao, who to the Soviet leader was thinking like a latter-day Stalin, basically always arguing from an inferior position. Khrushchev, on the other hand, wished to innovate and be flexible in the face of the shifting balance of power. The US could no longer roll back socialism: she had to accept the fact that the USSR could not be militarily defeated except perhaps at exorbitant cost. Mao even thought that after a nuclear war there would still be 300 million Chinese left.

Besides radically disagreeing on how to deal with the capitalist world, China and the Soviet Union quickly diverged on how communism was to be built. Mao was an innovative as Khrushchev, and the campaign 'let a hundred flowers bloom' was launched in 1957, basically meaning that differing views on socialism could contend with one another. Then in 1958 came the 'great leap forward' when China prepared to jump over socialism into communism. It consisted in setting up blast furnaces in back yards (dismissed as 'samovar industrialisation' by Khrushchev), building small steelworks in rural areas and organising peasants in strict communes. According to the Chinese Soviet wages were still calculated according to 'bourgeois principles', a jibe that stung the CPSU.

Khrushchev knew that better relations with the US would exacerbate Sino-Soviet relations but he still went ahead and declared on 31 March 1958 that the USSR was voluntarily suspending nuclear testing and the US responded in October 1958. Soviet testing recommenced in November 1958 but perhaps a bargain could be struck. In between Khrushchev again went to Beijing, on 31 July. The Chinese wanted help in their fight to occupy the offshore islands and Taiwan. However, when they began shelling Quemoy and Matsu in late August the Soviets only committed themselves to defensive help in the case of an American attack but no offensive aid was forthcoming. The Chinese could only be irritated by the knowledge that the USSR was not willing to risk a nuclear confrontation with the US on their behalf.

The last occasion, in public, when the Chinese endorsed Soviet policies was at the XXIst Party Congress. Soviet bait was a very substantial aid programme, almost all of which was to remain a dead letter.

A turning-point in Sino-Soviet relations occurred in the second half of 1959. According to the Chinese, the Soviets on 20 June 1959 unilaterally 'tore up the agreement on new technology for national defence, concluded between China and the USSR on 15 October 1957, [and] refused to provide China with a sample atomic bomb and technical data concerning its manufacture'.[22] Presumably the Soviet argument was that they would provide a nuclear umbrella for China but the Chinese could only understand this to mean that China was to remain in an inferior position *vis-à-vis* the USSR. The first flare up on the Tibetan-Indian border occurred on 9 September 1959 but the USSR, far from backing up the Chinese, took in effect a neutral stand. Then, in the same month, Khrushchev took off for the US and followed it up with a visit to Beijing. Mao had to endure lectures from Nikita Sergeevich, imbued by the Camp David spirit, on the statesmanlike qualities of President Eisenhower. Khrushchev asked for a Soviet base and a radio station to keep in contact with Soviet submarines in the Pacific.[23] The Chinese countered by asking for atomic data. Neither side got anything.

The parting of the ways came at the IIIrd Congress of the Communist Party of Romania in Bucharest, in June 1960, shortly after the collapse of the Paris summit meeting. Khrushchev continued his offensive at the Ist Congress of communist and workers' parties in Moscow, in November 1960. On both occasions the First Secretary was very aggressive and abused Mao personally but the Chinese countered skilfully. The most intemperate speech, however, was delivered by Enver Hoxha, the Albanian party leader. Albania had just gone over to the Chinese side presumably because she feared that the Soviet Union and Yugoslavia would reach agreement over her head for the incorporation of Albania in Yugoslavia.[24] The Sino-Soviet dispute was broadcast to the rest of the world at the XXIInd Party Congress, in February 1961. The Cuban débâcle delighted the Chinese and provided them with another stick with which to beat Nikita Sergeevich.

If Khrushchev was apprehensive about the Chinese procuring a nuclear potential then the prospect of West German hands on nuclear weapons gave him nightmares. His bargaining counter was Berlin. With the FRG in NATO there was the possibility that one day Bonn might threaten the GDR with these weapons. What was the USSR to do then? Certainly not give the National People's Army nuclear weapons, which would terrify Poland and Czechoslovakia. There was no way the FRG could defeat the USSR but she could drag the Soviet Union involuntarily into a war with the US. This was the chief fear in the Soviet mind. What could the Soviets offer the Americans to prevent them from providing Bonn with a nuclear capability? A nuclear free zone in central Europe, Poland, Czechoslovakia, the GDR and the FRG, as spelled out in the Rapacki Plan in 1957 and 1958. But it was of little interest to the US since it stopped the US placing short-range tactical nuclear weapons in the FRG. However, it did not affect Soviet long-range strategic nuclear rockets targeted on the FRG.

There followed the Berlin crisis which began on 27 November 1958 with a Soviet note proposing that West Berlin became a free, demilitarised zone. Agreement had to be reached within six months, otherwise the USSR would transfer East Berlin and her rights as an occupying power to the GDR. Then the US, the UK and France would have to negotiate rights of access with the GDR. Nothing came of this Soviet démarche. Ulam suggests that the Soviet government had wanted, in 1959, to 'be empowered to pledge that China would refrain from the production of nuclear weapons if for her part the United States would make a similar pledge about West Germany'.[25] Again not much of a bargain for the US since China was industrially in no position to produce sophisticated nuclear weapons and drop them on the US. However elementary short-range nuclear weapons could do great damage in the Sino-Soviet border area. Khrushchev needed foreign policy successes if the quarrel with the Chinese was to be patched up. If the US could be driven out of Berlin it could start a world-wide American retreat.

In his quest for success the First Secretary again went to the US, in 1960, but only to the United Nations. An impressive array of world leaders assembled but the only firework Khrushchev exploded was a proposal to turn the secretary generalship into a troika, one member coming from the socialist world, one coming from the capitalist and the third from the Third World. It turned out to be a damp squib as was his suggestion that the UN might care to move to Switzerland, Austria or the USSR. Hardly worth going so far to say so little. Nevertheless if Nikita Sergeevich made little impression as a statesman he was a huge success as an actor. He shouted, laughed and interrupted speakers and even banged his shoe on his desk during Harold Macmillan's speech. The debonair British Prime Minister, who was a past master at dealing with hecklers, turned the tables on Khrushchev. He calmly paused, then asked for a translation! Nikita Sergeevich's behaviour was very *nekulturnyi*. However, it was all premeditated. Careful examination of the shoe-bashing incident reveals that he was wearing two shoes at the time. The UN was not pleased and fined the Soviet delegation $10,000 for its *nekulturnyi* behaviour. Nevertheless, Nikita Sergeevich's acting appeared to have a serious side to it. He may have thought that the best way to scare off the Americans was to threaten them.

The First Secretary presented President John F. Kennedy with an ultimatum at their meeting in Vienna in June 1961. Conclude a peace treaty before the end of the year or West Berlin would become a free city and access routes would have to be negotiated with the GDR. Khrushchev thought he had the measure of the young President, the USSR began nuclear testing again with the greatest explosion ever, but no treaty was signed. On 13 August 1961 a wall across and eventually around West Berlin was put up by the GDR, who could not become a viable economic entity with an open door for those who did not want to build socialism – over three million had gone already. This was as far as it went: both sides accepted a compromise.

What was Nikita Sergeevich's goal in Cuba? He thought he could outmanoeuvre President Kennedy, score a foreign policy success *vis-à-vis* the US, raise his standing at home and quieten the Chinese for a while. But why take so many risks? He may have believed that the correlation of forces was shifting in favour of socialism and that his sabre rattling had contributed to the Bay of Pigs fiasco. Putting rockets on Cuba would consolidate the USSR's position. Another explanation would be to see the short-range missiles on Cuba as effectively checkmating US superiority in intercontinental ballistic measures. This would have established something like nuclear parity and would permit the Soviets to argue that the giving of nuclear weapons to Bonn was a warlike act.

The first step on the long road to a Strategic Arms Limitation Treaty (SALT) was taken on 25 July 1963 when the USSR, the US and the UK initialled an agreement to ban nuclear testing in the atmosphere, in outer space and under water. It did not include underground testing, a favourite with the Soviets, but it was a beginning. The Hot Line Agreement was also concluded in 1963 since the Cuban missile affair had demonstrated how difficult it was for the two governments to communicate during a crisis. All this and the growing Soviet addiction to American technology and grain could only exacerbate Sino-Soviet relations.

It can be seen that the US, China and Germany were the three countries uppermost in Khrushchev's mind. Soviet initiatives were plentiful but only limited successes were scored. China was the most irritating to deal with. In the polemics which flowed between them, the Chinese calling the Soviets 'revisionists' and 'social imperialists', the Soviets calling the Chinese 'dogmatists' and 'left adventurists' there was only one victor, the Chinese. Mao Zedong was a past master of the hyperbolic insult. On 11 May 1964 he said: 'The Soviet Union today is a bourgeois dictatorship, a dictatorship of the *grande bourgeoisie*, a fascist German dictatorship, a Hitlerite dictatorship, a horde of bandits, worse even than de Gaulle.'[26] The major Soviet weakness was that they were revisionists and anyhow they had forgotten the art of polemics, as they had ceased to practise them since 1929. For Khrushchev dealing with Mao was as painful as a mouthful of wisdom teeth all pressing on exposed nerves. Khrushchev conducted foreign policy along the same lines as internal policy, with impatience, bluster, threats, innovation, skill, dash and verve. He blew hot and cold, one moment he threatened the Americans with his rockets, the next he almost pleaded for an alliance. The USSR had to be seen to be strong but a country which attempts to blackmail others is not self-confidently strong. The First Secretary's threats were taken seriously and had the opposite effect from the one intended. President Kennedy was convinced that the US was lagging and so American nuclear potential was increased; the sputnik galvanised the US into attempting to land a man on the moon by 1970. All this forced the Soviet Union to respond, thus speeding up the arms race. Proportionately the burden was greater for Moscow: a conservative estimate would be that the Soviet GNP was about 60 per cent of the US GNP.

The Middle East[27]

By 1954 the American desire to establish a chain of alliances around the land frontiers of the USSR had produced NATO in the west and SEATO in the east. The missing link was an agreement binding together the countries of the 'northern tier', Turkey, Iran, Afghanistan and Pakistan. All these countries were non-Arab and so could be armed without affecting the delicate Arab-Israeli military balance. The other likely candidate, Iraq, was not contiguous to Israel. The first move was Iraqi-Turkish discussions and these eventually produced an agreement which paved the way for the Baghdad Pact. Turkey, Iraq and Pakistan formed the nucleus of the pact which became known as CENTO when Iraq withdrew in 1958–59.

The prominence of Iraq aroused feelings of jealousy in another Arab country, Egypt, since she regarded herself as the natural leader of the Arab world. Nasser was stung into action and discussions began, in January 1955, with the Soviet Union on the possibility of arms deliveries. This was a daring move since the West enjoyed an arms monopoly in the Middle East and the precedent of Guatemala was fresh in everyone's minds. The central American republic had acquired arms from eastern Europe in 1954 but before they could be put to use the government fell. The US demonstrated that she would not tolerate a pro-communist regime in the Americas.

Nasser announced to the world on 27 September 1955 that he had signed an arms agreement with Czechoslovakia in exchange for cotton and rice. This shocked the major Western Powers: in one move the USSR was ensconced on the Nile and at the very centre of the troubled situation in the Middle East. A long-cherished dream, the Aswan dam, appeared at last to be approaching reality. Naturally Egypt could not finance the project herself and the Soviet Union hinted, in October 1955, that she might be willing to help. The US was faced with a choice of either shouldering the main burden of financing the dam herself or standing back and watching Soviet economic as well as military penetration of Egypt. The US withdrew from the project, in July 1956, when the Egyptian ambassador informed John Foster Dulles that the Soviets had promised the money. D. T. Shepilov, editor of *Pravda* and later to become Foreign Minister, had visited Cairo in early July and besides establishing cultural relations had presumably encouraged the Egyptians to believe that the USSR was ready with the necessary credits. Nasser thereupon nationalised the Suez canal over the heads of its British and French owners and declared that the US$100 million revenues would help to build the dam.

Great Britain and France overreacted and colluded with Israel to attack Egypt and occupy the Canal Zone. Prime Minister Anthony Eden saw Nasser as a new Hitler and France was keen to prevent Egypt continuing to be the chief source of support for the Algerian rebels in their struggle for independence. Both saw their continued status as Great Powers at stake. The Soviet government contented itself with sending warning notes to the British and French governments.

Israel attacked on 29 October and the British and French followed suit on 5 November. The US, who had not been advised of the venture, reacted vigorously and demanded withdrawal. So did the UN Security Council but Great Britain and France used their veto there. The USSR could now make hay while the sun shone. Originally in a potentially dangerous position and not willing to risk a nuclear confrontation over Egypt, the USSR now adopted an aggressive stance *vis-à-vis* Israel,

Great Britain and France, and reminded the latter two powers that she had all the missiles necessary to wipe them out. The Soviet Union even proposed to the US that they should establish a condominium in the Middle East to drive out the aggressors.

The collapse of Great Britain and France as Middle Eastern powers, soon to be followed elsewhere in Africa and Asia, opened the door of opportunity to the USSR. Agreement was reached to build the Aswan dam and work began in January 1960. Industrial projects followed and by the summer of 1964 Khrushchev had sanctioned loans to the value of US$821 million.[28] The relationship, however, was never smooth. Nasser treated his home-grown communists badly and between 1959 and 1961 a vigorous anti-Soviet radio and press campaign was conducted.

The first Soviet loan to a non-socialist state was for US$3.5 million to build a grain elevator and flour mill in Kabul, on 27 January 1954. Afghanistan received a second loan on 5 October 1954 and by 1964 about US$500 million had been promised in the form of loans or grants. This made Afghanistan the largest recipient, in *per capita* terms, of Soviet credits and aid. The Soviets built highways, airfields, factories, provided Russian language teachers and so on. The total US commitment came to just over half the Soviet amount over the same period. Clearly Afghanistan because of its backwardness and its proximity to the USSR enjoyed a very high priority in Moscow.

An agreement for a US$87 million loan was reached with Syria in October 1957 but the relationship did not blossom.

In Iraq the coming to power of General Abdul Karim Kassem, in July 1958, signalled the end of the pro-Western orientation of that country, and fearing that the Iraqi example might spread the US landed marines in Lebanon and the British dropped paratroops into Jordan. This provided another opportunity for Khrushchev to rattle his rockets and play the role of defender of Arab interests. Loans were forthcoming, the first for US$137.5 million in March 1959, and the Iraqi-Soviet relationship was quite close. This was rather upset by the Ba'athist coup of February 1963 which resulted in the suppression of the CP of Iraq and the death of many communists.

After the fighting between the French and the Tunisians in July 1961 the Soviets offered Tunisia a loan of US$28.5 million but the relationship did not develop satisfactorily from a Soviet point of view.

North Yemen (Yemen Arab Republic), of vital strategic importance, received Soviet economic and military aid in 1961 and Morocco received military equipment in April 1962. Just over a year after gaining her independence Algeria received a US$100 million loan in September 1963 and this was followed by an even larger loan in May 1964.

The beginning of a *rapprochement* with Turkey was signalled by the US$168 million loan extended in April 1964. The Turks were vexed at the lack of support they were receiving from the West on the Cyprus problem.

A factor in extending credit and providing military hardware to so many states was the need to compete with the Chinese. They were particularly active in North Yemen. Hence Moscow in attempting to undermine the US position in the area and to reduce even further British and French influence had always to look over its shoulder to see what the Chinese were up to. Khrushchev discovered that the developing states always demanded more: influence in the short run was expensive. The long-term goal was to effect social changes which would produce regimes which would join the socialist camp, but in the Khrushchev era such a possibility seemed a long way off.

Asia

India occupied a special place in Soviet thinking in the 1950s. The major Third World power, she formed a natural bridge to the rest of the developing world. The USSR attempted even during the last days of Stalin to improve relations with a country with which the Tsars had historically little contact.

A five-year trade agreement was signed in December 1953 which exchanged machinery and industrial equipment for traditional Indian products. The signing of the agreement was timed to coincide with a visit by Vice President Richard Nixon to New Delhi, underlining Indian criticism of US approaches to Pakistan to join what later became the Baghdad Pact. Here was a community of interests, and the Soviet Union objected even more strongly than India to Pakistan's pro-Western stand.

The year during which Indo-Soviet relations really took off was 1955. First, in February, the Soviets announced that they would build a steel plant with a capacity of one million tons annually. This turned out to be Bhilai – the first blast furnace was blown in February 1959 and the plant was on full stream in early 1962; April saw the Bandung Conference co-sponsored by India and China; Jawaharlal Nehru arrived in the Soviet Union in June 1955 and was bowled over: 'I have left a part of my heart behind', he said on leaving; Khrushchev and Bulganin visited India in November–December and came down on the Indian side in the Kashmir dispute – a continuing commitment as the Soviet veto in the UN in 1957 and 1962 demonstrated.

These events underline the basis of relations. Economically Bhilai permitted the USSR to outdistance her British and West German competitors who were also building steel mills. India also benefited and the Soviet Union expanded her influence in the Third World.

The border dispute between India and China in 1959 placed the USSR in a difficult position. The unsuccessful uprising against the Chinese in Tibet had led to the Dalai Lama fleeing to India. Instead of siding with the Chinese and aiding a socialist country in a dispute with a non-socialist state as was expected, Khrushchev declared his neutrality but went further and overtly criticised the Chinese stance. 'It's [the conflict's] inspirers are trying to discredit the idea of peaceful co-existence between states with different social systems and to prevent the strengthening of the Asian people's solidarity in the struggle for the consolidation of national independence.'[29] Khrushchev, at just that moment, chose to announce a US$378 million credit for India's third FYP. The Sino-Soviet dispute was in the open.

Economically the Soviets again came up trumps in 1960. They offered India oil below the posted price but Western firms would neither refine nor market it. The upshot was that the Western oil monopoly was broken and India saved valuable foreign currency. The Soviets also prospected for natural gas and oil and found both where Western companies had failed. By 1966 about one third of India's oil was coming from these wells.

Late in 1961 and early in 1962 India turned to the USSR for military aid, especially for helicopters for her mountainous border area. The Soviet Union promised to build an aircraft factory in India to build MIG-21 fighters, a plane which the Chinese did not possess.

If economic and military relations were excellent the same could not be said of political relations. Nehru was wont to criticise the USSR and was very critical of the CP of India. Nevertheless India was defined as a 'national democratic state', in November 1960, underlining the Soviet belief that India was pursuing a non-capitalist line of development which would eventually lead to socialism. However new 'progressive' states were springing up: Egypt, Ghana, Indonesia and others and India was falling behind in Soviet eyes. Despite this sensitive military aid was extended to the Indians, which pointed to the Soviet Union's interest in securing India as an ally against China.

The Sino-Indian border conflict of October 1962 demonstrated this clearly. While the Cuban missile crisis was on the USSR remained neutral but once it was over and the Chinese had begun to pillory Khrushchev for his handling of the affair the Soviets swung right behind India. The major disadvantage of this policy, from the Soviet point of view, was that it pushed China and Pakistan closer together but the price had to be paid. In May 1964 India revealed that Soviet military aid since the 1962 border conflict had amounted to about US$130 million.[30] This angered the Pakistanis as much as it did the Chinese. It was only after 1964 that the Soviet Union began to tone down her support for the Indian stance on Kashmir and respond to Pakistan's susceptibilities in an attempt to secure a *rapprochement* with that country.[31]

Trade with the Soviet Union benefited India and she owed the USSR about US$500 million in March 1965.[32] Continuing interest in Indian industrialisation was demonstrated in April 1964 when the USSR stepped in to build the Bokaro steel plant after negotiations with the US had proved inconclusive.

Hence the Khrushchev era saw a marked advance in Indo-Soviet industrial and military co-operation but the country did not appear to be developing politically as the Soviet Union would have liked. This did not cause Moscow to despair since a Soviet goal in external relations has always been to establish a network of agreements, cultural, political, economic, military, which gradually bind the two countries together. Progress in one sector may lead later to progress in others as the web of relationships expands.

Sri Lanka only became receptive to Soviet overtures in September 1956 when diplomatic relations were established. An agreement on economic co-operation was signed in 1959. An iron and steel plant was envisaged, in July 1961, as the foundation of Sri Lanka's industrial programme. The ending of US aid in April 1963 further promoted relations with the USSR.

In South East Asia the Soviet Union concentrated initially on Burma and Indonesia, both decolonialised and neither in the American alliance system. An agreement on economic co-operation was signed by Burma and the Soviet Union in January 1957. The Technological Institute in Rangoon and a hospital in Taunggi were built and presented to the Burmese. However, they wished to repay the US$5–10 million cost in rice and began sending rice to the USSR in 1963.[33] Unfortunately for the Burmese the quantity necessary to clear was calculated in 1957 prices so they paid more than they anticipated since the world market price of rice rose. The Soviets also built a 206-room hotel on the shores of Lake Inya but the Burmese obliged them to instal Westinghouse airconditioning and Otis lifts. An Israeli firm even ended up managing the place.[34] Soviet experience here was not very happy nor did their shipment of cement in 1962 have the desired effect. Poor packaging and rain on the local quay produced something that was more like concrete than cement. 'If water makes it set, it is good cement', was the original Soviet reply.

Increasing xenophobia led to the Burmese decreeing that no foreigner could stay in the country more than twenty-four hours. This was bad for the hotel business but even worse for the Soviets, who had to concede that their efforts in Burma had produced very little.

Indonesia signed a trade agreement with the Soviet Union in August 1956 and military equipment arrived the following year. However President Sukarno, aided by the CP of Indonesia (PKI), turned anti-Soviet and, even worse, pro-Chinese in 1963. One estimate puts Soviet and East European military and economic credits at US$1,500 million.[35] Indonesia then joined China in labelling the USSR a European power and the Soviet Union was not admitted to the IInd

Afro-Asian Conference as a full member. Indonesia was an expensive way of discovering the vagaries of Third World politics. Eventually, on 30 September 1965, the PKI and some rebellious troops moved against the military but the army survived and it was the president whose days of influence were numbered. The PKI was literally chopped to pieces.

The 1954 Geneva Conference divided Vietnam in two but the north regarded it as an interim settlement. The defeat of the French at Dien Bien Phu in May 1954 by the Viet Minh had ended French power in Indo-China and had signalled the arrival of a powerful new fighting force.

The effect of Cuba passing into the Soviet orbit was to draw the Americans deeper and deeper into Indo-China in an attempt to prevent further Marxist-Leninist gains there. Gradually the US commitment to Laos, Cambodia and south Vietnam escalated to the point of no return.

In East Asia, Japan and South Korea were of immediate relevance to Soviet policy-makers. If American resolve should weaken in South Korea then the north might again be tempted to seize the whole of Korea by force. In Japan the lingering suspicion of the Soviet Union was compounded by the refusal of Moscow to listen to Japanese claims to the four southern islands of the Kuril chain, occupied by the Soviets and signed away by the Japanese in 1945. Hence the USSR had little success in her policy of weaning Japan away from her close relationship with the US.

Australia[36]

Australian-Soviet relations claimed world-wide attention for the first time in April 1954 when Vladimir Petrov, third secretary and consul at the Soviet embassy, asked for political asylum. What made Petrov's, followed by his wife's, defection sensational was that he was the top MVD man, responsible for non-military espionage, in Australia. He had a lot to tell and his revelations opened many eyes. Diplomatic relations with the Soviet Union were interrupted on 29 April 1954. The Australian Labour Party split and its anti-communist wing left, thus so weakening the party that it did not regain office until 1972. Then in February 1956 a Soviet base was discovered on an island off Queen Mary Land, in the Australian Antarctic Territory. The best the Australians could achieve was a freezing of territorial claims and a demilitarisation of the area.

Diplomatic relations were resumed on 21 July 1959 but there was little warmth or understanding between the two nations. Khrushchev hammered away at the UN in 1960 at Australian policies in Papua and New Guinea, demanding independence for these two territories. This became a constant theme in Soviet criticism of Australia. Relations became more strained when the new Soviet ambassador was declared *persona non grata*. He had recruited a member of the Australian security services so this time the government was clearly in the picture from the beginning.

The arrival in Indonesia of Soviet military equipment, including bombers, submarines and a heavy cruiser, caused some nervousness in Canberra, but Sukarno's leftward lurch towards China and his diminished prestige after the events of September 1965 defused that situation. The Sino-Soviet conflict worked to the benefit of Australia since Canberra could rely on the Chinese to oppose the expansion of Soviet influence in the area.

Africa

During the Khrushchev era the USSR amassed information, engaged in some trade and garnered experience the hard way in Africa. It gradually extended its diplomatic missions from 1958 onwards but only once, in 1960 in the Congo, could it be seen playing an important role in an African state. Its other favourites were Ghana, Guinea and Mali but by 1964 there was still no harvest. Cultivating the black continent in the late 1950s and the early 1960s was to produce fruit only in the late 1970s.

At the 1st conference of communist and workers' parties in Moscow in 1960 the concept of 'national democracies' was unveiled. These were states ruled by the bourgeoisie but which conducted an anti-imperialist foreign policy and whose domestic programme was basically democratic. This was extended, in 1962, when non-socialist states were classified under six headings, ranging from those in which the national bourgeoisie collaborated with feudal elements, e.g. Somalia, to those in which capitalism was strong, e.g. Zaire and Zambia, and to those in which feudalism still held sway, e.g. Ethiopia. One neat group of African states, Ghana, Guinea and Mali, was singled out for praise.[37] These nations were seen as anti-imperialist and a growing proletariat was forming in each of them. Good relations with these countries was based on good relations with the individual leaders, Kwame Nkrumah in Ghana, Sékou Touré in Guinea and Modibo Keita in Mali. In these states the public sector of the economy expanded and planning made its appearance. Nkrumah had a blind spot for economics and the fall of cocoa prices exacerbated the situation. Guinea opted out for the French African community when it was set up in 1958 so she needed friends and expertise. Economic success, however, was very limited. Lack of experience caused the Soviets to make egregious mistakes. A large case was unloaded in Guinea and everyone waited expectantly in the blistering heat to see what new wonder had arrived. When unpacked it stood there in all its pristine glory, a gleaming new snowplough!

Sékou Touré was not putty in Soviet hands. In December 1961 the Soviet ambassador was sent packing for becoming too involved in a teachers' strike and during the Cuban missile crisis Soviet jets *en route* to Cuba were not permitted to refuel at Conakry airport. It had been specially extended by the Soviets for just this purpose.[38]

In 1963 the concept of the 'revolutionary democrat' was introduced. This applied to leaders who while not Marxist were seen as leading their country towards socialism. Then followed the thought, derived from the experience of the October Revolution, that a socialist revolution from above could be successful due to the power and influence of the socialist camp. The proletariat could gradually be built up under its aegis. This reveals a striking belief in the influence of the individual leader in Africa, again a carry-over from Lenin.

The Soviets burnt their fingers in the Congo in 1960. When Lumumba sought Soviet military intervention he lost the sympathy of leading members of the UN secretariat and of the British and US governments. Dag Hammarskjöld, UN secretary general, who wanted to keep the super powers out of Africa, thought that Lumumba was providing the Soviets with a foothold there.[39] Lumumba was eventually dismissed and his successor Mobutu closed down the Soviet embassy. The USSR gave vent to her ire at the UN but she won little support as Africans favoured a strong UN.

And then there was the problem of the Chinese. They used their influence in the Afro-Asian movement to arouse suspicion about Soviet motives and became so intemperate in Algiers in March 1964 that they were rebuked by African delegates. The Soviets could counter on the economic plane since they were in a much stronger position to offer aid, trade and assistance.

Latin America

Until 1959 Latin America was of marginal interest to the Soviet Union. The US was the dominant power in the Americas and the Guatemala incident of 1954 demonstrated that she was determined not to allow a pro-communist regime on the continent.

The advent to power in Cuba of Fidel Castro, shortly after the fall of the Batista regime on 1 January 1959, opened up new perspectives. So cautious was the Soviet response that it was not until February 1960 that the man for all occasions, Anastas Mikoyan, dropped into Havana to sign a trade agreement. The Soviets were to take nearly 5 million tonnes of Cuban sugar over the next five years and to offer a US$100 million credit for economic aid.[40] Ché Guevara repaired to Beijing and signed an agreement which obliged the Chinese to buy one million tonnes of sugar in 1961. A US$60 million credit was also forthcoming.

The Bay of Pigs invasion in April 1961, a CIA-sponsored undertaking by Cuban exiles, long feared by Castro, moved the Cuban leader on the eve of the invasion to declare that the Cuban revolution was socialist. The Cubans needed arms to prevent a recurrence but the Soviets were careful not to give the impression that they had extended their socialist defence umbrella to cover the island. However Khrushchev eventually took the plunge and put Soviet rockets on Cuba, only 150 kilometres from the US, and this inevitably led to a confrontation with the US.

Castro was aggrieved when the rockets were dismantled. The Soviets made much of him to ward off Chinese accusations of 'capitulationism' over the missiles and to ensure that it was not China which benefited from the crisis. Castro was fêted in the USSR in April–May 1963 but Cuba was still determined to display some independence. She was more militant in her call for revolution in Latin America, she attempted to remain neutral in the Sino-Soviet conflict and she refused to sign the Nuclear Test Ban Treaty.[41]

NOTES

1. *Pravda* 7 March 1953.
2. Although the CC session took place on 14 March the change was only announced in *Pravda* on 21 March.
3. Michael Voslensky *Nomenklatura: Die herrschende Klasse der Sowjetunion* p. 390.
4. For a detailed account of the programme see Martin McCauley *Khrushchev and the Development of Soviet Agriculture: The Virgin Land Programme 1953–1964*. Unless otherwise stated all details of the programme are taken from this book.
5. John Armstrong *The Politics of Totalitarianism: The Communist Party of the Soviet Union from 1934 to the Present* p. 298; R. G. Wesson *Lenin's Legacy: The Story of the CPSU* p. 197.
6. Khrushchev was able to embarrass Molotov on an ideological point. The latter, in an address to the Supreme Soviet on 8 February 1955, stated that in the Soviet Union the 'foundations of a socialist society have already been built'. This, admitted Molotov later, could mean that a 'socialist society had still not been built in the USSR'. This 'mistaken formula' was politically harmful since it 'throws doubt on the presence of a socialist society which has already been built in the main in our country'. Molotov's letter, conceding this mistake, is dated 16 September and appeared in *Kommunist* no. 14, 1955, pp. 127–8. It is of interest that the same speech contains the orthodox formulation as well, stating that 'socialism has already triumphed in our country, in the period before the Second World War' *Pravda* 9 February 1955. Since someone as well versed in the niceties of Marxist-Leninist expression as Molotov would plainly not contradict himself in the same speech the only inference one can draw is that the 'orthodox' statement on socialism was inserted by Molotov's critics before publication.
7. Wesson, op. cit. p. 198.

8. Roy A. and Zhores A. Medvedev *Khrushchev: The Years in Power* pp. 111–13.
9. This account of the struggle and defeat of the Anti-Party group is based on Veljko Mićunović *Moskovske Godine 1956–1958* (Zagreb 1977). Mićunović was Yugoslav ambassador to Moscow during these years and was on good terms with Khrushchev. The latter granted him a ninety-minute audience on 5 July 1957 and gave him his version of the events which had just taken place. An abridged English version has appeared under the title: *Moscow Diary.*
10. *Pravda* 31 October 1961.
11. *Pravda* 6 March 1962.
12. Based on Alastair McAuley *Economic Welfare in the Soviet Union: Poverty, Living Standards, and Inequality.*
13. Priscilla Johnson *Khrushchev and the Arts* pp. 101–2.
14. Roy A. and Zhores A. Medvedev, op. cit. p. 139.
15. Michael Bourdeaux *Patriarch and Prophets: Persecution of the Russian Orthodox Church* p. 30.
16. Ibid. p. 31.
17. Ibid. p. 34.
18. Yakunin, head of the unofficial Christian Committee for the Defence of Believers' Rights, was charged with anti-Soviet propaganda and agitation and sentenced to five years' hard labour and five years internal exile in August 1980.
19. Michael Bourdeaux *Religious Ferment in Russia: Protestant Opposition to Soviet Religious Policy* p. 20. The new statutes are to be found on pp. 190–210.
20. Ibid. p. 39.
21. Khrushchev, in his memoirs, is very frank about the Chinese. 'We used to lie around a swimming pool in Peking, chatting like the best of friends about all kinds of things. But it was all too sickeningly sweet. The atmosphere was nauseating ... I was never exactly sure that I understood what he [Mao] meant. ... Some of Mao's pronouncements struck me as being too simplistic, and others struck me as being much too complex' (Strobe Talbott (ed.) *Khrushchev Remembers* pp. 429–30).
22. William E. Griffith *The Sino-Soviet Rift* p. 351; Adam B. Ulam *Expansion and Coexistence: Soviet Foreign Policy 1917–1973* 2nd edn, p. 611.
23. Talbott, op. cit. p. 433.
24. According to Khrushchev the Soviet Union discovered that the Albanians were negotiating with the Chinese through a member of the Albanian delegation. 'One of the Albanians, an honest woman, came to us and told us what was going on. I think she was strangled a short time later, poor woman' (Talbott, op. cit. p. 437).
    This was the first occasion on which Khrushchev had abused Mao at an international communist conference. However, at a conference of communist parties in Moscow in November 1957 the CPSU, in the person of Mikoyan, had insulted Mao. When the latter in his speech touched on the internal situation in the USSR Mikoyan got up, stared at the Chinese leader, then turned his back on him and appeared to be studying the wall.
25. Ulam, op. cit. p. 623.

26. Thomas Scharping *Mao Chronik: Daten zu Leben und Werk* p. 181.
27. Here taken to include Morocco and the Arab countries of north Africa in the west to Afghanistan in the east.
28. Marshall I. Goldman *Soviet Foreign Aid* p. 74.
29. *Pravda* 10 September 1959.
30. Goldman, op. cit. p. 105.
31. Richard B. Remnek *Soviet Scholars and Soviet Foreign Policy: A Case Study of Soviet Policy Towards India* p. 45.
32. Goldman, op. cit. p. 111.
33. Ibid. p. 142.
34. Ibid. p. 141.
35. Uri Ra'anan *The USSR Arms the Third World: Case Studies in Soviet Foreign Policy* p. 236.
36. This section is based on T. B. Millar *Australia in Peace and War: External Relations 1788–1977* pp. 340–9.
37. Christopher Stevens *The Soviet Union and Black Africa* p. 22.
38. Ibid. p. 23.
39. Ibid. p. 17.
40. Stephen Clissold (ed.) *Soviet Relations with Latin America 1918–1968: A Documentary Survey* p. 44.
41. Ibid. p. 52.

CHAPTER SEVEN

The Brezhnev Era

'THE BORDERS OF THE SOCIALIST COMMONWEALTH ARE INVIOLABLE'

INTRODUCTION

The long journey of the Soviet Union through revolution, war, civil war, the semi-bourgeois era of NEP, crash industrialisation and enforced collectivisation, the savage war of 1941–45, the harsh post-war years, the unending industrial and agricultural experimentation of the Khrushchev years, led those who survived to long for consolidation, calm, certainty, stability and a minimum of innovation. The moment was ripe for a careful consensus-seeking bureaucrat to lead the USSR. The man most suited by temperament and political instinct turned out to be Leonid Ilich Brezhnev. He was only the fourth Soviet leader in half a century, heir to the brilliant Lenin, the tyrant Stalin and the buffoon Khrushchev. What style of leadership would he adopt? There was no problem about deciding whom he wished to be compared with: even their patronymics are the same. But he lacked the intellectual penetration and the charisma of his mentor. Part of Lenin's charisma stemmed from his own personal modesty, but here Brezhnev and he part company. The latter was vain and enjoyed the trappings of office and ostentatious presents.

The collective leadership which took over from Khrushchev was headed by three men: Leonid Brezhnev, Aleksei Kosygin, the Chairman of the USSR Council of Ministers, and Nikolai Podgorny, who took over as Chairman of the Presidium of the USSR Supreme Soviet (President in fact) from Anastas Mikoyan in December 1965. Not far behind was Mikhail Suslov, a CC secretary since 1947, responsible for propaganda and relations with foreign communist parties. In fact he had made the speech condemning the Anti-Party group in June 1957, Zhukov in October 1957 and Khrushchev in October 1964.

The crisis in Czechoslovakia in 1968 propelled Brezhnev into international affairs and, although a reluctant invader, he gradually warmed to the task and became the Soviet spokesman on foreign affairs, pushing Kosygin aside. The latter was to concentrate on the formidable task of running Soviet industry, Brezhnev retaining overall responsibility for agriculture. Brezhnev, who had become Secretary General at the XXIIIrd Party Congress in March 1966, was clearly *primus inter pares* by 1972. The onset of détente increased his concern for international relations and he began to receive foreign leaders even before he became Soviet head of state.

Whereas Khrushchev had led from the front, Brezhnev led from the middle, in Archie Brown's phrase. On average during the 1970s he met foreign representatives on about one hundred days a year. He did not travel as much as Khrushchev, who was unwise enough to spend 135 days outside the country in 1964.

The increasing concern with foreign affairs came at a time when the Soviet Union was expanding her influence in the Third World. Sino-Soviet relations, however, remained as bad as ever. The USSR took full advantage of US discomfiture in South East Asia as well as indecision in Washington following Watergate. This was most marked in Africa where Moscow strengthened its position considerably in the 1970s.

Concern with external relations meant that there was not enough time for the Secretary General to be in day-to-day contact with the economy and here Aleksei Kosygin dominated industrial affairs. The role of the major technical ministries increased during the 1970s.

Brezhnev believed that his main forte was personnel policy. He was comrade Cadres. Hence policy-making was of secondary importance. The experience of Khrushchev was a warning to him that officials require something in return for their loyalty. Brezhnev never took great risks since he lacked the political imagination of a Khrushchev. He never tried to force legislation through the Politburo if there was a majority against it. He knew as a master *apparat* man that contentious legislation cannot be successfully implemented. Brezhnev consciously cultivated an aura of predictability. The nomenklatura knew where it was with him.

The role of the military also increased, not least in advising on foreign policy. The Secretary General kept the military-security complex happy and avoided the confrontations of the Khrushchev era.

Great care was taken to ensure civilian control over the military. Both the Ministry of Internal Affairs (MVD) and the KGB had very well-equipped units under their own command and there were also the frontier guards under KGB command. Arms dumps and nuclear installations were guarded by the KGB.

No major administrative reform was launched after 1964 and no important economic innovations surfaced between the late 1960s, when the Kosygin reform of 1965 ran into the sand, and 1979. Then in July 1979 changes aimed at switching the economy away from gross output as the main indicator of success for enterprises to 'intensive factors of growth' were announced. Technical progress, quality and labour productivity were highlighted. The slow growth in labour productivity in industry and agriculture, the slowdown in economic expansion in the late 1970s, the increasingly tight labour situation and the difficulty of expanding oil production to meet increased demand were just some of the problems which Brezhnev's successors had to tackle.

DOMESTIC POLICY

Brezhnev began as a member of a collective leadership in 1964 but had become *primus inter pares* (first among equals) by the early 1970s. By the mid 1970s he was the national leader. It took him longer than Khrushchev to establish his dominance but he chose to accumulate power gradually rather than adopt the high-risk strategy of his predecessor. Between 1964 and 1968 he had to play second fiddle to Aleksei Kosygin who, as Prime Minister, took the lead in economic reform and foreign policy. Brezhnev concentrated on building up the party *apparat,* oversaw culture and often involved himself in agriculture. He followed the standard technique of building up his 'tail' in Moscow by drawing in party and state allies from the Ukraine, Moldavia and Kazakhstan. Nikolai Podgorny was moved out of the CC secretariat in December 1965 and made President of the USSR. At the same time two Dnepropetrovsk contacts, Venyamin Dymshits and Nikolai Tikhonov, were brought to Moscow as deputy Prime Ministers. They were more conservative and less knowledgeable about the economy than Kosygin. Andrei Kirilenko joined the secretariat in April 1966 and set about unseating Aleksandr Shelepin. The latter was manoeuvred out of the secretariat in June 1967 and this strengthened Brezhnev's hold over this key body. This was effected by bringing in a galaxy of Brezhnevites to head important departments of the secretariat. He expanded his influence over the police and security forces by nominating Nikolai Shchelokov as MVD head in September 1966 and Yuri Andropov as KGB chief in 1967. Viktor Chebrikov became Andropov's deputy. Brezhnev's wartime colleague, Marshal Andrei Grechko, became USSR Minister of Defence in March 1967. Circumstances favoured Brezhnev. The 'Prague Spring' propelled Brezhnev into foreign policy since relations with socialist states were the party's responsibility. Kosygin was unhappy about the decision to invade in August 1968, and this diminished his authority. His 1965 economic reforms ran into the sand as a conservative, no-risks policy was adopted. Brezhnev stepped up to take over the foreign policy mantle and began to tour the world as if he were head of state. The XXIVth Party Congress, in March 1971, allowed him to consolidate his position and obtain a majority in the CC. The FYP adopted placed more emphasis on consumer goods production, a hallmark of the Brezhnev era. However, military expenditure also rose, and the pious hopes of faster growth of light industry never materialised. Heavy industry throughout the Brezhnev era grew more rapidly. At the congress Brezhnev was able to get four of his associates on to the Politburo. He did not replace Kosygin as Prime Minister since his colleagues observed the resolution passed at the Party plenum in 1964 which stated that no individual should hold the top party and government posts simultaneously. The cautious, consensual Brezhnev accorded more emphasis to interest groups than the erratic Khrushchev. Accordingly, in April 1973, three interest groups which had previously been excluded from the Politburo made it to the top. Marshal Grechko (Minister of Defence), Andrei Gromyko (Minister of Foreign Affairs) and Yuri Andropov (KGB chief) joined the top policy-making body. This leadership approach secured the stability which many sought but postponed hard decisions about economic and social reform. The decline of the Soviet Union set in at this time.

Brezhnev reached the apogee of his power in 1977. At the XXVth Party Congress in 1976 his personality cult reached new heights. He became a Marshal of the Soviet Union and was formally acknowledged Commander-in-Chief of the Soviet Armed Forces. A civilian, Dmitri Ustinov, succeeded Grechko as Minister of Defence on the latter's death in 1976. Brezhnev had to promote Ustinov marshal since the hierarchically minded military did not take kindly to him. A new 'Brezhnev Constitution' was promulgated in 1977, and he pushed Podgorny aside to become President himself. Podgorny left the Politburo as well. A close ally, Nikolai Tikhonov, became First Deputy Prime Minister in October 1976, and he gradually took over the government as Kosygin's health declined. Tikhonov succeeded Kosygin on the latter's death in December 1980.

Brezhnev suffered strokes in 1975 and 1977, and this accelerated his physical decline. He was forced to spend more and more time in the Crimea and to delegate policy-making to his colleagues and his chief of staff, Konstantin Chernenko. Brezhnev found it difficult to speak clearly. A cruel joke was that he spoke as if he always had kasha, buckwheat porridge, in his mouth. The final nail in Brezhnev's coffin was the ill-starred decision to intervene militarily in Afghanistan in December 1979. This increased international tension, led to many Western nations boycotting the 1980 Moscow Olympics, bumped up defence spending and cost the USSR prestige around the world. All this at a time when the economy had almost ceased to grow. Brezhnev's declining health and awareness was paralleled by the decline of the country. The struggle for the succession acquired a new dimension when Mikhail Suslov died in January 1982. Andropov quickly resigned as KGB chief and was able to get himself appointed to the CC secretariat. Brezhnev's protégé, Konstantin Chernenko, now had a formidable competitor. When Brezhnev died on 10 November 1982 it was Yuri Andropov who succeeded him.

The first of Khrushchev's 'hare-brained schemes' to go after the new collective leadership took over in October 1964 was the bifurcation of party, soviet, trade union and Komsomol regional organs into industrial and agricultural wings. This took place in November 1964 and reveals how strongly resented it had been. The new leadership also agreed to separate the posts of First Secretary of the party and Chairman of the USSR Council of Ministers. This was to avoid excessive concentration of power in the hands of one person.

The anxiety felt about the economy resulted in the CC plenum of March 1965 devoting its attention to agriculture. The wild reformism of Khrushchev was to be a thing of the past, the goal was to establish a stable environment for farm chairmen and directors to permit economic criteria to dominate decision-making. The medium- and long-term consequences of decisions were to be given much more thought than before. A promise was made to set procurements five years in advance and not to alter these amounts. Shortfalls and drought soon made it impossible to do so. Procurement prices for over plan deliveries rose.

Next came the turn of industry as the *sovnarkhozy*, dating back to 1957, were dismantled. They largely disappeared in the economic reform launched by Aleksei Kosygin at the CC plenum in September 1965. Functions were recentralised, accelerating a trend which had been evident during the last years of Khrushchev, and this meant the rebirth of many ministries and state committees. The aim of the reform was to reduce administrative interference in economic management. Success indicators were reduced in number and biased in favour of economic criteria such as sales and profits, and a charge on capital was introduced. A reform of wholesale prices, operative as of 1 July 1967, was announced.[1]

Another body which disappeared in late 1965 was the Committee of Party-State Control, established by Khrushchev in November 1962 to look into the malfunctioning of party and government organs and to check on the implementation of decrees. Its place was taken by a Committee of People's Control which was strictly limited to the state sector. The party has its own Committee of Party Control.

The whole move can be seen as one to downgrade Shelepin who was the chairman of the Committee of Party and State Control. He was the only Politburo member who was simultaneously a CC secretary and a Deputy Chairman of the USSR Council of Ministers. Since he was not made chairman of the Committee of People's Control he lost his position as a Deputy Chairman of the USSR Council of Ministers. Later Shelepin was made chairman of the All-Union Council of Trade Unions, a position a Politburo member could occupy but not one a CC secretary could hold. Hence Shelepin had to leave the secretariat. Brezhnev had neatly outmanoeuvred him. This in turn meant that Shelepin's supporters lost their positions. Semichastny, for instance, parted company with the KGB and became Deputy Chairman of the Ukrainian Council of Ministers.

The XXIIIrd Party Congress, which met in March–April 1966, saw further changes. Ever since October 1964 party officials had been voicing their opposition to the rates of turnover in party committees, at all levels including the CC and the Presidium, laid down by the party statute adopted at the XXIInd Congress in 1961. Brezhnev took their side at the congress and the offending rates were removed but a general clause was added stressing the intention of the party to promote energetic and competent young cadres. The Bureau of the CC for the RSFSR, set up at the XXth Party Congress in March 1956, also went. This could have been due to the fact that the RSFSR dominated Soviet life, and hence any decision affecting the largest republic would also affect the Soviet Union so there was no need to have parallel organs. It could also have resulted from the fact that the economic significance of the RSFSR had enhanced the influence of leaders of the Bureau such as G. I. Voronov and A. P. Kirilenko.

Brezhnev became Secretary General at the congress, a title held by Stalin between 1922 and 1934 and the Presidium became the Politburo once again. The threads which bound the party to the Khrushchev era were being visibly cut.

Such were the rumours that Stalin was going to be rehabilitated at the congress that some East European leaders interceded with the Kremlin and internally the cultural and technical intelligentsia sent letters to the Soviet leadership. The result was that Stalin was passed over in silence at the congress. Nevertheless the intellectual climate was perceptibly frostier. It was no longer as easy as before to get material which was critical of Stalin published and two writers, Sinyavsky and Daniel, were sentenced just before the congress convened. The former got seven years' and the latter five years' hard labour.

Another attempt was made in 1969 to repair some of the damage done to Stalin's image at the XXth and XXIInd Party Congresses. The ninetieth anniversary of his birth, on 21 December, was to be marked by a long, laudatory article and a photograph in *Pravda*. A statue was to be erected at his grave near the Kremlin wall and a special conference convened in the Institute of Marxism-Leninism. Georgia, of course, was to be the scene of special celebrations. None of this happened, due to pressure from East European parties, especially the Polish and Hungarian, and opposition within the USSR itself. The article which did appear was short and underlined the 'errors and perversions connected with the cult of the personality' rather than his contribution to socialism.[2] The original article was to have appeared in all the republican and East European communist newspapers and the order cancelling its publication only went out a short time before the presses were due to roll. Ulan Bator, 7–8 hours ahead of Moscow, was not informed, so the laudatory article and photograph appeared in the Mongolian language newspaper *Unen* on 22 December, stating that it had been reprinted from *Pravda* of 21 December.[3]

The Czechoslovak tragedy was partly set in train by Brezhnev himself. He flew to Prague in December 1967 and decided that Antonin

291

Novotny, head of the party and the State, was not worth saving. He could be sacrificed. This helped to undermine the authority of the party and when Alexander Dubček replaced Novotny as head of the party pressures to introduce far-reaching reforms proved irresistible. Democratic socialism was the goal but voices were raised which favoured political pluralism as well. Up till then Eastern Europe had really looked after itself, the economic reforms in the GDR, Czechoslovakia and Hungary, where the New Economic Mechanism was introduced on 1 January 1968, appeared to herald greater prosperity and contentment. The events of 21 August 1968, when the Warsaw Pact invaded, changed all that. Romania refused to join the advance and even feared Soviet intervention itself.

Where Novotny went Gomulka was not far behind. The riots in the Baltic ports of December 1970 consigned the Polish leader to oblivion. He had bungled food price rises and his mantle passed to Edward Gierek. With the unseating of Walter Ulbricht, the First Secretary of the SED, in May 1971 (this move had probably been agreed in Moscow during the XXIVth Party Congress), the East European political landscape took on a new look. The ideological and economic experimentation of the late 1960s was abandoned, and the fright of 1968 led to a predictable tightening of the reins. Conservative, safe policies were the order of the day and renewed emphasis on raising living standards an urgent priority. Innovation was risky and hence too dangerous.

The troubles in Eastern Europe erupted at a time when the USSR was actively pursuing a policy which culminated in détente in 1972. It needed grain from North America and technology from the advanced capitalist countries and, if possible, agreements limiting the production and deployment of nuclear weapons. Détente did not mean relaxation on the ideological front: indeed it meant a tightening up of censorship and more ideological rectitude. This led to an increase in dissent which, short of shooting all dissidents was now ineradicable.

Brezhnev enhanced the role of the party in Soviet society, thus continuing a trend set by Khrushchev. Membership reached 15.7 million at the XXVth Party Congress in February 1976. The proportion of workers grew slightly under Brezhnev and reached 41.6 per cent in February 1976. Over a quarter of party members by the early 1980s were graduates. As the party was keen to recruit from the technical intelligentsia this proportion grew. A determined effort was made to enrol female members; in 1976 about one-quarter of members were women. The party sought especially to recruit skilled workers – if they were female so much the better – and all those who were actual or potential decision-makers. Russians continued to dominate the party; they made up 61 per cent of the membership on 1 January 1976, even though they accounted for just over half the population. Most nationalities were underrepresented. The Moldavians stood out as they made up 1.1 per cent of the population in 1970 but only 0.4 per cent of party members in 1976. At the opposite pole were the Jews, who represented 1.9 per cent of party members but accounted for only 0.9 per cent of the population.[4]

Membership of the CC and the Central Auditing Commission revealed considerable stability. Whereas the re-election rate in 1966 was 73 per cent it rose to 83 per cent in 1976.[5] At the XXVth Party Congress about 90 per cent of full members were re-elected. Since places were found for capable younger people this increased the CC from 175 members in 1961 to 287 in 1976.

At the republican party level turnover during the Brezhnev era dropped sharply compared with the Khrushchev days. There was unparalleled continuity of office for those constituting the USSR Council of Ministers and party secretaries in oblasts, krais and autonomous oblasts and republics. Demotions became the exception rather than the rule. The great majority of promotions to first secretary were made by advancing a second secretary in the same oblast or krai. The practice of promoting the deputy was increasingly applied to the USSR Council of Ministers.[6] Khrushchev was wont to fill key party posts in the provinces with nominees from the CC secretariat but this ceased to be the case.

All this produced an ageing party and government elite. Whereas about 70 per cent of party members joined after 1952, only 17 per cent of the joint membership of the CC and the Central Auditing Commission came from this generation.[7]

The Politburo was a world of its own. By Brezhnev's death everyone was a pensioner except G. V. Romanov and Mikhail Gorbachev. Males qualified for a pension at sixty. Seven of the fourteen full members were over seventy. There were many changes in the Politburo under Brezhnev. Seven full members were promoted and three died. Eleven new men were elevated to full membership.

One of the demotions from the Politburo was connected with the new constitution of 1977. The incumbent President would not accept demotion to First Vice-President, a new post created by the constitution, to make way for Brezhnev to become head of state. So Podgorny had to go without so much as a thank you for all the services he had rendered the party and the State.

The new constitution replaced the 1936 Stalin constitution. It had been in the making ever since 1961 and expressed the realities of contemporary Soviet life. The role of the party, relegated to article 126 in the old constitution, was spelled out in article 6 of the new one. The USSR was a 'socialist state of the whole nation', reiterating Khrushchev's phraseology of the post-1961 period. Democratic centralism, always the guiding force for the party, was now extended to the state as a whole. The Presidium of the USSR Council of Ministers, which functioned without constitutional sanction, was now recognised. Soviets of working people's deputies became soviets of people's deputies, in line with the concept of the USSR as a state of the whole people. In line with the change made at the XXIVth Party Congress in 1971 of lengthening the interval between congresses from four to five years, to keep in step with the Five-Year Plans, the period between elections to the USSR Supreme Soviet and the Supreme Soviets of Union Republics was also changed from four to five years. Elections to local soviets were now to take place every two and a half years instead of every two years as formerly.

ECONOMIC POLICY

The innovations announced by Aleksei Kosygin in September 1965 which enhanced the role of management and encouraged the application of mathematical techniques among other things produced good results, especially where labour productivity was concerned, in the short term. Enterprises could actually release labour but only on condition that they found the redundant workers jobs elsewhere. However, by 1970 the trend towards more administrative direction from the centre was again reasserting itself. In 1973 industrial associations and *kombinaty* were set up to replace the ministerial *glavki*. Whereas previously an enterprise had been subject both to a main ministry and to several *glavki* of various other ministries, depending on its production profile, now the association grouped all the sections concerned with a certain area of industrial specialisation. The net result, if industrial output is the criterion of success, has not been encouraging.

Officially the eighth FYP (1966–70) saw a healthy increase in national income of 41 per cent and industrial output up 50 per cent. American estimates are, however, much lower (see Table 7.1). Agriculture was a long way behind. Poor harvests in 1965 and 1967 meant that the plan was underfulfilled. Actual growth was 21 per cent but looked good in comparison to the miserable 12 per cent increase of the 1961–65 period. However this was little comfort especially when it is borne in mind that gross agricultural investment during the eighth FYP was far in excess of that of the seventh FYP.

The ninth FYP (1971–75) was quite a different story. Industry and agriculture both failed to live up to expectations. Gross industrial production almost achieved the planned goals but the appalling performance of agriculture, which only grew 13 per cent instead of 23 per cent, meant that national income achieved was only 28 per cent compared to the 38.6 per cent hoped for. The ninth FYP was the first in which the growth of consumer goods output was planned to keep ahead of capital goods production but this never materialised and the consumer was relegated to second position as usual.

Agriculture suffered two bad harvests in 1972 and 1975. Both necessitated large imports of North American grain to feed the Soviet animal population. So skilfully did the Soviets manage their 1972 purchases that they ended up taking the American taxpayer for a very expensive ride. Not knowing the destination of the grain the US government lent the Soviet Union US$750 million for three years to buy US grain at a price which it was subsidising to the tune of US$316 million.[8] This meant, among other things, that the USSR could afford to buy about 30 million tonnes in Western countries. The 1975 harvest of 140 million tonnes was 70 million tonnes short of the target and the worst crop since 1963. The US government was awake this time and after 10.4 million tonnes had been bought imposed an embargo on further sales. The two governments signed an agreement obliging the Soviet Union to purchase 6–8 million tonnes annually for five years beginning on 1 January 1976 but permitting the Soviets to buy 7 million tonnes in any year without prior US approval. This ensured future supplies but it also underlined the fact that Soviet agriculture would not be capable of meeting domestic needs during the tenth FYP (1976–80). The agricultural performance during the ninth FYP was even more modest when one remembers that the Soviet population grew by about 5 per cent during the years 1971–75. Great priority has been afforded agriculture and whereas gross fixed capital investment averaged 23 per cent in the second half of the 1960s it rose to 26.5 per cent in 1973.[9] If investment going into branches supplying agriculture, machinery, fertilisers and so on is added then about one ruble in three was being invested in the agricultural sector in the second half of the 1970s.

The escalation of oil prices in 1973 and the commodity boom of 1974 turned the terms of trade in the Soviet Union's favour. Hydrocarbon (oil and natural gas) and raw material prices rose faster than those of finished products. This occurred at a propitious time for the USSR as huge imports of Western technology and grain, the fruits of détente, were just beginning. This also put the Soviet Union in a stronger position *vis-à-vis* her trading partners in Comecon. Instead of applying world market prices rolling five-year averages were to be used but in 1980 the full world market price was to apply. Increases were applied in 1975 even though there were agreements laying down fixed prices during the 1971–75 plan period. One of the countries hardest hit was the GDR which found that the terms of trade had turned sharply against it.

The tenth FYP (1976–80) continued the downward trend. The seriousness of the situation is quite clear from Table 7.1. A factor adding urgency to reform was the slowdown in the growth of labour supply. Whereas between 1960 and 1970 the labour force grew by 23.2 million, this dropped to 17.8 million between 1970 and 1980. Over the decade 1980–90 only 9.5 million joined the labour force.

Table 7.1 Economic performance 1955–87

	1955–65	1966–70	Average annual growth (%) 1971–75	1976–80	1981–83	1984–87
Population growth	1.6	0.9	0.9	0.8	0.9	0.9
Gross NP	5.4	5.2(5.0)	3.7(3.1)	2.7(2.2)	2.3	1.6
Industry	7.5	6.3	5.9(5.4)	3.4(2.6)	1.5	2.1
Agriculture	3.5	3.5(3.7)	−2.3(−0.6)	0.3(0.8)	4.2	0.8
Services	4.0	4.2	3.4	2.8	2.1	–
Consumption	4.7	5.3	3.6	2.6	1.7	2.4
Investment	9.1	6.0	5.4	4.3	4.2	3.0

Sources: 1955–80: US Congress, Joint Economic Committee USSR: Measures of Economic
Growth and Development, 1950–80 (Washington DC 1982); 1981–87: Handbook of
Economic Statistics (Washington DC 1983 and 1988); figures in brackets: recalculations from
1988 publication; Population: Narodnoe Khozyaistvo SSR, various years

Almost all of these were in Muslim areas where labour mobility was low. This exacerbated labour shortages in traditional industrial areas. The record 1978 harvest of 235 million tonnes was followed in 1979 by a disappointing one of 179 million tonnes about 47 million tonnes short of the target. This involved the USSR in purchasing over 20 million tonnes of grain, again for feed, in North America and elsewhere. Since the USSR was the second largest producer of gold in the world it benefited considerably from the sharp rise in the price of gold, about 75 per cent, in 1979. Its production was an estimated 410 tonnes and this on its own would have paid for all its grain imports in 1979. This however, proved to be unnecessary, as the US would only sell 8 million tonnes. Its hard currency debt in 1979 was about US$17,000 million but the continuing rise in hydrocarbon and raw material prices meant that it is a light burden to carry.

Every FYP has a project to capture the imagination and set the pulses racing. The tenth FYP had BAM, the Baikal-Amur Magistral, a 3,000-kilometre railway line linking eastern Siberia to the Pacific, just to the north of the Trans-Siberian railway. A line linking the two was built with Japanese help and this provided access to large deposits of coking coal in south Yakutia. BAM opened up sources of iron, copper and many other minerals with which Siberia is replete. As resources are depleted elsewhere so Siberia is taking over as the main storehouse. In 1980 Siberia provided almost half of all the oil extracted, 35 per cent of the natural gas output and 38 per cent of the coal and timber.[10]

SOCIAL POLICY

If a *per capita* income of 50 rubles per month was needed in 1967 to stay above the poverty line in the Soviet Union then 37.7 per cent of individuals and 32.5 per cent of families in that year failed to attain this level and hence were in need.[11] The incidence of poverty was not confined to rural areas and varied from republic to republic. Predictably the collective farm peasantry were the worst off. In 1965 about three quarters of the kolkhozniks had incomes of less than 50 rubles per month and a quarter earned less than half the minimum for subsistence. However, this situation changed rapidly, and by 1968 only 8 per cent of peasants received less than half the minimum but over 50 per cent were still below the 50 ruble mark. On the other hand about one fifth of kolkhozniks and their dependants lived in families enjoying incomes of over 75 rubles per month.[12] This was the other side of the coin. The great disparity between different regions of the Soviet Union continued to widen throughout the 1970s.

Hence there was some rural affluence and poverty was not confined to country areas. About half of those with *per capita* incomes below the official poverty line, 50 rubles, were state employees and their dependants.

Between 1960 and 1970 personal incomes in the USSR grew at an average rate of 6 per cent per annum.[13] Belorussia and Moldavia recorded a higher increase but in Azerbaidzhan it was only 5 per cent. Normally growth over the period 1965–70 was faster than during the early years of the decade. This meant that by 1970 personal incomes in general were above the official poverty line. In the five poorest republics, Turkmenistan, Uzbekistan, Kirgizia, Azerbaidzhan and Tadzhikistan, it was still below 50 rubles per head, and most people in these republics, accounting for about 10 per cent of the Soviet population, were poor.

The *per capita* total income of state employees – workers, office employees and so on – grew at an average rate of 5.4 per cent annually between 1960 and 1970.[14]

Kolkhozniks fared better. Their average annual *per capita* increase during the same period was 7.2 per cent.[15] Turkmenistan achieved a 10.4 per cent annual increase but it was from a very low base. Estonia, already a leader in 1960, averaged 9.9 per cent per year but Uzbekistan only averaged 3.9. This meant that in 1970 the average total income per kolkhoznik in the USSR had risen to 63 rubles 50 kopeks per month.[16] However there were great disparities between republics. In Estonia kolkhoznik incomes were over double the USSR average and in Latvia they were almost double. Uzbekistan, Azerbaidzhan, Kirgizia and Tadzhikistan were still below the 50 ruble per month minimum and Armenia was just above it. About 20 per cent of kolkhozniks were to be found in these republics.

In 1970 kolkhoz labour payments in the USSR accounted for 47.1 per cent of the kolkhoznik's total income.[17] However in Georgia it was only 23.4 per cent. The private plot brought in 34.5 per cent of income in the Soviet Union in 1970 but in Georgia it was as high as 54.5 per cent and in Lithuania it reached 46.9 per cent.

So successful was Baltic agriculture that in 1970 total income per head per kolkhoznik exceeded that of state employees in the three republics of Estonia, Latvia and Lithuania. The role of the private plot played a large part in producing this state of affairs but one should bear in mind that these republics contain some of the poorest land in the USSR. It is striking that the three republics which head the agricultural league are all non-Slav.

The right to a private plot was enshrined in the 1977 constitution and official policy was to encourage its well-being. Workers were also urged to cultivate small plots so as to improve their health and add to the supply of fresh fruit and vegetables. In 1974 private farming, always part-time, accounted for about one third of all man-hours expended in agriculture, and about one tenth of all man-hours worked in the national economy. In 1978 42.8 million families had a private plot and on 3 per cent of the arable produced 25 per cent of global agricultural output.

Table 7.2 Wages 1965–77 (in rubles)

	1965	1973	1977
All workers and employees in the State sector (excluding kolkhozniks)	97	135	155
Industrial and engineering technical personnel	148	185	207
Industrial workers	102	146	172
Industrial white-collar workers	86	119	142
Sovkhoz workers	72	116	138
Trade employees	75	102	117
Education	96	121	130
Kolkhozniks	—	—	100*

*Estimate. This is only for social labour and does not include income from the private plot. *Sources: Narodnoe Khozyaistvo SSSR v 1973 g (Narkhoz)* (Moscow 1974) pp. 586–7; *Narkhoz 1977* (Moscow 1978) pp. 385–6.

The five-day week was introduced in 1967 and at the same time the basic holiday entitlement was raised from twelve to fifteen working days. An even more welcome improvement occurred in 1968 when the minimum wage was raised to 60 rubles a month. Previously it had been below the minimum subsistence level. It led to a considerable drop in differentials between industries and within industries.[18] In some branches of industry the gap between the highest paid workers and those on the basic wage was reduced to about 20 per cent and on state farms it was even as low as 16 per cent or 10 rubles per month.

Some industries enjoyed substantial wage increases, for instance in construction wages rose by 25 per cent in 1969.[19]

The minimum wage was raised to 70 rubles over the period 1971–75 and those in health and education, predominantly female and badly paid, received increases of 20 per cent in 1972.

The increase in the cost of living can be taken at 1 per cent per year over the Brezhnev era. This meant that real wages increased by almost 50 per cent between 1965 and 1977. Industrial workers reduced the differential between themselves and the industrial and engineering technical personnel. Education lost ground fast.

The urban–rural differentials were now a thing of the past and special bonuses were paid to attract labour to the more inhospitable east and north. The kolkhoznik saw most of the legislation which discriminated against him amended since 1964. He now qualified for a pension at sixty and his wife at fifty-five, albeit smaller than that received by a state employee. The minimum pension was 12 rubles per month in 1965 but this was raised to 20 rubles by legislation in 1971. The kolkhoznik was expected to gain from his private plot even after retirement. Medical facilities were still not as good as in urban areas. In the early 1970s the countryside accounted for 40–45 per cent of the population but had to make do with 11 per cent of the doctors.[20] Education followed a similar pattern. Each kolkhoznik was provided with an internal passport during the 1980s and this removed the last great barrier on the road to urban–rural equality.

The knowledge that most of the poor were families with several children and that many of the poor were children led to the introduction of supplementary benefits in 1974. Families with a *per capita* income of less than 50 rubles per month are entitled to a supplement of 12 rubles a month per child until its eighth birthday.[21] Since 1,800 million rubles were disbursed during the first year, this would suggest that 12.5 million children qualified for aid or about one child in three in the USSR.

There was a great improvement in the diet of the Soviet population under Brezhnev. Protein intake increased and carbohydrate amounts dropped. However, by 1990 it still had not attained the pattern of food consumption recommended by Soviet dietitians. Despite the increase in the availability of food, popular dissatisfaction grew. The major reason for this was that real wages grew faster than food output. Whereas the annual growth of *per capita* food consumption, according to Western estimates, was 4.2 per cent between 1966 and 1970, this had fallen to 1.1 per cent between 1976 and 1980 but rose again to 4 per cent over the years 1985–87. According to official Soviet data, the share of a worker's income spent on food dropped from 35 per cent in 1970 to 28 per cent in 1986. Global Soviet agricultural output over the years 1950–80 rose by about 3 per cent annually, according to Gregory and Stuart, while population increase was around 1.6 per cent. This meant that net agricultural annual growth was about 1.4 per cent. The difference between this figure and the stated rise in *per capita* consumption was made up by imports. Whereas the USSR was a net exporter of grain during the 1960s it became a net importer from the early 1970s. For example, grain imports from the West rose from 12.1 million tonnes in 1975 to 41.8 million tonnes in 1985. Trade in meat and meat products was also in deficit over the same period, as was vegetable oil from the late 1970s onwards.

The retail price of meat and dairy products was heavily subsidised. This was due to the fact that increases in the procurement prices paid by the State to the farms was not passed on to the consumer to any appreciable extent. The subsidy was 6.5 billion rubles in 1965, but this had climbed to 20 billion rubles by 1979. This was an annual figure and not a cumulative total. It got to the stage where the price subsidy was greater than the declared defence budget.

Table 7.3   The Soviet diet 1966–90
(annual *per capita* consumption in kilograms; eggs, actual numbers)

	Meat	Fish	Milk	Eggs	Potatoes	Grain	Vegetables	Fruit
Health norm	82	18.2	405	292	110	115	130	91
Actual 1966–70	47	14.3	287	144	132	150	78	–
Actual 1976-80	57	17.3	318	227	116	139	92	39
Actual 1985	61	17.7	323	260	104	133	102	46
Plan 1990	70	19.0	330–66	260-66	110	135	126-35	66-70

Source: US Department of Agriculture, *USSR Outlook and Situation Report* (Washington DC, various years)

Increased living standards can be illustrated by looking at the sales of consumer durables. In 1965 only 24 per cent of Soviet households possessed a television set but in 1974 71 per cent enjoyed the privilege. Whereas 11 per cent of families in 1965 had a refrigerator, in 1974 56 per cent had. Over the same period those possessing washing machines jumped from 21 per cent to 62 per cent.[22]

Only just over a quarter of all worker families were living in housing which corresponded to the norm of 9 square metres per person of living space (excluding kitchen, bathroom and corridor) in 1967. At the same time over 50 per cent of urban households were living in substandard housing. The situation improved thereafter and if the total living space in 1977 was divided by the urban population the result was 12.3 square metres per person. Nevertheless about 40 per cent of Soviet families still shared flats in the mid 1970s. Waiting for a new flat can be frustrating and many families had to wait for ten years or more. Only those whose *per capita* living space was less than 5 square metres were put on the housing list. This meant that newly weds had to start married life with their in-laws. Since city soviets control only about one-third of the housing stock and the rest was owned by factories, ministries and co-operatives, the place of work assumed great significance when flat hunting. From 1957 onwards about 2.3 million dwellings were constructed annually, but this did not keep pace with the growth of the urban population. Hence the housing problem became more and more acute. In 1965 there was a shortfall of 142,097 dwellings but in 1974 this had jumped to 1,100,000.[23] The situation in the countryside where two fifths of the population live was even more difficult.

The short cut to a flat (houses were hardly ever built) was to join a housing co-operative and build your own. Banks were willing to lend the money, and the State, for obvious reasons, favoured this type of self-help. The majority of those who solved their accommodation problems in this way in urban areas were from the cultural and technical intelligentsia. In 1974 about one fifth of urban housing in the RSFSR was privately owned.

Rapid urbanisation produced appalling conditions in the major cities of the Soviet Union. The situation eased somewhat during the 1970s, but it was always necessary to obtain permission to move to a major city and without permission no housing was provided. Moscow, Leningrad and Kiev were the leaders in the field. Even there city budgets could not be based on need. There were just not enough resources to go round. Cities in the RSFSR fared better than elsewhere. At the end of the 1960s Russian cities, with about 50 per cent of the Soviet urban population, accounted for approximately 60 per cent of total city budget expenditure. In 1973–74 *per capita* urban expenditure in the USSR came to around 120 rubles but Russian cities averaged 178 rubles. If Moscow and Leningrad are excluded this figure falls to 160 rubles. In Kazakhstan expenditure per person was only 101 rubles despite the large number of children there.[24] Since city income depends on income tax, turnover tax, enterprise profits and so on the prosperous cities were getting more prosperous and the poor stayed poor. Moscow was in a special category and was favoured in every way from housing to the availability of vegetables in winter. The other cities can be divided into tiers with Leningrad and Kiev in the second category and so on. The lower down the scale a city was the less likely it was to meet even minimal standards for services and welfare. The 1970s saw an increasing inequality among Soviet cities and the regions they served. Resources were just not available to extend Moscow standards of urban comfort, modest as they were, to all Soviet cities.

The growth of the Soviet population slowed in the 1960s and 1970s and reached 262.1 million in 1979. There was steady migration from the north and the east to the south. Over the years 1954–63 1,511,000 people left the RSFSR and they were followed by a further 952,000 between 1964 and 1973.[25] Siberia lost about a million inhabitants during the 1960s and this trend continued during the 1970s. The Ukraine and Central Asia were the most sought-after areas of settlement.

301

Alcoholism was the major social problem in the Soviet Union. In Lithuania, for instance, one in eleven of the population overindulged and alcohol consumption per adult was about 26 litres, even higher than in France. Increasing alcoholism among pregnant women was one of the reasons why infant mortality in the USSR increased from 22.9 deaths per 1,000 live births in 1971 to 31.6 in 1976.

CULTURE

The passing of Khrushchev meant that the unpredictability went out of Russian literature. There was a struggle between those who wanted to publish some good and mildly critical works, thus carrying on the tradition of the early 1960s, and those who wanted to return to a more conservative, traditionalist literature. It took place in the late 1960s and by 1970 the conservatives had won hands down. Hence the decade of the 1970s passed without any outstanding works appearing officially inside the Soviet Union. However, the informed Soviet reader could augment his reading matter by getting hold of a copy of a novel, play or poem circulating in samizdat inside the country or procuring a literary work published abroad. The 1970s in Russian literature resembled to some extent the 1920s and 1930s when major writers were in exile and many of the important works were published abroad.

The struggle after 1964 centred on what direction writing should take. *Novy Mir,* edited by Aleksandr Tvardovsky, was on one side, espousing the view that literature involved telling the truth warts and all, and *Oktyabr,* edited by the orthodox Stalinist Vsevolod Kochetov who regarded *partiinost* or party-mindedness in writing to be of primary importance, on the other. *Oktyabr* believed in making life simple and painting everything in black and white, no morbid introspection for it. It was the natural ally of those in the party, the military and elsewhere who were keen to see Stalin partly or wholly rehabilitated. By the late 1970s this stark contrast between *Novy Mir* and *Oktyabr* no longer applied as the former was brought under stricter party control.

The letter signed by twenty-five leading members of the Soviet intelligentsia and soon joined by others arguing against the rehabilitation of Stalin at the XXIIIrd Party Congress obliged the cultural and scientific elite to decide on which side they stood. The letter may have had some effect as Stalin's name was not mentioned at the congress.

It became increasingly difficult to get material critical of the Stalin period published after 1964, although this was also true of the tail end of the Khrushchev period. Aleksandr Nekrich's book *1941. 22 Iyunya* was actually published in 1965 but was withdrawn after publication. He continued his work as an historian and put together the story of the deportation of the nationalities accused of collaborating with the Germans. If the party would not countenance the criticism of Stalin's unpreparedness in 1941 it was certainly not going to put up with the exposure of the illegalities of the deportation of non-Slav national minorities. Nekrich was later expelled from the party and eventually left the USSR.

A powerful voice opposing those historians and scholars who wanted to examine Soviet development critically was S. P. Trapeznikov, head of the CC Department of Science and Education. His book on collectivisation, published in 1967, summed up his views neatly. It was a whitewash job with all the imperfections painted out or ignored. It ran counter to the trend of the previous decade but it set the tone for years to come.

The anti-Stalin lobby was strong enough to cause the party leadership to have second thoughts about praising Stalin on the ninetieth anniversary of his birth in December 1969. However this may have been due more to fears of trouble in eastern Europe than to the impact of the Soviet intelligentsia.

The difficulty experienced in getting works published led to the appearance of samizdat or self-publishing. This usually circulated in typescript and practically anything could be obtained if one had the right contacts. Some of the samizdat found its way abroad to be published, sometimes without the knowledge or permission of the author. Gradually such writers as Aleksandr Solzhenitsyn, who only managed to get one article and one short story published internally after 1964, passed more and more of their work for publication abroad. *The Gulag Archipelago* appeared in this way and the gulf between Solzhenitsyn and the authorities (he was expelled from the USSR Union of Writers in 1969) widened until he was deported in 1974.

The shock of Czechoslovakia penetrated all spheres of Soviet life. It slowed down the economic reforms and resulted in safe, trusted, uncontroversial centralist policies. Culture was especially vulnerable as the lessons of Czechoslovakia were digested. Hence 1969–70 is a turning-point. Aleksandr Tvardovsky had to leave *Novy Mir* in 1970 and practically the whole of the editorial board was changed. Many who would not bend to the new wind of change were expelled from the USSR Union of Writers which meant that they could not publish in the Soviet Union. Some of those who emigrated were Valery Tarsis who left in 1966, Iosef Brodsky in 1972, Andrei Sinyavsky in 1973, Viktor Nekrasov and Vladimir Maksimov as well as Solzhenitsyn in 1974. Anatoly Kuznetsov defected in 1969 and died in 1979. Death also claimed Anna Akhmatova in 1966, Ilya Ehrenburg in 1967, Konstantin Paustovsky in 1968, Kornei Chukovsky in 1969 and Aleksandr Tvardovsky in 1971. Many of the household names thus passed from the scene either through the action of the State or Father Time. Among those who filled their places were a group of writers called the *derevenshchiki*, those who had or were living in the countryside and usually wrote about village life. They were very concerned about the future of the Russian nation and culture and wrote about the little man, or more often about the little woman. They included Yuri Trifonov, who became quite well known outside the USSR. Their main platform was *Nash Sovremennik*. Gradually this group became more nationalistic.

The Soviet reading public can be divided into several groups. Party members preferred *Oktyabr* which in turn was almost completely ignored by the intelligentsia and surprisingly unpopular among workers according to a survey conducted in 1967–68.[26] *Literaturnaya Gazeta* was read by all those with a serious interest in literature but the quality of the writing published was criticised. *Novy Mir* was also popular with these readers but workers were not taken by the journal. As a general rule the smaller the print run the more likely it was to print daring material. It was virtually impossible for a large circulation newspaper or journal to include risky works.

The art world also functioned at two levels. Officially the State required socialist realism and some artists spent part of their time on this and the rest on more *avant-garde* works. Some devoted themselves exclusively to post-socialist realism. Usually the authorities turned a blind eye if the artists paint for other artists but in September 1974 an open-air exhibition was broken up and many of the paintings seized. However the exhibition was held later.

Table 7.4   Soviet education 1960–87

	1960–61	1970–71	1983–84	1986–87
General schools	224,000	190,000	141,000	138,000
Pupils (million)	36.19	49.19	44.48	43.90
Graduates (million)	1.06	2.58	3.63	3.04
Specialised secondary schools	3,328	4,223	4,438	4,506
Students (million)	2.06	4.39	4.50	4.49
Graduates (million)	0.48	1.03	1.27	1.26
Vocational technical schools	3,684	5,351	7,624	8,020
Students (million)	1.06	2.38	3.77	4.18
Graduates (million)	0.74	1.64	2.52	2.58
Higher educational institutions	739	805	890	896
Students (million)	2.40	4.58	5.30	5.09
Graduates (million)	0.34	0.63	0.85	0.84

Sources: *Narodnoe Khozyaistvo SSSR v 1983 g.* (Moscow 1984) pp. 402, 484–504; *Narodnoe Khozyaistvo SSSR za 70 let* (Moscow 1987) pp. 422, 523–55

More and more young people gave up hope of getting into a university. A survey showed that whereas in the 1960s 90 per cent of those who had completed their secondary school education intended to go to university, the proportion in 1973–75 had dropped to 46 per cent.[27] This is understandable given the fact that universities at the end of the 1960s accepted 900,000 students annually but in 1977 this figure had dropped to 600,000. This caused many sons and daughters of workers and peasants to lose hope with the result that the proportion of students from the intelligentsia in universities is increasing. Over the period 1973–75 they accounted for 51.7 per cent of all new entrants and 70.2 per cent of graduates.

The difficulty in gaining entry to a university is clearly evident. University enrolment actually declined by the late 1980s at a time when the pool of potential students had never been higher.

Special schools for talented children increased under Brezhnev. They were in cities and were normally not boarding schools. Over three-quarters of the children in these schools were from the intelligentsia, and this in turn made it easier for them to enter high prestige institutions which trained graduates for careers in diplomacy, foreign trade and international relations.

Educational and cultural standards improved greatly in the USSR over the Soviet period, and this was accompanied by a longing for new experiences and new insights into the human condition. The Brezhnev regime was conservative and staid, and wished to avoid anything which would incite the public to oppose official policy. Hence, if *avant-garde* material remained private and was not flaunted before the world, the regime was quite tolerant. Outsiders were struck by the almost insatiable thirst of the average educated Soviet citizen for information, illustrating once again that information was a privilege, not a right, in the Soviet Union. As ideology concentrated on its imperative and emotive functions – letting everyone know what they were supposed to do and trying to excite them into doing it – thereby ignoring the intellectual needs of the population, a void developed in many people's lives. The plethora of slogans and placards in the end were counter-productive. People became so bored they were forced to think for themselves.

NATIONALITIES

An old Russian Jew with a long white beard is sitting on a park bench studying a Hebrew grammar. A KGB man peers over his shoulder and engages the old man in conversation.

KGB man: What is that book with the strange writing you are reading?

Old man: A Hebrew grammar.

KGB man: But you are not likely to go to Israel at your time of life.

Old man: Alas, you are quite right. I know that my dream of seeing the Promised Land will remain a dream. However they speak Hebrew in Paradise too.

KGB man: How do you know you are going to Paradise? What happens if you go to Hell?

Old man: Oh, I already speak Russian.

According to the 1970 census, Russians made up 53.4 per cent of the Soviet population, but this dropped to 52.4 per cent in 1979 and 50.7 per cent in 1989. The number of Muslims increased 25 per cent between 1970 and 1979, and by 1989 they made up 19 per cent of the USSR population.

These figures reveal that the net annual increase of the Soviet population (0.9 per cent annually since the 1970s) was almost exclusively non-Russian. Had the Soviet Union survived beyond 1991, Russians would increasingly have found themselves in a minority. The record for the greatest increase in population was retained by the Tadzhiks, with an extraordinary 45.4 per cent growth between 1979 and 1989. This has exacerbated economic and social conditions in one of the poorest of the Soviet republics. Emigration was the main reason for the decline of the Jewish population and the small growth of the German nation.

Table 7.5 National composition of the population (in thousands)

	1970	1979	1989	Percentage increase or decrease	
				1970-79	1979-89
Total USSR population	241,720	262,085	286,731	8.4	9.4
Russians	129,015	137,397	145,155	6.5	5.6
Ukrainians	40,753	42,347	44,186	3.9	4.3
Uzbeks	9,195	12,456	16,698	35.5	34.1
Belorussians	9,052	9,463	10,036	4.5	6.1
Kazakhs	5,299	6,556	8,136	23.7	24.1
Tatars	5,931	6,317	6,649	6.5	5.3
Azerbaidzhanis	4,380	5,477	6,770	25.0	23.6
Armenians	3,559	4,151	4,623	16.6	11.4
Georgians	3,245	3,571	3,981	10.0	11.5
Moldavians	2,698	2,968	3,352	10.0	12.9
Tadzhiks	2,136	2,898	4,215	35.7	45.4
Lithuanians	2,665	2,851	3,067	7.0	7.6
Turkmenis	1,525	2,028	2,729	33.0	34.6
Germans	1,846	1,936	2,039	4.9	5.3
Kirgiz	1,452	1,906	2,529	31.3	32.7
Jews	2,151	1,811	1,449	−15.8	−20.0
Chuvash	1,694	1,751	1,842	3.4	5.2
Latvians	1,430	1,439	1,459	0.6	1.4
Bashkirs	1,240	1,371	1,449	10.6	5.7
Mordovians	1,263	1,192	1,154	−5.6	−3.2
Poles	1,167	1,151	1,126	−1.4	−2.2
Estonians	1,007	1,020	1,027	1.3	0.7

Sources: 1970–79: based on Ann Sheehy, Radio Liberty Research no. 123/80 and calculated; 1989: *Naselenie SSSR po Dannym Vsesoyuznoi Perepisi Naseleniya 1989 g.* (Moscow 1990) pp. 37–40 and calculated. There are about 80 other smaller nationalities.

The new Brezhnev–Kosygin leadership continued Khrushchev's nationality policy but moderated the language used. At the XXIIIrd Party Congress in March 1966, Brezhnev referred to the drawing together of the peoples of the USSR but carefully omitted the concept of *sliyanie*. Although the term was still used in the scholarly literature Brezhnev avoided it and refrained from mentioning that the disappearance of all nations was the party's goal. To emphasise the progress made in drawing nations together Brezhnev, at the XXIVth Party Congress in March 1971, spoke of the emergence of a 'new historical community of people – the Soviet people'. Afterwards the General Secretary made it quite clear that he would brook no opposition to the policy of eliminating differences between nations. This became abundantly clear during the political and cultural purge of the Ukraine in 1972–73. The principal casualty was Pyotr Shelest, the First Secretary of the Communist Party of the Ukraine, who had played a leading role in the renewal of Ukrainian national assertiveness. About 1,000 bureaucrats, officials and academics were dismissed. Particularly hard hit were ideology, literature and history. The purge added impetus to the emergence of a Ukrainian dissident underground. Here the emphasis was not to escape from Stalinism but to evolve a distinctly Ukrainian culture.

The concept of the 'Soviet people' was officially promoted from the early 1970s. It was not a new formulation, as it had surfaced in the early 1960s. However, it gradually became synonymous with the period of 'ripe', 'mature' or 'developed socialism'. This had to be invented due to the realisation that communism was not round the corner but rather a long way off. Russians continued to take precedence among the nations of the Soviet Union. Brezhnev lauded the 'revolutionary energy, diligence and deep internationalism of the Great Russian people' which had earned them the 'sincere respect of the peoples' of the USSR.

Vigorous debate surrounded the new Soviet constitution, promulgated in 1977, especially over whether the federal structure of the Soviet Union should be retained. Brezhnev revealed that one lobby had advocated placing in the constitution the 'concept of an integral Soviet nation' and 'dissolving Union and autonomous republics'. The General Secretary was very discreet and warned that the 'objective process of the drawing together of nations' could not be artificially accelerated.

The expansion of education was extremely impressive, especially in the non-Russian areas. Over the years to 1970 the number of persons with incomplete secondary education (seven years of schooling) in the various republics evened out. The most dramatic increases were in the Central Asian republics and the least growth was recorded in Georgia. This was because the Georgians, together with the Jews, were and are the most educated nation in the USSR. Educational progress was much more marked in urban areas, with standards in the countryside still low. The number of non-Russian students in the tertiary sector grew very impressively. Whereas there were only 74,000 in 1927–28, this had grown to 506,000 in 1959–60 and to 2.22 million in 1980–81. It was only after Stalin's death that non-Russian student growth exceeded that of the Russian students. Hence the proportion of Russians among students continued to rise until the early 1950s but fell continuously afterwards. The result was that by the 1980s the distinctions between the developed and underdeveloped nations of the Soviet Union, as far as access to education was concerned, had almost disappeared. The Central Asians had caught up and in some cases had more students per 10,000 of the population than the Russians. However, as the Muslim population increased, so access to higher education became more difficult. Another reason for the slowdown, from the mid-1970s onwards, was economic decline. Exceptions to this were the Buryats and Kalmyks who, by the early 1980s, had caught up with the Georgians and Jews as regards the number of students per 10,000 of the population. As a rule, educational levels in autonomous republics lagged behind those in Union republics. This was partly connected with the fact that Russian was the language of instruction.

By the early 1980s, despite the great expansion of tertiary education, no non-Russian republic had trained elites in all walks of life. Culture, education and the social sciences were adequately covered, but science and technology were seriously underrepresented. This had profound implications for industrial development of, for example, Central Asia. As a consequence, industry was dominated by Russians and other Europeans. The situation in the autonomous republics was even more serious. A key reason for this was that courses in science and technology were taught exclusively in Russian.

The problem of language turned out to be the most acrimonious. The Brezhnev leadership vigorously promoted Russian as a medium of learning and intercourse. By the mid 1970s the Russian language press had been boosted and that of non-Russian publications cut back. In the spring of 1978 Moscow attempted to withdraw the constitutionally guaranteed status of Georgian, Armenian and Azeri as state languages in the new constitutions of the three Transcaucasian republics. In Tbilisi, the Georgian capital, thousands took to the streets and the central authorities gave in.

Undeterred, the Brezhnev leadership promulgated extensive legislation in 1978–79 to promote the teaching of Russian in non-Russian republics. The measures were intended to embrace all sectors of education and for the first time included kindergartens and nurseries. The process of language-learning was one-sided. No attempt was made to encourage the 23.9 million Russians living in the non-Russian republics to learn the local language. The extent of the problem can be gauged from the fact that only 0.2 per cent of Russians, according to the 1989 census, speak another Soviet language. The

promotion of Russian aroused increasing opposition, especially in the
Baltic republics, the Ukraine and Georgia.

The promotion of Russian was clearly related to the alarming
demographic trends. Russians were certain to become a minority in
the country in the early 1990s, and the low birth-rate of Russians and
the high birth-rate of Muslims meant that, for example, every sixth
national serviceman was Muslim. Most of them either did not or did
not want to understand Russian, the only language of command in the
Soviet armed forces. In the 1989 census only 23.8 per cent of Uzbeks
claimed a knowledge of Russian. In Tadzhikistan and Turkmenistan
the proportion was 27.7 per cent. The wooden spoon for knowledge
of Russian was held by the Beludzhi, with 4.6 per cent. However, there
were only 29,000 Beludzhi in 1989.

Improvement in educational standards made it easier for non-
Russians to enter the CPSU. However, progress was slower than in
tertiary education. For example, Russians continued to be overrepresented. In 1961 Russians made up 67.8 per cent of party membership
and Ukrainians 12.1 per cent. In 1982 the proportions were 59.8 per cent
and 16 per cent. According to the 1979 census, Russians accounted for
52.4 per cent of the Soviet population. In 1989, 58.6 per cent of party
members were Russian and 16.1 per cent Ukrainian at a time when
Russians only made up 51 per cent of the Soviet population. At this
date the number of Ukrainians, Belorussians, Georgians and Armenians
in the party corresponded more or less to their proportions in the
population. Underrepresented were Latvians, Lithuanians, Estonians
and Kazakhs, but Azerbaidzhanis, Moldavians and the peoples of
Central Asia were significantly underrepresented. Much of this can
be explained by the party penchant for recruiting graduates and those
living in urban areas. Jews were the most overrepresented in the party:
15 per cent of all Jews were communists. This was connected with
the fact that Jews live almost exclusively in cities and are highly
educated. Germans were among those severely underrepresented: only
4.4 per cent.

In the party Politburo the Khrushchev era was marked by the rapid
advance of non-Russians but this was reversed under Brezhnev and
the top party body became almost a Russian preserve after 1982. This
process was helped by the fact that Nikolai Ryzhkov, who joined
the Politburo in 1985, had by then changed his nationality from
Ukrainian (1974) to Russian (1979). Nikolai Tikhonov, Soviet Prime
Minister until September 1985, followed the same course between 1979
and 1984.

Native cadres in Central Asia made headway in all top party and
government functions in their republics and by the late 1960s occupied
over half of the positions. This progress was most marked in the Baltic
republics. In Lithuania, for example, the proportion of Lithuanians in
the Buros and Secretariat of the Central Committee rose to 87 per

cent in 1971 and 93 per cent in 1976. In the Council of Ministers 93 per cent of ministers were natives in 1975. Lithuanians made up about 79 per cent of the republic's population. Until 1972 only in Moldavia and Belorussia were the titular nations underrepresented in the CC Buros. Afterwards all republics registered overrepresentation of native cadres in top party bodies. This was very striking in the Ukraine where, between 1955 and 1972, 93 per cent of all Politburo members were Ukrainians. Over the same period, in the Tadzhik party, 72 per cent of CC Buro members were Tadzhiks. Comparable figures for Azerbaidzhan and Latvia were 87 per cent and 80 per cent.

As far as the top three positions are concerned (First Party Secretary; Prime Minister and Chairman of the Presidium of the Supreme Soviet) the general practice was that they were occupied by locals. Kazakhstan and Moldavia, during most of the Khrushchev period, are an exception to this rule. The post of Second Secretary (known as Moscow's arm), responsible for cadres, gradually became the preserve of Russians and Ukrainians. Until the late 1970s, in some republics such as the Ukraine, Belorussia and Transcaucasia, a local held this important post. This policy was to ensure Moscow control of the republican parties but was ineffective. Russians were drawn into local networks and came to serve republican interests. In autonomous republics the same cadre policy is observable except in heavily Russified areas where the First Secretary was a Russian and the Second Secretary a native. The same applies to the Chechen-Ingush ASSR and reveals the ongoing problem this area represented.

Two other key positions in the republics were held almost exclusively by non-natives: head of the KGB and head of the CC department for organisation and party work. This changed during the 1970s and by 1979 about half of the KGB chiefs were locals. This clearly contributed to the loss of control by the centre during the late Brezhnev era. However, by then the KGB leadership in Moscow had become as corrupt as the local organisations. Curiously, the CC secretary for construction and the head of the CC department for construction in all republics was always a Russian. On the other hand, locals dominated party offices concerned with propaganda, culture and education. The first secretary of the Komsomol and the head of the trade-union organisation were usually natives.

The Brezhnev era saw a marked preference for Russians in leading party positions. Of the 36 elected to full membership of the Politburo between 1950 and 1959 25 were Russian and five Ukrainian. Of the 20 elected between 1960 and 1969 13 were Russian and three Ukrainian. Of the 12 elected between 1970 and 1979 10 were Russian and none was Ukrainian. During the 1980s there were 17 Russians and 3 Ukrainians among the 23 new full Politburo members. This predilection for Slavs was also very noticeable in the CC apparatus. In 1980 among the leading 150 functionaries there were only three non-Slavs. There were also only 3 non-Slavs among the top 150 in the military. Some amendments were made under Gorbachev. Russians accounted for only 51.3 per cent of CC full and candidate members elected at the XXVIIIth Congress in July 1990. Ukrainians only made up 12.4 per cent. On the other hand, Tatars and Bashkirs did especially badly. Whereas there were almost 70,000 more Tatar than Georgian communists, in the CC there were 10 Georgian but only 2 Tatars. One Bashkir made it to the CC. Not one of the 110,000 Chuvash communists was elected.

It is curious that at the same time that Brezhnev was establishing Russian dominance of the Politburo he was promoting the close affinity of the Russian, Ukrainian and Belorussian peoples. The three Slav nations accounted for 189 million of the 262 million Soviet citizens in 1979. The Russians were attempting to maintain their dominance in the country by drawing in the other Slavs. Consequently, the Ukrainian and Belorussian languages came under greater pressure and these republics' histories were rewritten to stress the commonality of their historical experience. This included underlining the common blood links, the 'genetic affinity' and the fact that the Kievan-Rus state was the prototype of the USSR.

At the XXVIth Party Congress in February 1981 Brezhnev conceded that there were still nationality problems which needed addressing. One involved finding ways to utilise the growing labour surplus in Central Asia and the Caucasus. His remarks underlined the difficulty of persuading locals to move to labour-deficit areas. One solution he suggested was to improve the cultural facilities of those living outside their republics presumably to encourage more to migrate. The other topic raised the sensitive issue of minorities in non-Russian republics. Brezhnev pleaded for equal representation of all nationalities in a given republic. Positive discrimination in education had led to the promotion of locals to a point where they were overrepresented in party and government posts. Russians and other minorities began to doubt their future in an increasingly self-assertive world, especially in Muslim areas. He was implying that things had gone far enough and should be rectified. To leave no doubt he praised the 'disinterested assistance of the Russian people' *vis-à-vis* the non-Russian nationalities.

The thorny question of fusion forced its way to the top of the agenda during the last months of the Brezhnev era into the Andropov era. Andropov, as party leader, at celebrations to mark the sixtieth anniversary of the USSR in December 1982, came out unequivocally for fusion. He proclaimed that party policy was 'not only to bring nations closer together but to fuse them'. However, he acknowledged that experience had shown that the 'economic and cultural progress of all nations' was 'accompanied by the growth of their self-awareness'. The party would have to tread warily. Andropov had an intimate knowledge of the grievances of non-Russians, gleaned from his years as head of the KGB. Shortly afterwards he put blame on all sides and condemned national conceit and supercilious attitudes towards other nations. He even stressed that peoples without a national territory, such as Germans, Poles and Koreans, were full members of the Soviet family of nations. Andropov laid stress on the economic aspects of nationality policy and proposed greater economic integration and burden-sharing. This included greater mobility of labour outside republics.

In June 1983 Andropov and his heir apparent, Konstantin Chernenko, delivered addresses on the nationalities question but dropped the concept of fusion altogether. This was a tacit admission that proclaiming the goal of fusion was perceived to be too provocative. Chernenko, especially, searched for more skilful ways of saying the same thing. He complained again about the unwillingness of some nationalities to move from labour-surplus to labour-deficit areas. He also referred to the need for many Soviet citizens to improve their command of Russian. To this end a school reform, initiated under Andropov, envisaged competence in Russian as a hallmark of all those completing secondary education.

Andropov had little sympathy for Russian nationalism, which had been nourished by economic decline. He threw a sop to Muslims by promoting the diversion of Siberian rivers southwards to Kazakhstan and Central Asia. The spectre of water shortage haunted several republics, especially Kazakhstan, Uzbekistan and Turkmenistan, due to the profligate use of water to irrigate cotton and the population explosion. Predictably, the Russian nationalist lobby stepped up opposition to the project. They proposed that if the region conserved its water instead of wasting it there would be no need to engage in the ecologically and economically dubious exercise of diverting nature. The project was eventually shelved under Gorbachev, in April 1986. The Gorbachev leadership was alarmed at the huge cost of the operation, 55 billion rubles during its first five years, and the possible negative environmental effects of such a massive attempt to reshape nature.

DISSENT AND OPPOSITION

Dissent is limited to protesting about the imperfections of the present regime whereas opposition can be seen as wishing to replace the present regime with another. The Russian words for dissident and dissent, *inakomyslyashchyi* and *inakomyslie,* literally mean thinking differently without any connotation of having a political platform to put in the place of the existing one. Dissidents range from left-wing communists to fervent Russian nationalists, from minority nationalists who want their own people to decide policy to those who want socialism with a human face, with the emphasis on human rights, and to believers such as Baptists who have a completely different world view. Hence dissidents do not make up a conscious political movement, their goals are often mutually exclusive. They sometimes sharply criticise and fall out with one another.

Their numbers were a drop in the ocean of the Soviet population. A tentative estimate might be 8,000–9,000 political prisoners, about 10,000 dissidents, most concerned with human rights, still at large, and about 250,000 believers and members of various nationalities fighting for their rights – all told under 300,000.[28] They amassed mounds of samizdat documents, by 1979 about 4,000 had penetrated to the West. Jews, Germans and others wishing to emigrate have not been included since they did not wish to change the system but to leave it as quickly as possible. However, they could be called dissidents as long as they were in the Soviet Union.

Dissidents acquired an importance out of all proportion to their numbers. Since ideology concentrated on its imperative and emotive aspects there was a spiritual and intellectual void in many lives, especially among the intelligentsia. Dissident ideas may fill this void and this is what concerned the KGB. When samizdat material was sent to the West much of it was broadcast back to the USSR, thus greatly increasing the circles of those coming into contact with it. However there was a great gulf between the intelligentsia and the working class. This needed to be bridged before dissent could turn into opposition. Workers have protested and gone on strike against poor living standards and working conditions and a free trade union headed by a Ukrainian miner Vladimir Klebanov was even set up in late 1978. It appealed to the world labour movement but got little more than sympathy. Klebanov was incarcerated in a mental hospital in Dnepropetrovsk as a consequence. Here was an opportunity for the intelligentsia and the workers to link up but little came of it.

The Sinyavsky-Daniel trial, the invasion of Czechoslovakia, the Arab–Israeli wars of 1967 and 1973 and the Helsinki Final Act all provided impetus to dissent and brought forth new recruits.

The human rights movement had emerged by 1967. It owed its origin to the concern felt by some, usually from the ranks of the intelligentsia, at the turn of events after 1964. *The Chronicle of Current Events* made its appearance in 1968 and came out bimonthly, providing a forum and a focus for a wide variety of views and opinions. The journal developed a particular style, it concentrated on providing factual information on trials, harassment, the persecution of small nationalities and religious believers and the activities of the censorship and the security organs in the USSR. It printed as many names as possible, those who were being oppressed and those who represented the state organs. It regarded support and sympathy in the outside world as vital to its continued existence. It deliberately avoided polemics. Dissidents called for the Soviet constitution to be implemented and the Universal Declaration of Human Rights, which the Soviet Union has signed, to be observed.

Détente came in 1972 but with it came a crackdown on the *Chronicle* and its Ukrainian counterpart *The Ukrainian Herald*. The KGB was successful in silencing these voices, many sympathisers were warned off, others sentenced by the courts and some obliged to emigrate. A campaign followed aimed at two prominent dissidents, Andrei Sakharov and Aleksandr Solzhenitsyn, in the autumn of 1973. The result was that Solzhenitsyn was flown out of the country in February 1974 but Sakharov could not be harshly treated as American scientists made it clear that action against the Academician would adversely affect Soviet–American scientific links. The *Chronicle* reappeared in May 1974. The Helsinki Final Act led to the setting up of Helsinki monitoring groups in many parts of the country.

In the Ukraine twenty intellectuals were arrested and sentenced in 1965. Their case histories were recorded in the *Chornovil Papers* named after the person who had compiled the accounts. He was sent to a labour camp. Except for Valentin Moroz no prominent figure was arrested until December 1971. This was due to the influence of Pyotr Shelest, First Secretary of the CP of the Ukraine who was trying to come to terms with the dissident intelligentsia. His whole approach was seen as too conciliatory in Moscow and he was replaced by V. V. Shcherbitsky in May 1972. Then followed a hardline policy against dissidents, with many trials. *The Ukrainian Herald* was closed down but it briefly reappeared in 1974.

In Lithuania religion and nationalism are intertwined and provide the motive force behind dissent. *The Chronicle of the Lithuanian Catholic Church* appeared in 1972. A student engaged in self-immolation in May 1972 in protest against restrictions hindering religious and national expression. Riots in Kaunas followed.

Shelest was not the only First Secretary to go. Azerbaidzhan, Armenia and Georgia all changed their top party man between 1969 and 1974 as well. Corruption and nationalism were seen as too widespread and the new men had the task of putting matters right. The greatest problem was Georgia. V. P. Mzhavanadze, who was replaced by E. A. Shevardnadze, had been a very popular man in the republic, perhaps the most popular. He had been a complaisant First Secretary, turning a blind eye to corruption or, put another way, to the parallel or black economy, provided he benefited. He accumulated four dachas and became a ruble millionaire. Shevardnadze was made of sterner stuff. He had been Minister of the Interior from 1966 to 1972, and ordered the arrest of about 25,000 people on charges of corruption between 1972 and 1974. Of these 9,000 were party members. One Lazeikhvili, who can be described as the Georgian godfather, got fifteen years. Murder, arson and explosions followed. The opera house in Tbilisi was burnt down in 1973 – but those involved did the citizens a favour since it has been magnificently restored with some superb Austrian glassware included. An explosion occurred outside the Council of Ministers building in April 1976. Mzhavanadze was not put on trial nor indeed was any important party or government official. Their appearance in court would have discredited not only the party in Georgia but the CPSU as well. The Georgian samizdat journal *Golden Fleece* first appeared in 1975. Several Georgian dissidents were dealt with harshly by the courts in the late 1970s.

The current emigration of Soviet Jews which started its upsurge in 1971 partly as a result of détente and the influence of the Jewish lobby in the US, was not a new phenomenon. Previous waves of emigration occurred between 1923 and 1926, 1932 and 1939 and during the immediate aftermath of the founding of the State of Israel on 14 May 1948. The reasons which motivate a family which has grown up in the Soviet Union to pull up roots and leave for an uncertain life elsewhere are complex. Jews have historically been very mobile; during the 1950s, for instance, some Polish Jews were repatriated to Poland. There was an upsurge of anti-Semitism in the USSR in the wake of the Yom Kippur War of 1968, and this convinced some Jews that they would find it increasingly difficult to retain their distinct identity in the USSR. More than 200,000 Jews left during the 1970s. In the early years of the decade many were motivated by religious reasons and almost all emigrants went to Israel, but since then it would appear that a desire to better oneself materially has become an important factor. All Jews were given exit visas to Israel and travelled first of all to Vienna. Many emigrants sought a different destination after arriving in Vienna; for example, in 1976 48.9 per cent of arrivals did not go on to Israel. The policy of the Soviet government fluctuated from generosity to extreme meanness in the provision of exit visas. Moscow, of course, regarded every émigré visa as a motion of censure on Soviet society. Various devices, ranging from charging for an émigré's higher education, the so-called 'diploma tax', to arguing that many applicants were privy to state secrets – for example, recently demobilised military personnel – were employed to dam the flood. A major factor determining the flow of visas was the state of US–Soviet relations. In the aftermath of the Moscow Olympics, when the US-sponsored boycott led to some leading nations not competing, exit visas were very difficult to acquire.

Soviet Germans have benefited from improved relations between Moscow and Bonn and between 1971 and 1978 48,977 moved to West Germany. A few others preferred to settle in the GDR.

FOREIGN POLICY

Khrushchev's successors did not criticise the goals he had pursued in foreign policy. They thought that the country did not possess the means to carry through his policies successfully. Without nuclear parity and sea power there was little point in needlessly risking war. The USSR under Brezhnev and his colleagues had achieved nuclear parity by the late 1960s and was thus in a position to begin seriously to negotiate limits to nuclear armament. This, of course, did not please the Chinese. Improved relations after 1964 did not occur largely due to the personality and predilections of Mao Zedong whose opinion of the Soviet leadership was not high. The war in Vietnam was the main thorn in the flesh of better US–Soviet relations. Here the American attempt to link détente to a world-wide US–Soviet understanding failed since Moscow refused to put pressure on Hanoi. The ignominious American withdrawal from South Vietnam and the rise of Soviet influence in Africa soured détente for many Americans, as it appeared to be all one-way traffic. Nevertheless SALT I led to the signing of SALT II in June 1979. These agreements did not stop the arms race, but just directed it into other channels. If Soviet political power in 1964 was greater than its military potential the situation in the late 1970s was the reverse. Soviet superiority in some nuclear weapons systems and their coming of age as a sea power, allied to Western economic difficulties and the increasing vitality of non-capitalist modes of development in the Third World provided Soviet policy-makers with more options than they ever had hitherto.

All this began to change on 27 December 1979 when the Soviet Union started moving large numbers of troops into Afghanistan. Moscow claimed that Hafizullah Amin, the Prime Minister, had invited them in but he was killed by the Soviet Army during the subsequent fighting and was replaced by Babrak Karmal. Amin, however, was branded a reactionary and a traitor but Afghan relief at his passing was more than counterbalanced by the Soviet invasion. Those Afghans who had rebelled against Amin, the *mujahidin* (freedom fighters) now turned their guns on the Soviet army. It soon became abundantly clear that the Soviets had miscalculated the military situation. They were obliged to move in more troops and more advanced equipment. Something like eight divisions (about 85,000 troops) were in Afghanistan in July 1980. The military miscalculation was dwarfed by the political miscalculation. Washington, which had warned Moscow five times before the invasion that such a move would call détente into question, reacted strongly. The Soviets were to be permitted to import the 8 million tonnes allowed by treaty but the other 14.8 million tonnes of grain bought were embargoed. Sales of high technology were also affected. If the US was annoyed, so was the Muslim world. It called on the USSR to leave Afghanistan, SALT II disappeared from view and the US and China came closer together. Moreover China successfully tested an intercontinental ballistic missile with a range of 11,000 kilometres on 18 May 1980.

East–West tension increased in the wake of the rise of the Polish free trade-union movement, Solidarity, in 1980–81. One of the reasons why the USSR did not intervene militarily was the poor state of super power relations. The suppression of Solidarity in December 1981 by General Wojciech Jaruzelski and the Polish military lowered the international temperature further.

The United States and China

The Cuban crisis of 1962, the partial test-ban treaty of 1963 and US nuclear superiority led the Americans to the view that the Soviet Union would concentrate on internal development and desist from active involvement in revolution abroad. To Washington China was the greater problem and Vietnam the testing-ground. The partial test-ban treaty appeared to strengthen the Chinese case that Moscow was appeasing Washington and would not give high priority to aiding North Vietnam acquire the whole of the country. Zhou Enlai attended the celebrations marking the 48th anniversary of the October Revolution in Moscow but little progress was made in his talks with Soviet leaders. Kosygin went to Hanoi in February 1965 to discuss deliveries of war *matériel* and to counsel caution in relations with the South. A gradualist policy held out the prospect of winning the war there without sucking in large numbers of US troops and equipment. This Soviet advice had little impact as the US bombed North Vietnam for the first time while Kosygin was in Hanoi. The bombing was a direct challenge to Moscow and the communist world. Moscow had to step up military aid and the likelihood was that as North Vietnamese ability to fight a modern war increased so the course of the war would be dictated from Hanoi. Soviet attempts to pressurise the Vietnamese could only benefit Beijing. The USSR favoured a negotiated settlement but the men in the North were in a hurry and they were being egged on by the Chinese who would have been delighted by a US–USSR nuclear confrontation.

The cultural revolution threw China into turmoil from 1966 onwards. This revolution aimed at destroying the culture of the time. Moscow could only gain from Chinese weakness as the country turned its eyes inwards and away from foreign affairs.

The Arab–Israeli war of June 1967 brought the Soviet Union and the US together but on opposite sides. Aleksei Kosygin and President Lyndon B. Johnson met at Glassboro, New Jersey, but little emerged from the meeting. The Chinese predictably saw it as a plot to carve up the world. The US was more concerned with Vietnam and missed an opportunity to seize the initiative in the Middle East.

American and Chinese reaction to the invasion of Czechoslovakia varied. Whereas the Americans regarded it as an intra-communist affair not adversely affecting their interests (President Johnson shelved his proposed visit to Moscow and left it at that), the Chinese saw it as a manifestation of Soviet social imperialism. If they did not hesitate to invade Czechoslovakia, justifying their action by referring to their duty to defend socialism, might they not do the same elsewhere?

Clashes on the river Ussuri in March 1969 which resulted in the death of thirty-one Soviet border guards and many Chinese marked the lowest ebb of Sino-Soviet relations. The Soviets spread rumours that they were contemplating a 'surgical strike' against Chinese nuclear facilities.

In June 1969 a conference of communist and workers' parties met in Moscow with the Chinese, North Vietnamese and North Koreans failing to attend. Nevertheless there was no direct mention of China in the conference resolutions, indeed the basic document stated unequivocally: 'All parties have equal rights. At present, there is no leading centre of the international communist movement.'[29]

Four-Power discussions on defusing the Berlin problem once and for all got under way in May 1970, but Leonid Brezhnev was very suspicious of the motives of Walter Ulbricht, First Secretary of the SED. The latter wanted Bonn and the West to make far-reaching concessions but Brezhnev misread the East German leader's tactics. Brezhnev thought that Ulbricht was preparing to sell out to the West Germans and engineered his removal. Ulbricht had no support at home as the SED Politburo had written to the Soviet party leader to remove their leader. Erich Honecker, a more malleable leader, took over but in the course of time he was to prove a great disappointment. A Berlin agreement was reached in September 1971 but it really only affected West Berlin. It was ratified in June 1972.

If the Berlin problem could be solved so could others. The US desire to get out of Vietnam and the *volte face* in relations with China made détente between Moscow and Washington feasible. The USSR had to offer the US something tangible to ensure that Sino-American relations did not become too warm. President Richard Nixon's historic visit to China, at the initiative of the Chinese, took place in February 1972. Then followed, in September 1972, a visit by the Japanese Prime Minister Kakuei Tanaka and the establishment of Sino-Japanese diplomatic relations, Tokyo breaking its ties with Taiwan to make this possible. So a process was set in motion which saw the People's Republic of China enter the UN and the Security Council at the expense of the Republic of China. World-wide diplomatic recognition followed, culminating in full relations with the US in January 1979.

After Beijing came Moscow. There was a hiccough before President Nixon arrived in the Soviet capital. North Vietnam had escalated the war in the South and the US had replied by bombing the North and mining Haiphong. The Soviets turned a blind eye and the visit can be seen as marking the beginning of the end of the Cold War. Several agreements were signed including the Interim Agreement on Offensive Missiles and an Anti-Ballistic Missile Treaty to run for five years (SALT I) in 1972. There followed the Nuclear Accident Agreement, a joint space-trip in 1975 and so on. Together with the arms control agreement went a US promise to grant the USSR most favoured nation status and to extend her large credits. This proved very difficult as the US Senate wanted to link this concession to increased emigration of Soviet Jews. Henry Kissinger let it be known that Andrei Gromyko and he had come to an understanding and the Trade Bill was signed in October 1974. When the US Senate tried to make the unofficial agreement on Jewish emigration official, something Moscow could not do since it would have conceded the point that Soviet Jews were being discriminated against, the Soviet Union unilaterally abrogated the Trade Bill in January 1975 but declared that she still favoured détente. Leonid Brezhnev visited the US in 1973 and President Nixon was again in Moscow in 1974. The removal of President Nixon, a most perplexing event for the Soviet leadership to understand, did not mean the end of détente. President Gerald Ford journeyed to Vladivostok in November 1974 to sign a new agreement on nuclear weapons. The election of President Jimmy Carter and his commitment to human rights resulted in a cooling of US–USSR relations. The President also proposed that the SALT II negotiations should aim at lower weapon ceilings than those laid down at Vladivostok. This upset Moscow. Despite this SALT II was finally signed by the two presidents in Vienna in June 1979. Then came Afghanistan.

The Paris Agreement, initialled by Henry Kissinger and Le Duc Tho in January 1973 ended the war in Vietnam and allowed the Americans to leave that unhappy country. The North took the whole country by force of arms in 1975 and this left two other countries still in a destabilised state, Laos and Cambodia. The Khmer Rouge under Pol Pot took control in Cambodia, renamed Kampuchea, also in 1975, but became embroiled in border skirmishes which escalated in 1978 and led to the Vietnamese invading Kampuchea. China attacked Vietnam along their common frontier in January 1979 hoping to force the Vietnamese to withdraw some of their forces from Kampuchea, thus slowing down their progress there. Badly mauled, the Chinese withdrew in March 1979. Each side lost an estimated 40,000 men. By the terms of the Soviet–Vietnamese Treaty of Friendship and Co-operation of November 1978 both sides are obliged in case of attack to consult and to 'eliminate that attack'. The Soviets, however, restricted themselves to a verbal offensive. After China had withdrawn Soviet deliveries of war *matériel* to Vietnam were stepped up.

Despite the delicate state of Sino-Soviet relations the two sides began discussions aimed at improving relations in Moscow in September 1979, the first high-level discussions for more than a decade. However, they were soon discontinued. Desultory border talks have been going on for a decade as well and one result was that the Soviets lifted in 1978 the blockade they had imposed in 1967 which prevented Chinese vessels from sailing through the confluence of the rivers Amur and

Ussuri, near Khabarovsk. The blockade had been imposed to enforce
Moscow's reading of the 1860 Russo-Chinese Treaty. The Chinese had
acquiesced then but the Soviet attempt to enforce their interpretation
again at Chenpao or Domansky island on the Ussuri in March 1969
was unsuccessful. The Chinese victory there has kept their access to
the waterways open and they have made it clear that they would never
again yield to Soviet demands even if backed up by force.

Eastern Europe

Soviet concern with Eastern Europe can be looked at on three levels.
First, the area was part of the defence system of the Soviet Union
and was also a buffer zone. It also had to be capable of resisting a
resurgent West Germany. Eastern Europe in the twentieth century has
either been dominated by Russia or Germany. If Western political and
economic influence grew socialism would be seen to be in retreat and
this would have affected the face of Marxism-Leninism in the USSR
itself. Hence it could not be allowed to come about.

The Soviet decision to invade Czechoslovakia on 21 August 1968
was slow in coming and was only taken as a last resort. Shelepin,
apparently, voted against invasion.[30] The crisis had been brewing since
the spring and one explanation for Soviet slowness to make up their
minds would be that the situation was novel for everyone. What
was needed was a definition of sovereignty under socialism. What
were the limits beyond which a socialist state could not go without
ceasing to be socialist? The Czechoslovaks based their thinking on the
fundamental principles of the socialist commonwealth; the sovereignty
of member states, non-intervention in domestic affairs and equality of
nations. They understood that the only step which would place them
outside the socialist bloc would be a decision to leave the Warsaw
Pact on the analogy that the Hungarian decision to leave the Pact had
precipitated the invasion of 1956. Hence the Czechoslovaks reiterated
time and again their loyalty to the Pact. They just did not accept
that the Soviets had the right to define socialism on their own.
Even more confusing for the Czechoslovaks was the fact that some
of them were receiving private letters from members of the Soviet
Politburo encouraging them in their reforms. The Czechoslovaks
were idealistic, they were convinced that they were contributing to
the creative development of socialism. Socialism with a human face
was an expression of faith in its future. It should be stressed however
that the Communist Party leadership was split between those, headed
by Dubček, who wanted socialism to transform itself and those, such
as Indra and Bilak, who thought that things had gone far enough
and who opposed any fundamental changes. The media, especially
the TV, played an important role in stimulating debate. Censorship
was effectively abolished and plans to re-examine the sentences passed

on political undesirables after 1948 forced those who felt threatened into active opposition to the 'Prague Spring'. Although the names of those who signed the appeal to the Soviet Union have not yet been made known it is likely that some of these men and women were among them.

The Czechoslovak tragedy can be seen as a failure to communicate. Had the Soviets spelled out clearly the limits beyond which the Czechoslovaks could not go then it is likely that the whole episode would never have occurred. It was the slow Soviet response to the developing situation, compounded by poor intelligence reporting from the Soviet embassy in Prague, that exacerbated the situation and encouraged the Czechoslovaks to think that they could continue on the road they were taking. The Soviets were reluctant invaders. They knew that the Czechoslovaks would not fight and that the US regarded the quarrel as an intra-socialist one, not threatening vital US interests.

Socialism with a human face was causing problems elsewhere. Pyotr Shelest pointed to its appeal in the Ukraine and Walter Ulbricht saw banned German literature entering the GDR from Czechoslovakia. Significantly Kurt Hager, SED CC secretary for ideology, made the first virulent attack on the Prague Spring. The Soviet military were keen on intervention. The CPSU waited until it was convinced that the Czechoslovak party was no longer capable of bringing the country back on to the rails. Over 400,000 troops, overwhelmingly Soviet, occupied the country quickly leaving seventy-two Czechoslovaks dead. The Romanians refused to join the march on Prague and let it be known that they would fight if offered similar 'fraternal help' by Moscow. As an earnest of their intent Romanian border guards destroyed a Soviet tank. President Tito, who had visited Dubček shortly before the invasion, also had his people behind him.

The Czechoslovak episode gave rise to the Brezhnev Doctrine: the socialist commonwealth was duty bound to intervene whenever socialism was under threat in a member country. This was not new, but is as old as the October Revolution. However, it changed the mood of optimism in Czechoslovakia to one of despair and turned a country which had been pro-Soviet into one resentful of the Soviet connection. It soured relations with the outside world, halted any political or economic reforms in eastern Europe and slowed down economic reform in the USSR.

The Warsaw Pact changed as well. The occupation, a model of its kind, was commanded not by the commander-in-chief of the Pact but by the C-in-C Soviet ground forces. Four divisions were left behind after 'normalisation'. This increased Soviet strength in Eastern Europe to thirty-one divisions, there having been no Soviet troops in Czechoslovakia before the invasion. The Pact was streamlined and upgraded militarily and its structure was changed in 1969. A committee of defence ministers was established to advise the Political Consultative

Committee and a Military Council of the Joint Command came into being composed of representatives of all Pact states. On paper the ministers of defence were no longer subordinate to the C-in-C of the Pact but together formed the highest military body in the alliance. The Political Consultative Committee continued to be very active, taking the initiative in launching proposals for nuclear disarmament, reducing troop numbers and being involved in the Mutual and Balanced Force Reduction talks (MBFR) in Vienna.

The riots in December 1970 in Poland, the result of economic and political mismanagement, saw the replacement of Władysław Gomułka by Edward Gierek. Large food price increases had been announced just before Christmas giving the impression that Gomułka thought that everyone should be as abstemious as he. The Warsaw Pact did not invade, as Moscow knew that the Poles would fight. The riots led to increased emphasis being placed on consumer goods production everywhere, including the Soviet Union. As if it had learned nothing from the events of 1970 the Polish government again announced substantial increases in food prices in June 1976 and such was the unrest that the decree was withdrawn.

The Four-Power Agreement on Berlin also affected East–West German relations. Negotiations between the two German states produced the Basic Treaty, signed in December 1972 and effective as of 21 June 1973. The FRG recognised the GDR but the two states did not regard each other as foreign countries, exchanging permanent representatives and not ambassadors. This was a moment of triumph for the SED. At long last the GDR had become internationally respectable and by 1976 she enjoyed diplomatic relations with 121 countries, including the US. She became a member of the UN in September 1973 and of many other international bodies. All this was the tangible result of the Soviet connection.

The normalisation of the situation in Berlin and between the two German states were steps on a ladder which led to the Conference on Security and Co-operation in Europe in Helsinki in August 1975. The Final Act acknowledged the post-war frontiers in Europe and underlined the participants' desire to further détente. It also involved the socialist states committing themselves to observe human rights, increase the flow of information and so on. This encouraged dissidents throughout the bloc and Helsinki monitoring groups came into being.

The second European conference of communist and workers' parties convened in East Berlin on 29 June 1976 – the first had met at Karlovy Vary in 1967. The CPSU would have preferred the meeting earlier but French, Italian, Spanish, Romanian and Yugoslav objections to parts of the final text held up proceedings. The Soviets wanted to go further than the basic document of 1969 but the Romanian, Yugoslav and some West European parties would not recognise the hegemonial position of the CPSU in the world communist movement. The final document was accepted but not signed and it was not binding. However, as far as eastern Europe was concerned it was binding, leaving aside the obstreperous Romanians and Yugoslavs. Albania did not even attend. Détente, it was underlined, did not mean a slackening of the ideological reins, it meant a stepping up of ideological warfare with the bourgeois world.

Polish communism was in permanent crisis in the 1970s, and this led to a series of strikes against acute food shortages during the summer of 1980. The Solidarity trade-union movement emerged, headed by Lech Wałesa, and began to challenge the leading role of the Polish United Workers' Party, the communist party. It forced the party into concessions, including the right to strike, and became very confident about its ability to sweep away the communists. The election of Cardinal Karol Wojtyła as Pope increased the moral and intellectual authority of the Roman Catholic Church. However, the communists still retained the will-power to stay in command. It was the political military which came to the rescue of the party but at the expense of revealing the bankruptcy of civilian rule. General Wojciech Jaruzelski, a political general, brilliantly conceived and executed a coup on 13 December 1981, banned Solidarity and set about 'normalising' the situation. It was a Pyrrhic victory, since Solidarity supporters conspired to defeat all reform efforts of the new administration. Its legitimacy gone, communist rule sank into terminal decline.

There was some hope in Hungary, where János Kádár and the party, using the New Economic mechanism, in force since 1968, managed to arrive at a *modus vivendi* with the population. In Czechoslovakia the party was never able to 'normalise' the situation fully but did succeed in raising living standards. Dissent found expression in Charter 77, and there was a continuing concern for human rights and the implementation of the Helsinki Final Act. In the GDR, Rudolf Bahro, an SED member and convinced Marxist, published a withering attack on the SED regime in 1977. He was imprisoned, but expelled to the FRG in 1979. Many members of the cultural intelligentsia were also obliged to leave the GDR. Romania, under Ceauçescu, continued to defy the USSR from time to time. In 1978, Romania refused to increase defence spending by the amount agreed by the Warsaw Pact. There was a good reason for this: it could not afford to do so, but with one of the lowest living standards in Europe and one of the most Stalinist of parties Romania was just a nuisance and not a problem for Moscow.

Western Europe

The Berlin Agreement, West German treaties with Moscow and Warsaw and the Basic Treaty with East Berlin, and the Helsinki conference achieved one of the major goals of Soviet policy *vis-à-vis* Western Europe, the recognition of the *status quo* in Europe. The

FRG acceptance of the western frontier of Poland, the fact that Bonn no longer spoke for all Germans and West Berlin was not part of the Federal Republic, all the result of Willy Brandt's *Ostpolitik* which had been set in motion in 1969, went a long way towards solving the German problem. Moscow, ever since 1945, had been conscious of the economic weakness of eastern Europe and the economic revival of the FRG in the 1950s increased the fear of German power forcing through the political goals adopted in Bonn. Behind the FRG stood the North Atlantic Treaty Organisation (NATO). American dominated, its primary purpose was to dissuade the Soviet army from moving westwards, first and foremost into West Germany. The situation changed after 1969 when Moscow achieved nuclear parity with the US. Thereafter the fear was that the FRG might involve an unwilling US in a war with the east. Hence preventing Bonn acquiring its own nuclear weapons was a high priority. Could this be achieved by a policy aimed at reducing American influence in Western Europe, leading to the break-up of NATO? With the US having little military influence Moscow could aim at the Finlandisation of the area; dealing with each country separately, influencing the composition of governments, inhibiting moves which were inimical to Soviet interests and the strengthening of the communist parties of the region. Or would it be wiser to have an American nuclear commitment to Western Europe which would bind the West Germans tightly to NATO? Then the US could be encouraged to vouchsafe Bonn's good intent. The Kremlin, in the end, decided that keeping the US in Western Europe was the more advisable policy. It took comfort from the fact that the FRG signed the Nuclear Non-proliferation Treaty in 1969 and ratified it soon afterwards.

The defence of the post-war frontiers, the weakening of NATO and the European Economic Community were the main goals. A chink in NATO occurred in 1966 when France left and when General de Gaulle visited the Soviet Union he was fêted and shown space facilities, the first western head of state to be so honoured. But he would not recognise the GDR and could not be drawn into nuclear agreements. If NATO showed little sign of breaking up then its nuclear capacity had to be restricted. When the US offered her partners the neutron bomb in 1977 Soviet leaders and the media launched a vociferous campaign attacking this move. Washington withdrew its offer. A similar issue came up in late 1979 when the question of stationing US Cruise and Pershing 2 missiles in Western Europe in and after 1983 had to be decided. Leonid Brezhnev offered to withdraw 1,000 tanks and 20,000 troops from the GDR and to discuss the possibility of reducing the number of Soviet SS20 intermediate range missiles stationed in the western Soviet Union.

The invasion of Czechoslovakia led to many communist parties condemning the action. Those parties such as the Italian Communist

Party (PCI) and the French Communist Party (PCF) which had prospects of joining or becoming the government were in a quandary. If they showed proletarian solidarity it would adversely affect their standing with the electors so they came out against it, the PCI displaying more conviction than the PCF. The latter went so far as to abjure the dictatorship of the proletariat and entered into an electoral pact with the socialists but it did not last. Those parties which stressed democracy during the construction of socialism were labelled Eurocommunist. They criticised the Soviet and East European record on human rights, and this brought them into conflict with the CPSU. However, Eurocommunism turned out to be a transient phenomenon, and West European communist parties declined as rapidly as their sister parties in the east.

It looked for a time as if the Portuguese Communist Party would take power but in 1975 it shot its bolt and afterwards Moscow's eyes turned to the former Portuguese colonies in Africa, Angola, Guinea-Bissau and Mozambique.

The Soviet invasion of Afghanistan was sharply criticised by some West European communist parties, the Italian, British, Spanish, Belgian and Swedish being most outspoken. Moscow gained some solace from the fact that the PCF abandoned Eurocommunism and realigned itself with the CPSU. This was an attempt to widen the gulf between the PCF and the French socialists since the communist–socialist alliance had benefited the socialists almost exclusively.

The Middle East

Moscow's desire to strengthen itself militarily in its southern hinterland was fuelled by the inability or unwillingness of the US to establish better relations with the Arab world. The American commitment to Israel also took precedence. As the US gave up bases during the 1960s the USSR set out to acquire facilities. The Americans were not unduly worried. Besides their Sixth Fleet they had Polaris submarines in the Mediterranean which could hit a wide area. So the Soviets made a special effort to improve relations with all those states bordering on the Mediterranean, Syria, Egypt, Libya, Algeria and so on. The 1967 Arab–Israeli war was a disaster for the Arabs and underlined their need for advanced military technology and the men to operate it. The Soviet Union stepped neatly into the gulf between the Arab world and the US. Had Washington not been so engrossed with Vietnam a lasting solution might have been possible with Arab self-confidence at such a low ebb.

The Soviets made little progress in Algeria where Ahmed Ben Bella was replaced by Houari Boumédienne in June 1965 or in Libya after the monarchy was overthrown. Naval facilities were, however, acquired in Syria and Egypt. Not only did Cairo make Soviet ships welcome but it also granted air bases as well and thousands of Soviet military personnel poured into Egypt.

The high-water mark of Soviet–Egyptian relations were the years 1970–72. The Soviet and American search for détente made it less and less likely that Moscow would back a bellicose policy in the Middle East. Then President Anwar Sadat took the drastic step of ordering 21,000 Soviet advisers out of Egypt in July 1972. This hurt and astonished Moscow. With the Soviet Union recommending that the Arab–Israeli conflict be resolved by negotiation, something which was bound to favour Israel, Syria and Egypt launched the Yom Kippur War of October 1973. It caught everyone by surprise, destroyed the invincibility of Israeli military might and brought the two super powers back into the Middle East, on opposite sides.

President Sadat became convinced that the US was seriously interested in a peaceful solution to the Middle East conflict and this led to close US–Egyptian relations which discomfited Moscow. Peace negotiations between the Arabs and Israel became Israeli-Egyptian negotiations. Cairo was the butt of considerable Soviet criticism, internal and economic policies coming under special fire. Egypt was not satisfied with the limited quantities of Soviet arms and equipment which were arriving and spares were a problem. Relations reached a new low in March 1976 when Cairo tore up the Soviet–Egyptian Treaty of Friendship and Co-operation which dated back to May 1971. Egypt also ended the secret treaty of March 1968 which had provided the Soviet fleet with port facilities. Sadat had extended this agreement in the spring of 1973 for a further five years. The last Soviet ships left Alexandria, Marsa Matrub and Sollum in April 1976. Just how volatile Soviet–Egyptian relations could be can be gleaned from an incident on a Moscow dance floor when General Suleiman Ezzet knocked out the Soviet admiral commanding the Black Sea fleet for stating that the Egyptian naval contingent then in the Soviet capital contained American spies.

The signing in Washington of the Egyptian–Israeli peace treaty in March 1979 provoked fury in the Arab world and fuelled Soviet hopes that it would increase Egyptian isolation.

Algeria, which has had an unsuccessful Communist Party since the 1920s, Syria, Iraq, Afghanistan and the People's Democratic Republic of Yemen (South Yemen) were progressive states from Moscow's point of view. Nevertheless relations had their ups and downs during the 1970s. Relations with Turkey improved, mainly due to Turkish resentment at the low level of support it received from NATO countries in the Cyprus conflict. Libya, apparently as a result of warmer Egyptian–US relations, sought closer ties with the Soviet Union. In pre-1978 Iran the USSR supplied part of the country's defence requirements, Iran provided almost half of the natural gas needs of Azerbaidzhan, Armenia and Georgia, and Soviet involvement in Iran's industrial expansion was growing. A setback was the defeat of the Popular Front for the Liberation of Oman in the province of Dhofar in 1975. Moscow had backed the Front.

Considerable Soviet war *matériel* and personnel flowed into Syria during the 1970s but this did not lead to the two states seeing eye to eye on every matter. Considerable friction arose over Syria's intervention in the Lebanese civil war. The Syrians declined to sign a treaty of friendship on four occasions.

Iraq received the lion's share of her defence needs from Moscow and some of the equipment was very advanced. Trade was lively but Iraq, because of its oil wealth, could afford to shop around and on occasion bought Western technology in preference to supplies from the East. Relations were conducted within the framework of the Treaty of Friendship and Co-operation signed in April 1972. The Communist Party of Iraq was, in 1979, represented in the government but this did not prevent the ruling Ba'ath party from striking on occasions when it sensed its position to be under threat. In 1968 and again in 1978 communists were executed. In May 1978 twenty-three officers were shot for attempting to set up cells in the armed forces. Another batch of communists were executed at the end of 1978 for their activities in the civil service. Iraqi wealth and Ba'athist ruthlessness combined to restrict Soviet influence while securing what was needed for defence and industry.

South Yemen was the most pro-Soviet state in the Middle East. The ruling socialist party declared the country a Marxist republic in 1978 and modelled itself on the CPSU. There were many Cuban, East German and Soviet military and civilian advisers in South Yemen and the Soviet navy had port facilities in Aden. There was continual strife with the Yemen Arab Republic to the north and the assassination of the president there as well as the South Yemeni president in 1978 led to armed conflict. Bitter feuds in South Yemen led to many seeking refuge in the north and in Saudi Arabia. A Soviet–South Yemeni Treaty of Friendship and Co-operation was signed in October 1979. South Yemen was of considerable strategic importance to the Soviet Union, given the latter's position in Ethiopia.

Saudi Arabia was most concerned about events in South Yemen. The many Yemeni refugees in the country would have liked to see a different regime in power in Aden. The Saudis throughout the 1970s steadfastly refused to enter into diplomatic relations with the USSR.

The events in Iran in 1978–79 were as bewildering to the Soviets as they were to the rest of the world. Moscow had developed good relations with the Shah but these came under considerable strain when the Soviet Consul General in Tehran was expelled in September 1977. A senior army officer was executed in December 1977 for passing military secrets to the Soviets. The Tudeh party, the pro-Moscow

Communist Party, began to make some impact in late 1979, but this soon waned. However at the same time Iran abrogated the 1921 treaty under which the Soviet Union had the right to intervene militarily if her interests in Iran were threatened.

Afghanistan was Moscow's most favoured nation in the region. The USSR was intimately involved in the modernisation of the country. When the Democratic People's Party seized power in April 1978 after a bloody fight, it set about the task of making Afghanistan a socialist country. Its land reform was intended to end feudal practices but it aroused opposition among those whom it was supposed to help. They saw the party giving away land as a reward for loyalty to the regime. The Afghan President Nur Mohammed Taraki flew to Moscow in December 1978 and signed a Treaty of Friendship, Good Neighbourliness and Co-operation. He lost his position later to Hafizullah Amin. The civil war then increased in intensity. The Soviet response was to step up economic and military aid. Over one hundred Soviet personnel were reported dead by late 1979. The attempt to secularise the country, modernise the administration and the economy and make men and women equal was fiercely resisted. The massive Soviet intervention of December 1979 was prompted by the weakness of the Amin government and the possibility of an Iranian-style revolution in the country. This would have affected the Muslim population of Central Asia.

South Asia

The Indo-Pakistani conflict of August–September 1965 was the first opportunity afforded the new Soviet leadership of placing its imprint on the region. The two sides met in Tashkent in Uzbekistan in January 1966 with Aleksei Kosygin acting as mediator. On the surface it was a brilliant diplomatic success for the USSR. Pakistan was very disappointed by the outcome but the agreement did keep the peace for five years. The opportunity of prising Pakistan away from China had been missed. The Soviet Union became very circumspect in the Kashmir dispute and gradually edged away from Khrushchev's commitment to the Indian point of view.

The Soviet agreement to provide Pakistan with a limited amount of arms in the late 1960s was an attempt to weaken that country's ties with China and the US but the Indian public was not very understanding. Prime Minister Indira Gandhi did not allow this to harm relations with the Soviet Union and India's reaction to the invasion of Czechoslovakia was very measured.

Moscow judged it opportune in May 1969 to propose a pact of regional co-operation involving the USSR, Iran, Afghanistan, Pakistan and India. This had little prospect of success but it demonstrated to all that the Soviet Union wished to become the guardian power of the area.

The Soviets welcomed the split in the Congress Party in 1969 and Indira Gandhi's fine electoral victory in February 1971. Soviet help was stepped up. Then India and the Soviet Union entered into a Treaty of Peace, Friendship and Co-operation in August 1971. Pakistan, in the meanwhile, had been moving closer to China and when the Bangladesh crisis broke out and resulted in a renewal of hostilities with India in December 1971 the USSR was completely behind India.

Relations thereafter with India continued to improve until March 1977 when the election of the Janata coalition party under Morarji Desai threatened the smooth course of Indo-Soviet relations. Certainly the Soviet media abused the coalition in no uncertain terms before the election. Nevertheless Mr Desai soon discovered that his room for manoeuvre was limited given India's reliance on the Soviet Union for much of its defence needs and the close economic links which had been forged between the two countries. China was not able to make concessions which would have attracted India away from her close ties with Moscow. Before travelling to Beijing in February 1979 A. B. Vajpayee, the Foreign Minister, first flew to Moscow to assure the Soviets that India was not planning to break its close links with the USSR. Vajpayee broke short his stay in China, giving the invasion of Vietnam as the reason. Afterwards India sharply criticised China's action in going to war with Vietnam. Relations were at a low ebb. When Aleksei Kosygin came to New Delhi in March 1979 the Indians again condemned the Chinese invasion but would not recognise the pro-Vietnamese regime in Kampuchea. Several economic agreements were signed including expansion of the oil and steel industries. Indira Gandhi's return to power improved Indo-Soviet relations further, and India duly recognised the new regime in Kampuchea.

South East Asia

The death of Mao Zedong in 1976, the Chinese modernisation drive launched in 1977, the victory of the communists in Vietnam and Kampuchea in 1975 and the hostilities involving China, Vietnam and Kampuchea in 1978–79 profoundly altered relationships in the region. China's desire to become a developed country by the year 2000 altered its view of the world and made it a more attractive partner. This, however, increased rivalry between Moscow and Beijing. With Vietnam becoming a full member of Comecon in June 1978 and signing a Treaty of Friendship and Co-operation with the USSR in November 1978 Hanoi tilted towards Moscow and away from Beijing. Then it had ambitions to link Laos, Kampuchea and Vietnam more closely together. The Khmer Rouge took great exception to the fact that the Soviet Union had recognised the Lon Nol government and had maintained diplomatic relations with it during the civil war of 1970–75. Hence they looked to Beijing for aid and support. However the Pol Pot regime became involved in border skirmishes with the Vietnamese and this developed into full-scale hostilities with the Vietnamese occupying most of Kampuchea by the end of 1979. The Chinese action was not a success and only led to more Soviet war *matériel* for Hanoi.

Post-Mao China sought to establish better relations with all states in the area. Malaysia was very sensitive about China's influence given its Chinese minority, and Singapore, predominantly Chinese, was wary of Beijing's advances. Indonesia, which appeared to be heading for a resumption of relations in 1978, shied away in the end. Vietnam remained the only pro-Soviet state in the region.

East Asia

The Sino-Japanese Treaty of Peace and Friendship, signed in August and ratified in Tokyo in October 1978, was a great triumph for Chinese diplomacy. The Japanese accepted the treaty even though it contained an anti-hegemony clause which was clearly directed against the USSR. Japan and China concluded many economic agreements and Japanese expertise was of great value to China. South Korea will also benefit from this increasingly close relationship. The Soviet Union protested against the inclusion of the anti-hegemony clause but to no avail. Japanese–Soviet trade expanded throughout the 1970s with the Japanese investing in some projects in Siberia but the barrier to better relations was the ownership of the four southern islands in the Kuril chain signed away to Moscow in 1945. Japan wanted them back and this issue bedevilled relations between the two countries. In February 1979 Tokyo protested to Moscow about the construction of military bases on Etorofu and Kumashi, two of the islands. Dmitry Polyansky, the Soviet ambassador to Japan, dismissed the protest on the grounds that it was an attempt to interfere in internal Soviet affairs. The Soviet military build-up and the increasing strength of the Soviet Pacific Fleet only brought China, Japan and the US closer together, the exact opposite of what Moscow was trying to achieve.

Australasia[31]

Australian relations with the USSR improved noticeably after 1964. The war in Vietnam was of immediate pressing concern and the tendency was to blame China rather than the Soviet Union. Paul Hasluk, the Minister for External Affairs, expressed the view that the Soviet government was more concerned with internal development and might help in achieving a settlement in Vietnam, an illusion he shared with US policy-makers. The invasion of Czechoslovakia was a nasty shock and the appearance of the Soviet navy in the Indian Ocean was another unexpected event. Soviet diplomatic and trade ties with Malaysia and Singapore (neither state being friendly disposed towards Beijing due to their nervousness about the loyalty of their Chinese subjects), the establishment of a Trade Office and a shipping office in Sydney, and an increase in cultural and parliamentary contacts were indications that the goals being pursued by Moscow were not seen as inimical to the region.

The decision of the US to leave Vietnam led to the Sino-American *rapprochement* and détente with the Soviet Union. In 1975 the victory of the communists in Vietnam and Kampuchea, the increasing Soviet naval presence in the Indian Ocean and the expansion of the Soviet Pacific Fleet put a different complexion on things. When Prime Minister Malcolm Fraser went to Beijing in June 1976 he was given a very warm welcome and it became apparent that Australia's view of China had changed completely. Events in Indo-China in 1978–79 and the turning outwards of China which was accompanied by an expansion of Sino-Australian trade, especially purchases of grain, added impetus to the relationship.

Whatever affects Australia also affects New Zealand. Both countries were concerned about the upsurge of Soviet naval power. However, the improving Sino-Japanese relationship, the coolness of Japanese–Soviet relations and the desire of the US and China for closer ties kept the US nuclear umbrella extended in the eastern Pacific and Australasia continued to shelter under it.

Africa

The Brezhnev era started badly in Africa with the fall of Kwame Nkrumah in Ghana in 1966 and Modibo Keita in 1968 in Mali but after that the harvest began to ripen and by 1979 there was a solid phalanx of states which had declared that socialism *à la sovietique* was their goal: Guinea, Benin (Dahomey), Congo (Brazzaville), Guinea-Bissau, Angola, Mozambique and Ethiopia.

Relying on individual leaders – Africa never produced a Lenin – was not sufficient. Communist parties existed in countries such as the Sudan and South Africa but they were small and treated with suspicion by the authorities so it would be some time before they had the opportunity of taking power. Anyway in the Sudan the Communist Party was almost wiped out in the early 1970s. Hastening the exit of the colonial powers appeared to provide the best chances to influence events. The main targets were Guinea-Bissau, Angola, Mozambique, Zimbabwe (Rhodesia), Namibia and Azania (South Africa). If the Soviets hit on this so did the Chinese. So the two competed to aid the national liberation movement. The Chinese were in a good position in east Africa and in Zambia where they had

Table 7.6   Soviet, East European and Cuban technicians in Africa, 1977

	Soviet and East European	Cuban
Algeria	6,200	15
Angola	700	4,000
Ethiopia	250	400
Ghana	105	—
Guinea	710	—
Liberia	15	
Libya	15,000	—
Mali	375	—
Mauritania	60	—
Mozambique	500	400
Somalia	1,050	30
Sudan	125	—
Tanzania	165	200
Tunisia	650	—
Uganda	30	—
Zambia	125	—
Others	8,230	855
Total in all Third World countries	58,755	6,575
Total in Africa	34,290	5,900

Table 7.7   Soviet arms deliveries to Africa 1967-76

	Arms deliveries (millions of current US$)	Percentage of Soviet arms deliveries to Africa
Egypt	2,365	53.6
Libya	1,005	22.8
Algeria	315	7.1
Angola	190	4.3
Somalia	181	4.1
Nigeria	70	1.6
Sudan	65	1.5
Uganda	65	1.5
13 Others	160	3.6
Total	4,416	[100]

financed the building of the Tanzam railway which carries Zambian copper to Dar-es-Salaam for export. In the Nigerian civil war the Soviets supported the federal government and provided arms which the West refused to do while China supported Biafra diplomatically. This improved the image of the USSR in Africa's richest and most populous state.

The turning-point was the revolution in Portugal in 1974 and the subsequent decision to leave Africa. This meant that independence was to be granted to Guinea-Bissau, Angola and Mozambique where

Table 7.8   Soviet and Cuban military personnel in Africa 1977–78

	Soviet military advisers 1977	Cuban military personnel 1978
Algeria	600	35–50
Angola	500	19,000–20,000
Benin		20
Congo		300
Equatorial Guinea	50	100–400
Ethiopia	500	16,000–17,000
Guinea	125	300–500
Guinea-Bissau	50	200–250
Libya	1,000	100–125
Mozambique	200	500–550
São Tomé and Principe	—	75–100
Sierra Leone	—	'Small number' of security Advisers
Somalia	2,000*	—
Sudan	80†	—
Tanzania	—	100–300
Uganda	300	—
Others	2,515	

*Somalia expelled its Soviet military advisers in November 1977
†Sudan expelled its Soviet military advisers in June 1977

Table 7.9   Chinese arms deliveries to Africa 1967–76
(Millions of current US$)

Burundi	1
Cameroon	5
Congo	10
Egypt	5
Gambia	1
Guinea	5
Malawi	1
Mali	1
Mozambique	1
Rwanda	1
Sudan	5
Tanzania	75
Tunisia	5
Zaire	21
Zambia	5
Total	142

guerrilla warfare had been going on ever since the 1960s. In Angola the USSR stepped up its aid to the Movimento Popular de Libertação de Angola, the MPLA. Its leadership was made up of urban intellectuals, many of them of mixed race. Some of them were Marxists and they had close ties with the Communist Party in Lisbon. Holden Roberto's Frente Nacional de Libertação de Angola, the FNLA, drew much of its strength from the Bakongo tribe and received aid from China and the West. The Ovimbundu-centred União para a Independência total de Angola, UNITA, led by Jonas Savimbi, was backed by the South Africans as well as Zaire and other black states. The MPLA could not have won on its own. Aided by Soviet arms deliveries and about 17,000 Cubans it was unstoppable and by the spring of 1976 it had defeated its rivals. Angola was not the first country to receive Cuban military aid in Africa. Castro's desire to become involved had resulted in troops going to Guinea, Congo (Brazzaville) and to Guinea-Bissau. In the Middle East there were perhaps 3,000 troops from Cuba in 1973 and others arrived in South Yemen in the same year.

The slow transformation of the MPLA into a ruling party got under way and here the CPSU was of considerable help. The same pattern emerged in Mozambique. In both countries the GDR became actively involved in training party cadres, especially in propaganda and in providing military and security advisers.

Angola concluded a Treaty of Friendship and Co-operation with the USSR in October 1976 and Mozambique followed in March 1977. Both states signed similar treaties with Romania and Bulgaria, and with the GDR in February 1979. FRELIMO, the ruling party in Mozambique, also entered into agreements with the SED covering the years 1979 and 1980. On balance President Samora Machel and FRELIMO were willing to enter into much closer relations with the socialist bloc than President Agostinho Neto and the MPLA. However, Neto's death in September 1979 changed the situation. Angola became more dependent on the Soviet Union as the civil war dragged on.

The Soviet Union supplied the separatist movements in Eritrea and the Ogaden while its relations with Somalia were good. A Treaty of Friendship and Co-operation was signed in July 1974 and Soviet bases and port facilities became available. However, when the opportunity of becoming involved in Ethiopia appeared Moscow changed sides. For a time the Soviets tried to keep a foot in both camps but this proved impossible. Massive military aid was airlifted into Ethiopia to resist the Somali offensive in the Ogaden. General V. I. Petrov, deputy C-in-C Soviet ground forces headed the Soviet mission and General A. Ochoa, who had commanded the Cuban contingent in Angola, led the Cubans. In November 1977 President Siad Barre tore up the Somali–Soviet Friendship Treaty, expelled his Soviet advisers and asked Moscow to quit its Somali bases. In March 1978 the Somalis withdrew their troops from the Ogaden. Then Soviet and Cuban troops aided the Ethiopians in their struggle against the Eritrean secessionists. Ethiopia became socialist Ethiopia and President Mengistu Haile Mariam declared himself to be a Marxist-Leninist. Civilian and military advisers arrived from all parts of Eastern Europe.

Hence by the end of the Brezhnev era Soviet influence was strong in several African countries and the Chinese had been almost pushed out of Africa.

Latin America

Although the Communist Party of Cuba (CPC) came into being in October 1965 its Ist Congress did not convene until December 1975. The Congress elected a new Politburo, Central Committee and Secretariat and marked the transfer of political authority from Fidel Castro to the party and government, a process which had been under way since 1970. Until 1970 one can speak of Fidel Castro as the *caudillo*, all authority being vested in his person. Castro's 26 July movement and the armed forces gave expression to his decisions. Other political figures influenced policy, of course. The most influential was Ché Guevara who was killed in Bolivia in 1967. Guevara was keen on very radical revolutionary policies, using the peasants as a base and favoured moral over material incentives in the economy. Money was to be phased out. However, the harvest fiasco of 1970 when Castro had staked his reputation on achieving a harvest of 10 million tonnes (it fell short by a good 1.5 million tonnes) was a turning-point. Widespread labour absenteeism was leading to an economic impasse. The sovietisation of the revolution then began in earnest as the president had no other way to turn. Soviet and east European advisers came, economic aid was stepped up, all on the understanding that the country was joining the ranks of the Marxist-Leninist states. Another factor in this process was the increase in the influence of former People's Socialist Party members, the pro-Moscow Communist Party of the pre-1959 days. The CPC was becoming a mass party and had 270,000 members in mid 1978.

Cuba was made a full member of Comecon in July 1972 and Cuban and Soviet Five-Year Plans covering the years 1976–80 were co-ordinated. Thus the late 1970s saw closer and closer ties with the Soviet Union and Eastern Europe. Cuba became heavily in debt to these states and could not have sustained its level of development or living standards without them.

In foreign policy Cuba was unpredictable before 1970. Castro supported the Warsaw Pact invasion of Czechoslovakia but did not go along with all Soviet moves. However, the 1970s saw a new Cuba and its participation in Africa as a surrogate of the USSR had some impact on African developments. The non-aligned summit in Havana in September 1979 placed Castro on the world stage and his election as the movement's chairman for the next three years enhanced the Soviet position in the Third World.

The other country on the continent which looked for a time as if she was heading in the same direction was Chile. When Salvador Allende was elected president in 1970 his goal was a socialist revolution. Inflation, a weapon which Allende's Popular Unity coalition of socialists, communists and left-wing radicals hoped would destroy the bourgeoisie did nothing of the kind, but wiped out the socialist revolution instead. Allende's execution in the presidential palace in Santiago on 11 September 1973 terminated the experiment. The USSR provided very modest economic aid and counselled caution, an understandable attitude as Moscow was engaging in détente with Washington at the time. Castro gave the opposite advice and toured Chile to underline his point of view.

Much thought was given to improving economic relations between the socialist commonwealth and the Third World. A Comecon meeting in Bucharest in July 1971 adopted a comprehensive programme which aimed at a mutually beneficial division of labour. Ironically the country which displayed the greatest opposition to this was Romania. The Comecon decision followed the XXIVth Congress of the CPSU at which Aleksei Kosygin had elaborated the concept. It was also to include Third World countries. The Soviet Prime Minister was proposing a new type of economic relationship, one which involved a 'stable division of labour, counterposed to the system of imperialist exploitation'.[32] This socialist division of labour was roughly the counterpart of the law of comparative advantage in a market economy. The socialist world, especially Eastern Europe, needed to import increasing amounts of energy and raw materials. In order to guarantee supplies and to make the exchange mutually rewarding Comecon suggested that the socialist countries should help to build up the industrial infrastructure in the Third World countries they were trading with. These centres of development would involve vertically integrated plants, starting with raw materials and ending with semi-fabricates or finished products. The semi-fabricates could go to the socialist countries for finishing. This strategy was more realistic than that pursued under Khrushchev. It was a long-term policy and was restricted to those developing countries which have energy and raw materials to export. India was one of the countries in question and trade grew.

Trade turnover with the Third World expanded from 1,900 million rubles in 1965 to 8,333 million rubles in 1977, but as a percentage of total trade turnover it fell slightly. Third World trade was closely linked to the provision of Soviet economic assistance. Almost US$13,000 million was committed between 1954 and 1977 but only US$7,150 million was actually delivered.[33] About three quarters of the money committed was earmarked for the Middle East and South and South East Asia. There was an upsurge in arms deliveries to the Third World. Whereas the Soviets delivered on average US$300 million of military equipment annually to the developing nations between 1954 and 1967 this more than doubled during the following four years. It then escalated sharply and reached US$3,265 million in 1977.[34] Arms deliveries were worth US$14,145 million between 1972 and 1977. The distribution changed as well. Whereas until the early 1970s practically all Soviet arms deliveries were channelled to the Middle East and South and South East Asia, since 1975 Africa became a major recipient. Indeed in 1976 about half of all arms deliveries went there.

China made a great effort during the 1970s to outbid the Soviets in Africa and she committed US$1,882 million between 1970 and 1977 whereas the Soviets only came up with US$1,040 million over the same period.[35] However, Soviet arms deliveries in and after 1975 quickly nullified any advantage the Chinese may have gained.

THE RULING CLASS[36]

A ruling class came into being in the Soviet Union in the 1920s: the 'nomenklatura'. This word has two meanings: those posts which cannot be filled by the organisation concerned but by a higher organisation and the list of persons who occupy these posts or are qualified to do so. The origin of the nomenklatura goes back to Lenin who stated that in choosing officials reliability and political convictions should be accorded more attention than technical knowledge and administrative skills. Stalin put this into effect and it has remained so ever since. Hence technical ability still comes a poor third to a person's political reliability and devotion to the party.

According to the Soviet constitution members of the USSR Council of Ministers were appointed by the USSR Supreme Soviet or its Presidium; a Soviet ambassador was nominated by the Presidium of the USSR Supreme Soviet; a deputy minister by the USSR Council of Ministers; the director of an institute of the USSR Academy of Sciences, according to its statutes by the general assembly. Were these posts actually filled by the nominees of the organisations listed? No. The ministers and ambassadors belonged to the nomenklatura of the Politburo, the deputy ministers and directors of institutes were on the nomenklatura of the CC Secretariat. They made the decision and then it was formally adopted by the relevant organisation. The lowest-level nomenklatura was the bureau of the raion or city party committee, the middle-level nomenklatura was the oblast or krai party committee, the secretariat or the bureau of the CC, CPs of the republics, and the highest was the Secretariat or the Politburo of the CC, CPSU. The first rung on the ladder for a nomenklaturist was to be made head of an administration of a raion party committee. This was a salaried full-time job. Provided he did not commit any egregious mistakes he was in the nomenklatura for life. All promotions from then on would be to nomenklaturist posts. He could find himself working in the party, the government, the social organisations, academic institutions, industry or agriculture, the police, the KGB; in short in a post which the party regarded as important. This was one way of becoming a nomenklaturist. Others joined the nomenklatura because they possessed administrative, legal, technical, scientific or other skills needed in the running of the country. Collectively, nomenklaturists made up the ruling class and they took all key decisions in the USSR. Almost all were party members. The most brilliant specialist had to follow the instructions of the nomenklaturist responsible for him or her, even though the former may not have possessed any technical expertise.

The nomenklaturist system went back to the band of professional revolutionaries who instigated the October Revolution. This Lenin guard was later replaced by the Stalin guard. Hence the nomenklatura which was created by Stalin had Leninist foundations. The ideal nomenklaturist was a careerist who was willing to carry out every order the party gave him.

During the 1930s the nomenklatura expanded and those recruited corresponded to the social mix of the population, in other words, those of peasant origin dominated. Many ex-peasants turned their backs on the countryside and became contemptuous of peasants and village life. Hence it was during the 1930s that those of peasant origin numerically swamped those of working-class origin in the nomenklatura. Those who obtained good posts in the nomenklatura knew deep down that they were unqualified for the job. This realisation and their delight at such promotion made them very thankful to Stalin. They were willing to do almost anything to repay the trust placed in them. Here is one of the keys to Stalin's success.

Surplus value is produced in all societies in which there is a social division of labour. If a factory does not produce surplus value, i.e. profit, it goes out of business. Hence surplus value is not a phenomenon restricted to capitalism, it also exists under socialism. Lenin stated that surplus value under socialism does not flow into the pockets of the property owners but into the pockets of workers and only into their pockets. Stalin conceded in 1943 that working people created surplus value. According to the teachers of scientific communism it was the State which acquired the surplus value. The dominant institution in the State was the Communist Party and the nomenklatura dominated the Communist Party. Hence the nomenklatura controlled surplus value. It appropriated a greater part of the surplus value than its productive contribution to society justified. This resulted from the nomenklatura's control over the means of production. The nomenklaturist's standard of living was far higher than that of the average worker. Some workers could afford luxury goods, but only the nomenklaturist had constant *access* to them. He or she occupied much more than the fixed norm of 9 square metres of living space; the higher echelons had dachas, chauffeur-driven cars, access to special restaurants and grocery stores where there were no shortages, even of imported foods, a month in a sanatorium annually free of charge if so desired, and many other perks.

The nomenklatura provided power, status and material privileges to its members. Nomenklaturists were an elite, the key decision-makers. If income, status and power are seen as being structural and not transitional, the dominant grouping becomes the ruling class. The nomenklatura was this ruling class in the Soviet Union and indeed in all other Marxist-Leninist states. It was smaller than the bureaucracy and the intelligentsia but, of course, it contained many of its members. A nomenklaturist could not pass on his or her position to sons and daughters but could ensure that they got a good education and in this way enter the nomenklatura.

How large was the ruling class? Taking the figures provided by the 1970 census as a base the number of nomenklaturists in party, government and social organisation posts can be put at about 250,000. Then there are enterprise managers, sovkhoz directors and kolkhoz chairmen who numbered just over 300,000 in 1970. There were also about 150,000 nomenklaturists engaged in research in universities and elsewhere. Altogether there were just over 700,000 nomenklaturists in 1970. In 1982 the number was about 800,000. If the average nomenklaturist is assumed to have a wife and two children this meant that the ruling class in the Soviet Union consists of about three million persons or 1.2 per cent of the population.

The ruling class, although faithful to Stalin, suffered grievously during the 1930s. A large part of Khrushchev's secret speech at the XXth Party Congress was devoted to a catalogue of the unjustified repressions suffered by nomenklaturists under Stalin. The ordinary person was hardly mentioned. Khrushchev's incessant reforms in the end turned the nomenklatura against him. They wanted security of tenure as well as physical security. The Brezhnev era saw a flowering of the nomenklatura. Government by committee suited it. Each nomenklaturist had his or her defined sphere of competence, and such was the weight of tradition that Brezhnev's successors failed to reform the country. The small minority who favoured radical reform were nullified by the masses who feared radical innovation.

Nomenklaturists were the only people who could get away with telling jokes about the Secretary General. It is worthy of note that almost all jokes about Brezhnev present him as a man of decidedly second-rate abilities.

The Secretary General instructs one of his clever assistants to prepare a speech he is to make. It is to take him ten minutes to deliver. The assistant writes the speech but the next day Brezhnev is very angry. 'I told you to write me a ten minute speech but this one took me twenty minutes to read.' The assistant is very embarrassed. Very diffidently he replies: 'But, Leonid Ilich, I provided you with two copies!'

INTERREGNUM, OR ENTER AND EXEUNT ANDROPOV AND CHERNENKO

In his final years Brezhnev's loss of control was epitomised by the behaviour of his own family. His daughter Galina was rumoured to be having an affair with 'Boris the Gypsy', a man who had become an important official in the circus world. He decided who went abroad and who did not. Naturally, there was more to this than met the eye – diamonds and jewellery, to be more precise. Galina's appetite for the beautiful things of life was well-nigh insatiable and she clearly could indulge her fancy. After all, her husband, General Yuri Churbanov, was deputy USSR Minister of Internal Affairs. But there was another force in the land which took a jaundiced view of her cavortings – the KGB. Yuri Andropov, the ascetic *apparatchik* who had been running the political police for over a decade, had amassed quite a dossier on the misbehaviour of the Brezhnev clan. As KGB chief his main task should have been to protect the Secretary General, but his loyalty was to a higher body, the CPSU. A stroke of luck came his way on 25 January 1982 when Mikhail Suslov, the dry, severe guardian of ideological rectitude, died. Andropov now could see the goal of succeeding Brezhnev within reach, if he could replace Suslov as CC secretary for ideology. Meanwhile he began to undermine Brezhnev's position by arresting Boris and moving against Churbanov who was enmeshed in a huge corruption and bribery network. Journals even carried articles urging the Secretary General to go – in cryptic terms, of course. Brezhnev's loss of control over his family illustrated his loss of control over the country. He was also powerless to protect his family. On 7 November 1982, the anniversary of the October Revolution, he took the salute on the Lenin mausoleum in Red Square in an icy drizzle. This was an ill-advised move. Afterwards he was transported back to his dacha and died there on 10 November 1982. His chosen successor was Konstantin Chernenko, but Yuri Andropov, now a CC secretary, was named as chairman of the funeral commission. This almost guaranteed that he would succeed. He was confirmed as the new Secretary General by an extraordinary CC plenary session on 12 November.

Andropov, in the time-honoured fashion, set about replacing Brezhnev's 'tail' with his own. During his fifteen months in office he replaced one-fifth of all oblast or krai party secretaries, one-fifth of all USSR ministers and one-third of department heads in the CC secretariat. Many of the changes were long overdue, as complacency, inertia and corruption were widespread in the Brezhnev generation. The retail trade system and transport were special targets for his reforming zeal. His leadership style was in sharp contrast to that of the opulent, pompous Brezhnev. He cut back privilege and set out to meet workers on the shop floor. However, he lacked the easy-going charm of a Gorbachev and usually embarrassed his interlocutors. What does one say to a former head of the KGB? He cracked down on absenteeism, alcoholism, poor workmanship and the black market. His own health began to fail in mid 1983 and he dropped out of public view for the last 100 days or so of his life. He was dependent on a dialysis machine and there were some terrible jokes. For instance, he was the most switched on man in the USSR! Call Comrade Andropov, he will illuminate any problem! The jokes illustrated the fact that no one was afraid of Yuri Vladimirovich. The clamp down on absenteeism was good policy. However, it was undermined by officials entering shops, discovering many able-bodied men and women moonlighting, and offering to fine them on the spot so as not to need to report them either to their employer or the courts. It transpired that the 'officials' were merely conmen out to make a fast buck. The anti-alcohol campaign was well intentioned but vast sums were lost to the exchequer. No new sources of revenue were tapped, with the result that the budget deficit began to grow. Inflation began in earnest since there was no money market from which the government could borrow so as to balance its budget. It simply resorted to the printing press. Andropov's industrial and agricultural policy was also well conceived. It aimed at giving enterprises and farms more decision-making power. Unfortunately for him, the time was long past when such a policy would have the desired effect. The bureaucratic economy had become too inefficient.

Andropov was a cautious reformer and tried to render the planned economy more efficient. Under him a group of cautious reformers rose to prominence. These included Mikhail Gorbachev, Egor Ligachev and Nikolai Ryzhkov. Andropov wanted Gorbachev to succeed him, and added a paragraph to this effect to his report to a CC plenum which did not convene until after his death on 9 February 1984. Instead, on 13 February, Konstantin Chernenko was eased into the position of General Secretary and later became Soviet President and Commander-in-Chief of Soviet Armed Forces, all posts held by Andropov. The ageing Politburo had plumped for a non-reformer, a throw-back to Brezhnevism. The political elite had placed its own interests ahead of that of the country. However, Gorbachev became 'second' secretary and was to chair Politburo meetings when Chernenko was away or unfit. Eventually he may have chaired more Politburo meetings than Chernenko. The latter was terminally ill, suffering from emphysema among other things, when he assumed office. His state of health was demonstrated to the whole world at Andropov's funeral when he attempted to salute the coffin of the dead leader. He could only manage to get his hand half-way up to his shoulder. His address was garbled due to his difficulty in breathing. However, Chernenko did create a precedent in Soviet politics. He became the first politician to succeed as General Secretary after having previously failed. No one joined the Politburo under Chernenko. He surrounded himself with the non-reformers, and party privilege was again unrestricted. The military did not have things all their own way under Chernenko. The able, dynamic chief of staff, Marshal Nikolai Ogarkov, was moved sideways and replaced by Marshal Sergei Akhromeev, another formidable military man. Ogarkov was blamed for his aggressive promotion of the SS20 missile programme which had provoked Western counter-deployment and for the shooting down of a Korean jet, flight 007, with 269 passengers and crew on board, after it had strayed into Soviet airspace, in September 1983. The incident caused an international *furor* and increased tension between NATO and the Warsaw Pact. When Marshal Dmitri Ustinov died in December 1984 he was succeeded as USSR Defence Minister by Marshal Sergei Sokolov. This was a break with tradition. Ustinov, a civilian, was succeeded by a serving soldier. The Minister of Defence, ever since 1973, had been a member of the Politburo but Sokolov did not climb to the pinnacle of party power under Chernenko. However, he did under Gorbachev.

NOTES

1. Archie Brown and Michael Kaser (eds) *The Soviet Union Since the Fall of Khrushchev* 2nd edn p. 198.
2. *Pravda* 21 December 1969.
3. Roy A. Medvedev *On Stalin and Stalinism* p. 181.
4. Ibid. p. 317.
5. Robert E. Blackwell Jr, 'Cadres Policy in the Brezhnev Era' in *Problems of Communism* vol. XXVIII, no. 2, March–April 1979, p. 31.
6. Ibid. p. 36.
7. Ibid. p. 32.
8. Brown and Kaser, op. cit. pp. 227–8.
9. Gregory Grossman, 'An Economy at Middle Age' in *Problems of Communism* vol. XXV, no. 2, March–April 1976, p. 20.
10. Brown and Kaser, op. cit. p. 287.
11. Alastair McAuley *Economic Welfare in the Soviet Union: Poverty, Living Standards, and Inequality* p. 58.
12. Ibid. p. 61.
13. Ibid. p. 110.
14. Ibid. p. 138.
15. Ibid. p. 128.
16. Ibidem.
17. Ibid. p. 132.
18. Ibid. p. 206.
19. Ibid. p. 201.
20. Ibid. p. 368.
21. Ibid. p. 262.

22. Jerry F. Hough, 'The Man and the System' in *Problems of Communism* vol. XXV, no. 2, March–April 1976, p. 11.
23. Henry W. Morton, 'The Soviet Urban Scene' in *Problems of Communism* vol. XXVI, no. 1, January–February 1977, p. 76.
24. Carol W. Lewis, 'Comparing City Budgets: The Soviet Case' in *Comparative Urban Research* vol. V, no. 1, 1977, p. 50, and information provided at a seminar at the London School of Economics and Political Science on 9 May 1978.
25. Brown and Kaser, op. cit. p. 287.
26. Martin Dewhirst, 'Soviet Russian Literature and Literary Policy' in Brown and Kaser, op. cit. pp. 187–9. The first novel by a Jew in the USSR about the Holocaust there, A. Rybakov's *Tyazhelyi Pesok* (Heavy Sand) appeared in *Oktyabr* nos 7, 8 and 9, 1978.
27. *Sotsiologicheskie Issledovaniya* no. 2, 1977, pp. 42–51, quoted in *Sowjetunion 1978/79* (Cologne 1979) p. 98.
28. *Bericht des Bundesinstituts für ostwissenschaftliche und internationale Studien* no. 9, 1979, pp. 6–11.
29. *Pravda* 18 June 1969.
30. Michael Voslensky *Nomenklatura: Die herrschende Klasse der Sowjetunion* p. 379.
31. This section is based on T. B. Millar *Australia in Peace and War: External Relations 1788–1977* pp. 349–53, 424–5.
32. *Pravda* 7 April 1971.
33. Donald R. Kelley (ed.) *Soviet Politics in the Brezhnev Era* p. 241.
34. Ibid. p. 245.
35. David E. Albright (ed.) *Africa and International Communism* pp. 170–71.
36. Cf. Voslensky, op. cit., ch. IV. Alec Nove, 'History, Hierarchy and Nationalities' and 'Is there a Ruling Class in the USSR?' in *Political Economy and Soviet Socialism*. Jerry F. Hough *The Soviet Prefects: The Local Party Organs in Industrial Decision-making* pp. 29–30, 115–16, 150–55.

The Gorbachev Era

(12TH DECEMBER 1991) 'I HAVE ACHIEVED THE MAIN GOAL OF MY LIFE.'

During my period of office, I have been attacked by all those in Russian society who can scream and write . . .. The revolutionaries curse me because I have strongly and conscientiously favoured the use of the most decisive measures. . .. As for the conservatives, they attack me because they mistakenly blame me for all the changes in our political system.

(Count Sergei Witte, 1906)

If Vladimir Ilich Lenin was the father of the Soviet State, Mikhail Sergeevich Gorbachev was its gravedigger. Ironically Gorbachev, faced with dire problems as leader, sought to return to Leninist principles. Lenin, had he lived, would have strengthened the government *vis-à-vis* the party since he was becoming alarmed at the ever-expanding intervention of the party apparatus in the affairs of state. Gorbachev, facing the same problem, dipped into the 1924 constitution which had established the Soviet State, and followed Lenin's thinking about the soviets. The constitution envisaged the election of a Congress of People's Deputies. It, in turn, would elect a Supreme Soviet which would act as a parliament. Local government was to be soviet government. This never functioned as envisaged due to Lenin's death and the rise of Stalin. It also did not work under Gorbachev. The General Secretary succeeded in weakening the party apparatus but did not achieve his goal of strengthening the soviets as implementers of central policy. He was a master at increasing his own authority, and had the ability to dominate the decision-making process. He rapidly became the key decision-maker, mainly due to his skill at forging tactical alliances and cutting deals with the party and State barons. However, authority without power is impotent. Power is the ability to enforce the implementation of policy decisions, using coercion if necessary. Gorbachev, in this realm, was a dwarf. He never transformed the party *apparat*, the CC secretariat and local organs, into an effective weapon for the implementation of his policies of *perestroika, glasnost* and democratisation. On the contrary, at the XIXth Party Conference, in June 1988, Gorbachev set out to emasculate the secretariat and to deprive it of its key functions in the State. He wanted it to shed its economic functions and thereby to lose its right to intervene in the running of the economy. It was also to lose its dominance over the party. The secretariat had been the party's brain, and all key decisions had been taken there. Gorbachev also wanted to deprive it of its control of State legislative bodies. Soviets were no longer to be dominated by party officials. The party thereby lost its dominant role in the political process at the centre but gained its revenge on Gorbachev by consolidating its power at the periphery, where the weak soviets were no match for it. Hence there was a centrifugal flow of power from the centre to the periphery. This process had been under way ever since the death of Stalin, and the removal of Khrushchev underlined the power of the local party officials. The Brezhnev era further added to the flow of power to the periphery.

The locus of decision-making in the political process was to move from the party *apparat* to the soviets. The USSR Congress of People's Deputies convened in May 1989. One-third of the 2,250 deputies were elected from single-member constituencies, one-third were elected from nationality areas and the rest were nominated by social organisations, such as the Communist Party, trade unions, Komsomol and so on. Almost 88 per cent of deputies were communists, but by then the Communist Party was no longer a monolithic party. The congress elected from among its members a bicameral legislature, the Soviet of the Union and the Soviet of Nationalities. Each house had 271 members. Gorbachev chaired the proceedings, with Anatoly Lukyanov as his deputy. Among congress deputies were Andrei Sakharov and Boris Eltsin. Sakharov and his wife had been sent into exile to Gorky in 1980 and brought back to Moscow by Gorbachev. Eltsin had lost his post as First Party Secretary of Moscow and his candidate membership of the Politburo in October 1987. The congress afforded these two critics of Gorbachev a nationwide audience for the first time. Sakharov's moral authority shone through, as did Boris Nikolaevich's populist appeal. Predictably, Eltsin was not elected to the USSR Supreme Soviet, but a Siberian member surprised Gorbachev by proposing to stand down in Eltsin's favour. On live television, all Gorbachev could do was to ask for time to consider the matter. Gorbachev, a lawyer, consulted Lukyanov, a lawyer, and others, and they could find no legal objection. So Boris Nikolaevich used the Supreme Soviet as a national stage from which to attack party privilege and the slowness of reform under *perestroika* and to support claims for sovereignty by various republics.

The new pattern at the top was followed by each republic. Congresses were elected and Supreme Soviets emerged from them. The policy of *glasnost* had led to very frank speaking by the non-Russian republics, especially Georgia and the Baltic republics, Estonia, Latvia and Lithuania. Nationalists took over Supreme Soviets and immediately claimed sovereignty for their republic. This was made possible by communist parties splitting into pro-republican and pro-Union parties, with the former much larger. Gorbachev did all in his power to prevent

Eltsin becoming chairman of the Russian Supreme Soviet but all to no avail. A deputy could be simultaneously a member of the USSR Supreme Soviet and another republican Supreme Soviet. Eltsin used his new position to promote the sovereignty of Russia and other republics *vis-à-vis* the centre, attack the Communist Party and the shortcomings of *perestroika* and Gorbachev personally.

Gorbachev soon tired of the new-look USSR Supreme Soviet and cast his net ever wider in his search for a model. He eventually chose an executive presidency based on a mixture of the US and French presidencies. Again the constitution was amended to permit this new role and the word *'president'* entered the Russian official language. He decided he wanted a vice-president (the new word was *vize-president*, from the German, but there is no vice-president in the German system). Unfortunately for him, he chose Gennady Yanaev for this post. Later the USSR Council of Ministers was abolished and replaced by a cabinet (*kabinet* in Russian, from the French) headed by a prime minister (*premer ministr* in Russian, from the French). The deputy was called a *vize premer ministr*. The prime minister was subordinate to the president as in the French system, there being no such post in the US system. This verbal wizardry achieved what Gorbachev sought; it made him supreme decision-maker. His authority had never been higher. However, the power which accompanied the post of president in the US and France was not transmitted to him. His power or his ability to have his decisions implemented declined by the day. Here he made a crucial, perhaps fatal mistake. Whereas the US and French presidents derive their legitimacy from being directly elected, Mikhail Sergeevich did not dare take this risk. He had himself elected by the USSR Congress of People's Deputies. Had he stood for direct election he might have won and thereby become the people's president. He had no way of judging his own legitimacy, acceptance by the population of his right to lead the country.

Local soviet elections in March 1990 revealed how low the legitimacy of the Communist Party really was. Party officials had been encouraged by the General Secretary to stand for election, but many leading communist officials were defeated, some even when they were the only candidate (to be elected, a candidate had to obtain over 50 per cent of the votes cast). The leading casualty was Yuri Solovev, first secretary of Leningrad oblast and a candidate member of the Politburo. Eltsin's attacks on party privilege had reinforced the popular perception of a communist official as a parasite. As a result, the party *apparat* lost control of many key cities. There was no revolt by provincial party officials against Gorbachev. This was merely passive resistance. Even more ominous for communists was the annulment of article 6 of the constitution which had guaranteed the party the leading role in all institutions in the State. However, Russian communists forced

Gorbachev to concede the formation of a Russian Communist Party which would be dominated by the *apparat*.

On taking office Gorbachev was unaware of the parlous state of the Soviet economy. He had participated in discussion groups dominated by radical economists such as Abel Aganbegyan and the sociologist Tatyana Zaslavskaya. Their main thrust was against party interference in the economy. Enterprises should have much greater autonomy within an overall plan. They were not advocating the replacement of the planned economy by a market economy. Gorbachev devoted much energy to economic renewal and came up with the policy of *uskorenie* or acceleration. There were to be structural reforms but simultaneously growth of at least 4 per cent. Not surprisingly, results disappointed. Mikhail Sergeevich was to admit later that the first two years were wasted. Only with the Law on the Enterprise, in effect from January 1988, did reform really begin. However, this permitted enterprises to set many prices and also to decide what they paid their workers. Prices rose, wages shot up, far outstripping increases in labour productivity. Inflation climbed higher. Along with economic and social discontent came ethnic unrest. Had *perestroika* raised living standards, ethnic tension might have been contained. Instead, bloody conflicts in Nagorno-Karabakh, an Armenian-dominated enclave in Azerbaidzhan, led to calls from some communists and some military officers for stronger rule from the centre. A request for military help by the Communist Party of Georgia in April 1989 to disperse peaceful demonstrators in Tbilisi led to the killing and wounding of civilians. This proved to be a turning-point for the Georgian party and for Gorbachev. He had been out of the country when the attack took place but it ended any legitimacy the Georgian communists or Gorbachev had in Georgia. Nationalism took over. The bloody events in Baku in January 1990 when the military mowed down civilians, apparently to prevent Azerbaidzhan claiming independence, were followed by loss of life when the police stormed the television station in Vilnius, in Lithuania, in January 1991. Gorbachev claimed that the decision to attack had been taken by a local commander who had overreacted. However, he did not condemn the attack and no one was disciplined. After these events there was no turning back on the road to independence for the Baltic republics.

Lack of economic success forced Gorbachev to contemplate more radical policies. They centred on the problem of the market. What was a market economy and what did it imply for Soviet socialism and the Communist Party? One does not have to be a Marxist to work out that a market economy, in the Western sense, would have heralded the death of Soviet socialism and the power of the Communist Party. How could the General Secretary of the CPSU introduce a reform which signalled a return to capitalism? This was Gorbachev's cruel dilemma. The radical economists, Petrakov, Shatalin and Yavlinsky, told him there was no other way. Yavlinsky came up with a 400-day programme which was later transformed into a 500-day programme because it sounded better. A transition to a market economy lasting 100 days was elaborated and intended to begin when Gorbachev became executive president. If the pro-marketeers were for the fast track to the market, another group around Nikolai Ryzhkov, the Prime Minister, favoured the slow-track approach. The difference between the two was more fundamental. Yavlinsky wanted a Western-style market but the Ryzhkov group did not. They wanted a market on their terms. One of the terms was the absence of private property. Another was that the State should retain its dominant role in the economy. Prices should not be liberalised but should be carefully controlled. In other words, the Ryzhkov group wanted to have little to do with new-fangled Western economic ideas. They preferred a Soviet or Russian path. Gorbachev could never make up his mind. When he was with the proponents of the Western-style market he found their arguments convincing. After all, this was not surprising since all the richest countries in the world had market economies and that was why they were rich. When he joined Ryzhkov and the barons of industry he was told that a market reform would cause anarchy and a breakdown of society. The workers would not tolerate it. His usual response was to invite both groups to put their ideas together and come up with a compromise. This was akin to trying to mix fire and water or chalk and cheese. It could not be done. In the meanwhile the economy continued on its downward spiral. Inflation grew relentlessly as the government had recourse more and more to the printing press to pay its way.

When he became leader in March 1985 Gorbachev did not concentrate all his efforts on winning control of the CC secretariat and *apparat*. Instead, he turned his attention to accelerating economic growth, gaining control over the USSR Ministry of Foreign Affairs, the KGB and the armed forces, and promoting open criticism of the system, *glasnost* in action. He became very skilled at using the media to promote his policies and pressurising party officials to follow him. Since the arms race was crippling the country he needed a *rapprochement* with the West, first and foremost with the US. His 'new political thinking', which emphasised the interdependence of states, the abandonment of an ideological approach to Soviet foreign policy-making and arms reduction, was brilliantly successful. When Andrei Gromyko, known as 'Grim Grom' or 'Mr Nyet' (No), the long-serving Foreign Minister, was kicked upstairs in July 1985 and made USSR President, Gorbachev placed Eduard Shevardnadze, First Party Secretary in Georgia, and not blessed with a perfect command of Russian, in charge of the Foreign Ministry. Mikhail Sergeevich was clearly going to play a leading role in foreign policy. Over time Gorbachev became a world statesman, the most successful Soviet leader ever internationally, voted *Time's* Man of the Year and awarded the

Nobel Peace Prize. Summits with Presidents Reagan and Bush became a way of life, as did arms limitation and disarmament treaties. He struck up close relationships with Prime Minister Margaret Thatcher and Chancellor Helmut Kohl. The revolutions in Eastern Europe were allowed to run their course in 1989 without the intervention of Soviet military power. Gorbachev, inadvertently, promoted German unification. When in East Berlin in October 1989 to celebrate the fortieth anniversary of the founding of the GDR he conspired to unseat Erich Honecker, the party leader. He also warned East Germans that 'history punishes those who arrive late'. His intention was to promote *perestroika* in the GDR, but his words were seized upon by the opposition to undermine communism in the GDR. When Lothar de Mazière, GDR Prime Minister at unification, thanked him later for this remark he declared, with an embarrassed smile, that he had never intended his words to be interpreted in the way they were.

Germans will always be grateful to him, as will East Europeans, but the Soviet military were deeply hurt and frustrated by his foreign and security policy. They accused him of giving away Eastern Europe and allowing the unification of Germany. To them this meant surrendering all the gains of victory in 1945. Gorbachev also secured the withdrawal of Soviet troops from Afghanistan. His relations with the military were always subject to tension.

Gorbachev was a latter-day Witte. Witte had saved the monarchy from war and revolution in 1905 but was obliged to resign the following year. He was discarded by Tsar Nicholas II before he could deal decisively with the problems of a decaying empire. When Gorbachev took his leave of the Soviet people on 25 December 1991 he did so a saddened and chastened man. The Soviet Union, which he had tried so valiantly to reform in his own image, was about to pass into history. The Communist Party had been banned.

Vitaly Korotich, editor of *Ogonyok*, graphically catches Gorbachev's style: 'Gorbachev treated this country as my wife treats cabbage. He thought that to get rid of the dirt, he could just peel off the top layer of leaves. But he had to keep going until there was nothing left.'

Gorbachev had a clear agenda before he took office in March 1985. In a speech on 10 December 1984 he spoke of the need to effect 'deep transformations in the economy and the whole system of social relations', to carry through the '*perestroika* of economic management', the 'democratisation of our social and economic life' and '*glasnost*'. He stressed the need for greater social justice, a greater role for soviets and more participation by workers at the workplace. His intention was to set in motion a revolution, controlled from above. His reforms quickly reached their limits. What was Gorbachev to do? Draw back or allow fundamental changes which would lead to a wholesale redistribution of power within the State? Gorbachev backed off. His intention was not to effect fundamental changes but to make the existing structures function more efficiently. The Leninist State and the centrally planned economy were to remain. It was to be an elite revolution, putting more efficient cadres in place, and was to be peaceful. Gorbachev carried on where Andropov had left off: efficiency and discipline, greater say for enterprises and more use of technological innovation. As a product of the Khrushchevian era he instinctively rejected the Stalinist legacy and searched for a more humane socialism. However, he never had a clear vision of how political, economic and social reform would interact and gell to become a critical mass for progress. Only his foreign-policy goals were clear. He was greatly impressed on his foreign travels by Western material wealth but appalled by the gulf which separated the socialist and capitalist worlds. However, he failed to comprehend the reasons behind the West's economic success.

The impetus for reform came from the politically active part of the CPSU and society. However, opposition to *perestroika* was also fiercest among the same group. The reformers knew that the party and State *apparat* were past masters at blocking reforms which they perceived to be inimical to their interests. The only way to drive through a reform was to use a battering ram. Khrushchev had been very daring in his innovations but had been rebuffed. The Brezhnev era merely saw the icing on the cake being dusted, not changed. What tactics would the new leader adopt? During the first three years Gorbachev promoted reform by launching a series of thrusts. Each time he encountered opposition from party conservatives he retreated and sought another route to advance. According to Aleksandr Yakovlev, one of the architects of *perestroika* and its main theorist, the revolution from above reached a crossroads at the XIXth Party Conference in June 1988. The General Secretary was faced with a stark choice: to advance and transform *perestroika* into a 'genuinely popular democratic revolution, go to the limits and really afford society total freedom' or to rein back, remain a communist reformer and stay within the well-known milieu of the bureaucracy. Yakovlev saw various dangers for *perestroika*: it could be suffocated by Stalinist reaction or Brezhnevite conservatism or be hi-jacked by officials mouthing its slogans while they redistributed power among themselves.

The choice was between genuine or controlled democracy. Fyodor Burlatsky states that in early 1988 he was a member of a small group under the chairmanship of Anatoly Lukyanov. The latter proposed adopting the two-stage approach to the election of a parliament contained in Lenin's 1924 constitution. Legal authority was to be vested in local soviets. The relationship between the party and the soviets was left vague. Burlatsky proposed direct elections of the parliament, president and vice-president on a multi-party basis but claims that everyone opposed this except Yakovlev. Gorbachev could have effected a political revolution but, true to his low-risk strategy, chose Lukyanov's variant. In March 1990 Gorbachev again could have transformed Soviet politics. Article 6 of the constitution, affording the Communist Party a monopoly on power, had been discarded at the CC plenum in February 1990. He decided against direct election of the president. Again his reluctance to take risks surfaced.

Unfortunately for Mikhail Sergeevich, he had opened Pandora's box. Public, social and political forces, awakened by *perestroika*, could not be regulated from above. If Gorbachev would not claim them as his constituency, then others would. Nationalism became a major force in all republics. Since the Communist Party would not move towards democracy, radical members abandoned it and formed their own groupings. Boris Eltsin emerged from this process as the strongest challenger. After being humiliated by the party in 1987 he had only one route back, via the Russian parliament. His election as chairman of the Russian parliament in May 1990 was a turning point for Gorbachev. Eltsin became a pole of attraction for frustrated radical reformers. In August 1990 Gorbachev appeared to have taken on board a modified version of the 500-day programme, and hopes were high that a Gorbachev–Eltsin tactical alliance could push through a really radical economic reform and get *perestroika* on its way. Hopes were dashed in October when Gorbachev backed off, alarmed by the warnings of party conservatives and the military-industrial complex about the dangers of social strife if the reform were implemented. Yakovlev sees the retreat as a catastrophe for Gorbachev. Reactionaries and conservatives began to launch open attacks on the President and *perestroika* from the autumn of 1990.

I am convinced that the rejection of the 500-day programme served as an encouraging signal to them. It was a mistake with momentous consequences. It demonstrated that *perestroika* was prepared to retreat under pressure.

In retrospect, Gorbachev admitted that he should have committed himself strongly to a pact with the democrats at this vital juncture. Instead, he moved to the right and parted company with Yakovlev and Eduard Shevardnadze. The latter's emotional resignation speech in December 1990 warning of the danger of an imminent dictatorship did not cause the President to rethink. He also dismissed Vadim Bakatin, the liberal USSR Minister of Internal Affairs, because of, among other things, disagreements over the use of force to deal with nationalist opposition. He was replaced by Boris Pugo, a former KGB chief in Latvia. The way to the murders of Vilnius was open. Gorbachev genuinely did not know about the order to attack until afterwards but as Commander-in-chief of the Soviet armed forces he should have asserted his authority. Lithuania had declared independence in March 1990 but this was never accepted by Gorbachev. He could not cope with nationalism and would not accept that the Baltic republics could leave the Soviet Union. Keeping all fifteen republics in the Union was a sacred duty to him.

Gorbachev was fed slanted KGB reports about the security situation. The aim was to convince the president that a crackdown was necessary. A special target was Boris Eltsin and when the Russian parliament convened on 28 March 1991 the military moved on to the streets and sealed off the centre of Moscow. Gorbachev was told of an attempt to storm the Kremlin but Yakovlev ridiculed this suggestion in conversation with him. The troops were withdrawn. It had been the dress rehearsal for the coming attempted coup.

Gorbachev travelled the world in search of economic aid and invited himself to London in July 1991 when the IMF was meeting there. He was offered associate status but no hard cash. Time was running out for him economically, as well as politically. He finally reached agreement with Eltsin and eight other presidents (the leaders of Estonia, Latvia, Lithuania, Armenia, Georgia and Moldova were the absentees) about a new federation which envisaged greater autonomy for the republics and a significantly reduced role for the centre. The treaty was to be signed on 20 August 1991.

Like Stalin before the German attack in 1941, Gorbachev could not plead ignorance about his enemies' intentions. After Vilnius he backed away from the use of bloody force to maintain the Union. However, he participated in discussions with the instruments of coercion about how to restore Communist Party control. One option which was discussed was a crackdown. Anatoly Lukyanov played a leading role in such deliberations and was in favour of the iron fist being applied. Gorbachev never committed himself to such a course of action but may have given the impression that he was willing to go along with such a move. Rumours had been rife since early summer about the military acting. The only thing in dispute was the timing of the coup. Even President George Bush telephoned to mention that he had heard that a military coup was in the offing. Gorbachev took it all in his stride and set off for his summer vacation at his luxury dacha at Foros in the Crimea. On 18 August 1991 a delegation arrived and demanded his resignation as President. Gennady Yanaev, the Vice-president, was to take over the presidency. Gorbachev refused and the ill-managed coup attempt, masterminded by Anatoly Lukyanov and General Vladimir Kryuchkov, got under way on 19 August. It collapsed on 21 August. The hero of the hour was Boris Eltsin. Hearing of the *putsch* about 6.30 am he set off by car from his dacha outside Moscow for the White House, the Russian parliament. He held a Russian flag in one hand and dared the troops to arrest or shoot him. He made it to the White House just after midday on 19 August. When Gorbachev came back to Moscow the political landscape had changed beyond recognition. However, the President had not perceived this and at his press conference after his return talked about working with the democratic elements within the Communist Party. This was the kiss of death and when Gorbachev addressed the Russian parliament later Eltsin humiliated him and banned the Communist Party with the Party's leader claiming that the Russian President did not have the power to do so. On 24 August Gorbachev resigned as Party leader. In September 1991, the Baltic republics left the Soviet Union. On 8 December 1991 Russia, Ukraine and Belorussia formed the Commonwealth of Independent States. In Alma Ata on 23 December another eight joined. It was all so simple. Whereas Gorbachev had insisted that the formula be 11 + 1, the 1 being the centre, Eltsin and the others agreed the formula should be 11 + 0; there would be no centre. No centre meant no job for the President. On 25 December 1991 he resigned as President and the USSR was laid to rest. In a farewell meeting with reporters on 12 December Gorbachev declared that he had attained his main goal in life. 'The rest . . . well perhaps someone will come and do it better. But you must understand, I wanted to succeed. What's special about me is that I can't admit defeat.'

The world had benefited from Gorbachev's six years and nine months in office. One is tempted to dub him Comrade Serendipity which according to the *Oxford English Dictionary*, is the 'faculty of making happy and unexpected discoveries by accident'. Through his actions he buried communism in the Soviet Union and Eastern Europe and promoted the unification of Germany. From his point of view all this was an accident since he had set out to resurrect communism. However, this accident made many happy.

GORBACHEV AND HIS TEAM[1]

There appears to have been a tacit agreement among Politburo members that on Chernenko's death Gorbachev would take over. However, in March 1985 some of them had got cold feet. One of these was Grigory Romanov, formerly party leader in Leningrad and on Chernenko's death CC secretary for the military economy. Another was Viktor Grishin, the Moscow party leader, known locally as 'the godfather' because of the high incidence of corruption in the capital. Egor Ligachev later confirmed that a power struggle had taken place, and that Gromyko, party Control Commission chairman Solomentsev and KGB boss Chebrikov ensured that Gorbachev prevailed over Grishin. Ligachev, although then not a member of the Politburo, also claimed that he played a significant role in the General Secretary's victory. This alludes to his role as CC secretary in charge of organisational party work. He carefully selected the CC members, who were invited to the hastily convened CC plenum on 11 March 1985 which elected Gorbachev leader. The Politburo which convened after Chernenko's sudden death was also incomplete. Dinmukhamed Kunaev, Kazakh party leader, and Vladimir Shcherbitsky, party leader in the Ukraine, were absent. Neither would probably have voted for Mikhail Sergeevich. Shcherbitsky also missed the CC plenum. Significantly, there was no vote. The new General Secretary became leader by 'general consent'. Ligachev became 'Second' Secretary as a result of the Politburo authorising him to chair secretariat meetings. He was also responsible for cadres and ideology. Thus Gorbachev started with a considerable handicap, and it meant that all personnel changes would be the subject of intense bargaining and horse-trading.

Gorbachev turned out to be a skilful horse-trader. In April 1985 Ligachev became a full member of the Politburo and was replaced as head of the department of party organisational work by Georgy Razumovsky. One to Ligachev. Gorbachev's nominee was Aleksandr Yakovlev, who became secretary for propaganda and overseer of the media. His task was to expand the limits of *glasnost*, and protect creative writers and journalists against Ligachev's ire. Gorbachev managed to make Yakovlev a CC secretary at the XXVIIth Party Congress in February–March 1986 (Razumovsky also became a CC secretary), a candidate member of the Politburo in January 1987 and a full member in June 1987. These were significant moves in his campaign to dilute Ligachev's power. Chebrikov reaped his due reward and became a full member of the Politburo in April 1985. In July 1985 Romanov left the Politburo and secretariat because of 'ill health' (a transparently thin excuse given his appetite for women and drink) but Boris Eltsin, First Party Secretary in Sverdlovsk, and Lev Zaikov, First Party Secretary for Leningrad oblast, became CC secretaries. In this way Ligachev brought a viper into his nest.

In July, Gorbachev managed to get Gromyko elected President and Eduard Shevardnadze appointed Foreign Minister. The latter also became a full member of the Politburo. This was rewarding for Gorbachev because Shevardnadze shared some of his radical views on *perestroika*. In September 1985, the octogenarian Tikhonov made way for Nikolai Ryzhkov as USSR Prime Minister. Grishin and Konstantin Rusakov left the Politburo and the secretariat in February 1986, and at the congress the following month there were wholesale changes in the CC. Zaikov, protecting the interests of the military-industrial complex, advanced to full Politburo membership. Eltsin left the secretariat and became a candidate member of the Politburo on becoming Grishin's successor, and there were five new CC secretaries, including Yakovlev. One of the newcomers was Aleksandra Biryukova, the first woman in the top leadership since Ekaterina Furtseva. About 52 per cent of the newly elected CC were fresh appointees.

The first direct evidence that Gorbachev and his allies had moved on to the offensive against the existing party order surfaced at this congress. The centre of contention was Boris Eltsin, who shocked the delegates by strongly criticising the privileges of the party *apparat*. Among his targets were the special shops for the nomenklatura, which had also been attacked in *Pravda* on the eve of the congress. Ligachev rose to the bait and denounced the *Pravda* article in vitriolic terms and the raising of the issue in the first place. Gromyko supported him. The battle-lines had been drawn. Henceforth Ligachev would become the principal defender of the rights of the party *apparat* and of the existing order in general.

In late July 1986 Gorbachev delivered a speech in Khabarovsk which revealed his frustration at the failure of *perestroika* to date. He came to the conclusion that a political reform was necessary to supplement the economic reform. However, so strong was resistance with the party *apparat* that it would take him two years to overcome it. At the end of 1986 Gorbachev sought to win over the intelligentsia when he had Andrei Sakharov and his wife brought back from Gorky. Gorbachev had sought in vain to convene a CC plenum on cadres but achieved his goal in January 1987. At it he talked of the build-up of 'crisis phenomena' in Soviet society and proposed the democratisation of the party in order to overcome the crisis. One of those promoted at the plenum was Anatoly Lukyanov, who joined the secretariat as a CC secretary. He and Gorbachev had been fellow law students at Moscow University in the early 1950s and also Komsomol activists together. Yakovlev's promotion to full membership of the Politburo during the first half of 1987 sowed confusion over who was to provide guidance to the press, he or Ligachev. Yakovlev encouraged the radical media and many of the central propaganda organs to pressurise the conservative establishment. Gorbachev was winning over the intelligentsia. Ligachev was furious and by July was denouncing the 'scum and debris' which had surfaced under *perestroika*. Gorbachev boldly defended the innovative journalists and spoke of 'socialist pluralism' for the first time. He was then on safe ground, since most of the 'plural' (non-party line) views supported him and not Ligachev. In August Gorbachev went off to the Crimea for his holidays but Ligachev, now temporarily in charge in Moscow, and Chebrikov, the KGB chief, got down to some work. They attacked the notion of socialist pluralism and defended Stalin's bloody collectivisation programme. This retreat into history was designed to prevent Gorbachev, in his keynote speech, at the seventieth anniversary of the October Revolution in November 1987, from backtracking on socialist agriculture. Stalin was having a bad time and undoing collectivisation risked setting in motion an unstoppable surge of reform which could unravel the Stalinist legacy.

These attacks and the sensational Eltsin affair forced Gorbachev to retreat in October 1987. During his time as Moscow party leader Boris Nikolaevich had engaged in a furious confrontation with Ligachev. The latter had objected strongly to Eltsin's damaging attacks on party privilege and his populist policies. Ligachev had successfully frustrated Eltsin's attempts to remove many insubordinate and corrupt officials and to obtain compensation from central ministries in Moscow for the burden they imposed on local services. Eltsin adopted the suicidal tactic of challenging Ligachev at the CC plenum in October 1987 (there was a Politburo rule that its divisions should not be revealed at CC plenums). Gorbachev had had forewarning of Boris Nikolaevich's feelings but had asked him not to bring the Ligachev issue up at the CC. Gorbachev, as a consequence, abandoned Eltsin and sharply criticised his personal failings. Boris Nikolaevich was thrown to the wolves of the Moscow city party committee and they savaged him in exemplary Stalinist fashion. Eltsin also had to leave the Politburo, thereby reducing radical support for *perestroika* there. Eltsin had been drummed out of party politics but was given a post in construction with the rank of minister, and this permitted him to stay in Moscow. His harsh treatment by Gorbachev and the party had unexpected consequences. It strengthened immensely his public appeal and made him the natural leader of the radical constituency. Ligachev, buoyed up by his total party victory over Eltsin went off to Paris where he revealed that he, not Gorbachev, chaired meetings of the CC secretariat. The announcement was nicely timed as Gorbachev was soon off to the UN in New York. The whole world was now aware that a duumvirate, the General Secretary and Ligachev, was running the country. In later transpired that Lev Zaikov, another conservative CC secretary, chaired the secretariat when Ligachev was away.

The conservatives had another stick with which to beat Gorbachev. Ethnic riots had occurred in Alma Ata and other Kazakh cities after Dinmukhamed Kunaev, Kazakh First Party Secretary, had been removed in December 1986, accused of corruption and replaced by a Russian, Gennady Kolbin. Worse followed in early 1988 when the bloody dispute of Nagorno-Karabakh burst on to the country's front pages. This Armenian-dominated enclave in Azerbaidzhan wished to join Armenia, but Moscow could not accede to its wish since it would have resulted in scores of other territorial disputes being placed on the agenda. The conservatives hammered him for provoking the conflict by not putting limits on *glasnost*.

The long-simmering confrontation between managed *perestroika* (Ligachev) and radical *perestroika* (Gorbachev) erupted on to the pages of *Sovetskaya Rossiya* on 13 March 1988. A letter by Nina Andreeva, a Leningrad teacher, strongly defended the Stalinist legacy. This clarion call against radical *perestroika* had been submitted to the newspaper some time before, had been rewritten with the help of Ligachev's supporters and then published when Gorbachev was away from Moscow. For three weeks the course of *perestroika* hung in the balance. Several Soviet newspapers reprinted the letter. Finally, a sharp rebuttal was published in *Pravda*, penned by Yakovlev. It rejected the notion that Andreeva was the author and referred to the contents as an article. Ligachev consistently denied responsibility for the letter's publication but he committed a grave mistake by allowing his overzealous supporters to go so far. He was defeated in the

Politburo in April and this prepared the ground for his humiliation at the XIXth Party conference in June 1988.

The Party conference emasculated the secretariat by depriving it of its main functions. Eltsin was given the floor by Gorbachev to berate Ligachev, and one delegate attacked Andrei Gromyko (USSR President) and Mikhail Solomentsev (chairman, Party Control Commission). Ligachev, on the defensive, revealed that Gromyko, Solomentsev, Chebrikov (KGB chairman) and he had been behind the election of Gorbachev as party leader. What a treacherous comrade Gorbachev had turned out to be! The General Secretary had a satisfying July. First, Eduard Shevardnadze transformed Soviet foreign policy by declaring that the link between it and the class struggle had been severed. Foreign policy was to be based on national interest and not on ideological foundations. Many in the West read this as crafty disinformation, but Shevardnadze and Gorbachev meant what they said. Secondly, Gorbachev won Politburo support for condemnation of Stalin's collectivisation programme. This opened the door to family farming. Ligachev riposted in August by reiterating the class basis of Soviet foreign policy and his opposition to decollectivisation. In September Gorbachev made spectacular gains. A CC plenum divested Ligachev of his supervision of cadres and ideology. A new cadres commission, one of six new CC commissions set up to replace the previous sections, was headed by Razumovsky, now directly under Gorbachev. Ligachev had to make do with the commission on agrarian policy. Here Gorbachev had not got his way. However, Ligachev no longer chaired the secretariat. Moreover, it appears to have met very seldom. The General Secretary chaired the meetings of the CC commissions but they were never quite sure what their functions were. Gromyko and Solomentsev left the Politburo, Vladimir Kryuchkov took over the KGB from Chebrikov and 'Grim Grom' Gromyko ceded the presidency to Gorbachev. Mikhail Sergeevich certainly was on the crest of a wave. However Ligachev, now out of the secretariat, had more time for the Politburo and remained Gorbachev's deputy there. Chebrikov, although he had lost control of the KGB, took over the CC legal affairs commission, and retained his Politburo seat. This gave him major influence over new legislation on law and order and how the existing law was applied: an unwelcome appointment for legal reformers. Chebrikov also liaised, on behalf of the leadership, with the instruments of coercion, the KGB, MVD and the military. He was also made responsible for nationality relations with the non-Slav republics.

The rules of political discourse were changing. Gradually, the pretence of Politburo unanimity was being chipped away. The altercations between Eltsin and Ligachev at the XIXth Party conference was a watershed. Henceforth it was possible to subject individual members of the Politburo to criticism and to call them to account. This was seized upon by radical journalists and editors, and Eltsin was also given free rein. Initially he had to content himself with sounding off to the foreign press but he eventually broke through into the central Soviet press. This could not have happened without at least Gorbachev's tacit approval. Presumably he believed that this would drive *perestroika* forward and that he would benefit most. This provoked heated debate within the Politburo, with Ligachev and the conservatives calling for party discipline to be reimposed. Under the old rules a member of the Politburo was a protected species and could not be criticised outside Politburo meetings. The only exception to this was when he was facing political death. Eventually, in March 1989, the Politburo conservatives managed to obtain a majority to oblige Gorbachev to discipline Eltsin for the harm he was causing the party. Gorbachev sidestepped this by setting up a party commission to look into the matter. Before it could report, Boris Nikolaevich won a resounding victory in elections to the USSR Congress of People's Deputies and this buried the issue. The battle to retain Politburo immunity from public criticism had been lost.

The other factor, which was to have devastating consequences for the party, was the emergence and gradual legitimation of informal movements and popular fronts. During the Brezhnev era unofficial culture flourished due to widespread access to foreign broadcasts and music. Videos, tapes and cassettes spread Western culture, especially pop, widely. Informal networks expanded everywhere to discuss problems of mutual interest. The wooden nature of Marxism-Leninism with its unwillingness to become involved in debate, even with party members, meant there was a huge constituency for novel political and social ideas. Latent protest broke surface for the first time during elections of delegates to the Party conference in June 1988. Most local party leaders organised the elections as they had always done, in their favour. This time round there were loud protests, sometimes covered by the central press. The most egregious offenders were sacked from their party offices. The informal associations had scented blood, and a protest wave against local party organisations built up during the autumn of 1988. The most vigorous were in the non-Slav republics, where the disparate organisations banded together into national or popular fronts. The Baltic led the way, and for the first time in Soviet history these republican groups could legitimately cross-fertilise with one another. Links were quickly established between the Baltic, Moldavia and Transcaucasia. Local communist leaderships began to come under increasing pressure from their local popular front. Elections to the USSR Congress of People's Deputies in March 1989 provided popular fronts and informal groups with an enormous boost. They were able to function outside effective party control for the first time. Party officials were obliged to stand for election. If defeated they were ripe for purging. The most prominent casualty was Yuri Solovev, First Party Secretary of Leningrad oblast and a candidate member of the Politburo.

Gorbachev was able, in July, to engineer his removal. Gorbachev and his supporters were able to dominate the congress, when it convened in May, and the subsequent elections to the USSR Supreme Soviet. The congress was televised live and became a hit with viewers. Andrei Sakharov, Boris Eltsin and other radicals skilfully used it to radicalise the population over the heads of the local party *apparat*. So addictive did viewing become that proceedings had to be recorded and put out in the evening. This meant that many weary people turned up for work the next day.

Gorbachev's new role as Chairman of the USSR Supreme Soviet clashed with that of party leader. This mirrored the tension between the Politburo and the Supreme Soviet. The latter was functioning in Moscow, and taking decisions which had previously been the prerogative of the Politburo and local party organs. However, new-style local soviets, which were to implement the decisions of the Supreme Soviet and to run local affairs, did not emerge. This was critical, since simultaneously the authority of the local party *apparat* had been diminished. This led to a power vacuum in many areas and exacerbated economic and nationality tensions. The local party *apparat* had traditionally co-ordinated state activities and supervised resource allocation at the local level. These local Party officials became a vociferous chorus in 1989 and subjected Gorbachev to sharp criticism at each CC plenum. In April 1989 a CC plenum obliged those members who had lost their jobs to proffer their resignations. Since Gorbachev was not influential enough to remove those members in jobs, the CC remained basically hostile to him. At a CC plenum in July Ligachev, Zaikov and (significantly) Ryzhkov revealed that they sympathised with the predicament the *apparat* found itself in as a result of Gorbachev's policies. Ryzhkov had previously sided with the General Secretary and this had been of major significance during the row over the Andreeva letter. Gorbachev's more radical stance was putting him in a minority in the Politburo. The plenum also saw Ligachev supporters stoutly defending him and desiring a return to the old-fashioned secretariat. This revealed their lack of political perception, which was eventually to lead to their demise. They did not attempt to seize the initiative and claim leadership of the emerging democratic forces. The pool of officials who shared Gorbachev's views was very small, and this was illustrated by new appointments in 1989. Party leaders in Moscow, Leningrad and the Ukraine changed, but the new men were hardly an improvement on the old. In Leningrad Boris Gidaspov, presumably a Gorbachev appointee, turned out to be a spokesman for the military-industrial complex, Russian national resentment, a Russian Communist Party and a thorn in Gorbachev's side.

The massacre of twenty civilians by the military in the Georgian capital Tbilisi in April 1989 severely damaged Gorbachev's power and legitimacy. The decision to accede to the Georgian Communist Party's request for the use of force to clear demonstrators was taken while Gorbachev was absent from Moscow. It appears to have been inspired by Ligachev and Chebrikov. By September 1989 Gorbachev was able to split the conservatives and remove Chebrikov and Vladimir Shcherbitsky, the last relic of the Brezhnev past, from the Politburo. The price he paid was the promotion of Vladimir Kryuchkov, head of the KGB, to full Politburo membership, jumping over the candidate stage. Kryuchkov turned out to be a conservative and only a tactical ally, until, that is, August 1991. Gorbachev only just prevented the formation of a Russian Communist Party, one full of *apparatchiks* angry at his policies.

The autumn of 1989 brought a harvest of despair for the communist regimes of Eastern Europe. One after the other they collapsed under popular pressure. Gorbachev encouraged the process by undermining the staid, conservative leaders who were resisting *perestroika*. This was clearly evident in the German Democratic Republic. Erich Honecker, the GDR President and SED General Secretary was a long-term critic of Gorbachev's policies and had censored his utterances in the early *perestroika* years. On the occasion of the fortieth anniversary of the GDR, in October 1989, Gorbachev repaired to East Berlin and put the finishing touches to the removal of Honecker. Egon Krenz was the compromise candidate as Hans Modrow was not in the SED Politburo. Krenz turned out to be a lame duck and presided over the rapid dissolution of the GDR. Gorbachev afforded the Germans one valuable service: he ordered the Soviet military not to get involved and also prevented the use of the GDR people's army. The East European security catastrophe challenged the foundations of the new thinking in foreign policy and for the first time put Gorbachev and Shevardnadze under real pressure. Soviet radicals called for the annulment of article 6 of the USSR constitution which guaranteed the CPSU a monopoly of political power. Lithuanian nationalists in the Communist Party of Lithuania began trying to disengage from the CPSU and to take Lithuania out of the USSR. The example of Eastern Europe was a powerful stimulus to nationalist ambitions. If the USSR would not use force to keep communists in power in Eastern Europe, would force be deployed to keep the Soviet Union together? Had not Gorbachev on many occasions maintained that military force would not be used to resolve political conflict?

Gorbachev came under concerted fire at the CC plenum in December 1989 and angrily defended himself. He was finding it more and more difficult to get the Congress of People's Deputies and the Supreme Soviet to take the decisions he favoured. They became less radical and began to correspond to the conservative consensus in the Politburo. This was particularly evident in economic policy, where Abalkin's modest market reforms aroused strong opposition from Ryzhkov, who carried the day in the Politburo. This appears to have been the moment when Gorbachev and Ryzhkov parted company. Gorbachev was pursuing a centrist line and fell into the classic trap of appeasing all but pleasing no one. He refused to identify the right as the main barrier to progress and thereby frustrated his radical supporters who wanted the party to be downgraded further and the legislature and presidency strengthened. At the CC plenum in February 1990 he appeared to be siding with the radicals. He obliged the members to endorse the removal of article 6 from the constitution. To many of them this was tantamount to political suicide, but party discipline held. This move legitimised the emerging political pluralism inside and outside the party. Clearly Gorbachev thought that he could cut deals with the various groups and parties which would enhance his position. This turned out to be quite false since these groups and parties proved too radical for Gorbachev. The plenum also acceded to Gorbachev's wish to establish an executive presidency. He expected to be popularly elected, thereby enhancing his ability to dragoon the demoralised party *apparat* as he thought fit. He was planning to launch an offensive against party recalcitrants at a party congress in July. The threat of a split in the ranks of the party became a possibility with the formation of the Democratic Platform faction within the CPSU in January 1990. Yakovlev and Eltsin supported this group. A democratic Russia electoral alliance formed to contest the elections to the RSFSR Congress and to city soviets. It made spectacular gains at the expense of the party *apparat*. Cities such as Moscow and Leningrad fell to the radicals. Thus began a tug of war between the incoming radicals and the old *apparat* for control of economic decision-making. This was another reason for economic decline. Gorbachev became Executive President in March 1990 but did not risk going to the people. Nevertheless, only 1,329 voted for him, 495 voting against and 426 abstaining. A presidential council was set up to advise him and a council of the federation, consisting of the chairmen of the republican Supreme Soviets, was also established. Mindful of the lack of enthusiasm in the party for his policies, he clung on to his post as CPSU leader.

Gorbachev presided at the opening Congress of the Russian Communist Party in June 1990. Ivan Polozkov, an uninspiring *apparatchik*, was elected First Secretary. The XXVIIIth CPSU Congress – and the last – met in July. Politburo members had to give an account of themselves, and several announced their retirement. There were fireworks from Colonel General Albert Makashov, commander-in-chief of the Volga-Urals military district. He issued a clarion call for the party to return to its roots and vitriolically attacked *perestroika* and *glasnost*. Other military leaders at the congress applauded enthusiastically. Clearly, there was considerable tension between Gorbachev and the military. Vladimir Lysenko, a leader of the Democratic Platform, proposed that Lenin be removed from his mausoleum and 'given a decent Christian burial'. Gorbachev was re-elected as General Secretary with 1,116 out of almost 5,000 delegates voting against. A new post of Deputy was created and Gorbachev managed to get Vladimir Ivashko, the conservative Ukrainian leader, elected instead of Ligachev. The latter declared that he would not stand for re-election to the Politburo. Game, set and match to Gorbachev. The new Politburo was enlarged and consisted of all republican party leaders and seven CC secretaries. Those holding government posts, Eduard Shevardnadze, Nikolai Ryzhkov, Dmitry Yazov and also Vladimir Kryuchkov, were excluded from the Politburo. Hence the Politburo was downgraded and was to restrict itself to party affairs. New party rules were adopted and greater autonomy was afforded regional organisations.

There was always tension between Gorbachev and the military. He was determined to reduce the defence burden and to break the dominance of the general staff over defence and security policy. Shevardnadze was used as a knife and wounded the military deeply. Gorbachev took a centrist position, as was his wont. The Tbilisi massacre of April 1989 transformed the situation and led to a polarisation of relations between most of the top military and most of Gorbachev's supporters. The killings were blamed on internal troops and the military by a Congress of People's Deputies commission but on the demonstrators by the military. Gorbachev used his authority as party leader to convince the congress, which had a conservative, pro-military majority, to adopt a motion condemning the use of force against the demonstrators, but it declined to adopt the report's condemnation of specific actions by the military and central party leadership. *Sovetskaya Rossiya* published the military prosecutor's findings, which whitewashed the military. Military intervention in Baku in January 1990, which resulted in over 100 civilian deaths, sharpened tensions between civilians and the military. The latter had moved to crush the Azerbaidzhani popular front, whereas Vadim Bakatin, the liberal USSR Minister of the Interior, and Shevardnadze and other Gorbachev supporters, wanted to arrest the leaders who were organising violence and to negotiate with the rest. Chief of the General Staff General Moiseev vented his anger at Gorbachev's policies in *Krasnaya Zvezda* in March 1990. He was particularly annoyed by the fact that he and other military men had not been allowed to speak at the CC plenum in February 1990 or at the session of the Congress of People's Deputies in December 1989. Rising ethnic violence forced Gorbachev to compromise with the military. An indication of this was the promotion of General Yazov to marshal in April 1990. Previously Gorbachev had removed all marshals from active duty. He promised the military more weapons and to address the many grievances they had.

Gorbachev's backtracking on economic reform in the autumn when he abandoned plans to introduce the 500-day programme led to many supporters deserting him for Eltsin. It also encouraged the conservatives. Rumours of a military coup circulated, and Gorbachev's inability or unwillingness to protect Shevardnadze from the arrows of the military, in particular, led the Georgian to resign his post as Foreign Minister in December. In a highly emotional speech he warned of the threat of dictatorship.

NATIONALITIES

Gorbachev had little understanding of nationality affairs when he became leader. As party leader he placed the cohesion of the Soviet Empire above all else. The Kazakh riots of December 1986 shocked him, as he had supported Ligachev's proposal to remove the corrupt Kunaev and replaced him with a Russian who was amenable to central direction. Moscow was wont to regard all the indigenous party elites, especially in the Muslim republics, as corrupt.

There was a lot of embezzlement, and the Uzbek cotton scandal was only the tip of the iceberg. The Uzbeks had been fiddling the books and had been paid vast sums for mythical deliveries of cotton. The locals looked at it differently. They regarded Moscow as an imperial power which was out to exploit them. Their first national duty was to fleece Moscow. Gorbachev and Ligachev thought the problem could be solved by sending Russian and Ukrainian officials to take over. How naïve they were! The other person who was determined to bring the natives to book was KGB boss Chebrikov. He was responsible for many of the coercive policies adopted by Moscow and had a hand in the Tbilisi massacre. He authored the CC document of August 1989 which threatened the Baltic secessionists with dire consequences if they did not desist. *Glasnost* and democratisation promoted the articulation of old hatreds and resentments. Only some of these concerned the Russians.

Gorbachev hoped that greater participation in the political process, firmly guided by the CPSU, would greatly strengthen the Soviet Union. Instead, it blew it up. One of the reasons for this was that the communist leaderships in the Baltic – Estonia, Latvia and Lithuania – and Transcaucasia – Azerbaidzhan, Armenia and Georgia – were gradually submerged under nationalist sentiments and found themselves following the national fronts rather than leading them. In 1988 the leaders of the three Baltic parties had been changed, and the new men told to keep in step with national sentiments so as to ensure popular support for the Communist Party. Gorbachev's response to the take-over of the Communist parties by the nationalists was to attack them for surrendering to anti-Russian sentiments. He was indeed naïve if he thought that communists could dominate local politics by promoting Moscow's policies.

Eventually the local parties seceded from the CPSU, but a rump, mostly consisting of Russians, remained loyal to Moscow. Thus each Baltic republic had two Communist parties. The most abrasive and confrontational course was pursued by Lithuania and the most malleable by Latvia. Lithuania had the fewest Russians and Latvia the most. The challenge to Moscow went through various stages: claims for economic self-accounting; then declarations of autonomy: then sovereignty; and finally independence. They all declared independence between March and May 1990. One argument deployed was that the Baltic states had been illegally incorporated in the USSR in 1940. In January 1991, Soviet paratroops and MVD troops attacked the television tower in Vilnius, the capital of Lithuania, leaving fourteen dead and many injured. This bloody episode ended any doubts the Baltic republics had about seceding from the USSR.

It also irreparably damaged Gorbachev's legitimacy since he failed to condemn the killings. His hopes of fashioning a new federal Soviet State out of the old USSR were doomed to failure, at least in the Baltic. Gorbachev was deeply embroiled in the bloodletting. Since the autumn of 1990, he had participated in discussions with the military, KGB and the MVD about using coercion to halt the disintegration of the USSR. Gorbachev found himself in a quandary after the shootings. He may not have given the order to shoot, but neither did he order the forces of coercion to desist. More ominous for Gorbachev was the fact that Boris Eltsin flew to Tallinn, in Estonia, to confer with Baltic leaders, and condemned the use of force in Vilnius. He called on Russians, called up on Russian territory, not to obey orders to use force to resolve inter-ethnic conflicts. In a bid to gain support for a new federation Gorbachev called a referendum, the first in Soviet history, in March 1991. He got his majority, but astute local leaders had added their own questions. One of these asked Russian voters if they were in favour of a directly elected Russian president. The answer was 'yes', and in due course Boris Eltsin was elected President of Russia. Boris Nikolaevich now had a formidable institutional base from which to attack Gorbachev. Russia claimed sovereignty over everything on its territory and adopted market reforms ahead of the USSR. A war of laws developed between Russia and the USSR and between other republics and the USSR. Eltsin conducted his own foreign policy towards other republics and recognised the sovereignty of other republics and their rights to secede from the USSR.

ECONOMIC POLICY[2]

The economic stagnation of the late Brezhnev era was the result of many factors: the exhaustion of easily available resources, especially raw materials and the growing structural imbalance due to the distorting effects of the incentive system. It reduced initiative and encouraged fewer and fewer to do an honest day's work. The policies of *perestroika* must carry much of the blame for the plight of the economy. Gorbachev admitted in 1988 that the first two years had been wasted and that he had been unaware of the depth of the crisis when he took over. Since Gosplan had no model of how the economy functioned, the various reforms attempted were shots in the dark. Perhaps no one had an overview of the whole economy.

Soviet gross national product (GNP) was almost stagnant during the first four years of *perestroika*. Unemployment remained about 4 per cent of the labour force, almost all in the labour-surplus areas of Central Asia and the Caucasus. Open inflation remained low until 1989. Underlying trends, however, pointed towards systemic failure. Shortages, endemic to all planned economies, became serious from the mid 1980s. By mid 1990 over 1,000 consumer goods were very seldom on sale. Rationing became widespread, with most goods being sold at the point of work. Queueing became the national pastime: a 1990 estimate put it at 30–40 billion man (or rather woman) hours a year. The only commodity that was not in short supply was money. This was due to a rapidly growing budget deficit, first evident in 1987. Then the law on the state enterprise, effective from January 1988, permitted managers to increase wages to cope with the tight labour situation. Increases were far in excess of productivity growth. The State Bank lost control of monetary growth. The plan for 1990 was for an increase of 10 billion rubles, but it turned out to be about 28 billion rubles. Social benefits rose by 21 per cent in 1990 as a result of the USSR Congress of People's Deputies voting to increase a whole raft of benefits, notably pensions. Since there were no resources to meet this extra expenditure the budget deficit grew, as did the money supply.

Responsibility for the budget deficit rests fairly and squarely on the shoulders of the Gorbachev leadership. Traditionally, the deficit had been 2 or 3 per cent of GNP. The years 1985 and 1986 changed all that. Gorbachev's desire to achieve faster growth-acceleration resulted in the 12th Five Year Plan (1985–90) being returned three times to Gosplan with orders to raise targets. In 1986 the budget deficit rose to 6 per cent of GNP. By 1988 it was up to 10 per cent and the subject was out in the open. The law on the state enterprise reduced the powers of the ministries, and also the number of bureaucrats was cut back sharply. Those left were simply overwhelmed by the work load. Rising nationalism, ethnic strife and regionalism led to the economy fragmenting into scores of mini-economies. They all pursued policies of economic autarky. Barter was widespread. Ukraine introduced coupons and Moscow ration cards.

Foreign trade suffered. Lower oil prices and economic fragmentation led to the hard currency debt rising from US$25.6 billion at the end of 1984 to about $80 billion by the end of 1991. Imports from the West were cut back sharply over the period 1985–87. These were mainly consumer goods. People protested and imports from the West rose by almost a half between 1987 and 1989. As a consequence, by 1989, the USSR could not service its hard currency debt on time. Recalculations of Soviet economic performance by Soviet statisticians scaled down Soviet achievements. The official view was that Soviet national income was about 64 per cent of the US level in 1988. Gorbachev, in a speech in October 1990, implied that the real figure was about 40 per cent. Another estimate put the real level at about 46 per cent in 1970, declining to 40 per cent in 1987.

The Gorbachev leadership suffered from wishful thinking in economic affairs. When Leonid Abalkin, at the XIXth Party conference in June 1988, stated the plain truth that the country was still suffering from stagnation, Gorbachev and others scolded him and adopted a motion stating that economic decline had been halted. The advent of the USSR Congress of People's Deputies made it virtually impossible for the Gorbachev leadership to adopt austerity measures. The deputies wanted to spend, spend, spend. Gorbachev never came up with a viable economic policy, nor a mechanism to implement economic decisions.

FOREIGN POLICY

If Gorbachev's domestic policy failed, his foreign policy was a brilliant success – that is, from the West's point of view. He and Shevardnadze formed a famous team and won the trust and affection of many world leaders – an unprecedented occurrence for Soviet leaders. In 1990 Gorbachev was awarded the Nobel Peace Prize for his contribution to the ending of the Cold War. His message was the message the world wanted to hear. No ideology in foreign, defence and security policy-making. The world is interdependent; no state can increase its security if it undermines the security of another. If the world did not unite the planet was in danger. Eliminate all nuclear weapons by the year 2000. Establish a system of comprehensive security. Soviet military doctrine was to be based on reasonable sufficiency. At the UN in December 1988 he praised its role in promoting international peace, a sea change in Soviet attitudes. He announced a reduction of 500,000 in the Soviet armed forces over the following two years. A major reason for disarmament and a reduction of international tension was Gorbachev's perception that military expenditure was crippling the USSR.

The first Reagan–Gorbachev summit took place in Geneva in November 1985 and the next in Reykjavik in October 1986. At the latter, the Soviets overplayed their hand, demanding agreement on all points, including abandonment of the strategic defence initiative

(SDI), a space-based defensive shield. The meeting in Washington, in December 1987, was historic. A whole range of nuclear weapons, land-based intermediate and shorter-range missiles, was to be eliminated. This was the INF treaty. SDI was passed over in silence. In Moscow, in May–June 1988, INF was signed but differences remained, mainly over verification. Bush–Gorbachev relations were warm. There were two historic agreements: on conventional disarmament, signed in Paris in November 1990, the CFE treaty, and the strategic arms reduction treaty, START, in July 1991. However, opposition by the Soviet General Staff sabotaged the CFE treaty and the demise of the Soviet Union halted progress on START. The new super power relationship resulted in Shevardnadze voting, in the UN, for military intervention in Kuwait in early 1991. This was painful for Moscow because Iraq had been an ally. Gorbymania broke out in Europe, especially in Germany. He was mobbed in China in the spring of 1989 and this severely embarrassed and alarmed the ageing Chinese leadership. They ruthlessly suppressed those calling for *perestroika* in China shortly afterwards. One of the agreements reached at Geneva concerned the withdrawal of Soviet troops from Afghanistan. The last man left in February 1989. Brezhnev had blundered into Afghanistan, did not possess the willpower to acknowledge the mistake and hostilities slowly escalated; Andropov recognised the dangers and began to slow down the pace and seek a platform for withdrawal; Chernenko, confirming his pedigree as an archetypal Soviet bureaucrat, escalated the conflict in a vain attempt to find a military solution; Gorbachev, slowly scaled down hostilities in preparation for a solution of the conflict. The official number of dead was put at 13,833, with 11,381 dying in combat; about 11,500 emerged from the war as invalids. Altogether about 750,000 Soviets (*afgantsy* in Russian) took part in the operation. The experience left an indelible mark on all participants. Officially the war cost around 80 billion rubles between the years 1979–88. This amounted to about 2 per cent of declared Soviet defence spending over the period.[3] The goal of the new thinking in foreign policy was to strengthen socialism around the world. This mission failed and the Soviet Union's allies at its demise were poor Third World states, every one of them a liability.

THE COUP

Why did the coup fail? On paper it should have succeeded. Most people were disenchanted with *perestroika* since they had seen a steady decline in their living standards. The party *apparat* was sullen and resentful. The military was depressed at the loss of Eastern Europe and civilian hostility. Several republican leaders, including those in Azerbaidzhan, Tadzhikistan, Turkmenistan and Uzbekistan, came out in support of the coup. Many others prevaricated while only President

Akaev of Kyrgyzstan came out strongly against it. Many provincial newspapers printed the communiqués of the Yanaev commission.

So why did it not succeed? Astonishingly, it was poorly planned and executed. The guiding light was Vladimir Kryuchkov, KGB head. The lessons of the brilliant coup in Poland in December 1981 were forgotten. The fatal tactical error was failure to identify and deploy loyal troops. It was assumed that orders would be obeyed. Troops had moved ruthlessly against civilians in Tbilisi, Baku and Vilnius. What was different this time was that troops, overwhelmingly Russian, were being ordered to move against Russians. Had Asian troops been deployed they would probably have mown down Russians with gusto.

Even Kryuchkov found that he could not rely on KGB troops. He, as USSR KGB chief could give orders to the head of the Russian KGB. However, he in turn, was under the authority of Boris Eltsin. Placed under great pressure by members of the Russian government, he decided eventually to ignore Kryuchkov's orders. Some of Kryuchkov's own USSR KGB officers were not loyal. A major sent an open fax to a leading Russian democrat and USSR people's deputy in London, warning her that she would probably be arrested at the airport if she returned to Moscow.

The strategic error committed by the plotters was their inability to understand the radical political and social transformation which had been under way since 1985. It was no longer credible to announce that Gorbachev had retired for 'health' reasons. Eltsin and the democrats seized the opportunity afforded by the incompetent plotters to organise effective resistance in Moscow. Anatoly Sobchak did the same in St Petersburg. Eltsin stressed that the coup was aimed primarily at Russia. There were significant divisions between top military and KGB officers. For instance, some KGB officers informed Eltsin about the employment of KGB marksmen and how they would try to gain entry to the White House. World statesmen condemned the coup and warned that aid would be cut off.

NOTES

1. Harry Gelman, *Gorbachev's First Five Years in the Soviet Leadership*.
2. Anders Åslund, 'Gorbachev, *Perestroyka*, and Economic Crisis', *Problems of Communism* Vol. XL, no. 1–2, January–April 1991, pp. 18–41.
3. A Russian joke illustrates the bitter civilian attitude to the war. An officer is giving a pep talk to some young recruits before they leave Moscow for Afghanistan. He hammers home the message that the mujahedin are ferocious fighters and that the recruits will have to be on their mettle to beat them. On their shoulders rests the honour of the Soviet army and the motherland. In order to encourage them he promises that every man who brings in the head of a guerrilla will receive a medal. The plane

lands and the soldiers disembark. Later the same evening the officer lines them up for inspection. Every man is carrying a head under his arm. The officer glances at them and is absolutely horrified. 'But, but lads . . . this is Tashkent!'

The Afghan imbroglio is often compared to the Vietnam war, another conflict in which a super power blundered into a conflict it little understood in an attempt to maintain the *status quo* in the East–West confrontation. The Americans lost about 40,000 men in Vietnam but there were already over half a million troops there by 1970 whereas the Soviets never deployed more than 150,000 at any one time. This reveals that Soviet casualties, per 1,000 troops deployed, were higher than those of the US in Vietnam.

CHAPTER NINE

Why Did the Soviet Experiment Fail?

The October Revolution changed the world and shook the existing order to its foundations. It set in motion a societal experiment which resulted in the USSR becoming a super power. During the early years of the revolution, in the late 1940s, the late 1950s and during the mid 1970s it appeared to many of its competitors – first and foremost the United States – that Soviet power was on the march and might challenge successfully for world leadership. Looking back it reached its zenith of power and influence in the mid 1970s. Thereafter an astonishing collapse set in and the State which had set so many hearts fluttering – out of excitement or nervousness – ceased to exist at the end of 1991. Its failure has changed the political geography of the world.

The State which set out to abolish the State failed to evolve a society capable of constructing an economy which was able to satisfy the aspirations of its members. On paper a planned economy, deploying all the potential of the country in the pursuit of material growth, should have been able to perform better than the ups and downs of the capitalist economies. The primary reason for the destruction of the Marxist socialist dream was Marx's inability to understand the fundamental importance of the market in generating secular growth. The Communist Party mobilised the resources of the country during the 1930s in the pursuit of rapid growth of heavy industry, energy and transport. Success was such that its military potential made it possible to defeat Germany. Stalin and many communists can be forgiven for believing that they had found the key to political and economic success.

Ironically, at its apogee the Stalinist system was revealing the cracks which were later to undermine the foundations of the USSR. The very success of industrial expansion rendered it more and more difficult to manage the system from the centre. Khrushchev perceived the dangers and the challenge but could not find any solution. Without a formal market the economy became more and more wasteful and inefficient. An army of bureaucrats had been brought into existence to run the State in the interests of the leader. However, this nomenklatura or ruling class, once freed from the murderous uncertainty and arbitrariness of the Stalin era, closed ranks and became an interest group which gradually ran the USSR according to its own lights. Brezhnev, the *apparatchik par excellence*, presided over this nomenklatura but discovered that he could not significantly alter its behaviour. Markets are to be found in all societies and cannot be legislated out of existence. In the Soviet Union since the market was taboo it was replaced by the bureaucratic market. The bureaucrats traded options among themselves and allocated resources according to their preferences. The party was the co-ordinator but found from the 1950s onwards that the task was beyond it. The system was so complex, with so many conflicting interest groups, that no one had a comprehensive overview of what was going on. So delicate was the mechanism developed under Brezhnev that when Andropov and Gorbachev began to tinker with it, it broke and could not be repaired. Understanding how and why this mechanism came into being and how it functioned is a fascinating study. The mechanism could not be successfully reformed so as to generate secular economic growth. It had to give way to the market. The following are only a few points towards an explanation.

The first attempt to eliminate the market was undertaken under War Communism. Lenin, like Marx, was fascinated by the machine and thought that if a factory could be run like a machine so could a whole economy. Hence the problem was purely organisational. Provide the leader at the centre with all the relevant information he needed, and a master plan could be evolved. This approach was deeply paternalistic and envisaged everyone carrying out the orders of the centre. War Communism collapsed and almost brought down Soviet Russia. Stalin's industrialisation drive was ruthlessly paternalistic and exploited everyone in the interests of the State. Again, the model was a machine factory transferred to embrace the whole economy. Growth rates under Stalin were the highest ever achieved in the Soviet Union. This was because he was able to mobilise the resources of the State and society, employ coercion, and achieve some startling growth rates. Another reason was that the USSR began at a low level of *per capita* output so growth initially was dramatic. Stalin also had the incentive that if resources were used effectively his prestige and power would expand along with that of the country.

There were two main sources of capital for the huge amounts of investment needed in the 1930s: foreign financial institutions and the Soviet people. He chose the latter and depressed consumption to a level barely sufficient to keep body and soul together. He targeted heavy industry, partly for strategic reasons. Science and technology were also high on his list of priorities. Technology was not very complex in the 1930s and the Soviets found it possible to buy whole enterprises from the West. For example, Henry Ford built and equipped the largest tractor plant in the world at, appropriately enough, Stalingrad, the city of Stalin. Bureaucrats were needed to carry out the will of the leader. They, in turn, needed a vast amount of information from enterprises about their potential. When this information was processed at the centre orders were handed down to enterprises about what and how they should produce. This was fine as long as the economy was small and compact. Information-gathering about retail trade and agriculture, for example, was much more complex, since these sectors covered a huge area. The planners at the centre always wanted to know the true production potential of the inputs which every factory received. Inspectors were sent from Moscow to assess this. However, since the penalty of failure was so severe under Stalin, enterprise managers had an interest in concealing the true potential so as to obtain 'soft' plans, those which could be more easily achieved. They also sought to conceal reserves.

Theoretically the planners would have favoured several competing factories producing the same product but the nature of planning made this illogical. Why produce the same goods in several factories, why not concentrate output in one and produce something else in the next? The desire of Stalin to achieve huge growth rates meant that resources were always in short supply and never enough to meet the plan. Managers had to collude in order to survive. They had to co-operate among themselves and barter scarce goods and inputs wherever possible. The Soviet economy was in a critical state in the late 1930s due to excessive demands being made by the leader. Quality inevitably suffered and gave way to quantity. Production plans were expressed in physical units: for example, in tonnes. It was natural to favour heavy goods and to neglect light goods. As the economy grew and became more complex it became impossible for planners to know accurately the production potential of each enterprise and to hand down detailed plan targets. They had to be aggregated at the top and then disaggregated by middle-level bureaucrats and further broken down at the enterprise level. The wishes of the planners could be flouted successfully. The war strengthened the role of enterprises. Malenkov, for instance, was responsible for aircraft production. In order for his ministries and subordinate enterprises to achieve their targets they had to integrate their efforts as never before. Regional enterprise associations came into being, with the ministries and branch industries playing key coordinating roles. Party officials supervised the whole.

After the war the ministries in Moscow were not as powerful as they would have liked since the links forged by enterprises remained. Khrushchev dissolved most of the industrial ministries and replaced them with the *sovnarkhozy* in 1957. This strengthened regionalism and enterprise co-operation. Every enterprise had an interest in reducing the range of products it produced since that cut down the hassle of getting all the inputs necessary for production. There was a finite quantity of inputs, decided by the planners, but because of imperfect information, it was never adequate. Bureaucratic permission had to be obtained to get anything since money was passive and not active.

Some things could be bought, but not everything that was needed. Enterprises took to exchanging inputs and goods among themselves.

This system reached its apogee under Brezhnev. A vast bureaucratic system was needed to regulate the economy which was made up of thousands of mini-systems, each regulating the production of a particular good. As the economy grew, so did the bureaucracy to cope with it. It became so complex that no one had an overview of it. It was impossible to gather the information to do this. Hence the Brezhnev economy was one in which thousands of sub-economies functioned, each pursuing its own interests. There were thousands of interest groups, encompassing enterprises, ministries, regions, cities and so on. The major force was the military-industrial complex, which had first call on resource allocation. So intricate did the system become that it had, naturally, a strong bias against innovation. This was because innovation involved remaking the web of contacts necessary to make the new product. The military sector was an exception to this. Those who had novel ideas were normally unable to get them into the production cycle. The uncertainty of the supply system led to enterprises getting larger and integrating production. Kamaz, the largest truck plant in the USSR, produced about 150,000 lorries annually at Naberezhny Chelny in Tatarstan. It had its own foundry, tyre plant and so on. The natural trend towards monopoly meant that a particular input or product could often only be obtained from one factory in the USSR.

The above process, over time, reduces the power of the party leader to direct the economy. By the time Gorbachev took over in 1985 the Politburo had limited influence over economic policy. Indeed, the changes they did introduce exacerbated the situation. Hence Ryzhkov's pleading for slow, incremental, managed change fitted the logic of the situation. However, this was not a solution, merely an attempt to prolong a dying system. Under Khrushchev, Brezhnev, Andropov and Gorbachev there was considerable desire to reform from above. However, the reforms were always proposed by economists who were not involved in day-to-day production. Workers sometimes welcomed proposals for change. Hence the constituency for change consisted of those at the top and the bottom. Those in the middle, the ministries, enterprise managers and so on resisted change. The bureaucrats who actually ran the economy could effectively sabotage any reform which they perceived to be inimical to their interests.

One can speak of a bureaucratic aristocracy which runs a bureaucratic market[1] in its own interest. Centrifugal flows of power to the periphery are inevitable. Each region, each republic develops its own bureaucratic aristocracy regulating its own bureaucratic market. Who integrates and coordinates these various hierarchies? Theoretically it should be the party, but the task was beyond it. Institutional sclerosis sets in and eventually this disease becomes terminal. The speed of decline depends on how dysfunctional the bureaucratic markets become. They all pursue their own separate interests which in turn cause irreparable damage to the country. An example from the retail sector will illustrate the lack of integration and innovation: Moscow's bread.[2] Five mills deliver flour to twenty-four bread factories and thirty-eight bakeries: they in turn produce an average of 2,400 tonnes of bread a day for 1,420 ordinary and specialist bread shops for the capital's 9 million inhabitants. Bread has to be ordered daily by the shops. If the order does not get through between 7 a.m. and 3 p.m. the shop gets no bread the next day. There is no such thing as a standard order. A standard white loaf stays fresh for about sixteen hours from the moment it leaves the oven. Even if dispatched quickly, loaves reach the shops with only a few hours of freshness to spare. One hitch, and the whole batch is stale. The shop has no way of replenishing its stocks for perhaps a day. Customers have to find another shop with fresh bread. Queues are the inevitable result. The obvious solution is to wrap the loaves in plastic bags. This prolongs freshness to two or three days. However, no factory makes plastic bags. Whereas 95 per cent of food is packaged for sale in advanced market economies, in the former USSR it is about 2 per cent. Most Russian shops have a three-tier queueing system: once to make sure the bread is available; then to pay for it and get a slip; then collect it. Bread factories have various departments: milling, transport, production and so on. Everyone is a specialist on his or her own department. No one has an overview of the whole process. No one has the task of coordinating the various processes and rationalising them.

The same applies, *a fortiori*, to the Soviet economy. Some brave souls did try to rationalise the system but found that there were so many links in the chain that they gave up in frustration. Every official is subordinate to his or her superior and to all those superior to them. So the request has to go up and down again with the result. A key component is to convince a superior official that a decision is necessary. The usual response is to take no decision. If the decision is positive then the whole process begins once again since the necessary resources have to be provided. If manufacturing is involved changes have to be made to production plans and so on. Quick decisions and quick results are ruled out. Disruptions anywhere along the chain slow the whole process. An ingenious system involving myriads of personal networks was built up. It was always part of the deal that if official A helped official B then B had to do something for A in return. The Soviet economy favoured monopoly and specialisation. Most air-conditioning equipment is manufactured in Azerbaidzhan; almost all bicycle chains come from Lithuania, and so on. If the Balts are vindictive, Russian factories can only produce bicycles without chains.

Japan and Italy have the highest level of political and financial corruption in advanced market economies. In Japan the liberal democrats (LDs) have been in power for decades, and in Italy the Christian

Democrats (CDs) have been Italy's leading political party and have been in every government since 1945. The power of patronage has led to a situation where most public offices have been filled by the CDs' nominee. In Japan the LDs are the public face of big business, top civil servants and the banks. Hence in both countries governments are traditionally weak. Even in a well-functioning democracy, a feeling of creeping omnipotence overtakes a party which has been in power for about a decade. The Conservative Government in Britain, under Mrs Thatcher, showed signs of this in the late 1980s. It would have been a miracle had the CPSU been an exception to this rule.

The monopoly of power of the CPSU, expressed in theory in every constitution and in practice by banning all other parties and eliminating all factions within the party, made it impossible for the CPSU to develop into a democratic party. The same process which occurred at State level took root within the party. Networks developed and a bureaucratic market emerged. In the early years the Politburo was the only institution where democracy prevailed. This was a tender plant since discord at the top had to be masked from the public because of the narrow support base enjoyed by the Bolsheviks until the late 1920s. Stalin and his cohorts ensured that debate in the Politburo, in the sense of opposing Stalin's priorities, was gradually stifled. By the mid 1930s, Stalin's goals prevailed. Party officials built up their own networks in self-defence and self-interest. Stalin was aware of this and collected information through his own personal secretariat, under Poskrebyshev. He employed trouble-shooters to break through networks and resistance. Kaganovich was one of the most ruthless, Molotov was not far behind. After Stalin's death no one acquired or was allowed to acquire the master's powers. Khrushchev was astute enough, by using the party *apparat*, to outmanoeuvre Malenkov, who relied on a government base. The victory over the Anti-Party group in 1957 sealed the victory of the party *apparat*. It retained its pre-eminence until the late Gorbachev era. Tatyana Zaslavskaya, a leading sociologist, saw it as parasitic and a brake on efficiency. Khrushchev recognised the dangers of creeping omnipotence and the corrupting power of patronage, but the *apparat* was stronger than he. Brezhnev was an *apparat* man, and under him it flourished as never before. Officials luxuriated in privilege and power. A classic example was Viktor Grishin, the Moscow party leader. So arrogant and secure did he feel in the early 1980s that he had no objection to revelations about housing corruption in the capital. Brezhnev was so long in power that practically all public posts changed hands during his leadership. It might have been thought that the nomenklatura in 1982 was Brezhnev's nomenklatura. However, his own physical decline in the mid 1970s led to his cohorts arranging appointments in their own interests. Brezhnev was strikingly impotent during his last years to force government and party bureaucrats to improve their performance.

Ideological fervour was considerable in the early years of the revolution and the first Five Year Plan. Socialism was a moral and physical goal and inspired hundreds of thousands. Stalin simplified Marxism and made it digestible. His fear of Trotsky and other strands of Marxism caused him to seek a rigid interpretation and to force this on everyone. This was successful in the 1930s when there was a common enemy, fascism, and the USSR could be cut off from the rest of the world. The war changed all that. Many educated Soviets came into contact with capitalism for the first time and discovered that the USSR was not the most advanced country on earth. Khrushchev was a true believer and a fundamentalist. He was convinced that freewheeling debate about socialism and communism was bound to benefit the party. Instead it undermined party authority since many party and non-party members involved in the debate were better educated than party officials. Khrushchev's attitude to culture was that it was a battalion in the class war. Creative thinkers were appalled by this crudity, and Nikita Sergeevich's clamp-down on the creative intelligentsia alienated many and strengthened the growth of an unofficial culture. Even under Khrushchev there was a tacit agreement that an intelligent person could think anything he or she liked providing these ideas were not communicated to the general public. Brezhnev became a figure of ridicule for the educated and the intellectual, and moral authority of the party rule was lost.

Marxism-Leninism as an ideology proved quite incapable of reacting creatively to the changing environment. It is surprising that the ideology, which was an obligatory subject for all students, remained a wooden subject devoid of intellectual content. The subject was taught by rote. Students needed to acquire a knowledge of the party's view of the world. The party filled up with careerists. About 80 per cent of party members in 1991 were in the party to further their careers. As the USSR opened up to the outside world under and after Khrushchev, foreign ideas, many of them inimical to socialism, began to penetrate the country. Little attempt was made to integrate those which were socialism-friendly into the ideology. Each discipline, whether it was social psychology or law, developed on its own. Those involved were not concerned about working out the implications for Marxism-Leninism, that was someone else's task. Even in ideology there was no overall co-ordination.

The very educational system, which was geared to producing mediocre graduates who would not undermine the system, failed. Lack of access to information stimulated the more gifted to find out more. Psychologically they were being moulded to give greater credence to surreptitiously acquired information. Networks of like-minded searchers after Western knowledge grew up. The experience of *glasnost* demonstrated the frustrations of the population. Permission always had to be sought from an official. Lack of control over personal lives sapped initiative and produced apathy. The party did not recognise that the growing level of culture among the population meant that the party's word carried less and less credence. It was usually stated that an official had requested to be relieved of his post due to ill health. Something more implausible would have been difficult to conceive in a country in which the official was tsar. Ideological preconceptions held back economic growth. Opposition to the market and family farming undermined agriculture. Khrushchev, in a bid to force farm workers to concentrate on socialist agriculture, penalised the private plot and the family cow. Many peasants got rid of the cow and went to the shop to buy milk, milk products and meat. Needless to say, the supply was quite inadequate to meet demand. He relaxed his measures later, but by then it was too late. Peasants, or rather their wives, preferred to watch television in the evening to looking after the cow.

The defence burden did much to cripple the USSR. No one will ever know the exact cost of the instruments of coercion because of the accounting system used. One objective of this system was to hide the real cost. Russia always suffered from a fortress mentality due to its open frontiers in the west. Marxism reinforced this, and the Soviet Union became a bastion of world socialism. Stalin's main priorities during the Five Year Plans was to make the USSR militarily impregnable. The best scientists were creamed off for work on military research and development. The military-industrial complex, about a third of the economy, had first choice of every resource. It also contained within itself all high-tech industries, and these were designed to serve defence and security. President Reagan set out to increase the US defence budget so significantly that the Soviets would have to follow suit. In so doing they would irreparably harm their economy since it was less efficient than that of the United States and only about half its size. By the mid 1980s keeping up with NATO was crushing the USSR.

Imperial Russia was an empire and so was the Soviet Union. By 1989, about 48 per cent of the population was non-Russian, with the likelihood that there would be a majority of non-Russians by the end of the century. Yet the country was run by Russians in the interest of Russians. Stalin, a Great Russian nationalist, knew that religion, nationalism and regionalism could destroy his revolution from above. He solved the problem in his lifetime but left a cancerous growth to his successors. Moscow always preferred a fusing of the population but could not always say this. Ironically, the federal Soviet State, designed by Lenin to overcome nationalism and regionalism, fostered it. Had the USSR been as rich as America or Saudi Arabia, then the State might have held together. However, economic decline, the inevitable result of the bureaucratic market, sealed its fate. The irony of the Soviet Union supporting national liberation and national self-determination abroad while denying it to its own citizens could not last for ever. The deportation of fifty-eight nationalities, embracing 3.5 million persons, in the 1930s and 1940s, to the more inhospitable parts of the Union, rankled. Where to put the Crimean Tatars and the Germans after liberation proved to be an insoluble problem.

Marxism in theory has been a pole of attraction for many workers and intellectuals. It has been one of the major ideologies of the twentieth century. Marxism in practice has failed everywhere. There is no Marxist economic model capable of competing with capitalism. The latter has benefited greatly from competition with socialism. Other sources of inspiration will now be necessary to soften the edges of capitalism. Marx's main work is *Das Kapital*. A free translation of this is money. He provided a critique of nineteenth-century British and French capitalism, but, apart from stating that the dictatorship of the proletariat would gradually fade away into a classless socialist society, he provided no thoughts on how a socialist society could be constructed or function. Marxist socialism has always been more attractive to underdeveloped societies than to advanced market economies. Perhaps an exception to this was the German Democratic Republic. The ruling Communist Party had a choice of retaining elements of the market, but turned its back on this in 1958. The reasons for the abject failure of the GDR economic model are still to be elucidated. Why should a country, starting from a German base, have failed so miserably? The absence of democracy does not explain the failure of Marxist economics. The thriving East Asian economies do not practise democracy in the Western sense but have developed models worthy of emulation by underdeveloped states. Marx did not hit the mark.

NOTES

1. V. A. Naishul, *The Supreme and Last Stage of Socialism*.
2. *Financial Times*, 8 April 1992.

Select Bibliography

See bibliographies to separate chapters below

GENERAL

Alt, H. and Alt, E. *The New Soviet Man* (New York 1964)

Armstrong, J. A. *The Politics of Totalitarianism: The Communist Party of the Soviet Union from 1934 to the Present* (New York 1961)

Arutyunyan, Yu. V. *Sotsialnaya Struktura Selskogo Naseleniya SSSR* (Moscow 1971)

Atkinson, D. *The End of the Russian Land Commune, 1905–1930* (Stanford CA 1983)

Bajanov B. *Avec Staline dans le Kremlin* (Paris 1930) (see Baschanow below)

Barron, J. *The KGB* (London 1974)

Baschanow, B. *Ich war Stalins Sekretär* (Frankfurt-am-Main 1977) (see Bajanov above)

Besançon, A. *The Rise of the Gulag: The Intellectual Origins of Leninism* (New York 1981)

Brezhnev, L. *Tselina* (Moscow 1978)

Bronfenbrenner, U. *Two Worlds of Childhood* (New York 1973)

Brown, E. C. *Soviet Trade Unions and Labor Relations* (Cambridge MA 1966)

Carew Hunt, R. N. *The Theory and Practice of Communism* (London 1950)

Carmichael, J. *Trotsky: An Appreciation of His Life* (London 1975)

Carr, E. H. *A History of Soviet Russia* 14 vols (London 1979)

Carr, E. H. *The Russian Revolution from Lenin to Stalin 1917–1929* (London 1979)

Carrère d'Encausse, H. *Decline of an Empire: The Soviet Socialist Republics in Revolt* (London 1980)

Carrère d'Encausse, H. *Une Revolution, Une Victoire: L'Union Soviétique de Lénine à Staline 1917–1953* (Paris 1972)

Churchward, L. G. *The Soviet Intelligentsia* (London 1973)

Clissold, S. (ed.) *Soviet Relations with Latin America 1918–1968: A Documentary Survey* (London 1970)

Colton, T. J. *Commissars, Commanders and Civilian Authority: The Structure of Soviet Military Politics* (Cambridge MA 1979)

Connor, W. D. *Deviance in Soviet Society* (New York 1972)

Connor, W. D. *Socialism, Politics and Equality: Hierarchy and Change in Eastern Europe and the USSR* (New York 1979)

Conquest, R. (ed.) *Religion in the USSR* (London 1968)

Davidson, J. *Indo-China: Signposts in the Storm* (Singapore 1979)

Dawisha, K. *Soviet Foreign Policy Towards Egypt* (London 1979)

Degras, J. (ed.) *Soviet Documents on Foreign Policy* 3 vols (London 1951–3)

Deutscher, I. *Stalin* (London 1949)

Dewhirst, M. and Farrell, R. (eds) *The Soviet Censorship* (Metuchen NJ 1973)

De Witt, N. *Education and Professional Employment in the USSR* (Washington DC 1961)

Dukes, P. *October and the World: Perspectives on the Russian Revolution* (London 1979)

Dziewanowski, M. K. *A History of Soviet Russia* (Englewood Cliffs NJ 1979)

Erickson, J. *The Soviet High Command: A Military-Political History* (London 1962)

Fotieva, L. A. *Iz Vospominanii o Lenine* (Moscow 1964)

Friedgut, T. H. *Political Participation in the USSR* (Princeton NJ 1979)

Gaponenko, L. S. (ed.) *Revolyutsionnoe dvizhenie v russkoi armii 27 fevralya – 24 oktyabrya 1917 goda: Sbornik dokumentov* (Moscow 1968)

Garthoff, R. *Soviet Military Policy: A Historical Analysis* (London 1966)

Gilboa, Y. A. *The Black Years of Soviet Jewry 1939–1953* (Boston MA 1971)

Gilison, J. M. *The Soviet Image of Utopia* (Baltimore MD 1975)

Goldman, M. I. *Soviet Foreign Aid* (New York 1967)

Granick, D. *The Red Executive: A Study of the Organization Man in Russian Industry* (New York 1961)

Gregory, P. *Russian National Income, 1885–1913* (Cambridge 1982)

Gregory, P. R. and Stuart, R. C. (eds) *Soviet Economic Structure and Performance* (New York 1990)

Griffith, W. E. *The Sino-Soviet Rift* (London 1964)

Griffith, W. E. (ed.) *The Soviet Empire: Expansion and Détente* (Lexington MA 1976)

Hahn, W. G. *The Politics of Soviet Agriculture 1960–1970* (Baltimore MD 1972)

Hayward, M., and Labedz, L. (eds) *Literature and Revolution in Soviet Russia 1917–62* (London 1963)

Hill, R. J. *Soviet Political Elites: The Case of Tiraspol* (London 1977)

Hingley, R. *The Russian Secret Police* (New York 1970)

Hoensch, J. K. *Sowjetische Osteuropa-Politik 1945–1975* (Düsseldorf 1977)

Hough, J. F. *The Soviet Prefects: The Local Party Organs in Industrial Decision-Making* (Cambridge MA 1969)

Hough, J. and Fainsod, M. *How the Soviet Union is Governed* (Cambridge MA 1979)

Jain, R. K. *Soviet South Asian Relations 1947–1978* 2 vols (London 1979)

Jones, E. and Grupp, F. W. *Modernisation, Value Change and Fertility in the Soviet Union* (Cambridge 1987)

Joravsky, D. T. *The Lysenko Affair* (Cambridge MA 1970)

Khruschchev, N. S. *Memoirs* (see under Talbott)

Klinghoffer, A. J. *The Soviet Union and International Oil Politics* (New York 1977)

Knight, A. W. *The KGB: Police and Politics in the Soviet Union* (London 1988)

Kochan, L. *The Jews in Soviet Russia since 1917* 2nd edn (New York 1973)

Kolkowicz, R. *Institutions in Conflict: The Soviet Military and the Communist Party* (Princeton NJ 1967)

Krawchenko, B. *Social Change and National Consciousness in Twentieth-century Ukraine* (London 1985)

Kusin, V. V. *From Dubček to Charter 77: A Study of 'Normalisation' in Czechoslovakia 1968–1978* (Edinburgh 1978)

Lane, D. *Politics and Society in the USSR* (London 1978)

Lapidus, G. W. *Women in Soviet Society: Equality, Development and Social Change* (Berkeley CA 1978)

Lenin, V. I. *Collected Works* 4th edn, 45 vols (Moscow 1963–70)

Lenin, V. I. *Polnoe Sobranie Sochinenii* 5th edn, 55 vols (Moscow 1959–65)

Lewin, M. *Lenin's Last Struggle* (London 1975)

Lewis, R. A. *Science and Industrialisation in the USSR: Industrial Research and Development 1917–1940* (London 1979)

Lewis, R. A. Rowland, R. H. and Clem, R. S. *Nationality and Population Change in Russia and the Soviet Union: An Evaluation of Census Data 1897–1970* (New York 1976)

Lewis, R. A. and Rowland, R. H. *Population Redistribution in the USSR: Its Impact on Society 1897–1977* (New York 1979)

Lieven, D. C. B. *Russia and the Origins of the First World War* (London 1983)

Lunacharsky, A. *Revolyutsionnie Siluety* (Moscow 1923)

McAuley, A. *Economic Welfare in the Soviet Union: Poverty, Living Standards, and Inequality* (London 1979)

McCagg W. O. Jr. *Stalin Embattled 1943–1948* (Detroit MI 1978)

McCauley, M. (ed.) *Communist Power in Europe 1944–1949* rev. edn (London 1979)

McCauley, M. *Marxism-Leninism in the German Democratic Republic: The Socialist Unity Party (SED)* (London 1979)

McCauley, M. (ed.) *The Russian Revolution and the Soviet State 1917–1921: Documents* rev. edn (London 1980)

McCauley, M. and Waldron, P. *Octobrists to Bolsheviks: Imperial Russia 1905–17* (London 1984)

McNeal, R. H. (ed.) *Resolutions and Decisions of the Communist Party of the Soviet Union* 5 vols (Toronto 1974–82)

Macdonald, H. *The Soviet Challenge and the Structure of European Security* (Aldershot 1990)

Mackintosh, J. M. *Strategy and Tactics of Soviet Foreign Policy* (London 1962)

Makepeace, R. W. *Marxist Ideology and Soviet Criminal Law* (London 1980)

Mandelstam, N. *Hope against Hope* (London 1971)

Matthews, M. *Class and Society in Soviet Russia* (London 1972)

Medvedev, R. A. *Let History Judge* (London 1973)

Medvedev, R. A. *On Socialist Democracy* (London 1975)

Medvedev, R. A. *On Stalin and Stalinism* (London 1979)

Medvedev, Z. A. *The Rise and Fall of T. D. Lysenko* (New York 1969)

Medvedev, Z. A. *Soviet Science* (London 1979)

Millar, T. B. *Australia in Peace and War: External Relations 1788–1977* (Canberra 1978)

Milyukov, P. N. *Rossiya na Perelome* 2 vols (Paris 1927)

Morozov, B. M. *Partiya i Sovety v Oktyabrskoi Revolyutsii* (Moscow 1966)

Moses, J. C. *Regional Party Leadership and Policy Making in the USSR* (New York 1974)

Nicolaevsky, B. I. *Power and the Soviet Elite* ed. J Zagoria (New York 1966)

Nogee, J. L. and Donaldson, R. H. *Soviet Foreign Policy since World War II* (New York 1981)

Nove, A. *An Economic History of the USSR* (London 1969)

Nove, A. *Stalinism and After* (London 1975)

Nove, A. *The Soviet Economic System* (London 1977)

O'Dell, E. *Socialisation through Children's Literature* (Cambridge 1979)

Perrins, M. 'Rabkrin and Workers' Control in Russia 1917–34', *European Studies Review* vol. 10, No. 2, April 1980.

Pethybridge, R. W. *The Social Prelude to Stalinism* (London 1974)

Pinkus, B. *The Jews of the Soviet Union: The History of a National Minority* (Cambridge 1988)

Pyataya. *Konferentsiya Vsesoyuznoi Kommunisticheskoi Partii (b) 26 Oktyabrya – 3 Noyabrya 1926 g* (Moscow-Leningrad 1927)

Ra'anan, U. *The USSR Arms the Third World: Case Studies in Soviet Foreign Policy* (Cambridge MA 1969)

Ranger, R. *Arms and Politics 1958–1978: Arms Control in a Changing Context* (New York 1979)

von Rauch, G. *History of Soviet Russia* 6th rev. edn (New York 1972)

von Rauch, G. *The Baltic States* (Berkeley CA 1974)

Remnek, R. B. *Soviet Scholars and Soviet Foreign Policy: A Case Study of Soviet Policy Towards India* (Durham NC 1975)

Rigby, T. H. *Communist Party Membership in the USSR 1917–1967* (Princeton NJ 1968)

Rosenfeldt, N. E. *Knowledge and Power. The Role of Stalin's Secret Chancellery in the Soviet System of Government* (Copehagen 1978)

Ryavec, K. W. (ed.) *Soviet Society and the Communist Party* (Amherst MA 1978)

Schapiro, L. *The Communist Party of the Soviet Union* (London 1966)

Scharping, T. *Mao Chronik: Daten zu Leben und Werk* (Munich 1976)

Scott, H. and W. *The Armed Forces of the USSR* (London 1979)

Serge, V. *Vie et Mort de Trotsky* (Paris 1951)

Service, R. *Lenin: A Political Life* 3 vols (London 1985–93)

Service, R. *The Russian Revolution, 1900–27* (London 1986)

Seton-Watson, H. *The Imperialist Revolutionaries: Trends in World Communism in the 1960s and 1970s* (London 1980)

Shst. Sezd VKP(b) (Moscow-Leningrad 1930)

Shub, D. *Lenin* (London 1966)

Simon, G. *Nationalismus und Nationalitätenpolitik in der Sowjetunion* (Baden Baden 1986)

Smirnov, G. *Soviet Man: The Making of a Socialist Type of Personality* (Moscow 1973)

Stalin, I. V. *Sochineniya*, 13 vols (Moscow 1946–51); 3 vols (Stanford CA 1967)

Stevens, C. *The Soviet Union and Black Africa* (London 1976)

Stites, R. *The Women's Liberation Movement in Russia: Feminism, Nihilism and Bolshevism 1860–1930* (Princeton NJ 1991)

Strauss, E. *Soviet Agriculture in Perspective* (London 1969)

Stuart, R. *The Collective Farm in Soviet Agriculture* (New York 1973)

Suny, R. G. *The Making of the Georgian Nation* (London 1988)

Talbott, S. (ed.) *Khruschchev Remembers* (London 1971)

Talbott, S. (ed.) *Khruschchev Remembers: The Last Testament* (London 1975)

Tarschys, D. *The Soviet Political Agenda: Problems and Priorities 1950–1970* (London 1978)

Treadgold, R. W. *Twentieth Century Russia* (Chicago IL 1964)

Trinadtsatyi Sezd VKP (b) Mai 1924 goda (Moscow 1963)

Trotsky, L. *Lenin* (New York 1925)

Trotsky, L. *Literatura i Revolyutsiya* (Moscow 1923)

Trotsky, L. *Ma Vie* 3 vols (Paris 1930)

Trotsky, L. *Permanent Revolution and Results and Prospects* (London 1962)

Trotsky, L. *The Revolution Betrayed* (New York 1937)

Trotsky, L. *The Stalin School of Falsification* (New York 1937)

Trotsky, L. *The Suppressed Testament of Lenin* (New York 1935)

Tucker, R. C. *Political Culture and Leadership in Soviet Russia from Lenin to Gorbachev* (Brighton 1987)

Ulam, A. *Expansion and Coexistence: Soviet Foreign Policy 1917–1973* 2nd ed (New York 1974)

Ulam, A. *Stalin* (London 1974)

Ulam, A. *History of Soviet Russia* (New York 1976)

Uldricks, T. J. *Diplomacy and Ideology: The Origins of Soviet Foreign Policy 1917–1930* (London 1979)

Vanneman, P. *The Supreme Soviet: Politics and the Legislative Process in the Soviet Political System* (Durham NC 1977)

VKP(b) v Resolyutsiyakh 8 vols (Moscow 1936)

Volin, L. *A Century of Russian Agriculture from Alexander II to Khrushchev* (Cambridge MA 1970)

Voslensky, M. *Nomenklatura: Die herrschende Klasse der Sowjetunion* (Munich 1980)

Voslensky, M. *Nomenklatura: Anatomy of the Soviet Ruling Class* (Oxford 1984)

Voznesensky, N. *War Economy of the USSR in the Period of the Patriotic War* (Moscow 1945)

Wädekin, K-E. *Privatproduzenten in der sowjetischen Landwirtschaft* (Cologne 1967)

Walicki, A. *A History of Russian Thought: From the Enlightenment to Marxism* (Oxford 1988)

Weber, G. and H. *Lenin* (London 1980)

Wesson, R. G. *Lenin's Legacy: The Story of the CPSU* (Stanford CA 1978)

Wiles, P. J. D. *The Political Economy of Communism* (Cambridge 1962)

Wistrich, R. (ed.) *The Left Against Zion: Communism, Israel and the Middle East* (London 1980)

Za Leninism Sbornik Statei (Moscow–Leningrad 1925)

Zaleski, E. *Stalinist Planning for Economic Growth 1933–1952* (London 1980)

CHAPTER 1

Abraham, R. *Alexander Kerensky: The First Love of the Revolution* (London 1987)

Anweiler, O. *The Soviets: The Russian Workers', Peasants' and Soldiers' Councils 1905–1921* (New York 1974)

Avrich, P. H. (ed.) *The Anarchists in the Russian Revolution* (New York 1973)

Brovkin, V. N. *The Mensheviks after October: Socialist Opposition and the Rise of the Bolshevik Dictatorship* (London 1987)

Browder, R. P. and Kerensky, A. F. (eds) *The Russian Provisional Government 1917: Documents* 3 vols (Stanford CA 1961)

Bunyan, J. and Fisher, H. H. (eds) *The Bolshevik Revolution 1917–1918 Documents and Materials* (Stanford CA 1965)

Chamberlin, W. H. *The Russian Revolution 1917–1921* 2 vols (New York 1965)

Daniels, R. V. *The Conscience of the Revolution: Communist Opposition in Soviet Russia* (London 1960)

Debo, R. K. *Revolution and Survival: The Foreign Policy of Soviet Russia 1917–18* (Liverpool 1979)

Deutscher, I. *The Prophet Armed: Trotsky 1879–1921* (London 1954)

Elwood, R. C. (ed.) *Reconsiderations on the Russian Revolution* (Cambridge MA 1976)

Ferro, M. *October 1917: A Social History of the Russian Revolution* (London 1980)

Ferro, M. *The Russian Revolution: A Social History of the Russian Revolution* (London 1985)

Fitzpatrick, S. *The Commissariat of the Enlightenment: Soviet Organization of Education and the Arts under Lunacharsky* (Cambridge 1970)

Fitzpatrick, S. *The Russian Revolution* (Oxford 1982)

Gerson, L. D. *The Secret Police in Lenin's Russia* (London 1976)

Getzler, I. *Kronstadt 1917–21: The Fate of a Soviet Democracy* (Cambridge 1983)

Gill, G. J. *Peasants and Government in the Russian Revolution* (London 1979)

Hasegawa, T. *The February Revolution: Petrograd 1917* (Seattle WA 1980)

Kaiser, D. H. (ed.) *The Workers' Revolution in Russia, 1917; The View from Below* (Cambridge 1987)

Katkov, G. *The Kornilov Affair: Kerensky and the break-up of the Russian Army* (London 1980)

Keep, J. L. H. *The Debate on Soviet Power: Minutes of the All-Russian Central Executive Committee of Soviets: Second Convocation October 1917–January 1918* (London 1979)

Keep, J. L. H. *The Russian Revolution: A Study in Mass Mobilization* (London 1976)

Kenez, P. *Civil War in South Russia 1918: The First Year of the Volunteer Army* (Berkeley CA 1971)

Kenez, P. *Civil War in South Russia 1919–1920: The Defeat of the Whites* (Berkeley CA 1977)

Koenker, D. *Moscow Workers and the 1917 Revolution* (Princeton NJ 1981)

Leggett, G. *The Cheka: Lenin's Political Police* (Oxford 1981)

Malle, S. *The Economic Organisation of War Communism, 1918–1921* (Cambridge 1985)

Mandel, D. *Petrograd Workers and the Soviet Seizure of Power (July 1917–June 1918)* (London 1984)

Mawdsley, E. *The Russian Revolution and the Baltic Fleet* (London 1978)

Mawdsley, E. *The Russian Civil War* (London 1987)

Pipes, R. *The Formation of the Soviet Union: Communism and Nationalism 1917–1923* rev. edn (New York 1968)

Rabinowitch, A. *Prelude to Revolution: The Petrograd Bolsheviks and the July 1917 Uprising* (Bloomington IN and London 1968)

Rabinowitch, A. *The Bolsheviks Come to Power: The Revolution of 1917 in Petrograd* (New York 1976)

Radkey, O. H. *The Agrarian Foes of Bolshevism: Promise and Default of the Russian Socialist Revolutionaries: February to October 1917* (New York 1958)

Radkey, O. H. *The Election to the Russian Constituent Assembly of 1917* (Cambridge MA 1950)

Radkey, O. H. *The Sickle Under the Hammer: The Russian Socialist Revolutionaries in the Early Months of Soviet Rule* (New York 1963)

Reed, J. *Ten Days that Shook the World* (Harmondsworth 1966)

Reshetar, J. S. *The Ukrainian Revolution 1917–1920: A Study in Nationalism* (New York 1972)

Rigby, T. H. *Lenin's Government: Sovnarkom 1917–1922* (Cambridge 1979)

Rosenberg, W. G. *Liberals in the Russian Revolution: The Constitutional Democratic Party 1917–1921* (Princeton NJ 1974)

Rosenberg, W. G. (ed.) *Bolshevik Visions: The First Phase of the Cultural Revolution in Soviet Russia* (Ann Arbor MI 1985)

Schapiro, L. *The Origin of the Communist Autocracy: Political Opposition in the Soviet State First Phase 1917–1922*, reprint (London 1978)

Schapiro, L. *The Russian Revolution of 1917: The Origins of Modern Communism* (London 1984)

Schapiro, L. and Reddaway, P. (eds) *Lenin: The Man, the Theorist, the Leader: A Reappraisal* (New York 1967)

Service, R. *The Bolshevik Party in Revolution 1917–1923: A Study in Organisational Change* (London 1979)

Shukman, H. *Lenin and the Russian Revolution* (London 1967)

Skocpol, T. *States and Social Revolutions: A Comparative Analysis of France, Russia and China* (London 1979)

Smith, C. F. *Vladivostok under Red and White Rule: Revolution and Counterrevolution in the Russian Far East 1920–1922* (Seattle WA and London 1975)

Smith, S. A. *Red Petrograd: Revolution in the Factories, 1917–1918* (Cambridge 1983)

Sukhanov, N. N. *The Russian Revolution 1917: Eyewitness Account* edited, abridged and translated by J. Carmichael, 2 vols (London 1958)

Ulam, A. *Lenin and the Bolsheviks* (London 1966)

Volobuev, P. V. *Ekonomicheskaya politika vremennogo pravitelstva* (Moscow 1962)

Wade, R. A. *The Russian Search for Peace February–October 1917* (Stanford CA 1969)

Wade, R. *Red Guards and Workers' Militias: Spontaneity and Leadership in the Russian Revolution* (Stanford CA 1983)

Wheeler-Bennett, J. W. *Brest-Litovsk: The Forgotten Peace, March 1918* (London 1963)

Wildman, A. K. *The End of the Russian Imperial Army: The Old Army and the Soldiers' Revolt (March–April 1917)* (Princeton NJ 1980)

Wildman, A. K. *The Road to Soviet Power and Peace* (Princeton NJ 1988)

CHAPTER 2

Cohen, S. F. *Bukharin and the Bolshevik Revolution: A Political Biography* (New York 1975)

Danilov, V. P. *Rural Russia under the New Regime* (London 1988)

Deutscher, I. *Prophet Unarmed: Leon Trotsky 1921–29* (London 1959)

Erlich, A. *The Soviet Industrialisation Debate 1924–1928* (Cambridge MA 1967)

Fitzpatrick, S. (ed.) *Cultural Revolution in Russia 1928–1931* (Bloomington IN and London 1978)

Fitzpatrick, S. *Education and Social Mobility in the Soviet Union 1921–1934* (London 1979)

Gorodetsky, G. *The Precarious Truce: Anglo-Soviet Relations 1924–27* (London 1977)

Kenez, P. *The Birth of the Propaganda State: Soviet Methods of Mass Mobilization* (Cambridge 1985)

Knei-Paz, B. *The Social and Political Thought of Leon Trotsky* (London 1979)

Stalin, J. *Leninism* (London 1942)

Taylor, R. *The Politics of the Soviet Cinema 1917–1929* (London 1979)

Tucker, R. C. *Stalin as Revolutionary* (London 1974)

Tucker, R. C. (ed.) *Stalinism: Essays in Historical Interpretation* (New York 1977)

Tumarkin, N. *Lenin Lives! The Lenin Cult in Soviet Russia* (Cambridge MA Harvard 1983)

White, S. *Britain and the Bolshevik Revolution: A Study in the Politics of Diplomacy 1920–1924* (London 1979)

Wistrich, R. *Trotsky* (London 1979)

CHAPTER 3

Andrle, V. *Workers in Stalin's Russia; Industrialisation and Social Change in a Planned Economy* (Brighton 1988)

Bailes, K. E. *Technology and Society under Lenin and Stalin: Origins of the Soviet Technical Intelligentsia 1917–1941* (Princeton NJ 1978)

Chew, A. F. *The White Death* (East Lansing MI 1971)

Conquest, R. *The Great Terror: Stalin's Purge of the Thirties* (London 1968)

Conquest, R. *Harvest of Sorrow: Soviet Collectivisation and the Terror-Famine* (London 1986)

Conquest, R. *Stalin: Breaker of Nations* (London 1991)

Davies, R. W. *The Industrialisation of Soviet Russia:* Vol. 1, *The Socialist Offensive: The Collectivisation of Soviet Agriculture 1929–30;* Vol. 2, *The Soviet Collective Farm* (London 1980)

Davies, R. W. *The Soviet Economy in Turmoil, 1929–30* (London 1988)

Deutscher, I. *Prophet Outcast: Leon Trotsky 1929–40* (London 1963)

Filtzer, D. *Soviet Workers and Stalinist Industrialisation* (London 1986)

Gill, G. 'Political Myth and Stalin's Quest for Authority in the Party' in T. H. Rigby, A. Brown and P. Reddaway (eds) *Authority*, Power and Policy in the USSR (London 1980)

Kemp-Welch, A. 'Stalinism and Intellectual Order' in ibid.

Kemp-Welch, A. *Stalin and the Literary Intelligentsia* (London 1990)

Kuromiya, H. *Stalin's Industrial Revolution: Politics and Workers, 1928–32* (Cambridge 1988)

Lampert, N. *The Technical Intelligentsia and the Soviet State: A Study of Soviet Managers and Technicians 1928–1935* (London 1979)

Lewin, M. *Russian Peasants and Soviet Power: A Study of Collectivization* (London 1968)

McCauley, M. *Stalin and Stalinism* (London 1983)

McNeal, R. *Stalin: Man and Ruler* (London 1988)

Orlov, A. *The Secret History of Stalin's Crimes* (London 1954)

Sholokhov, M. *The Soil Upturned* (Moscow 1934)

Siegelbaum, L. *Stakhanovism and the Politics of Productivity in the USSR, 1935–41* (Cambridge 1988)

Tucker, R. C. (ed.) *Stalinism: Essays in Historical Interpretation* (New York 1977)

Tucker, R. C. *Stalin in Power: The Revolution from Above 1928–1941* (New York 1990)

Vaughan James, C. *Soviet Socialist Realism: Origins and Theory* (London 1973)

Viola, L. *The Best Sons of the Fatherland: Workers in the Vanguard of Soviet Collectivisation* (Oxford 1987)

CHAPTER 4

Conquest, R. *The Nation Killers: The Soviet Deportation of Nationalities* (London 1970)

Correspondence between the Chairman of the Council of Ministers of the USSR and the Presidents of the USA and the Prime Ministers of Great Britain during the Great Patriotic War of 1941–1945 2 vols (Moscow n.d.)

Erickson, J. The Road to Stalingrad: Stalin's War with Germany (London 1975)

Erickson, J. The Road to Berlin (London 1983)

Grigorenko, P. Memoirs (London 1983)

Harrison, M. Soviet Planning in Peace and War (Cambridge 1985)

Lubachko, I. S. Belorussia under Soviet Rule, 1917–57 (Kentucky 1972)

Mackintosh, M. Juggernaut: A History of the Soviet Armed Forces (London 1967)

Mastny, V. Russia's Road to the Cold War: Diplomacy, Warfare and the Politics of Communism 1941–1944 (New York 1979)

Misiunas, R. and Taagepera, R. The Baltic States: The Years of Dependence, 1940–80 (London 1983)

Nekrich, A. The Punished Peoples: The Deportation and Tragic Fate of Soviet Minorities at the End of the Second World War (New York 1978)

Pospelov, P. N., et al. Great Patriotic War of the Soviet Union 1941–1945 (Moscow 1974)

Rubin, B. The Great Powers in the Middle East 1941–1947: The Road to the Cold War (London 1980)

Seaton, A. The Russo-German War 1941–45 (London 1971)

Streit, C. Keine Kameraden: Die Wehrmacht und die sowjetischen Kriegsgefangenen 1941–1945 (Stuttgart 1978)

CHAPTER 5

Alliluyeva, S. 20 Letters to a Friend (London 1967)

Conquest, R. Power and Policy in the USSR (London 1962)

Davies, R. W. The Socialist Offensive: The Collectivisation of Soviet Agriculture, 1929–1930 (London 1980)

Davies, R. W. The Collective Farm (London 1980)

Dunham, V. S. In Stalin's Time: Middle Class Values in Soviet Fiction (Cambridge 1976)

Dunmore, T. The Stalinist Command Economy: The Soviet State Apparatus and Economic Policy, 1945–53 (London 1980)

Hahn, W. Postwar Soviet Politics: The Fall of Zhdanov and the Defeat of Moderation (Ithaca NY, Cornell 1982)

McCauley, M. The Origins of the Cold War (London 1983)

Tucker, R. C. Stalin in Power: The Revolution from Above 1928–1941 (New York 1990)

Zhdanov, A. A. On Literature, Music and Philosophy (London 1950)

CHAPTER 6

Bourdeaux, M. *Patriarch and Prophets: Persecution of the Russian Orthodox Church* (London 1975)

Bourdeaux, M. *Religious Ferment in Russia: Protestant Opposition to Soviet Religious Policy* (London 1968)

Cohen, S., Sharlet, R. and Rabinowitch A. (eds) *The Soviet Union since Stalin* (London 1980)

Johnson, P. *Khrushchev and the Arts* (Cambridge MA 1965)

Krushchev, S. *Khrushchev on Khrushchev: An Inside Account of the Man and his Era* (Boston MA 1990)

Linden, C. A. *Khrushchev and the Soviet Leadership 1957–1964* (Baltimore MD 1966)

Linz, S. J. (ed) *The Impact of World War II on the Soviet Union* (Totowa, New Jersey, 1985)

McAuley, M. *Labour Disputes in Soviet Russia 1957–65* (London 1969)

McCauley, M. *Khrushchev and the Development of Soviet Agriculture: The Virgin Land Programme 1953–1964* (London 1976)

McCauley, M. (ed.) *Khrushchev and Khrushchevism* (London 1987)

McCauley, M. *Nikita Sergeevich Khrushchev* (London 1991)

Matthews, M. *Education in the Soviet Union: Politics and Institutions since Stalin* (London 1982)

Medvedev, R. A. and Z. A. *Khrushchev: The Years in Power* (London 1977)

Mićunović, V. *Moscow Diary* (London 1980)

Tatu, M. *Power in the Kremlin* (London 1969)

CHAPTER 7

Abir, M. and Yodfat, A. *In the Direction of the Gulf: The Soviet Union in the Persian Gulf* (London 1980)

Adams, J. S. *Citizen Inspectors in the Soviet Union: The People's Control Committee* (New York 1978)

Albright, D. E. (ed.) *Africa and International Communism* (London 1980)

Alekseeva, L. *Soviet Dissent: Contemporary Movements for National, Religious and Human Rights* (Middleton, CO 1985)

Allworth, E. (ed.) *Nationality Group Survival in Multi-Ethnic States: Shifting Support Patterns in the Soviet Baltic Region* (New York 1977)

Amann, R., Cooper, J. and Davies, R. W. (eds) *The Technological Level of Soviet Industry* (New Haven CT 1977)

Andropov, Y. V. *Speeches and Writings* (Oxford 1983)

Azrael, J. R. (ed.) *Soviet Nationality Policies and Practices* (New York 1978)

Benningsen, A. and Broxup, M. *The Islamic Threat to the Soviet Union* (London 1983)

Benningsen, A. and Enders Wimbush, C. *Mystics and Commissars: Sufism in the Soviet Union* (London 1985)

Bloch, S. and Reddaway, P. *Russia's Political Hospitals: The Abuse of Psychiatry in the Soviet Union* (London 1977)

Bociurkiw, B. *Religion and Atheism in the USSR and Eastern Europe* (London 1975)

Brown, A. 'The Power of the General Secretary of the CPSU' in T. H. Rigby, A. Brown and P. Reddaway (eds) *Authority, Power and Policy in the USSR* (London 1980)

Brown, A. and Kaser, M. (eds) *The Soviet Union Since the Fall of Khrushchev* 2nd edn (London 1978)

Conquest, R (ed.) *The Last Empire: Nationality and the Soviet Future* (Stanford CA 1986)

Dallin, A. (ed.) *The Twenty Fifth Congress of the CPSU: Assessment and Context* (Stanford CA 1977)

Donaldson, R. H. (ed.) *The Soviet Union in the Third World* (London 1981)

Dornberg, J. *Brezhnev* (London 1974)

Dunlop, J. *The Faces of Contemporary Russian Nationalism* (Princeton NJ 1983)

Ellis, J. *The Russian Orthodox Church: A Contemporary History* (London 1986)

Fisher, A. W. *The Crimean Tatars* (Stanford CA 1978)

Fleron F. J. Jr (ed.) *Technology and Communist Culture: The Socio-Cultural Impact of Technology Transfer under Socialism* (New York 1977)

Ginsburgs, G. and Rubinstein, A. Z. (eds) *Soviet Foreign Policy Towards Western Europe* (London 1978)

Horn, R. C. *The Soviet Union and India: The Limits of Influence* (New York 1981)

Hough, J. F. *Soviet Leadership in Transition* (Washington DC 1980)

Jacobsen, C. G. *Soviet Strategic Initiatives: Challenge and Response* (New York 1979)

Jones, C. D. *Soviet Influence in Eastern Europe* (New York 1981)

Kaiser, R. G. *Russia: The People and the Power* (London 1976)

Karklins, R. *Ethnic Relations in the USSR* (Boston MA 1986)

Kelley, D. R. (ed.) *Soviet Politics in the Brezhnev Era* (New York 1980)

Kerblay, B. *Modern Soviet Society* (London 1983)

Lapidus, G. (ed.) *Women in Russia* (Brighton 1978)

Levesque, J. *The USSR and the Cuban Revolution: Soviet Ideological and Strategic Perspectives 1959–77* (New York 1978)

Lewis, C. W. and Sternheimer, S. *Soviet Urban Management: With Comparisons to the United States* (New York 1979)

392

London, K. (ed.) *The Soviet Union in World Politics* (London 1980)

McCauley, M. (ed.) *The Soviet Union after Brezhnev* (London 1983)

Makepeace, R. W. *Marxist Ideology and Soviet Criminal Law* (London 1980)

Matthews, M. *Privilege in the Soviet Union: A Study of Elite Life Styles under Communism* (London 1978)

Medvedev, Z. *Andropov* (Oxford 1983)

Millar, J. R. (ed.) *The Soviet Rural Community* (Urbana IL 1971)

Morton, H. W. and Tokes, R. (eds) *Soviet Politics and Soviet Society in the 1970s* (New York 1974)

Nove, A. *Political Economy and Soviet Socialism* (London 1979)

Park, D. *Oil and Gas in Comecon Countries* (London 1979)

Rabinovich, I. *The Soviet Union and Syria in the 1970s* (New York 1980)

Reddaway, P. *Uncensored Russia: The Human Rights Movement in the Soviet Union* (London 1972)

Reddaway, P. 'Policy Towards Dissent since Khrushchev' in T. H. Rigby, A. Brown and P. Reddaway (eds) *Authority, Power and Policy in the USSR* (London 1980)

Ruble, B. and Kahan, A. *Industrial Labor in the USSR* (New York 1979)

Rush, M. *Political Succession in the USSR* 2nd edn (New York 1968)

Rywkin, M. *Moscow's Muslim Challenge: Soviet Central Asia* (London 1982)

Sen Gupta, B. *Soviet Asian Relations in the 1970s and Beyond* (New York 1976)

Skilling, H. G. and Griffiths, F. (eds) *Interest Groups in Soviet Politics* (Princeton NJ 1971)

Smith, G. B. *The Soviet Procuracy and the Supervision of Administration* (Alphen aan den Rijn 1978)

Smith, H. *The Russians* (London 1976)

Smolansky, O. M. *The Soviet Union and Iraq 1968–1979* (New York 1981)

Steele, J. and Abraham, E. *Andropov in Power* (Oxford 1983)

Strong, J. (ed.) *The Soviet Union under Brezhnev and Kosygin* (New York 1971)

The Soviet Union 1973 (London 1975)

The Soviet Union 1974–75 (London 1977)

The Soviet Union 1975–76 (London 1978)

The Soviet Union 1976–77 (London 1979)

Tökes, R. L. (ed.) *Dissent in the USSR: Politics, Ideology and People* (Baltimore MD 1975)

Valenta, J. *Soviet Invasion of Czechoslovakia 1968: Anatomy of a Decision* (Baltimore MD 1978)

Vardys, V. S. *The Catholic Church, Dissent and Nationality in Soviet Lithuania* (Boulder CO 1978)

Weinstein, W. and Henriksen, T. H. (eds) *Soviet and Chinese Aid to African Nations* (New York 1980)
White, S. *Political Culture and Soviet Politics* (London 1979)
Willerton, J. P. *Patronage and Politics in the USSR* (Cambridge 1992)
Zaslavsky, V. *The Neo Stalinist State* (Brighton 1982)

CHAPTER 8

Aganbegyan, A. *The Challenge: Economics of Perestroika* (London 1988)
Bourdeaux, M. *Gorbachev, Glasnost and the Gospel* (London 1990)
Dawisha, K. *Eastern Europe, Gorbachev and Reform: The Great Challenge* (Cambridge 1988)
Frankland, M. *The Sixth Continent: Russia and the Making of Mikhail Gorbachev* (London 1987)
Gelman, H. *Gorbachev's First Five Years in the Soviet Leadership: The Clash of Personalities and the Remaking of Institutions* (Santa Monica CA 1990)
Goldman, M. *USSR in Crisis: The Failure of an Economic System* (New York 1983)
Gorbachev, M. *Perestroika: New Thinking for our Country and the World* (London 1987)
Haynes, V. and Bojcun, M. *The Chernobyl Disaster* (London 1988)
McCauley, M. (ed.) *The Soviet Union under Gorbachev* (London 1987)
McCauley, M. (ed.) *Gorbachev and Perestroika* (London 1990)
Marples, D. *The Social Impact of the Chernobyl Disaster* (London 1988)
Medvedev, Z. *Gorbachev* (Oxford 1986)
Sakwa, R. *Gorbachev and his Reforms* (Oxford 1990)
White, S. *Gorbachev and After* (Cambridge 1991)
Ziegler, C. E. *Environmental Policy in the USSR* (London 1987)

CHAPTER 9

Naishul, V. A. *The Supreme and Last Stage of Socialism* (London 1991)

Maps

POLAND

BALTIC SEA

CZECHOSLOVAKIA

FINLAND

ESTONIA

KARELIAN ASSR

WHITE SEA

NOVAYA ZEMLYA

LITHUANIA

MOLDAVIA

BELO-RUSSIA

LATVIA

RUSSIAN

NENETS N.O.

ROMANIA

UKRAINE

Moscow ●

KOMI ASSR

YAMAL NENTES N.O.

CHUVASH ASSR

MARI ASSR

BLACK SEA

MORDVA ASSR

TATAR ASSR

UDMURT ASSR

KHANTY MANSI N.O.

KABARDINO-BALKAR ASSR

BASHKIR ASSR

ABKHAZ ASSR

GEORGIA

KALMYK ASSR

NORTH OSSETIN ASSR

S F S R

ADZHAR ASSR

ARMENIA

DAGESTAN ASSR

CHECHEN INGUSH ASSR

TURKEY

CASPIAN SEA

ARAL SEA

KAZAKHSTAN

NAKHICHEVAN ASSR

KARA KALPAK ASSR

GORNO-ALTA A.O.

AZERBAIDZHAN

TURKMEN-ISTAN

Lake Balkhash

IRAN

UZBEKISTAN

KIRGIZIA

TADZHIKISTAN

GORNO-BADAKHSHAN A.O.

AFGHANISTAN

Map 1.   Political-administrative map of the USSR until 1991

Autonomous Soviet Socialist Republics (ASSR)
Autonomous Oblasts (A.O.)
National Okrugs (N.O.)

CHUKOT
N.O.

KORYAK
N.O.

TAIMYR
N.O.

YAKUT
ASSR

SEA OF
OKHOTSK

EVENKI
N.O.

KURIL
ISLANDS

SAKHALIN

UST-ORDYN
BURIAT
N.O.

BURYAT
ASSR

Lake
Baikal

JEWISH
A.O.

HAKASS
A.O.

MANCHURIA

TUVA
A.O.

MONGOLIA

JAPAN

CHINA

KOREA

0   500 mls

0   500 km

397

Map 2. The Civil War

Map 3. The German invasion of the USSR 1941–42

Map 4. The Allies close in on Germany

Areas of Allied bombing, 1942-44

Operation 'Overlord' June 1944, and the follow-up in France

Operation Anvil, August 1944

Battle of the Bulge, December 1944-45

Allied advances through Italy, to December 1944

Soviet advances, 1943 to the end of 1944

Soviet advances, January and February 1945

A-L   Alsace and Lorraine

0 _____ 500 mls
0 _____ 500 km

FINLAND

Leningrad

BALTIC SEA

E. PRUSSIA

Minsk

POLAND   Warsaw   USSR

Oder

BOHEMIA-MORAVIA

R. Vistula

UKRAINE

SLOVAKIA

HUNGARY

Budapest

CRIMEA

ROMANIA

BLACK SEA

CROATIA

Belgrade

SERBIA

BULGARIA

ALBANIA

GREECE

USSR in 1938

Acquired by USSR 1939–45

Soviet satellite states

Communist but not Soviet satellites

0   400 mls

0   400 km

Map 5.   Soviet territorial gains in Europe 1939–49

Map 6. The Soviet Union and the Middle East

Countries with Friendship Treaties
with the Soviet Union

CHINA

0   200 mls
0   200 km

NORTH VIETNAM

Dien Bien Phu

BURMA   Hanoi
                                    Haiphong

Luang Prabang

Gulf of
Tonkin

LAOS

17th Parallel

Hué

THAILAND   Da Nang

R. Mekong

Pleiku   Qui Nhon

CAMBODIA
(KAMPUCHEA)

Nha Trang

SOUTH
VIETNAM
Bien Hoa
Phnom Penh
Saigon

Vung Tau

Cai Ngai

| | Communist state of
North Vietnam

| | Areas under communist*
control by mid-1960s | | Further areas under communist
                                              control by 1973

➡ Communist supply route to the
South (the Ho Chi Minh Trail)   Areas conquered by communists
                                              by April 1975

➡ US invasion at Cambodia,
April to May 1970   *Qui
                                     Nhon*   Major bases in South Vietnam

➤ South Vietnamese invasion of
Laos, February 1971   ■ US air bases in Thailand

*Pathet Lao in Laos, Khmer Rouge in Cambodia, and Vietcong in South Vietnam

Map 7. War and the advance of communism in Indo-China

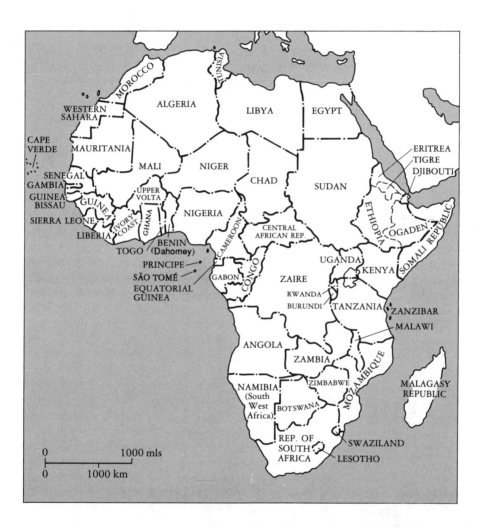

Map 8.   Africa in 1980

Map 9. The Commonwealth of Independent States (CIS) from 1991

Index